Film and Its Techniques

Film

RAYMOND SPOTTISWOODE

illustrations by Jean-Paul Ladouceur

nd Its Techniques

erkeley and Los Angeles 1957

UNIVERSITY OF CALIFORNIA PRESS

UNIVERSITY OF CALIFORNIA PRESS, BERKELEY AND LOS ANGELES, CALIFORNIA
CAMBRIDGE UNIVERSITY PRESS, LONDON, ENGLAND
COPYRIGHT, 1951, BY THE REGENTS OF THE UNIVERSITY OF CALIFORNIA
PRINTED IN THE UNITED STATES OF AMERICA

FOURTH PRINTING, 1957

for Francesca

The Cinema is an art. It is the first and only new art form to be discovered by man within recorded history. He could not have discovered it earlier because it is the child of the industrial revolution. It is the one positive creative discovery of the machine age, for it depends for its existence on machinery, chemical processes and electricity. It is an art because it represents the end of that quest for representation of life in movement which began when the cave men of Altamira painted leaping figures on the walls of their caverns. Despite the sound track, it is an art because it is visual.—Basil Wright.

Foreword

T HIS BOOK is the outcome of many years of documentary film production in the United States, Canada, and Great Britain. Within recent years, film production at all levels has become so specialized that it is difficult for a writer to gain enough practice in all its many branches to infuse a book such as this with the warmth and vividness of personal experience. It is my good fortune to have worked for several years, first as Producer and then as Technical Supervisor, at the National Film Board of Canada. This is an organization which has gathered under one roof all branches of film making, and has united them in a happy combination of creative and technical skills. It is to my friends at the Film Board—too many to name them all—that I owe the largest debt of gratitude.

For the final revision of the book, Mr. Ross McLean, then Canadian Government Film Commissioner, gave me free access to all the Film Board's technical departments with their wealth of experience in documentary production. This was a courtesy which I cannot sufficiently acknowledge.

Among the members of the Board's staff, Mr. Gerald Graham, Director of Technical Operations, gave me valuable help in collecting this information, and the benefit of his technical experience in annotating the manuscript; Mr. Harry Randall offered most detailed suggestions on both the first and last drafts of the text, and I have gained much by incorporating very many of his ideas; Miss Margaret Ellis has allowed me to draw on an unpublished paper on negative cutting; and Mr. Norman McLaren, a pioneer in all branches of animation and in the development of synthetic sound, has made most fruitful suggestions in the chapter on animation, where the analysis of techniques is largely his.

M. Jean-Paul Ladouceur has proved himself much more than an illustrator—he has been a collaborator whose grasp of technical principles has often made it possible to replace an unwieldy page of text by a picture.

[ix]

There are many outside the Board to whom I am almost equally indebted. The original inspiration of this study I owe principally to Mr. J. A. Maurer, Engineering Vice-President of the Society of Motion Picture Engineers, 1947–1950, whose insistence on the highest technical standards has done so much to put the 16 mm. film on the same professional basis as 35 mm., thus immeasurably advancing the cause of the nontheatrical film of ideas.

I wish also to thank Mr. Roger Barlow for his patient instruction in the arts of the camera, and Professor Kenneth Macgowan, chairman of the Department of Theater Arts, University of California, Los Angeles, for adding to the text something of his own wide knowledge of the film as an art and a science. Mr. W. H. Offenhauer, Jr., has read and commented on an early draft of the book. Mr. David Brower, of the University of California Press, has combined the editing of a difficult manuscript with a keen insight into the practical problems of photography. Mr. Arthur Knight, formerly assistant curator of the Museum of Modern Art Film Library, has given me invaluable help in preparing the index of films. The booklist in turn owes much to the assistance of the Museum's librarian, as well as to Miss Margaret Cohen, librarian of the British Film Institute, London, and to my friend, Mr. Gene Fenn, of Paris.

Finally, I wish to add a more personal word of thanks to two friends, Guy Glover and Norman McLaren. Others have paid tribute to their contribution to the art of the film; I wish only to record their infinite patience in helping me to wrestle with the compression of so large a subject into the covers of a single book. For its many omissions and shortcomings, neither they nor any of the other helpers I have mentioned must be held responsible.

Since this is an introductory study to the science of film, it has not seemed necessary to weigh down the text with detailed references to the basic technical literature. References, in fact, are confined to sources which, because they are very old or very new, may not be familiar to the reader. Film examples have been chosen with a view to their easy availability in 16 mm. form. An index of films, with names and addresses of distributors, will be found at the end of the book.

RAYMOND SPOTTISWOODE

Contents

Introduction

Until very recently, professional film making was a closed occupation confined to the few writers and technicians who, in only a few score cities throughout the world, had learned skills which were as jealously guarded as the secrets of a medieval craft. Indeed, the atmosphere of a craft guild prevailed in every branch of film making. The new worker graduated through a long apprenticeship; he was narrowly specialized to a single task; and there were few who could command the financial resources needed for production and at the same time learn its technical skills.

In the citadels of Hollywood and London, little has changed today. The writer is still kept at a distance from the cutter, the cutter from the cameraman, the cameraman from the sound mixer. The barriers which divide them cannot be broken down until the organization both of capital and labor becomes more flexible. But outside these impenetrable walls, a new army of film makers has sprung up. Aided by the lighter weapon of the 16 mm. film, they are able to move to and fro with great ease and shoot where they will. Their arrows have found a mark not reached by the heavy cannonades of the theater film.

It was World War II, with its demand for training films, indoctrination films, morale films, and information films, that put an impossible strain on the old machinery for turning out film makers. But even before the war, the rise of the documentary film, with its imaginative projection of facts, had made this new medium accessible to large numbers of groups in society which were anxious to communicate and exchange ideas. Educators wanted to bring the world into the classroom. Scientists needed a tool of analysis which could enlarge the powers of the eye. Government was on the lookout for a way of explaining the new relationships in society which had made citizenship a more responsible charge on the individual. So, in a hundred different ways, film has come to be a means of communication to which ordinary people turn as naturally as to the pamphlet, the book, the poster, the newsletter, and the radio broadcast.

[1]

It is to train people in these manifold uses of film that many universities and technical schools have of recent years begun to give courses in cinematography. Lately these courses have been entered by thousands who have elbowed their way onto the bandwagon of television, knowing that, for all the stress which the new medium puts on the advantages of immediacy, it cannot dispense with the creative and manipulative faculties of film. Not all who have taken these courses intend to make movies or television a technical career. Many will reach executive or administrative positions, or will see in the motion picture a valuable aid in other fields of knowledge. But all must learn, as part of their training, a large number of new skills, manual as well as mental, which are more complicated than in most of the arts because the film is a meeting ground for many arts and sciences. Writing, scene design, stage direction, costuming, are paralleled by technical contributions from optics, electronics, organic and physical chemistry, many of which even today are scarcely out of the laboratory. Moreover, the film as a medium now has a large literature of its own. The student should make himself familiar with the techniques developed in many countries and over many years for conveying feelings and ideas through a medium very different from any of the earlier arts.

It would be impossible to compress so wide a field of knowledge within the covers of a single book. The aim of the present volume is much more limited. It is an attempt to get at the root of enough of the technical problems of film to start the newcomer well on his professional way. He will not go far, however, before he discovers that scale has a powerful bearing on the relative importance of the machinery of film production. If he has recently graduated from the ranks of the amateur, the movie camera will be in the forefront of his mind, and he will have only a hazy conception of the processing laboratory and the technique of sound recording. But if he is a worker in Hollywood or another major production center, processing and sound recording will be familiar operations. He will be more interested in new developments such as three-dimensional film or the relationship between the movies and television. Again, some limiting of the field will be necessary. The amateur is already well supplied with reference books, while the experienced professional has reached a vantage point where expert information from his own colleagues will suffice to start him along fresh lines of inquiry.

Little guidance, however, is available to the newer medium-size units of production: the government departments, the regional film services, the film units of the armed forces, the school and university groups which are at once mastering a new art and applying it to practical film making, the companies producing advertising and public-relations films—in short, the studios and production units devoted primarily to the making of informational and other types of fact film. It is to the learner in these fields of film production that the present study is chiefly directed. It therefore lays less stress on advanced studio techniques, and more on the practical problems likely to be encountered by the smaller production unit. These units are often in a state of expansion and change, so that the film maker's power to make his own way depends on his grasp of new techniques. He cannot count on established procedures, as can the worker in the big studio. He must often help to lay down these procedures, and that needs a firm grasp of fundamentals.

Though techniques and practices may differ according to the scale of production, underlying principles remain the same. Here this study has a more general application. It describes the successive stages through which all films must pass on their way from the script to the screen. It defines in simple terms most of the technical phrases which a person would meet if he were handling the financial or administrative affairs of a film-making organization, or were newly apprenticed to one of its production or technical departments. It also sets out to explain some of the practical hazards which are known by bitter experience to the professional film maker, but which often rise up unexpectedly to harass the newcomer to film.

In spite of the interlocking of technical and creative functions in all parts of the smaller production unit, some distinctions are necessary. Various departments of film making, such as processing and sound recording, have become highly specialized. Every film maker should know the elements of these techniques, but only the operators need to study their principles in detail. On the other hand, the technicalities of scripting and editing, of elementary camerawork, of lighting and exposure, of negative handling and animation, should be mastered by everyone who aspires to professionalism in film, unless he is content with the specialization of the bigger studios. Here, the new film maker will expect a more detailed treatment, and more practical guidance in the routines which experience has shown to be helpful.

Film making is an unusual blend of the mechanical and the creative. Those who encounter it for the first time—be they sponsors or students—are often discouraged by the long sequence of technical processes which rise to hamper and thwart the transference of their ideas to the screen. There is in this medium none of the satisfying directness of writing, painting, or composing. Film is refractory, and will only yield its satisfactions to those who accept and master its strict disciplines. Hence, while concentrating principally on the science of film, we may hope through this study to further a much more important aim—the use of film as a tool for communicating ideas.

I

Л_Л

Mapping the Route

THE TERRITORY which we shall have to traverse in this book is in many places rough and difficult. In the lowlands of film the reader must hack his way, machete in hand, through dense jungles of technical terms which rise on every side to block his progress. When he has at length climbed the foothills and reached the upper slopes of his subject, he may well find himself short of breath in the rarefied atmosphere of chemical, optical, and electronic theory. There he will discover that sensitometric curves shoot off at unexpected tangents, beams of light are whittled down to less than a thousandth of an inch in thickness, lens coatings are measured in fractions of an optical wavelength, while electrons buzz provocatively round his bewildered head.

Before setting off on such a journey, the reader may well ask for a map sufficiently small in scale to chart his route from one end to the other, from the start of a film to its presentation before its ultimate audience. Such a map, greatly simplified in detail, is provided by this preliminary chapter.

The type of film we shall be discussing goes by a number of general names, such as fact film, documentary film, or film of ideas; and many specialized names, such as publicity film, educational film, industrial film, scientific film, etc. All these films are characterized by their relatively short length, a primary audience outside the movie theaters, and a primary aim of informing, educating, or influencing people, rather than simply entertaining them. We shall refer to these films by the name that happens best to suit the context.

In the film of ideas, the germ of the idea is the initial starting point. Usually it will originate in the mind of someone who is not himself a professional film maker, but who feels that film, better than any other medium, will convey his purposes to the audience he wishes to reach. It may originate with an individual or a group: the board of directors of a company, a commanding officer in the army, a school principal, the public-relations officer in a govern-

[5]

ment department, a member of a university faculty. We will call this person or group of persons the Sponsor.

To carry out his ideas, the sponsor will summon a member of a film making company, who may be its president, its sales manager, a script writer, or anyone else actively engaged in its affairs. We will call this person the Producer.

Sponsor and producer therefore meet together to give this germ of an idea a first embodiment in film form. It may happen that the sponsor, in his enthusiasm for film, has chosen the wrong medium for presenting his ideas. Perhaps they would be more effectively conveyed in a pamphlet or a film strip, which is simply a set of lantern slides on film. If this is true, the producer will be wise, even if it is contrary to his immediate interest, to say so. Film is one of the most expensive of the media of communication. It seldom costs less than a thousand dollars a minute, and may run to two or three times that figure, even in a simple documentary film. Its distribution outside the theaters is at present difficult and slow.

However, if film is definitely decided on, the sponsor and producer will go along together. Their association, if continued no further than a single film, will last three to four months. During that time, all sorts of unexpected troubles may befall. The sponsor may dislike the script, and fail to reach agreement with the producer on it. The film may take much longer to produce than the contract allows. When it is finished, it may not meet the sponsor's expectations. It may even leave behind it a trail of legal action and unpleasantness which will take years to clear up. In this event the sponsor is likely to steer clear of films in the future.

On the other hand, the relations between sponsor and producer may grow increasingly cordial as the film goes along. Films are a meeting ground for many interests—dramatic, literary, musical, scientific—and the sponsor must indeed be dull if he does not take some pleasure in the progress of his film, provided always that he and the producer understand one another's problems. Indeed, one of the objects of this book is to explain to the sponsor some of the vexatious technical difficulties which the producer must surmount; for though it becomes the latter's legal responsibility to overcome them successfully and deliver the film, they are often so great that he is forced to ask for consideration and even assistance from the sponsor.

We shall have occasion to repeat again and again that film making, no matter how technical a process it is, is also much more than technical. It is an assemblage of very human abilities and frailties, so that, for instance, a single mistake by an assistant working in the dark depths of a developing laboratory may destroy the work of days of patient effort by members of the production team. Often no one can be blamed for the mistake. Film making, even in Hollywood, is a precarious balance of uncertainties.

Once, then, the idea for the film is agreed on, the sponsor is almost certain to ask what it will cost. Since short films have been made for as little as a hundred dollars and as much as several hundred thousand, it is obviously impossible to take an average. However, on the basis of his experience and what he knows of the sponsor's requirements, the producer should be able to quote on the spot a figure within 25 per cent of the correct one. He will afterwards, of course, have the picture accurately budgeted on the basis of the first script, and should then be within limits of 5 per cent above or below the actual cost. Very often the sponsor has a fixed ceiling, which he is willing to state, whereupon it only remains to tailor the film to a known figure. The interesting subject of film budgets and fiscal control is, however, outside the scope of this book, and we shall say no more of it.

Closely connected with the cost of a film is its length, and here the producer is on surer ground. Very few fact films are less than 10 minutes long, or more than 40 minutes. Those which are expected to reach the movie theaters tend more and more to be one-reelers (10 minutes), so that they can be wedged into a double-feature bill. The wholly *nontheatrical* [1] film tends to be of two- to three-reel length (20 to 30 minutes), since a 40- or 50-minute film is difficult to combine with others into a program which, because of the concentrated attention demanded by the documentary picture, should not exceed 75 or 80 minutes in total length.

Armed with a knowledge of the approximate cost and length of the proposed film, and some insight into the sponsor's intentions, the producer is ready to commission a first script or *outline* of the film. It is at this stage, or shortly afterwards, that the contract between producer and sponsor is usually signed. Normally, this contract provides for part payments to be made at carefully specified stages in the film's production. The stages most easily defined are: signature of contract; commencement of shooting; completion of a *rough cut;* completion of *fine cut;* delivery of the finished film and printing materials. It is not necessary, or indeed usual, to select all these points for making a payment; three or four payments are the general rule. The contract also contains nonperformance clauses, safeguards on copyright, and other protections for the sponsor. But his main security is the reputation of the producer he has chosen.

Next, the producer and sponsor meet to discuss the outline, and it is at this stage that a close meeting of minds is vitally important. If there is already a hidden divergence of opinion as to the scope or purpose of the film, it may widen as production goes ahead, only to be revealed when a great deal of money has been spent and it is too late to make any changes.

1 Technical terms are italicized throughout the book on their first appearance. If they are defined more fully on a later page, they are there italicized a second time. All terms so italicized are defined in the Glossary at the end of the book, either separately or within appropriate groupings: e.g., *step printer* will be found under *printer; overexposure* will be found under *exposure.*

Some basic principles of script writing are set out in chapter ii, which also discusses the styles of the film of ideas. Although the outline will be in simple story form, it may already reveal an approach which is peculiar to film, and this will develop increasingly as the script assumes its final shape (see, for instance, the excerpt given in figure 2-2, p. 16). The sponsor will naturally read the script very carefully in order to safeguard his investment in the production, but it is essential that he try to read it with an imaginative eye. The more original the film is to be, the more unconvincing the script may appear to the layman. It is difficult even for the film maker to equate written word and visual image; it is ten times more difficult for a sponsor who tends to pay exclusive attention to the narrative or commentary, which he supposes will carry the chief brunt of his ideas.

We have, for convenience, spoken of the sponsor as if he were a single person, but very often he is a multiple entity. There will be colleagues on the board of directors, or public relations experts, or seniors in the government hierarchy, or fellow committee members, to consult and satisfy. However necessary it is to seek the opinion of these persons, the sponsor should remember that good films cannot be made by committees. Film making is an art which can no more be practised by laymen than can writing a symphony, or playing championship tennis, or designing the Empire State Building. Because a film is compounded of words and photographs, with which everyone claims an intimate familiarity, the script on which it is based is often pawed over and spoiled by unskilled hands.

Many a potentially good film has been ruined, long before it was hatched out of a script, by the sponsor's obstinate insistence on an approach to his subject totally unsuited to the film medium. Examples are not difficult to cite, but an outstandingly bad film, which illustrates almost all the faults detailed in chapters ii and iii, is readily available in *The Bank Note Story*,[2] a film which should be screened for all sponsors who show an excessive liking for the spoken word. The unending stream of narrative in this film, full of words with much sound but little meaning, is paralleled by an unrelated series of images of the most melancholy monotony. Not a moment of suspense arrests the attention. No ripple of humor breaks the flat surface. The shots flow on without interest, without connection. Yet the film is technically by no means incompetent or amateurish. It may have started out in life with high hopes. But the dead hand of uninspiring sponsorship lay heavy on it at the end.

As the script is progressively tightened up and clothed in technical terms, the producer is concerned with a multitude of production problems. He may decide to shoot the film in the studio, which will often save time and money

[2] Source references to this and other films mentioned in the text will be found in the Index of Films at the end of the book.

over shooting in real places. On the other hand, studio construction, especially in a low-cost picture, frequently sacrifices the sense of reality which is the chief asset of the documentary film. This should be a matter of careful discussion between sponsor and producer. A number of studio techniques are discussed in chapter xii, among them methods of lighting, background projection, prescoring, playback, and dubbing.

The producer must also make up his mind whether to shoot in color or black and white, in standard theater 35 mm. film, or nontheatrical 16 mm. film. Thirty-five mm. film can be reduced to 16 mm. for ultimate release, but 16 mm. film cannot be satisfactorily enlarged to 35 mm. Hence a film which may secure theater release should be shot in 35 mm. However, 35 mm. color processes are not yet in general use by the smaller unit, because of their high raw-film and printing costs, and the long processing delays they entail. Color films are therefore usually shot in 16 mm. on either Kodachrome or Ansco Color. The special characteristics of color processes are discussed in the first part of chapter ix, and 16 mm. techniques in the second part of the same chapter. At the end of that chapter will be found a concise summary of the different gauges of film used in motion picture production.

After a number of consultations between sponsor and producer, the shooting script is ready for final agreement. Since this script will govern the direction, the editing, and the sound recording of the film, it is a detailed and often highly technical document. The division of the page into two vertical columns enables the visuals (the picture images) to be separated from the sound; while camera directions such as CU, LS, MS, and DOLLY (*close-up, long shot, mid shot,* and *traveling shot*) signal to the director what effects are intended. The shooting script is often mimeographed and passed around by the sponsor for criticism; but it would serve almost as little purpose to ask a layman to comment on a complicated will, the score of an opera, or a patent specification. The further the script proceeds, the less helpful is lay comment. It is at the beginning, in laying out the contents and terms of reference of the film, that the ideas of the sponsor and his associates are of utmost importance.

One of the determinants of the script will be the admissibility of dialogue, sometimes referred to in film parlance as sync dialogue or lip sync ("sync" is an abbreviation of synchronous or *synchronism*). It may seem strange that dialogue, which has been the merest commonplace in entertainment films for twenty years, should be regarded as anything peculiar or difficult. However, as will appear in chapters ii and iii, the equipment for sync sound shooting is expensive and burdensome compared to that used for silent shooting. However, the widespread use of magnetic tape recorders (discussed in the latter part of chapter x) promises to lighten and simplify the task of dialogue recording.

The producer is now ready to go ahead with his shooting, and proceeds to assemble a director, cameraman, and crew (end of chapter ii). The actual shooting, whether on *location* or in the studio, centers round the *camera,* which has not fundamentally changed since Edison made his first films in the "Black Maria" of 1895, but which has gained so enormously in refinement and detail that it has become an instrument of the highest precision. The camera, as it is adapted for field work, for the studio, and for combat, is described in detail in chapter iii, along with the principal accessories which make shooting more convenient, and the theory of the exposure meter.

During the period of shooting, the sponsor is often out of touch with the producer, unless he has been asked to provide facilities or supply a technical consultant to the unit. This is as it should be; the director is now in charge of the special processes of film. Some sponsors, however, send a kind of watchdog along on location, or station him in the studio, to oversee the unit in its carrying out of the approved script. From what has already been said, it is clear that this practice is highly undesirable. Hired crank turners are never good film makers.

Exposed film is rushed back from location or studio to be developed and printed in the *laboratory,* and it is then sent to the *cutting room* where it is put in script order and assembled on *reels.* The process of cutting (chapter iv) is highly important and creative. Film as a medium has its own laws and guiding rules, and the very same strips of celluloid can be edited into a tense and gripping film, or into a film which drags out its monotonous length. The sponsor has usually stipulated in the contract that he should see and agree to the *rough cut,* or first rough assemblage of his film. Here again, a good deal of mutual forbearance is called for. The screen appearance of the film will be indescribably rough. It will either have no sound, or a dialogue track which bumps in and out unexpectedly. There will be none of that smooth visual continuity which later results from the inclusion of *fades* and *dissolves;* some shots will be missing, replaced by opaque *leader* or titles which read "Missing scene." The attractive photography may be blemished by grease pencil marks and accidental *scratches* picked up in the cutting room. There will be no *main titles* or *animation* sequences.

In fact, the screening of a rough cut resembles in many ways the first fitting of a new suit at the tailor's. Lacking pockets, with the sleeves pinned to the coat, the trousers without cuffs, and chalk marks everywhere, the suit is not an attractive sight. However, the buyer who has risked a hundred dollars on a tailor's reputation is usually much less apprehensive than the sponsor who has ten to twenty thousand dollars invested in his new film. Suit and film have other points of resemblance. While the suit can be shortened or lengthened, taken in a little and generally made to fit, it cannot be turned into an overcoat or a tuxedo. The sponsor who suddenly discovers (as many do) that the film is totally different from what he wanted, is similarly out of luck. He can,

however, suggest minor alterations; one sequence may be increased in emphasis, another toned down; shots which now for the first time seem desirable can
be added; objectionable shots may be removed; and the commentary still
remains to be written. A discussion follows the screening. The sponsor usually
feels some disappointment mixed with his elation, but the producer assures
him that the film will present a much more attractive appearance at its next
or *fine cut* stage.

Various other streams of material are now converging on the cutting room.
The *stock shot* library (equivalent of the newspaper morgue) supplies footage
on historical events and remote geographical areas. Its work is described in
chapter v. To give added interest to the film, and to explain some abstract or
complex process, it is common practice to include one or more animation
sequences. Though the commonest animated films are the cartoons seen in
theaters, the animation in documentary pictures is usually produced by
methods which are much simpler, though just as effective. These are dealt
with in the first part of chapter vi. It must not be supposed that either the
stock shots or animation sequences are afterthoughts. Their roots go back to
the script itself, and both film researcher and animation artist may prove
themselves creative workers of first importance.

During all these processes, film has been passing through the laboratory,
which *develops, prints,* and *duplicates* it. Since film is the basic stuff of film
making, the laboratory, which alone works on the actual film image, can
make or destroy the picture. Yet many film makers have only the haziest idea
of what goes on in its dark depths. If interested enough to investigate, they
are hampered by the cramped quarters which the laboratory usually occupies,
by the difficulty in seeing what is going on, and by the confusing combination
of chemical and physical processes. Chapter viii therefore deals rather extensively with laboratory techniques, explaining how the outside world is
satisfactorily reproduced in photographic tones, and how the development
and printing of millions of feet of film is held to close standards of accuracy.

When the film has undergone further pruning, compression, and rebal-
ancing, the sponsor is once again summoned back to see it as a fine cut. To
the producer it will seem a different picture, so much improvement has it
undergone in passing from a rough cut to a fine; but the less practiced eye of
the sponsor may notice little change. True, library footage and animation
sequences will now be included, and the continuity will seem rather better.
But all the roughnesses mentioned earlier will remain.

Impatient at the long time taken to finish his picture, the sponsor may now
show a strong desire to present it to his colleagues and friends. He should be
firmly discouraged. He might as soon appear in his club in the chalked and
pinned-up suit, and expect to receive praise for his good taste in clothes. None
the less, minor changes in the visuals may still be made, and there is always

the commentary or narrative to reinforce points insufficiently emphasized by the picture.

Though a detailed commentary will have been written for the shooting script, it will almost always require extensive revision or complete rewriting when the fine cut has been approved. This is because the director will have brought back sequences which do not exactly correspond to the script. Some scenes may have had to be omitted as unpractical, new ones will have taken their place. Stock shots will not accord exactly with expectations. In the cutting room, rhythm and thus length will have altered. The commentary is therefore pulled to pieces, reëxamined, and built into a new shape.

Here the sponsor often sees his opportunity to put back what he feels has been omitted from his original framework of ideas. The contract usually assures him a final veto over what goes into the commentary, which corresponds to his control of the shooting script. If he makes use of this power, he should exercise the utmost restraint. More documentary films have been spoilt by an overloaded commentary than by any other single fault. *The Bank Note Story,* already quoted, bears witness to the unhappy consequences. Film is a highly condensed medium. It strikes into the audience's mind by two channels, the eye and ear. The picture, as now represented by the fine-cut *workprint,* is itself in all probability a miracle of compression. The average length of the *shots* may be only ten seconds, so that the eye is constantly being charged with new impressions. Now the ear is to be bombarded with an equal variety of information projected from the sound track. This is more than the mind can stand. It rebels. It closes down those twin entrances, the eyes and ears. The audience's attention has gone. The film is addressing an audience of dummies.

The moral is simple. If the producer is a good one, as we have been tacitly assuming all along, he will know how much narrative the film will stand. If he wishes a whole sequence to go by without a single spoken word, to the accompaniment of sound effects or music, it is because he knows that the audience must be relaxed after digesting a difficult complex of ideas. Silence is as important a constituent of a film as sound itself.

While the narrative is being written, the negative of the film (or *original,* if it is in color) must be matched to the workprint which has resulted from the cutting process. This matching, and the preparation for it, is the subject of chapter vii. At the same time, the *optical effects* (fades, dissolves, etc.) are got ready, shot in a special *optical printer,* and finally inserted in the film (second part of chapter vi).

By this time (preferably much earlier), the composer for the film's original score will have been selected, and will have screened and studied the film with the director and producer to insure the utmost understanding of what it is that his score can contribute. If, on the other hand, the musical accompaniment is to be pieced together from library sources, it will become the sound cutter's responsibility.

The cutter will now be engaged in preparing the various sound tracks for the film, of which there are likely to be between three and eight. The sync dialogue (if any) will account for one of these, the commentary a second, the music a third, and the remainder will carry sound effects. This power of film to separate the world of sound into its elements is one of its greatest creative assets. To each kind of sound is allotted a separate *sound track*, the name for the thin ribbon of *emulsion* (or magnetic material) which carries the sound *modulations*, and is itself part of a band of film exactly like that bearing the picture image. This process of cutting and synthesizing a new world of sound is described in chapter xi, and chapter x examines the nature of sound and the methods of recording it on film.

When the tracks have been prepared, they must be *re-recorded*, or mixed together in the proper proportions and transferred to a single and ultimate sound track. Since this is the last creative process through which the film is to pass, the sponsor sometimes again avails himself of his right of supervision. The earlier warnings apply in full force. The first run through of the film and its sound tracks results in a babel of sound, perplexing and often downright painful to the ear. The *mixer* must get to know the film; under the skilled guidance of the editor he must explore what is on each sound track, fading up now one and now another to hear how it sounds, much as an expert chef will dip his ladle into one after another of a row of steaming saucepans to savor the contents.

The film and its sound tracks are rehearsed several times before the mixer is ready for a *take*. Two or three hours of hard work may be spent on re-recording ten minutes of film. But film making is too complicated a process to hustle. A dozen things may yet go wrong. The expert is patient; it is the novice who becomes more and more impatient, and cannot understand why so much time is spent on so apparently simple a process.

Now at last the film is ready to be finally printed and projected (chapter xiii). Producer and sponsor sit down together for its first screening. All is tension and uncertainty. Does it justify the high hopes which were set on it? Will it stir its audiences, hold their attention, make them think and act? Those who are present at this screening seldom know. They are too close to the film, they have lived with it too long. It must go out into the market place to be seen and discussed, to meet the people for whom it was made, who are not merchants of ideas but plain ordinary folk. Theirs is the final judgment.

Thus, after a brief glimpse at the technical future of film (chapter xiv), we reach the end. And now we must return to the beginning.

II

How a Film Starts

ONCE IT HAS ceased to be merely an idea, the plot or plan of a film is almost always embodied in a script. This term, however, covers a great variety of forms and stages. Each script, for instance, starting with an idea, becomes in turn a *synopsis,* a *treatment,* and a *shooting script,* according to the degree of its development. At each stage it will differ as well according to the purpose to which it is to be put. A feature film, for instance, is built according to the common rules of continuity which have prevailed on the stage for more than 2,000 years. Dialogue tends to dominate action, and the script therefore details the dialogue with only cursory reference to what the camera sees and how it moves. Figure 2-1 indicates this resemblance between stage and film script. The documentary film—or, more generally, the film of ideas—is not straitjacketed by those Aristotelian unities which keep their ancient grip on Hollywood. It moves in a freer world of allusion and juxtaposition, creating its own framework of time and space. This is exemplified by the page of script shown in figure 2-2, taken from a film in which the camera and the narrator are identified as one, the two together interrogating a series of characters who address the lens directly, whether speaking to the narrator or to one another. A third type of film script is represented in figure 2-3, in which the narrative is spoken by a single voice and represents an editorial comment on the accompanying visual scenes.

Whatever form it takes, the script of a fact film must be solidly based on research. An entire book may have to be combed to yield its essence in a single line of commentary or dialogue. An odd fact culled from a foreign radio broadcast or an eighteenth-century manuscript may prove to be the linchpin of an entire sequence. Thus the scripting process may seem akin to the research job a writer might do in preparing an article for a specialized journal or a radio program. Yet when the work of research is done, the script still has far to go.

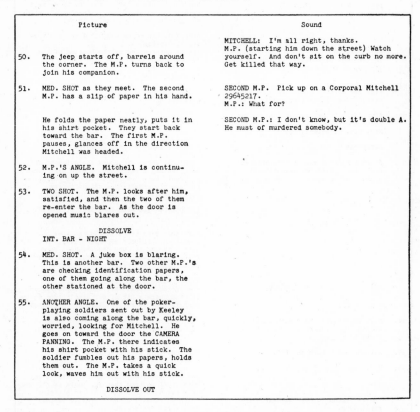

Picture	Sound
	MITCHELL: I'm all right, thanks. M.P. (starting him down the street) Watch yourself. And don't sit on the curb no more. Get killed that way.
50. The jeep starts off, barrels around the corner. The M.P. turns back to join his companion.	
51. MED. SHOT as they meet. The second M.P. has a slip of paper in his hand.	SECOND M.P. Pick up on a Corporal Mitchell 29645217. M.P.: What for?
He folds the paper neatly, puts it in his shirt pocket. They start back toward the bar. The first M.P. pauses, glances off in the direction Mitchell was headed.	SECOND M.P.: I don't know, but it's double A. He must of murdered somebody.
52. M.P.'S ANGLE. Mitchell is continu- ing on up the street.	
53. TWO SHOT. The M.P. looks after him, satisfied, and then the two of them re-enter the bar. As the door is opened music blares out.	
DISSOLVE INT. BAR - NIGHT	
54. MED. SHOT. A juke box is blaring. This is another bar. Two other M.P.'s are checking identification papers, one of them going along the bar, the other stationed at the door.	
55. ANOTHER ANGLE. One of the poker- playing soldiers sent out by Keeley is also coming along the bar, quickly, worried, looking for Mitchell. He goes on toward the door the CAMERA PANNING. The M.P. there indicates his shirt pocket with his stick. The soldier fumbles out his papers, holds them out. The M.P. takes a quick look, waves him out with his stick.	
DISSOLVE OUT	

Fig. 2-1. Excerpt from a typical Hollywood film script. Note the resemblance to a play script. (From the script of Crossfire, screenplay by John Paxton, based on the novel, The Brick Foxhole, by Richard Brooks. Copyright, RKO Pictures, Inc.)

Film has at its command all the resources of sound, but is first and foremost a visual medium. Consequently, a script should never be a mere literary construction of words, with a list of shots added as an afterthought. Figure 2-4 shows a small section of two scripts which convey an identical idea by contrasting methods. The first excerpt is written in the style of an editorial or a textbook. Its leading ideas are all in verbal form, the shots which accompany them being merely a nondescript assemblage of visual counterparts to the commentary, which in turn is abstract and difficult for the listener to grasp. "Early decades," "principles of democratic society," "a competitive economy," "stability," "security"—these are words which the film is poorly suited to convey. It speeds along at an unvarying pace, and the moviegoer, unlike the reader of a book or newspaper, cannot go back and run over a difficult passage

89.	M.S. Passenger finishing his meal and polishing his glasses.	PASSENGER: If these people haven't got dollars to pay us with, why should we send good American stuff our of the country without getting anything useful in return?
		NARRATOR: Anything useful? I've been trying to explain..... (He is interrupted by the hooting of the locomotive)
	SWISH PAN TO	
90.	The freight locomotive. Camera dollies up as Engineer beckons.	ENGINEER: You can't convince that guy by talking to him.
91.	L.S. Large piece of equipment on flat car covered with tarpaulin and marked "Made in Switzerland".	Why don't you find out where that shipment's going And hurry up! We're not going to be here all night.
92.	C.U. "Made in Switzerland" sign. Pan to second shot marked "to: Midwest Mfg. Co., Cleveland, Ohio."	
	SWISH PAN TO	Sound of rapidly passing train.
93.	Door of Midwest executive's office. Door opens revealing executive at desk. Camera moves in toward desk.	NARRATOR: Whew! That was the quickest trip to Cleveland I ever made. (Pause and change of tone) Hope you don't mind the intrusion, but are you expecting a shipment from Switzerland?
		EXECUTIVE: You mean it's here?...Where?... When?...
		NARRATOR: Take it easy, old man - we only saw it on a flatcar 800 miles away. But what's the deal? Why did you have to get it from Switzerland? Don't we make every kind of machine right here in Cleveland?
		EXECUTIVE: No, I'm afraid not, nor even in the United States. Not many people realize it, but quite a bit of our specialized equipment is made in Europe. Some of our largest - like that monster you saw on the flatcar -
94.	C.U. Executive's hand with chain draped over fingernail coming into shot.	and some of our smallest. Now these chains - You won't find "Made In America" on them.
95.	Extreme C.U. Chain on nail.	The ones this size come from abroad.
96.	M.S. Executive at desk smiling.	Ha-ha-ha. You look surprised - why, I bet you your ten year old son could list a lot more stuff we need than you could at his age - both raw materials and finished articles invented since you and I went to school.
	Camera begins to move backwards towards door.	Hey, where are you going?
		NARRATOR: To settle accounts with our friend in the dining car.
	SWISH PAN TO	
97.	M.S. Dining car. Waiter approaches. Passenger's table with coffee pot. Waiter nods and removes coffee pot.	Remove that coffee! It's from Brazil and the gentleman doesn't approve of foreign products....
98.	C.U. Passenger, cigar in hand. Cigar vanishes, and Passenger looks amazed. Necktie vanishes. Passenger looks at wrist.	And that cigar, sir - it was made in Havana. Surely you aren't going to smoke that! (Musical ping) What's this? A silk necktie? Away with it! (Musical ping) Are you aware that the works in that handsome watch on your wrist came from (slight pause).........
99.	C.U. Watch on wrist. Watch vanishes.	Switzerland? (Musical ping)
100.	C.U. Passenger's jacket which is drawn back to reveal lining.	And your suit, sir - I understand your embarrassment - (pause).....................
101.	Extreme C.U. Label in lining. "Made in Great Britain".	... but off with it! (Musical effect)

Fig. 2-2. Excerpt from an argumentative film script. Note the nonillusionistic use of the camera and the screen world. (From the script of Round Trip, sponsored by The Twentieth Century Fund and produced by The World Today, Inc.)

Picture	Sound

1. Pan along Greek mountain coastline to city.
2. Girl walks through Greek garden gate.
3. Handing tiles up ladder to roof.
4. MCU Old man handling clay.
 	
5. Greek woman spinning.
6. MCU man nails timber to roof.
7. CU woman spinning.
8. Down shot - men place tiles on roof.
9. CU men placing tiles on roof.
10. MS men place timbers on roof.
11. MLS men laying bricks on foundation.
 	
Screen time: 47 seconds.
	Narrator: Beyond the oceans - along the shorelines of the Old World - a day of hope is slowly dawning.
	   All through these battered lands, men's hearts are lighter than they were: hands are once more busy.
	   (Music swells, then fades under voice.)
	   In East and West - in Europe and in Asia - the broken threads of life are being joined again.
	   (Music swells, then fades under voice.)
	   Everywhere, the long tasks of patching the old, building the new, are bravely under way.
	   (Music swells again.)

Fig. 2-3. Excerpt from a narrative film script. The careful continuity of the visuals, and the echos between commentary and picture, serve to weld the two into a truly filmic relationship. (From the script of Lifeline, sponsored by UNRRA and produced by The World Today, Inc. Production: Stuart Legg.)

Picture	Sound

19th century engraving showing early textile factory.
 	
Scenes from the depression: bread-lines, locked gates, long lines of job applicants, etc.
 	
Picket lines, police breaking up strike meeting.
Pile of legislative papers on table in different languages.
 	
Approximate screen time: 45 secs.
	Narrator: Since the early decades of the last century, the growing tendency to industrialization put into practice in ever-increasing degree the principles of a competitive economy first enunciated by the Physiocrats and Adam Smith.
	   But as the years passed, the instability of such an economy also began to manifest itself. Granted freedom to choose his employment - one of the basic principles of a democratic society, - the worker found that much of the time there was no employment to choose. He had bartered security for freedom; and, risking his freedom, he now sought to regain security through the strife and factionalism of labor disputes.
	   Many governments capitulated to the workers' demands, and began to enact labor legislation which was more or less socialistic according...............

Fig. 2-4a. Excerpt from a verbalistic film script. Lack of "vertical" visual relationship combines with verbal abstraction to produce a nonfilmic and ineffective sequence. Points to Note: (a) The thin and inadequate visuals. (b) The lack of "vertical" connection between visuals, leading to sequential weakness. (c) The number of abstract terms in the commentary. (d) The use of antitheses, symmetrical clause construction, and other rhetorical devices which have no visual counterpart or significance. (e) This type of commentary gives rise very easily to semantic confusions: e.g., rhetorical antithesis between "freedom" and "security" implies their incompatibility in society; "socialistic" has the same meaning as "socialist" but adds pejorative overtones.

[17]

Picture	Sound
62. Pan across roofs of factory district. There are many chimneys but no smoke or other sign of activity. DISSOLVE TO	Narrator: The furnaces had gone out. The streets were silent. The hum of life had died down. Music, with perhaps a wordless choir, carries the sense of desolation and hopelessness, then dies out.
63. Pan down factory building to deserted street. At a corner, a small crowd has gathered and is being harangued by a labor leader.	A distant sound of voices. On the cut, the tumult builds suddenly into an angry roar, from which one masterful voice stands out.
64. M.S. the strike meeting. Bill [an unemployed worker introduced in previous sequences] strolls up, hands in pocket, and listens.	
65. C.U. labor leader speaking.	Labor leader:.....There must be no concessions, no giving way before half-measures. The employers need us more than we need them. If they try to throw the blame on us for the lack of coal, the shortage of steel, we have an answer.
66. M.S. Bill, hands still in pockets. As he drifts away from the meeting, the camera dollies with him, picking up the quizzical look in his face. Whether he agrees with the speaker – or condemns him for his threat of violence, - the camera does not reveal.	He is greeted by a roar of applause from the crowd. The voices die down gradually, and the music takes up. It mingles the marching sounds of the procession (see Shot 67) and the exultation of the workers with a feeling of the conflict in Bill's mind.
67. Reverse shot down the street. Far in the distance (Bill still in fgd.) a workers' procession with banners moves along a cross street and disappears. DISSOLVE TO	Music continues.
68. M.S. Bill, deep in thought, has wandered into a park. He sits down at the base of a stone structure which rises out of sight. The camera pans up from the seated figure to reveal the base of a statue and then the statue itself. It is that of a great reformer (Lincoln, no doubt, if only for recognizability), who seems to be looking down on the puzzled figure below with compassion and not a little humor. The camera continues to pan up, eventually coming to rest on the sky. DISSOLVE TO	The music quietens, and the sound of voices can be heard again, though very far away.
69. Still shot of sky (must closely match end of previous shot). Pan slowly down onto dome of Capitol in Washington, then to rest of building. Hold for 20 ft., then DISSOLVE TO	The distant clamorous voices now mix into a more ordered and disciplined buzz, which in turn is silenced by the sharp stroke of a gavel. A voice, resonant and authoritative, begins to recite: Voice: Resolved by the Senate and House of Representatives of the United States of America in Congress assembled..... (complete with opening text of Social Security legislation.)
70. Interior.........	

Approximate screen time: 1 min. 40 secs.

Fig. 2-4b. Excerpt from a well-visualized film script. Tight visual connections and a sparing commentary help to impart conviction. Points to note: (a) Visuals have plenty of life and vitality, granted adequate direction. (b) Greatly improved visual continuity. (c) Commentary held to a minimum, and sentences kept short and simple. (But note that any concepts not conveyed by implication are lost altogether. E.g., if shot 62 has been cleverly contrived—perhaps by some architectural emphasis, or an early date on a factory pediment—it will bring the spectator's mind back to the Industrial Revolution and its social consequences. But if these ideas are missed, there is no way of driving them home and setting them in the general argument, as in the script of fig. 2-4a. (d) Technical again. Furthermore, the eye is more receptive and retentive than the ear, and it is folly to throw away the visual advantages of film by subordinating the picture to the sound. The ear is easily wearied by a monotonous, sermonizing speech. A film based on the first script would weary its audience to distraction long before it had run out its course.

The second script, by comparison, is simple, concrete, and above all, visual. It keeps interest alive by the continuity of a story, and by supplementing commentary with dialogue, random voices, natural sound, and music, all these elements being balanced against one another like the instruments of an orchestra.

In short, a script should not be the translation of a word concept into a visual concept. It should be the record of a visual concept in words which are then translated back again into visual impressions by the director and his camera.

These principles, obvious enough when stated, are equally essential to the making of a good entertainment film and a good factual film—but they are often ignored in the making of fact films, because of the intractability of the subject matter. It is hard to render "economic equilibrium" or "regional self-government" or "civic responsibility" into visual terms. Yet there is no substitute for the hard process of thinking all these things through into concrete visual images. The raw material of film is the stuff of the outside world, the world of green things, of land and sea, of human beings and the places where they work and live. It is not the mental world of concepts and beliefs. But because these are the mainsprings of human action, the film maker must search for the physical things and events in which this inner world manifests itself— the casual words which reveal motive, the symbols of achievement or defeat, the buildings or aspects of nature which have taken on a human significance.

---

devices: (1) the violent sound cut between shots 64 and 65 to heighten the impression of anger, compared to the slow dying away of the same sound over shot 66, as Bill walks puzzled away; (2) use of camera panning to reveal ideas successively (shot 68); (3) use of similar sounds (but with different emotional overtones) used as the sound transition between shots 68 and 69, coupled with a similar visual transition using the neutral sky as a bridge between two completely different locales. (e) While the script guides the director to the effect that is wanted, it does not limit him unduly. (E.g., shot 63 might be most effective if the camera were about 40 feet above street level, so that it could start by looking up at the smokeless chimneys and end by looking down on the workers' meeting. But this might be physically impossible to accomplish on location, and the director's hands must not be tied.)

The outer world is everywhere stamped with the mark of what is going on within. It is the task of imagination to see these hidden signs, select them, record them in words, and shape them to the peculiarities of the camera and microphone. This is the basis of good script writing.

When the writer turns his attention to sound, he is faced with the widest possible gamut of choice. Speech includes dialogue, free or nonsynchronized voice, and choral effects; the whole world of music and natural sound is at his disposal, including notes which no musical instrument can play but which can be handwritten on the sound track, and sounds which have been artificially accelerated, retarded, or reversed. Again we find that the feature film, obeying for the most part the continuity of the stage, makes scant use of the manifold possibilities of film. Therefore the script writer need detail little else but the dialogue, with only rare and incidental reference to other sound elements. But the writer of scripts for the film of ideas has wider responsibilities, stemming from his much greater available choice of styles. He is wise if he plans and provides for as much of the varied sound track as possible right from the beginning of the film—even though much alteration will be needed as the film develops. Since, in these more complicated types of film, sound and picture are interdependent, it is dangerous to assume that any important component can be added as an afterthought. This is like writing a play without regard to the sets, or a piece of music with no thought of the orchestra which is to play it.

Wherever dialogue or complex sound predominates, the script writer in preparing his shooting script should thus define every single shot in terms of visuals and sound. This helps him to visualize concretely the final outcome of the film, and it also helps the director, whose responsibility it is to realize the script in speech and action.

While dramatic films should be planned to make the fullest use of the resources of film, instructional films often call for a simplification of the sound track because their themes must be stated in direct and simple terms. The limiting case is the use of commentary alone, but the writer should beware of the pitfalls exemplified in figure 2-4a, where the shots accompanying the commentary have no "vertical" relationship, or visual connection with one another.

These, then, are some of the basic requirements of all script writing for the film of ideas. Remember that film is a visual medium. No matter how abstract the subject matter, it must be manifested and made concrete before it is put on film. The research on which this visualization is based must be comprehensive, detailed, and exact. Sound and music must be regarded as an integral part of film, not as an appendage or an afterthought to make the film run more smoothly.

CATEGORIES OF STYLE IN THE FILM OF IDEAS

Granted that all these necessities have been taken care of, the script writer for the fact film has yet a wide enough choice before him. Here it is only possible to sketch some of the styles of presentation he may adopt, with their range of usefulness and limitations. It must be remembered that practical examples of films will seldom fall exclusively into a single style. Animation sequences, for instance, are inserted in realistic films; short dialogue passages occur in narrated pictures; lyrical and descriptive sequences are alternated. This classification is therefore somewhat abstract and unrealistic, but it serves to draw attention to the components of style which the film maker can ill afford to ignore. Starting at the naturalistic end of the scale, we have:

1. The classical documentary film.—The film in which observation outruns interpretation is commonly considered the "purest" style of documentary.[1] At its best, this results in a blunt, convincing style of film, usually accompanied by realistic dialogue and sound effects, which has been most highly perfected in England.[2] The long series of United States State Department films, beginning with *The American Scene,* is an attempt to achieve the same end without the use of dialogue, which was precluded because of the need of translating these films into many different languages. However, the substitution of narrative for dialogue removes much of the sense of actuality, while retaining the rather drab literalness which is the chief defect of the pure documentary film.

2. The eyewitness film (Le film témoin).—Because of the limitations of "pure" documentary, more dramatic styles have been evolved, which have culminated in a kind of film developed by the Italian school of directors. These eyewitness films penetrate reality by means of a shrewd and ironical insight, which is yet based on a very exact observation of everyday things. The camerawork tends to be plain, not to say drab, with a sense of randomness, almost of accident. The true atmosphere of the out-of-doors registers

1 While credit for the development and social exploitation of the documentary film is justly given to John Grierson and his followers in England (1929-   ), it should be remembered that they were by no means the originators of the documentary philosophy. This honor belongs to those early pioneers, the brothers Lumière, who broke away from the artificialities of Edison's first films to establish a realistic style of film making. Such phrases as *ils ont pris la nature sur le vif* and *la nature prise sur le fait* were already current in film criticism in 1895, and were summed up in the instruction given to Lumière's cameramen, "*Ouvrez vos objectifs sur le monde.*" The films which these men brought back from distant parts of the world were the forerunners of the modern documentary, not of the newsreel. See Georges Sadoul, *Histoire générale du cinéma,* Paris, 1946. Vol. I, pt. 2, chaps. 2–6.

2 Examples are: *Housing Problems,* Elton, 1935; *Cumberland Story,* Jennings, 1947; *Children Learning by Experience,* Thomson, 1947.

itself on the film, which is thus redeemed from the glassy monotony of the studios. The characters seem to have been caught off guard; they behave instead of acting; their speech will occasionally stumble and repeat itself as in real life. Yet with all this there is an impalpable quality which springs from the personality of the director himself.[3]

3. The lyrical documentary film.—Many film makers who have wished to eschew dialogue for reasons of artistic purpose or technical disability, moved away from naturalism toward symbolism or a more interpretative realism. In able hands, this has unlocked many of the most interesting secrets of the cinema.[4] The danger of this lyrical style lies in vagueness and rhapsody. Unless the imagery is vivid, the rhythms strong and at the same time supple, the sound rich and evocative, nothing issues but rhetoric, for which the *avant-garde* has already got a bad name. It is of course much easier to sustain a sequence in a lyrical vein than a whole film, and there are few pictures which do not attempt at least one passage into the poetry of film.[5]

4. The editorial film.—A long step away from naturalism, both in presentation and content, is taken by the editorial film, which divorces strips of celluloid from their context in the real world, and juxtaposes them according to the ideas in the producer's head, exactly as if they were verbal concepts.[6] The danger of this style of film making is that it tends toward a mere illustrated lecture, the visuals simply describing what the narrator is saying, without vertical connection between them, as discussed above. However, the more skillful film makers relieve the monotony of editorializing by giving the visuals a scope and sweep of their own, and by alternating narration with dialogue and with short lyrical passages in which music is used to sustain the mood of the film.

Most educational films are in an editorial style, adapted to a purely expository purpose. Here the chief object is clarity, and other kinds of effect (valuable in films for adults) must often be sacrificed so that the rate at which knowledge is imparted is slowed down to the rate at which children can absorb it. The concentration of the film medium is so remarkable that those who make films (and even more, those who pay for them) often try to squeeze the maximum amount of information into the minimum of screen time. This

[3] Examples are: *Open City, Paisan,* and *Germany—Year Zero,* Roberto Rossellini; *Tragic Hunt (Caccia Tragica),* de Santis, 1947; *The Illegals,* Meyer Levin, 1948; *The Quiet One,* Myers, 1948.

[4] Examples are: *Song of Ceylon,* Wright, 1935; *Night Mail,* Wright & Grierson, 1936; *The Plow That Broke The Plains,* Lorentz, 1936; *Man of Aran,* Flaherty, 1934; *The River,* Lorentz, 1937; *Louisiana Story,* Flaherty, 1948.

[5] Interesting examples, because they occur in an instruction film, are to be found in the admirable *Your Children's Sleep,* Brian Smith, 1948.

[6] Examples are: *The March of Time,* 1934–　　; *This Modern Age,* 1942–　　; *This Is America,* 1941–　　; *World in Action,* 1940–45.

tendency, always regrettable, has come in for vigorous criticism from school-teachers, especially in the lower grades.[7]

5. *The argumentative film.*—So far, although in lessening degree, the film styles we have discussed have kept up a certain continuity of actuality. This may be expressed, in a variant of Lumière's phrase, by saying that "they open a window on the world." In the argumentative film, however, this illusion of observing reality is deliberately destroyed, and the screen becomes a consciously used device for interesting and amusing the audience. The technique was brilliantly employed by Olsen and Johnson in the movie version of *Hellzapoppin* (1942), and a more serious application is illustrated in figure 2-2. Here the camera is a participant in the action, and by means of *swish pans, push-over wipes* and other technical devices, the characters confront one another through the medium of the screen, beckon to the camera or wave it away, and in general play fast and loose with space, time, and the medium itself. Credit for the invention and development of this promising technique belongs almost exclusively to Paul Rotha, the well-known English producer and writer.[8]

6. *Cartoon and animation films.*—The cartoon film occupies a rather ambiguous position on our arbitrary scale, since, although it forms the first clear break with the world of actuality, it can enforce a credibility of its own. Thus a film of Walt Disney may be more naturalistic than a film of Paul Rotha. Again, small children do not distinguish in their minds between animated films and films of real life. Nevertheless, the powers of animation to simplify and stylize the portrayal of reality entitle it to a separate section. Every script writer knows the moment when his subject matter becomes so dense or abstract that to portray it in terms of actuality is either impossible or absurd. The answer is animation, and the writer is usually ready to accept all the succor it can give. For if actuality is the arithmetic of film, animation is its algebra, concealing individual differences under a uniform and generalized formula. The early films of Philip Ragan show to what lengths this can be carried. Seldom have economic principles been so brilliantly schematized; but seldom has the screen been put to so lifeless and impersonal a use.[9] Animation excels in materializing (*a*) the impossible, (*b*) the invisible, (*c*) the abstract,

[7] The best examples of the Canadian *World in Action* series demonstrate the extraordinary powers of condensation latent in the film medium. By the use of shots which seldom last more than two or three seconds, and by ingenious counterpoint of sound, some of these 20-minute films have been so charged with information and opinion that the audience can remember scarcely a single clear idea when the performance is over.

[8] Rotha's best known films are: *World of Plenty*, 1943; *Land of Promise*, 1945; *The World Is Rich*, 1947. There appear to be no full-fledged American examples of this technique except the author's *Round Trip*, 1947.

[9] The later Ragan films (e.g., *Stuff for Stuff*, 1948) show a much more human and interesting approach.

(d) the secret, (e) the ludicrous, (f) the fantastic and grotesque. It is a good servant but a bad master.

7. *Avant-garde and abstract films.*—The *avant-garde* is not strictly a style, for it is simply that which is ahead of current styles. Many of the innovations of the French *avant-garde* period (1927–1931) have passed into common film usage, even in conservative film places like Hollywood—just as the mural designs of the Bauhaus may now be seen in the tearooms of the Bronx. None the less, experimental film techniques have as much to offer the film maker today as ever before, for film is an infinitely various art form, which in fifty years has only begun to develop the main outlines of style. Among films thus ahead of the times are those of Jean Vigo [10] (produced nearly twenty years ago, but pointing to still undeveloped expansions of the cinema's powers); of Norman McLaren, whose multitude of styles has included hand-drawn films (made without a camera), complex superimposition, the metamorphosis of painting, stereoscopic films, and synthetic sound and music; [11] of the Whitney brothers, who are also trying to find new combinations of cameraless visuals and unplayed sounds; [12] of Philip Stapp, an artist turned film maker who is exploring the animation of the unanimated and the close relationship between color, sound, and image.[13] These are all lone, almost solitary, workers who know that though the accepted roads in film must be trodden by many people together, coöperating to a single end, there are still narrow paths which only the untrammeled artist can hack out. The most mechanical of the arts interposes the most obstacles between the artist and his aim—between the vision seen and the image bodied forth. The lone animator and experimentalist, like the director-cameraman, tries to compass all the stages of film making at a single bound. He works slowly, and what he produces may be hard to grasp, but he is moving toward a liberation of the cinema as fundamental as the change which overtook Western painting with the discovery of the laws of perspective.

Scripting of the kinds of film we have just outlined involves an intense effort of visualization. It is the worst films which are the easiest to script, simply because they imitate established arts and techniques of presentation. Many films which purport to be films of ideas are in reality no more than radio or stage plays, or travelogues, or simply platform lectures illustrated by lantern slides. Naturally, script writing is not wholly *sui generis*. It demands a penetration of character, a quick and lively ear for dialogue, a knowledge of situation and command of suspense, which are common to other dramatic

[10] See *Apropos de Nice, Zero de Conduite,* and *L'Atalante.* Vigo died in poverty in 1934 at the age of 29.

[11] See *Love on the Wing,* 1938; *C'est l'aviron,* 1944; *Little Phantasy,* 1947; *Fiddle-de-Dee,* 1947; *Chalk River Ballet,* 1949; *Begone Dull Care,* 1949.

[12] See *Opus 1–Opus 8.*

[13] See *Boundary Lines,* 1947; *Picture in your Mind,* 1949.

arts. If we have here chiefly emphasized the peculiarities of film, it is because they are so frequently forgotten.

WHERE THE FILM COMES FROM

When scripting is finished, there are three sources for the material needed to give it tangible form as a movie (figure 2-5). In the earliest stages of writing, it should be decided what use to make of new material shot for the picture, of animation (something created out of nothing), and of existing (stock) footage by recourse to the film library. All these sources are important and require treatment in turn. Unless a film is to consist wholly of animation, most of its footage will almost always be shot especially for it, since an audience will pick out familiar stock shots as readily as clichés in a politician's speech. Unhappily, many striking and irreplaceable shots, like those of Pacific landings in World War II, the German fire raid on London (the shot with the cross in the foreground), and closeups of historic characters like Gandhi, Lenin, and Trotsky, are greeted by melancholy groans from the audience when an editor is foolhardy enough to include them in his film. We will therefore consider first the shooting of new material.

In the smaller production unit, shooting most often takes place on *location*, or in the places where things actually happen. It may be useful to follow such a unit, and see how many people comprise it and what their duties are.

Throughout this book, unless specific exception is made, reference to production embraces both *35 mm.* (theater standard) and *16 mm.* (nontheatrical standard) practice. For all too long, a distinction has been drawn which places 35 mm. on the professional side, 16 mm. on the amateur. It is imperative now to break down this barrier by joining the two gauges in a single survey, save where arithmetic or procedure call for separate mention. But it is important at the very beginning to dispel the idea that the use of 16 mm. film confers upon production a miraculous simplicity and cheapness. What actually makes film production expensive is the reaching of professional standards. Once these are achieved, it will be found that 16 mm. film introduces marked but by no means startling economies in capital and operating costs.

THE UNIT

The production unit is the technical group responsible for converting a script into a length of uncut film. It is the tool by which the image is impressed. It manipulates the medium to record a small section of the visual and audible world, and also adapts this small section of the world to the peculiarities of the medium. Both these tasks are delicate and complex. Before the unit goes on location, it is often wise to send a representative on

Fig. 2-5. The three sources of film material.

ahead, charged with making arrangements, selecting places for shooting, estimating the difficulties of recording sound, insuring adequate power supplies for lighting, and in general providing for work to start immediately the unit arrives. Sometimes the script writer does these things, sometimes it is the director himself, sometimes the unit manager. Usually the cost of such an advance trip is money well spent. The size of a location unit will depend upon the budget of the film, whether a union or a nonunion crew is chosen, and the type of film which is being made (figure 2-6). The nucleus of any unit will consist of the following: a *director*, a *first cameraman*, a *second cameraman*, and a *unit manager*. If much lighting is to be done, one or more electricians will also be needed, while sound recording will require a *mixer*, a *recordist*, and a *mikeman*. A slightly more elaborate unit will add a second camera assistant, a *script girl*, and perhaps a *still cameraman*. The electrician(s) may be put in charge of a *gaffer* and the props of a *grip*. Thus, without exceeding the limits of a modest scale of production, a location unit may expand from a basic 4 persons to 8 or even 12. While a unit in a studio will be able to dispense with the unit manager, it will usually add an *assistant director*.

It must not be supposed that it is impossible to achieve professional results with smaller units. The solitary director-cameraman with his 16 mm. or ultra-light 35 mm. equipment is still a figure to be reckoned with. But shooting under complex conditions, and achieving the standards of quality expected

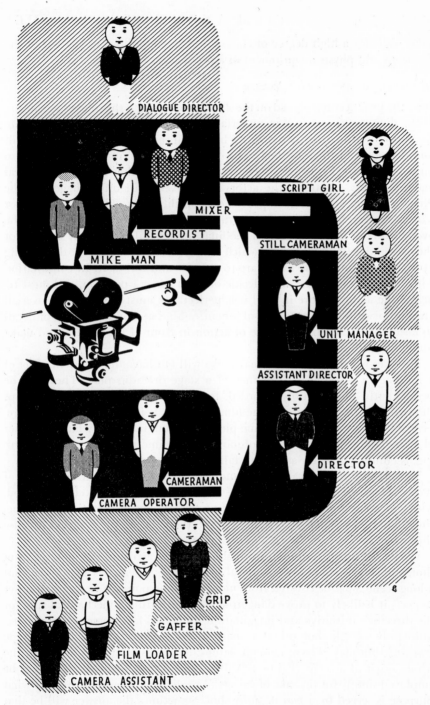

Fig. 2-6. Basic and supplementary units for location shooting.
Basic unit: Black area. Supplementary unit: Shaded area.

today, calls for a high degree of elaboration, as the following analysis of the functions and physical equipment of a production unit will show.

THE DIRECTOR AND UNIT MANAGER

Once the producer has agreed on the shooting script, it is the sole responsibility of the director to realize it in material terms, that is, to get it onto the film. No matter how brilliantly the writer has visualized his ideas, the director will find that some of them cannot be carried out as the script prescribes, and so must be presented in some other way. And on the other hand, the physical materials—sets, locations, the actors themselves—will often suggest to the director's mind all sorts of improvements on the script. The skillful director will take advantage of these opportunities, while never losing sight of the over-all line of the script. His is the final responsibility for each setting, for the pace and action of the scene which takes place in it, and for the dovetailing of each scene into those which are to precede and follow it. In consultation with the cameraman, he must decide on each camera position, and must rehearse the action before it until it is perfect. He must have enough over-all grasp to plan the shot sequence of an entire film; and enough grasp of detail to fasten onto the smallest piece of action in front of the camera and make something significant out of it.

Mistakes which the director may make will not have the transient effect of a mistake in a single performance of a stage or radio play. They will be permanently and indelibly recorded, to be repeated hundreds and perhaps thousands of times, wherever the film is shown. It is for this reason that repeated *takes* are made of the same piece of action, until every fault, whether of acting, dialogue, dovetailing of movements, camerawork, or sound recording, is eliminated as far as human fallibility—or the budget—allows.

The art of direction cannot be taught in a book, though the rudiments of it can be learned by anyone who will study movies, the bad as well as the good, with sufficient attention. But there are a few axioms of direction still sometimes laid down which deserve to be set in their proper place, either because they never had any application or because they are long out of date.

1. The old adage that each scene should be covered in long shot, medium shot, and close-up has only one useful application: it serves as a reminder that a long scene must be covered from more than one point of view. In all other respects it is likely to prove dangerous by substituting a mechanical rule for the director's initiative and imagination. In actual fact, some scenes may require only a single shot, others as many as ten or twelve. Frequently, a single *trucking* shot may present enough significant points of view to bring out the whole spirit of a scene (figure 2-7). But camera movement should never be employed simply for the sake of variety. The director should ask himself what purpose is served by a *pan* or *dolly* shot. Sometimes the answer will be that

Fig. 2-7. The camera "rule of three" contrasted with a
dolly shot.

the movement links together two points of interest in a continuous motion; sometimes it will surprisingly reveal something that was hidden before; sometimes the camera movement itself can convey a physical sensation which the director is trying to put across. But it is considerations of this sort, and not mere rules of three, which should govern the kind and number of angles used to cover a particular scene.

2. It is often said that various rules of pictorial composition should govern the setting up of a scene before the lens—the heads of speakers should be about one-third of the screen height from the top of the screen, the chief point of interest should not be set symmetrically in the center of the frame, and so on. Just as no artist worthy of the name pays any attention to these mechanical rules, so should they be ignored in setting up a shot in the camera (figure 2-8). Each shot should be judged on its merits, and in relation to the dynamic pattern contributed by movement within the shot and by movement of the camera itself.

3. In revolt against the dead and empty shots of some conventional directors and cameramen, there has been a recent tendency to demand that every shot in a film be packed with action. As a result, most shots in information films have people walking in from the left, running by from the right, and circulating around in all parts of the shot not otherwise occupied with movement. This artificial frenzy is often dignified with the term "planes of action." In reality, it is the significance and not the quantity of action which determines the success of a shot. A single lifted finger may be more dramatic than a skyful of airplanes.

4. In consulting with the cameraman on camera movement, the director is often confronted with a flat refusal when he wishes to pan or dolly at other than a slow, even speed. But in point of fact, rapid and even jerky camera movements are sometimes extremely effective, and the director should know where to call for them. It took Hollywood nearly forty years to discover that actual shaking of the camera would help to give the feeling of a violent explosion; and it was not until the war that it was proved in commercial theaters that cameras held in the hand while walking, running, or traveling on skis could produce remarkably powerful shots.[14] *Swish pans,* or very rapid and blurred camera movements from side to side, may be used to denote a sudden shift of attention, or a character frantically searching with his eyes for a way of escape, or again may form an interesting kind of transition from one shot to another. Shots in which the camera moves across a room while jerking and reeling unsteadily have been used in feature pictures to convey a sense of drunkenness or delirium.[15]

[14] E.g., the dolly shots in the boxing ring in *Body and Soul,* 1947, taken by the cameraman, James Wong Howe, on roller skates.

[15] See, for instance, *Great Expectations,* David Lean, 1947.

Fig. 2-8. Avoiding conventional rules of composition within the frame.

These few examples may serve as reminders to the new director that rules, especially in a new art like film, are made only to be broken, and that the best guide is his own taste and judgment.

Harassed by having to control so many human and mechanical factors, the director needs an extra person to handle the administrative duties of his assignment. In the studio these are usually the province of an assistant director; on location, of a unit manager whose function it is to see to the making of arrangements, check the dispatch and arrival of film, plan living accommodation and transport, pay the bills, and keep the accounts. A good unit manager is often the making of a good unit. He must be firm and yet equable in disposition, capable of dealing with emergencies and handling people of every rank and temperament, and above all bent on keeping the whole unit, including the director, up to the shooting schedule set by the studio.

THE CAMERA AND ITS CREW

A standard movie camera, whether 35 mm. or 16 mm., requires many adjustments before and during its operation. First it must be set on a *tripod* [16] and placed in the position which will give the desired angle on the scene. The tripod head must then be leveled in two directions at right angles to one another, so that the camera will always remain level, even when it is panned. Next the camera has to be precisely *framed* so that its field of view embraces neither more nor less than the director and cameraman in consultation agree to be desirable, having regard for the action and the psychological effect aimed at. This will almost always involve a trial-and-error process of looking through the *viewfinder* with different lenses in place. Most cameras are fitted with three or four lenses, and many have an equal number kept in reserve to meet unusual conditions.

If there is doubt where the camera should be placed the director may find it useful to detach the viewfinder and move around the set with it, to see what the shot will look like with different lenses and as seen from different angles and heights. This often saves moving a heavy camera from place to place. Whether the director can look through the viewfinder and camera without hurting the cameraman's feelings is a matter of personal relations, and is a point which should be settled before production starts rather than on location or on the studio floor.

When the preliminary decisions have been arrived at, there are many fine adjustments to make to the camera. In the first place the view obtained by looking directly through the lens must be transferred to the *monitoring* viewfinder, since in few types of camera is it possible to see the picture during shooting through the lens which is actually taking it. The viewfinder must therefore be adjusted (by *matting down* or otherwise) for the lens in use; and if the subject is close to the camera, it must further be adjusted for *parallax*. If the layout of the shot calls for panning or dollying, this action must be rehearsed a number of times to secure absolute smoothness (and noiselessness, if dialogue is being recorded) and also to insure that framing is perfectly correct throughout the camera travel. To make sure that this travel is smooth, it is often necessary to lay down camera *tracks* for the dolly or boom to run on. These are made of wood or metal, usually of channel section to guide the dolly wheels. If the camera and the subject approach or recede from one another, it will probably be necessary to *follow focus* during the action. This involves smooth and skillful adjustment to keep the subject in sharp focus throughout the shot.

16 For definitions of other types of camera mount, see Glossary under *high hat, velocilator,* and *boom*. See also *friction head* and *gyro*.

Another series of adjustments relates to the lens and the amount and quality of the light it lets in. A rapid reading on an *exposure meter* enables the amateur to set his lens *diaphragm* for a proper exposure, but the professional will proceed much more cautiously. His exposure meter provides a useful check on his own instinctive sense of what the lens *aperture* should be. But he will devote much more time to determining the quality of the light [17] and its distribution over the scene in front of him. A large variety of *filters* enables him, when shooting out of doors, to alter the image which would result from exposure through the lens alone. If the sky will register on film as a featureless white, he can use a filter to darken it and make clouds more visible. This kind of compensation can be applied with subtlety to provide under- and overcorrection, the latter extending so far as to produce night effects by day. Other filters can soften or increase *contrast,* lessen haze, and produce fog effects.

The cameraman in the studio can control lighting effects at will. Even out of doors, lighting can be influenced by the choice of angle in relation to the sun, and by the use of reflectors to redirect sunlight and brighten areas which would otherwise fall into deep shadow.

Since a 35 mm. camera and tripod may weigh as much as 150 pounds, appreciable effort will be needed to move it from one setup to another. A quite normal succession of shots may call for the camera to be mounted on its tripod for one shot, moved down to the ground on a high hat for the next, and set on a dolly for the third. To make these changes rapidly is work for two people; delays here hold up the whole unit. Sixteen mm. equipment has the advantage of much greater portability; but all the other settings and adjustments mentioned require just as much manpower on the smaller type of camera, for they hinge on the complexity and professionalism of the shots to be taken.

It is for these reasons that it is regular practice to use a *first cameraman* (in studio productions often called *director of photography*), who consults with the director on the type of shot required to translate the script into film, plans the dollying, panning, or *boom* movements, and above all decides how the shot is to be lighted. Except on a very small unit, he neither operates the camera nor physically carries out any of the lighting.

The *second cameraman* (or camera operator) actually makes the initial settings on the camera and controls it during the shot. He is helped by the *first assistant cameraman,* who is usually entrusted with following focus, and if necessary by a second assistant. Sometimes a *film loader* is used to load *magazines* with unexposed film and unload exposed film into cans.

[17] It is here assumed that the cameraman is shooting in black and white. Some of the problems of color photography are discussed in chapters iii and ix.

GRIPS AND GAFFERS

Obviously, a camera unit of such size and complexity will require very efficient auxiliary services if it is to shoot enough film each day to justify its high
operating cost. If the unit is shooting with *props,* as it usually will be, whether
on location or in the studio, it will need the services of a *grip,* whose business
it is to have on hand all the props that are needed, and to make those last-
minute adjustments and alterations which are discovered when the camera
is ready to turn.

In the studio, the carrying out of the cameraman's lighting plan is in the
hands of a *gaffer* and his staff of electricians. The gaffer does not usually
handle the lights himself; but he is a past master in the art of placing lights
and using *gobos* and *barn doors* and the various diffusers by which light can
be softened, directed, and redistributed.

THE SOUND CAMERA AND ITS CREW

Sound recording adds a further complication to location work, for the small
unit must economize on staff here as elsewhere, and usually cannot afford a
man for each separate job. The *mixer,* who is in charge of the sound crew,
will often not find the acoustics to his liking if he is recording in an enclosed
space which has not been specially designed for the purpose. He must therefore determine how to deaden (or, less often, liven) this space by artificial
means; and from long experience he will be able to apply the properties of
ready-to-hand materials—plywood sheets, rugs, blankets, etc.—to improve
the acoustics of the scene.

But the mixer's task is not merely the negative one of removing imperfections. He has the responsibility of producing a recording in which the wanted
sounds are as clear and prominent, and the unwanted sounds as inaudible,
as his skill can make them. He must be adept at controlling wind noises out
of doors and diagnosing a multitude of resonances and reverberations which
will interfere with the good quality of his recording.

The mixer usually works with headphones at a movable *console* or *tea
wagon* on the set; but he may occasionally *monitor* with a loudspeaker from
the *sound truck* which carries equipment to a location, and which in certain
studios is used in place of fixed equipment.

The task of recording sound on film is entrusted to the *recordist,* who has
charge of the *sound camera* and its associated multiplicity of amplifiers, *compressors, filters,* etc., each with many adjustments and a routine of highly expert maintenance. The microphone is in charge of a *mikeman,* who has the
skillful and delicate task of keeping it always in the position from which it
will pick up the dialogue of the person speaking most clearly and usually most
loudly. This he accomplishes with the aid of a *sound boom,* a kind of elaborate

fishing rod on the end of which the mike is mounted. A multiplicity of controls enables him to run the microphone in and out, twist it around and alter its angle, so that he can follow dialogue as it passes from character to character, often as they are moving about the set.

THE SCRIPT GIRL

In a unit of the size and specialized function we have been describing, it would not be surprising if the script—the simple cause of all this complication—were to be neglected, save for occasional reference, by a director who may feel that he can lay out the action his own way much more successfully than a mere writer could have envisaged it. But however many changes in the script may be made during production, it is the script girl's job to keep track of them, and to prompt the director in matters of completeness and continuity. If she has been successful, when the film comes to be laid out in the cutting room for assembly, there will be no vital connective shots missing, no directions of movement confused and tangled, no changes in the character of some conspicuous object like a man's tie in scenes which were shot days apart but which are now to be welded into immediate relationship.

DUTIES OF THE UNIT

To avoid unnecessary expense, voice tests of characters should be made ahead of time, and acoustics of rooms and buildings worked on before the arrival of large numbers of people who may object to being kept waiting. It is usually desirable to plan alternative interior sequences which may be shot if bad weather prevents the camera crew from going out of doors. A long spell of bad weather will seriously upset the timetable and budget of any unit which relies on getting exteriors, and ample allowance should be made in the cost estimates if the film is being shot in an uncertain climate.

Enough has been said to show why even the moderate-sized production organization has often to muster a sizeable crew to translate a script into film. Obviously films can be made, and made professionally, with smaller crews. Sound can be dispensed with in shooting, a light camera used to simplify the setups, and much of the paraphernalia of sets and props may be eliminated. But script and shooting must be carefully tailored to one another if the film is to be both economical and effective. One of the chief tasks of the newcomer to film is to learn the art of what is possible.

It would be a mistake to imagine, however, that a film unit's responsibilities end with the carrying out of its technical duties. These are so numerous, so complicated, and often run so far into the night, that there is a natural tendency to ignore all but the film itself. This is often the source of much unintended bad feeling on location. A film unit arrives in a small town. It rounds up the characters it needs, organizes its shooting, disrupts the traffic, offers prints and stills of the film when finished as payment for services, then blows out of town and is never heard from again. Unlucky the film maker who ever again wants to put that town in a movie! But had the unit manager consulted the mayor on his arrival, had he taken the local newspaper editor into his confidence, worked out his street shooting plans with the police, written down the names and addresses of all to whom he promised payment in kind, and sent the prints and stills as soon as the film was finished, what a gain there would have been in coöperation and even useful publicity. And how different the reception of the next movie maker to pay the town a visit!

The careless production unit may also run into serious legal difficulties if it films people without securing adequate clearances from them. It may not be difficult for an aggrieved person to prove that his appearance in a film has caused him to suffer loss of reputation, and in this event he will be able to hold up distribution of the film or exact substantial damages from its producer. All people who are easily recognizable in shots should be asked to sign properly drawn up clearances before the camera turns, and the unit should be prepared with a supply of these formidable-sounding documents, a specimen of which appears in figure 2-9.

FILM AND ACTUALITY

Such, in brief, are the mechanical reasons for the large units entailed by film production. But there is another reason too. When the author or the dramatist, the artist or the reporter, looks over a scene which he wants to record, he can very simply alter it in any way he chooses as he transfers it to the written page or canvas. This is because the synthesis he makes is primarily a mental synthesis. But the film maker, especially if he is working in the realist tradition, has a much more difficult problem. Out of the untidy and miscellaneous happenings of real life he must pick the essential elements of a scene, discarding what he does not need, selecting and molding the rest, and knitting the whole together into a compact and coherent image. And it is upon the physical world itself that this creative synthesis must be wrought.

The relation between film and reality will confront the film maker again and again. When movies were first invented, they were valued just because they came so close to reproducing real life. When they recorded Queen Victoria's funeral or the early stages of building the Panama Canal, it still seemed amazing to audiences that the real event was happening over again before their eyes. So in these early films the camera was simply set up in a fixed position in front of the scene, and the cameraman cranked away as long as anything interesting was happening in front of his lens. The shots produced in this way were very long, and sometimes for several minutes there would be

Dated:

Magnificent Pictures, Inc.,
4500 Larrimac Drive,
Peoria, ILLINOIS.

Gentlemen:

    The undersigned, for good and valuable con-
sideration, hereby releases you, your successors,
representatives and assigns, and all persons privy
to, or claiming by, through, or under you, from any
and all claims, demands, and causes of action of
every nature and kind arising out of or connected
with the photographs of the undersigned taken by
you or your representatives and the use thereof as
you may deem fit and the undersigned hereby consents
that you take such photographs and that you may use,
reproduce, and publish the same in the manner and
context and with such sound and dialogue as you deem
advisable.

        Very truly yours,

Fig. 2-9. A legal waiver.

no change of "angle," as we should say today. This literal rendering of a scene is usually called *naturalism*.

Meanwhile, many directors were beginning to realize that the powers of film were much more varied and interesting. Chief credit for this discovery has latterly been accorded to the Frenchman, Georges Méliès, who as early as 1896 was producing imaginative dream films and all kinds of magic displays far removed from the documentary cameraman's simple records. Georges Sadoul, however, in an interesting analysis of Méliès' style,[18] has shown that this former professional magician was bound by all the conventions of the

18 *Op. cit.*, vol. 2, chap. 10.

stage, and invariably places his camera in the position of a *monsieur de l'orchestre*, who viewed the stage from an ideal central position. Méliès' discoveries thus lay within the film frame. The powers of cutting seem to have been discovered independently about the year 1900 by two English film makers, George Albert Smith and James Williamson, both of Brighton, who used close-ups and a well-developed discontinuity of image two years before Edwin S. Porter produced his famous *Life of an American Fireman* and *The Great Train Robbery*, the films on which his claim to the same discoveries has been based.

The ambition of these early showmen was to make money by surprising and amusing their audiences with the tricks of a new medium. Yet to them—the Frenchman within the film frame, the Englishmen and the American within the realm of cutting—we owe important and lasting aesthetic discoveries. They opened the way to a creative interpretation, as distinct from a literal rendering, of reality, and thus became the parents of the school of film *realism*.

The director is pressingly concerned all the time with the responsibility of interpreting and not merely recording. He and his crew work long hours, repeating pieces of action until they are perfect, sharpening the point of some important incident, building up a scene by the massing of elements which must often be brought together with the greatest patience and effort. If the camera were only a recording instrument, shooting would still be difficult, but not one-hundredth as difficult as it actually is. The creative use of the camera means selecting and molding what goes on in front of it. And this means interrupting work on location, getting people released to repeat a piece of action over and over again, and generally upsetting the activities of a school, a farm, a small town, a factory, or whatever it may be.

Professionalism in film is largely a matter of ceaseless attention to detail. In the small unit, where the individual cannot help being something of a jack-of-all-trades, this calls for an encyclopedic range of knowledge which can come only from many years' experience. The system of apprenticeship common in the unions and thus in the commercial studios is well designed to hammer in every detail of the craft. But hitherto this apprenticeship has been on too narrow and specialized a basis to produce good all-round film makers. It has waited for the smaller production units of the university, the documentary group, and the regional film board to realize the aim of over-all training combined with unremitting concentration on the details of technique.

III

The Camera

THE PRIMARY tools of the film maker are the camera and the microphone. These are the sense organs through which he must channel his impressions of the world. Their superficial resemblance to his own eye and ear may lead him to assume an identity which does not exist. The human eye is an organ of infinite mobility and subtlety. It is constantly on the move, observing, relating, comparing, picking out a small detail here, and there enlarging its field of attention to include a vast panorama. Moreover, we see not with our eye but with our eyes. Had we the single eye of the Cyclops, or the fly's multifaceted eyes, or the sideways-staring eyes of the hare or the horse, our world would be almost unrecognizably different. The two and one-half inch separation of our eyes gives us a strongly marked perception of depth—a perception which can be brought home by shutting one eye, not on the world itself, but on a stereoscopic photograph of it. The scenes in which we live have such a familiarity that three-dimensional vision is scarcely recognized as a thing in itself. But a one-eyed man will tell you how hard it is not to bump into walls on an unfamiliar staircase, or make a misjudgment in stepping off a sidewalk.

The camera is like the one-eyed man. It has no direct means of suggesting depth but only inferential means like perspective and parallactic movement. Unlike the eye, the camera lens has a fixed and narrow frame of vision. Unlike the eye, it often sees on a surface unresponsive to color. Nevertheless, it is through the needle's eye of the camera that the director must funnel the impressions that he wants to convey.

Let us imagine that this is his first job. In his excitement he will attribute to the inanimate scene all his own feelings, together with those of his characters, and a thousand things that he knows or senses about them. But when, a few days later, he sits in a projection room watching what he has just shot unfolding coldly in front of him, he will scarcely believe his eyes—almost

[39]

nothing of what he saw so recently has come out on the screen. What seemed to vibrate with life is flat and insipid. The jokes that were so amusing would not now raise even the faintest smile. That massive pile of girders and concrete which, in the sunlight and fresh with the sense of his own discovery, seemed to him the symbol of energy and growth, is reduced on the screen to a flat and awkward jumble of unimpressive lines. The director—who now goes back to his job with a new humility and respect for his medium—had supposed that what he saw and felt the camera's eye would automatically record. But the camera can lie. It has no knowledge of what goes on outside the frame. It still records for the most part in black and white. It makes what is solid flat. Set woodenly before a scene, it cannot be compared with the director's eye, which moves to and fro, coördinating one focus of interest with another, narrowing its gaze to concentrate on a detail, then suddenly expanding it to put the detail in its proper setting.

ADAPTING THE CAMERA TO ACTUALITY

To make the camera live, the director must see with its eyes—eyes that are governed by laws of optics which he must master and work with. When he has done this, he will find that the camera is almost as flexible an instrument as the eye, though very different in its properties. In its various adjustments and accessories, he will discover counterparts to the mental powers of observation which enable him to select and emphasize the important details of a scene.

The simplest device for selecting and emphasizing is called *camera angle.* Any lens which the cameraman may be using has a fixed angle of view.[1] That is to say, if the camera is set up at a certain place and pointed in a certain direction, there will be a cone (cut off by the camera's rectangular mask) within which objects will be visible to the camera, and outside of which they will not be visible to it. The position from which the camera thus views a scene can be altered at will, and is commonly, though rather loosely, called the camera angle. In the very early days of movies, the camera was set up at eye or shoulder level and pointed horizontally at the scene to be photographed. Cameramen were afraid to tilt their cameras up and down, because they knew that this produced a distortion of perspective which was considered bad practice by still photographers.

Soon, however (and the freedom won by the arts in the last forty years may have had its influence), directors and cameramen began to start pointing their lenses in different directions, discovering that each camera angle produced a

[1] Excepting the *zoom lens,* a lens of variable focal length, and hence of variable magnification.

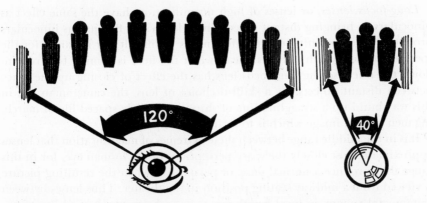

Fig. 3-1. Fields of vision of the eye and the wide-angle lens. Note the much wider field of vision of the eye, and the gradual tapering-off in the region of indirect vision. The camera lens cuts off sharply at the edges of the field.

different psychological effect. Shooting up at a person from his feet made him look overpoweringly tall; shooting down from above him reduced him to insignificance. And beyond these obvious tricks lay a wealth of more subtle devices brought about by varying the camera angle.

The director must learn, therefore, how the placing of his camera, near or far, high or low, affects the appearance of his scene. When he has mastered the possibilities of a single lens shooting from a fixed position, he can go on to study the consequences of using lenses of different magnifying power.

Wide-angle lenses, or lenses of low magnification, are those which include the widest possible field. In cramped quarters these lenses are often invaluable in making up for the sense of "all-aroundness" which the eye enjoys over the camera. But even the wide-angle lens is like an eye in blinkers. Including the field of indirect (or indistinct) vision, the eye can see a field of about 120°; the widest-angle lens in common motion picture use embraces a field of only about 50° (figure 3-1). When projected, a shot made with a present day wide-angle lens is seen to distort parallel lines near the edges of the field, an effect which cannot be eliminated until better lenses are produced, as they will be soon. Panning with an extreme wide-angle lens produces a curious effect of a quite different kind. Lines which appear parallel in the center of the scene develop an increasing curvature as the camera movement brings them toward the edge. As this goes on continuously, the net effect is that the actually solid scene assumes a plastic and warped appearance which is very unrealistic and requires sparing use. This bending of the field is an effect of perspective and cannot be eliminated by better lenses.

Long-focus lenses, or lenses of high magnification, have the same effect as binoculars in bringing distant objects into close view. But just as binoculars produce a foreshortening effect which makes it difficult, for instance, for the spectator to see which horse is ahead when the field is coming toward him down the track, so the long-focus lens has the effect of closing up the space between distant objects. By a skillful choice of lens, the cameraman can in this way build up a straggling line of ships or a widely spaced file of marching men into an image which is towering and impressive.

It is in the middle range between these extremes of magnification that lenses approximate most closely the space perceptions of the human eye; for in this range they produce a normal sense of perspective when the resulting picture is viewed from a midway seating position in the theater. Thus lenses between 35 mm. and 50 mm. in focal length (see p. 54) are commonly used in 35 mm. cameras when a naturalistic rendering of a scene is needed. Long- and short-focus lenses are used either when the scene is inaccessible (too far or too near to be compassed adequately by normal lenses) or when some distortion of appearance is desired for artistic reasons.

The position of the spectator in the theater is intimately related to the perspective of the image which he sees. A scene as shot by the camera is faithfully reproduced only when the spectator looks along the axis of the projector lens, and when the screen subtends at his eye the same angle that the scene as framed by the camera aperture subtended at the camera lens. Thus, ideally, the spectator should shift his position in the theater whenever the cameraman has altered the focal length of his lens. However, approximately midway between screen and back wall of an average theater is a seating area where perspective effects are not unduly distorted.

The effect of varying spectator viewpoint in relation to the focal length of the camera lens is shown in figures 3-2a and 3-2b. Both these drawings look distorted when held at a normal reading distance from the eye. But if *a* is held still with its center about three inches in front of one eye (the other being closed), and if *b* is looked at from a distance of about ten feet, normal perspectives are obtained on both. The reason is that *a* corresponds to a view of a tennis court taken with a very short-focus (wide-angle) lens, *b* with a very long-focus lens. It will be noticed that there is no single position from which both of these shots can be viewed satisfactorily. In fact, the apparent focal length of the camera lens can be decreased by sitting close to the screen and increased by sitting farther away, so that those who like wide-angle shots should occupy the unpopular seats close up to the movie screen, while those who like telephoto shots should choose the equally unpopular seats at the very back of the house.

The distortions here referred to are quite distinct from those obtained by viewing the movie screen from one side. These cannot be compensated by any movement of the spectator toward or away from the screen. The same considerations apply to spectators sitting far below the axis of the projector beam, even if they are on the center line of the theater.

Panning and *tilting* the camera (that is, moving it horizontally and vertically), confer on it many additional powers of the eye. Slow movement can convey the grace and strength of a breaking wave or the curve of a hand on a potter's wheel. Fast movement of the camera whirls the spectator's eye along with it. The scene breaks into dazzling horizontal bands as if the camera were being flung through space. The director will discover, too, that movement of the whole camera restores some of the sense of three-dimensional space, lost by seeing with a single lens and projecting onto a flat screen. By moving the camera, he makes objects in different planes appear to move past one another, and this is associated with the three-dimensional experience of everyday life.

Again, the mood of a scene—the lowering of the sky, for instance, or the piercing sharpness of a pilot's vision—can often be contrived with the aid of *filters* when these effects exist only in the director's imagination.

There is no reason why the camera should be confined to its standard speed —that is, that the speed of shooting should be the same as the speed of projection. *Slow motion,* which involves taking pictures faster than they are projected, and *fast motion,* which involves taking them slower, have their place in the intelligent modification of life as it goes by. The speeding up of the movement of clouds will give an entirely different emotional feeling to a scene; the slowing down of a commonplace motion, like the sweep of a sower's hand, will add a force and dignity to it which is a function of the mind, not the eye.

This possibility of varying speed in either direction may be likened to a "time microscope" and a "time telescope." Slow motion is a means of expanding the scale of time so that, for instance, an action which goes through its entire cycle in one second can be made to occupy eight minutes on the screen. Contrarily, actions spread over long intervals of time, which the eye could not possibly compass as a single movement, can be squeezed into a few seconds and so be made to appear continuous; examples are the growth of plants and the transition of insects from one stage of development to another.

ADAPTING ACTUALITY TO THE CAMERA

So far we have seen only how the director can call for adjustments of the camera to modify the channel through which his living scene has to pass. But that scene must itself be altered to meet the camera's needs. The shape of the frame dictates the shape of the action. If this action is to fix attention, it must be boldly conceived. The director must learn to use his diagonals to give

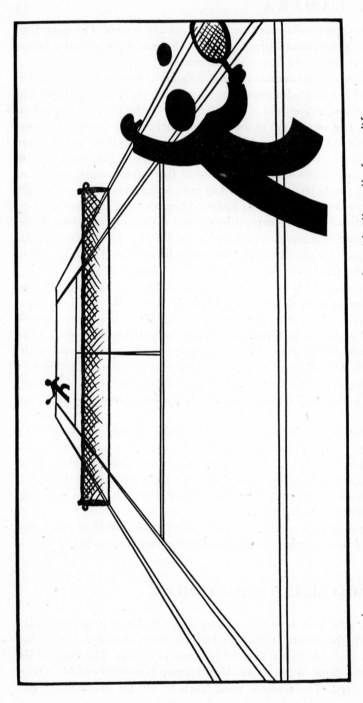

Fig. 3-2a. Each different focal length of camera lens ideally calls for a different seating position of the spectator along the centerline of the theater. This picture of a tennis court "shot" by a very-short-focus (wide-angle) lens must be viewed with the eye not more than three inches from its center if the distortions are to be corrected. It will then resemble the player's view of the court. (Swiveling the eye will make the ball appear to be circular.)

Fig. 3-2b. This picture of a tennis court "shot" by a lens of very long focal length must be viewed from a distance of ten feet or more if its perspective is to appear correct. It will then look like a view of the court taken from a distant window.

strength to the frame. He must learn how to place heads at the very top and bottom of the screen—as well as in their usual position two-thirds of the way up. And because the eye grasps each scene so rapidly, he must make sure that its content is always relevant and interesting. *Cutting* (or the following of one scene by another on the screen) has proved time and again that an audience can grasp a simple movie shot in as little as a second. Few shots, even in a feature picture, run for more than twenty or thirty seconds on the screen. The capacity to compress and concentrate his material is one of the hallmarks of a good movie maker. A Preston Sturges or René Clair will make something of every flicker of his characters' eyelids. In fact, you can forget the main characters and look exclusively at the crowd faces and the props, the costumes and the architecture, and you will still enjoy his film. You can even shut your eyes and listen to the sound track and feel that every second is packed with wit and meaning.

These are just a few of the camera's battery of tricks—tricks which have a real creative function when they are used to hammer out a concept of a scene which is much more purposeful than the flat reality.

HOW THE CAMERA WORKS

The magnificently elaborate studio cameras which photograph multimillion dollar productions today are basically little different from the old black box with the crank handle which turned out the comedies of Chaplin and Mack Sennett a generation ago. In fact there are *camera movements* designed in those days which have never been excelled, and which are still the standard for steadiness and durability.

Yet in all other respects great advances have taken place in camera design during the past thirty years. The camera has become specialized to many new jobs (figure 3-3). There is the *hand camera* or *field camera,* used by most of the makers of information shorts who are accustomed to working with small units, often under difficult out-of-door conditions. While almost always mounted on a tripod, this type of camera is often suitable for hand holding, and is light enough to be moved from place to place by a small crew.

The *combat camera,* a product of World War II, was designed mainly for hand holding, and was planned to be even more compact and self-contained than the field camera. The Germans were most successful in designing this type of camera.

The *studio camera,* silenced to produce the minimum interference with sound recording, has all the features needed to give swiftness of adjustment in making complicated studio shots.

There are also a multitude of specialized cameras, some designed for high

Fig. 3-3. Basic types of standard 35 mm. camera. Characteristic appearance of the studio, the field, and the combat camera.

speed (slow motion), some for three-color photography, some for time lapse (fast motion) and other scientific uses like the tracing of oscillographic records. But there are a number of basic components common to almost all movie cameras.

If the lens were simply to trace images on a long steadily moving band of film, it is easy to see that these images would be nothing but a blur.[2] Only by taking separate and distinct pictures of moving scenes can these scenes be recorded sharply. Hence the movie camera is essentially a machine for taking pictures intermittently, the separate, spaced-out pictures afterward being fused together in the observer's brain. *Persistence of vision,* a sort of mental hangover, prolongs the image of what the eye is seeing. In this way a rapid succession of slightly different still pictures deceives it into thinking that it has seen real continuity of movement. If the eye were entirely sober, there would be no movies.

When a scene is being photographed, the film is held stationary in the camera. At the end of each exposure, the film is moved rapidly forward a distance equal to the height of one picture (or *frame*), a shutter meanwhile shutting off the light to prevent blurring, and the next frame is exposed. During this next exposure the film is again held stationary, after which it moves forward once more. The motion of the film is intermittent (figure 3-4). The motor system that operates the intermittent mechanism is called the *drive.*

DRIVE AND SPEED RANGE

Modern cameras are driven either by electric or spring motors. Electric motors are almost always used when power is available; even on location 110-volt

---

[2] An exception is the oscillographic camera. Here the image is already a sharply focused line which the moving band of film simply stretches out longitudinally. This type of camera therefore has no need of either shutter or intermittent motion.

Fig. 3-4. Arresting the world by intermittent motion and intermittent lighting. Two methods of stopping movement with the movie camera: continuous lighting of the scene with a film moved forward and obscured intermittently; intermittent lighting of the scene with very brief flashes and a film moved forward continuously (stroboscopic cinematography).

motors can be run by radio "B" batteries of the heavy-duty type. Six-volt and 12-volt electric motors are also in common use. They are usually powered by automobile batteries; but, where weight is a consideration, "hot-shot" batteries form a convenient substitute and can be counted on to drive several thousand feet of film before becoming exhausted.

Spring drive eliminates heavy batteries and hence is more convenient in field cameras; its disadvantages are lack of power to drive large film magazines, and short running time. Most spring motors will drive only about 50 feet of 35 mm. film, and often need winding up at awkward moments when it is essential to get an action shot. There is, however, one type of camera [3] which will run 170 feet on its clockwork motor without a rewind.

Different types of camera have different ranges of speed, although the standard speed of 24 frames per second is invariably a fixed point in this range. Studio cameras designed mainly for dialogue work are often confined to this speed by the type of motor fitted to them. Field cameras usually have a speed range between 8 and 48 frames per second, while high speed cameras of conventional design will run up to about 130 frames per second.

[3] The Newman-Sinclair camera; it will also continue to run during rewinding.

Above this speed, *continuous motion* cameras take over. These produce a stationary image by means of a simple device called an *optical compensator,* in which a rotating slab of glass displaces the image in the same direction and at the same speed as the film motion, so that over a short distance there is no relative movement between the two (figure 3-5). Continuous motion cameras can be made to run up to the enormous speed of 8,000 frames per second on small gauges of film.

Another method of "stopping" rapidly moving objects is to light them intermittently for very brief periods (usually between one and ten microseconds), the repetition rate of the flashes determining the number of frames per second recorded. Since the moving object is illuminated by flashes so short that it appears virtually stationary, the record can be made on a rapidly moving film without a shutter. This is known as *stroboscopic* cinematography, which gives good results in the speed range between 100 and 1,500 exposures per second (figure 3-4).

Very much higher speeds may be attained with cameras which consist of a revolving drum around which the film is wrapped in a spiral path. The film is then exposed by a row of small lenses, and the whole supply may be consumed in less than a thousandth of a second. In addition, the image may be dissected so that its depth is greatly reduced and its width correspondingly increased, with the result that a given film velocity corresponds to a much greater number of frames per second than normal. A camera of this type has been constructed to record at the rate of ten million images per second, while by other image-dissection methods

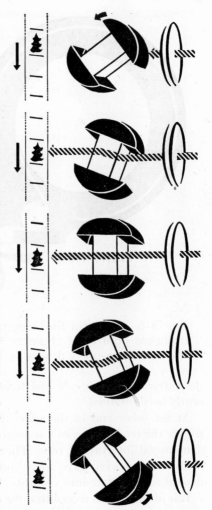

Fig. 3-5. Continuous motion shooting and viewing: the optical compensator. If the incoming ray of light is made to pass through a slab or prism of glass of the proper thickness, it will, over a certain distance, be refracted or bent in such a way that it "keeps pace" with the traveling film. Thus an unblurred image will be photographed or viewed on the film.

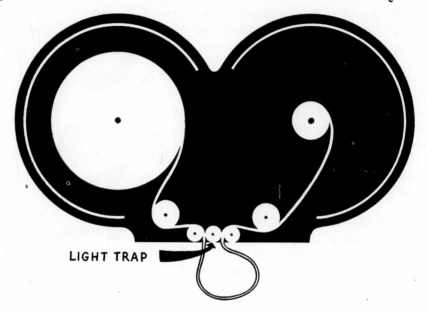

LIGHT TRAP

Fig. 3-6. A typical film magazine. The Mitchell film magazine is a double light-tight chamber mounted externally to the camera; the film take-up is driven by a belt.

the extraordinary rate of one hundred million images per second has recently been attained.[4]

At the other end of the scale, time-lapse mechanisms are devices which trigger the release lever of a standard camera to expose a single frame at predetermined intervals of time. These intervals range from a few seconds to many hours or even days, according to the slowness of the action which it is desired to accelerate into visibility.

It is of interest to record that the possibilities of time-lapse and high-speed cinematography had been widely explored 40 years ago. In 1910, for instance, a German professor at the Berlin Military Academy was taking pictures at the rate of 30,000 per second as a part of his ballistic researches.

FILM MAGAZINES

The film magazine is the light-tight chamber in which film is kept wound up, and from which it passes to the body of the camera to be exposed (figure 3-6).

[4] The high-speed movie camera is admirably treated in two collections of papers published by the Society of Motion Picture Engineers, entitled *High-Speed Photography*, of which the first volume (129 pp.) appeared in March, 1949, and the second (163 pp.) in November, 1949. See also K. Shaftan, "A Survey of High-Speed Motion Picture Photography," *JSMPTE*, May, 1950, pp. 603–626, and M. Sultanoff, "A 100,000,000 Frame Per Second Camera," *JSMPTE*, Aug., 1950, pp. 158–166.

In most American designs of camera the exposed film then returns to the magazine, where it is rewound, and is afterward unloaded in darkness. A number of European cameras, however, make use of separate magazines for film supply and take-up. These are often known as Debrie-type magazines, from the name of the French camera which first popularized them. Standard sizes of magazines for 35 mm. cameras are 100, 200, 400, and 1,000 feet, the two latter sizes being interchangeable on most American field and studio cameras. Standard 16 mm. magazine sizes are: 50, 100, 200, 400, and 1,200 feet. The 100-foot 35 mm. magazines are usually of the kind in which the film is bought loaded on a spool which can be inserted in the camera in daylight. The film then winds itself, after exposure, on another spool which can be removed in daylight, the outer layers at beginning and end being protected by several turns of blank film. Other types of magazine used in 35 mm. cameras must be loaded and unloaded in darkness, which on location is often accomplished in a *changing bag,* a black bag equipped with light-tight sleeves into which the cameraman can insert his arms.

FOCUSING AND VIEWFINDING

The image on the film is the fact of central importance in camera design. The lens produces this image on a plane called the *focal plane,* and great care must be taken that it is focused perfectly sharply, and that the film frame occupies precisely the plane of the image. The focusing and composition of the image can be accurately accomplished only if the cameraman can see this image exactly as it is to be formed on the film. In very simple cameras, there is no means of accomplishing this; focusing must be done by a lens scale of distances, and composition by a viewfinder mounted close to the shooting lens, but nevertheless not "seeing" precisely the same field of view, because of *parallax.*[5] More advanced cameras have an arrangement for substituting for the film behind the lens a small ground glass screen forming an image which in turn can be enlarged and viewed through a *focusing microscope.*[6] This is usually accomplished by a method perfected in the Mitchell camera: the lens turret remains fixed to the tripod, while the body of the camera shifts or racks over by the twist of a handle so that the ground glass takes the place of the film aperture behind the lens which is in the shooting position. Just before shooting, the body of the camera is shifted back again; if the cameraman forgets to do this, there will be nothing on the film. With this system the film image cannot be viewed while shooting actually takes place, so that the cameraman must watch the action through a *monitoring viewfinder,* which has to be adjusted for parallax on close shots (figure 3-7).

[5] Hold up a ruler vertically at arm's length and, with one eye shut, cover a certain point on the opposite wall with the ruler while looking through the other eye. Then change eyes and look at the ruler again. Its position will appear to have moved. This difference between the apparent positions of an object as viewed from different points is called *parallax.*

[6] Sometimes incorrectly called a *focusing telescope.*

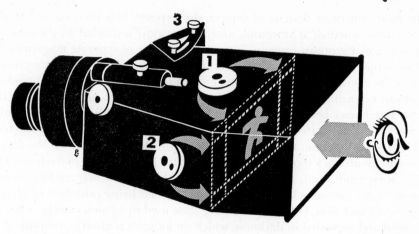

Fig. 3-7. A typical monitoring viewfinder. Note the large erect image, the two knurled knobs (1 and 2), for adjusting the field of view to that of lenses of different focal length, and the swinging device (3) for parallax adjustment.

Some advanced studio cameras have an arrangement whereby the lenses and the monitor are geared together so that both are focused simultaneously, while a set of cams (one for each lens) connected to the lens-focusing control automatically adjusts the monitor for parallax.

In certain foreign camera designs, advantage is taken of the translucency of film to place a focusing microscope directly behind the film in the aperture, thus eliminating parallax error at the source. However, *greyback antihalation* stock, now almost universal, provides a dim and murky image which is hard to focus on. A third method, first applied in the German Arriflex camera, makes use of the shutter to provide the cameraman with an image identical to that "seen" by the film. The shutter blades, which revolve between lens and film, are mounted at a 45° angle to the film plane, and their front surfaces are silvered. They thus act as a mirror which reflects light on a small piece of ground glass so placed that the light path from it to the lens is the same length as that from the lens to the film. The result is that film and ground glass "see" the same lens image alternately. Therefore, when the ground-glass image has been enlarged by a focusing microscope, it can be used for focusing, for composition, and for monitoring, and no separate monitor finder is necessary. This arrangement is known as a reflex viewfinder (figure 3-8).

The image on the ground glass of a focusing microscope is always the same size, no matter what focal length of lens is being used. The monitor viewfinder, on the other hand, usually has an optical system of fixed magnification,

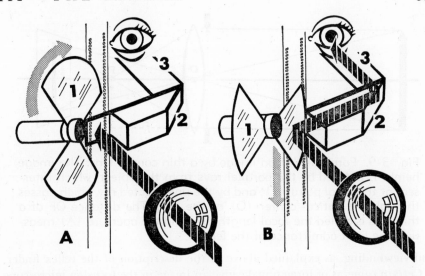

Fig. 3-8. The reflex viewfinder. Light entering the camera lens alternately exposes the film (A) and, when the film is being pulled down (B), strikes a mirror-faced shutter (1), from which it is reflected onto a ground-glass surface (2) where it forms an image, which in turn is magnified by a focusing microscope (3) and seen by the camera operator.

so designed that when the widest-angle lens available is in use, the image just fills the finder. This image may, and indeed should, be quite large—say 2 by $3\frac{1}{2}$ inches—so that it can be watched by both eyes together. If the finder is to be matched to a lens of longer focal length—i.e., higher magnification—the full field is usually masked or matted down, either by opaque cells with cutout rectangles of the proper size, or by wires which stretch across the field vertically and horizontally to indicate its limits. With very long-focus telephoto lenses, this system becomes inconvenient because the finder field shrinks to such a small size.

In some camera finders, a compromise is made by having constant image size for all the shorter-focus lenses, but a size which is smaller than the fixed magnification finders provide. The problem is not serious in the design of studio cameras, which seldom make use of lenses outside the 25–75 mm. range, having field areas with a ratio of 9 to 1. Even one-ninth of the full finder field is not too small an area to view comfortably. On a field camera, however, 9-inch (225 mm.) lenses are not uncommon, and these would call for a field only one-eightieth of the full area of a masked-down finder. Here, the most satisfactory solution for the field camera is to use the same lens for shooting

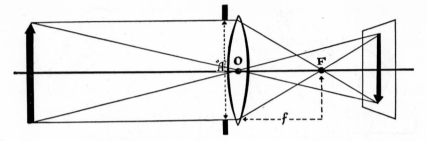

Fig. 3-9. Formation of an image by a thin convex lens. The image height is defined by the parallel rays from the object, which intersect at the focal point (F), and by the unrefracted ray which passes through the optical center (O) of the lens. The distance OF of a thin lens is called the focal length (f), and the aperture (A) measures the light admittance of the lens.

and viewfinding, as explained above in the description of the reflex finder.

Certain cameras of foreign make give an image in the focusing microscope which may be upside down, reversed, or both. This is both inconvenient and unnecessary. The image should be as seen by the eye, and sharp and clear to the extreme corners of the field. There should be an adjustment for individual eyesight, while an additional magnifier for very close inspection of the center of the image is an advantage.

LENSES

The lens differs from the human eye, but it also has points of resemblance. When objects are very small or very far away the eye needs the help of a magnifying glass or a telescope. The camera also needs lenses of different magnifying power if it is to do justice to the range of objects of vastly different size which may confront it. The eye has a pupil which expands and contracts to fix the amount of light which can strike its sensitive surface or retina. The camera lens is equipped with a very similar *iris* or *diaphragm*. The parallel between eye and lens, though often overworked, helps to emphasize the fact of observation, which is one of the keys to good direction and camera work.

To gain a real understanding of lenses and how they work, the reader should consult an elementary text on optics, since there is space here for only the briefest outline of image formation. All camera lenses are of the converging (convex) type; that is, they form a real image on the side of the lens opposite the object, as shown in figure 3-9.[7]

[7] If the reader has any difficulty in remembering which is a concave and which a convex surface, he has only to recall that a concave surface caves inwards, so that a convex surface is one which bulges outwards. Lenses which have the same properties on both outer surfaces are known simply as concave or convex. "Mixed" lenses are called "concavo-convex," or "plano-concave (-vex)" if one surface is flat.

The lens shown in the diagram is called a thin lens, and is used only for simplified demonstrations. It serves no useful photographic purpose, for it suffers from a number of faults known as *aberrations*, the most serious of which are:

Spherical aberration.—The rays passing through the periphery or rim of the lens come to a focus closer to the lens than the axial rays. (Focal length different for peripheral and axial rays.)

Chromatic aberration.—Rays of different colors do not come to a focus at the same point. (Focal length different for each color of the spectrum.)

Astigmatism.—Distortion of off-axis rays such that either vertical or horizontal lines in the image can be brought into sharp focus, but not both.

Curvature of field.—The image of a plane object lies on a curved surface, instead of in a plane, so that the whole object cannot be brought into focus at once. (Focal surface not a plane but a curved surface.)

Distortion.—The image of a square object is shaped either like a barrel or a pin-cushion—these accordingly being the names given to the two types of distortion.

To eliminate all these aberrations is impossible, since in the present state of lens making correction for one is likely to increase another, and the large relative apertures demanded in modern camera lenses tend to increase them all. Correction is accomplished by combining converging (convex) with diverging (concave) elements, the curvature of the surfaces being made somewhat independent by the use of glasses of different refractive index, that is, light-bending power. Lens designers sometimes require several years to carry out the calculations on a single series of lenses, so difficult is it to combine a high degree of all the desirable qualities in a single objective.

As can be seen from figure 3-9, camera lenses have two basic characteristics, their focal length and their aperture, these being related to form their relative aperture (or speed). Since in a film camera the image always remains the same size—i.e., the size of the frame of film—even though the lens is changed, it is the focal length of the lens, which determines its field of view, and therefore also its effective magnification on the frame. On a 35 mm. film camera, lenses of 25–35 mm. focal length are considered to be of short focus (wide angle), 40–50 mm. lenses are normal, and 75–500 mm. are long focus (telephoto).

Now suppose that for the 35 mm. frame we substitute a 16 mm. frame. The lens image is of course circular, and the frame rectangle is symmetrically inscribed in it, as shown in the diagram. Hence the frame diagonal' is also a diameter of the circle, and it is thus apparent that it is the length of the diagonal of the frame which determines the effective magnification with

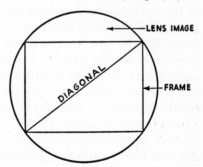

a lens of any given focal length. The diameter of the 35 mm. frame measures 1,073 mils (i.e. thousandths of an inch), and that of the 16 mm. frame measures 504 mils, or approximately one-half. Thus any given focal length of lens gives about twice the magnification on a 16 mm. frame, and hence equal magnifications are obtained when the 16 mm. lens has a focal length one-half that of its 35 mm. counterpart. Sixteen mm. wide-angle lenses are therefore in the 12–18 mm. group; normal lenses, 20–25 mm.; and long-focus or telephoto lenses, 35–250 mm. Millimeters are easily converted into inches by remembering that 25 mm. equal approximately one inch.

In the simple lens diagram of figure 3-9, the object lies in a single plane, and consequently, if the lens has no curvature of field, the image will also lie perfectly flat in the focal plane of the lens. However, practical camerawork is not confined to the shooting of flat objects like maps or pictures. Real solid objects produce an image which also has depth, though a depth enormously reduced by the geometry of the lens. We have seen how the eye has a "temporal tolerance" known as persistence of vision, which enables it to overlook the discontinuities in time which form the very condition under which film can be made. If the eye did not possess this property, it would be necessary to shoot film at an infinite number of frames per second; and this of course would be impossible. The eye has the same kind of "spatial tolerance," which enables it to overlook blurrings of the image in space, and see these blurs, if small enough, as sharp points. If the eye did not possess this property, but had an infinitely high power of discrimination, movies, and for that matter still photographs, of other than plane objects could not be satisfactorily made, the reason being that the eye would see a blurring of every object which was not precisely in the focal plane.

The depth of focus of a lens is twice the distance (D) the film can be moved from the plane of precise focus before an image point becomes unacceptably blurred. D is close to one-thousandth of $f \times N$, where f is the focal length of the lens, and N is its f/number. Thus a two-inch lens working at $f/2$ calls for the film plane to be within 0.004 inches of its correct position, evidence of the great accuracy required in camera construction. In practice, D is governed by the maximum acceptable diameter of blur circle, or *circle of confusion* as it is frequently called. This diameter, in turn, depends on the use to which the image is to be put. A circle 1/100 inch in diameter is frequently quoted as satisfactory for still pictures, a diameter of 1/250 inch being sought for more critical work. But because of the high magnification of the image on movie film when it is shown on the screen, nothing larger than 1/500 inch is sufficiently sharp for 35 mm. film and for 16 mm. film a circle with a diameter of 1/1000 inch is necessary. Tables will be found in *The American Cinematographer's Handbook* and elsewhere, showing the depth of field for lenses of different focal lengths and different apertures. The formation of the circle of confusion is shown in figure 3-10.

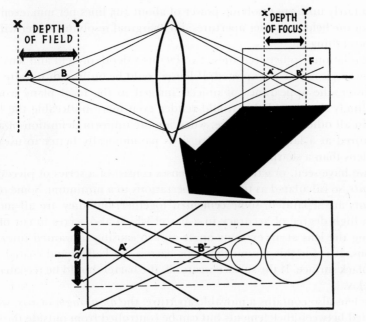

Fig. 3-10. Imaging a solid object on the film plane. A'
and B' are the image points corresponding to two axial
field points A and B. If the largest tolerable circle of confusion is represented by **d**, and F is the plane of the film,
F can be moved through a distance X'Y' before the circle
of confusion becomes unacceptably large. This is therefore known as the depth of focus. The corresponding
range of object distances (XY) is called the depth of
field.

In all practical lenses, even the image of a flat object on the focal plane is
not perfectly sharp. This condition, corresponding to the most perfect performance of which the lens is capable, is commonly measured, not in terms of
the blur circle, but of *resolving power*. Resolving power is defined in terms of
the fineness of parallel black lines, spaced by white lines of equal width, which
can be separated in the image. It is commonly measured in lines per millimeter, and is a concept of great importance throughout the photographic
process.[8] High quality camera lenses working at apertures of about $f/2.3$ will

[8] This is because the real world has the appearance of being a perfect continuum, the human eye having an effective resolving power much higher than can be obtained by the
photographic process under the best possible conditions. (*See* R. M. Evans, *An Introduction
to Color*, New York, Wiley, 1948, pp. 99–100.) Every photographic step, in fact, introduces
some determinate loss of resolving power, these losses often accumulating into a serious deterioration of the image. This is one reason why every part of the film-transmission system
must be designed with scrupulous care.

yield a fairly uniform resolving power of about 105 lines per mm. even at the edges of the field. At wider apertures, the marginal resolving power will show a serious falling off.

The relationship between these two factors—depth of field and lens resolving power—is rather unexpected. If lenses could be built with infinite resolving power, the appearance of objects imaged in the focal plane would be exceedingly sharp, and this would render even more noticeable the lack of focus in all other objects. Hence, when a more uniform definition of a scene is required at a large lens aperture, it is paradoxically better to use a soft-focus lens than a sharp one.

As we have seen, practical camera lenses consist of a series of pieces called *elements,* so calculated as to reduce aberrations to a minimum. Some of these elements are separated, some cemented together, but they are all mounted with a high degree of accuracy in a barrel which also serves to cut off light entering the lens at an extreme angle and so causing unwanted internal reflections. It is for this reason that lens barrels are baffled and coated with a matt-black surface. If the surface wears off, the barrel should be recoated without delay.

The lens also contains a movable aperture, the *diaphragm* or *iris,* which is mounted between the elements but can be controlled from outside the barrel. The purpose of this diaphragm is to act as a variable *stop* which decreases at will the amount of light actually falling on the film. The object of *stopping down* is (*a*) to prevent overexposure of the film, and (*b*) to secure greater depth of focus, for, the smaller the aperture in relation to the focal length (i.e., the lower the *speed* of the lens), the greater is the range of distances within which objects can be brought into sharp focus.[9] Thus speed and depth of focus are in inverse ratio.

The speed (or light-admitting capacity) of a lens is usually measured in a rather unsatisfactory way by its *f/number*—the focal length of the lens divided by its effective aperture or light-admitting diameter. Thus an *f*/2 lens has an effective aperture equal to half its focal length. If it is a 50 mm. lens, its aperture will be 25 mm. An *f*/11 lens with a focal length of 5½ inches has an effective aperture of ½ inch, and so on.

These *f*/numbers, however, do not directly indicate the relative speed of different lenses. This is because the light-admitting properties of a lens depend on its area, which in turn is proportional to the square of the diameter or aper-

---

[9] Stopping down a lens also tends to improve its definition, because the stop blocks off the periphery of the lens, where the corrections for aberrations are least effective. However, as the aperture is progressively reduced, a counteracting effect begins to set in. This is a result of the bending or diffraction of light rays when passing through very small apertures, which is described in textbooks on optics. The optimum aperture for definition depends on the design of the lens, but usually lies between *f*/5.6 and *f*/18.

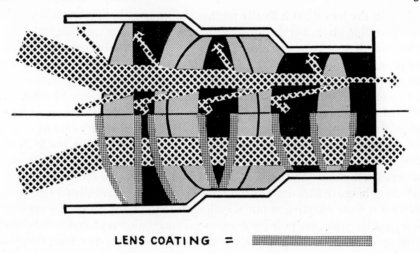

LENS COATING   =

Fig. 3-11. Loss of light at the glass-air surfaces of a lens. The upper half of the diagram shows how the incoming light beam is attenuated by losses due to successive reflections at air-glass surfaces, whereas in the lower half the coated lens passes the light through undiminished. (Light losses are exaggerated for the sake of clearness.)

ture. Hence, it is the squares of the f/numbers which inversely indicate lens speeds. An $f/2$ lens admits not two but four times as much light as an $f/4$ lens, because 4 divided by 2 and squared equals 4. It is therefore said to be four times as fast. In order to make the series of stops engraved beside the diaphragm lever indicate double or half the exposure at each change of stop, adjacent numbers have been chosen of which the squares are in the ratio of 2. The most commonly used series is: $f/1.4$, 2, 2.8, 4, 5.6, 8, 11, 16, 22, and 32. Another series often seen on European lenses is $f/1.6$, 2.3, 3.2, 4.5, 6.3, 9, 12.5, 18, 25, and 36. Lenses are always rated by their maximum effective apertures, which may not fall precisely in these series.

Most modern lenses are of large aperture, the extra light admittance serving to compensate for slow color films and finer-grain black-and-white emulsions. To correct aberrations, wide-aperture lenses must be built up out of three or four elements, so that a single lens may contain six or eight air-to-glass surfaces, at each of which light is lost by reflection, as shown in figure 3-11. This loss of light often amounts to between 30 and 40 per cent, and may even reach 50 per cent, whereupon the actual speed of the lens becomes a full stop less than the rated speed. In addition to lost light, some light may be reflected to and fro in the lens until it finally reaches the film, there to cause *flares* and a general veiling glare over the image which results in loss of contrast.

A means of decreasing surface reflection is now commonly applied to camera and projector lenses of the better sort. This is the *antireflective coating*, a thin film of transparent magnesium fluoride deposited by a vacuum process on the surface of the glass, which splits the reflected light into two equal beams, one reflected from the *interface* between lens and coating, the other from the surface of the coating itself. The refractive index of the coating material is such that the first *node* in one reflection coincides with the first *antinode* in the other, producing a cancellation which redirects the reflected energy through the lens itself. Since the action of the coating depends on refractive indexes and since these are functions of the wavelength of the transmitted light, cancellation is more effective at one wavelength than at any other. To even out these imperfections, the point of maximum cancellation is placed in the center of the spectrum (green region). Viewed by reflected light, therefore, the coating appears minus-green or magenta.

Antireflective coatings reduce reflection at each surface from about 5 per cent to about 0.5 per cent (figure 3-11). The slight color discrimination just noticed does not prevent their use even with well corrected color processes. The latest coatings resist abrasion and moisture fairly well. However, since they are less than four-millionths of an inch thick (one-quarter of a wavelength of light), they should be treated with the greatest care, and should never be touched with the fingers or roughly cleaned.

Since the f/number of a lens is of purely geometrical derivation, it takes no account of reflection, absorption, or scattering of light by the lens. Allowance can be made for these imperfections by correcting the f/number with a special ratio factor, often designated by the letter T (transmission). This factor is so defined that a lens rated at T-4 (its real speed index) passes the same amount of light as an imaginary f/4 lens having 100 per cent transmission. But if a lens of the same diameter and focal length transmitted only 50 per cent of the light which fell on it (an example by no means extreme), it would have a real speed index of T-5.6 to set against its claimed f rating speed of 4. Exposures made with this lens on the f rating basis would therefore be a full stop too low. T-ratings are likely to oust the older geometrical ratings as soon as standards of measurement have been agreed on.

Unlike f/numbers, T-ratings are not true lens constants. Wear of antireflective coatings, surface scratches, loss of blackening in the lens barrel, will reduce the effective T-number. The remedy is periodic recalibration of the lens.

Lenses, in short, should be regarded as variable-characteristic transmission systems, the transmission at any one time being a function of determinate geometrical, physical, and chemical factors. As a rule, the fidelity of this transmission system will be governed solely by the geometrical factors, and will therefore remain constant throughout the life of the lens. On the other hand, the efficiency of the system will depend also on the physical and chemical factors, which will undergo slow but substantial changes with time.[10]

This brief treatment of lens optics has shown that the lens, for all its seeming simplicity and ruggedness, is a complex and delicate instrument which requires exceedingly careful treatment. Lens surfaces should never be touched with the fingers, nor cleaned with miscellaneous objects such as rags, handkerchiefs, or tissue paper. Dust and grit should be removed only with a fine camel's hair brush. If grease spots are unavoidably formed on the lens surface, they may be removed with a small medical-cotton swab dipped in pure acetone. Both swabs and acetone can easily be bought at drug stores. Lenses should be wiped only with a soft lintless cloth, cotton swab, or special paper tissue.

Particles of dust on the lens surfaces, however carefully cleaned off, are bound to be damaging in the long run, and lenses should consequently be protected at all times when not in use by well-fitting rubber or metal lens caps. When a lens is dismounted for packing, a cap should be used to cover the rear element also. The removal of elements from lenses, except by expert optical technicians, is strongly to be discouraged. The spacing of elements is adjusted to minute limits of accuracy, and any variation of the pressure with which they are screwed in is likely to produce visible errors in the focus or correction of the lens.

Cameramen are sometimes asked to give a routine test to used lenses. Accurate tests are exclusively the business of an optical laboratory but the following simple checks may prove useful. Testing procedures within the capacity of an ordinary studio are described in Cox, *Optics*, pp. 217–257 (see Bibliography, p. 489).

INSPECTION TESTS

1. Look at the make and type of lens, usually engraved on the recessed part of the barrel surrounding the front element. Experience will show whether the lens was a good one when new.

2. Check the focal length and aperture markings, and make sure that both characteristics are suited to the work the lens will be called upon to do.

3. Examine the lens mount and make sure there is no play or rattle when the barrel is moved in and out by means of the focusing lever.

4. Check the diaphragm (a) by looking inside the barrel and making sure that none of the movable leaves are broken or missing; (b) by sliding the control back and forth and feeling for roughnesses which will indicate particles of grit in the mechanism.

5. Inspect the front and back surfaces of the lens and make sure that the glass is not chipped at the edges. Some old lenses show small occluded air bubbles which do not affect image quality.

6. Note whether the matt black covering the inside of the lens barrel is in good condition, together with the cement which holds the lens elements in their mounting rings. Also be sure that the elements are firm and do not rattle.

[10] See the very complete "Report of Lens Calibration Subcommittee," *JSMPE*, Oct., 1949, pp. 368–378, which contains a full bibliography.

PERFORMANCE TESTS

1. *Lens centering.* Make a 1/10 inch pinhole in a card, backlight it with a 25-watt bulb, and set it up 10 to 15 feet from the camera. Examine the image through the focusing microscope on ground film in the aperture, or, failing this, on the ground glass. Focus the pinhole in the center of the field, then very slowly turn the lens in both directions. If the shape of the patch is not circular, and changes as the lens turns, the lens is badly centered and should be rejected. Repeat with the pinhole in other parts of the field.

2. *Definition on lens axis.* Repeat the pinhole test, examining the image shape and clearness with great care. If the lens is well corrected for spherical and chromatic aberrations, the pinhole will come cleanly and sharply into focus. Uncertainty about the precise focus position is a bad sign.

3. *Focus scales.* Place the pinhole at precise measured distances from the film plane, focus carefully and check scale readings. For greater accuracy, expose frames of film at positions staggered slightly on either side of visual focus and examine negative under microscope.

4. *Resolving power.* Set up lens charts at appropriate distance to give at least 50 lines per mm. on film. Shoot, develop and examine negative to make sure that marginal definition is at least 25 lines per mm. Use the finest-grain emulsion available.

THE ZOOM LENS

We have seen that since, on a given size of film, all lenses form the same size of image, the magnification of a lens will depend on a single constant, its focal length. In this way, lenses can be ranged in order from the extremest wide-angle to the longest telephoto. Disregarding such extremes, it is still necessary, when shooting an average film, to have at hand a minimum of three lenses, and to have five or six is much more convenient. Each of these separate lenses, differing essentially only in focal length, is an instrument of high precision, containing six or eight elements, a baffled barrel, an iris diaphragm, and a focusing mount, all assembled and calibrated with the utmost accuracy. Three good lenses may, in fact, cost as much as the carcass of the small field or combat camera which carries them.

It is not surprising, therefore, that the ingenuity of lens designers has long been taxed by the problem of designing a lens of variable focal length, which would not only eliminate the multiplication of individual lenses, but would make possible interesting variable magnification or zoom effects.

However, so formidable are the difficulties of designing even a fixed focal length lens of impeccable quality that the problems of adequately correcting aberrations in a lens of variable focal length have proved well-nigh insuperable. Only three *zoom lenses* have ever reached the American market, the Bell and Howell, the Astro, and the Zoomar, of which the last alone is available today. Even the Zoomar, which represents an immense step forward in the elimination of multiple sliding elements and cams, is normally available only for 16 mm. cameras, and at wide apertures cannot compare in definition with the best lenses of fixed focal length.

Rated at a maximum aperture of $f/2.9$, the 16 mm. Zoomar lens has two ranges of zooming, one of them obtained with a small auxiliary lens which can be screwed to the front element. The two ranges of focal length are 17–53 mm. and 35–106 mm., the overlap allowing the cameraman to cover in what appears to be a single shot the whole range, 17–106 mm., provided that in the section where the overlap occurs, the camera and the subject are motionless, and the speed of zooming on the two sections is accurately matched.

The Zoomar lens consists of two long coupled barrels placed side by side, the second acting as a viewfinder and in principle giving the same field of view as the main lens at all magnifications. In practice, it is not safe to rely exclusively on the viewfinder, and the lens should be used on cameras which make provision for lining up the scene through the shooting lens and a focusing microscope. Zooming is effected by a means of a long lever mounted below the lens barrels. Its movement is oil damped, making possible the slowest of zooms with the greatest smoothness. The focusing and diaphragm controls of the Zoomar lens are perfectly normal, the same aperture and focusing settings obtaining all the way through the range of zoom effect. However, to obtain an image quality which enables zoom shots to be intercut with normal-lens shots, it is necessary to stop down the zoom lens to $f/7$ or smaller, which is often inconvenient or impossible when shooting in color.

Continuous improvement of the Zoomar lens is proceeding, and the next few years may see it begin to replace sets of normal lenses, while adding the important extra tool of variable magnification. It is here that interesting aesthetic effects arise which have not yet been sufficiently studied. We shall see in a later chapter how zoom effects have always been obtainable in the optical printer by taking a shot of fixed magnification and rephotographing it frame by frame with the camera approaching it little by little. This effect, which can be achieved even more easily by animation, is familiar to every moviegoer from the shots of newspapers and headlines which suddenly rush up out of the distance until they fill the screen.

Where the subject is flat, like a newspaper, this technique is perfectly effective; but where it has depth, it becomes apparent immediately that objects do not seem to be moving past one another, that in fact there is no parallax between them. This rapidly destroys the illusion of reality, for parallax is one of the chief means of overcoming the actual flatness of the film image. For this reason, zoom shots must be very carefully planned.

The least satisfactory kind of zoom is frequently to be seen in newsreels, when the frame embraces a whole football field, let us say, as seen from high up in the stands, and then quickly zooms down to a small group of players. In spite of the great change of magnification, the effect is not that of traveling through space; it is little more than that of dissolving from an ordinary long shot to a close up. Let us suppose, however, that at almost maximum magnification, our zoom lens is framing the same small group of players. The camera pans up to the stands just behind, a simultaneous slow zoom using the remaining magnification giving the impression that the camera is moving in on a few spectators to watch their reaction. Then, at slightly greater speed, the zoom control is pulled back, and the camera is simultaneously panned and tilted upwards. If these movements are skillfully coördinated, it will seem as if the camera itself were moving upward and sideways through empty space above the field, in order to get a full general view of the stands and the game. Let us suppose that at the end of this maneuver some zoom range still remains. The camera is, in fact, mounted behind some kind of arch which can only be framed by a very wide angle shot. As this arch comes unexpectedly into view at the end of the zoom, it creates an irresistible impression that the camera has actually withdrawn through it, passing by its very walls.

Thus we have the following elements: (a) a fixed magnification section of the shot at the beginning, which makes the audience think that nothing surprising will happen; (b) a slow zoom and pan in, which gives the searching, groping effect produced by actual camera movement, thus helping to annul the absence of parallax; (c) a highly complicated zoom-plus-pan-plus-tilt which adds still further to the illusion of reality of camera movement; (d) a completely surprising element, the arch, which seems to give a final confirmation to the swooping, aerial character of the shot.

While all these elements cannot be present in every zoom shot, it is extremely important to bear in mind the principles they rest on, and especially the necessity of zooming slowly. The zoom shot may easily degenerate into a mere technical trick, which will pall on audiences as quickly as the exaggerated use of wipes in editing some fifteen years ago. Used, however, with a real understanding of its technical capacities and limitations, the zoom shot can be a powerful artistic tool.

LENS TURRETS AND ACCESSORIES

On almost all cameras except the very largest and the very smallest, the lenses are mounted in clusters of three or four on a turret, a revolving device which serves to bring the wanted lens in front of the aperture. A three-lens turret on a 35 mm. camera may be equipped with 25, 50 and 75 mm. lenses, or 35, 50 and 100 mm., or any other combination which suits the cameraman's needs. The only limitation is that a very-long-focus lens will obstruct the field of view of an adjacent wide-angle lens. Since lenses are readily demountable, it is easy to alter the combination in the field.

It has been found that camera noise readily seeps through a lens turret and tends to interfere with dialogue recording. For this reason some of the latest sound cameras have returned to the old single-lens panel, since in the

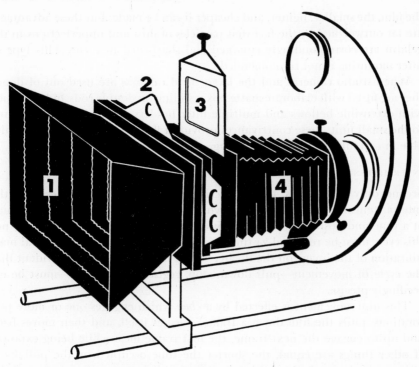

Fig. 3-12. The matte box. Running on rods attached to the front of the camera, it consists of a sunshade (1) ridged to minimize reflections, a series of filter and matte holders, as at 2 and 3, and an extensible bellows (4) for varying the shielding of the lens.

studio labor is plentiful and action does not have to be caught on the run.

The most important lens accessory is the *filter*, which is discussed in chapter ix since it is difficult to understand how filters work without some knowledge of the theory of color. Lenses should be readily fitted with filters and shaded from direct sunlight if they are to work efficiently. On small hand cameras, both filter and sunshade must usually be screwed into each separate lens. Larger cameras, however, are equipped with more or less elaborate *matte boxes* combined with a single large lens shade. The term "matte box" originally referred to the holder for mattes or masks used in the days of silent pictures to produce special effects, before the perfection of the optical printer. The term outlived its application and now refers to a fixed filter holder, behind which the lenses rotate on their turret (figure 3-12).

Some cameras make provision for mounting gelatin filters in a holder in a narrow slot between shutter and film. Obviously, the nearer the filter lies to the film, the smaller, lighter, and cheaper it can be made; but these advantages are far outweighed by the fact that particles of dust and imperfections in the gelatin are correspondingly enlarged and sharpened in focus. This type of filter mounting is not recommended.

When studio cameras and the larger field cameras are used out of doors, they are fitted with elaborate matte boxes sliding on double rods and equipped with extensible bellows and multiple filter holders. Though often irritating to the small unit, these contrivances provide a flexibility of operation invaluable in careful and accurate shooting.

INTERMITTENT MOVEMENT

Second only to the lens, the most critical part of a camera's design is the intermittent movement, the device which carries the film downward a frame at a time and positions or registers it during the moment of exposure. Since this cycle must be repeated 24 times every second, and since the vertical magnification of the image on the theater screen may reach 500, it is evident that the cycle of movement—pull down, stop, register, pull down—must be exceedingly precise.

This film movement is effected by a *claw* which engages one or more perforations, pulls the film down a frame, releases itself, and then moves back and up to engage the next frame, the first frame meanwhile being exposed. If other things are equal, the shorter the time occupied by the pull-down process, the better is the mechanism, since this leaves a greater part of the cycle for exposure of the film. But it is also most important that the film be accelerated and slowed down smoothly to avoid tearing of perforations, especially at high speeds. For these reasons, the best intermittent mechanisms are complicated arrangements of cams and eccentrics, machined with very great accuracy. Though little larger than a matchbox, they cost several hundred dollars. However, this is a small price to pay for the mechanism which positions the celluloid strip that every day may record action costing hundreds of thousands of dollars. Figure 3-13 shows a very simple intermittent mechanism having pilot pins but only a single claw instead of the usual one on each side.

The standard of accuracy in the 35 mm. motion picture industry has been set by two film movements—the Bell and Howell, designed nearly forty years ago, and the Mitchell. Both of these employ *pilot pins* to position the film, that is, pins having the same height as the film perforations, which engage these perforations when the pull-down action is complete, and thus hold the film steady while it is being exposed. In the Bell and Howell camera, these pins are fixed to the frame, and the film is pushed onto them and subsequently lifted off. In the Mitchell camera, the pins are mounted on a plunger, which thrusts forward to engage the perforations, one on each side of the frame.

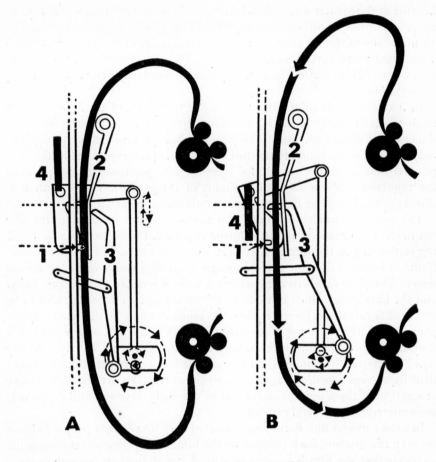

Fig. 3-13. A simple intermittent movement. Diagram A shows the film at rest, the pilot pin (1) engaged in a perforation, the back pressure plate (2) pressing the film flat against the aperture plate, and the claw (3) moving up and in to engage a perforation. A few moments later, as in B, the plate (2) has relaxed its pressure, causing the film to leave the pilot pin, and the claw is starting to pull it down, while obscured by the shutter (4), in preparation for the next exposure. Note the expansion and contraction of the film loops above and below the aperture.

Several other cameras, such as the British Newall and the Vinten, and the French Eclair and the Debrie, have similar intermittent mechanisms.

However, there is a school of thought which holds that, especially with 16 mm. film, registration pins may actually contribute to image unsteadiness because of the greater dimensional changes of the acetate base, which is more hygroscopic than its nitrate counterpart used for 35 mm. negative. The Maurer 16 mm. camera, for instance, is now designed without the pilot pins which were fitted to an earlier model. However, the pull-down claws act as their own means of registration, since they pause momentarily before withdrawing from the film.

In a camera with pilot pins, mechanical steadiness of the image can be made virtually absolute, leaving the film material itself as the only source of dimensional variations. Both pilot pins fill their perforations vertically, but only one pin is machined to the full width of its perforation. This, the "big pin," is thus alone responsible for sideways film positioning, and provides the reference axis for all measurements of image shift, which, with low-shrinkage stock, can be held to a few ten-thousandths of an inch.

The transport mechanism must also make provision for holding the film flat in the focal plane of the lens during exposure. Even a microscopic bending or twisting of the film in the aperture, or alteration in its position from frame to frame, will show up as a greatly magnified *weave* or *flutter* on the screen. The plate in which the aperture is formed is called the *aperture plate;* and the back plate which can be opened on a hinge to allow the film to be threaded is called the *pressure plate.* To make the film lie in a perfectly flat plane, it is necessary to apply pressure to it back and front, on the soft emulsion surface as well as on the hard base. Since the film is not merely traveling rapidly but traveling intermittently, so that its peak speed is much higher than its average speed, the aperture and pressure plates are a prolific source of *scratching,* the bane of cameramen in the early days and still frequently encountered on some field cameras.[11]

In most cameras film flattening is assured very simply by a proper balance between the side and back pressure on the film, these pressures remaining the same whether the film is moving or still. A few designs incorporate a more complicated *intermittent pressure* device, which clamps the film securely when it is at rest and then freely releases it for transport to the next frame.

The aperture and pressure plates are slightly recessed all over the picture area, except for the narrow rim round the aperture itself, so that the film is held principally by its outer edges. This militates against scratching, but if the plates become pitted, scraps of emulsion will collect in them, which soon

11 When a print is being looked at, it is usually possible to distinguish scratches in the print itself from scratches printed from a negative. Because small scratches rapidly become filled with dirt, print scratches are black, whereas negative scratches printed onto the print will be white. The only intentional scratches are those which are placed on prints from *stock-shot* libraries to prevent their unlawful duplication. These scratches are made by a mutilator; they are heavy and run down the middle of the screen. A print thus scratched is called a *scratched print.*

build up and harden until they touch the film surface and irreparably damage it. Guide rollers are also undercut across the picture area, and it is important to keep them free running and clear of emulsion.

During the pull-down period, the film is blocked off from the lens by a shutter, thus preventing blurring of the image with incoming light. The angle of the shutter blades is calculated to cover the film only during motion, so not to waste precious time available for exposure. Hence the size of the shutter angle is a measure of the efficiency of the pull-down mechanism, and a direct indication of the available exposure at any camera speed.[12] Many professional cameras have an outside shutter adjustment, by which the shutter angle can be progressively reduced from its maximum to zero. This provides the cameraman with a means of adjusting his exposure independently of the lens iris, which is occasionally useful when it is required to control the depth of focus of a shot within narrow limits, or when the lens iris does not provide a small enough stop for holding down brilliant sunlight on a fast film. A variable shutter angle can also be used to reduce stroboscopic flicker effects (see p. 76).

The original purpose of the adjustable shutter was to provide for *fade-ins* and *fade-outs*. With a windback of the film it made camera dissolves possible, a useful arrangement twenty-five years ago when optical printers were uncommon and when duplication was an inefficient process. The technique is now obsolete, save for direct 16 mm. shooting in production centers where 16 mm. optical printing facilities are still not available.

The intermittent movement is completed by a simple device. If film were to be run directly from a continuously turning sprocket to the pull-down mechanism, it would immediately tear. This is because the claw, when engaged, must move the film forward much faster than its average or sprocket-driven speed, in order to make up for the periods when it is at rest. Consequently the film would have to travel at two different speeds at once, which is impossible. Again, when the film emerges from the aperture and is at rest, it cannot at the same time be traveling round a sprocket at its average speed. This dilemma is resolved by the use of *loops,* or slack sections of film which alternately expand and contract to allow for the difference of motion. One loop is formed above the aperture and one below. Practice will show that if a loop is too small, it will snatch the film and tear the perforations; if too large, it will flap about, hit the surrounding mechanism and perhaps make the film movement in the aperture unsteady. All intermittent film mechanisms require loops.

12 Shutter angles vary quite widely in practice—between 135° and 230° in commonly found commercial designs. Exposures with different shutter angles and shooting speeds can be rapidly calculated, or they may be found in tables in the *American Cinematographer's Handbook.*

Fig. 3-14. A new conception of the movie camera: the Cameflex-Eclair. The camera carcass (A) has been reduced from its old box-like form to a light-alloy casting which carries the three-lens turret (B), the film magazine (C), and the reflex viewfinding mechanism which terminates in the eyepiece (D). The electric driving motor (E), with built-in rheostat and switch, has shrunk to a very small size. The magazine, which is clamped onto the camera without manual threading and even when the motor is running, can be

THE CHOICE OF A CAMERA

Studio cameras.—The studio camera, costing upward of $20,000 when completely equipped and mounted, is a major item in the expenditures of any moderate-sized production unit. It should therefore be chosen with the utmost care, after examining the specifications and performances of all available machines. In particular, methods of silencing vary greatly, and adequate silence is sometimes secured by devices so clumsy that control of the camera becomes awkward and slow. Since silencing is necessary for direct dialogue recording,[13] studio cameras—which alone are silenced—must often be taken into the field. Here compactness and convenience are imperative, for the smaller unit cannot manage many setups if it has to haul a very heavy camera and dolly from place to place.

Field cameras.—These cameras are much lighter than their studio counterparts, but the best of them—the Mitchell and the Bell and Howell, for instance—have movements of equally high accuracy. When fitted with good lenses, they are capable of turning in a complete production fully equal to studio standards of camera quality. The less good machines on the list given below are used as second-line cameras, or in places where only a hand-held camera can be operated.

Combat cameras.—In our present condition of permanent war, it is not surprising that much thought has been lavished on a type of camera which

---

either of 30 meters capacity, as shown, or of 120 meters. The reflex eyepiece can be swiveled through a wide angle to suit any position of the cameraman's head. The lenses are angled outwards from one another so that a long-focus lens will not interfere with the field of a wide-angle lens mounted in an adjacent socket. Complete with small magazine, film, lenses and motor, the camera weighs less than 12 pounds, and can therefore be fitted, with its friction head, to clamp mountings as at (F) attached to doors, mouldings, brackets, fences, etc. At the same time, the camera with its head (G) can be removed from (F) at the turn of a single screw and placed on a light tripod. The basic camera design lends itself with little change to 16 mm. shooting, filming of the television image (with a 340° shutter opening), underwater photography in a streamlined shell guided by a diver, and synchronized silent operation for sound shooting. (Courtesy M. Coutant and Etablissements Eclair.)

[13] Indirect, or *playback*, methods of dialogue recording, which do not require silenced cameras, are described in chapter xii.

should be equally suited to tripod and hand use, much more adaptable than the older field cameras, and capable of producing negatives of studio quality which can form the bulk of a feature picture. Two of these cameras, the French Cameflex [14] and the German Arriflex, have proved outstandingly successful.

Sixteen mm. cameras.—Professional 16 mm. production demands even higher camera standards than required in 35 mm. Attention should therefore be fastened on the details of design, with special attention to viewfinding, since the smaller image is harder to examine critically when shooting. Only the finest lenses should be bought, but these will be wasted if the intermittent mechanism is not built to very close tolerances. Many will regret the increasing size and weight of professional 16 mm. cameras, since one of the outstanding advantages of 16 mm. has been its mobility, which favored small and inexpensive shooting units. Modern 16 mm. cameras are almost as difficult to carry and set up as the heaviest of the 35 mm. field cameras described below; they are more cumbersome than the 35 mm. combat cameras.

If the choice of a unit falls on a combat or light field camera, the results may at first fail to meet expectations. The very ease of operation is a snare. The simplicity of moving from one setup to another, with the camera ready to shoot a few seconds after the tripod has been placed, invites both director and cameraman to skimp the rehearsal of whatever action is to go on before the lens. If there is awkwardness of composition or action, it is easy to think that another equally hurried setup will make it good. But though the camera may be dragged from one position to another, and a great footage of film exposed, calm review later in the projection room (often too late to reshoot) may show that all the shots are haphazard, and that extra coverage has merely multiplied the sense of carelessness.

The studio or heavy field camera is by contrast slow and difficult to move around. But once set up, there is a strong argument for contriving the action as compactly and expressively as possible, if only to save sweat and toil.

CHARACTERISTICS OF LEADING MAKES

The list which follows comprises most of the cameras in common professional use in North America and Europe, and outlines the salient points of each.

STUDIO CAMERAS (35 mm.)

1. **Mitchell (N.C. Model).** A silenced camera of conventional design and exceptionally good workmanhip employed as standard equipment in most American and many European studios. Four-lens turret, variable 175° shutter, shift-over viewfinding with excellent optical system, large-view monitoring finder, pilot-pin movement with constant pressure. Two-compartment external magazines.

2. **Mitchell (B.N.C. Model).** Virtually an N.C. model within a sound-deadening

---

14 Now known in America as the Camerette. See André Coutant and Jacques Mathot. "A Reflex 35 mm. Magazine Motion Picture Camera," *JSMPTE*, Aug., 1950, pp. 173–179.

shell, sufficient space being left for the characteristic Mitchell rackover. Single-lens bayonet mounting (no turret) to reduce noise transmission. Specially silenced pull-down mechanism. Automatic parallax-correcting monitoring viewfinder.

3. **Newall.** A British version of the N.C. Mitchell. There are virtually no differences between the two machines.

4. **Vinten (Everest II).** An ingenious and compact British design, which cleverly combines features from the Debrie and Arriflex cameras with several original devices. Shutter (170°) with improved reflex finder, eliminating parallax complications at the source. Controls split between back and side of camera, with camera assistant operating lens diaphragm and focus, the latter coupled to a built-in range finder. Single interchangeable lens. Camera cover is also blimp. Side-by-side magazines. Pilot-pin constant-pressure movement.

5. **Debrie.** A prewar camera of advanced design, of which production has now been resumed. Great compactness has been attained, but at the expense of ruggedness and simplicity. Direct viewfinding through the film when shooting, 180° shutter, pilot-pin movement with intermittent pressure. Separate internal magazines mounted side by side.

6. **Twentieth-Century Fox.** A comparatively recent design which is not radically different from the Mitchell. Four-lens turret, 200° shutter. For direct viewfinding, camera rotates through small arc instead of racking over. Silenced pilot-pin pull-down mechanism with constant pressure. Automatic parallax-correcting monitor finder. Mitchell-type magazines. Camera is self-silenced.

7. **Galileo.** An extremely refined Debrie-type camera of Italian design with very compact and complicated follow-focus and parallax-correcting mechanism.

FIELD CAMERAS (35 mm.)

1. **Mitchell (Standard Model).** The camera from which the N.C. model was evolved. The design is essentially the same, but no noise-reducing features are incorporated.

2. **Bell & Howell (Standard Model).** Though one of the oldest machines in service (and no longer in production), this camera is fitted with an intermittent movement of the highest precision, which is matched by the rest of the mechanism. A rackover conversion job is essential, as the original direct viewfinding system is very primitive. Four-lens turret, 170° shutter, pilot-pin movement with intermittent pressure.

3. **Bell & Howell (Eyemo Models K, L, M).** A widely used hand camera of simple design. One-hundred-foot daylight-loading film spools, 55-foot spring drive, single-lens mounting or turret, 160° fixed shutter, simple pressure pull-down movement without pilot pins, no viewfinding through the lens, small-image monitoring finder. Larger models add 200-foot or 400-foot magazines, electric-motor drive, and direct viewfinding, but only at the cost of simplicity and compactness.

4. **Newman-Sinclair (Model G).** A compact rectangular camera of British design, built up of duralumin plates. Individual lenses on interchangeable sliding panels, 170° shutter. Pilot-pin movement with intermittent pressure, 200-foot internal magazines, double spring motor driving 170 feet of film on one wind. Weight, with film, 22½ pounds. Direct viewfinding of erect image through back of film, and focusing on ground glass with small parallax error. Built-in monitoring finder has internal footage counter and spirit level.

5. **Debrie.** Several prewar models in use, with 170° shutters, single-lens mounts, viewfinding through the film when shooting, rather inadequate monitoring finders. Four-hundred-foot magazines (raw stock must be specially Debrie wound, emulsion out). Some models have pilot-pin registration, others not.

6. **Akeley.** An old type of hand-cranked camera still giving magnificent service in the hands of newsreel cameramen. Designed primarily for exteriors. Dual-lens plate carrying picture and finder lenses close together, no parallax correction, simple pull-down movement without pilot pins or intermittent pressure. Two-hundred-foot built-in magazines, 230° shutter. Camera is easily recognizable by its circular shape.

7. **Vinten (Model H).** A British camera of a design generally similar to the Mitchell Standard. Four-lens turret, 170° variable-angle shutter. Rackover direct viewfinding by displacing film instead of camera. Large-image external monitoring finder. Pilot-pin movement with constant pressure. External double-compartment magazines.

COMBAT CAMERAS (35 mm.)

1. **Arriflex.** German. An exceptionally well-designed and compact camera for rapid field work. First camera to incorporate the reflex viewfinder. Three-lens turret, 130° shutter, 200-foot external gear-driven magazines, 12-volt motor drive, built in *tachometer,* simple pull-down movement without pilot pins or intermittent pressure.

2. **Cameflex.** French. Introduced in 1948, this camera is of excellent design and workmanship. Reflex finder with flexible eyepiece. Variable 200° shutter (230° shutter also available). Constant-pressure movement without pilot pins. Three-lens turret with diverging lens mounts, so that there is no interference between the longest- and shortest-focus lenses. Interchangeable 30- and 120-meter magazines. Spring or electric motor (6 volt) drive. Speed range, 8–32 frames per second. Total weight with 3 lenses, 120-meter magazine, and electric motor: 14 pounds.

SINGLE-SYSTEM SOUND CAMERAS (35 mm.)

1. **Akeley.** A silenced camera used chiefly for newsreel interview shooting. Three-lens turret or 2-lens plate, 225° or 280° shutter, pilot-pin movement with constant pressure. Mitchell-type magazines. Adaptable to various types of recording galvanometer.

2. **Mitchell (Single-System).** An adaptation of the Mitchell (N.C.) described above.

3. **Wall.** A somewhat similar design to the Mitchell (N.C.).

PROFESSIONAL CAMERAS (16 mm.)

1. **Maurer.** A partly silenced camera with electric-motor drive, and 200-foot, 400-foot, or 1,200-foot gear-driven magazines. Three-lens turret, 235° variable shutter, constant-pressure movement without pilot pins. Mitchell-type rackover direct-focusing system, with large-image monitoring finder. Weight, ready to shoot, with tripod: 40 pounds.

2. **Mitchell ("16").** A partly silenced camera which closely follows the specifications of the N.C. model. Weight, ready to shoot, with tripod: 55 pounds.

3. **Auricon-Pro.** A self-blimped camera fitted with 115-volt single-phase synchronous motor drive, and 200-foot magazines. Constant-pressure movement without pilot pins, 175° fixed shutter. Single-lens mount, no focusing through lens. Parallax-correcting, large-field viewfinder. Weight: 22 pounds.

4. **Kodak (Cine Special).** Though designed for the amateur (and therefore lighter, somewhat cheaper and built with less precision than the machines listed above), this camera has seen professional service for many years. Two-lens turret, 170° variable shutter, constant-pressure movement without pilot pins. Spring drive, 38 feet on one wind. One-hundred-foot built-in magazine, 200-foot external magazines and electric-motor drive available. Nonsilenced. Direct focusing through prism which clears itself automatically when camera starts. Very small reversed image, and small monitoring finder. Weight, ready to shoot, with 12-pound tripod: 22 pounds.

5. **Bell & Howell (Specialist).** A rather clumsy expansion of the Filmo 70-D camera. Four-lens turret, 204° fixed shutter, constant-pressure movement without pilot pins. Spring or electric motor drive, 100-foot, 200-foot, or 400-foot magazines. Nonsilenced. Mitchell-type rackover direct-focusing system, with small-image monitoring finder having a parallax adjustment. Speed range, 8–64 frames per second.

6. **Bolex.** Swiss. A compact, high-precision camera designed for the amateur but usable by the professional. Three-lens turret, 190° shutter, constant-pressure movement without pilot pins. Spring drive, with 18-foot capacity. Speed range, 8–64 frames per second. One-hundred-foot daylight-loading spools. Nonsilenced. Direct focusing through lens, but not in shooting position, and with very small reversed image. Small-image monitoring finder with parallax correction.

SINGLE-SYSTEM SOUND CAMERAS (16 mm.)

1. **Auricon-Pro.** Identical with the Auricon-Pro camera described above, except that it is fitted with galvanometer for producing unilateral variable-area track. Weight: 22 pounds.

CAMERA FAULTS

It may be convenient to collect in one place a list of the principal faults to which cameras are liable, in order that the newcomer to film may learn to identify them as accurately as possible when he sees his *dailies* on the screen.

1. Scratching.—Trace back immediately to negative, to eliminate printer and projector scratches on the positive. Negative scratches may also derive from the developing machine and printer rather than from the camera. Scratches may be either on the base or emulsion side of the film, the former being as a rule less serious because the hard base is more resistant to scratching than the soft *emulsion*. Camera scratches can usually be traced to a pile-up of emulsion on the aperture or pressure plate which results from insufficient cleaning out of the camera. Dust in the *light traps* (or light-tight openings) of magazines is a less frequent source of scratches. A scratch near the side of the frame can often be eliminated by optical enlargement (see chapter vi, p. 150).

2. Unsteadiness.—Unsteadiness of the image on the screen is often extremely difficult to trace to its source. First eliminate printer unsteadiness by projecting the negative; then eliminate projector unsteadiness by having the picture framed so that the *frame line* appears on the screen. If this line is perfectly steady, the projector is not contributing to the image unsteadiness. The term *weave* is often applied to side-to-side movement and *flutter* to fore-and-aft movement (apparent movement at right angles to the plane of the screen, causing rapid defocusing). The simple term *unsteadiness* is usually reserved for up-and-down movement. Some causes are: wear of the pilot pin(s), if any; upset relationship between side and back pressure on the film (if constant pressure); loops too small, or occasionally too big. Simple 35 mm. camera movements cannot be expected to give the rock-steady images achieved with pilot pins, especially after the camera has been in use for several years. However, with 16 mm. cameras, pilot pins do not give the same guarantee against image unsteadiness, because of the more variable *shrinkage* of the film.

3. Flare.—Bright areas of light marring the camera image are called flare. They normally arise when the lens is pointed close to a bright light source, owing to spillover of light striking the front surface of the lens. Coating greatly reduces the tendency to flare, but it can only be prevented by adequate shading of the lens.

4. Fogging.—Light leaks in the camera will almost certainly expose the film and cause fogging. If the fogging is exclusively along the edge of the film (*edge fogging*), it is likely to originate in the magazine, where the tight winding of the film reduces unwanted exposure across its full surface.

5. Blurred pans and stroboscopic effects.—The familiar but very irritating effect of spoked wheels revolving backward on the screen derives from the essentially stroboscopic or intermittent character of the motion picture. Rapid cyclical events (e.g., the movement of spokes) are likely to be reproduced in jumbled form, for the camera only picks out isolated moments from the continuum of reality. Certain rapid serial movements, like pans across railings or brightly lighted venetian blinds, produce very unpleasant flickering effects, due to the conflict between continuous movement and intermittent reproduction (cf. Zeno's paradox of the arrow). Flickering pans can be somewhat improved by increasing the shutter angle, so that each exposure is longer and the image more blurred. But the best remedy is to avoid this type of shot whenever possible.

6. Unsharp focus.—In nine cases out of ten, out-of-focus shots appearing on the screen are the result of incorrect focusing by the cameraman, and are therefore not camera faults. However, if focusing has been effected by setting the lens calibrations to the distance measured to the principal object, it may be that these calibrations are themselves at fault. Occasionally, this is due to some remediable defect: either the lens mount is not firmly secured in the camera, or the barrel, fitting into its mount on a multiple-thread screw, has been screwed in along the wrong thread. If an obvious defect such as this cannot be found, the camera should be sent for repair by an expert.

7. Travel ghost.—When the camera shutter is incorrectly synchronized with the movement of the film, the film will be exposed to the lens image while it is starting to move or is just about to stop. The photographed image will therefore be blurred, and will show a ghostly picture accompanying the wanted picture. This is known as *travel ghost.* The simple remedy—resynchronizing the shutter—can usually be effected without much difficulty.

8. Static.—Cameras in use under field conditions will often develop static electricity by the rubbing of the film against the aperture and pressure plates. If a discharge takes place across the emulsion surface, its luminosity will cause an exposure and an image will appear when the film is developed. As a rule this image can be recognized by its brush or crowsfoot pattern, and it is of course impossible to separate it from the wanted image. Static is favored by excessive aperture pressure on the film and by low temperature and humidity. Until the film is developed, there is no way of knowing whether the image has been spoiled by static. With well-designed cameras, static is only to be feared at extremely low temperatures.[15]

ACCESSORIES TO THE CAMERA

Various pieces of associated equipment are needed to make the camera work effectively, and some of these require brief description here.

BLIMPS

The blimp is a soundproof covering for the camera which prevents camera noise from reaching the microphone when recording dialogue. Since studio crews are apt to be large, heavy blimps do not inconvenience them, and therefore little has been done to make blimped cameras more manageable. As the table of 16 mm. cameras will show, silencing is still too often an afterthought, and heavy blimps, costing as much as a thousand dollars, may have to be added to cameras that are already too expensive.

In the best designs, the blimp is an integral part of the camera housing, and therefore does not interfere with the controls. However, there is only one 16 mm. camera with this type of blimp, and it has compensating disadvantages. If a standard blimp has to be bought, points to watch are: (*a*) insulation beneath the camera to isolate vibration from the tripod or other mount; (*b*) counterweighting and easy raising of the blimp to make internal adjustments; (*c*) ability to change magazines without taking off the blimp; (*d*) sturdiness of the follow-focus and parallax-correcting mechanism (most of these make use of a grooved drum rotated by a length of piano wire which frays and breaks after continued use if the device is not very well designed).

Most commercial blimps are satisfactory when tested with a new camera, and this is how they are most often demonstrated. But cameras, like other mechanisms, get noisier as they get older, no matter how carefully they are maintained. The buyer is wise, therefore, to test a blimp with a camera which has been used for some time, and not with a new one.

CAMERA MOUNTINGS

Supports for the camera include the tripod, high hat, baby tripod, dolly, velocilator, and boom or crane. The tripod is a development of the still-camera

---

[15] Static is occasionally produced by maladjusted printers. When a print is being screened, static marks show up black if they are in the print only, white if (as is more usual) they are printed through from the negative.

tripod. Points to notice in its design are: sturdiness of the legs, ease of adjusting height, spirit levels for leveling, and above all construction of the *head* on which the camera is mounted (figure 3-15). There are three types of tripod head in general use: the *geared head,* the *friction head,* and the *gyro head.* The geared head has separate worm-gear drives for panning and tilting, these being operated by crank handles. It is little used in the field, where quick pans may need to be made, and where the cameraman must be able to pan as well as operate the camera. Frequently, however, velocilators and booms are fitted with geared heads of massive construction for use in the studio.

The friction head makes use of simple frictional resistance to provide steadiness of panning. In experienced hands it can give exceedingly satisfactory results, but only if it is of good design. Points to watch for are: (*a*) the diameter of the friction element should be ample; (*b*) the movement should be free from the slightest roughness; (*c*) the vertical and horizontal locks should be capable of adjusting tension to fine limits. If it is to support a heavy camera, the friction head should be fitted with springs as a counterbalance.

The gyro head (as it is rather inaccurately called, since it has no perceptible gyroscopic effect) consists of a geared drive rotating a comparatively heavy

Fig. 3-15. A field tripod with friction head. The tripod legs are calibrated for rapid leveling, and are easily tightened by knurled knobs. The friction head carries spirit levels, levers for locking both the vertical and horizontal motions, and of course a socket into which the panning handle can be fitted and a platform for the camera.

flywheel at stepped-up speed when the camera is panned or tilted. The inertia of the flywheel provides exceedingly steady movement, especially when starting and stopping, and thus removes one of the main bugbears of the camera novice. The gyro head, however, which was designed in the early days of movies to allow the operator to crank his camera by hand and pan it simultaneously, has today fallen into neglect. This is partly because the extra mechanism is heavy and expensive, partly because the expert cameraman can pan smoothly with a friction head.

The *high hat* is a miniature fixed tripod, usually made as a single casting, which stands about six inches high. A standard tripod head fits into the top of the high hat, while holes in its feet enable it to be secured to some rigid object like the floor of an airplane. Intermediate between the tripod and the high hat is the baby tripod, which resembles an ordinary tripod save that its legs are much shorter.

A *triangle,* consisting of a three-armed piece of metal which is really "triangular" is frequently used to hold the tripod legs and prevent their sliding apart on smooth surfaces (figure 3-16).

The *dolly,* a term loosely used for any kind of camera conveyance, is more properly confined to a lightweight, often three-wheeled, platform on which a camera tripod can be mounted. Its main purpose is to move a heavy camera from setup to setup without putting the operator to the task of lifting it; the dolly, when in place, is raised from the floor with jacks to hold it steady. In the field the dolly is often pressed into service by small units for traveling shots, although most dollies are too flimsy to provide smooth movement with a heavy camera and two cameramen aboard. But they are easy to carry on a station wagon when compactness and light weight are important.

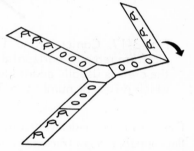

Fig. 3-16. The triangle. Triangles hold the tripod feet in sockets and thus prevent them from sliding apart on smooth surfaces. The triangle arms are usually double-hinged for compactness in carrying.

The *velocilator* is a more elaborate type of dolly containing machinery (usually hand operated) for raising, lowering, and swinging the camera. The maximum available height from lens to floor is usually between six and seven feet, and the minimum height about one and a half feet. Velocilators are designed to support the heaviest cameras and blimps, and are of the utmost use in sound studios. Sturdiness is of the greatest importance in choosing a design. Some velocilators are too shaky to allow the camera to be moved rapidly up and down while shooting; but all of them allow perfectly smooth dolly and

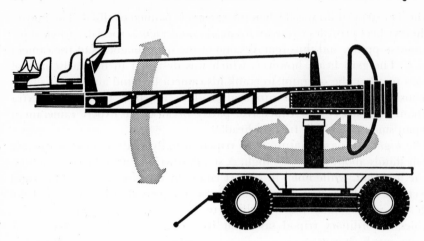

Fig. 3-17. Camera crane. The crane is so designed that the camera platform remains horizontal in all positions. The variable weight of the crew is usually counterbalanced by a weight box at the rear in which different numbers of heavy metal weights are placed.

pan shots to be made, while carrying a crew of two. If the floor surface is not flat enough, camera tracks must be laid down.

The term *boom* or *crane* covers a number of devices, some little bigger than a velocilator, others designed for exterior work and reaching as high as forty feet above the ground. In almost all designs, the boom is driven along on the floor by electric motors, since from three to six men would be needed to push it. But the raising, lowering, and swinging movements are usually operated by hand, as this gives more sensitive control (figure 3-17). The weight of crew and equipment is accurately counterbalanced by movable weights.

TROPIC HEAT AND ARCTIC COLD

The movie camera, like its human operator, is designed to work best at moderate temperatures. In both tropic and arctic climates it needs special preparation if it is to give good service.

In the tropics the film itself is the chief sufferer. Molds, whose spores are air-borne, settle on the sensitive surface if it is exposed for long to the surrounding air. The resulting spots damage or destroy the photographic image. Film should therefore be purchased in special tropical containers. In these it is wrapped in thick tinfoil and placed in a metal container which is itself wrapped and placed in another metal container along with a quantity of desiccant. Film should not be allowed to remain in the camera longer than is absolutely necessary. As soon as a roll is exposed, it should be taken out and returned to its double container. Color film is especially likely to be affected by heat, and should be placed in an icebox whenever possible to prevent deterioration of the image.

When both temperature and humidity are very high, the film, being hygroscopic, will take up moisture and swell at the same time that the emulsion softens. The joint effect will be a dragging of the film under the pressure plate of the camera, combined with a stripping off of the emulsion. When this occurs, the pressure should be relieved somewhat by loosening the springs, and a small quantity of desiccant should be placed in the camera itself to absorb moisture there and in the magazines.

Metal parts of the camera which are not chrome plated or properly enameled are very likely to rust in the tropics, and should be kept well greased for protection. Sound recording equipment may be attacked by fungoid growths, causing insulation breakdowns, and should therefore be properly tropicalized.

In arctic latitudes the cameraman suffers more than his equipment. There his chief problem is to keep alive while handling delicate instruments requiring adjustments almost impossible to make when wearing thick gloves. Chamois-leather face masks with slits for eyes and mouth help to solve the problem of applying the skin to freezing metal when viewfinding. Silk gloves under leather gloves make it possible to load and unload film in changing bags.

It is equally important to make the camera operate with the least possible difficulty, for the cameraman must often keep ahead of a moving column of men or vehicles, and must therefore be able to travel faster than they no matter how cruel the cold. Winterizing a camera involves taking it apart and removing all traces of regular machine oil and grease. A special "Hi-Lo" aviation grease may be obtained for lubricating gear trains in the drive mechanism, and oils are also available which remain fluid down to temperatures of —80° F. A mixture of kerosene and sperm oil may be used down to —40° F. Since the lenses are the most exposed parts of the camera and the most difficult to adjust with gloved hands, diaphragms and focusing barrels should be run dry. Large-aperture long-focus lenses may give another kind of trouble, for the area of the glass is so great that contraction in extreme cold will break the cement, loosening the lens and making it useless. In four- to six-inch focal lengths, an aperture of $f/4.5$ or $f/5.6$ is safe at —40° F.

Even when the camera is properly greased and oiled, its internal friction will probably have increased. Some makes of spring-driven camera have insufficient power to overcome this resistance, and consequently will not run at the required speed. Though electric motors usually have a greater reserve of power, the batteries which drive them in the field undergo a serious drop of voltage at low temperatures. More current has to be drawn from them, and they require frequent recharging. Where ample battery power is available, electric heating pads may be placed round the camera, and especially round the motor, to keep it running freely. A blimp may be an advantage in cold weather, since it acts as an effective heat insulator. A small heating element placed under a blimped camera will maintain the mechanism at a normal running temperature when the outside air is slightly below freezing.

When film is cold it becomes brittle, and static electricity is likely to be generated where there is rubbing contact. Threading of the camera should be done carefully to prevent broken sprocket holes, and heavy spring tension on the aperture plate avoided. If the camera has a rackover device, its positioning pin may "freeze" into its socket. The only remedy is to machine the pin down to a loose fit at normal temperatures.[16]

THE PROBLEM OF EXPOSURE

We have already considered several of the adjustments by which the camera must be adapted to the external world: its mounting and movement, its framing and focusing. Underlying all of these is the problem of exposure. How is the image of the scene to be adjusted in intensity to match the narrow limits of the photographic film? This problem must be solved by use of the exposure meter, the most important mechanical guide the cameraman has to insure correct operation of his camera. Yet the exposure meter's indications are by no means automatic, and must be modified by the results of experience.

Essentially, an exposure meter is a means of relating four variables: light intensity, film speed, exposure time, and lens aperture. Since the meter determines only one of these variables—light intensity—two of the remaining variables must be ascertained by the cameraman. The final variable can then be calculated on the meter. Since the film stock has usually been selected to cover a considerable period of shooting, the cameraman is left to juggle with exposure time and lens aperture. But in movie work, as we have seen, the shooting speed and the shutter opening—which together determine the exposure time—remain, for all practical purposes, constant. Hence, the exposure meter, once properly set up, will read directly in lens apertures. If the illumination of a scene cannot be accurately controlled, as for instance out of doors, the cameraman must either alter the aperture setting or place a *neutral density filter* before the lens. If lighting is perfectly controllable, as in the studio, the cameraman may prefer to work at a constant lens aperture. He

16 See also, C. C. Shirley, "Navy Photography in the Antarctic," *JSMPE*, Jan., 1949, pp. 19–29.

will then increase or decrease the illumination of the scene until he reads the wanted aperture setting on his meter.

The exposure meter, like the combination of lens and film, forms a kind of eye, and, like the eye, embraces a certain field of view. Instead of forming an image, however, the exposure meter merely integrates the incoming light on the surface of a *photoelectric cell* (conveniently abbreviated to *photocell*), which generates a current proportional to the light falling upon it. The size of this current is indicated on a *microammeter,* which is read by the operator and is often graduated in *foot-candles.*

In some convenient position on the meter is mounted a calculator which relates the four variables, light, film speed, exposure time, and lens aperture. As already stated, the calculator is used in movie work to set the film speed and exposure time, after which the light reading determines the lens aperture. The calculator is a mechanically simple attachment; all that can be expected of it is that its markings be clear and easy to read.

As in everything photographic, the theory underlying the use of this simple instrument is extremely complex. How is one to insure, for instance, that the exposure meter "sees" the same field of view as the lens, when the lens may be interchanged to give a wide or narrow angle of vision? And how to settle on one exposure, when the scene is full of gradations from very bright to very dark, and when many of the objects in it are far too remote to be approached with the exposure meter? Moreover, what about differences of color? Will not objects of the same brightness but of different color give different readings on the exposure meter? And how will these differences relate to the color response of film, when *orthochromatic* emulsions respond much less to green and red than *panchromatic,* and *infrared* emulsions respond to radiations which scarcely affect an exposure meter? What does "correct exposure" mean? How much latitude will there be toward overexposure and underexposure? Why are there so many kinds of film speeds—Din and Scheiner, H. & D., Weston, G.E., A.S.A., and others? Why not establish a single scale which everyone can agree on? And how about the laboratory? Will not differences in development upset the findings of the exposure meter?

Answers to all these questions cannot be expected so early in our inquiry, but the attentive reader will be able to piece them together before he has reached the end.

Since the *photovoltaic cell* is common to the majority of exposure meters it requires some preliminary comment. While its *spectral response* is not unlike that of the eye, which in turn is fairly closely paralleled by panchromatic film, there are some important differences between the color sensitivity of the three light-sensitive devices. For instance, the human eye has a comparatively low sensitivity to the blue and violet end of the *spectrum,* the exposure meter a much higher sensitivity, and photographic film a higher sensitivity still. This is why, when the exposure of a scene is guessed by eye, the film will usually be found to be overexposed; and why the exposure meter itself will give a lower scale reading than is warranted. Again, the photovoltaic cell has practically no response to infrared radiation, and cannot be used as a guide to the exposure of infrared sensitive film. Finally, and most important, owing to the relatively low red sensitivity of even panchromatic film emulsions, they will respond less to light from a tungsten (filament-type) light source, the radiations of which are rich in yellow and red, than to daylight, which is rich in blue and violet. Consequently, a film emulsion must be given a lower exposure index for tungsten than for daylight, in order to boost the exposure and compensate for the lower photographic efficiency of the film.

Exposure meters are in general of two types: *incident-light meters* and *reflected-light meters*. These types differ more in the use to which they are put than in their mechanical construction (figure 3-18). Since reflected-light meters are by far the most commonly used, they will be described first.

Reflected-light exposure meters.—When an exposure meter is pointed at the scene to be photographed, it records the light reflected from that scene. Since the total amount of reflected light picked up by the meter will differ greatly according to the angle of view embraced, the *acceptance angle* of the meter should ideally be the same as that of the lens which is to shoot the picture, so that identical cones of light are funneled into photocell and lens. Practical exposure meters never have more than two acceptance angles—a wide and a narrow—the latter achieved by placing a slot, honeycomb, or grid over the cell. Even these two arrangements are not strictly alternative, for the device which narrows the angle also cuts off light and calls for reading on a different meter scale. Thus the design is a compromise, and can give correct results only with intelligent use.

If the scene includes a large expanse of sky, the meter should be pointed slightly downward, or it will accept too much sky light. If the foreground of the shot is in shadow, and it is desired to expose for sunlit areas beyond, the meter will accept too much of the shadow light and indicate too large an aperture. The meter should therefore be carried out into the sunshine. If a person's face is the most important thing in a shot, the meter should be held no more than a foot from it to eliminate light reflected from other objects. However, the operator should be careful not to cast his own shadow on the subject, but only on the meter. It is assumed that the brightness of the face lies more or less midway between the brightness of the lightest and darkest objects in the scene. This will almost always be so, but due allowance must be made if the face is deeply tanned or very pale.

The reflected-light meter can also give useful information by being pointed at subsidiary objects in the scene. For instance, if there is an area of shadow in which details are supposed to be visible, it should not have less than one-

Fig. 3-18. Types of exposure meter. At the left is a Sixtus meter. Top center, a General Electric meter and calculator, with light masks to permit its use as an incident light meter. Center left, a Weston meter. Center right, the Norwood Director, the first meter designed especially for incident light readings. At the right is shown the S.E.I. Photometer, an extinction-type meter with a very narrow acceptance angle and a high ratio of maximum to minimum measurable exposure. Bottom left, a General Electric foot-candle meter. Bottom center, the light sensitive element of a General Electric exposure meter. Bottom right, the Weston Photromic cell.

fiftieth, and preferably not less than one-thirtieth, of the brightness of the brightest area. If the film in use is Kodachrome, shot for *duplication,* this brightness ratio should not exceed 20 to 1, it being remembered that the newer commercial Kodachrome, having a lower inherent contrast, has a greater latitude than regular Kodachrome.

The virtue of the reflected-light meter is that it takes into account the varied reflecting powers (called *reflectances*) of the surfaces in the scene, and thus measures the light which actually enters the lens and exposes the film. Its weakness is that it seldom collects light from the same area as the lens, and is therefore likely to have large margins of error if incorrectly used. The virtues and defects of the incident-light type of exposure meter are of somewhat different kind.

Incident-light exposure meters.—The incident-light meter measures the illumination falling on the subject, and consequently is pointed in the opposite direction from the reflected-light meter—either at the camera itself or at the source of light. As a result, and this is its chief merit, it receives a sample of the light which falls on the object and contributes to its illumination and disregards the light which falls elsewhere in the scene. The use of this type of meter assumes an accessible central object of predominant importance. The popularity of the human face as a subject for photographs—especially in commercial studios where incident-light meters are chiefly used—makes this assumption a sound one.

If the meter is to be pointed directly at the camera, it should have a hemispherical light collector with an acceptance angle of 180° to receive light from every direction which contributes to the building up of the film image. In this way the meter gives a single over-all illumination reading. The Norwood was the first commercial meter built to this specification; the design is of course so arranged that the more angular the direction of the incident light, the smaller is its contribution to the meter reading.

Many cameramen, however, prefer to evaluate the contribution of each light source separately. Recent models of the G.E. meter are supplied with multiplying masks or mattes, so that illumination from light sources as brilliant as the sun can be measured on the same scale as the faintest shadow lighting. The masks reduce the light intake to the cell by a factor which is then used to multiply the exposure indicated on the meter. By pointing the meter in turn at the source of *key, filler, and back light,* the lighting contrast can be accurately built up to conform with the cameraman's experience of what it should be.

The chief weakness of the incident-light meter is that it takes no account of varying subject reflectances. If the subject is a dense black or a brilliant white, the meter gives the same reading, for it is turned in the opposite direction. The cameraman must therefore learn to estimate the reflectance of different objects, since exposure indexes have been computed for use with reflected-light meters on average scenes. If the meter is pointed at a grey card of about 18 per cent reflectance placed at the subject position (incident-light technique), the reading will be nearly the same on average scenes as that obtained from the camera position by the reflected-light technique. Skin has a reflectance of about 35 per cent so the exposure index must be divided by 2 when the cameraman points the meter at his hand (a common procedure) held in the position of the subject.

Thus, the reflected-light technique (used with meters adapted to it) excels in open-air settings where the subject matter is inaccessible or diffused in space; the incident-light technique (with the proper meter) excels when the subject is accessible and compact, and when its reflectance can be estimated and the sources of light are controllable.

The former conditions tend to prevail in documentary camerawork of the classical Flaherty and Lorentz school; the latter in feature-film production (exterior as well as interior) and in the newer styles of documentary. Most experienced cameramen learn to use both techniques and supplement the information they provide with acquired skill and judgment.

FILM SPEEDS AND EXPOSURE INDEXES

Of the four variable factors which enter into exposure computation—light, shutter opening combined with shooting speed, lens aperture, and film speed —all but the last have been discussed. Film speed and its measurement have long been a matter for debate, and various criteria have found their champions at different times and in different countries. Today, thanks largely to the work of the American Standards Association and the Eastman Kodak Company, it appears as if unanimity will at last be reached.

The most useful determination of film speed has proved to be in terms of that minimum exposure of the film under test which, developed under specified conditions, will yield a print of highest quality. Thus the problem of establishing standards breaks down into four parts: a psychophysical problem, essentially statistical in its solution, of determining what prints from what negatives reach an agreed level of acceptability (the classical work here was accomplished by Dr. Loyd Jones of Eastman Kodak); [17] second, a spectroscopic problem of devising a reproducible source of artificial sunlight (accomplished by Davis and Gibson in the United States); third, a sensitometric problem of giving the exposure results a precise meaning (here also the work of Eastman Kodak has been embodied in the new standard); lastly, a processing problem of establishing exactly reproducible conditions of film development (mainly the work of the A.S.A. committee).

Note carefully that this standard [18] applies only to daylight exposure, and further, cannot be used in shooting reversal or color film; its extension to these conditions will require many more years of work.

The new speed numbers are identical with the old Kodak film speeds, but are not immediately applicable to exposure meters. This is because an *ex-*

[17] Fully reported in the *Journal of the Franklin Institute*, Oct.–Dec., 1939.
[18] *American Standard Method for Determining Photographic Speed and Exposure Index* (Z38.2.1–1947).

posure index or *exposure number* must afford an adequate margin above
minimum exposure to allow for errors in lens-aperture and shutter-speed
calibration, which are particularly serious with cheap amateur equipment.
The A.S.A. Exposure Index has been arranged to lie almost midway between
the familiar Weston and G.E. numbers, and in fact is less than half a stop
removed from either of them. This enables the new indexes to be used with
meters having Weston or G.E. calibrations. Between all three scales of numbers there is a linear relationship; that is, a simple multiplier will convert one
scale into another. A.S.A. film-speed determination has been adopted in Great
Britain [19] as well as in the United States, and there is a good chance of its
international adoption within a few years. Most film stocks and exposure
meters are now rated according to the new exposure numbers.[20]

An introduction to the sensitometry of film speed and its measurement
must be deferred to chapter viii, where it follows the discussion of the graphical representation of exposure and density.

The close relationship between the cameraman's calculations and the film
he uses is exemplified by the problems which exposure poses. In every detail
of shooting, however, the cameraman must remember that the image he is
engrafting on film is a *latent image*. The most powerful microscope or X-ray
is unable to reveal it; it cannot even be subjected to direct chemical analysis.
Only proper development by the laboratory—to which the film passes next—
can make visible and permanent what the cameraman has taken such pains
to record accurately. If a perfect dovetailing of effort between the two is
wanting, their collaboration can succeed only by accident. One misunder-
standing by the cameraman may impair all the good work of the laboratory,
and one error by the laboratory may irreparably damage the precious strip
of images, on every foot of which many hundreds of dollars may have been
spent.

The cameraman is usually the main liaison between the production unit
and the laboratory, for his concern with his film does not end when it is neatly
wound in his exposed magazines. It does not end until he has seen a satisfactory print on the screen.

Under studio conditions, the exposed negative is developed and printed
the night after it is shot, so that prints can be screened before shooting starts

[19] British Standard *1380*. By mutual agreement, Great Britain will use a logarithmic series
of exposure numbers, which advance 3 units for every doubling of the numbers on the
American scale. These logarithmic numbers are distinguished by being marked in degrees (°).

[20] For further information, see *Exposure Indexes and How to Use Them*, Eastman Kodak
Co., 1947. This pamphlet does justice to the problems of film exposure, which remain complex notwithstanding the introduction of the new A.S.A. indexes. For an excellent, though
less recent, study of exposure, see P. K. Turner, *Photographic Exposure*, London, Pitman,
1940.

the next day. For this reason, these prints are called *dailies;* because they are rushed through the laboratory, they are sometimes called *rushes.*

Since the laboratory enters into every stage of production, we shall take up the cutting room and the cutting process before returning to see how the film is developed and printed.

IV

ЛЛЛЛЛЛЛЛЛЛЛЛЛЛЛЛЛЛЛЛЛЛЛЛЛЛЛЛЛЛЛЛ

The Cutting Room

AT THE END of the last chapter we saw the exposed film—now unloaded from its magazines and placed in light-tight cans—as far as the door of the laboratory. During the night it is developed and printed, and in the morning the print is screened for the producer, director, editor, and cameraman. Thereafter the print goes to the cutting room, where it is worked on for a period at least as long as that required to shoot the picture.

The editing or cutting process is peculiar to films, and it is in the cutting room that we can most easily get an idea of what film is really like. Just as a carpenter must not only know the theoretical properties of wood, but must get the feel of saw and chisel, drill and plane, against an actual material, so the film maker should learn the peculiar and often provoking characteristics of his own medium. In the smaller production unit, many people are able to get their first training in the cutting room—or they may have graduated from an amateur cine club where the editing of their own camera footage has become second nature. The worker in a large studio is at a great disadvantage, for he may reach the highest levels in his own branch of the profession, and yet lack even the slenderest acquaintance with this most basic of all the creative processes of film.

The cutting room is the place where film is assembled—that is to say, where a new order in the shots is brought out of the random order in which they have hitherto existed, and a new creative life is given to them. It is an obvious characteristic of film shooting that there is no necessity to film the scenes in the order in which they are finally to appear on the screen. It is a less obvious characteristic of film that the juxtaposition of two shots and their accompanying ideas can give rise to a third idea which has no physical embodiment.

This is the root of the film editor's power. Instead of dealing with intractable lumps of reality, he deals with highly tractable pieces of film. By clever intercutting, he may so arrange shots of a weeping child, a violent explosion, and a blazing house that his audience will think that the child has lost his home and family through bombing. Yet the shots may in truth depict something quite different. The child may be a Brooklyn kid who is crying over the loss of his pet kitten; the explosion may be that of a wall of rock dynamited ten years before to make a railroad cutting in New Zealand; the fire, a peacetime accident in Buenos Aires. Film has therefore two great powers: it can produce a new synthesis of space and it can produce a new synthesis of ideas.

This facile power of film to create an illusion of reality out of nothing may lead to an irresponsible sense of power among editorial film makers who know that a well-stocked film library will furnish them with the materials for constructing any interpretation of world affairs they have a mind to impose, without regard to outward actuality or inner truth. What, then, is reality in film? Is it no more than a literal joining of fact to fact? Or is it an interpretative synthesis of pieces of film, guided by the film maker's own perception of the truth? But in that event film becomes as much a subjective art as painting or writing, or any other art which has never made the cinema's bold claim of pictorially representing reality as it really is. And should not this alter the whole status of film in the public's eyes? Should it not induce a much more critical watchfulness in the movie audience, and a much more responsible awareness in the documentary director of his power of creating and therefore distorting the truth? These are interesting paths of exploration which belong not to the science but to the sociology of film.

Enough has been said to show that a medium with such immense capacities for building a new framework of reality is obviously not to be upset by a mere rearrangement of the order in which the pieces of a story are shot. The last shot may have been made first, the middle section at the end, and the beginning shot in the middle. Before he essays his more creative tasks, the editor must sort these pieces of film and arrange them in the proper script order.

THE ARITHMETIC OF FILM

In the first ten minutes the apprentice will discover that the smooth continuity of film actions on the screen is built up of a multitude of small images, separate from one another and each of them perfectly stationary, placed in succession on a long strip of film. These still pictures, he will notice, are each about four-fifths of an inch wide and three-fifths of an inch high on a piece of 35 mm. film, with the individual picture or frame crosswise to the length of the film (figure 4-1). That is to say, the pictures can be seen right way up when the strip of film is held vertically. One side of the film is dull and the other side is shiny. The shiny side is called the *base,* and the dull side is

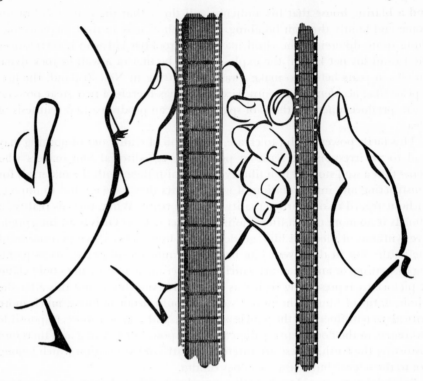

Fig. 4-1. How 35 mm. and 16 mm. film look to the editor. Note Academy masking on 35 mm. film. The 35 mm. film is a print, and the 16 mm. film a reversal dupe.

called the *emulsion* side. The base is made of a cellulose substance, and has no photographic properties. Its function is to support the thin coating of light-sensitive emulsion on which the photographic image is registered. While the thickness of the base will range from 4½ to 5½ mils, the thickness of the emulsion will be about ½ mil.[1]

In the cutting room 35 mm. film is always wound and run with the emulsion side uppermost, in order to see the picture the right way round and to avoid scratching the delicate emulsion, since it is then facing away from the steel surfaces on which it travels, and the cutting table on which it may drag.[2]

[1] One mil is one one-thousandth of an inch.

[2] Though for the most part these surfaces are undercut or recessed beneath the picture area (except on sound-recording and reproducing drums), the undercut is often very shallow. Consequently a small piece of emulsion or dust may project upward sufficiently from the undercut surface to touch the film. Were the emulsion to face downwards, it would then be scratched. This sometimes happens in 16 mm. moviolas, synchronizers and projectors, where the emulsion position may call for the film to be faced downward in threading.

Standard film is 35 mm. (1⅜ inches) wide, and is universally known as "35 mm. film." Along both sides of the film are punched holes called *perforations* or *sprocket holes,* of which there are four on each side of each frame. Perforations are of two kinds, *negative* (or *Bell and Howell*) and positive, the former distinguished by having curved sides, the latter straight sides. Cameras (and optical printers which use camera movements) have been designed with sprockets which fit film having negative perforations, and that is why these perforations continue in use. Much thought has been given to the design of perforations which can be positioned on both positive and negative sprockets, and one of these (the Dubray-Howell) will probably be adopted, and will eventually replace both present perforations. The purpose of perforations is to engage with pilot pins and sprocket teeth on many film-driving mechanisms, thus insuring good steadiness and registration. It is easy to see the importance of extreme accuracy when it is realized that each ⅘ inch by ⅗ inch picture may have to be projected on a screen forty feet wide by thirty feet high, or a magnification in area of more than 300,000 times. Even under this terrific enlargement, there must be no visible wobble of the image. This order of magnification is easier to grasp when the starting area is larger. It is as if a Rubens canvas measuring twelve by nine feet were to be enlarged to the size of one hundred and seven city blocks.

Down the left-hand side of 35 mm. film, as the image is held upright with the emulsion facing him, the cutter will see a narrow black or transparent band, approximately one-tenth of an inch wide. When the final *composite print* is made for projection in a movie theater, this space will be occupied by the *sound track* which is synchronized to the picture images. All modern cameras are built with an *Academy mask,* which since the introduction of sound has cut off the sound track area on one side of the film, and a band above and below the frame sufficiently wide to restore the rectangular proportions of the screen image. Some very old cameras are still equipped with their original *silent apertures,* but their viewfinders must of course be Academy masked, or parts of the wanted image would disappear in printing and projection.

In the projector, the individual frames travel past the aperture (with intermittent motion, as we have seen) at a rate which has been standardized all over the world at 24 each second. As exactly 16 of the frames are contained lengthwise in each foot of film, 1½ feet of film pass the projector aperture per second, or 90 feet per minute, which is therefore the standard speed of 35 mm. film.

According to North American practice, positive film is always wound on *reels*—metal spools with a small hub and spoked side pieces, about 10 inches in diameter. (According to European practice, film is simply wound up in rolls on itself, usually against detachable metal discs called *flanges.*) When these spools are wound tightly up to their full capacity, they will hold about 1,000 feet of film, though for practical purposes the length is limited to about 900 feet, which will take ten minutes to project. This is the unit known everywhere as a reel of film, and is the unit of measurement for the length of films. Thus a two-reel short is a film between 1,800 and 2,000 feet long, running about twenty minutes, while an eight-reel feature is about 8,000 feet long and runs an hour and twenty minutes. Reels are stored in circular cans about 10½ inches in diameter, and these too are familiar sights throughout the world.

It has been said with justice that the most standard thing in existence is a piece of 35 mm. film. With its accompanying sound image, it can be projected in Patagonia or Siam as effectively as on Broadway or Piccadilly. If there were countries which spaced their film perforations 60 to the foot instead of 64, or standardized a film speed of 20 frames per second, universal projection of movies would be impossible.

Having now ousted its European rival, the 17½ mm. gauge, 16 mm. film bids fair to become as universally accepted a standard for film projection as 35 mm. Since it travels more slowly than 35 mm. film, and has a different system of perforation, a new arithmetic is needed. Table 1 compares the two gauges of film in professional use.

THE CUTTER'S TOOLS

Mechanically, cutting is a simple task, and the cutter's tools are simpler than the tools of any other production department, script writing alone excepted. The *cutter* (or *editor*) needs a pair of scissors to cut the film, a *splicer* to join it together again, a pair of *rewinds* for running reels back and forth, and a *moviola* on which to screen the picture. To handle film which is not wound on reels, the cutter will find it convenient to use a flange or plane face against which the film is wound up. Some studios use split reels (sometimes called open-face reels), one side of which is detachable, which combine the advantages of normal reels and flanges.

In many documentary films, the picture is shot first and the sound added later, when cutting is complete. But dialogue films require simultaneous sound and picture cutting, which in turn calls for more equipment. The moviola must have a *sound head* attached to the picture head, and a *synchronizer* is necessary to hold the picture and sound tracks in proper relation to one another..

The cutter's tools are completed by a number of bits and pieces such as paper clips, rubber bands, grease pencils, etc., without which cutting would be seriously slowed down. And finally, if the film is inflammable, specialized furniture is needed in the cutting room (figure 4-2).

TABLE 1

COMPARISON OF 16 MM. AND 35 MM. FILM

Characteristic	35 mm.	16 mm.
Standard speed (feet per minute)	90	sound ....36 / silent 24
Standard frame repetition rate per second	24	sound ....24 / silent 16
Frame line modulation frequency [a]	24 cps	———
Sprocket hole modulation frequency [b]	96 cps	———
Number of perforations per frame	8 (4 each side)	sound ....1 / silent 2
Frame size (camera aperture)	$0.631'' \times 0.868''$	$0.294'' \times 0.410''$
Frame size (projector aperture)	$0.600'' \times 0.825''$	$0.284'' \times 0.380''$
Ratio of projected frame areas	4.59	1
Number of frames per foot	16	40
Footage for 10 minutes running time (1 reel)	900	sound ....360 / silent 240
Maximum practical footage per reel for printing and recording	960	380
Maximum reel capacity (feet)	1,000	400
Standard reel size (feet)	1,000 [c] / 2,000 [d]	100 [e] / 200 [e] / 400 / 800 / 1,200 / 1,600 / 2,000
Position of film in camera	Emulsion faces lens	Emulsion faces lens
Position of film in projector	Emulsion faces light	Emulsion faces lens or light [f]

a Hum produced by frame lines (or their image) entering sound track.
b Hum produced by perforations (or their image) entering sound track.
c Standard for production.   d Standard for release.
e Camera spool also used in cutting.   f See chapter ix.

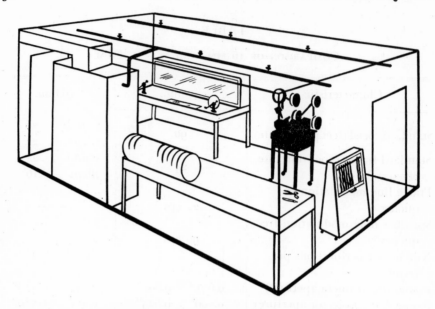

Fig. 4-2. The cutting room. The 35 mm. cutting room is fully sprinklered and the steel safety cabinet is connected to the sprinklers and to a fume vent. The bin is of special safety design, and there are exits at both ends of the room. The main cutting bench is furnished with light boxes and rewinds, and a sound moviola stands on the floor.

THE MOVIOLA

Since a piece of film consists of a long strip of separate pictures, nothing but a blur would result if the editor merely wound it through rapidly while looking at it against the light. Film has to be viewed intermittently—that is, each frame must appear stationary while it is being viewed, and must then be moved on and replaced by the next picture while this blurring action is screened from the viewer's eyes, exactly as in a projector. The moviola is, in fact, a projector for one person (figure 4-3).

Whereas the camera makes use of a claw to provide intermittent motion, the moviola, like the 35 mm. projector, drives the film through a device with slotted arms which, from its shape, is known as a *Maltese cross*.

The film, as it goes through the *gate* or picture aperture, is by turns moving and stationary. But as it comes off the *take-off spool* and as it winds up on the *take-up spool*, it must run smoothly to avoid snatching and tugging. If the film went straight from the intermittent to the continuous sprocket it would be ripped apart, for when the intermittent was stationary, the continuous

Fig. 4-3. The moviola. The silent moviola is a simple shutterless film viewer, driven by a motor (1). An intermittent sprocket (2), actuated by a Maltese cross movement (3) drives the film past the lens (4). Loops at 5 and 6 take out the intermittent motion for the continuous drive sprocket (7). The picture is properly framed by moving lever (8).

sprocket would be moving and thus would tug at the film and tear it. To avoid this, as we have seen, intermittent machines like moviolas, projectors, cameras, and step printers, make provision for two film loops, one before and one after the intermittent, which alternately take up the slack and feed it out again.

The moviola has a variable-speed motor so that it can be run very slow or very fast. The fast speed is useful for running quickly down to a point in the middle of a reel, the slow speed for pinning down some significant movement to an exact frame, or for identifying precisely on a sound track the beginning or end *modulations* of a word, as in sound cutting and *spotting*. The moviola also has a simple reversing switch, so that film can be run backward as easily as forward. Moviolas, like projectors, must include a *framing device*. A picture is said to be *in frame* when the frame lines (the lines which divide one frame from another) are not visible at the top or bottom of the screen. The framing device pushes the viewing aperture up or down to make it correspond with the area of the screen. For simplicity the standard moviola, made by the Moviola Company, dispenses with a shutter. While this increases the brightness of the image, it leads to a blurring of vertical lines, especially bright lines. In fact, moviolas should never be used for judging photographic quality.

Like all pieces of film machinery, moviolas require proper handling. They should never be reversed while running forward,[3] but should be brought to rest first. They should be oiled with a few drops of oil at regular intervals, and should be kept in good mechanical order.

Sometimes, for speed, the cutter will want to look through an entire reel of film faster than it can be safely run on the moviola. He will then use a *viewer,* a simple device containing only one moving part, a revolving slab of glass which acts as an optical compensator (see figure 3-5). The absence of intermittent motion makes it possible to run film through the hand viewer at a fairly high speed without danger of damage to the film, provided that the viewer is in good mechanical condition, correctly threaded, and mounted on the table in proper alignment to avoid twisting the film. Accelerate the film slowly when starting the rewind; otherwise the perforations may be damaged. The hand viewer is very useful for finding shots quickly in large masses of film.

THE SPLICER

Film splicing can be done very simply. All that is actually needed is a piece of blotting paper, a paper clip to hold one of the sections of film being joined, a razor blade, and a bottle of cement. This primitive method of splicing has long been abandoned in favor of the *hand splicer* and the *machine splicer*. Neither of these is really an automatic instrument, like a sausage machine; you can't just put an unspliced roll of film tacked together with paper clips into one end and get it out properly spliced at the other end. All the machine does is to hold the two pieces of film and bring one of them down on the other in the proper relative positions (figure 4-4). As the pieces overlap, emulsion on one would be in contact with base on the other. These substances would not join together. Hence the emulsion must be scraped off along the overlapping area, the surface of the celluloid softened with cement and the two

___
[3] On the sound models, this is prevented automatically by a centrifugal switch.

Fig. 4-4. The machine splicer. Foot treadles raise and lower the upper blades which clamp the sections of film to be joined in exact relationship to one another.

pieces held firmly together. They then become one, so that a film splice is like a weld and not like a glued joint. Splicing is speeded up if the temperature of the splice is higher than room temperature; machine splicers and some hand splicers therefore include an electrical heating element which should be left on night and day since several hours are required to produce the correct temperature.

If commercial film cement cannot be bought or does not prove satisfactory, the following simple formulae may be tried (the measures are given in terms of parts by weight):

For Nitrate Base		For Acetate Base	
Scrap film	15	Cellulose-acetate base	12
Camphor	3	Methyl alcohol	20
Acetic acid (28°)	1	Acetone	60
Acetone	60	(Use special cement for the new tri-	
Methyl alcohol	20	acetate base)	

These cements may be thinned with acetone to the desired consistency.

The film manufacturers are at present changing the chemical structure of the base rather frequently as they try to find a completely satisfactory acetate base. These bases may require different cement formulae, especially the high-acetyl base introduced early in 1949. If splices are found to come apart after all proper procedures are carried out, the film manufacturer should be consulted.

The more volatile elements in film cement tend to evaporate, thus reducing its strength. The cement bottle should be kept tightly screwed up when not in use, and the cement should be changed every day.

The strength of a splice bears no relation to any extra pressure brought to bear by the swinging arms of a machine splicer: consequently, these arms must never be lowered with a bang. A fifty-dollar repair job is poor compensation for a splice which isn't even any stronger than usual. The beginner should practice splicing until he has thoroughly mastered it. Good practice is to frame cut ten feet of film—that is, cut out every alternate frame. This produces eighty splices in a row; to make these in forty-five minutes is fast work. The best test of a splice is to try to tear it apart. If it has been properly made, it will be stronger than the rest of the film, because at the joint the film is almost twice as thick.

Splices are made in various widths, the commonest 35 mm. widths being $\frac{5}{32}$ inch (the *positive splice*) and $\frac{1}{10}$ inch or $\frac{1}{16}$ inch (the *negative splice*). It is a common delusion, often fostered by projectionists, that the strength of a good splice increases with its width. Actually, the two factors are within wide limits independent, and as the negative splice is quicker to make since it involves less scraping of emulsion, it is gradually replacing the positive splice in cutting. However, a poor positive splice is stronger than a poor negative splice, and provides a larger margin of safety.

Machine splicers are much faster and more uniform in their results than hand splicers, and are accordingly strongly recommended. All splicers should be kept in scrupulously clean condition by applying acetone at frequent intervals (say between every fifty splices) to all the operating parts. This will dissolve the clogged pieces of emulsion, which can then be wiped out of the way. Razor blades and paper clips must never be used to scrape the operating surfaces, as they will produce minute scorings even in the hardened steel.

If there is any possibility that paper clips have been left in a spliced reel, it should be carefully checked through before projection. Clips can seriously damage a projector if they are drawn into the revolving mechanism, an accident which may also destroy several feet of film before the machine is stopped.

BITS AND PIECES

Though the moviola and the splicer are the most important of the cutter's tools, he needs a number of bits and pieces before he would consider his cutting room properly equipped. Film is quite easy to tear, and if the cutter doesn't mind wasting frames, he can just tear it across. But for all accurate cutting, a pair of scissors is used, so that there can be no doubt which frame line the splice is to come on.

Film must often be marked to identify a frame. Running it backward and forward in the moviola, the cutter will hit on a spot where he thinks a scene should start or finish. He lifts up the hinged viewing lens of the moviola and makes a mark on the film in the aperture with a grease pencil, sometimes called a china-marking pencil. This kind of pencil makes a very clear mark (usually in red or black) on the emulsion side of the film, which is the side the cutter always has uppermost since it shows the picture the right way round. *Sync marks* on music and effects tracks are also made in grease pencil, as we shall see later.

Film is usually fastened together in the cutting room with clips preparatory to splicing it. These are ordinary paper clips which are slid over the two pieces of film. It is impossible to prevent the rough edges of the clips from scratching the soft emulsion. This does not matter on the positive print, but for negative assembly, clips must never be used unless the film is first wrapped with a protective layer of paper. To avoid this complication, the negative is very often assembled with *patches*—small pieces of cardboard or celluloid with projecting teeth on either side which engage in the perforations of the two pieces of film to be assembled. These are sometimes called Mercer clips, after their inventor.

The 1,000-foot rolls of film (400-foot in 16 mm.) which reach the editor from the laboratory are for convenience broken down into shots or groups of shots before being reassembled in their proper order. This breaking down is accomplished most easily with a *horse*—a pair of parallel uprights separated halfway up by a horizontal spindle on which the roll of film is placed. The separate small rolls are prevented from unwinding by fastening them with rubber bands, and are marked with a shot number or other description for easy identification on the cutting bench.

Winding of film is done on a pair of *rewinds,* which are set up at either end of the cutting bench, usually with a translucent *light box* in between, over which the film can be easily examined. *Positive rewinds* have a high gear ratio so that a reel of film can be rewound on them very quickly; *negative rewinds* have a low gear ratio to discourage improper handling of the master film.

FILING PROCEDURE

In spite of the relative simplicity of cutting equipment, the actual man-handling required in cutting a film is very great. Thirty thousand feet of 35 mm. film, with an equal amount of sound track, may be required to make a picture which will eventually be three reels long on the screen. This means that sixty large cans of film may have to be wound through. The physical weight of these cans will be about three hundred and sixty pounds, and they will need a lot of moving around in the course of one day's cutting. If a reel is wound *head-up* (with the beginning on the outside), the wanted shot will usually—owing to the cussedness of film—be found at the end; while if the reel happens to be wound *tails-up* (with the end on the outside), the wanted shot will still be found on the inside. Both reels will need rewinding—a back-breaking business if it has to be done for several hours every day.

Faced with these mechanical difficulties, the newcomer may be inclined to grow careless about the time-consuming tidinesses of film. If he finds a shot in the middle of a reel, he will cut out the shot but not bother to rewind the reel to the end and put it away in its proper can. He will simply leave it out on the cutting bench divided between two reels. If he expects to need shots from thirty cans of film during the day, he will leave the thirty cans on his bench within easy reach. If he has to unwind rolls of trims (cut-out sections of shots), he will let them hang on the bins, no matter how much loose film has already accumulated. And if he should strong-mindedly wind up a loose shot, he will decide that it is far too much trouble to label it and put it away in its proper can.

A person who acts like this will save minutes at the time, but lose hours and perhaps days later on. Quite apart from the fire hazard these bad practices create, they will hopelessly confuse the film which is being edited. If each foot of film among a hundred thousand feet is to be at the cutter's immediate command, he cannot be too careful about the mechanical organization of his material. In addition to the labeling of individual shots, it will almost always be worth his while to make up a book in which every shot is listed by scene number and code number, and also described, so that there is perfect cross-indexing between the script and the cans in which the production is kept.

The law provides that all *nitrate film,* when not in use, is to be kept in fire-proof storage cabinets which must be provided in every cutting room. These cabinets should have self-closing doors, sprinklers, and explosive vents communicating with the outside of the cutting room. Like all cutting-room furniture, they must be made of steel. As little film as possible should be taken out of these cabinets at any one time.

Some film, of course, has to be at the cutter's elbow while he is assembling his reel. He will take one of the small rolls off the bench, run it through the moviola, cut it down to approximately the right length, and if he has no immediate need for it, will hang it on a *bin.* This is most often a circular container of fiber or steel, above which is mounted a rack with vertical or horizontal pins for holding the film by its perforations. Since the film is loosely piled in the bin and therefore very dangerous, it should be wound up and put away in cans every evening as a precaution against fire. This may be very inconvenient, however, and bins have been designed with sliding steel sides, counterweighted to make closing easy, which securely protect the film.

FILM ON FIRE

There is a last important point about the mechanics of cutting which cannot be repeated too often. Standard 35 mm. negative film, and all but the most recent types of 35 mm. positive film, makes use of a base of cellulose nitrate, on which the light-sensitive emulsion is coated. Such film is therefore called *nitrate film*. Cellulose nitrate is a substance very closely akin to guncotton in its chemical composition. Indeed, apart from the presence of certain *stabilizers,* and a somewhat lower degree of nitration, there is virtually no difference between the two. Film is thus midway between an inflammable and an explosive substance; and when the stabilizers have evaporated, as they will do if the film is stored at too high a temperature, film is liable to self-ignition (spontaneous combustion). It is therefore a good rule to take particular care of film which is dry and brittle, as may be recognized by its tendency to curl. It can be exceedingly dangerous.

A film fire in a cutting room can be dangerous and terrifying. Suppose a cutter is rewinding a roll of film when it catches fire from a spark or from contact with a hot radiator. The flame races along the piece of film and ignites the rolls at either end. These blaze fiercely, and the flames jump to a bin a few feet away which is heaped with loose film. Instantly, with a tremendous roar, this film catches fire, and soon the closed cans in the neighborhood are heated to the combustion point and violently burst open. All this happens within ten to twenty seconds. If the cutter is wise, he will have already taken to his heels, slamming the door behind him. Unless the sprinkler seals break at once, the whole cutting room will soon be an inferno of blazing film; if the room is not of fireproof construction, the flames may quickly spread to adjacent rooms, which are probably cutting rooms also. If a fire starts in a storage vault, normally containing about a million feet of film, the damage can be extremely serious unless the huge explosive force released is harmlessly channeled away. If combustion is imperfect, because it takes place in the presence of an inadequate volume of oxygen, the consequences may be just as serious. The burning and smoldering film generates enormous volumes of poisonous gases, mostly nitrous and nitric oxides, which are likely to prove fatal even if inhaled in small quantities. The fire at the Cleveland Clinic in 1929 resulted in over a hundred deaths, all from fumes, none from burns. If a free explosion occurs, the quantity of poisonous fumes is less but the gases generated reduce visibility over a large area, making fire fighting very difficult.[4]

The film industry owes its excellent safety record to the fact that it has regulated its own operations with extreme care. Except in conditions of emergency, film production and storage are only carried out in buildings designed for the purpose and protected by a score of safety devices such as sprinklers, vapor-proof electric fixtures, and automatic alarms.

No matter how many safety devices there may be, the ultimate responsibility for avoiding fires rests with the individual. In the cutting room, this means an ingrained habit of good housekeeping, including among other things the following:

1. Never have more than the minimum amount of film outside safety cabinets.
2. Keep doors closed all the time to prevent the spread of fire.
3. Turn off moviola and bench lights when not in use to prevent their reaching a dangerous temperature, which might ignite stray pieces of film.
4. Put all scrap film in immersion barrels, which wet the film and so make it less inflammable.
5. Have scrap film removed from the cutting room every day and properly disposed of.

All film producing organizations should have a carefully planned fire warden system, which, by means of frequent, unrehearsed fire drills, has made everyone aware of what he has to do should fire break out. If a fire starts in a cutting room, the occupants should leave immediately, closing the doors behind them. It is false courage to stay and fight the fire with extinguishers inside the room. Film fire is just not that kind of fire.

THE PSYCHOLOGY OF CUTTING

The newcomer sits down for the first time at his cutting bench, rather apprehensive—as was the director the first time he stood behind a camera—at the threat of so many mechanical obstructions to the realization of his ideas. If he has read anything of the history of movies, there are likely to be two crosscurrents of thought in his mind. First is the style of editing developed in the classical Russian silent films like *The Battleship Potemkin* and *Mother*. This is often called dynamic cutting, because it largely disregards the regular continuity of story cutting, and substitutes the film's particular ability to relate together things which may have occurred far apart. The pursuit of the heroine by the villain in a typical western is a simple example of dynamic

---

[4] The latest available information on the decomposition of film is to be found in James W. Cummings, Alvin C. Hulton, and Howard Silfin, "Spontaneous Ignition of Decomposing Cellulose Nitrate Film," *JSMPTE*, Mar., 1950, pp. 268–274.

cutting. A shot of the heroine galloping along on a horse, immediately followed by a shot of the villain galloping along, gives rise to the instinctive feeling that one is being hotly pursued by the other, even though the two shots bear no real spatial relationship to one another. This synthesized space is sometimes called *filmic space*.

The Russians eagerly took up dynamic cutting, and soon found that it was especially applicable to their new revolutionary films. They began to claim that cutting was the most important thing in film making. In other fields, they said—in painting a picture of the real world, in representing stage plays, in reproducing speech and music—film plays second best to the older arts. But cutting provides something totally new. It adds the separate heroine and villain into a new idea—the chase. It makes out of the explosion and the weeping child (shot years and thousands of miles apart) something completely different from both—the effects of mass bombing.[5]

Dynamic cutting thus starts with the idea that film can be made much more exciting by breaking the world down into carefully selected bits, than by recording long, uninterrupted stretches of action.

The other style of cutting, which we may call *continuity cutting,* starts with quite a different idea—that film has a story to tell, and that it will tell this story most clearly if there is a recognizable continuity of movement and dialogue. Carried to extreme lengths, this would mean that a film would simply reproduce a stage play, with little or no change of angle or introduction of parallel action. And that, of course, is exactly the point of critical attack for the exponents of dynamic cutting. However, they, in their turn, found that by going to extremes, they made a film abrupt and choppy unless it was followed with the most concentrated attention by an audience ready to jump imaginatively over all sorts of difficult gaps.

Thus, in practice, cutting has come to be a combination of dynamic cutting and continuity cutting. All intermediate stages exist between one extreme and the other, the story film favoring continuity cutting and the fact film dynamic cutting, merely because of the different type of film material used in the two kinds of film. In recent years there has been a healthy interchange between the two. The makers of fiction films have swung back to a freer use of visuals, helped by their search for realistic backgrounds and by the documentary training which many of their directors received during the war. The makers of fact films in turn have found that story development often gives a more personal interest to a film than the relationship of blocks of explanatory footage. For each particular film the right method must be found.

So our newcomer, faced with his many neatly wound rolls of film, each

[5] This type of cutting, often called *montage* (see Glossary for its present studio sense) appealed especially to the Soviet directors because of its parallel with their Hegelian dialectic; the famous thesis, antithesis, and synthesis.

labeled with a description or shot number, will come up against one obvious fact: he must discover for himself the laws of film—the dynamics of converting assorted bits of space into a single sequence of time.

To translate the bits of film at hand into not merely physical, but psychological units of time on the screen is the inexperienced cutter's first problem as he decides where to start and finish his initial shot. Twenty seconds may seem to him a short enough time, as time goes in daily life. He multiplies twenty by 1½ (since, as we saw before, 1½ feet of film are projected each second), rather nervously chops off a shot thirty feet long and winds it up on a neighboring rewind.[6] Maybe it's an establishing shot of a town. The next shot called for in the script shows a street in this town, down which a character walks to enter his office building. This seems to call for a fairly leisurely inspection on the screen. Half a minute, the greenhorn knows, flies past quickly enough when you are reading an interesting magazine story. This should just about do to introduce the street and the character and get him in through the door of his office building. So forty-five feet comes off one of the rolls on the table and is attached with a paper clip to the roll forming on the rewinder. And so it goes on. Our newcomer won't pay overmuch attention to the way the camera is moving; apparently its only purpose is to keep some character or important object in the middle of the shot. On the other hand he will follow this character around like a shadow, and will not let him off the screen for a single second in the edited film. Every movement will be there so that our beginner may avoid that first of the editor's terrors—a jump, an obvious loss of continuity in the action. Finally, after a surprising number of hours' work, the new cutter has finished a full reel. He wearily splices it together— not yet rating an assistant—and has it projected.

In the theater he gets as much of a shock as did the novice director when he sat down to watch his first day's rushes. First of all the film is unutterably slow. That establishing shot, which he knows lasts only twenty seconds, seems to go on and on for hours. The street shot is so unbearably wearisome that he has time to read the signs on all the stores and watch a farmer getting out of his jalopy half way down the street, long before our character has got himself into his office building and closed the door. The simple failure to notice the direction of the camera's movement proves just as disastrous. Cutting from a pan one way to a pan the other way produces a clashing effect quite the opposite of the smooth flow of action the cutter wanted. And as for his insistence on avoiding anything which could possibly be called a jump—that seems to have been quite thrown away; for it is now obvious that he could have taken all sorts of liberties with time and space without upsetting the audience in the least, in fact with a great saving of tedious footage.

That this discouraging contrast between film and reality was well recog-

[6] His arithmetic must, of course, be altered if he is cutting 16 mm. film.

nized long ago is shown by an amusing passage from an early work on film.[7] "When the films are developed and a trial positive is struck for projection before the powers that be, to receive official approbation and sanction to enter the market, the critics in the private projecting room sometimes fail to see eye to eye with the cinematographer, and deem this and that to be lacking in the essentials which render a film attractive to the public. Accordingly, these sections are eliminated. From 300 to 3,000 feet may be destroyed in this manner."

In cutting it is very much easier to describe what is bad than to define what is good. This is because cutting is a matter of artistic perception, and with each film it is necessary to make different judgments. As we have seen, two styles of cutting predominate. Cutting a continuous story consists mainly of selecting the best takes of each shot and joining them together in script order so that the psychological intentions of the director are most sensitively brought out by the interplay of different camera angles. Of course, the more difficult rhythms of fast and slow, rest and climax, play their parts. But that the whole process is not an exceptionally responsible and creative one will be realized by anyone who looks at the credit titles of the next feature picture he sees, and notes how far down the list the name of the editor appears. Many editors in Hollywood and elsewhere are men of talent, who lament the little creative scope afforded them by present methods of making commercial films.

The editor of information films is usually in a much better position, though his pay will be less and his audience smaller than those of his Hollywood colleague. In compensation, he will have a larger share in the picture's success, for many of the basic effects will be of his designing. Montage is still at the bottom of most of this kind of cutting, for though violent juxtapositions of single shots are seldom used, whole sequences are placed alongside one another to provide overtones of meaning by their contrast. The less the continuity imposed by the flow of a story, the more freedom the editor has to develop the special rhythms and properties of film construction. But even when a story ties down the general line of the picture there is a sound track which can be used with great freedom to get away from a literal rendering of the scene.

SYNC

On rare occasions, the direct sound for a film is recorded on the same piece of film as the picture itself. This is called *single-system recording,* and its very few advantages show up only in newsreel interviews and hurried television production. The reason is that it is impossible to secure a fine enough grain structure and proper sensitometric control when the picture image is to be recorded on the same piece of film. Single-system recording also imposes

[7] F. A. Talbot, *Moving Pictures: How They Are Made and Worked*, Lippincott, 1912.

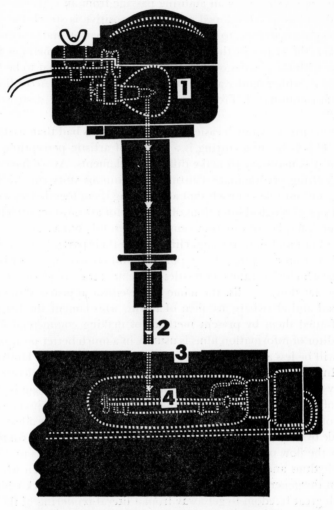

Fig. 4-5. A moviola sound head. Light from an exciter lamp (1) is directed in a thin beam through a slit (2) onto the sound track (3), the slit being at right angles to the direction of the track which is coming up through the page. After passing through the sound track, which acts as a variable light stopper, the light beam strikes the sensitive surface (4) of a phototube, in which it sets up currents corresponding to the fluctuating intensity of the beam.

limitations on the editor (unless he makes a separate sound print), because sound and picture are not recorded parallel but with a staggered separation of up to twenty frames.

Normally, the sound is recorded on a separate piece of film called a sound track.[8] This film is of exactly the same size and standards as the picture film, and can be run on the same machines. The sound record itself occupies only a narrow strip along the side and just within the sprocket holes, the rest of the area of the film being blank. We shall see later on how sound is recorded on film.

In the cutting room, the sound is played on a sound head, a mechanism coupled to the *picture head* of the moviola and driving the film at the same speed (figure 4-5). In this way *synchronism* is achieved. Imagine two people talking in front of the camera, which is to make both a picture and sound record of them; that is to say, they are to appear on the screen exactly as in real life. Before the start of the dialogue scene we are shooting, the camera assistant claps a pair of wooden *clapper boards* [9] in front of the camera after it has got up to speed. One frame of the picture records the moment when the clapper sticks come together; a sharp modulation representing the resulting bang appears on the sound track. When these two are placed parallel with one another, the film is said to be in synchronism, or *in sync* (pronounced "sink"). This is the basic means of synchronizing, which is one of the fundamental necessities of sound-film making.

Suppose for a moment that, through some mechanical defect, the sound camera is going a little slower than the picture camera. After the scene has been taken, the sound and picture tracks (a convenient colloquialism covering both strips of film) are developed and printed and turned over to the editor, who proceeds to synchronize them with the aid of the picture and sound records of the clappers, as explained before. As the sound camera is running slow, the editor will find that, though he may start the two tracks in sync on his moviola, they will very soon get out of sync. The sound track will be shorter than the corresponding picture film, with the result that when the last word of a sentence has been spoken, the speaker's lips are still seen to be moving. It has been found by experiment that most people can detect an error of synchronism on speech when it exceeds two frames either ahead of or behind exact correspondence, or a total latitude of four frames. When it is considered that a sound shot may run as long as ten minutes or 16,000 frames, it will be seen that an error of only $\frac{1}{40}$ of 1 per cent can be tolerated. This is

[8] This term is ambiguous, for it describes (correctly) the narrow sound image and (colloquially) the whole band of film which carries the image.

[9] Also called *slate boards* and *take boards*. The large studios have now replaced this primitive device with an electrical interlock system in which sound and picture tracks come up to speed in exactly the same distance from a punched sound sync mark and a miniature nonclapping slate board attached to the camera. This eliminates noise and waste footage.

another reminder of the extraordinary accuracy which has to be achieved in all film mechanism.

After the previous day's rushes have been synced, they are sent back to the lab for *coding* in a *coding machine,* a device which prints a series of key numbers along the edge of the film. These numbers run from the *start mark* of the action to the end of the reel, and are repeated from the start mark of the dialogue reel.[10] In this way what is effectively a foot-by-foot series of sync marks is placed on the reels, enabling sound and action to be synced up even when the tracks have been cut into small pieces. In the major studios, these numbers are made to correspond to designations in the script, and they must be entered shot for shot in the log book which the cutter keeps.

So useful are these numbers that much dialogue can be cut without any other means of maintaining synchronism; but when complicated *overlaps* are being made, in which several tracks have to be handled simultaneously, it is more convenient to use a synchronizer (figure 4-6). This instrument consists of a freely rotating shaft to which are rigidly attached two, three, or four sprocket wheels, on which the same number of film tracks can travel, their perforations meshing with the teeth on the sprocket wheels, so that the tracks move simultaneously, always maintaining the same position in relation to each other.

Thus, by the end of this part of the editing process, the cutter has one or more reels of positive picture film, called a *workprint* or *cutting copy,* and usually a dialogue track which synchronizes with it. Each reel of workprint will contain on the average between 80 and 150 shots, depending on the style of shooting and cutting. A feature film shot with stagey slowness might contain less than 50 shots per reel, and a war film made by montage methods of cutting might have as many as 250. The average shot length of the feature is only 13 seconds, which will seem short enough to anyone unaccustomed to film tempo. But in the war film, the average shot stays on the screen for less than three seconds, a time so short that few shots can be held much longer, since, to maintain the average, others would then sink below the threshold of visibility. These figures are worth pondering as further evidence of the striking difference between film and drama.

When the workprint is projected, it looks very much like the finished picture, save for the scratches it may contain, and the frames which may be missing. If frames or longer sections of the workprint are damaged, they must be replaced in order to make the print safe to project, for torn perforations are a frequent cause of breakage and may even lead to fire. Replaced sections of film must be made the exact length of the original. Otherwise, when the nega-

10 Code numbers are often called footage numbers and edge numbers, but these terms are properly reserved for the numbers which are photographed into the negative stock by the manufacturer and printed through to the positive to enable negative and positive to be matched.

Fig. 4-6. The four-way synchronizer, or "fourway." Four large sprockets fixed to a common spindle hold the film tracks in precise relationship while they are wound to and fro by the rewinds at either end. A footage counter counts the feet in either direction, and marks on the nearest sprocket count the frames from a start mark which is often described as "zero-zero" (0–00).

tive of the film is matched to the positive, there will be a discrepancy which can only be put right by an undesirable jump cut or an alteration in the frames at the beginning or end of the shot. If one or more sound tracks are synchronized to the picture, the consequences are even more serious, for replacement errors will put the subsequent part of the reel out of sync.

Breaks in picture and sound track may be temporarily made good by *leader* (blank film), but picture leader should, and sound leader must, be replaced by *reprints* before the final re-recording of the film. From every point of view it is desirable to keep the workprint in good condition, and great care should be taken not to kink or step on the film, or pick up dust on the sound track by dragging it across the cutting room floor.

At this stage the film has no sound except the dialogue track, none of that smooth blending of music, sound effects, and speech which will characterize it when it is finally seen in the movie theater. These extra sound elements are also added in the cutting room, and to them we shall return in a later chapter.

THE CUTTING UNIT

Up to this point we have assumed that the editor of a film is a single person, who plans the cutting sequence, carries it out, and handles all the cutting room chores. A small unit may indeed impose all these tasks on one person, who may be the film's director as well, but he will certainly not be able to work very fast. As the production unit enlarges, it subdivides responsibilities. There will be an editor, who physically edits the film. Over him there may be a supervising editor who is in charge of several productions, under him an assistant editor, who looks after the film material, searches for shots, does the physical work of assembly, and helps on the synchronizer. Finally, one or more cutting room assistants splice film and carry cans. This small job has often been the start of big careers.

Either the editor or his assistant must maintain daily or even hourly touch with the laboratory, checking on the progress of rushes or material for optical effects, ordering library shots, reprints, and so on.

THE FILM TAKES SHAPE

Film cutting is a stage-by-stage affair. First comes the assembly of the material in the proper order. For each shot, several takes (repeat shots of a piece of action from the same camera position) may have been printed, even though it is customary for the sake of economy to eliminate as many unwanted takes as possible before printing. *Assembly* involves whittling down the takes to the best one of each shot, and eliminating any obviously unwanted action. The assembly is then screened and the cutter, usually with the director or producer, makes notes on the flow of action and on alterations in the sequence of incidents. Reel by reel the cutting of the film is refined. In its early stages the film is usually referred to as a *rough cut,* and in its later stages as a *fine cut.* Frequent projections are necessary, since, among other things, the size of the screen image has an appreciable effect on the tempo of cutting. Dead passages may seem on the moviola to have been eliminated from the cutting of a particular reel. Projected on a large screen, however, the magnified size of the image will make the details so much easier to grasp that the cutting will often seem slow. The cutter then takes his picture and dialogue back to the moviola and works over them again. In this way the film is gradually compressed into its essential footage, and every waste frame eliminated from every single shot. Taut cutting is just as important in an orthodox Hollywood feature as it is in a *March of Time* or other documentary.

Finally, before the picture (or *action*) reels of his workprint are completed, the cutter must decide what fades, wipes, and other *special effects* he needs, and when these and the titles have been completed, he must cut them in.

We started this chapter with a picture of the editor cutting and screening his first film. Many an editor and director of much longer experience have been discouraged at the sight of the first assembly of a new picture. They discover with dismay that there is no coherence between sequence and sequence, even between shot and shot, no forward progression of interest. The story limps and drags. It is one of the most convincing demonstrations of the power of cutting as an art to watch a film gain in clearness and dramatic intensity at successive screenings.

In the months that follow his initial failures, the cutter learns—as does everyone who begins to get a grasp on a new medium—that that medium has all sorts of rules of its own. Film has a tempo measured in seconds and not minutes; it has a rhythm of fast and slow which enables the cutter to plot a satisfying curve of his picture in terms of rest and climax. He learns to use movement within the frame—sometimes in the same direction, sometimes in opposite directions in successive shots—and to relate this to movements of the camera itself. He masses his shots as between close-ups and long shots, getting the feel of each for the kind of mood it will convey.

And all the time he becomes more conscious of the overtones which each juxtaposition of shots and sequences will convey. The Russian directors were right in insisting that two shots do not merely add up to A plus B; they produce a new element, C, from the fusion of A and B.

In cutting a picture, the editor will never forget its relation to sound. If a commentary is to be added, he will search for shots which will illustrate verbal images he intends to use; or, better, the picture may suggest key phrases to his mind. This "sparking" from one to the other gets away from the monotonous technique in which the commentary is a mere explanation of what happens on the screen, or else an abstract lecture bearing little relation to the visuals. The editor should also have from the beginning a clear idea of where he is going to call on music, where he will throw extra weight to sound effects, and where the picture may be given extra dramatic impact by running in complete silence. As sound and picture have a complementary relationship, anything which affects one will affect the other too. An editor who has arranged things so that his most exciting visual sequence coincides with an immense crescendo of music and effects and at the same time requires explanation from the commentator will have produced nothing but an inarticulate din.

For this reason, the screening of a workprint, with or without dialogue, requires a constant effort of imagination. The editor must ever be on the alert to plan his cutting in order to take greatest possible creative advantage of the various sound elements which can only be added at a later stage. One of the keys to good picture cutting is the intelligent anticipation of sound.

V

⊓⊔⊓⊔⊓⊔⊓⊔⊓⊔⊓⊔⊓⊔⊓⊔⊓⊔⊓⊔⊓⊔⊓⊔⊓⊔⊓⊔⊓⊔⊓⊔⊓⊔⊓⊔⊓⊔

The Library:
Indexing Time and Space

SOMETIMES it is impossible to secure in the film studio or on location the shots demanded by the script. The film maker must then have recourse to the *film library*, sometimes called the *stock shot* library to distinguish it from libraries in which completed pictures are stored.

The importance of the *film library* varies greatly with the kind of film-making organization. It is least in the big commercial studios, which film their fictional dramas almost entirely on *sound stages,* reckoning that it is easier to fabricate reality than go out and find it. But even here it is useful to have on file a large range of exterior shots, called *establishing shots,* of foreign countries and famous places. It is just another example of filmic space, that if a real shot of the city of Morocco is dissolved into a detail shot of the Casbah inaccurately reconstructed in a studio many thousands of miles away, the spectator will be irresistibly driven to think that the second shot is just as realistic as the first.

Newsreels have developed the idea of the film library much further. As with the newspaper morgue, there is hardly an important event or personality of the last thirty years in any country on the globe which cannot be found in its files. Scarcely any two film libraries are alike, and almost all of them have different systems of cataloguing. Indeed the system usually goes with the librarian, and some libraries have four or five different systems which they have inherited from the past running simultaneously.

The library has two vitally important tasks. First is the actual physical storage of film. Film often has great archival value, and consequently requires as careful treatment as documents or other properties which are to be preserved for hundreds of years. Second, the library must keep track of the entire contents of its film storage vaults, often amounting to twenty or thirty million feet. The tracing of individual shots in this immense footage requires a very high degree of organization, especially when new material is constantly coming into the library, and other shots are being sent for *papering* or *cording off* in production departments.

STORING FILM

Because of the high combustibility of nitrate film, film storage is a technical problem of some difficulty, as a mere list of the requirements for storage vaults will show (figure 5-1). According to the standards of the National Board of Fire Underwriters, each vault may not exceed 750 cubic feet in volume (giving space for about a thousand cans); it must have a vent with an area exceeding a stated minimum; it must have a sprinkler system with not less than twelve heads (if the vault is full size); these heads must be separated by baffles, and all film kept below the level of the sprinklers; double doors, one of them automatic, are to give entrance to the vault; the lights are to be of vaporproof type, with switches outside the vault; the temperature inside must never exceed 70° F. In addition to these and many other stipulated requirements, all vault vents should end at least fifty feet from the nearest building, or point straight up in the air, clear of any adjacent roof; external baffles should be provided between one vault and another, to prevent an explosion from carrying into an adjacent vault; and continuous ventilation of the vaults by extractor fans should be arranged for. Finally, if the film is of archival value and expected to last for several decades, each reel should be stored horizontally in a separately vented container; its hypo content must be less than about 0.02 milligrams per square inch; and the humidity as well as the temperature of the vault must be carefully adjusted to prevent excessive shrinkage.

THE FILM ENCYCLOPEDIA

The most general way of indexing a library is merely to list the cans it contains, together with their individual contents. This system is entirely adequate for nonproduction purposes, and it is generally used in *film exchanges*—regional centers from which pictures are distributed to movie theaters. In these exchanges it is essential to know the whereabouts of all reels of film at all times. Consequently, there is usually a very thorough card-index system to check prints in and out. There is also a system of *inspection,* which provides for release prints to be wound through and checked for damage at frequent intervals. This information is also marked on the index cards.

Production organizations require much more detailed cataloguing of ma-

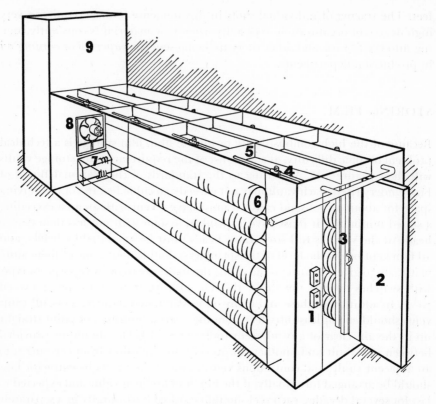

Fig. 5-1. A vault for storing inflammable film. Electric switches for the vault are mounted outside (1) to reduce sparking hazards. A steel door (2) provides a first line of protection in case of fire, and a safety door (3) slides to when released by a fusible link. An 8-head sprinkler system (4) is ready to dowse the film, while baffles (5) direct water downward onto the cans (6). The radiator (7) is protected by a well-spaced grille, and a fan (8) draws fresh air under the door and expels it outside. This fan is mounted so that it will fall outward if an explosive pressure builds up in the vault, a pressure which will then relieve itself through the large vent (9) into the open air. Vault shown holds 750 cans.

terial in their libraries, because they are likely to make use of individual shots buried in reels of film. The first step involved is to make *synopses* of each film in the library. These are brief summaries which give a clue to the kind of material the films contain. Next comes the making of dope sheets, a procedure which is known as *shot listing*. Here the film and its sound track are first screened by the librarians, who thus gain a clear idea from the commentary or dialogue what it is about. They then go through the picture shot by shot, usually on a hand viewer, writing down the contents of each single shot.

Considerable knowledge and political acumen are needed in indicating the context, and picking out important people from the background, of material of foreign origin. Though the man in the center of a shot may today be the premier of a Balkan country, the next few years may see him liquidated and replaced by the second man from the right in the fourth row. The good shot lister is the one who also looks at the fourth row.

After the dope sheets have been properly indexed, the cross-indexing begins. This is the most difficult part of the whole business. On the one hand it is possible to ignore all but a very few cross-references—e.g., personalities, countries, general headings, and so on—a method used by one of the largest newsreel libraries in the United States. It has the great merit of speed in filing, so that the library runs little risk of getting behind, in spite of the thousands of feet of new film which pour in every week. On the other hand, it makes almost psychic demands on the librarian in charge. One has to look under the general heading of Buildings to find swimming pools, statues, and the Unknown Soldier; under Geography to find harbors; under Aviation to find smoke screens, and so on. At the other extreme it is possible to list every single shot of every film on a separate card, breaking down the cards into as many classes as may be needed by cross-indexing cards. This makes the cataloguing of new footage a very slow business, and also increases the number of steps the librarian must take when requested to find a shot of a particular kind. Most libraries try to compromise between these extremes (figure 5-2).

There is, however, one recently introduced system which combines the utmost accuracy of classification with high speed in finding shots. It operates by means of punched cards—familiar from their use by banks and other large businesses. These cards contain about eighty vertical columns and twenty horizontal classifications. Each shot in the entire library has a card, and each card will provide 80 times 20, or 1,600 designations of a shot. This is far more than would ever be needed. The card also contains a sample frame of the shot attached to one corner. The system also needs a multiple-brush sorter, a machine which will pick out the cards according to the position of the punch marks at a rate of 24,000 an hour.

Suppose it is desired to find a shot of Russian guerillas marching through mountainous country on a cloudy day. The librarian gets out all the cards marked "Soldiers"—a main classification—and sets the sorting machine for Russian, guerillas, mountains, and cloudy weather. The available shots conforming to this specification will then be automatically selected in a few minutes, and the sample frame will tell the librarian or editor which is the best shot of the group for his particular purpose. A simple entry on the chosen card tells him further what vault, rack, and can the shot is to be found in.

```
01-510-P-10                    -2-
GATEWAY TO ASIA

Content:
13.30E G35687-671 LS   Across water (house on hill in bgd.)
                       birds swoop over water - pan right
                       as birds fly out over water.
14.30E G35672-700 VCS  Beautiful flowers (dahlias)
15.10E G34563-615 MS   Trucking shot as camera moves along
                       road through avenue of trees at even
                       tide.
16.13E G60287-311 VCS  Flower (white - possibly bleeding
                       heart).
17.14E G40178-202 MS   Tilt down from top of Douglas fir to
                       bush to logs on ground.
18.14E G40206-240 VHS  Pan along tops of trees in dense
                       bush - pan covers deep wooded gorge
                       with mountains in bgd. where pan
                       stops.
19.14E G40241-273 VHS  Same as 18.
20.14E G40277-311 VHS  Looking down on river gorge - two
                       men being towed up river on raft.
```

a

```
Flowers
   SEE ALSO    displays - flowers




   04-510-P-1
   01-510-P-8-10
   10-519-P-2
   X5-P-1
   14-010-P-2
   10-023-P-1-2-3
   13-040-P-4
   13-052-P-1
   14-100-P-1
```

b

Fig. 5-2. Stock shot library indexing cards. Card **a** is a breakdown by shots, or small groups of shots, of unused material assembled for the film Gateway to Asia. The indication "01-510-P-10" gives the position of this reel of shots on the vault shelves. Note shot identification by negative numbers. Card **b** shows how a library classification "Flowers" enables shots 14 and 16 in **a** to be traced.

This is probably the most perfect indexing system so far devised, but because of the high cost of the equipment, and the difficulty of changing over a large library from one system to another, it has not so far made much headway. Also, of course, it needs expert operators to make it work, and so cannot be handled even in emergency by people from other departments. But this is not wholly a disadvantage.

We have spoken so far as if only complete films were shot-listed in the library. But actually—barring dialogue shots—all the unused material (called *outs*) from every production, if of any general interest at all, is catalogued in the library. Most libraries retain the negative of this *stock footage* intact, simply ordering master positives and dupes of wanted shots. But this may lead to the use of the same shot in different pictures, and sometimes in different and even opposite contexts—an embarrassing consequence of the powers of filmic space. To prevent this, some libraries give out the original negative of stock shots and forbid the duping of finished films.

As negatives are easily damaged by constant handling, especially when run through hand viewers, some libraries make up matched *viewing prints*. These are ordinary black-and-white prints matched to the rolls of stock-shot negative, but, unlike the negative, they can be projected and handled. When a shot is wanted, the viewing print is run through and *papered* or *corded off*—that is, small slips of paper are inserted in the roll or short pieces of string are tied through the perforations to mark the beginning and end of the wanted shot. The corresponding negative is then papered or corded off to match and sent to the lab for duping, or cut out and used, according to the practice of the library.

Libraries are often tied in closely with the shipping department, and made responsible for checking all film in and out of the studio. They must also know the whereabouts of all negatives and master positives which may be sent to outside laboratories for printing. Finally, they may be put in charge of the checking and repair of all reels of film projected in the studio or sent in from elsewhere.

One measure of the importance of a department is the confusion it can create if it becomes disorganized. By this test the library rates high.

VI

⨅⨆⨅⨆⨅⨆⨅⨆⨅⨆⨅⨆⨅⨆⨅⨆⨅⨆⨅⨆⨅⨆⨅⨆⨅⨆⨅⨆⨅⨆⨅⨆⨅⨆⨅⨆⨅⨆

Synthesizing Space and Time

H ITHERTO, the material which we have sought for our film, whether captured on the spot or taken from library storage, has been the brute stuff of reality, modified, it is true, by many of the optical resources of the camera, worked upon by the director's imagination, and even reconstructed where necessary on the studio floor, but in the result still recognizable as the world of everyday event. One of the principal attributes of this world is movement. In the film it assumes an even greater significance, because film has no abstract language, and cannot express without infinite labor many of the concepts which spring so readily to the writer's mind, and flow onto his page. This very paragraph, for instance, though it expresses ideas of no great complexity, lies beyond the cinema's power to convey to an audience's eye. Hence, rejecting the impossible and seizing instead upon what it can so magically accomplish, the cinema, as Basil Wright has said, has achieved "the end of that quest for life in movement which began when the cave men of Altamira painted leaping figures on the walls of their caverns."

Movement, then, is the cinema's breath of life. And in the world of life, which is also the world of film, movement is present in a range and profusion past the mind's or the eye's power to grasp. A stroke of lightning flashes from cloud to earth in twenty or thirty millionths of a second. No one has ever seen it as it moved; all we see is its luminous channel through the air. The sweep of an airplane's propellor and the beat of a humming bird's wings appear to us a scarcely perceptible blur. At the other end of the scale, flowers open and close too slowly for the eye to see. Glaciers make their way imperceptibly down the mountain slopes. A farmer will neglect his hillside, and it will be his son who, when he tills it a generation later, first notices the channels of erosion which the rains have scoured out. And the vast canyons and gorges which the rivers are digging deepen at a pace perceptible only to the eye of God.

The camera has wonderfully brought this range of speeds within the scope of human vision. We can watch a bullet lazily bursting a soap bubble, a plant frantically scurrying through childhood to full maturity. Cameras have lately been designed which can shoot ten million pictures in a second. By time lapse, as we have seen, individual frames can be taken at long intervals, and there is theoretically no limit to the slowness of the movement which can thus be accelerated until it becomes visible. But if we take as a workable minimum the exposure of one frame in each twenty-four hours, the range of speeds which the camera can bring to a single speed on the screen is extraordinarily large.[1] Its ratio is 1 to 864,000,000,000. No small achievement for an instrument which was invented only sixty years ago!

All matter is in motion. The buildings in which we live are weathering away, our bodies wrinkle and grow old, rust and fungus attack the objects of daily use. These are movements which even the camera cannot see; and where this is the only movement we may call the object static. It then does not matter how long we keep the camera's shutter closed between each exposure of film; nothing will have changed before the lens. Hence a person may walk into the scene, move what is there, and get out of sight again, without the camera ever being aware that anything has happened.

Forty-five years ago, this simple idea was a closely guarded secret of its discoverer. The first animated film, *The Haunted Hotel,* was made in the United States in 1906 by Stuart Blackton. A bottle of wine poured itself into a glass; a knife raised itself from the table and cut a sausage and a loaf of bread; tools went on working without any operator in sight; all this with no sign of wires, trapdoors, or any of the other paraphernalia which movies had borrowed from the practitioners of magic. When this film arrived in Paris, then the world's film production center, it created consternation. The finest technicians of Pathé, Gaumont, and the other studios crowded into the small projection rooms and screened the film over and over again. The producers had set them a time limit for discovery of the secret; competition between France and the United States was intense, and *The Haunted Hotel* was achieving a prodigious success in America. The time limit passed, the film still remained inexplicable. At length it was Emil Cohl, who was to become the originator of the animated cartoon, who pried this secret from the screen.[2]

Single-frame animation (sometimes still called "one turn, one picture") means simply that the film is exposed one frame at a time, instead of continuously. Actually, as we have seen, no film exposures are continuous. The movie camera is by its nature a time analyst. But whereas normal film photography

---

[1] Excellently and amusingly demonstrated in the short film, *Wonder Eye,* Glover, 1946.

[2] This story is told by Georges Sadoul, *Histoire général du cinéma,* vol. 2, pp. 477–480. Sadoul relates that at that time single-frame animation became known as *"le mouvement américain."*

spaces the exposures about one twenty-fourth of a second apart, single-frame photography enables the intervals to be stretched to minutes, hours, and days.[3] During these intervals, any desired change may be introduced into the camera's field of view. Its object may be displaced, added to, reduced, or replaced. Single-frame photography therefore enables the artist to telescope time, and simultaneously bring new movements into the world of static objects. This was the great secret which Stuart Blackton discovered, and it is a secret which belongs peculiarly to film.

There is another method by which intervals of time can be bridged. The *dissolve* is a device for overlapping two shots in such a way that, while the first fades out from full intensity to darkness, the second scene seems to emerge out of the first. If, now, the two scenes are substantially different, though having an underlying uniformity, a long dissolve will serve to bridge the gap between the first and the second, whereas a cut would introduce a harsh and intolerable jump. Several styles of animation make use of dissolves as transitions or "time bridges."

ANIMATING THE INANIMATE

It is often convenient to think of the scene before the camera as hidden in darkness until the cameraman causes it to be lighted in any way he pleases. Thus, lighting is itself a means of bringing a scene to life, and since the light can move and play over the scene, it is a means of imparting movement.

The camera has its own power of movement. It can pan, now quickly, now slowly, over the world before it, relating one thing to another, and by turns hiding and revealing in order to create dramatic suspense. Thus, when the world of reality has been frozen, the movement of the camera can bring it back to life.

In short, when we have eliminated movement from the world before the camera, we can reintroduce it by moving either the camera or the lighting. These are the logically simplest means of *animation,* the technical term in film for bringing the inanimate to life.

From these borderline examples of animation, we can move toward devices to which the term animation is more commonly applied. Panning the camera across a still object, or moving it closer or farther away, is equivalent to moving the object in relation to the camera. Indeed, it is often as difficult for the audience to know which is taking place as it is for a railroad traveler to know

---

[3] This basic similarity between normal shooting and single-frame animation is recognized by the old term for the former process—animated photography. "What Is Animated Photography?" is the title of the first chapter of F. A. Talbot's *Moving Pictures, How They Are Made and Worked,* published in 1912. The author devotes nine pages to explaining how remarkable is the phenomenon of persistence of vision which has made movies possible.

whether his train or that on the next platform is moving. Since it is the object as a whole which is being displaced, we may call this technique "animation by displacement."

Now if the animated object, instead of being displaced, is partially replaced by something new, we have another kind of animation, which may be called "animation by partial replacement." Common examples are the boundary lines which animate into place in geographical sequences, and the creeping lines which indicate the routes of expeditions. In these examples the body of the line remains where it is, but is constantly added to.

Often, however, displacement and partial replacement will not suffice to produce some wanted movement. The object must be completely replaced. Almost all film cartoons are made by this method, since the objects and characters are drawn on separate sheets of celluloid (called *cells,* for short), which are changed from frame to frame. We will call this "animation by total replacement."

This scale of techniques moves step by step away from actuality in finding new ways of synthesizing movement: that is, animating the inanimate. We are speaking here of the technical means; and this scale is in no way to be confused with the scale of effect on the audience, stretching from simple representation (the imitation of life) at one extreme to pure abstraction at the other. On this scale of effects, any point may be arrived at by many different techniques; and the technique most removed from reality—*cell animation*—is often used to produce the most realistic, or at least naturalistic, effects. The naturalism of the means, in short, has nothing to do with the naturalism of the effect. The two must be considered separately.

Up to this point we have ignored the number of dimensions in which the objects of animation are to be constructed. Film is at present a two-dimensional medium; that is, it is able to represent depth only by inferential means, of which the most important are perspective (recession of lines and planes) and masking (the passing of one object behind another). If, then, the solid world is to be represented on a flat plane, what purpose is served in the synthesis of movement by using a superfluous dimension in front of the lens which the film plane will afterwards annul? On the scale of effects, the answer is very often: none. And indeed this is the basic reason for the lack of success of the puppet film. Productions by the Walt Disney studios during the past ten years have seemed to audiences just as solid and realistic as the best puppet films, which have on the other hand lacked the marvelous fluidity of two-dimensional animation. None the less, on the scale of techniques it is important to distinguish between two- and three-dimensional methods, since convenience and style of effect often dictate the use of one or the other.

Thus the various systems of animation can be conveniently summed up as follows.

CATEGORIES OF ANIMATION

Two Dimensions   *Three Dimensions*

1. MOVEMENT OF CAMERA AND LIGHT

a. Panning and zooming on a flat surface like a map.
b. Moving light beams over a flat surface, and varying their intensity or color.

a. Panning and zooming over real life objects, puppets, statues, etc.
b. Moving light beams over models, sculpture, etc.; changing their color and direction.

2. DISPLACEMENT

a. Flat paper and metal cutouts.
b. Single- and multiple-jointed cutouts.
c. Moving shapes of string, thread, chain, etc.

a. Movement of complete objects such as plates, chairs, matches, cigarettes.
b. Jointed objects like dolls, mannikins, puppets.

3. PARTIAL REPLACEMENT (ADDITIVE AND SUBTRACTIVE)

a. Scratch-off and paint-on techniques.
b. Chalk and blackboard technique.
c. Pencil, pastel, and paint techniques.
d. In and out movement of pin shadows.

a. Building up and paring down of blocks of clay, plasticine, cheese, etc.
b. Molding putty, clay, chewing gum, or flexible plastic.

4. TOTAL REPLACEMENT

a. Cell animation.
b. Hand-painted movie film (cell = frame).
c. Perforated movie film (cell = frame).
d. Frameless handpainted movie film.
e. Replaceable cutouts.

a. Changing heads of puppets for different facial expressions, while bodies are animated by displacement.

This classification may help to put cell animation in clearer perspective as only one out of many methods of bringing the inanimate to life. Most of these methods depend on an important mechanism, the animation camera and stand, for their transference to movie film. After describing it, we shall return to a more detailed analysis of the categories of animation.

THE CAMERA IN ANIMATION

The animation camera is essentially no different from any other movie camera, since its purpose is the same: to record intermittently an almost instantaneous cross-section of the outside world. However, the animation camera has certain special requirements of its own. Registration must be extremely precise, since the very smallest shake in an animated object will be noticeable, while multiple exposures (superimpositions) will show up an even more objectionable relative shake between objects. In 35 mm. practice, Bell and Howell and Mitchell movements are almost universal, and are widely used in 16 mm., where they are joined by Maurer and even Kodak Cine Special cameras. The film movement of the camera is controlled from a switch panel. It may be either forward or backward, uninterrupted (though usually at a reduced speed of about 8 frames per second), or by single-frame exposure, the time of exposure being of course rigidly uniform.

By closing the shutter, film may be made to travel in either direction without exposure, and often, in fact, is shuttled back and forth many times during the shooting of a single sequence. Since frame-by-frame control of the image is required in animation, the normal footage counter is replaced by a frame counter, and the camera operator receives from the animation department a detailed log sheet explaining just what is to be done, frame by frame.

To produce a dissolve, a fade-out is made by gradually closing the shutter, after which the film is wound back with shutter closed to the start of the fade-out, whereupon a fade-in of the same length is started, with another piece of art work in front of the lens. Thus the fade-out and the fade-in are exactly overlapped.

The superimposition may be considered as a dissolve in which the rate of growth and decay of the dissolved images is zero. In other words, the two (or more) images remain simultaneously visible in a constant intensity relationship to one another. One image may be faint and the other strong, and so they will continue as long as the animator pleases.

The animation camera is fitted with a single lens of the highest quality of definition, which has an accurately calibrated iris, and the camera shutter is also closely calibrated for fades and dissolves. Though it is seldom necessary for two-dimensional animation, there is usually some provision for viewfinding through the lens, often by a prism which "sees" through the cutaway back of the pressure plate. The more convenient rackover arrangement is really not required, since the field of view of the lens at different distances from its subject is accurately known, as we shall see in a moment.

For convenience, the animation camera is almost always mounted vertically, looking down at its subject matter, a position which enables the art work to be laid flat, where it can most easily be handled. Puppets, however, and other solid objects are shot with a horizontal camera. The stand which holds the camera is called an *animation stand* (figure 6-1). Since this stand usually provides for movement of the camera toward and away from its subject matter (a movement known as *zooming*), it is familiarly called a *zoom stand*. The zoom is effected either by hand or by motor—the former for single-frame effects, the latter for uninterrupted film movement. The motor zoom provides for several speeds, either by a gearbox or a continuously variable speed drive. The calibrations on the vertical pillars of the stand correspond with precisely

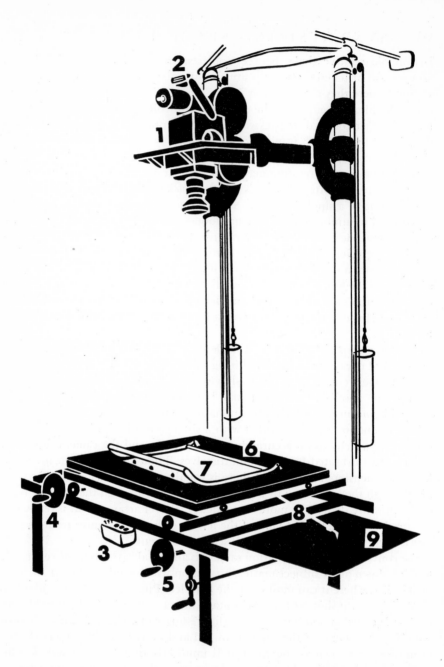

Fig. 6-1. The animation stand or zoom stand. Massive uprights anchored to the wall insure rigid alignment of the camera (1), equipped with a single-frame mechanism (2) operated from a switchbox (3). Handwheels (4 and 5) provide movement in two

known field sizes on the table beneath, thus obviating frequent viewfinding.

Directly under the camera lens is mounted a table on which the art work is placed, and this table can be moved in either of the two horizontal dimensions by means of accurately calibrated handwheels. Thus the animation stand provides perfect four-dimensional control in terms of the X-, Y-, Z-, and time-axes.

When cells are being animated (two-dimensional method 4, a), they are placed in a platen which holds them flat in perfect registration, since it is most important to avoid stray light reflections which might be thrown into the lens if the surface were crinkled.

The movable table is often provided with an extension arm carrying a pointer which travels over a fixed board (figure 6-1, 8 and 9), to which an irregular line diagram can be pinned. By turning the handwheels on the table so that the pointer exactly follows this line, any move sketched on the diagram will be reproduced on the table. Suppose that the animation camera is shooting an aerial photograph intended to represent the bomber pilot's view as he flies in over a target (two-dimensional method 2, a). The plane is supposed to swerve in to the right for its run, after which, at a prescribed point, it is hit by ack-ack fire. The animator traces a line drawing of the required movement, after carefully examining his photograph. He pins this drawing to the fixed board, lines up the camera and sets the pointer. Between each exposure, he turns the handwheels to keep the pointer dead on the line, the wheel controlling the right swerve at first predominating, and the photograph afterward traveling in a straight line under the camera lens. To represent the impact on the plane of the unseen ack-ack fire, which jars it in midflight, the animator has introduced an abrupt zigzag into his line. In following this zigzag with the pointer, he in fact traverses the photograph sharply to one side of its previous course, then sharply to the other, each movement occupying only a few frames. When seen on the screen, this jolt of the photograph (which is interpreted by the audience as being the bombed city) will seem instead to be a jolting of the plane itself. If there is an accompanying sound of ack-ack fire on the sound track, the illusion will be complete. The movement we have been describing can be perfectly controlled, allowing any speed of build-up and decay, and any amplitude of movement the animator desires. All has been planned previously and laid down on the diagram, which the camera operator has only to follow in conjunction with his shooting log.

---

directions of the table (6), which is fitted with a platen (7) for holding cells. An extension arm (8) holds a pointer over a board (9) to which a travel diagram can be pinned, enabling the cameraman to plot zig-zag movements of his animation table.

Among the many other devices which can be fitted to animation stands must be mentioned a projector which throws an image from beneath onto a sheet of ground glass in the plane of the table. The film in this projector can be advanced frame by frame, so that if cell animation is to be combined with live action, the two can be exactly related under the camera. A simpler arrangement enables the camera itself to act as a projector, like an enlarging stand. Film (negative or print) is threaded into the camera, and a small lamp housing is slid into place behind the aperture. This housing contains a prism device which directs the light beam through the cutaway back of the pressure plate, as in the direct viewer already described. Thus an image of the film is formed on the table below. This type of projector, though simple, is inconvenient, since shooting and projection cannot be carried on simultaneously, or even in quick succession, for the projected film must be removed from the aperture and the unexposed film threaded up before shooting can begin.

The crew which mans the animation camera will vary greatly according to the work it has to do. Cell animation by itself, as we shall see, reduces shooting to a mechanical function, requiring only an expert and efficient routine. Other types of animation require the presence of the artist, who must collaborate closely with the cameraman in solving the host of problems which will arise in each new production. This is often called "animation under the camera." Standards of cleanliness and dustlessness in the animation camera room are identical to those demanded by negative matching, and the reader is referred to chapter vii for further information.

The animation camera and stand, simple as they are, together form an instrument of rich and boundless flexibility. If few animators have made full use of its resources, it is because they have been cramped by the stereotype of cell animation. The alternatives are at every film maker's command. A film, *C'est l'aviron* (*Chants Populaires N° 6*), which was made in 1945 by Mc-Laren, and hailed by Picasso as opening up new avenues in the cinema, was in fact produced by the very simplest of means (two-dimensional method 1, *a,* plus superimpositions and a single use of two-dimensional method 2, *a*). The haunting, dreamlike quality of this short piece, and its blending of northern woods and streams with the nostalgic memories of the singer, sprang from a perfect insight into the relation between subject and technique.

The other tools of the animator are many, but it is more convenient to consider them one by one as we discuss the techniques themselves.

THE CATEGORIES OF ANIMATION

Method 1, a. Movement of camera over flat surfaces and over objects.—The simplest type of animation consists in movement of the camera over a stationary object. The example which will come most readily to mind is a zoom in on a map or newspaper to bring a place or a piece of news into sudden prominence. This simple application of the technique has many variants, but there are other more interesting possibilities. Some of these may suggest themselves from a study of the film, *C'est l'aviron,* referred to above. This film was made by painting a series of pictures on large cards which were placed under the camera. As the camera zoomed down, each of these scenes appeared to come nearer and nearer, finally dissolving into another scene which was farther away and also zooming in. Since other successions of scenes appeared simultaneously in superimposition, the total effect was of passing through innumerable planes of scenery. The film was based on an old song chanted by the Canadian *voyageurs* as they paddled through the wilderness, and the apparent movement was imparted to a canoe, the prow of which was seen at the bottom of the screen moving rhythmically up and down, by cutout (two-dimensional method 2, *a*). The singer's reveries were imaged in the center of the screen, and these images were of constant size, the transitions from one to another being effected by dissolves with an ingenious use of similar shapes (metamorphosis).

Other interesting uses of this technique are found in Philip Stapp's films, *Boundary Lines* and *Picture In Your Mind.* Stapp often employs painted panels in which the perspective is so designed that, as the camera moves slowly in, the spectator seems to enter into the painting and not merely move toward it.

When we turn to the three-dimensional world, we find that this method of animation is exceedingly common. Basically, in fact, any pan shot in any film over a stationary landscape is a form of animation. Animation interpenetrates reality. There is a borderland where the camera, through its peculiar creative powers, is able by itself to give meaning and movement to that which is static. This can be seen displayed most fully in a remarkable eight-reel German film, *Michelangelo: The Life of a Titan* (Oertel, 1940), which was almost wholly animated by this means, since it portrayed real life but contained no living characters. The camera itself recreated the Italian scene. By panning over contemporary drawings, dissolving through into actual buildings, moving circularly round Michelangelo's sculpture, it wrought a powerful transformation of these objects into living things. Indeed, the measure of its success is the difficulty of conveying in words effects which are so essentially filmic.

Method 1, b. Movement of light beams over flat surfaces and over objects.— Very little use has been made of this technique in either two or three dimensions. The fade-out and fade-in may indeed be thought of as elementary examples, and in occasional film sequences moving beams of light are made to play over a fixed scene in order to isolate some object of importance. The film

Michelangelo contains a remarkable sequence in which the sculptor tells about his own work. As he starts to speak, the screen is in darkness, but when he begins to describe the labor and agony of creation, a faint beam of light slowly appears and moves searchingly over the screen until it falls upon an unfinished head still partly hidden in the marble. Here the light pauses and grows in intensity, producing a powerful effect of the sculpture coming to life out of the stone, which is given even greater urgency by Michelangelo's words.

This technique is perhaps most consistently used in a film study of primitive and modern sculpture called *Shapes and Forms* (Hoellering, 1949). Throughout this 25-minute film, which has no commentary, statuettes and other small objects are made to revolve while beams of light progressively unmask and obscure them.

Method 2, a. Displacement of unjointed cutouts and objects.—Movement of the object in front of the lens (displacement) is the simplest means of panning with an animation camera, since the table carrying the art work can be traversed with micrometer accuracy. Hence, shots in which the camera zooms in and at the same time moves across a map, are commonly made by a combination of methods 1 and 2. A more interesting use of this technique is to be found in *Boundary Lines*. A sequence in this film traces the growth of weapons across the centuries from the bow and arrow to the atom bomb. Here, a long pageant of the life and architecture of different epochs was prepared on a continuous painted panel, which was slowly traversed under the camera. At the same time a stationary cell which carried the painting of the arrow seen near the beginning (two-dimensional method 4, *a*) was mounted above the panel. Though the arrow remained still and the background moved, it seemed to the audience by the natural association of objects that it was the arrow which was moving, while the background stood still. After traversing scenes of primitive man, the arrow entered the breech of a medieval cannon and emerged as a cannonball. These transitions were effected by scratch-off and paint-on (two-dimensional method 3, *a*) during the passage through the cannon.

One of the commonest displacement techniques is the cutout. A cutout is no more than a shape cut out of a thin sheet of paper, metal or plastic. The human figure in its most elementary form can be represented by a simple unjointed cutout. However, it is essential that the cutout be made of thin material, so that it does not cast an edge shadow. It must lie flat, so that no bends or wrinkles betray its composition.

In three dimensions, the synthetic movement of whole objects before the camera is usually effected by single-frame animation. Many amateur "table-top" films are made by this method, where knives and forks, pens, ink bottles, and small unjointed figures seem to come magically to life and move around without human intervention. That this technique can, however, be made to yield the most elaborate and subtle effects is proved by a recent English film, *The Story of Time* (Signal Films, 1949). Working almost wholly by total displacement of solid objects, the makers of this film have achieved a smoothness of motion beyond comparison with the films of Starevich and George Pal, early experimenters in this field. It is also interesting to note that this 10-minute film, though powerfully aided by music, has no narration, the continuity being carried along entirely by association of ideas and visual fluidity of the images.

Method 2, b. Displacement of jointed cutouts and objects.—The addition of jointing to cutout figures greatly increases the flexibility of screen movement. Joints at the elbows, shoulders, knees, and thighs (eight joints in each figure) make possible a good representation of walking, dancing, and gesticulating. Cutouts save the expensive multiplication of cells, since the same cutouts will serve for a whole sequence or even for a whole film, it being necessary to change only the backgrounds. The movements of the cutout figures are carefully planned in advance, and faint calibration marks made on the backgrounds, which the camera will not pick up. Often, if the figures are dancing, the same calibrations will serve for several cycles of action, but these must be arranged in exact synchronization with a prerecorded music track, which has been analyzed into beats and measured.

To offset their simplicity, cutouts have some seemingly ineradicable shortcomings. They are of little use in representing the lip movements of speech, except in profile. They can represent movement only in the plane of the screen, unless the animator resorts to a replacement technique which soon lands him in the same complications as cells. Again, since each position of the cutout is clearly registered on a frame, it is impossible to introduce the blurring which is inseparable from the recording of all actual movement with intermittent camera motion. As we saw in an earlier chapter, too narrow a camera shutter opening produces individual frames which are too sharp, and these, when the camera is panning, add together to produce an intolerable shuddering or shivering of the object as seen on the screen. This is why the movement of cutouts seems jerky and unreal, and in fact the cutout is most useful when realism is not attempted, but when a certain stylization or simplification is given to the characters. Indeed, no animation technique should be rejected merely because it fails to give a good imitation of life. Its limitations and possibilities should be carefully studied, and used as a frame within which to create the film or sequence.

A method of shooting may be noted here which is applicable to other techniques as well as to cutouts. The *light box* is a device which is placed on the animation table and consists of a panel of diffusing glass illuminated from below. If all the light comes from this source, and if the figures are black, they will appear as silhouettes. Lotte Reiniger's films, which used jointed cutouts in many sequences, were made by this method.

The jointing of solid objects makes for a similar improvement in flexibility. A three-dimensional counterpart to cells would involve so much labor that animators will go to almost any lengths to make their creations realistic by increasing the flexibility of their forms. The Czech film, *A Christmas Dream,* is an excellent example of the fluidity which can be, but seldom is, achieved with puppets.

Method 2, c. Displacement of chain and string figures.—There are many other ways of producing an illusion of life by a mere displacement of objects. For instance, if a piece of chain, thread or string is laid on a table and shaped into the form of a face, it may be pushed little by little into a change of expression, or even, by gradual metamorphosis, into the representation of a completely different object. These and like devices lend themselves to very economical methods of animation.

Method 3, a. Partial replacement: scratch-off and paint-on and corresponding three-dimensional techniques.—In real life, displacement is only one of the simplest manifestations of movement. Growth and decay are also made visible by movement, and these processes are represented by a whole series of animation techniques. These are the more important in that film has an uncanny power of telescoping time, so that the growth of years or centuries or aeons can be convincingly compressed into a few minutes on the screen.

Foremost among these techniques of growth or partial replacement is the method known as *scratch-off.* Suppose we wish to represent on a map the spreading out of America's international trade routes across the world. While this could be done with cells, it would mean drawing the routes over and over again in slightly progressed positions. Instead, it might be thought that the routes could be painted on little by little, the camera turning one frame at each step. But in practice it is very difficult to paint along a precise route, adding exactly the same small slab of paint each time. There is also a delay while waiting for the paint to dry. The routes are therefore painted first in their entirety, usually on a piece of glass placed over the map, which is in fact a cell. Then the animation camera is run *backward* while the routes are scraped off little by little in accordance with predetermined calibrations to establish the speed of the action. When the film is finally run forward in the projection room, the routes will seem to appear out of nothing and smoothly run from the United States toward the other countries of the world. An alternative to running the camera backward is to turn the map top to bottom, making north south and south north and animating in the direction opposite to normal. Occasionally, scratch-off and paint-on techniques are combined, as in the sequence from *Boundary Lines* already cited.

These techniques are invaluable when showing the growth or decay of a single element in the subject, like a route, a frontier, or a pointing arrow. Scratching off paint a frame at a time is, however, a rather tedious process, and it is sometimes possible to achieve the same result by masking or unmasking. If, for instance, a white line (e.g. a graph of sales) is to progress gradually along a black background, it is easy to mask the line with a thin sheet of matt-black card, and unmask it a frame at a time after each exposure of the film. If the edge of the mask throws back any light, or if slight imperfections are visible on its surface as it moves, the trick is revealed and the effect fails. In chapter viii it will be explained how high-contrast film emulsions, developed to a very high *gamma*, destroy practically all rendering of grey tones. Hence, if the surface of the mask is not perfectly matt, and shows greyish patches under reflected light, a high-contrast emulsion will still yield a uniform black.

A further refinement is to make use of "black light" techniques. Certain types of paint have recently been developed which fluoresce (i.e., give out visible light) under the impact of ultraviolet (UV) radiation, the direct effects of which are invisible to the eye. These paints are used on the instrument dials of certain automobiles, and also on a kind of decorative wall panel which is beginning to appear in the newer movie theaters. The illuminant is a lamp rich in radiation at the blue end of the spectrum, covered by a filter which excludes almost all visible light but passes the ultraviolet. (A great part of its total energy is wasted by the filter, so that it becomes very inefficient.)

This paint and lamp provide a selective means of shooting two separate objects in the same field, with no alteration save a change in the lighting. Let us suppose that a map is drawn with ordinary paints, and that an arrow is supposed to appear, pointing to one of the countries on the map. The arrow will be painted into the map with fluorescent paint, taking care that it precisely matches in shades the surrounding areas of ordinary paint. When the map is exposed to white light, the arrow will therefore not be seen. After the requisite footage has been shot, the film in the camera is wound back (with shutter closed) to the point where the arrow is supposed to fade in. The regular lights are switched off, and the UV lights switched on. The fluorescent arrow now shines with a visible light, and when the camera runs forward again, an additional exposure of the arrow is obtained, whereas the rest of the map remains in darkness. When the print of the map is screened, the arrow will appear to grow out of nothing into visibility.

Many extensions of this technique will occur to the reader. If, for instance, a title or arrow is painted in fluorescent paint, and a black mask is used to cover and uncover it, there will be no possibility of the mask becoming visible, even when the film which "looks" at it has a low-contrast emulsion. This enables different shades of grey to be registered on other parts of the shot under normal lighting, which would be impossible to accomplish otherwise without resorting to laborious scratch-off.

These fluorescent techniques are also useful in color shooting, but they have gained little ground as yet because of their very poor luminous efficiency.

The three-dimensional counterpart of scratch-off and paint-on is the building up and paring down of blocks or figures of malleable material like clay, plasticine, and putty. Possibly because of the difficulty of applying and removing exact amounts of material from soft substances, this technique does not seem to have been used very often. Situations which call for it may be better handled by a replacement technique.

Method 3, b. Partial replacement: chalk and blackboard techniques.—The use of chalk on a black background lends itself to very simple and often effective animation techniques. A chalk line can be removed or added to even more simply than a painted line by scratch-off or paint-on. Since it is usually white on black, the chalk line can be very easily animated by masking and unmasking. Chalk animation lends itself best to a simple caricature style resembling children's blackboard drawings. Granted a sufficiently light and skillful touch, quite long sequences will hold the audience's interest.[4]

Here it may be appropriate to describe a technique which is applicable to cells, cutouts, chalk drawings, and other kinds of animation, and which greatly reduces the labor of drawing. It is sometimes called the "Baby Weems" technique, after the sequence of that name in Walt Disney's *The Reluctant Dragon*. This was the story of the infant prodigy who put his parents right on controversial issues, confounded the scientists, and finally ran for President while still in diapers. The whole episode was told in still pictures, yet it was so dramatically conceived in terms of action caught in mid-air and cuts between successive phases of motion, that the total effect was one of violent movement and activity. Since large drawings were used instead of cells, the cost of making the sequence was much reduced.

Animators, unlike directors of live action, work in long, continuous passages of film, and therefore tend to ignore the dynamic powers of cutting which can create a sense of movement, build suspense, and bring elements of the story into a new relationship. The original "Baby Weems" sequence is a useful reminder that cutting can save the animator a lot of time.

Method 3, c. Partial replacement: pastel and putty techniques.—If a drawing in crayon (pastel) or very soft pencil is lightly smeared, its shape will be changed. What happens is that some of the opaque particles in the material are transferred by means of the fingertips to another part of the card on which the drawing is made. Thus the relative density of different parts of the drawing can be altered, and its shape changed as required. This technique does not lend itself very well to single-frame animation, because of the difficulty of controlling the changes. However, by a series of long dissolves, a gentle and

---

[4] E.g., the sequence showing the planning of the United Nations headquarters building in Manhattan in *Clearing The Way*, Burger, 1948; animation by Schwartz and Hilberman.

gradual transition from one phase of a scene to another can be effected. Examples are: *Là-Haut sur ces montagnes* and *A Little Phantasy,* both by Norman McLaren. There are sequences of add-on animation in both of these films, which show how readily it can be combined with pastel. Similar effects can also be achieved in color (e.g., *La Poulette grise,* McLaren, 1948).

This pastel technique is at its best in atmospheric changes of scene, where cloud shadows play over the landscape, night alternates with day, and the painter's moods are given rein in gradually transforming a shape of mist into an ominous bird, or the profile of a mountain range into the recumbent figure of a naked girl. Here we can sense the immediacy which some of the less orthodox systems of animation can achieve. The artist sees his work grow and take form under his eyes. If he is dissatisfied with one effect, he can immediately improvise another. He enjoys the freedom of the painter and the composer. This is a far cry from the elaborate animation factories in which cartoon films for the theaters are produced.

However, there are many studios where this animation under the camera is economically impossible. Overhead and labor costs are often so high that camera time must be reduced to a minimum, which usually necessitates shooting cells and simple scratch-off. A production unit is fortunate which combines good equipment with low costs, and can give the artist freedom to choose his own style of animation.

Translated into three dimensions, the pastel and chalk techniques would yield a method of molding putty, clay, or flexible plastic into ever-changing forms. These possibilities have been little explored.

Method 3, d. Partial replacement: moving pin shadows.—That new systems of animation may be evolved in seemingly inexhaustible variety will appear from the description of another technique, originated by the French artist, Alexander Alexeieff. Returning to his home one day with a bag of large headless nails, Alexeieff happened to notice that, as he held a bunch of the nails in his hand, they cast oblique shadows on the table. The farther out the nails projected, the longer the shadow became, so that the shadow could be made to grow or shrink by pushing the nails out or in. This gave Alexeieff, who is one of France's foremost etchers, the idea of creating a "living engraving" by means of single-frame camera exposures of a board of movable pins. He therefore set about constructing such a board in which more than a hundred thousand pins were mounted side by side in rows to form a large surface which consisted of almost nothing but pin heads. The camera and lights were set in fixed positions, and the image on the board (which was mounted vertically like a picture, but in the middle of the studio) was created by pushing pins out, using pressure on the back of the board, and pushing them in with pressure on the front. The subtlest modulations of light, shade and shape could be accomplished by delicate, localized movement of the pins. At each new setting, a single frame of film would be exposed. By this means was produced the famous *Night on Bare Mountain* (Alexeieff and Claire Parker, 1932), to a setting of Moussorgsky's music. Later, Alexeieff constructed another board containing more than a million pins, but he has so far used it to produce only a single very short film, *En Passant*. Though technically more perfect, it lacks the imaginative impulsion of the earlier film.

Method 4, a. Total replacement of cells and puppet elements.—It is only now that we arrive at a discussion of cell animation, which a great majority of actual film makers would regard as the only effective animation technique. Nor is this altogether to be wondered at. Almost all that the average film maker and filmgoer calls animation—that is, the cartoons he sees in the theaters—are made by the cell method, although it is only in the United States that this has been brought to full perfection by the mechanization of its many stages.

The great advantage of cells is that they set almost no technical limit on what can be accomplished in the way of movement. Every effect described in the preceding pages of this chapter could have been produced on cells, as can many that are impossible by any other method. However, the elaboration and cost involved in cell animation are such that there are very few places in the world where it is practiced. When costs rise, the big animation studios are the first to feel the pinch, and even the Walt Disney plant has been compelled in recent years to transfer most of its activities to live action. The niceties of style and taste proved, in so complex a medium, altogether too expensive. The field has been abandoned to the units which for the most part are content to grind out a poor, mechanical product.

This technique which is at once so fluid and flexible, and yet so mechanized and costly, is essentially very simple. The *cell* (abbreviated from "celluloid") is as a rule a transparent piece of that substance, standardized in size and so perforated that it fits over the registration pins in a platen beneath the animation camera. Since the cells are transparent, backgrounds, foregrounds, and different characters may be separated (figure 6-2). Thus all that remains stationary in a sequence may be painted on a cell or cells which stay fixed in position during the shooting of that sequence. The moving characters must of course be painted fully for each frame (in single-frame animation) on separate cells which are replaced frame by frame. That is, after each exposure they are removed, and fresh cells substituted on the pins. It is this which gives rise to the tremendous labor of cell animation. Twenty-four separate drawings are required for each screen second, and 1,440 for each minute, in addition to the background cells, even if only one cell is to be changed each frame. The labor of drawing and painting the cells may be reduced by exposing each set of cells on two frames of film, or even three, these processes being called *double-* and *triple-frame animation*. Unless the movement is sufficiently slow,

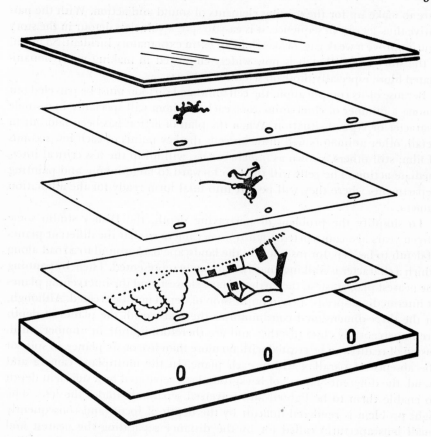

Fig. 6-2. A simple sequence of cells. Registration is insured by a system of pins and holes (the oblong holes allow for expansion of the celluloid under the heat of the lamps). The lowest cell carries the background, since this drawing will be changed least frequently. The upper two cells carry two characters, whose movements are required to vary independently.

use of these devices will give the animation that jerky quality which it is the great merit of cells to be able to eliminate.

Owing to the high cost of cell animation, it is imperative to lay out the story of the film on a *story board*. This is a large board, or series of boards, on which is pinned in sequence a set of sketches depicting the main points of the story and showing how they will ultimately appear on the screen. Usually there is a conference at which the writer and the artists appear and tell their version of the story based on the sketches, often adding a wealth of pantomime and gesture to make up for the missing elements of sound and action. With the narrative thus set out in sequence, it is easy to spot a valueless detour in the story line, improve a weak gag, or sketch in an extra explanatory incident. So useful is the story board that it is now widely employed in making many nonanimated films, especially those on scientific subjects.

Because of its complication, the cell-animated cartoon must be parceled out among a number of chief animators, each of whom will specialize in a single character or type of situation. When the plan of action has been laid out in detail, other animators will draw on cells the key points of each few seconds of film; still others, known as *in-betweeners,* will fill in the less critical intermediate action. The cells will then go forward to large inking and painting departments where they will be put into final form ready for the animation camera.

To simplify the problem of portraying depth, the Disney studio some fifteen years ago constructed a *multiplane* camera so that the different planes of depth to be seen, for instance, in the landscape background to a road along which a character is walking, may be separately represented. Then, by panning the nearest plane fastest, the farthest plane slowest, and the intervening planes at intermediate speeds, a vivid impression of depth may be created. Although, in the three-dimensional continuum of the real world, the planes of depth are imperceptibly close together and are therefore infinite in number, an illusion of reality can be created with no more than five or six planes, in spite of the absence of parallax within each plane. In the multiplane camera and stand, the different "layers" of background are separated by a sufficient depth to enable them to be lighted and traversed separately under the lens. The light problem is rendered difficult by the depth of focus (and consequently small lens aperture) called for by the distance separating the nearest and farthest planes. Much simpler multiplane devices can be built in the smaller studio; designs will no doubt occur to the ingenious reader. Multiplane effects, if well planned, will give an illusion of depth almost equal to that of a good puppet film.

Cell animation has certain great advantages in the representation of rapid movement. The continuous movements of the outside world are necessarily replaced by discrete steps in the intermittent camera, and the illusion of continuity when the film is projected results in large measure from the blurring of each exposure. This is why fast movements, which call for very short exposures in the still camera, are best represented in the movie camera by comparatively long exposures. Displacement animation by cutouts cannot reproduce this blurring, but a blurred movement can be portrayed on a cell with the utmost simplicity. Thus the character called "Thumper" in Disney's *Bambi,* a young rabbit which thumped its feet on the ground, was represented with a foot in the up position, the same foot in the down position, and one or two cells showing a very blurred foot in between. The illusion of rapid movement was perfect.

The use of cells is of course not confined to complex cartoon films. Even the smallest animation departments will often have recourse to them, when the possibilities of simpler methods fail. Lip movements in speech, for instance, are almost impossible to reproduce by other means. Cyclical movements, like the falling of rain, water flowing through a pipe, and a revolving wheel with spokes, may be repeated indefinitely with a small series of from four to twelve cells. Cell animation is thus frequently used in technical sequences, where action repeats itself; scratch-off may also be applied to the cells.

In short, cell animation is an indispensable tool of the film maker, but should never be allowed to blind him to the many other resources of the animated film.

The method of replacement is widely used in three-dimensional animation, though in a way not closely analogous to cells. Frequently, the animator needs to show a change of expression on the face of a puppet. He has therefore prepared in advance a large set of heads of the same size and appearance, save that a smile or frown or whatever it may be progresses over the series of faces little by little, as if on cells. The heads are made easily detachable, and the animator places one after another on his puppet, exposing a new frame of film each time. Thus the facial expression changes progressively. The same technique can be applied to the lip movements of speech, though these are so complex that it is difficult to represent them on puppets with any accuracy.

Puppet animation is thus basically a combination of displacement (for motion) and total replacement (for expression). Examples: The Russian feature film *The New Gulliver* (Ptushko, 1934) and George Pal's Dutch and American pictures.

Method 4, b. Total replacement by hand painting of film.—The cell and the film frame are both transparent pieces of celluloid. They have the same shape and the same appearance, and differ only in size. The animation camera is merely an elaborate means of converting one into the other. It was therefore inevitable that animators should evolve the equation, cell = frame, and thus at a stroke discover a new type of animation which abolishes the camera. This technique may be called hand-painted animation, since the animator draws directly on the film with pen or brush, frame by frame. The limitation of the method is of course the exceedingly small size of the 35 mm. frame, which is less than an inch wide and precludes very detailed drawing, or very exact registration of succeeding images.

At the same time, hand-painted animation increases creative immediacy to its very limit, enabling the artist to improvise spontaneously with the greatest speed and freedom. Norman McLaren, the originator of the pastel technique,

Fig. 6-3. The artist draws directly on film. With the film held lightly in a cutaway camera aperture, the artist draws on it in ink, a dopesheet at his side indicating the musical rhythms and the sequence of movements required. The film is advanced a frame at a time by a treadle. In a more elaborate development of this machine, an optical system images the immediately preceding frame below the frame being drawn, so that the artist knows exactly what differences of position to introduce.

alone has used this method consistently and successfully (figure 6-3). Perhaps the best example is his first hand-painted film, *Love on the Wing* (1938), but *Five for Four* (1943), and *Dollar Dance* (1943), are also brilliant examples of an infectious gaiety and witty transformation of images which must be credited to the elimination of cluttering machinery between the artist and his work.

Method 4, c. Total replacement by perforated film.—A very simple animation technique, effective within its narrow limits, consists in punching holes of different shapes, frame by frame, in a length of opaque leader. The patterns thus produced may be accurately synchronized to a prescored sound track, and the perforated leader may be used as a mask for spraying color on clear film, or as a traveling *matte* for letting colored light through a printer onto unexposed color stock. This system seems to have been first developed by Wolf Koenig in Canada; it is of outstanding simplicity, requiring no camera and little other equipment.

Method 4, d. Total replacement by frameless hand-painted film.—If, instead of drawing an image on each frame of film, the artist draws in pen or brush lengthwise down a strip of film, an altogether different effect will be obtained. This may be called frameless animation, since the normal division of film into frames is ignored. Because of the intermittent projection of film, each "frame" is imaged separately, so that the screen appearance of such a strip of film is totally different from its appearance when held in the hand (figure 6-4). This technique, the invention of Len Lye, was first used by him in the film *Colour Box* (1935). It has since been developed by Norman Mc-Laren, as in the films *Fiddle-de-Dee* (1947) and *Begone Dull Care* (1949). Though completely abstract (nonrepresentational), these frameless films have a spontaneous good humor and warmth, their complex patterns and textures of moving lines and forms dancing in intricate relationship to the music track. These are the simplest of films to produce. They of course require no camera and no processing, and are made by pegging lengths of emulsionless 35 mm. film to a long board, and painting it by means of all the ingenious devices which occur to the animator as he goes along.

It may be wondered why this type of animation falls into the class of "total replacement." It does so because the image on each frame is different in essence from the images on the preceding and succeeding frames. Nothing has been displaced or partially replaced. It is a totally new image which can, however, be most conveniently produced by a mere extension of the lines and patterns on preceding frames.

Method 4, e. Total replacement by cutouts.—We have already seen (method 2, *a*) that simple displaced cutouts are incapable of realizing motion at right angles to the plane of the screen, since the size of the cutout remains constant, instead of increasing or decreasing as it would do in real life if it advanced toward the spectator or receded from him. However, by the method of replacement, it is possible to make up a series of figures of gradually increasing or decreasing size, the substitution of one for another thus producing an appearance of fore-and-aft movement when shot by single-frame animation. This is merely an extension of the cell principle, but without the means of registration which cells afford. The method is therefore seldom used in extended sequences or films. It can be seen to great advantage in a short film based on atomic motion, *Chalk River Ballet* (McLaren, 1949), in which the dance of the spheres in interstellar space achieves an astonishing appearance of motion

Fig. 6-4. Frameless animation. Though the frame lines are ignored in this type of animation, exact and intricate correspondences
are possible between visuals and music.

in depth, though in fact the spheres were flat discs cut out in a long series of
smaller and larger sizes, and all moved on a single flat surface.

SUMMARY AND EXAMPLES

Thus in skeleton form there now emerges an outline of the animator's
methods. For simplicity, each technique has been considered separately, although in practice several may be combined in the same sequence or even in
the same image. And because this is a book on the science of film, not its style,
little has been said of the aesthetics of the animator's art.

Animation begins where reality leaves off; or, to adapt Clausewitz's phrase,
it is a continuation of reality by other means. Animation can conjure up the
fantastic, create the ridiculous and absurd, symbolize the many by the few,
telescope aeons into seconds. Whatever can be imagined in form and movement, the animator can make visible. Yet, with all these creative powers, the
animated film has all too often become a mere imitation of life. As the machinery of animation has grown, costs have risen and larger markets have had
to be found. On the principle of the lowest common denominator of taste,
cartoons have become increasingly vulgar and stupid. Demand, however, has
still failed to keep pace with costs of production, and today less cell animation is produced for the theaters than at any time since the coming of sound.

Animators are therefore thrown back on their own resources to evolve new
methods if they are to keep an old art alive. Especially in the smaller centers
of production there is a chance to break new ground and push the frontiers
further back. We will end this short account of animation by two examples of
what can be done on fairly modest budgets, given talent, imagination, and
freedom from narrow restraints.

Picture in Your Mind (Philip Stapp, 1949) is an animated film in color
which traces with a wealth of overtone and image the history of race prejudice
from its dark beginnings in the primitive mind. It opens with a series of dissolved shots in tones of grey, portraying desolate landscapes and recumbent

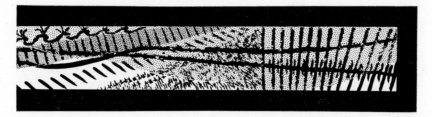

Fig. 6-4. Frameless animation. The continuity of the image drawn on the film surface produces an effect which would be almost impossible to achieve by any other means.

figures. "What hour of history is this? . . ." asks a voice. "The dawn? . . . The first faint stirring of civilization? . . . Or . . . are these the shadows of dusk before the last long night? . . . The dying embers . . . The silent end . . ."

Then occurs the following sequence, which is here analyzed in detail, so that the reader can see how some of the techniques described are blended together to carry out the dominant idea of the film.

VOICE	DESCRIPTION AND TECHNIQUE
A woman's voice sings an archaic chant: "Over the barren lands flowers will have possession . . . Deep shades of ancient days . . . Full of hate and oppression . . . In the brightness of joy fade away and are gone . . ."	LS of a plateau gashed by deep canyons. Gay yellow daisies appear here and there in the landscape. (Painted on successively in pastels, and dissolved in.) The scene dissolves into a dark nebulous shape with the rays of a white flower in the center. The flower grows through successive dissolves in richness, size, and complexity. (All this by pastel paint-on.)
Narrator: "Which future? The bright or the dark? . . . The future is up to you . . ."	The red and orange heart of the flower is transformed into an image of small white stars on a dark background, which quickly fades out. (Metamorphosis of still images.)
Voices: "Who? Me? Am I my brother's keeper?" *Narrator:* "Yes . . . You . . . And me . . . And everyone . . . everywhere . . . Because the sum of all our thoughts and actions will decide Which future, And see! Among all the people who give life and movement to our globe there are a hundred ways of life for which men have died.	Fade in panel showing a Chinese man, cut to a Mexican woman, cut to an American farmer. An open space, one man on it. Another dissolves in, then another and another. (The men were made in the form of fixed cutouts.) The camera zooms back, and the group of men (which is circular in outline) metamorphoses into the center of a many-pointed star (produced by spangled white and black dots of paint). These come and go (black dots painted to white, white to black), and almost at once transform the star into a moon and crescent, this into a pentagram and so on into an eagle and a lion

VOICE	DESCRIPTION AND TECHNIQUE
	(the whole transformation lasting only 10 seconds). Meanwhile, dark clouds pass by in the background (by superimposition of pictures on long panels traversed under the lens).
"The time is here to ask instead . . . How can we live? How can we live together on our congested earth? There is no easy answer, There is no easy way, But in our search we can look backward in time to our common origin . . . to the spark of life in the primeval waters."	The last scene dissolves to a representation of the heart within the body, which goes rhythmically in and out of focus to the sound of a heart beat. The camera zooms in through a long dissolve to a painted background of desolate marshland, and so zooms on through other scenes of desolation, finally panning down over seaweed deep into the sea.

As in all good animation films, there is here a close interweaving of sound and image. The score of *Picture in Your Mind* resulted from close collaboration between artist and composer. The music and the sketches for the visuals grew and changed together. Both the score and the narrative and other voices were recorded before the picture was shot, so that a perfect counterpoint could be established between them. In place of the hundreds of animators of different grades, inkers, painters, etc. required to make a cell-animated cartoon, the artist and a single assistant did all the art work and supervised all the shooting of this 15-minute film. The gain in creative control over the medium was incalculable, but the saving in cost was by no means so spectacular. The high cost of camera time and the slowness of making such a film made its total cost at least one-half that of a similar length of cell-animated film.

Our second example is altogether different, and shows how animation and real life shooting can be combined in a single image without recourse to difficult optical printing processes and trick effects. There are of course many such effects which cannot be carried out by any simple means. However, the producer and his associated technicians may be able to figure out all sorts of ingenious devices once they begin to explore the many resources of film.

Dependency (Anderson, 1949), is the third in a series of films on psychiatric problems in everyday life which has included *The Feeling of Rejection* and *The Feeling of Hostility* (Anderson, 1947 and 1948). The leading character of *Dependency* is a young man named Jimmy who is unable to make his own way in the world, but must hang for support and guidance on his wife, mother, and friends. At length he is persuaded to take his problems to a doctor, who asks him to recall some of the incidents of his childhood. Among these, Jimmy mentions his father's frequent refusals to take him out fishing. "No, you're too young, Jimmy," the father would always say. "I'll take you when you're older." Jimmy often dreams of this, and one day he describes the dream to the doctor.

Jimmy, about ten years of age, is standing in a rowboat. He is dressed in a magnificent outfit like his father's, complete with crimson plaid shirt, a hat bristling with fishing flies and lures, and waders reaching up to his thighs. The rod he holds is like his father's too, and with it he is reeling in what proves to be an enormous fish. Jimmy's father is sitting in the stern of the boat. He is dressed, as was Jimmy himself in the previous flash back, in an old pair of jeans and a shabby straw hat. For a rod, he uses a branch, and his line is a piece of string from which dangles a bent pin. The father looks unhappy and ridiculous, the son proud and triumphant as he lifts a great silver-spangled fish from the pool. "Don't rock the boat!" Jimmy cries severely as his father lurches out of the way of the swinging fish.

The dream ends and the scene dissolves back to the doctor's office where the adult Jimmy is sitting.

This simple dream, which needs little analysis for the audience since the context makes its meaning clear, was shot in the following way. The scene described was presented in actuality. The boat, however, was set on a shooting stage (actually the stage of a theater), and under it was draped a matt-black cloth covering the whole stage. The back of the stage was also hung with black. Lighting was at floor level to represent the rays of the setting sun. The establishing shot was made at a distance of some forty feet with a 35 mm. lens, so that the image of the boat was quite small. The lens was only just above the level of the "water." The closer shots were also imaged against the black backgrounds. Thus a print from the negative showed nothing but the boat and the action in it.

The negative was afterwards transferred to the animation camera, and projected downward on the table, following the procedure already described. On a large card on the table the artist (who had been present to advise on the shooting) made a pastel drawing showing the surface of the lake on which the boat was supposed to drift, with the boat's reflection and that of Jimmy and his father mirrored in it. He also sketched in for his own reference the part of the frame occupied by the boat and the two characters, to keep this clear of drawing. He then prepared in pastel a number of cards. On the card which already represented the lake he painted a background of vague mountains touched by the setting sun. The other cards were backgrounds for the closer shots, and portrayals of mist which was to drift across the face of the lake. This art work occupied about a day.

Shooting was then started. The first background shot was placed beneath the camera, the water surface in proper registration with the position formerly occupied by the image of the boat's side. As the film in the camera was advanced according to an accurate log sheet, the pastel surface of the drawing was smeared to alter the shape of the clouds and mountains like the images of a dream. At each change, the film in the camera was wound back and the altered scene was dissolved in. By this means, the floating shapes were made to take the form of an ominous black bird with wings outspread over little Jimmy in the boat. In a moment this image had melted away.

By planning that several layers of mist, each shot separately on the same length of film, should pass the camera at different speeds (the nearest the fastest), the artist increased the sense of depth across the lake, so that the boat, no longer anchored in a black void, would seem to be drifting along the calm surface. A further trick was used to save art work, so that only one set of mist cards was needed. These mist cards, also sketched in pastel, were first shot with the camera close to the table. The cards were gradually traversed by the handwheels, a new card being dissolved in when the length of the first one was exhausted. Then the camera was raised up higher on the zoom stand, the film was wound back again, and the same cards were shot at a lower rate of traverse. The extra height reduced the height of the floating mist shapes, and so made them appear smaller. This whole process was repeated for a third layer of mist. The shooting of this sequence occupied a full day.

Such multiple superimpositions in the camera require an accurate knowledge of exposure which is to be gained only by experience.[5] Each exposure is a fraction of the full amount, so that the total number of exposures will add up to that amount. The greater the *latitude* of the emulsion the better.

The remaining closer shots of the sequence were handled in the same way, and the negative was unloaded and processed. Finally, the original sequence and its matching animated sequence were superimposed in a device called an optical printer, to which the rest of this chapter is devoted.

SHOOTING AT SECONDHAND

The optical printer, though usually under the same supervision as the animation stand, is a completely different kind of mechanism. It produces the effects known as fades, dissolves, superimpositions, and wipes, as well as many other modifications of the straight shot which comes out of the camera. A fade is said to occur when a shot gradually disappears into blackness or appears out of blackness. Fades are used at the beginning and end of *sequences* (i.e., film chapters). Dissolves (sometimes called *lap dissolves*) consist of a superimposition of two shots, in which the second shot gradually begins to appear over the first, the first shot at the same time gradually disappearing. This effect is commonly used to indicate a lapse of time or a crossing over to another piece of action which is occurring simultaneously elsewhere. Wipes take place when a second shot appears and wipes the first off the screen along an easily visible

[5] Berthold Bartosch, creator of the almost legendary film, *L'Idée* (1930–1934), is said to have superimposed as many as thirty images on a single strip of film.

line, which may run from top to bottom or from side to side, or may spiral out from the center of the screen or burst in with the jagged edges of an explosion. Soft-edge wipes are those in which the line of demarcation between the two shots is blurred.

The optical printer (sometimes loosely called an optical camera) is a re-photographing device (figure 6-5). That is, the object in front of the camera is not a piece of real life (as in the studio or on location), nor is it a cell or title card (as in the animation department); it is simply another strip of film. This photographed film is usually a positive, so that when it is rephotographed a negative results. Though a positive, it is not an ordinary print, like a daily print, but is a special *master positive* having reduced contrast, very-fine-grain characteristics, and correspondingly reduced speed. Positives for optical print-ing (*optical positives*) are preferably made on *step printers* with pilot-pin registration (see chapter vii). The section of film to be photographed travels slowly frame by frame through a device called a *tailgate*, which is often a camera stripped of nonessential parts. Thus the light-tight magazine is usually removed and replaced by conveniently mounted spindles, since protection from light is not needed. The lens, the monitor viewfinder, the side door of the camera and the rackover mechanism (if any) are also dispensed with. The most important section of the camera left in position is the intermittent move-ment, which must be of the highest precision, employing pilot pins. The move-ment is driven by a shaft from the photographing camera, so that the two can turn together at the same speed. The frame of film in the aperture of this tailgate is backlighted from a light source of high intensity, often employing a mercury arc.

The photographing camera (also an instrument of high precision) is set up facing the tailgate on a lathe bed on which it can slide to and fro. Its lens is mounted separately on a slide, a long bellows connecting it with the camera. This separation is needed in order that the camera may film the frame in the tailgate full size ($1:1$), or even enlarge a section of it to full frame area.

In the $1:1$ position, the master positive would be reproduced as a negative without modification. If, however, the camera shutter is gradually closed, the film in the camera will receive a lesser and lesser exposure as it travels along, until finally no image will be formed on it. This is how fades are made. Now suppose that, after fading a shot out, the exposed film is wound back in the camera with shutter closed to the precise frame on which fading had been begun. The first shot is now taken out of the tailgate and a second substituted, a previously marked frame being put in the aperture. Camera and tailgate then turn slowly together again, and at the same time the shutter is gradually opened until it is fully open, at the same speed at which it was previously closed (therefore exposing the same length of film). This procedure gives rise to a dissolve, since the total exposure on the film remains constant, one tail-

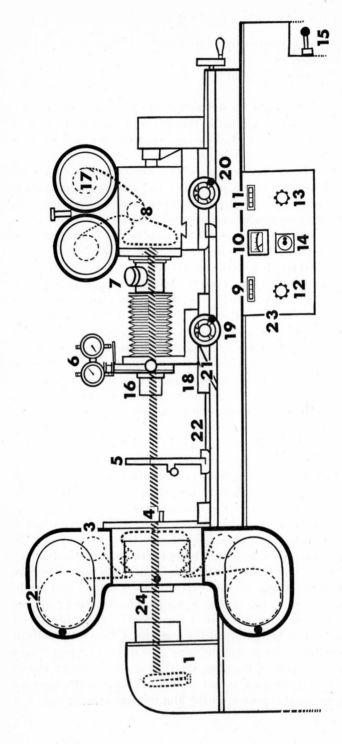

Fig. 6-5. An optical printer. An optical printer consists essentially of only two parts: a projector (2)
through which moves intermittently a length of film;
and a camera (8) which photographs the image on
this film. The projection lamp (1) focuses a beam of
light on the film in the aperture (4) of the projector
(2). The lens (16) of the camera (8) is focused on
the image in this aperture, thus rephotographing it
on the film in the magazines (17). The purpose of
all the other devices in the optical printer is to make
this rephotographing operation as flexible as possible,
so as to introduce image modifications of various
kinds, as explained in the text. In bipack contact with
the projected film in 2 it is possible to run various

[148]

kinds of mattes and masks on film, such as wipe mattes, as shown at 3. Movable masks may also be placed in the projected light beam at 5, a holder which enables these masks to be traversed or rotated in different planes with micrometer accuracy. The camera lens (16) may be moved off center vertically or horizontally by vernier screws, the exact travel of these movements being read on gauges (6). To secure different magnifications between the projected film and the camera film (as in optical zooms), the camera and lens can travel toward or away from the projector, either under hand adjustment from controls (19 and 20), or by a motor drive with different speeds, which are engaged through zoom control lever (15). Focusing of lens (16) is achieved automatically as it travels by means of an arm (21) which is held in contact with the profile of a cam (not shown) lying horizontally beside the rails (22). These rails, widely spaced and rigid as the bed of a lathe, carry the camera, the lens unit, and the mask holder (5). Precise setting-up is effected by looking through viewing aperture (7), and swinging a mirror into the light path of the optical system.

The printer's electrical controls are operated from a panel (23). The light output of the lamp (1) is read on an exposure meter unit (24) which bleeds off a small part of the total light. This light output can be set to a predetermined value by adjustment of a rheostat (13), the lamp voltage being read on the meter (10). The functions of the printer are selected by a knob (12) which enables the projector or camera film movements to be operated separately, or to be locked together in synchronous travel. The film can be moved backward or forward with equal ease with the aid of a switch. Alternatively, the knob (12) will bring into gear a skip-motion mechanical drive, which prints every second or every third frame at will, when it is desired to speed up the action in a shot. Other settings of 12 cause each frame to be photographed twice or three times, in order to slow down action. By stopping the projector alone, action can be frozen. The center control (14) enables the driving motor to be speeded up to wind the film forward or back to a predetermined frame. Projector frames are counted on a Veeder counter (9) and camera frames on another Veeder counter (11). In this way a perfect tally is kept with the operations log sheet.

(NOTE. This diagram has been simplified by the omission of many essential parts, notably in the electrical and mechanical drives to the different units of the printer.)

gate shot fading out in exact proportion as the other fades in. This gives the effect on the screen of one shot gradually disappearing, and the other gradually appearing over it and taking its place.[6]

Wipes are produced by means of traveling mattes, lengths of film containing areas of black and transparent film so arranged that in successive frames the line of demarcation gradually shifts to produce the effect needed. Wipe mattes may either travel through the tailgate in contact with the master positives; or they may be placed in a second tailgate, usually hand driven, placed closer to the camera lens and having an open back.

By setting up camera and tailgate to equal size (1:1), and photographing only alternate frames of the master positive, action is speeded up to twice its normal rate. Similarly, by photographing every frame twice, action can be slowed down to half its normal rate, while by printing every second frame twice, action shot at the old *silent speed* of 16 frames per second can be rephotographed to project at the *sound speed* of 24 frames per second.

By focusing the camera on only a part of the frame in the tailgate, magnification can be secured. This is often useful for eliminating a scratch which runs close to the edge of the frame. By extending this technique a zoom effect can be achieved, somewhat as if the camera which originally made the shot had traveled in rapidly toward its subject. This is done by zooming the optical printer camera toward the tailgate while film is running through both, the change of focus being sometimes made automatically by a cam contour. The disadvantage, of course, is that the graininess of the film is greatly increased by a large amount of zoom magnification. The optical printer can produce many other trick effects—such as *pushovers, flipovers,* and optical distortions —which cannot here be described for lack of space.

The technique just described is called *projection printing,* because an image of the frame to be reproduced is projected on the frame of unexposed film in the camera aperture. There is a considerably less flexible technique, mainly confined to the making of fades and dissolves, which is briefly described here because it calls for less elaborate equipment than projection printing.

In the *bipack method,* the tailgate is dispensed with, and two films are run through the camera aperture in contact with one another, emulsion to emulsion, using a special bipack magazine. One of these films is the negative raw stock, the other a roll of master positive (called "roll A") containing the first shot of all the dissolves to be made, or as many as can be contained in a 400-foot reel, which is the capacity of most bipack magazines. In place of the second shots, leader is inserted, cut to exactly the right length. Roll B con-

---

[6] Thus dissolves are essentially overlaps of shots, and this is why they are sometimes called lap dissolves. Often dissolves are made with the fade-out starting after the fade-in of the following shot has already begun, if this is necessary to avoid a dip in screen brightness in the middle of the dissolve, caused by the particular taper of the shutter control.

sists of the second shots making up the dissolves, with leader replacing the first shots. Roll A is placed in the camera, which is then run forward, and the fades, in and out, are made in the proper places. Next, the shutter is closed and the film wound back to the start mark. Roll B is inserted in the place of roll A, and the camera again goes forward, and its appropriate fades (which are the opposite of those in roll A) are made in the proper places. The exact frames at which all these fades are to start and finish have been laid out in a detailed log sheet, and must tally with the frames which are counted off on a Veeder counter driven from the optical camera. If these procedures have been correctly followed, and if the rate of shutter fading has been correctly timed, perfect dissolves will result. Since a fade-in or a fade-out is a simple single-shot operation, these fades are usually placed at the end of either roll A or roll B.

The effectiveness of an optical department will largely depend on the accuracy with which workprints are marked up by the editors. It is usual to indicate by a line in grease pencil the length of the effect desired; the nature of the effect is indicated by a number at the center splice which corresponds with a table of effects which the studio has standardized. The workprint is then itself used to match the optical positives in a synchronizer. Alternatively, a log may be prepared in which the starts and ends of effects are indicated in terms of negative numbers which are common both to the workprint and the optical positive (having been printed from the same negative). This method allows the cutter to keep the workprint while opticals are being made.

The beginner should heed an often repeated warning when he wishes to set up overlapping effects like wipes and dissolves. The splice between two dissolved shots indicates the center of the dissolve. But to get the overlap, an extra piece of negative, equal to half the full length of the effect, must be available on each shot. If, for instance, the cutter were to use, as the frame where he chose to splice, the first frame the camera had exposed, and then asked for a three-foot dissolve, there would be no negative on this shot to overlap, and the dissolve could not be made. Hence the cutter's first task is to make sure that he has enough unused footage on the ends of each pair of shots to allow overlapping. This task is greatly simplified if he has kept an accurate record of all shots in the picture by code number, and in addition has filed the trims systematically. Lastly, he must clearly mark the workprint according to some uniform method agreed to by the optical department.

VII

∏_∏

The Irreplaceable Negative

W̲E̲ H̲A̲V̲E̲ S̲E̲E̲N̲ how the workprint of a film contains material from three different sources. Cameras shoot part of the footage in the studio and on location; the library supplies some from its files; and some comes from the filming of inanimate objects like maps and title cards or the rephotographing of other shots with special modifications such as fades and dissolves.

The workprint is a positive.[1] It is like the succession of snapshots in a photograph album—pleasant to look at, but valueless if a great many copies have to be made. The whole essence of film lies in its power of being multiplied almost indefinitely. Until a feature picture has been reduplicated hundreds of times for running in thousands of theaters before millions of people, it has little chance of returning its original cost, which may amount to two or more million dollars. Hence, like the amateur who puts his negatives away in an envelope ready for reprinting, the professional must have his own negative,[2] amounting to many hundreds of thousands of feet, accurately and safely filed away in the film library.

When the workprint has been finally approved by the editor and producer of the film, it goes to the *negative cutters,* whose duty it is to pick out the negatives (or reversal originals) for every shot in the film, and cut them to match exactly with the shots in the workprint.

Before investigating how this is done, it will be well to return for a moment to the cutting room and find out how the workprint is marked up by the editor or his assistant. The workprint is like a map of the finished film. Optical

[1] For discussion of the accompanying sound track, see chapter xi under the heading, "Mechanics of Sound Cutting," p. 329.

[2] The term "negative" is often used loosely to mean all original camera footage, even though with reversal color processes such as Kodachrome and Ansco Color, the original is a positive. The reason is, of course, that professional film making had been established on a negative-positive basis for forty years before reversal processes became widespread. Because of the confusion which often arises from describing two opposite things by one term, we shall use here the more cumbersome but exact phrase "negative (or reversal original)."

effects, for instance, must pass once through the negative department for making master positives, and once for final cutting into the negative. Many damaged shots will have been replaced, especially in the smaller unit, by leader rather than reprints. The negative cutter must be instructed, by marks, what to do with these and other alterations in the workprint. Though there is no accepted marking for workprints, the following system is clear, simple and reliable.

A piece of leader, or *slug*, which represents a missing part of a shot, should be marked thus if the shot is to continue through it:

and thus if the shot terminates with the leader:

and thus if the cut is to occur in the stretch of film indicated by the leader:

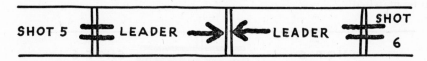

A fade-out followed by a fade-in is marked thus:

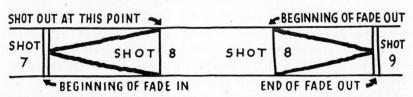

These and all other optical effects must be measured out on the workprint and marked to their exact length.

A dissolve is marked thus:

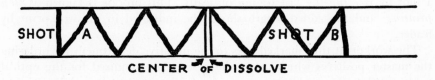

A wipe is marked thus:

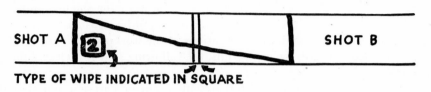

TYPE OF WIPE INDICATED IN SQUARE

The number in the small box corresponds to some standard designation used by the firm or department which will make the effects.

If some frames have been cut out of the middle of a shot, a *jump cut* will result. Occasionally, when there is no movement in the shot at this point, the jump cut is used to bring together more closely the action at the start of the shot and at the end. This kind of jump cut is marked thus:

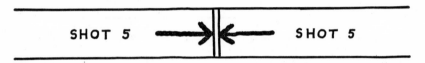

When, however, the jump cut results from the editor's carelessness in replacing lost frames, it should be marked thus when the workprint is sent in to be matched:

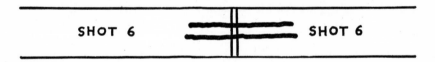

The negative cutter, working from the beginning of the shot, will then continue the shot in the negative (or reversal original) uncut past this point, where it will of course become out of sync by the length of film which has disappeared in the jump cut. It will then be cut at the splice to the next shot.

When a shot is to be reversed, that is, turned over so that the top side is on the bottom, in order to reverse the direction of action, this must be written on the workprint. Such a shot has to be passed through the optical printer to bring the emulsion back to the proper side, and also to change the position of the Academy sound track mask. Occasionally it will be necessary to lengthen a shot by *freezing* the last frames optically. This process is known as *step printing,* and the added length should be indicated in the workprint by leader.

The workprint thus marked goes to the negative department for ordering the master positives which, as we have seen, are required for the optical printer. When the workprint returns for final negative cutting, the print of the optical effects may not have been cut into it, because of lack of time. The negative cutter must then once again make use of the markings to cut the optical negative (or dupe).

Before negative cutting, the cutter usually makes a shot list which numbers the shots in the film from beginning to end, and lists the edge numbers, a description of the shots, the source, and the footage. The purpose of the shot list is to enable all material from the same source to be grouped together, and to make sure that nothing has been forgotten.

Armed with the shot list, and with the negative (or reversal original) of the film gathered together and broken down into numbered rolls of convenient size, the negative cutter is able to start work. The clue to cutting is the existence of an *edge number* (also called a *footage number* or *key number*) which is printed on one side of every foot of most 35 mm. film stocks, as shown in figure 7-1. The only commonly used types of film which are not numbered are those upon which release prints are made, since these films are never used for further printing stages and consequently do not need identification marks of their own. As a relic of their amateur origin, 16 mm. original materials are normally not supplied with footage numbers; but these can—and should— be obtained by special order.

The edge number is printed through a small slit in the printer alongside the picture aperture, through which the printing and printed films pass, emulsion facing emulsion, as we shall see in more detail in the next chapter. If, therefore, the printing roll is printed from the wrong end, the numbers on it will be on the side of the film opposite to the edge number aperture, and the edge numbers will not print through. This will give the negative cutter a great deal of trouble later on, for each unnumbered shot will have to be painfully matched by eye—that is, by looking at the action.[3] A simple rule determines whether the roll to be printed should be sent in head up or tails up:

NEGATIVE
If the numbers are on the sound or masked side, print head up.
If the numbers are on the non-sound-track side, print tails up.
POSITIVE
If the numbers are on the sound or masked side, print tails up.
If the numbers are on the non-sound-track side, print head up.

If there is no track or masking, the position which the sound track would occupy if it were there is on the left on positive film when the film is held with the image right way up and the emulsion facing the observer, and on the right on negative film.

With a properly prepared workprint, edge-numbered negative which is broken down, labeled, and arranged in order, and a good shot list, the nega-

---

[3] Uncountable man- (and woman-) years are wasted annually because of the inexplicable failure of the film manufacturers to edge number all 16 mm. original materials in the same way that 35 mm. materials have now been numbered for close on thirty years.

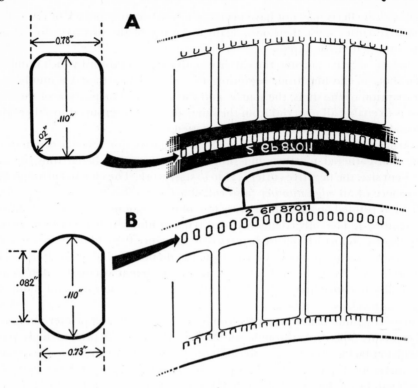

Fig. 7-1. Matching negative and positive 35 mm. film on a synchronizer. At A is seen the positive film with the standard dimensions of the positive perforation and at B the matching negative film with the dimensions of the negative perforation.

tive cutter should be able to cut and splice a reel of negative (or reversal original) in from three to five hours, depending on the number of shots. The tools required are the same as for positive sound cutting—a synchronizer, a pair of double rewinds, scissors, and cardboard or celluloid patches. If the negative is spliced as it is cut, the patches will not be needed.

What has been said so far about the mechanics of negative cutting gives little feeling of its peculiar flavor, which results from the irreplaceability of all original material. This original film is the film maker's most valuable possession. Indeed in a very real sense it is his only possession. For as, in the first place, the ribbon of exposed film winds up inside the camera, it holds in invisible storage all that the cameraman, the director, and the producer have so painstakingly painted on it in tones of light and shade or color. The set has been built, the lights arranged with infinite care, the characters rehearsed in their parts, the sound engineer satisfied. At last the camera turns, and the film, to any outward eye unchanged, passes into the take-up magazine. The work of hours and perhaps days of planning and design, or the good fortune of a few moments of actuality which can never be repeated, has now been crowded beyond recall onto a fragile strip of celluloid. And when the picture is at last edited, recorded, and ready for the first print to be made, the producer has nothing to show for the thousands or millions of dollars he has invested, except a picture negative or other original stored in from one to twelve cans, together with the same number of cans of sound track. A small suitcase will easily carry a picture that may have cost as much as the latest jet bomber, and a match could destroy it in a few moments.

There are many less drastic ways by which this destruction can be effected —or at least by which the original film can, little by little, be spoiled during the many handlings which it must receive during production. The image on a frame of 35 mm. film is only one-half a square inch in size, the 16 mm. image less than a quarter as big, and formed in metallic silver. Yet it is not the sort of silver image which on an Italian mirror or Spanish sword hilt has withstood centuries of handling. It is an image formed of millions of separate particles of silver suspended in a soft gelatin layer half a thousandth of an inch thick. A mark or scratch of no greater depth than this will damage or completely destroy the emulsion and with it the irreplaceable image.

It is the delicacy of the negative-cutting process that gives it the peculiar flavor we have spoken of. A kind of ritual surrounds it. There must be no haste, no short cuts. Everything in its proper order and at its proper speed. A few examples of the effects of seemingly trivial carelessness must suffice.

A careless winding up of a roll of negative, followed by pressure on the edges to make it lie flat, will produce cross scratches or *cinch marks* which cannot be removed. The same goes for an accidental thumb mark on the emulsion surface, or the scratching of a fingernail. The application of too much heat will make the negative soften and run. The mere rubbing of one piece of film across another, however lightly, may cause abrasions to the emulsion surface. A particle of dust allowed to rest on this surface, and then pressed in by an adjacent turn of film, will leave a permanent hole in the emulsion. All these blemishes are very small, but when magnified in area some 300,000 times, to the size of the largest theater screen, they become very large indeed.

The preservation of the negative (and reversal original) requires thoughtful planning and scrupulous care. Among the many important points to be observed, the following are outstanding.

1. Originals should be confined to two places only: the library and the negative-cutting department (as a section of the laboratory). In the library the originals should always be kept in cans, and stored if possible at a constant medium temperature and humidity.

2. Handling of the originals should be confined to the negative-cutting rooms (and the associated laboratory), which must be designed for a minimum ingress of dust. Air conditioning is almost essential; but if unprocurable, the windows should be covered with extremely fine (100 gauge) metal screens. Members of other production and laboratory departments should be excluded as far as is practicable, to avoid the continual coming and going which brings in dust on the soles of the feet and disturbs concentrated work.

The negative-cutting rooms should be painted white with washable paint, the ceilings should be low enough to be easily cleaned, and inaccessible dust-collecting corners and crevices should be avoided. Unless cutting is to be confined to 16 mm., cutting tables and cabinets must be of metal, and should be paneled to make dusting easier. Each room, in short, should look like a hospital ward. To remove the last traces of dust from the air, a Precipitron or other similar electronic dust precipitator may be installed, though the price is at present rather high.

3. The surface of each cutting table should be frequently dusted and kept absolutely spotless. The inside of bins, and other areas difficult to dust carefully, should be lined with detachable covers or spread with soft tissue paper.

4. The negative cutters should wear white uniforms and white gloves when they are working, and these should be washed at frequent and regular intervals.

5. Original films should always be handled by the edges. When they are fitted on synchronizers and taken off again, rough contact between film and metal must be carefully avoided.

6. Original film should never be assembled with metal clips, unless paper is inserted both over and under the clips so that they are completely covered.

7. The viewing of original films on projectors and moviolas should be strictly forbidden, as the most precise adjustment and expert maintenance cannot guarantee that they will not abrade the film. Thirty-five mm. negatives are in fact never projected, except in newsreel plants where quality must be sacrificed to speed. However, this ban on projecting negatives has always been reinforced by the practical difficulty of judging the appearance of a reversed image. With reversal materials, where the original is a positive, it is quite otherwise. A director, or even a cameraman, will screen his Kodachrome or Ansco Color original without a tremor, excusing his action if he has to by saying that he will only do it once. One projection may be enough to put fine but irreparable marks on the film, which will be visible throughout the life of the finished picture. This practice of projection is thoroughly bad, and should not be tolerated.

The continuous-motion film viewer is not to be classed with the projector as a potential damager of film. It has fewer revolving parts, no intermittent motion, and, being operated by hand, it can be stopped instantly at the least sign of trouble. Therefore, while use of a viewer with originals is strongly deprecated, it can be excused in an emergency.

The foregoing seven basic rules for the handling of original films apply also to duplicating materials, such as library footage and optical effects, since other negatives or positives will be printed from them to be intercut with the original film, from which they should ideally appear indistinguishable. Indeed, since they go through one or two additional processes, these secondary materials require even greater care than the originals if they are to show no visible deterioration.

Thus, in short, while most other production departments modify or add to the film in some vital way, the negative department's chief care is to add nothing and to take away nothing from it, but to preserve untouched the irreplaceable image and its scarcely less delicate support.[4]

---

[4] Differences in practice between the handling of 16 mm. (reversal) and 35 mm. (negative) materials are discussed in chapter ix under the heading "Matching Originals," p. 242.

VIII

⎍⎍⎍⎍⎍⎍⎍⎍⎍⎍⎍⎍⎍⎍⎍⎍⎍⎍⎍⎍⎍⎍⎍⎍⎍⎍⎍⎍⎍⎍

The Laboratory:
Studio Grand Central

IN ALL THE production processes thus far described, and the many others required before the picture is complete, film passes and repasses through the laboratory—or the lab, as it is colloquially but universally called in the industry. The newcomer will tend to think of the lab in the terms most familiar to him from amateur photography, that is, the development and printing of film. These, it is true, are at the bottom of most of the lab's activity, but it is the essential extra functions and services which give it the quality of a studio Grand Central.

Figure 8-1 shows in summary form how these functions are organized. The Lab Superintendent has charge of a number of semi-independent departments. The Office routes and reroutes the many orders that come in, and works closely with the Accounting Department. A Cleaning Department prepares the negatives and other materials for further processing—a generic term which covers all lab operations. A Control Department supervises the many chemical and physical processes within the lab, and tests the variable characteristics of the processed film. A Timing Department is required to even up the variations in the cameraman's exposure to produce a smooth and well-balanced print. Printing concerns itself with the high-speed transference of an image from one piece of film to another, which next requires Development. Chemical Mixing looks after the supply of the solutions which are pumped to and from the developing machines. These are grouped together into two further departments, one concerned with 35 mm. film, the other with 16 mm. When the film comes off the developing machines, it must be inspected to see that no mistakes have been made, no unsuspected damage caused.

Not only must the superintendent dovetail the daily working of all these departments; he must be ready to answer the complaints and demands for

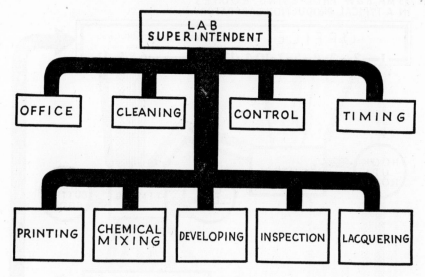

Fig. 8-1. Organization plan of a typical laboratory.

extra speed which reach him all the time from production departments. These result from the many times that film must be immobilized in the lab during production, which makes it appear as the chief cause of all delays. That there are good reasons for the film being held up in the lab may be seen from figure 8-2, which shows the processing routes in a typical 35 mm. production laboratory. Unless the reader is already familiar with lab practice, he may conveniently concentrate on the broad outlines of film flow, leaving the details of the diagram for further study when he has finished this chapter.

Development, it will be noticed, is at the center of the process, flanked on both sides by control. Positive (print) development is preceded by timing and printing. All finished material is inspected. Everything that requires a second lab process must return to the office and be fed once again through the whole system. If the lab can switch the many different kinds of film onto the right track, shunt them to and fro without confusion, and finally bring the proper coaches to the platform alongside the producer, all within the space of a few hours, it will indeed have deserved the name of studio Grand Central.

The technical functions carried on in a laboratory are fairly complex, and to the beginner difficult to grasp. Dealing as they do with the chemistry and physics of film, they have much less contact with the world of ordinary experience than direction or camera work or even cutting. Unless the underlying principles of processing are well understood, a visit to a laboratory will seem rather like a visit to the catacombs—a strange world of darkness and mysterious happenings.

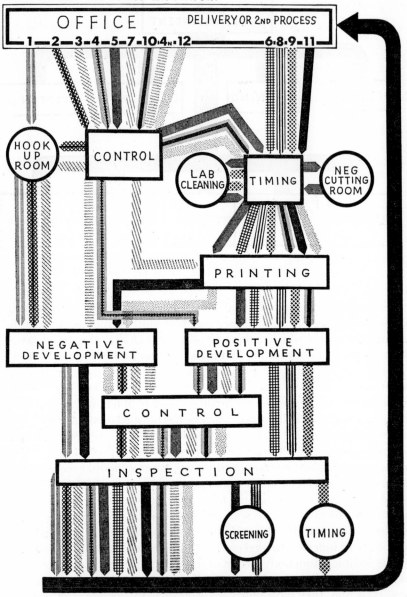

Fig. 8-2. For detailed explanation see foot of facing page.

THE IMAGE APPEARS

All lab processes stem from the very simple operations carried out by any amateur who develops and prints his own film. The simplest kind of apparatus, which the amateur uses, is a series of shallow trays in which the solutions are placed. The first tray contains the developing solution. The strip of exposed film is drawn backward and forward through the tray, while the solution is agitated as much as possible so that fresh developer is constantly brought into contact with the surface of the film. This must be done in total darkness or in a faint light of a color to which the negative is comparatively insensitive—usually red or green. The next step is to rinse the negative in water in order to remove all trace of developer and so stop the development process.

At this stage the latent image on the film produced by the original exposure in the camera has been made visible by development. But if it were to be exposed to light it would rapidly vanish. What is the reason for this? Light-sensitive emulsions consist basically of a *silver halide* suspended in gelatin. Silver halides are compounds containing metallic silver combined with one of the halogens—bromine, iodine, chlorine, fluorine—and have a peculiar characteristic which is the basis of photographic chemistry. When light strikes them, it produces a change which is visually quite undetectable. But there are certain chemicals called *developing agents,* which have no effect on the silver-halide emulsion if it has not been exposed to light, but which, if the emulsion has been exposed, reduce it to pure metallic silver. If, therefore, a surface coated with light-sensitive emulsion is exposed to a scene containing varying highlights and shadows, an invisible image of it (called the latent image) will be formed on the emulsion. When developing agents are allowed to flow over the emulsion they will discriminate between the exposed and unexposed parts, attacking the former and reducing them to silver, but leav-

Fig. 8-2. 1. Original picture negative for development. 2. Single-system sound negative for development. 3. Double-system sound negative for development. 4. Animation high-contrast positive (negative image) for positive development. 4n. Negative opticals for negative development. 5. Picture and sound release negatives for composite printing. 6. Negative opticals for print. 7. Negative sound track for print. 8. Negative picture for print. 9. Picture negative for master positive. 10. Composite negative for master positive. 11. Master positive for dupe negative. 12. Composite master positive for dupe negative.

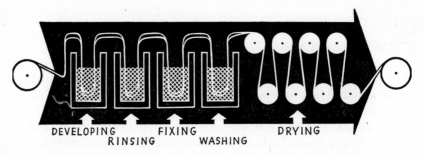

DEVELOPING   FIXING   DRYING
RINSING   WASHING

Fig. 8-3. Processing sequence in a continuous developing machine.

ing the latter untouched. If we now look at the film under a faint light, we shall see an image on it, formed in silver. But if a bright light were turned on, it would immediately expose the hitherto unexposed areas of silver halide, enabling the developer to attack them and reduce them to silver. This is equivalent to making the image disappear, for it now consists of undifferentiated silver all over. An over-all exposure of this kind is called *fogging*.

In order that the image may be exposed to a bright light without danger of its suddenly vanishing away, it is necessary to *fix* it. In the developing agent we found a chemical which would single out the *exposed* silver halide and attack it, reducing it to silver. Now we want a chemical which will attack only the *unexposed* silver halide and wash it away. This chemical is called *sodium thiosulphate,* commonly known as *hypo.* By immersing the developed film in a solution of hypo, we clear away all the unexposed silver halide, leaving an image consisting of nothing but silver suspended in gelatin.

The hypo now contains a quantity of silver. If in a large scale laboratory the used hypo is thrown away, much money is lost. Hence a process called *silver recovery,* which electrolytically plates or chemically precipitates the silver in the hypo, is often applied to the circulating system. The pure silver thus recovered is sold, and at the current price the proceeds will usually pay for all the chemicals used in the laboratory.

If hypo were to be left in the emulsion, it would gradually bleach out the image. Consequently, the film must next be thoroughly washed in running water, and then must be dried, either by hanging in a room at ordinary temperature or preferably by passing a current of warm, dry air across it. The negative is now ready for printing. Thus, in brief, the exposed film has to be developed, rinsed, fixed, washed, and dried (figure 8-3).

Basically the development process is quite simple, involving only the reduction of silver bromide or iodide to metallic silver to form the opaque image; the bromine and iodine which are released immediately combine with other elements present to form soluble salts which wash away. The developing agent is a reducing agent, and a reducing agent is simply a substance which is able to convert a metallic salt such as silver bromide to the free metal, which is itself oxidized to form another compound.

WHAT GOES INTO A DEVELOPER AND WHY

The developing agent is by far the most important element in a developing solution. But to provide the conditions necessary to make it work properly, other substances are needed, and the complete developer will contain (1) one or more developing agents, (2) a preservative, (3) an alkali, (4) a buffering agent, (5) a restrainer.

To these may be added auxiliary constituents such as antifogging agents, wetting agents, and foam repressers. The statement which lays down the relative volume of these chemicals, and usually advises on the order in which they are to be mixed, is called a *formula,* in this case a *developing formula.* The different components which go to make up such a formula act separately and so can be considered one by one. But this is only a first stage of approximation, for complex cross-reactions also take place. Even today, in spite of lengthy and brilliant researches in photographic chemistry, there are still gaps in our knowledge.

1. Developing agents.—These are the most important materials to be found in any developer. While certain inorganic chemicals possess the property of reducing silver halide, they are not used in film processing because of their slow speed and staining properties. Instead, a long search through the vast field of organic chemicals has revealed a number of organic developing agents which have been successfully used in different branches of photography. But only two of them are today widely used in film processing. One of these, *monomethylparaminophenol* (usually known by the trade names of *elon, metol, photol,* or *rhodol*) is a very rapid and energetic developer which brings out fine detail in the image but is somewhat lacking in contrast. The other, *parahydroxybenzene (hydroquinone,* sometimes abbreviated to HQ), acts more slowly to give images of great contrast and density but somewhat lacking in detail. By blending these two agents it becomes possible to combine the advantages of both, and to provide within certain limits images of high or low contrast and density. In a developing formula for high-contrast positive prints the ratio of hydroquinone to elon will be much higher than in a formula for low-contrast negative development.

Developers containing metol and hydroquinone are generally known as *MQ developers.* Two points regarding their use must be borne in mind. First, the effect of hydroquinone falls off very rapidly as the temperature of the developing solution is reduced below the normal 65° F, until at about 50° F it becomes practically inoperative. Since metol is much less sensitive to changes of temperature, the effect of reducing the temperature of the developing solution is not merely quantitative but qualitative, i.e. the predominance of metol at the low temperatures will tend to give an image lacking in contrast.

Second, hydroquinone will act only in a solution of relatively high alkalinity. Consequently, its effect is very slight in solutions of low alkalinity, such as those frequently used to develop variable-density sound track.

2. *Preservatives.*—Since developing agents, being reducing agents, must have a strong affinity for oxygen, they must be protected from aerial oxidation in the processing tanks. For this purpose *sodium sulfite* is usually added. It combines with the developing agents to form complex sulfonates, which maintain their reducing properties but resist oxidation. The quantity of sulfite added is limited by two factors: (*a*) it slows the developing action, and (*b*) it has a strong solvent action on the gelatin emulsion and would tend to dissolve away both exposed and unexposed silver halide before development had properly started.

3. *Alkali.*—The developing agents reach their maximum practical effectiveness within certain narrow ranges of acidity or alkalinity. As a general rule it may be said that acid baths are slow, and that solutions develop to a given density and gamma faster as they become more alkaline. To achieve the desired activity, alkaline substances such as *sodium tetraborate (borax)* and *sodium carbonate* are added. The effect of these activating agents must be carefully controlled to avoid sudden and unexpected accelerations of developing speed, tending to cause grainy and overdeveloped negatives.

4. *Buffering agents.*—During the life of a developing solution, changes in chemical activity take place because of, among other things, dissolved silver-halide content and aerial oxidation of hydroquinone. These changes tend to unbalance the activity of the developer, making it necessary to add a *buffering agent*—a compound which dissociates slowly to counteract changes in acidity or alkalinity. Borax (an alkali) is often used to counteract acidity and therefore increase the activity of the developer. Contrarily, boric acid is used to counteract alkalinity and so decrease the activity of the developer. Buffering is also used to adjust the activity of a developer to suit the speed range of a particular developing machine. For example, if a negative stock is found to develop to the required gamma in seven minutes, and if the equivalent of eight and a half minutes developing time is needed in this machine to give adequate fixing when the film reaches the hypo tanks—then careful buffering with boric acid will reduce the speed of development by the required amount.

5. *Restrainer.*—Freshly mixed developing solutions will cause a slight chemical fogging (i.e. produce a density not caused by light exposure). To combat this, *potassium bromide* is usually added to the new bath. After processing has started, sufficient potassium bromide is formed in the bath as a reaction

by-product from the bromide contained in the emulsion to render further addition unnecessary. Indeed, it would be unwise to go on adding potassium bromide, since it tends to depress the image density, and thus causes a falling off in contrast and a general appearance of underexposure on the negative. In some formulae, *citric acid* and *potassium metabisulfite* are added as restrainers.

These, then, are the basic ingredients which will be used to mix the developer. While, in theory, large variations can be introduced into the quantities of the ingredients used, and a satisfactory image still be obtained, in practice the choice is much more limited. This is because with machine development, unlike hand development, only a certain range of developing times is available and this range will vary widely according to the design of the machine. Not only will the variable-ratio drive set an upper and lower speed limit, but the difference in number of racks available for fixing and for developing, the amount of turbulation in the developing tanks, the degree of aeration of the developer—these and many other factors will result in different performances from the same formula in different machines. For this reason, the formulae recommended by the film manufacturer are only intended as a guide, and must be modified to suit the equipment in any particular laboratory.

WHAT GOES ON IN A DEVELOPING MACHINE AND WHY

The processes of development are the same whether film has been exposed in the simplest Kodak or the most complicated movie camera. But the developing machinery designed around each of these processes is altogether different, for it is suited to physical convenience and to the accuracy of control desired. Plate- or cut-film cameras expose each picture separately; roll-film cameras usually take eight to sixteen pictures on a roll; Leica-type cameras take about thirty-six pictures. But in a thousand feet of 35 mm. movie film there are sixteen thousand pictures, and this presents complicated new mechanical problems to the designer of *processing equipment,* as developing machinery is usually called. Tray development is quite out of the question. Tanks in which the film is wound statically on large racks or spools become very cumbersome if long lengths have to be developed. They were used in the early days, under the title of *rack-and-tank* development, but are now obsolete.

The answer to the problem is the *continuous developing machine,* which today is universal except in the smallest laboratories (figure 8-4). This type of machine can take many forms, but in all of them the film is driven continuously through the different solutions.

In some designs the film runs up and down vertically between pairs of

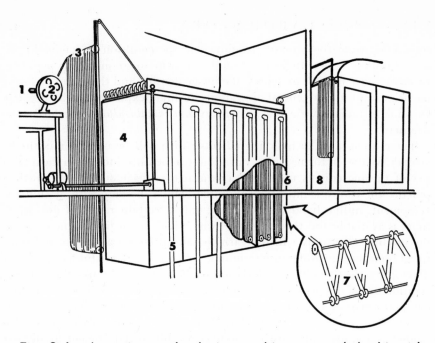

Fig. 8-4a. A continuous developing machine: wet end. At this end of the machine the film is developed, either in darkness or very subdued light. A table (1) holds the exposed but undeveloped reels of film which the operator receives through a light-trap from the room where they are unloaded from magazines. The reel is then mounted as shown at (2) and passes onto an elevator (3), the lower spindle of which is able to ride upward freely, so that film can continue to feed into the tanks (4), even when (2) remains stationary for a minute or so, as it must do when a new reel is being spliced on. The processing tanks are fed with fresh solution from pipes at the bottom on the far side (not shown), and the overflow is returned through the circulating system by other pipes (5). At 6 is shown a cutaway section of the tanks, wherein the film racks are threaded as shown at 7, where the individual spools are shown with exaggerated separation for clearness. After washing, excess moisture is removed from the film by a squeegee, and it then passes through a light trap into the dry end of the machine. At 8 is seen an additional elevator which comes into play if there is a break in the drying cabinet, thus preventing loss of film through total stoppage and overdevelopment.

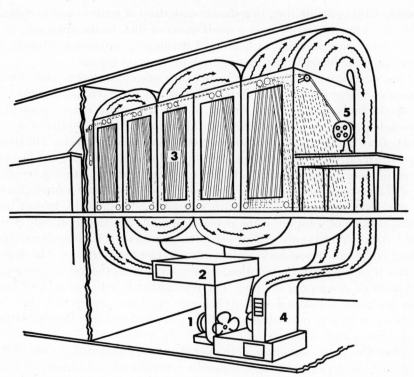

Fig. 8-4b. A continuous developing machine: dry end. The dry end of the machine serves no other purpose than to dry the film under precisely controlled conditions of temperature and humidity. A blower (1) forces air into a chamber (2) where banks of heating elements raise it to the correct temperature for the drying cabinets or dryboxes (3). Note that the air first enters the cabinet where it will pick up the most moisture. After passing through the last cabinet, the moist air returns for recirculation through a dehumidifier (4) where it is deprived of its excess moisture. The dried film winds up on a reel (5). (The mechanism shown in these figures is greatly simplified.)

horizontal spindles, and each strand of film is surrounded by a narrow tube through which the solution is passed. This insures constant movement of the solution past the film. Carrying this a step further, machines have been designed in which the film does not pass through tanks or tubes, but is sprayed with solution from a series of fine jets. The difference, in fact, is very like the difference between a bath and a shower. In a bath by far the greater part of the water never touches the body at all, while the water close to it may actually become saturated with dirt. In a shower each drop of water comes in contact with the skin and carries away a small quota of dirt. In the same way, in a spray developing machine each drop of developer contributes its quota to developing the image before passing back to the main supply.

Most developing machines are not of such advanced design, and merely consist of a large number of strands of film passing up and down in tanks full of developing solution. These strands of film are wound round spools and sprockets (or rollers in *sprocketless* machines) on horizontal spindles at top and bottom of the tanks, something like strands of wool in a skein. The structure which carries each pair of spindles is called a *rack,* and there may be two, three, or more racks in each tank. In order to increase the agitation or *turbulation* of developing solutions near the film, a submerged spray is often placed in the developer tanks and fed with solution under pressure. In fact, the whole volume of solution in the developing tanks is being constantly circulated. At a rate of twenty gallons per minute or more, it is pumped to circulating tanks and thence back again to the developing machines. The object of this is to *replenish* the solution, thus making good the loss of developer sustained in developing the film. The replenisher is fed from a *bleed tank* into the main circulating tank. When new solutions are needed, they are made up in *mixing tanks,* from which they are pumped into the circulating tanks to start their travel round the circulating system.

When film passes out of the developer into the rinsing tank, or out of the wash into the drying cabinets, it is usually sprayed with compressed air from very fine nozzles to remove droplets of liquid and prevent them from being carried over into the next section of the machine. To keep the film from fogging, the tanks so far mentioned must either be self-enclosed or contained in a dark or dimly lighted room which is therefore called the *dark end* or *wet end* of the machine. The film image having by now been fixed, the film can pass into the *drying cabinets* or *dryboxes* which are known as the *dry end* of the machine. As this section of the machine can be brightly lighted, it is sometimes called the *light end.* In the drying cabinets the film continues to pass up and down in long skeins, but it is now subjected to a current of warm dry air. The air must not, however, be too hot (lest it cause *reticulation,* or breaking up of the emulsion) or too dry (or the base will curl unduly and become brittle). Finally, the film is wound up on a reel and is ready for use.

Thus, in an over-all view, exposed film comes off a spool or reel at the dark end of the machine, is driven continuously through a series of tanks and cabinets, and finally is wound up on a spool at the far end.

Developing machines vary greatly in capacity. Small negative machines may develop 20 feet per minute, or 1,200 feet in an hour—large positive machines 200 feet per minute or 12,000 feet in an hour. This is more than twice as fast as film runs in a projector.[1] The speed can be adjusted within wide limits, as a rule, to develop different kinds of stock to different degrees of contrast. This is because the faster the film is run, the shorter the length of time it stays in the developer; the slower it is run, the longer it stays in the developer. The relation between developing time and contrast is one of the basics of lab control.

CONTROLLING THE IMAGE

Film emulsions, as we shall see in a later section, have many different characteristics, such as speed and resolving power, color sensitivity, and inherent graininess. These are "built-in" and the laboratory has very little control over them.[2] There is only one characteristic of film stocks which can be very much altered in development. This is contrast, or the degree to which variations in the brightness of the original subject are reproduced as variations in the tone of the photographic image, a point which the mere snapshotter seldom considers at all. If asked about it, he would probably reply that correct reproduction was in some way automatically assured. Yet it is everyone's experience that scenes taken in brilliant sunlight often show a dullness which does not correspond at all to the actual range of highlights and shadows. And on the other hand snapshots taken on dull days may reveal an equally unexpected snap and clarity which seem to render the scene more clearly and sharply than it appeared to the photographer's eye.

This may be imagined more clearly by taking a simple example (figure 8-5). Suppose a card is set up with a grey scale painted on it. Suppose this scale, while showing a gradation of tones of grey, does not go so far as black in one direction nor so far as white in the other. Suppose this card is photographed

---

[1] Compact developing machines of radical design with capacities of 25,000 feet per hour are now in active construction, and will find wide use in newsreel printing and intermediate-film television. High-temperature developers of greatly increased activity fully develop the image in five seconds, or about one-fortieth of the normal time. So short a stay in the developer greatly reduces the moisture absorbed by the film, which may in consequence be dried by a multiplicity of hot-air jets or infrared lamps at greatly accelerated speed. The abrupt changes of temperature to which film is subjected when entering and emerging from such a machine would cause orthodox emulsions to reticulate and part company from the base. New film stocks, now in the final stages of development, incorporate base and emulsion materials of much better physical characteristics than any obtainable before. See Clifton M. Tuttle and Fordyce M. Brown, "High Speed Processing of 35 mm. Pictures," *JSMPTE*, Feb., 1950, pp. 149–160; and J. S. Hall, A. Mayer, and G. Maslach, "A 16 mm. Rapid Film Processor," *JSMPTE*, July, 1950, pp. 27–36. The new conception of film processing suggested by these methods is ably discussed in C. E. Ives and C. J. Kunz, "Simplification of Motion Picture Processing Methods," *JSMPTE*, July, 1950, pp. 3–26.

[2] This is further discussed later in the chapter.

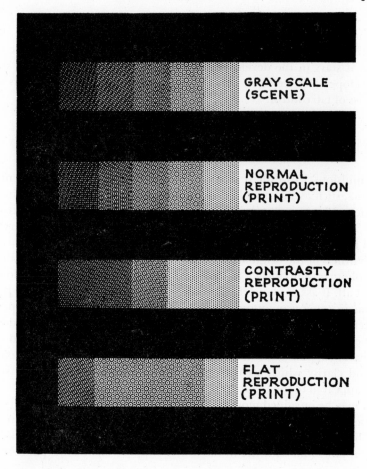

Fig. 8-5. Reproduction of a grey scale in black and white.

in the ordinary way with a normal camera exposure, and the negative is developed and printed. We would probably expect that the result would show a scale of greys exactly like the one on the card; that, in general, the scale of tones in the print would be exactly the same as the scale of brilliance in the original scene. This is called *normal reproduction* and is the usual goal of the photographic process. But if this happened, it would only be by most unlikely coincidence; there would be nothing automatic or inevitable in it. It might well happen, for instance, that the darker half of the scale had become quite black, losing all its internal gradations; while the light end was an undifferentiated white. On the other hand it might be found that the plainly visible steps in the original scale had been transformed into one practically indistinguishable tone of grey. These are of course extremes. But results of this general character have technical names: the first are called *contrasty,* the second *flat.*

Thus contrast is a neutral term, simply denoting the variations of light and shade in the reproduction of a certain scene. *Contrastiness* refers to what is usually an error in reproducing this scene, in which these differences of light and shade have been exaggerated, the bright parts becoming too bright and the dark parts too dark. Contrastiness is often noticed in real life, even though it is not usually recognized in these terms. If you are looking at a scene lighted full in front by the sun just as it is going down,[3] you will notice that the sky is brilliantly light, while objects in the foreground appear merely in silhouette. Conversely, in a mist, where the light is so diffused that it is coming equally from all directions, everything is reduced to a monotonous tone of grey. In photographic terms, such a scene would be called *flat.* The measure of contrast is denoted by the Greek letter γ (gamma).

To see how speeding up and slowing down the developing machines—decreasing and increasing the degree of development—is related to the control of contrast, it is necessary to know a little about the composition of emulsions.

It is enough to say here that a piece of film base coated with emulsion does not have an entirely uniform surface. If looked at under a high-power microscope it would have the appearance of a pointillist painting by Seurat in which the stippling effect produces an appearance of a picture only when viewed at some distance. The stipplings correspond to *clumps* of light-sensitive grains in the emulsion, and the much smaller particles of paint to the actual microscopic grains themselves.

Some of the grains are more sensitive than others, some grains lie deeper in the emulsion than others. Consequently, exposure to a weak light produces conversion of only the surface grains and those which are most sensitive. A strong light will penetrate deep into the emulsion, converting grains lying beneath the surface.

When the developer gets to work, it at first acts like the weak light and affects only the surface grains, whether in the less-exposed or in the more-exposed areas, reducing them to silver. Soon, it has reduced all these surface grains uniformly to silver, producing an image which is flat, in the sense defined above. If development were stopped at this point, and the film fixed, the resulting image would be flat, no matter how much contrast there had been in the original camera exposure.

But now suppose we let development continue. In the least exposed areas none of the deep-lying grains have been exposed, and here further development will produce no further effect. In the exposed areas, the developing

[3] I.e., in the technical sense, *backlighted.*

solution will gradually diffuse into the emulsion and convert to silver those of the deep-lying grains which have there become exposed. The more silver-halide grains are reduced to silver in any small area, the greater the opacity in that area, because metallic silver is opaque.

For reasons which will soon appear, opacity is measured logarithmically and called *density,* and it thus becomes one of the fundamentals of film measurement. Hence the longer development is continued the more contrast will appear between the less- and more-exposed areas; the greater will be the density difference between these areas.

This increase of contrast with development does not continue indefinitely, and a point is finally reached at which further development produces no further increase of contrast. This is called *gamma infinity* for the particular stock and developer. But within the limits of zero development and gamma infinity, it is within the power of the lab control department to produce any degree of contrast it likes. It can make an ordinary well-lighted scene look as if it had been shot in a Scotch mist, or at the other extreme, in a silhouette studio. Obviously, a department with such powers has a large responsibility in maintaining good quality. It has to adjust individual gammas to close-set limits (using a technique called *sensitometry*), and to do this must maintain elaborate physical and chemical checks on the developing equipment.

SENSITOMETRY AND THE FILM CHARACTERISTIC

Sensitometry may seem a remote and abstract subject for the beginner to study. But actually it has a close practical bearing on conditions he will meet almost every day. How, for instance, is the smooth and attractive balance of photographic tones achieved in the labs of the big commercial studios? Why is so much amateur shooting—especially in color—so harsh and contrasty and lacking in detail? Why are dailies developed in a small lab in hot weather likely to be grainy? To what degree is it possible to "cook" an underexposed negative? How can one distinguish on the screen between underexposure and underdevelopment? Or between overexposure and overdevelopment? Why are optical effects often much more contrasty than the appearance of the original materials and their development in the lab would seem to warrant?

This is the kind of question which can be satisfactorily answered only on the basis of a knowledge of sensitometry and gamma control. The expert still photographer who has moved on to films is often scornful of the scientific method because he knows that he can produce irreproachable negatives and prints without even a mention of logarithms or tangents. But what he often forgets is that during the few minutes when he controls development of his single negative by expert visual inspection in the dark room, a large film processing machine is developing more than 6,000 separate 35 mm. pictures or 15,000 16 mm. pictures. If the fate of these frames were to be risked on a mere intuitive judgment, film making would fall into chaos, so numerous are the combinations of variable factors in a continuous developing system.[4]

"A characteristic" is often used in technical jargon to mean "a characteristic curve," and this in turn merely means the curve which shows the relationship to each other of two important factors. A graph of an automobile's performance, for instance, might indicate speed along one axis and time along the other. A line drawn through the established points would be the characteristic curve, and might show that in 10 seconds, starting from rest, the automobile could reach 45 miles per hour, in 20 seconds 60 miles per hour, in 35 seconds 75 miles per hour, and so on.

For any complicated device like an automobile or a piece of film, there are likely to be many important characteristic curves; but it is the relationship between exposure and resulting negative density which is of paramount importance in photographic sensitometry. It is this curve which is known as "the film characteristic." We have seen that the greater the exposure of a piece of negative film, the greater the density produced in it. This is because increasing light intensities convert an increasing amount of silver halide in any small area to opaque silver, thus reducing the amount of transmitted light, which is tantamount to an increase of density. Hence, we may assume that there is a relationship between the two variables, exposure and density, for any particular emulsion. This relationship can be graphed as shown in figure 8-6.

The curve we have drawn is sometimes known as the H & D curve, after the two English researchers, Hurter and Driffield, who laid the foundations of scientific sensitometry more than fifty years ago. It is more explicitly known as the *D log E curve*.

We have seen that, in addition to exposure and density, there is a third important variable, development time. If several identical pieces of film are exposed to the same uniform light intensity and then developed in the same solution for different lengths of time, the longer-developed pieces will have the higher densities. And if the test is repeated with a gradation of light intensities in the scene, an increase of contrast will occur with increasing length of development. If, therefore, we draw a characteristic curve for some convenient minimum developing time, say seven minutes, and then another for nine minutes and another for twelve, we shall soon have built up a family of curves which will represent the behavior of the emulsion under a variety of conditions (figure 8-7). The composition of the developer can change both

---

[4] E.g., temperatures of developer, hypo, and wash; pH of these solutions; chemical activity of developer and rate of replenishment; speed of machine; all these may vary independently.

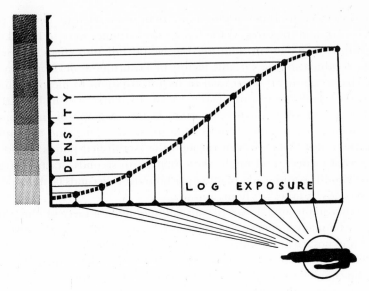

Fig. 8-6. The film characteristic.

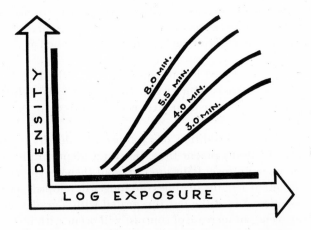

Fig. 8-7. A typical family of characteristic curves.

the slope and the shape of the curve, and so forms a fourth variable. It is customary, however, to state the type of solution and the temperature of development specified for the tests, thus eliminating this variable factor.[5]

5 For further illustration, see the excellent Kodak handbook, *Motion Picture Films for Professional Use,* or the pamphlets issued by other manufacturers of motion picture film.

WHY EXPOSURES AND DENSITIES ARE MEASURED LOGARITHMICALLY

The reader will notice from figures 8-6 and 8-7 that exposures are measured on the horizontal axis of the characteristic curve, increasing in the usual way from left to right, whereas densities are measured on the vertical axis, increasing upwardly.

A new kind of scale here enters the picture. Most people who are not scientists have been accustomed all their lives to using a linear scale, i.e., one in which all the units are equal, like the inches marked on a foot rule. This type of scale is perfectly satisfactory for measuring distance, time, speed, and many other things. In fact, such linear units occur so frequently that many people forget that other kinds of units can exist at all. Yet musicians, for instance, use almost instinctively a quite different kind of scale—one in which the intervals are measured by ratios and not by equal additions. The human ear is pleased by combinations of sounds whose frequencies progress in certain ratios, and it finds no particular significance in additive intervals. Semitones, tones, and octaves are multiplying intervals or *logarithms*. An increase of one octave does not correspond to an addition to the pitch of so many vibrations per second. It multiplies the pitch in vibrations per second by two.

The reason composers used this logarithmic scale long before logarithms were invented is because the ear operates according to a logarithmic law. It attaches equal importance to equal frequency ratios, no matter what band of frequencies they comprise: the octave from 50 to 100 cycles comprises only 50 cycles; the octave between 4,000 cycles and 8,000 cycles comprises 4,000 cycles. It is the same with volume. The ear responds with smaller and smaller increases of sensation as volume is raised, and here too it is sensible to use a logarithmic unit, the *decibel*.

The eye, also, responds in a logarithmic way to increases of brightness. In other words, to produce an arithmetical increase of sensation, a geometrical increase of brightness must be provided. In simple terms, if a room is lit up by a 40-watt bulb, a distinct increase of brightness will be seen when a second 40-watt bulb is turned on, a smaller increase with the next 40-watt bulb, and a still smaller increase with the next one. To produce equal increases of sensation, successive steps will need two bulbs, then four, then eight, and so on. Hence it is logical to use a kind of exposure scale in which equal spaces on the paper represent not equal exposure increases but powers of those increases. This is what is called a logarithmic scale, and common logarithms are based on the number 10 and its powers (i.e., 10^2, 10^3, 10^4, etc.). The indices 2, 3, 4, etc. are known as logarithms to the base 10, and since the product of powers is obtained by adding their indices ($10^2 \times 10^3 = 10^5$, *not* 10^6), multiplication can be effected by adding logarithms. This is why busy and lazy people use slide rules.

Since brightness and opacity are simple opposites (imagine opaque cells being held before the light bulbs we have just mentioned), the eye will react in the same way to both—that is, logarithmically. Hence, it would seem convenient to use a logarithmic unit of opacity (O). This is *density,* which is defined as being equal to $\log_{10} O$.

THE RELATION BETWEEN CONTRAST AND THE CHARACTERISTIC CURVE

We can see at a glance that the characteristic curves of figure 8-7 are inclined to the exposure axis, some steeply, others at a slighter angle. All these curves have a long, straight (or almost straight) part in the middle, but their slope flattens off both at the top and bottom. These rounded parts of the curve are called the *shoulder* and *toe* respectively. By looking at the exposure axis it is easy to see that the toe corresponds to the low exposures or shadows, and the shoulder to the high exposures or highlights.

This use of the term "exposure" deserves some looking into, since it may not be familiar to the average cameraman, whether amateur or professional, who is accustomed to say, "I gave that scene an exposure of a fiftieth of a second," meaning that his shutter was open on a scene for that length of time, irrespective of the balance of lighting in it. *Exposure* in the technical sense is measured by multiplying the intensity of light acting on the emulsion by the time during which it acts. Since the average scene contains a multitude of lights and shadows, it will produce in the camera a corresponding number of different exposures. It is the sum of these thousands of different *point exposures* that the exposure meter evaluates (figure 8-8).[6] The meter would give exactly the same reading off two scenes of equal total brightness, in which one was a surface of uniform brilliance, while the other contained every gradation of brilliance from an extreme highlight to an intense shadow. Yet the difference between these scenes would be of paramount importance in deciding how they were to be photographically reproduced. Sensitometry, therefore, must concern itself with the individual or point exposure, or with the exposure of uniformly illuminated areas.

Figure 8-9 shows on the right a circular object (an oil tank) which is lit from one side by the sun, so that the surface it presents to the camera lens in front of it is gradually shaded from brightness on the left to darkness on the right.

---

6 There is, however, one type of exposure meter on the market, the S.E.I., which is capable of evaluating point exposures. This meter, manufactured in England, is of the extinction type, in which a small spot in the field of view can be brightened or darkened until it exactly matches its background, whereupon it disappears or is extinguished. In the S.E.I. meter, the spot subtends at the eye an angle of less than $0.5°$, which corresponds to the width of a man's tie at eight feet, or the trunk of a tree a hundred yards away. The meter thus effectively reads point exposures. The exposure scale is also exceptionally long, having a range of a million to one or 0.01 to 10,000 foot-lamberts. When these point brightnesses are combined with the usual range of lens apertures, the resultant exposure times range from 1/500,000 second to 2 hours and 47 minutes.

Fig. 8-8. Concept of a point exposure. Cameraman sighting a small intensely illuminated area in the scene with a special exposure meter having a very narrow angle of acceptance, like the S.E.I. Photometer shown in figure 3-18. This small area (or "point") will give rise to a much higher reading than a normal exposure meter will show for the scene as a whole.

We may therefore call this scale of brightnesses the *object brightness scale.* (Of course, except in special objects like this, the bright and dark areas are scattered about, and the scale cannot be so simply abstracted. But it is there just the same.) In the camera, as the figure shows, this object brightness scale becomes an *exposure scale,* since exposure is measured by the product of point brightness and the time during which this brightness is allowed to act on the photographic emulsion.[7] It might at first be thought that the object brightness

[7] In the most recent textbooks on photographic theory, the 1943 recommendations on terminology of the Colorimetry Committee of the Optical Society of America have been adopted. According to these recommendations, optical terms are broken down into three groups: physical, psychophysical, and psychological, the second group referring to the visual perceptions of standard observers under defined conditions. The full terminology is described in the *Journal of the Optical Society of America,* 33 (1943), 544 and is explained very clearly in R. M. Evans, *An Introduction to Color,* chaps. i and iv. Since optical terms are used only in a few sections of the present book, the old popular terminology has been retained. Thus brightness, as here referred to, is a psychophysical concept which would now be called *luminance,* and the object brightness scale would be the *luminance scale.*

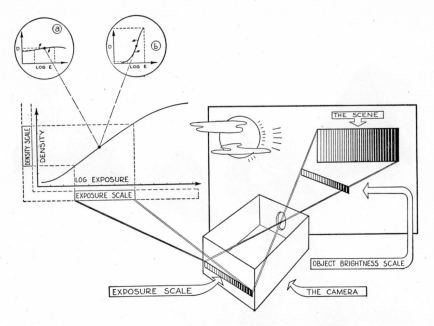

Fig. 8-9. The scale of brightness of the scene, the scale of point exposures in the camera, and the scale of densities on the negative.

scale, or range of brightnesses in a scene which is being photographed, would be identical with the scale of brightnesses which illuminates the negative emulsion, and which in conjunction with the time element of the shutter, forms a scale of exposures or exposure scale. The object brightness scale is merely transferred through the shutter and lens to the film plane, but in this process—and quite independent of the film characteristic—it suffers a contraction often amounting to 4:1. In other words, the exposure scale may be no greater than one-quarter of the object brightness scale.

As we saw in chapter ii, not all the light rays entering the camera lens contribute to forming the image. Some of them strike the inner surfaces of the lens elements at such an angle that they are reflected back rather than being refracted through; some are reflected from the inner surfaces of the lens barrel. Light which does not contribute to the image and is not harmlessly absorbed inside the camera will reach the film as an over-all flare or fog. In any well-designed camera and lens system, this stray light is insufficient to produce a recognizable fog; but it nevertheless results in a reduction of contrast which is equivalent to reducing or compressing the exposure scale.

Even more important than stray light in the lens is the effect of the inner surfaces of the camera itself. The rays of light which pass through the lens at an extreme angle do not contribute to the image, but strike the walls of the camera, which for that reason are coated with absorbent black. Even the "blackest" blacks, such as soot, and carbon black or lampblack, have, however, a reflectivity as great as 5 per cent. Of course, if stray light reaches the film only after two or more internal reflections, its intensity will be reduced to 0.05^2 (1 part in 400) or less, assuming that the blackened surfaces are in uniformly perfect condition, which is seldom achieved in practice. But if some light spills on the film after a single reflection, the effect will be much more serious.

Let us suppose that the unwanted light reaching the film amounts to only 3 per cent of the light forming the image; for every hundred units of wanted light, there will be three units of stray light. Now suppose we are shooting a scene with an object brightness scale of 100:1. Over the plane of the film there will be a suffusion of three units of stray light, and in the darkest part of the image there will be one unit of image-forming light. Thus the intensity of this darkest part will be $3 + 1 = 4$ units, and since the brightest area receives 100 light units, the illumination ratio on the negative (i.e., the exposure scale) is 100:4 or 25:1.[8] But this is only one-quarter of the object brightness scale.

If the same reduction were effective whatever the magnitude of the object brightness scale, satisfactory tonal reproduction would be hard indeed to achieve. For instance, a 10:1 ratio would be reduced to 2.5:1 on the exposure scale, a flattening difficult or impossible to compensate by raising the negative-positive gamma product. However, a very little arithmetic will show that this built-in "light compressor" is fortunately nonlinear in action. It is assumed in table 2 that maximum brightnesses in the scene remain the same.

TABLE 2

Object brightness scale	1000:1	100:1	50:1	10:1	5:1
Spillover onto film (in per cent)	3	3	3	3	3
Exposure scale	32:1	25:1	20:1	7.7:1	4.3:1
Compression ratio	31:1	4:1	2.5:1	1.3:1	1.1:1

That more work has not been done to eliminate this "light compressor" is due to two main reasons: (a) there are many other contrast limiters in the over-all motion picture process; (b) the compressor acts as a useful buffer or

8 The addition of the three stray light units to the brightest area only raises this ratio to 25.7:1. Consequently, this effect is ignored in the table.

cushion at the very start of this process. In the latter respect it offers an interesting parallel to the *volume compressor* amplifiers which are now an important part of all film recording systems: the action of both compressors is to compress more strongly at the upper end than in the lower and middle parts of the scale.[9]

Having seen how the exposure scale is produced, we can now investigate its relation to the characteristics of the negative emulsion. This emulsion has a characteristic curve like the ones we have already seen; and, under given conditions of development, it has a determinate shape and position in relation to the density and log exposure axes. The D log E curve can be drawn, as shown, in proper relation to the exposure scale, which is expressed in logarithmic units and here projected for convenience outside the camera. The unit of exposure is the unit of light intensity (the meter-candle) multiplied by the unit of time (the second), and called the meter-candle-second or mcs.

In figure 8-9 the exposure scale exactly fits and fills the straight part of the characteristic curve. If the range of object brightnesses is very great, however, the exposure scale may at one or both ends stretch beyond the straight part of the curve. Or again, it may be displaced as a whole toward the shoulder or the toe of the curve. We shall soon see the significance of these possibilities.

Notice that the exposure scale will produce on the negative film a scale of densities which may conveniently be called the density scale.[10] This scale is arrived at, as shown in figure 8-9, by drawing vertical lines upward from the two ends of the exposure scale until they meet the curve, and then drawing horizontal lines to meet the density axis. The uprights at the ends of the exposure scale are said to be projected onto the curve; and the part of the curve which is thus cut off is said to be intercepted. The density scale may be said

[9] The movie theater is no more a completely dark box containing the movie image than is the camera. The camera at least contains no source of light, but only suffers from internal reflections. The movie theater has a number of lights under the balcony and in alcoves, which serve to guide latecomers to their places. These still further reduce the image contrast, and it is easy to calculate that, if the camera and theater spillovers are each 3 per cent, and if the over-all processing and projection gamma is unity, an object brightness scale of 100:1 will be reduced to a mere 14:1 at the eyes of the moviegoer. A great improvement in photographic quality may, in fact, be noticed by running a picture in an entirely dark projection room. It is to be hoped that theater design will be improved by the adoption of "black light" and directional fixtures, so that the necessary light is shone where it is needed, and not into the eyes of the audience or onto the screen.

Were this to be accomplished, it would be found that the camera light compressor serves a useful purpose, for it (*a*) reduces the latitude requirements of film, (*b*) makes processing much less critical, and (*c*) conceals faults in projection, such as shutter flicker and insufficiently reflective screens.

The parallel process of volume compression in sound recording is accomplished only by the use of an expensive and complex electronic instrument; it is fortunate that brightness compression in picture recording requires nothing more than a layer of imperfectly absorbing lampblack.

[10] Provided always that we have fixed the type of emulsion, the developer, and the time and temperature of development.

to be reflected from the exposure scale through the medium of the characteristic curve. This is a very common type of graphical construction, much used
in sensitometry.

Now imagine (figure 8-9, *a*) that we take the intercepted part of the characteristic curve and pivot it clockwise around its center point until it is almost
horizontal. In the process, the projection of this intercepted part on the
density axis will shrink, and when the curve is horizontal the density scale
will shrink to zero. This simply means that all brightnesses in the original
scene will be represented by a single density in the negative. And this is no
other than the extreme case of flatness previously discussed, now demonstrated clearly in graphical form.

Next (figure 8-9, *b*), let us pivot the characteristic curve around counter-
clockwise so that it becomes steeper and steeper until it is vertical. In the
process, the projection of the intercept will cut off larger and larger lengths
on the density axis, until finally the density scale becomes infinite. This in
turn corresponds to our previous extreme of contrastiness.

Neither of these extremes can be realized in practice—but the graphical
construction demonstrates that the degree of contrast imparted by development can be found by measuring the slope of the characteristic curve. If the
slope is steep, contrast is high; if the slope is gradual, contrast is low.[11]

PRACTICAL SENSITOMETRY

These curves and constructions are by no means confined to the pages of a
textbook. A visit to the control department of any well-run lab will prove
that many characteristic curves are drawn and measured every day, and that
the whole operation of the developing system is guided by them. The procedure is as follows. At the start of each day, a short strip of the type of film
to be developed (say camera dailies) is torn off a roll in the dark and placed
in a sensitometer. A sensitometer is simply a device for making a series of exposures in *steps* on a small length of film—graduated from a very short to a
very long exposure, or from a very low light intensity up to a very high intensity. When the time of exposure varies, the instrument is called a *time-*

[11] A reader with a slight acquaintance with trigonometry will notice at once that the
slope of the straight part of the D log E curve is represented by the tangent of the angle (δ)
which the curve makes with the horizontal. This in turn results from dividing the density
scale by the exposure scale as we have defined them, the exposure scale being expressed in
logarithmic units. Thus: density scale $\div$ exposure scale $=$ tan $(\delta) =$ gamma (γ).

The theory of tone reproduction can of course be pushed on as far as the positive material and so to the final appearance of the finished print. Also a subjective tone-reproduction
curve can be tentatively constructed, which takes into account the characteristics of the eye.
A very lucid restatement of the elements of the tone theory is to be found in T. H. James
and George C. Higgins, *Fundamentals of Photographic Theory*, New York, Wiley, 1948.

scale sensitometer; when the intensity varies, it is called an *intensity-scale sensitometer.* The Eastman Kodak IIb sensitometer, standardized throughout North America, is of the time-scale type. On a piece of film about ten inches long, it produces twenty-one steps of differing exposure by illuminating the film through slots of varying length in a revolving drum. The ratio of the longest to the shortest of these slots or apertures is 1,024 to 1, giving a corresponding ratio of exposures. The slots increase in length logarithmically, each being 1.41 ($\sqrt{2}$) times as long as the preceding one. Consequently, a log scale of exposures can be drawn on graph paper having equal divisions.

This sensitometer, though it performs a very simple function, is an elaborate instrument designed with immense care and built to the highest standards of precision. This is necessary because errors in sensitometry are reflected throughout the entire developing process and will upset every other type of control.

The exposures made in the sensitometer on a strip of film are the counterpart of the exposure scale shown in figure 8-9. Since the strip is to be used for determining gamma, it is called a *gamma strip* or *control strip.* The gamma strip is next put through the developing machine, spliced in the middle of a long piece of leader. When it has reached the end of the machine, which may take thirty minutes or more, it is taken off, and its developed image placed under a densitometer, which measures the density of each step. There are several kinds of densitometer. In one of the simplest types, the Eastman Densitometer, the density of the film sample is compared with a standard density scale or wedge formed on a disc which can be turned with the thumb. The field of view in the eyepiece is arranged to form an outer ring whose density is that of the film sample, and an inner dot whose density can be varied by rotating the wedge. When the wedge is rotated so that the spot is neither lighter nor darker than the surrounding area, but blends into it, the diffuse density of the sample can be read on a scale attached to the wedge. This is known as a *comparator densitometer,* and resembles the extinction type of exposure meter already described.

In *photoelectric densitometers,* a light source throws a beam through the film sample onto the surface of a photoelectric cell. This is a device which emits electrons and so generates an electric current proportionate to the intensity of the light which falls upon it. Accordingly, if this current is measured (usually after amplification) by a sensitive milliammeter, it will indicate the amount of light falling on the photocell. Consequently, since the density of the film sample is measured by the logarithm of its light-stopping power (opacity), the meter can be directly calibrated to read densities.

It now only remains to plot the results. The lab is equipped with special graph paper, on which the horizontal axis of the D log E curve is marked 1 to 21 to correspond with the steps on the gamma strip, while the vertical axis indicates density in the usual way. It is only a matter of moments to plot the curve from the densitometer readings. Finally, the operator places against the straight part of the curve a small celluloid device called a *gammeter*, which is graduated in tangents and so reads gammas directly.

The graph paper is immediately sent through to the control superintendent, who, helped by long experience, can derive a great deal of useful information from it. If the curve is satisfactory in shape, and shows adequate density at the center (step 11), but indicates too high a gamma for the stock, the superintendent will give orders for the developing time to be reduced by so many seconds, this time being derived from a *time-gamma curve*. The developing machine is then speeded up by the requisite amount. If the gamma is too low, the procedure is exactly the opposite. If the step-11 density is too high or too low, it indicates that the developing temperature and/or chemical activity of the developer is too high or too low also. The chemical and control departments then go into action to correct these conditions.

These are some of the more interesting dynamics of sensitometry. But sensitometry also makes possible some useful static analyses, which can be discussed but briefly here because of space limitations.

PRACTICE AND THEORY DIVERGE

As sketched thus far in this chapter, the theory of sensitometry oversimplifies the facts. Straight-line sensitometry exists only in the pages of textbooks, and while perfectly well adapted to control, fails when applied to interpretation. The first thing to notice is that the toe of the negative material reaches upward into what is commonly thought of as the straight part of the curve, while at the lower end it tapers off very gradually. Movie cameramen have recently begun to explore the artistic possibilities of what is called *low-key* lighting, that is, lighting in which the key or general illumination is kept at a low intensity. Thus in areas of the subject which are not highlighted or brightly lit up, the shadows are deep—that is, the negative densities are low. This is sometimes called *toe exposure*, since much of it falls on the toe of the curve, but it must be remembered that the highest exposures will reach well up into the straight part of the curve, although never encroaching on the shoulder. *High-key* lighting, in which the basic illumination of the scene is greater, tends to result in negatives with a shorter exposure scale, and more nearly conforms to the older ideal of straight-line rendering.

This prevailing absence of straightness in the characteristic curves of both negative and positive materials means that the lab control department must be as much concerned with the shape as with the slope of the curves. In particular, it is found that the bromide (restrainer) concentration in the developer must be accurately maintained if the toe of the negative curve is to be kept long and well-rounded. In a well-run lab, development times for differ-

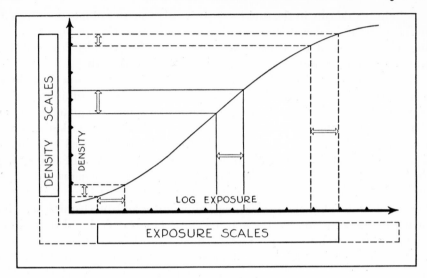

Fig. 8-10. Overexposure and underexposure and their relation to contrast.

ent film stocks remain almost constant, and therefore any sudden change revealed by readings of gamma strips will alert the chemical analysis department.

Subject to these cautions, useful conclusions of both practical and theoretical value can be drawn from simplified characteristic curves with respect to over- and underexposure, latitude, and emulsion speed.

THE EFFECTS OF OVER- AND UNDEREXPOSURE

Figure 8-10 shows what happens when the exposure scale is shifted too far down into the toe or up onto the shoulder of the D log E curve. It can easily be seen that if we take a certain span of exposure, represented by the double-headed arrows, this span will always correspond to the same span of densities so long as it is reflected from the straight part of the curve. Shift the exposure span up to the shoulder or down to the toe, however, and the span of densities will be compressed. This means that tonal contrasts will not be faithfully reproduced. The curve shows that overexposure results in, (a) too high an average density (a heavy negative) which is difficult to print because an excessive amount of light is required to push through the highlights; (b) a lack of contrast in the highlights, often noticed in an unpleasant chalkiness in skin tones. *Underexposure,* on the other hand, results in, (a) too low an average density (a thin negative), thus showing up the faintest abrasions on the surface; (b) a lack of contrast in the shadows, which have a muddy instead of the

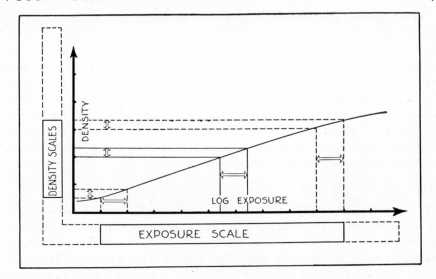

Fig. 8-11. Latitude and its relation to contrast.

generally desirable rich black appearance when the negative is so printed as to avoid excessive brightness in the highlights.

LATITUDE

The 1,000 to 1 brightness ratio of some original scenes is compressed in the camera into the much more manageable ratio of 50 or 100 to 1. This is a ratio of exposures which can easily be accepted by modern negative emulsions, and in fact errors of more than a full stop on either side of the optimum will not result in serious over- or underexposure. The wider is this range of tolerance, the greater is said to be the *latitude* of the emulsion. Conversely, if the exposure is correct, an emulsion of greater latitude will accommodate a longer exposure scale.

Figure 8-11, if contrasted with figure 8-10, shows how, other things being equal, a lower gamma will provide a greater latitude. This is because a flatter slope will enable the exposure scale to be reflected by the usable part of the curve with much less compression at shoulder and toe. It is one of the reasons why negative emulsions are developed to low gammas (usually between 0.55 and 0.65).[12]

[12] Mathematically inclined readers will sense that "perfect" reproduction is secured only when the over-all gamma from object brightness scale to theater screen is 1 (unity); i.e., the over-all characteristic curve will be inclined at 45° to the axes (tan 45° = 1). Only then will the original brightness ratio of objects be reproduced as an equal ratio of screen brightnesses. Since γ over-all $= \gamma_1 \gamma_2 \gamma_3 \ldots$, it might be expected that a negative of $\gamma = 0.65$ should be printed to a gamma of about 1.54, since $0.65 \times 1.54 = 1$. However, the action of "contrast

While gamma has some effect, latitude is primarily a "built-in" quality of the emulsion. Latitude is increased if the emulsion is comparatively thick, so that there are many layers of light-sensitive grains. This is because the degrees of density which can be produced in any one small area depend on the number of layers of grains which have been rendered developable by exposure. Extra layers of grains thus provide a sort of cushioning effect, allowing more light to be absorbed to produce an increasing conversion of grains. A very thin cushion looks all right until you sit on it. It then goes down flat all at once. But a thick springy cushion has many degrees of compression with which to respond to the weight of the person sitting on it.

SPEED

We can now see how a practical emulsion speed index may be arrived at. It is "inversely proportional to the minimum exposure which must be incident upon the negative material, from the scene element of minimum brightness in which detail is visible, in order that a print of excellent quality can be made from the resultant negative." [13] "Visible" is further defined in terms of a normal person at the camera position, and the scene is assumed to be of normal brightness contrast. This definition, as was said in chapter iii, can be evaluated only in psychological terms, i.e., by submitting many hundreds of prints to the judgment of a panel of qualified observers.

The results of the most thorough tests, carried out by Dr. Loyd Jones of the Eastman Kodak Company, can be translated into sensitometric terms in the following way (figure 8-12). Plot the D log E curve for the specified conditions of negative material, illumination, exposure range, developer, etc., as prescribed in Z38.2.1–1947. Assume an exposure scale of 32:1 (log 32 = 1.5).[14] Move the length AB (1.5 on the exposure axis) toward the right until the gradient of the curve at the low end of the range is 0.3 of the tangent of the average slope of the part of the curve intercepted by the exposure scale of 1.5 units. In other words, tan a $\div$ tan b = 0.3. When this position has been found,

compressors" calls for a rather higher negative-positive gamma product (in the neighborhood of 1.3). This is commonly secured by developing the print to a gamma of about 2.1. Since, as we have seen, the working parts of film characteristics are actually curved, gammas, which are based on straight lines, are erroneous. It is therefore more realistic to consider *gradients* (G), which are the instantaneous values of the slope of a curve, measured by the tangent at the given point. Thus we may say more correctly that G over-all $= G_1 G_2 G_3 \ldots$

However, it must be emphasized that while sensitometric theory underlies all practical film development, theoretical results must be modified by the results of experience, since the eye, the ear, and the mind are the final judges. Film is a psychophysical science: much of it lies in the twilight zone between physics and psychology. The true scientist is not a person who makes statements of rigid exactness all the time; he is a person who adjusts the exactness of his statements to the precision or imprecision of his knowledge.

[13] ASA Z38.2.1–1947, p. 9.

[14] $32 = 10 \times 3.2 = 10^1 \times 10^{0.5}$. Adding power indices (logarithms) to multiply, we have log $32 = 1.5$.

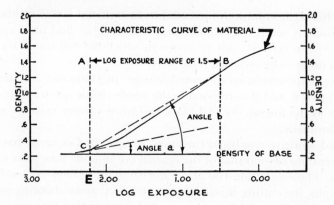

Fig. 8-12. Determination of American Standard
Speed.

E is the minimum satisfactory exposure, 1/E is the American Standard Speed, and 1/4E or Speed/4 is the American Standard Exposure Index.

Outside the lab, sensitometry is one of the least understood aspects of film making. In spite of its difficulties it deserves more widespread study, for it holds the key to many problems of image and sound-track quality, as well as being indispensable to an understanding of color processes.

NEGATIVES AND POSITIVES

The still photographer and the newcomer to motion pictures are accustomed to think of celluloid film chiefly as a material used for taking pictures in a camera. This is because still pictures are usually printed not on film but on paper, and the movie amateur sends his film to a processing plant for development, and gets back the same piece of film to put in his projector. To both, in fact, the difference between the color response of emulsions is more familiar than the functional distinctions demanded by the professional movie maker. We may therefore conveniently start with color and its reproduction in monotone. The four commonest types of color sensitivity are: blue-sensitive (*colorblind*), orthochromatic, panchromatic, and infrared.

Blue-sensitive emulsions have the natural sensitivity of the silver halides, and were invented by the Frenchman Nicephore Niepce in 1816. They are still the cheapest to produce, and are perfectly adapted to types of film which can be exposed to artificial light in the reproduction of black-and-white tones on other pieces of film (i.e. duplication). If exposed to colored objects in sunlight, colorblind film will, when printed, record as black everything which is not blue.

Orthochromatic emulsions (invented in Britain and Germany about 1875) are additionally sensitized to green and yellow. They find little application today except in certain color processes in which the red image must be excluded in order to be recorded separately.

Panchromatic emulsions (invented in 1906 in Germany) are additionally sensitized to red, and thus respond to the whole visible spectrum in much the same way as the human eye. All black-and-white camera negative emulsions are panchromatic.

Infrared sensitive emulsions (invented in 1907 in Germany) have a sensitivity extending beyond that of the human eye into the long-wave end of the spectrum. These emulsions are also sensitive to blue. They are used in aerial photography for cutting through haze, and they make shooting possible in darkness, which is useful in espionage and in recording the spontaneous reactions of theater audiences.

Crosscutting these divisions by color response is another classification of film by function. Many of these functional differences stem from the need for *duplication*. Suppose that the film maker has in mind a piece of negative which he wants to use in the cut negative of his film, but this piece is a valuable property of the library, which wishes to preserve it intact, or of someone who will license its use but refuses to sell it outright. What does he do? From the library negative it is possible by ordinary printing processes to make a positive—but a positive with special characteristics called a *master positive* because copies can be made from it. From this master positive he in turn, by ordinary printing, makes a negative called a *duplicating negative* (more commonly a *dupe negative* or just plain *dupe*). This gives him two more kinds of film. Next, since negatives are master records with reversed tonality, it is necessary to make *black-and-white prints* for projection purposes. Since these prints are released or distributed in theaters, the stock on which they are made is often called release-print positive. Lastly, sound recording requires another special type of film stock.

Thus black-and-white film may be conveniently grouped into five broad types, (1) picture negative, (2) duplicating positive, (3) duplicating negative, (4) release-print positive, (5) sound-recording positive.

The balance of qualities to be looked for in these types of film must be based on the qualities to be desired in all film emulsions.

1. Film should be fast; it should have a sensitivity or speed which enables it to respond to light of very low intensity.

2. Film should have a low graininess; it should be free from the tendency to show on the screen the particles from which the image is composed. This bad quality can often be noticed when one is sitting fairly close to the screen, and especially when looking at shots containing large areas of light sky.

3. Film should have a high *resolving power,* which means an ability to distinguish between very fine lines drawn close together and which determines the clarity and detail of the image.

4. Closely allied is the desirability of a good *sharpness of image,* defined by the steepness of the density gradient at the boundary between black and transparent areas in the image, and highly important in variable-area sound recording.[15]

5. Film should be free of *halation,* or the tendency to show a fringe or halo round objects shot against a brilliant light.

Unfortunately, in the present state of the art, it is impossible to combine all these good qualities in one emulsion. Indeed, a heavy stress on one quality may necessitate the almost complete abandonment of another. The design of emulsions not only demands a rare knowledge of organic chemistry and a high manipulative skill, but also a delicate sense of balance between many conflicting factors.

This is how the balance is commonly struck in the five principal types of black-and-white photographic emulsion used in motion pictures:

1. Picture negative.—Good reproduction of color in monotone (panchromatic response) and high speed are the most important characteristics of picture negative. Color response is important because nothing can be done to correct a tonal deficiency in the original negative. Speed is important because the movie cameraman suffers under the handicap of having to shoot at 24 pictures per second, or with an exposure which is seldom more than $\frac{1}{50}$ second.

High emulsion speed is at present incompatible with very fine grain. Hence, picture negative must put up with comparatively severe graininess, and also with relatively poor resolving power and sharpness of image. If very fast lenses and good lighting are available, speed can be safely sacrificed, thus enabling the emulsion chemist to reduce graininess and improve resolving

---

[15] The relationship between graininess, resolving power, and sharpness of image is likely to cause confusion. Though their effect tends in the same direction, these three factors are by no means identical; they are independent variables and have different causes and significances.

Inherent graininess refers to the graininess of the image developed in a stated standard developer under correct conditions. It may therefore properly be considered a "built-in" characteristic of the emulsion. Actual graininess can be increased by overdevelopment or by incorrect choice of a developer. It can also be somewhat reduced by the use of special fine-grain developers, for which many exaggerated claims have, however, been made, and which are not as a rule suitable for motion picture use because of their high cost and low contrast.

Graininess is due, as has been said, to the degree of nonhomogeneity of grain clusters and clumps. The special developers which improve graininess do not, however, favor the second of the three factors, resolving power. This is aided by contrastiness in the subject matter and development, and by thinness of the emulsion layer.

Failure to produce sharpness of image, the third factor, is due to random reflections of light (scattering) from grains in the emulsion. Hence this factor is favored by low exposures confined to surface grains, and by the use of a yellow-dyed emulsion.

power. For this reason, film manufacturers almost always produce two or more picture-negative emulsions, and the cameraman should choose the slowest which allows adequate exposure at the stop he wants to use.

Picture negative must be protected against halation, and this is usually done by incorporating a grey dye in the base (known as grey base), which absorbs light that has passed through the emulsion, and so prevents it from being reflected to form a secondary image.

2. Duplicating positive.—To make satisfactory duplicating or master positive prints, it is essential to lose as little as possible of the original quality. The prime requirement is therefore the finest possible grain and the highest resolving power. The consequent low speed matters little, since artificial lighting is used in printers, and can be made as brilliant as is needed. Moreover, in simply transferring an image from one piece of film to another, light of any desired spectral composition can be used. Therefore duplicating-positive emulsions are usually blue-sensitive only, since this is the cheapest and simplest type of photographic sensitization.

One type of duplicating-positive stock, now obsolescent, is called *lavender* or *blue print* from the color of its base. Modern duplicating positive stock is of much finer grain and is glossy and slightly brownish in appearance. The terms lavender and *fine-grain positive* should be avoided and replaced by the more general terms *picture master positive* and *sound master positive*.

3. Duplicating negative.—This film stock is also used for duplication only, and so requires the same characteristics as duplicating positive. The emulsion, however, is usually made panchromatic to increase its speed by enabling it to respond to all the spectral energy in the light source, and not merely to its blue-violet component.

4. Release print positive.—Release printing is merely another duplicating process—one step farther from the original negative. Therefore it too requires the same characteristics as the duplicating stocks—fineness of grain and high resolving power—and suffers from the same drawback of low speed. Since release prints must be printed as rapidly as possible, however, some fineness of grain is sacrificed in the interests of higher speed. Release-print stocks are sensitive to blue light only.

5. Sound recording positive.—Sound recording, as we shall see later, is carried out by two radically different methods—*variable area* and *variable density*—demanding different types of emulsion. For variable-area sound, new stocks have been developed which give exceptionally high sharpness of image and very strong contrast between the black and the transparent areas. For variable-density recording, considerable latitude is needed. This is increased by development to a very low negative gamma, usually around 0.4, and this in turn calls for the use of special developing solutions of low activity. Recently, emulsions have been produced which give a sufficiently low effective gamma when developed in ordinary picture-negative solutions. In other respects, both systems of recording need the same characteristics—low graininess, high resolving power, freedom from halation, and enough emulsion speed to be usable in existing equipment.

Negative emulsions are commonly developed to a low gamma (around 0.5 to 0.6) since this increases latitude and reduces their tendency to excessive graininess. In order to produce an over-all gamma approximating 1.0 (unity), the positive emulsions which are printed from negatives must be developed to a gamma of about 2.0. The development of film emulsions to two such different orders of contrast calls for different types of developing solution. Negative solutions are comparatively weak in strength and develop negative emulsions to the proper gamma in from 6 to 14 minutes. Positive developing solutions, which contain a higher percentage of an active developer, produce their proper positive gammas in about 2 to 4 minutes. Variable-density sound track calls for an even lower gamma than the normal negative—between 0.35 and 0.45. Very often a negative-type solution of still further reduced developing strength is used to develop variable-density sound negatives. These weak solutions bring with them a number of difficult practical problems of control, and it is for this reason that the latest types of emulsion for recording variable-density track have been adapted to development in picture-negative solutions.

The types of emulsion described in this section (save those used for release printing) are normally supplied on an inflammable cellulose-nitrate base in the 35 mm. standard. Apart from its safety advantages, an acetate base insures a very much longer print life in storage, and should be ordered in preference to nitrate when prints are being made as archival records. Accelerated aging tests indicate that acetate base is equal to the purest types of paper used for making permanent records.

Cellulose-acetate prints must always be ordered for cutting in rooms which do not comply with safety regulations. The combustibles divisions of city fire departments have no jurisdiction over places where acetate film is handled, and therefore can demand no greater provisions for safety than in a building where film is not handled at all. However, in certain parts of the country, obsolete laws continue to make no distinction between acetate and nitrate film, thus hampering production and projection.

The current standardization of a safety-base film for all 35 mm. release printing in North America and the United Kingdom will greatly reduce the hazard of fire in theaters. It has taken many years to develop an acetate base with good wearing and other physical qualities, but this goal has at last been achieved, a price slightly higher than that of nitrate base being the only remaining disadvantage of the safety stock. Nonetheless, thousands of millions of feet of nitrate film still exist in storage vaults and stock-shot

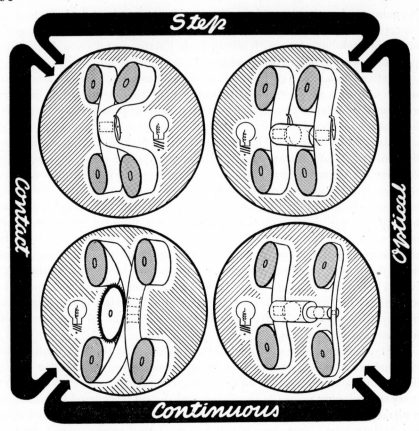

Fig. 8-13. The four types of film printer.
　　　　Step-contact.　　　　　　　Step-optical.
　　　　Continuous-contact.　　　　Continuous-optical.
(Small claw in upper diagrams indicates intermittent movement.)

libraries, and must represent a continued though diminishing danger for many years unless proper safety precautions are observed.

THE PRINT COMES OFF

Printing consists essentially of the transference of a photographic image from one piece of film to another. There are four types of printer in common use, this number being arrived at by combining two sets of two principles, as shown in figure 8-13. Printers may be either *continuous* or *step:* that is, the printing and printed films may either move along at uniform speed, or may be advanced intermittently a frame at a time, as in a camera. Again, printers may be either of the *contact* or *optical* type: that is, the printing and printed films may either be in contact with one another while printing takes place, or they may be separated by an optical system which transfers the image from the printing to the printed film, with or without modification. Four types of printer result from these combinations: the continuous-contact, the continuous-optical, the step-contact, and the step-optical.

THE CONTINUOUS-CONTACT PRINTER

The continuous-contact printer consists basically of a large sprocket wheel, round an arc of which the two films travel in close contact, emulsion to emulsion. This sprocket is hollow, and carries the films past a nonrotating aperture of adjustable width. At this aperture, a light shining through the printing film exposes the printed film, the exposure being greatest where the density of the printing film is least, and vice versa. This is why densities or tonalities are reversed in printing.

As the two films are in motion while exposure takes place, slippage between them is always possible, although the curvature of the sprocket allows for a slightly different *pitch* (or center to center distance between perforations) on positive and negative film.[16] However, if the shrinkage proves to be more or less than the printer was designed for, slipping is bound to occur, and this is especially serious in sound film where very fine lines have to be printed. Hence it is important in printing rooms to control accurately the two factors —temperature and humidity—which affect the shrinkage of film.

Continuous-contact printers usually run at 70 to 200 feet per minute, and are used for almost all release printing and for most duplicating work. Production continuous printers print sound and picture in separate operations, although both operations can be performed on the same machine with a simple adjustment of aperture. Release printers usually have two printing heads, so that sound and picture can be printed simultaneously to form a combined print.

THE CONTINUOUS-OPTICAL PRINTER

The object of interposing an optical system between printing and printed films is usually to enlarge or diminish the image. Since the continuous principle provides high speed, the continuous-optical printer serves to print 16 mm. sound tracks from 35 mm. originals. One-to-one optical systems also have their uses. By physically separating the printing and printed films, it is possible to make both travel with an extremely steady motion, and to avoid the slippage inseparable from contact printers. Hence we find that 16 mm.–

16 This is to allow for shrinkage in processing.

16 mm. sound printers of the highest quality employ 1:1 optical systems, and will print frequencies as high as 12,000 cycles with little loss.

THE STEP-CONTACT PRINTER

The step printer (whether of the contact or optical type) is much like a camera or projector. The printing and printed films are pulled down one frame at a time, usually by a claw device, and held in front of a frame-sized aperture while exposure takes place.

Like all intermittent mechanisms the step printer works slowly, usually between thirty and forty feet per minute. It has the advantage of printing only when the film is at rest, so that no slippage between the two films can occur. This makes it useful for work involving a very high degree of accuracy, such as prints for *process projection,* master positives for optical effects, and color *separation negatives.*

In the step-contact printer the two films are held in close contact at the aperture during the printing operation, as in a bipack camera. The printer also has a framing device, something like that of a projector or moviola, which is precisely adjusted for each film to be printed so that the illuminated area of the film frame is symmetrical with the aperture. In this way, the frame lines will be properly placed on the printed film. When this adjustment is not correctly made, the printed frame lines overlap, and become wider than they should be. This produces a "ledge" or "window-sill" at the top or bottom of the frame when projected. This is often seen on much-duped footage.

THE STEP-OPTICAL PRINTER

Step-optical printers have already been seen at work (chapter vi) making fades, dissolves, and other modifications of the film image. In this type of printer the image is transferred from negative to positive and vice versa by a lens system, rather than by having light strike the two films while in contact. It is thus simply a rephotographing operation, and in fact its extra complexity is seldom justified except when some modification in the original film is called for. Just as, in a photographic enlarger, the distance between the printing film and the paper to be printed can be varied to produce different degrees of enlargement, so the optical printer enables the distance between the printing and printed films to be changed—or of course to be rigidly set at some predetermined separation.

MULTIPLYING THE ORIGINAL NEGATIVE

The process of duplication is common to all film work. Strictly speaking, the transference of an image from any piece of film to any other piece of film is called duplication, but the term is not used for straight printing from a negative to a release-print positive.

There is a good deal of understandable confusion about the terms "negative" and "positive" when applied to emulsions and images. It is easy to think that negative and positive emulsions will produce only corresponding types of image. This is wrong. Since tonalities are reversed in printing, the tonality depends solely on the number of stages the film has passed through, not on the kind of stock used. Except in the *reversal* process, only positives can be printed from negatives, and only negatives from positives.

Sometimes, in fact, positive images are printed on negative film, and negative images on positive film. For instance, most sound cameras record a negative image, but register it on a positive emulsion. Again, it is often necessary to make duplicate copies of workprints in the later stages of production. These scoring dupes, as they are sometimes called, are used for synchronizing music and effects sound tracks, while the negative is being edited from the original workprint, which carries footage numbers. This makes it possible for several processes to be carried on at the same time. Since perfect quality is not necessary and economy is the chief consideration, the solution is to print or dupe the workprint to the cheapest kind of stock available—release-print positive. In this way also a negative image appears on a positive emulsion. In animation, art work is sometimes done in reversed tonalities, so that a positive image appears on a negative emulsion.

SNOWBALLING ERRORS

In the printing and processing of duplicates, errors rapidly accumulate. Faults like graininess which are below the threshold of visibility may easily be raised above the threshold if they are introduced in the intermediate processes. To get from an original negative to a print from a dupe calls for six processes: (1) print original negative to master positive, (2) develop master positive, (3) print master positive to dupe negative, (4) develop dupe negative, (5) print dupe negative to black-and-white print, (6) develop black-and-white print.

In the three processing stages, not only may graininess become objectionable, but contrast may be pushed too high. A rather high degree of contrastiness gives a print what photographers call "snap"—a crispness and projection which may hide a number of faults. The tendency is, therefore, to raise gammas slightly above the optimum; that is, the optimum for well-exposed negatives. But if this contrastiness is introduced into every processing stage, its results will increase geometrically, since the gammas of the individual stages are multiplied to produce the over-all gamma. Printing losses accumulate in a similar way. A single operation in a continuous printer is likely to result in a loss of 30 per cent (0.3) of the resolving power of the film through slippage and imperfect contact, leaving an efficiency of $(1 - 0.3)$ or 0.7. Where three printing stages are involved, this means that the over-all efficiency will be $(0.7)^3$ or only 34 per cent. Thus, if the original camera negative had a resolving power of 60 lines per mm. the release print would have a resolving power of only 20 lines per mm., even assuming that no resolving power was lost in the three processing stages. A step printer is similar to the contact-printing frame used by still photographers, in which maximum uniformity of contact is assured by carefully controlled pressure, and slippage is impossible. Even here, losses in a single operation are likely to be around 10 per cent, an over-all efficiency of 73 per cent, or a final resolving power of about 45 lines per mm. in the example given above.

To the losses in processing and printing must be added those which will arise if there is carelessness in handling the film during any of the stages of duplication. If particles of dust are present on the original negative, they will print through onto the master positive, and will then become an irremovable part of that print. Likewise, dust on the master positive will be added to the marks already present on it, and will become part of the dupe negative. And so on through the final stages of release printing. What applies to dust applies also to scratches, cinch marks, graininess, reticulation, *developing streaks, directional development* marks, and all other possible blemishes on the film.

No more need be said to prove that the most scrupulous care and attention must go into the making of film duplicates. In particular, printers, gamma control, and physical handling of the original and intermediates must be lifted to the highest standards. Emulsions of the finest grain and resolving power must be used at every stage. But these are no panacea. They must be supplemented by all other available measures of mechanical precision and human skill. It is small wonder that only in very recent years has it been possible to make from a production dupe a print which is to the layman practically indistinguishable from a print from the original negative.

IRONING OUT BRIGHTNESS CHANGES

Since film shots are commonly made under varying light conditions, negatives are of varying densities, despite the efforts made by the cameraman to equalize his exposures. If all his shots appeared on the movie screen directly printed through from their original negative density, the effect would be exasperating beyond words. As an extreme example, a person might walk into a room, apparently in the deepest shadow, and a second later his head appear in close-up so brilliantly light that the eye would be dazzled. The sense of screen reality would disappear, and with it the psychological effect of the film.

To match these densities before printing is the task of the *timer*. His job is to determine the proper light intensities for each shot on the printer so that he may compensate for different densities in the negative. Or, if a negative is being printed, then it is the positive which has to be timed. It might be thought that this timing could be done automatically by some kind of photocell device which recorded the total amount of light passing through the frame at any moment and set the printing intensity accordingly. Such devices have been tried, but have not worked well in practice because of the numerous psychological factors which have to be taken into account in timing. For instance, a human face is often the thing on which attention should be focused in a shot, even though this face occupies only a small part of the whole frame. An automatic device would time the shot for the average light intensity of the scene. Only human judgment could pick out the small wanted detail— the face—and time the shot to give it greatest prominence. Sometimes whole sequences of ordinary daylight photography must be specially darkened to produce a night effect, and this too requires subjective judgment. Consequently, there is no substitute for the timer's skill, and timers often work for ten or fifteen years to reach the top of their profession.

In assessing printing exposures the timer allots to each shot a *printer light,* usually numbered from 1 to 21. (The higher numbers correspond to the higher lighting intensities.) To give the timer an opportunity of seeing how each shot looks under all timing conditions, i.e. from very dark to very light, 21 adjacent frames of each shot may be printed as a test strip on the 21 printer lights by a machine called a *timer* (unfortunately the word is the same as for the human timer, so the machine is often called a *Cinex printer,* though this is simply a trade name).[17]

When the strips have been exposed and developed, the (human) timer sets them up in a row against a lighted panel and compares them. This enables him to pick out the correct printing lights by direct comparison, and see at a glance how an entire sequence will appear on the screen. In this way waste of footage on test prints is reduced. The Cinex strips are also invaluable guides to the cameraman, who picks them up with the day's rushes, notes the lights his shots are printing on, and can judge their effect even when he disagrees with the timer's judgment.

The timing lights decided on by the timer and entered on a *timing card* are translated into different light intensities in the printer. In the simplest system, the timer clips a *notch* in the edge of the film which actuates a trigger device on the printer. Step printers, which travel very slowly, are usually arranged so that the intensity of the light can be varied by switching in one of 21 resistances, which reduce the voltage applied to the light. The switching is accomplished by a *light-change board* in which the light changes required

[17] In most machines, the even-numbered lights are omitted, and the strip of only 11 frames results, called a *Cinex strip.* This is more convenient to handle.

in a reel can be preset; in one typical board, pegs are used to preset the light changes. A bar then drops down from the top, one level at a time, actuated by the notches, and brings the right resistance into use.

It takes an appreciable time for the intensity of a light to change from very brilliant to very faint or back again, due to *thermal lag,* so that if light shots are immediately followed by dark ones and vice versa it takes several frames for the proper light intensity to "catch up." This is a very irritating defect. For the same reason, light-change boards are not adapted to high-speed printing. Continuous printers, which travel faster than step printers, usually, therefore, have a light source of constant intensity. The amount of light reaching the film is controlled by a shutter.

In the type of printer still most commonly used,[18] the shutter is set by the operator from the timing card, the notch comes along and sets off a relay which brings the shutter to the right setting, the hand control is shifted to the next position by the operator, and so on.

In either type of printer, if a single shift is passed over accidentally, the whole of the rest of the reel will be *mislighted.* To overcome this difficulty, a more elaborate machine makes use of a timing strip or *matte* which is punched out by the timer in much the same way as a player-piano roll. The matte is then put in a special device in the printer where it travels along, usually at one-tenth the printer speed, actuating the shutter automatically as it goes. This avoids the disadvantages of both the systems just described. But printers using traveling mattes are complicated and expensive. They are confined, as a rule, to the mass production of release prints.

Finally, there is a type of printer in which the lights cannot be changed at all while the print is being run off. Usually such a printer runs at a very high speed—between 120 and 200 feet per minute—at which it would be difficult to make even a shutter work satisfactorily. Of course original negatives cannot be printed on a machine like this because of their varying density. But if a master positive from such a negative is very carefully timed, and the few residual errors removed in timing the dupe negative, a *one-light dupe negative* will emerge. The printer light needs only to be set to produce the wanted density, and the print can be run off without possibility of mislighting.

ROUTING THE TRAFFIC

So far we have imagined a sort of "freezing" of the lab, so that its individual bits of machinery could be looked at separately. Actually, it is a whirl of

---

18 The Bell and Howell. Another example of an instrument whose fundamental design goes back to the early days of movies, and which has required little modification to fit it for the most accurate modern practice.

ordered activity all day long and most of the night, for the lab is the studio department which comes nearest to the methods of the assembly line. How near it comes will depend on the scale and character of its activities. To see this concretely, it may help to look briefly at three representative labs—the first processing a million feet of film a week, the second a million feet a month, and the third a million feet a day.

The simplest kind of lab is one devoted to the making of release prints only. It will use one kind of stock and one developing solution, and its printing and developing machines can be made to run continuously with practically no attention. If studio negatives are being printed, they will be of fairly uniform density, so that little time is wasted making *sample prints*—that is, prints used to correct errors in timing. Probably, also, only one out of every five release prints will need to be inspected. Sensitometry can be held to a minimum since there are so few variable factors to go astray. A well-run lab of this kind can easily process a million feet of film a week with a staff of no more than twenty people.

The lab of a fairly small producing organization which goes to the other extreme and does no release printing may well not exceed an output of a million feet a month, or only a quarter of our first lab. But to produce this much smaller output, much larger and more complex resources are needed. Instead of the one emulsion and the one developing solution, it will need perhaps nine emulsions and three developing solutions made up to different formulas.

Three negative emulsions may be used by cameramen in the studio and the field, two further emulsions will be needed for duplicating, two more, with special characteristics, in the optical and effects departments, another for sound recording, and another for printing dailies and sound tracks. The negative emulsions will need one developing solution, the positive emulsions another, and variable-density sound recording a third. In a small lab there may be fewer developing machines than solutions. This means pumping one solution out of the tanks and another into them, unless the machines contain dual developing tanks. Again, when a machine is changed over from developing one kind of emulsion to developing another, a gamma strip has to be run through to learn whether the developing gamma is correct. This also takes time, as the strip must travel through the machine by itself, which may take thirty or forty minutes before actual development of film can go ahead. All in all, a great deal of time is consumed if the number of emulsions exceeds the number of developing machines.

The control machinery must also be much more complicated in a production lab than in a lab devoted entirely to release printing. There must be temperature controls and equipment for chemical analysis and accurate sensitometry. Inspection of negative requires constant and expert scrutiny. If positive film is spoiled, it can always be replaced at the mere cost of the stock. But original picture and sound negative has the whole cost of a production wrapped up in it, and may be worth hundreds of dollars a foot.

Traffic management comparable to that of a railroad system will be needed in this kind of lab to route all the separate orders rapidly. A single short film may accumulate several hundred lab orders in a couple of months' production. If this is multiplied by fifty productions going on simultaneously, it gives some idea of the volume of traffic.

This sort of lab is doing well if, with a staff of forty, it processes a million feet of film a month.

Small labs may well process much less footage than this, and still have to tackle all the difficulties of a production schedule. Having a reduced revenue, they may not be able to install all the controls nor institute all the analyses we have mentioned. But, especially if they can avoid being swamped with work, they can still carry out enough checks to maintain excellent quality. A sensitometer, a densitometer, a *pH* meter, a well-planned but simple circulating system—these, and a chemist with a good nose, can produce first-rate results with a minimum expenditure of money.

The very large lab has the best of both worlds. It processes enough release footage to keep the wheels turning fast all the time, thus getting the financial advantages of mass production. This pays for the special equipment and auxiliary services needed to give first-rate development of negative, duplicating stocks, and sound tracks. There can be so many developing machines that drastic speed changes with their attendant delays are virtually eliminated. A very large lab may thus develop a considerable amount of special production work and still reach an output of a million feet a day.

It must be borne in mind that these are only representative examples. In fact, practically no two labs are exactly alike. But in assessing lab requirements for any particular kind of work, it may be helpful to bear in mind these three examples of how to get out a million feet of film in a day, a week, and a month. A processing plant is a cross between a busy railroad station and a research laboratory. The practical demands made on it will decide in which direction it inclines.

IX

░░

Production Techniques:
Color and 16 mm.

THE NORM of professional production is still the 35 mm. film shot in black and white. Even today not more than 15 or 20 per cent of the theater films produced in North America are in color, and in other countries the percentage is very much less. The growing use of 16 mm. film has until recent years been almost entirely confined to prints for distribution; most of the pictures thus distributed have been shot in 35 mm. because it is the standard for professional camera and editing equipment. Spurred, however, by the availability of excellent 16 mm. color materials, producers are now turning to the use of the smaller-gauge film right through from shooting to editing and release. While the basic principles of production remain unchanged, modifications in technique have often tripped up the unwary and given 16 mm. film an undeservedly bad name. Some of the basic differences between standard production and the use of color and 16 mm. film are discussed in the following pages.

Although the principles of color photography were first clearly stated by Clark Maxwell nearly a hundred years ago, there are now only half a dozen color processes by which actual objects can be satisfactorily recorded in movement for the theater screen. This is in part the result of the very severe intrinsic difficulties which research workers have encountered in meeting the requirements of the film maker. There is no need to stress again the many characteristics of film which are scientifically contradictory, and which can be met only by compromise even in the simpler techniques of black-and-white reproduction. But even when these obstacles to the development of the color film have been taken into consideration, it still seems that the small number of successful color processes has resulted from the monopolistic structure of industry in both capitalist and communist economies. The vast resources of

I. G. Farben in Germany, which produced Agfacolor,[1] and the brilliant research, aided by Eastman Kodak, which underlies the success of Technicolor, have very naturally accrued solely to the advantage of those corporations. Having watched the rise and fall of scores of competitive processes in the course of the past twenty years, they have no doubt drawn the conclusion that color cinematography requires such complicated and delicate control that it cannot be handled by a multitude of suppliers, as can black-and-white. The practices of the Technicolor Corporation are the logical consequence. This corporation provides the raw stock, manufactures and rents the special cameras, trains and hires out cameramen, supplies a color expert to advise on costumes and set design, does the processing and special effects, and finally makes the release prints on all productions in three-strip Technicolor. The user is bound, by contract and lack of alternatives, to buy these services from the corporation.

None the less, he gains many technical advantages, as may be seen by contrasting two average productions filmed in the esentially similar processes of Kodachrome and monopack Technicolor. The enormous difference in technical quality is not principally due to the disparity in budgets; it is due to the failure of the small-scale color user to appreciate the close tolerances to which he must work, and the attention he must give to matters of detail. He is apt to regard color merely as a garnish to his tale. Seldom does he think back to fundamentals and reëxamine the mechanism of color photography.

WHAT IS COLOR?

Color, like sound, is one of the basic and indefinable elements of sensation.[2] Like the word "sound," the term "color" is applied to the physical means of arousing the sensation as well as to the sensation itself. Like sound, color is associated with wave motion. But here the general resemblance ends, for whereas sound is conveyed through an elastic medium—usually the air—in longitudinal waves of considerable length, light is conveyed by electromagnetic wave motion, independent of physical material in its path, and its waves are extremely short, varying in length between 390 and 750 millionths of a millimeter.[3] The longer wavelengths correspond to the yellow, orange, and

---

[1] An offshoot of this process, known as Ansco Color, is produced in the U.S. by a former affiliate of I. G. Farben, at present operated under government control. Since the defeat of Germany and the collapse of I. G. Farben, the Agfacolor process has been taken over by the Soviet Union. The monopoly has merely changed hands.

[2] The theory of color vision, which lack of space here confines to a bare mention, is treated in clear and fascinating detail in Ralph M. Evans, *An Introduction to Color*, already referred to.

[3] Or millimicrons (mμ). Color wave lengths are often expressed in Angstrom units (A), which are ten times smaller than millimicrons.

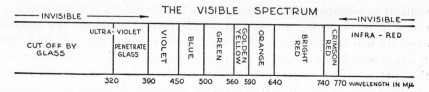

INVISIBLE ────────────▶		THE VISIBLE SPECTRUM						◀──INVISIBLE──
CUT OFF BY GLASS	ULTRA-VIOLET / PENETRATE GLASS	VIOLET	BLUE	GREEN	GOLDEN YELLOW / ORANGE	BRIGHT RED	CRIMSON RED	INFRA - RED
	320 390	450	500	560 590	640		740 770	WAVELENGTH IN Mμ

Fig. 9-1. The visible spectrum and its invisible border regions.

red part of the spectrum, the shorter wavelengths to the green, blue, and violet (figure 9-1).

Bordering the visible spectrum at its lower end is the ultraviolet radiation, which has marked photographic and physiological effect. Bordering it at the upper end are the infrared rays, which account for heat radiation. This spectrum is only a small part of the whole *electromagnetic spectrum*, which embraces the entire band of electromagnetic-wave phenomena from the shortest cosmic rays to the longest radio waves, with wavelengths ranging from a trillionth of a millimeter to many miles. The exploration of this gigantic span of phenomena in little more than a generation must rank as one of the greatest historical achievements of the human mind.

The minute part of this gamut of waves called the visible spectrum is important because the human eye is sensitive only to the radiations it comprises, and because the eye reacts to different parts of this spectrum by the sensation called *color*. The color of an opaque object is the color of the light it reflects. If, without spectral discrimination, it reflects most of the light falling upon it, it is said to be white; if only part of it,

Fig. 9-2. The color of transparent and opaque objects.

grey. If it reflects a good deal of green, and absorbs most of the blue and red, it is called green, etc. (figure 9-2).

FILTERS

If an object is transparent, the light it absorbs will not affect the eye. It is the light which it transmits which gives it its color. *Filters* are therefore made of a transparent substance (gelatin or occasionally glass) so colored that they absorb that part of the spectrum which the user wishes to restrain, thus emphasizing the spectral color which the filter transmits. Because a smaller quantity of effective radiation now strikes the film, the exposure must be increased; the factor of increase (as compared to some standard light such as sunlight or tungsten) is called the *filter factor*. If sunlight is allowed to traverse a light-green filter and fall on a blue-sensitive emulsion, the effective exposure will be very low and the filter factor consequently very high. But if a panchromatic emulsion is substituted, the filter factor is reduced many times. Hence, filter factors are significant only if the color response of the emulsion is specified. If a panchromatic emulsion is exposed to sunlight through a red filter, the filter factor will be fairly high. If tungsten light of equal intensity is substituted for the daylight, the filter factor will decrease, because the tungsten radiation is richer in yellow and red. Therefore, filter factors must also be referred to a specified light source.

A very few examples of filters and their uses must suffice. Colorblind film is sensitive only to blue and blue-green (up to 500 mμ), the colors corresponding to the longer wavelengths having no effect on it. No filter can therefore give it a realistic value response.[4] Orthochromatic film has been additionally sensitized to green and yellow-green, but is disproportionately sensitive (as compared to the eye) to blue and violet. Hence a blue-absorbing filter like the K2 will even up response at the expense of effective film speed (filter factor approximately 2). Panchromatic film has been additionally sensitized to yellow, orange, and red, though excessively so as compared to the eye. Thus, full correction requires a filter which absorbs some of the blue and some of the red extremes of the spectrum, and is therefore predominantly green in color (e.g., the X1 and X2). Finally, suppose that the cameraman wishes to produce a night effect in daylight on panchromatic film. Since the sky is bright by day and dark by night, it is the principal object requiring color correction. To determine the filter characteristics needed, we must know the spectral composition of light from blue sky: this predominates in violet and blue, but also contains substantial amounts of green, yellow, orange, and even red. If we chose a filter which completely absorbed all these colors, there would of course be nothing recorded on the film. An adequate compromise would be a filter absorbing blue, green, and yellow (i.e., red in color). Thus a *night filter* is a deep-red filter (e.g., a 25A, a 29A, or a 72) which has a very large filter factor (usually about 15) and produces a violent value distortion, especially if the negative is somewhat underexposed. This, however, is not objectionable in night scenes, because moonlight already exaggerates the "cold" colors.

The nomenclature of color filters has grown up haphazardly, and is altogether uninformative and confusing. The terms X1, X2, K1, K2, 72, 25A bear no relation to the characteristics of the filters. A bold attack on this tangle of numbers and letters was made during the war by a committee of the American

---

[4] Note that it is common practice to refer to the color response of a black-and-white emulsion, even though the emulsion cannot record colors, but only the equivalents of colors on a monochromatic scale of densities. These black-and-white equivalents are conveniently called "values" when there is danger of ambiguity.

Standards Association. It resulted in the drawing up of a simple and rational system for specifying the optical characteristics of filters, which is now available as standard Z52.61–1945. It is greatly to be hoped that manufacturers will adopt this system, which enables the user to read off the characteristics of a filter at sight—provided, that is, he has a nodding acquaintance with spectrograms and how to read them. These may be studied in any textbook on photographic theory, or in the data book on filters published by Eastman Kodak.

ADDITIVE COLOR PROCESSES

The visible spectrum can be divided into three primary colors: blue, green, and red. It was the English physicist, Clark Maxwell, who showed in 1855 that if a colored scene were separately recorded on three black-and-white negatives through filters which transmitted the blue, green, and red sections of the spectrum (and together transmitted all the visible light), the scene could be built up again in its original colors by projecting positives from the three negatives through the same filters and superimposing them on a screen. This is called the *additive method* of color reproduction because it adds together the primary components of color; and the three separate negatives on which the color is analyzed by means of filters are called *separation negatives*.

The additive process is in theory the most perfect form of color reproduction, for it requires no dyed images in the film emulsion, the color residing merely in simple and easily reproducible filters attached to camera and projector.

In spite of these advantages, additive color processes have made little headway in motion pictures, though intensive research is applied to them sporadically when a new company enters the field or when an old monopoly is threatened.

In some additive processes (e.g., Thomascolor), the frame is physically divided into sections, each photographed through a color-analyzing filter.[5] This process has the unique disadvantage of multiplying by four the area magnification from frame to screen, which introduces many difficulties of definition and resolution. These are removed by the *lenticular* process, long under development by Eastman Kodak,[6] in which color analysis is achieved with the aid of embossings on the film base which make up a network of minute lenticules (or miniature lenses) by which each small pencil of rays entering the

[5] Since the frame and its subdivisions must be rectangular, there are actually four subimages produced by four-color analysis, instead of the more usual three colors.

[6] A Kodak lenticular process was available to the public for a few years under the name of Kodacolor—not to be confused with the current still picture process which bears the same name. The original Kodacolor was withdrawn in favor of Kodachrome.

camera is imaged on the emulsion through a banded three-color filter placed over the main lens. In this way, three-color separation is obtained laterally. By projection of the film back through a banded filter an additive synthesis is achieved because the observer's eye cannot resolve the small unitary color elements.

Both these systems have the disadvantage of requiring special filters on camera and projector. Lenticular film is also extremely hard to duplicate satisfactorily. Additive color processes in which the system of color analysis and synthesis is wholly contained in the film itself are known as *screen processes*, of which one, Dufaycolour, was at one time applied to motion pictures with some success but has now fallen into disuse. The back of the film is coated with an immense number of minute red, blue, and green filters or screens, the proportions of the three colors being such that there is no resulting color when the film is viewed at a distance. In some screen processes the filters have a random arrangement, which makes reproduction almost impossible. But in the Dufay process the filters are arranged in a regular grid, called a *reseau*, so that duplicates can be made by exact registration. This, however, tends to introduce a "shot silk" effect, which is called moiré.

Film is threaded in the camera with the base and its filter grid toward the light, so that the light reflected from each small patch of color in the scene is filtered according to its blueness, greenness, and redness before it reaches the emulsion. Thus the image is formed in silver opacities corresponding to the original colors, and it is only necessary to reverse these into transmittances to recreate the original colors when the film is viewed by transmitted light. The photographic process known as reversal is accomplished by giving the film a second exposure and redeveloping it. If the film is then projected, the transmission of each minute group of three colored filters through the emulsion over it will correspond to the brightness of the original light reflected from the corresponding small patch of color in the scene. However, the mesh of the reseau, the light lost in the screen, and the dilution of color resulting from overlapping filter transmissions, tend to make the system inefficient, in spite of its many attractions.

SUBTRACTIVE COLOR PROCESSES

All remaining practical color systems used in motion pictures are of the *subtractive* kind. The method of color analysis used in taking the pictures is exactly the same as additive analysis: breaking down the scene into primary colors. The synthesis used in reproduction is, however, quite different, and employs the secondary colors, or the colors obtained by subtracting the primaries from the visible spectrum (figure 9-3).

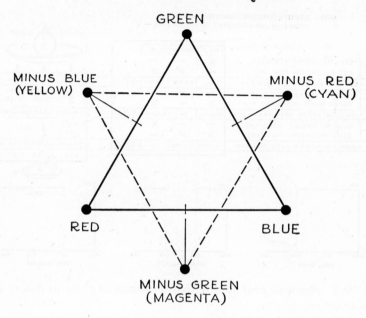

Fig. 9-3. The color triangle: primary and secondary colors.

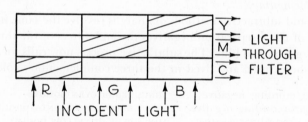

Fig. 9-4. Absorption by secondary color filters.

Subtracting primary color	Leaves secondary color	Therefore called	Or
Red	Green & blue	Blue-green or Cyan	Minus-red
Green	Red & blue	Magenta	Minus-green
Blue	Red & green	Yellow	Minus-blue

The absorption of secondary-color filters may be still further simplified in a block diagram, in which shaded squares represent absorption and white squares transmission (figure 9-4). As the figure shows, a yellow filter absorbs

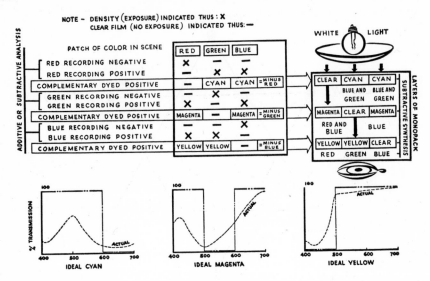

Fig. 9-5. Analysis and subtractive synthesis of color in theory and practice.

blue, a magenta filter green, and a cyan filter red. These pairs are therefore called *complementary*.

Additive and subtractive methods of analysis involve the same initial steps: the making of three separation negatives through filters of the three primary colors—red, green, and blue. The subtractive process now calls for three color positives to be printed and dyed in the three complementary colors:

> RED-recording negative......MINUS RED or CYAN positive
> GREEN-recording negative....MINUS GREEN or MAGENTA positive
> BLUE-recording negative.....MINUS BLUE or YELLOW positive

When the cyan, magenta, and yellow positives are placed over one another in exact registration and projected, the colors of the original will be reproduced. The reason for this is best seen by following the course of a red, green, and blue patch in the original scene through the reproduction process (figure 9-5).

Thus, in the subtractive color process, each of the three color components in the original scene is reproduced by the absorption or subtractive action of the images recording the other two color components.

This simplified analysis calls for secondary-color filters having the characteristics shown in the lower part of figure 9-5 (solid line). But whereas the ideal primary-color filters can be fairly accurately matched by existing dyes, the secondary filters fall far short of perfection and their characteristics resemble the dashed lines in the figure. While the yellow filter is fairly good, the magenta is poor, and the cyan even worse, satisfying less than 50 per cent of the theoretical requirements. It is easy to see that the magenta dye does not completely absorb green, and is a very poor transmitter of blue. The cyan dye absorbs much of the green and blue it is supposed to transmit, and transmits part of the red it is meant to absorb. This is the chief reason for the imperfection of the subtractive process. It is not, however, irremediable, and can be improved by the complicated technique known as masking.[7]

PACKING UP THE COLOR

The terms monopack, bipack, tripack, one-strip, two-strip, and three-strip can easily become confused, since, for instance, an integral tripack can also be called a monopack. This is what the terms mean in their application to the camera:

TERM	DESCRIPTION	EXAMPLE
Monopack	Three emulsions superimposed on one base. Also called an integral tripack.	Kodachrome Monopack Technicolor
Bipack	Two emulsions, each on a separate base, exposed in contact with one another.	Cinecolor
Tripack	Three emulsions, each on a separate base, two exposed in contact, and one separately.	Three-strip Technicolor
One-strip	Same as monopack.	
Two-strip	Same as bipack.	
Three-strip	Same as tripack.	

THE MONOPACK OR INTEGRAL TRIPACK

Seemingly, the simplest way to obtain subtractive color reproduction is to combine the three recording emulsions on one base, thus producing an *integral tripack* or *monopack*. At present the only satisfactory motion picture processes of this type in commercial use in any part of the world are: for 35 mm., Technicolor, Ansco Color, Eastman Color Negative and Positive, and Agfacolor; for 16 mm., Kodachrome and Ansco Color.

Figure 9-6 depicts the structure of a typical monopack. Actual films may exhibit slight differences in the arrangement of filters and light stoppers.

[7] The recently developed science of colorimetry and the modern theories of subjective and objective color reproduction are outside the scope of this study. The interested reader is referred for an introduction to Evans, *op. cit.* and for a more mathematical account to Joseph S. Friedman, *History of Color Photography*, Boston, American Photographic Publishing Co., 1945, chaps. 1–3.

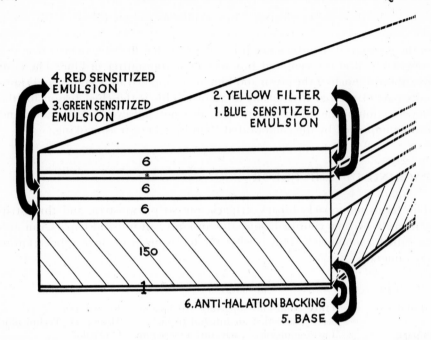

Fig. 9-6. Diagrammatic cross-section of an integral tripack. The number in the center of each layer represents its thickness in microns, or thousandths of a millimeter.

Layer 1.—Blue-sensitized (colorblind) emulsion. Exposed directly to the incident light, this layer has the key speed for the whole pack.

Layer 2.—Yellow filter acts as stopper to prevent penetration of blue rays to lower layers. This filter may be incorporated as a dye in the green-sensitive layer.

Layer 3.—Green-sensitive emulsion. Must be speeded up to compensate for the loss of light in layers 1 and 2.

Layer 4.—Red-sensitive emulsion. May incorporate a red-dye stopper to eliminate green rays. Must have highest possible speed to overcome loss of light in layers 1, 2, and 3.

Layer 5.—The film base has its usual function of acting as a support to the emulsions, and may be of the nitrate or acetate type.

Layer 6.—The antihalation backing prevents reflection of light with its consequent fringing and causing of double images.

The three emulsion layers, when combined, must have the same equivalent speed—that is, incident white light must produce a normal exposure in each of them. Thus the speed of the pack is the speed of the most unfavorably placed emulsion layer, which is why monopacks are essentially slow. More-over, development of the pack must result in the same gamma and density being acquired by all three color-sensitive layers. It will be evident why the making and processing of monopack film is exacting and expensive, and why very precise exposure is called for.

The Agfacolor and Ansco Color tripacks are unique among motion picture films in that the color-forming substances remain fast in the emulsions during the stages of silver development, and do not have to be added separately at the later stage of color development. This makes processing comparatively simple, though about eleven operations are still required, as against three or four for black and white.

The first stage is to develop the blue-, green-, and red-recording images in an ordinary black-and-white developer. No color is formed, and normal silver images result. The pack is then reëxposed with white light, and the reversed (positive) [8] images developed in a color-forming developer which precipitates dyes in the three layers proportionately to the density of these images. All the silver halide is now reduced to metallic silver, and the silver is finally removed by the reducer, leaving an image which is formed in the three complementary colors.

In the Kodachrome tripack, the color-forming substances are not incorporated in the emulsions, and consequently each color has to be developed separately. First of all, as in Ansco Color, three negative black-and-white images are developed. The remaining (unexposed) silver halides retain their spectral sensitivities, so that when red light is shone through the base, it effects only the lowest (red-sensitive) layer. The positive image is then developed in a dye-coupler developer which forms cyan. Next the pack is exposed to blue light on the top and developed in a dye-coupler developer to form a yellow positive. Finally, the green-sensitive center layer of the sandwich is exposed and developed to yield a magenta positive. When the silver has been removed by bleaching, a subtractive color transparency remains, exactly as in the Ansco Color process. This Kodak technique is known as *differential reëxposure,* and it is not hard to understand why the manufacturer insists on retaining control of processing.

The arrangement of the color layers is now as follows:

ORIGINAL FILM	COLOR POSITIVE
Blue sensitive	Yellow image (Minus blue)
Green sensitive	Magenta image (Minus green)
Red sensitive	Cyan image (Minus red)

[8] If the reader is not familiar with the method of producing a positive from a negative image in the same emulsion, he should read the description of the reversal process given on pages 235–237.

Thus, when the monopack is projected, it will, subject to technical imperfections, reproduce the colors of the original, as previously explained in figure 9-5.

The process described is known as a reversal process, because the film exposed to the original scene produces correct colors upon development and reëxposure instead of the reversed colors resulting from the simpler *negative-positive* process. However, it is easy to see that, by omitting the reëxposure and redevelopment stages, the film will appear as a negative in terms both of density and of color values. Thus red in the scene is represented by white light minus red, that is, blue-green or cyan. Similarly, cyan is represented by red, green by magenta, and blue by yellow. When printed and developed, the image will be restored to its true colors and tonalities. This technique is important because the reduction in the number of processing stages makes possible, for the first time, development in the producer's laboratory, with much saving of time and temper when a difficult production is under way.

Historically, the first successful negative-positive color process was Agfacolor, introduced in Germany in 1939 and taken over by the Soviet Union in 1945. The Agfa technicians developed means of accurately timing release prints which were greatly superior to those produced by direct reversal printing.[9] The quality of the results is attested by the many German feature films produced during the war, though on this evidence most observers would judge Agfacolor to be inferior to the much more complex Technicolor process.

Early in 1950 Eastman Kodak announced the first American negative-positive color process for motion pictures, which so far remains unbaptized with any memorable name. The color negative (Type 5247) has the same arrangement of color-sensitive layers as Kodachrome, but is developed to form a complementary image. Development can be carried out in a modified standard machine, a total of eight processes occupying an elapsed time of about seventy-five minutes. The film is color balanced for 6000° K, and has an ASA speed rating to daylight of 12. Lighting contrast should be kept low, the film must be stored in a cool place, and development should follow exposure as rapidly as possible.

Type 5247 prints to Color Print Film Type 5381, the colored couplers in the negative acting as automatic color correcting masks which help to make good the deficiencies of the dyestuffs, as explained elsewhere. Color correction filters must be inserted in the printer optical system to compensate for errors in color balance caused either by variations in the stock or by deviations from the proper color temperature during exposure. It will no doubt require two or three years, as in Germany, to devise really satisfactory means of color timing on a production basis.

[9] This feature of Agfacolor is very well described by Wilhelm Schneider, *The Agfacolor Process*, FIAT Final Report No. 976, Washington, D.C., 1946.

Development of Type 5381 is in eleven stages and occupies about sixty minutes. Physical precautions are the same as for the negative material, save that the storage temperature must be even lower (40° F for long periods). Minor points of interest are these: Type 5247 is the first 35 mm. negative material to be standardized on acetate base; Type 5381 is the first film to be standardized with the new Dubray-Howell perforations.

This new Eastman color process is of capital importance, for it simplifies the problem of processing (hitherto confined to a few central stations), and lowers the cost of making color release prints in small numbers. The negative-positive process will consequently see its first successes in the field of industrial films and commercial shorts, where the higher cost of large print orders is of less importance, and where there is less need of refined and complex optical effects. These present obstacles in all color processes which do not permit the making of separation negatives; successive duplication from monopacks at present entails a serious degradation of color. In its greater latitude of exposure and timing, however, a negative-positive process still shows to great advantage over a reversal process such as Ansco Color.

In short, over the next few years, those films which have had to be produced in 16 mm. Kodachrome for lack of an economical 35 mm. color process can now be shot on Eastman color negative and developed locally. Films which have hitherto been produced in Technicolor will continue to be so produced, for the technical lead established over many years will not be lost overnight.

BIPACKS

Only a two-strip process will serve the purpose of a two-color analysis, since there are no integral bipacks on the market. The *two-color* process is based on a compromise principle of color analysis into two sections of the spectrum —one emulsion recording blue and green, the other yellow, orange, and red. The reproduction of green in two-color processes is markedly inadequate, and all remaining colors tend to have a harsh, unpleasant quality absent from good three-color reproduction.

In *two-strip* or *bipack* photography, two films are exposed simultaneously, passing through the camera aperture in close contact. Facing the lens is the base side of the front film, which contains a minimum amount of grey die to reduce halation without unduly affecting speed. The emulsion of this front film is orthochromatic, and it records the blue and green light reflected from the subject. To prevent this blue and green light from continuing on and exposing the adjacent second emulsion, the first emulsion is overcoated with a thin orange-red filter layer. The emulsion of the second film is panchromatic, and records the rest of the spectrum. The camera problems attending the use of two- and three-strip film are discussed in a later section.

The two exposed black-and-white films, having been removed from the camera, are developed in the normal way in an ordinary laboratory, twice as much footage, of course, being required for any given screen time as with black and white. The two-color separation negatives can then be printed to separation positives; but they are usually transferred immediately to the release print, which receives its complementary colors by the *dye-toning* process.

Since two-color photography is not restricted by patents, it exists under a large number of trade names. All these commercial applications are basically similar, though differences may occur in the method of making release prints.

TRIPACKS

The three-strip process is commonly associated with the name of Technicolor, a corporation which, by intensive development and controlled use over a period of many years, has brought it to an unequalled pitch of perfection.[10] In this type of process, as "three-strip" implies, the three color images are formed on three separate strips of film. The Technicolor camera (described more fully in a later section) makes use of a colorblind film to record the blue image, and two panchromatic films to record the green and red images. These films, made by Eastman Kodak, have exceptionally low shrinkage, so that subsequent registration of the three images may be exact to less than one-thousandth of an inch. After exposure, the films are developed to an equal contrast to form separation negatives, from which separation positives are printed on special stock in a projection printer. The remainder of the process is concerned with the method of release printing, which we will now examine.

RELEASE PRINTING

Of major importance in all color processes—affecting speed, simplicity, and cost—is the method provided for release printing. The total film footage in release prints is vastly in excess of the total footage employed in a film's production, and its cost (stock plus processing) is an appreciable deduction from the gross receipts of the picture. Speed is important because prints must often be made at short notice, while processing simplicity enables prints to be struck off from dupes in foreign countries, reducing freightage and often

10 Since published information on Technicolor is somewhat scanty, the following references may prove useful: J. A. Ball, "The Technicolor Process of 3-color Cinematography," *JSMPE*, Aug., 1935, pp. 127–138. C. G. Clarke, "Practical Utilization of Monopack Film," *JSMPE*, Nov., 1945, pp. 327–332. Friedman, *op. cit.*, chap. 5, "Camera Patents," and chap. 26, "Imbibition and Dye-Transfer Processes." Detailed references to original patents are given as an aid to those in search of further information. Winston Hoch, "Technicolor Cinematography," *JSMPE*, Aug., 1942, pp. 96–108. Technicolor Corporation, *Detailed Information on Shooting*. Memoranda issued to cameramen and revised from time to time. See also, W. T. Hanson and F. A. Rickey, "Three-Color Subtractive Photography," *JSMPE*, Feb., 1949, pp. 119–132.

eliminating burdensome customs duties on the importation of positives.

Unfortunately, these valuable economic advantages are not combined in any one process. The cheapest methods of printing satisfactory color are currently inadequate to meet the increasing demand for color prints and are confined to a very small number of producing centers.

DYE TONING

This is one of the oldest color reproduction processes applied to movies, having been perfected in the formerly well-known Brewster Color. It is now used in the making of two-color 35 mm. prints from bipack negatives, and three-color 35 mm. prints from separation negatives originating in an animation camera or made from 16 mm. monopacks. Cinecolor is today the largest exponent of this process.

If a clear piece of emulsion-coated film is immersed in a solution of a basic dye, the dyestuff will not hold to the film and can be easily washed off. If, however, the gelatin has first been treated with certain substances known as *mordants,* the dye forms an insoluble pigment and adheres to the film. The most important mordants are certain iron salts, copper iodide and other iodides, and the thiamino compounds of which thiourea is an example. These substances will combine with the silver in a photographic image to form silver salts.

An image is printed from each of the two separation negatives (in a bipack process) on the two sides of a *duplitized* film, the three films being held in exact register. The two silver images are then mordanted and dyed with complementary colors. Since the dye formation will at all points be proportional to the amount of mordant present, which in turn is proportional to the original amount of photographic silver, which in its turn corresponds in one separation negative to the amount of blue and green reflected from the subject, and in the other to the yellow and red, a true color reproduction will result within the unsatisfactory limits of a two-color analysis and synthesis.

Three-color dye toning operates on the same principle, but the necessity of making an integral bipack on one side of the film complicates it considerably.

Duplitized (double-coated) film adds to the cost of release printing, and is disliked by projectionists because it has two soft surfaces, of which the lower is particularly likely to become dirty and scratched during projection. When duplitized film is spliced two scraping operations are necessary (figure 9-7).

MONOPACK PRINTING

The most obvious method of printing from a monopack is to print on another monopack film as the release-print material. Ordinary black-and-white print-

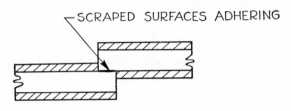

Fig. 9-7. Splicing of duplitized film.

ers can then be used, and the release print can be developed in the same developing machines as the original camera film.

If this camera film has been developed by reversal as a positive, the release print must also be reversed. If the camera film has been developed without reversal to a color negative, the print, also without reversal, will yield a color positive, exactly as in negative-positive black-and-white photography.

Monopack printing is used in several commercial processes; negative-positive with 35 mm. Agfacolor; and reversal-reversal with Kodachrome prints from Kodachrome originals, 35 mm. Ansco Color, and 16 mm. Ansco Color.

There are a number of disadvantages which combine to make monopack printing less attractive than it appears at first sight. In the first place, monopack printing stock is almost or quite as expensive as shooting stock, since it contains the same three layers and separation filters. Black-and-white release-print stock, on the other hand, costs less than one-third of the price of negative stock.

Secondly, developing times are very long, so that larger machines than any now available for black-and-white development would be required for processing the millions of feet of film which pass into theatrical distribution. Even the less pressing demands of 16 mm. production entail long delays in developing and printing.

Finally, printing control for color and contrast correction is neither so simple nor so flexible with monopacks as with separation negatives. If the three color-sensitive layers remain superimposed, they can be independently controlled only with masks or colored light beams to compensate for the poor characteristics of the complementary filters incorporated in the stock.

Thus, on the one hand, monopack printing saves and simplifies equipment; on the other, it increases the cost of release prints and hampers color control, especially over optical effects, background projection, and any other second-remove processes which depend for their success on exceptionally accurate laboratory manipulation.

THE TRANSFER PROCESS (IMBIBITION PRINTING)

This printing process was devised to overcome some of the difficulties of monopack printing. It provides flexible color and contrast control, greatly reduces print costs and provides a high speed of operation. The many technical problems it entails have been overcome, notably through the efforts of the Technicolor Corporation, but only at the price of confining all release printing to two centers, Hollywood and London.

Imbibition printing is used commercially with 35 mm. Technicolor (3-strip), 35 mm. Technicolor monopack, 35 mm. Technicolor blow-up from 16 mm. Kodachrome originals, and 16 mm. Kodachrome prints from Technicolor originals.

In its most general terms, the transfer process consists in converting separation negatives into gelatin relief images called *matrices,* the physical depth of which at any point corresponds to the image density, which in turn corresponds to the brightness of the elements of the original scene in terms of their three-color analysis. The gelatin forming the relief images is so treated that it will absorb or imbibe dye in proportion to the depth of gelatin present —hence the term *imbibition.* The three matrices are then dyed magenta, cyan, and yellow, and each brought into contact with a treated blank film, into which the dye transfers. During this process exact registration must be maintained, and the transfer dye must not diffuse beyond the edges of the relief, or a blurred image will result. When the three dye images have thus been superimposed on the blank, the picture is complete. The printing of the separation positives and the making of the matrices allows an admirable degree of control, while the final blank is a cheap and convenient receiver of the dyed image, which is all on one side of the film, and which, since it does not require development, can be applied after the sound track has been laid down in black-and-white silver.

In rather more detail, the process is carried out as follows. The separation negatives are printed on three special films which will form the reliefs. These films are developed in a *tanning* developer, which hardens the gelatin only where the image has been formed. At this point the nonhardened, nonimage-bearing gelatin is still present. Next, the matrix is bleached, washed, and fixed to recover the silver. Then comes the etching process, in which the matrix is plunged in hot water to dissolve the untanned gelatin and wash it away. Finally, the tanned gelatin forming the relief is set and hardened. The matrix is now ready. During the printing of the matrix, very accurate control of contrast can be exercised. It has been found that the incorporation of yellow dyes decreases the contrast, while exposure to green light increases it. Thus, any desired contrast in the relief can be secured at the printing stage by the use of filters.

The matrices are now loaded with dye which is transferred to a blank prepared to imbibe it and already printed with the silver image of the sound track. Transfer machines have been devised which handle long lengths of film at a time. But since several minutes of close contact are required for the dye to be fully transferred, these machines must be very different in design from continuous printers.

The matrices can be replenished with dye and used over and over again to make many release prints, until finally they become clogged and the transferred image begins to lose quality. Registration during the transfer, as at every exposure and printing stage, must be very precise, or *fringing*, a particularly objectionable defect, will appear in the final print.

BLOW-UP

Applicable to any of the release-printing methods described is the technique of blow-up from 16 mm. to 35 mm. Starting with a Kodachrome or Ansco Color original, separation negatives of 35 mm. width are produced by enlargement in an optical printer, using tricolor filters to separate the images. These separation negatives are then printed on a single film in one of the ways already described, or by some other process.

The final appearance of blow-up material on the screen depends very largely on original quality. Much 16 mm. color is shot carelessly by specialists in other fields who may—through their occupations or hobbies—find themselves in a position to get footage which is out of the reach of professional cameramen. This film material can only find its way to theater screens by enlargement to 35 mm. color, where the faults in the original appear under great magnification, for the 16 mm. frame has but one-quarter of the area of a frame of 35 mm. film.

When blow-up is planned, the greatest care must be taken at the 16 mm. stage. As far as possible, lighting must be controlled to avoid excessive contrast, the camera must be fitted with a steady intermittent movement, the aperture framing must conform to standard, and the processed film must never be projected. Even when all these precautions are taken, blow-up seldom provides more than passable quality on the screen. In appearance, it is usually better than two-color reproduction, but falls far short of three-color processes, even when they are in monopack form.

Blow-up, in short, is as satisfactory a method as can be expected for accomplishing something which it is usually better in the first place not to attempt.

MASKING

We have already seen (p. 211) that, owing to the imperfection of the secondary-color dyes in current use, color dilution takes place whenever a dye image is formed during the process of subtractive synthesis. Reference to figure 9-5 will show, for instance, that the cyan image transmits less than half of the blue and green rays which it should transmit perfectly. The magenta image fails to transmit part of the blue. Only the yellow dye approaches perfection. The result of the inadequacy of the cyan and magenta dyes is that the positive cyan image records some blue and green, and the magenta some blue, which have no counterpart in the original scene and merely serve to deteriorate the color rendering.

These spurious positive images can be neutralized by the use of like negatives called *masks,* printed in ordinary black and white. For instance, a negative cyan mask can be printed and developed to a gamma and density which will enable it to stop the tripack's cyan image. A negative magenta mask will similarly stop the magenta image. If the two masks and the tripack are then superimposed in exact registration, a blue separation negative can be obtained as if through filters having perfect transmission characteristics. The same technique can be applied to the other two primary separations.

The complexity of this process has made it difficult to apply to motion pictures, but some type of masking is almost a necessity in all-monopack processes like Ansco Color, in which as many as three successive subtractive images may need to be formed (original film, intermediate duplicate, and release print).

In practice, mask printing requires a step-optical printer having excellent registration characteristics and therefore slow speed. The proposed technique is to apply masking only to production of the intermediate duplicate, which is then said to be *conformed.* This dupe is printed to the release print in a standard contact printer, the loss at this stage not being corrected.[11]

SOUND REPRODUCTION

If the sound track is formed in a colored dye, instead of in silver densities, the proper reproduction of sound is difficult to achieve. A sound track is essentially a variable light obstructor interposed between a constant light source and a light-sensitive device known as a phototube in such a way that the variable light obstruction of the film effects the greatest possible change in the phototube current.

Now suppose that the phototube "sees" red and infrared light very efficiently, but is almost blind to green and blue light. Suppose further that the sound track is printed in red. the nonprinted parts being transparent. Since the phototube is almost as sensitive to red light as to white (for it is blind to all other components of white), the variations of the sound track printing will

[11] See Duerr and Harsh, "Ansco Color for Professional Motion Pictures," *JSMPE*, May, 1946, and T. H. Miller, "Masking: A Technique for Improving the Quality of Color Reproductions," *ibid.*, Feb., 1949, for short accounts of this process. Also Friedman, *op. cit.*, for an excellent general description of masking techniques with further arithmetical examples.

be almost invisible to it. There will be little effective variable light obstruction and consequently little variation in current. The moviegoer listening to the sound track will hear only a faint murmur of dialogue accompanied by a thunderstorm of frying, hissing, and crackling noises.

Though exaggerated for the sake of clarity, this is essentially what happens with many colored sound tracks. The phototube in universal theater use at present is highly sensitive to red and near infrared, where the greater part of the exciter lamp energy is also concentrated. Thus, since an opaque silver image is an almost perfect light obstructor for all colors, light source and phototube are well matched in the reproduction of black-and-white sound tracks.

Unfortunately, however, most dyes used in color processes are virtually transparent in the near infrared region (700–900 mμ), even the cyan, or minus red, increasing rapidly in transmission at the edge of the visible spectrum. To remedy these difficulties with the existing type of phototube, many ingenious solutions have been proposed. Among the most notable are:

Technicolor.—A silver track is laid down and printed prior to dye transfer. This provides a perfect solution at the expense of an extra process.

Kodachrome.—A silver-sulfide track is laid down during processing by edge treatment of the track with a fluid. While this also provides a satisfactory solution, the edge treatment is an extremely delicate operation, since the boundary line cannot wander more than $15/1000$ of an inch. It no doubt adds appreciably to the cost of printing.

Ansco Color.—After several years of experiment, a silver-sulfide track applied by edge treatment has been adopted, as in Kodachrome.

Cinecolor.—Ferric-ferrocyanide is one of the very few dyes which are absorptive in the near infrared, and it is also suitable for forming the cyan image. This method cannot, however, be applied to other than dye-toning processes.

Gasparcolor.—On a duplitized film, the cyan dye is absent from the sound track area, and a silver sound track may be deposited. The superimposed yellow and magenta images on the other side of the film form a red filter which freely passes the effective red radiation from the lamp to the red-sensitive phototube through the parts of the track not covered by the silver image.

These complex methods of printing sound tracks would be rendered unnecessary if magnetic recording and reproduction were to become universal; or, with optical recording, if a blue-sensitive phototube were installed as standard in all theaters. A tube with these characteristics was developed in Germany shortly before World War II and is now manufactured in the United States. The motion picture industry has given little encouragement to its adoption, as may be seen in the excellent chart, "Characteristics of Color Film Sound Tracks," prepared by the Society of Motion Picture and Television Engineers and reproduced in their *Journal* for March, 1950, p. 377.

CAMERA MODIFICATIONS ENTAILED BY COLOR

Monopack.—Monopack stock (35 mm. or 16 mm.) has the advantage of requiring no structural modifications in the camera. It is most important, however, that the lenses have excellent definition at the large apertures at which they will be called upon to work (owing to slow monopack speeds), as well as the best possible correction for color.[12] The narrow latitude of monopack also calls for calibration of all lens apertures by actual transmission test, since the calibrations on lens barrels are often in error by as much as half a stop, which is the maximum permissible departure from correct exposure. The camera should be in excellent mechanical condition, and should be regularly checked for small particles of film in the aperture and light traps. The high shooting cost of color makes these precautions advisable for economic reasons alone.

Bipack.—Bipack cameras are also essentially standard camera designs, the Mitchell and the Bell and Howell being almost exclusively used in this country because of their excellent registration of the two films. Aperture pressure must be reduced to allow free passage of the films, and, since the front film is exposed through its base, the exposure plane (at which the two emulsions are in contact) is moved back a distance of 3.5 mils. This entails moving the plane of the focusing-microscope ground glass through a like distance, and altering the index mark on the lens focusing mounts to new positions. Bipack magazines are of double-tiered construction, and rather clumsy and slow to load. They are usually built in a 400-foot size, which is almost as large as a standard 1,000-foot magazine. The lens requirements for bipack are as strict as for monopack, or stricter. The stock used consists of one special orthochromatic and one special panchromatic film.

Three-strip.—Except for the little-used British Tricolour camera, the Technicolor camera alone is available for shooting three-strip live action. All Technicolor pictures are shot on fewer than forty cameras, owned and maintained by the corporation in Hollywood and London. This close control

12 Because the refractive index of glass is not the same for all wave lengths (cf. Newton's experiments with prisms), the colors of the spectrum are not brought to a focus on a single plane by an uncorrected lens. An *achromatic* lens brings two colors into focus in the same plane, and an *apochromatic* lens (used for copying), three colors. Even when a lens is color corrected, focusing for infrared calls for the lens to be moved forward one quarter of one per cent of the focal length from the position of visual focus.

is imposed by the exacting routines needed to secure precise registration of the image on three separate films. So well have these routines been devised and executed that color fringing is all but imperceptible on the largest screens. The camera has two aperture plates, with synchronized pull-down movements, set at right angles to each other (figure 9-8). In the L-shaped space so formed is mounted a glass cube composed of two half cubes, the *interface* being *sputtered* with gold to form a *semireflecting mirror*. The film which travels through the normally placed aperture is exposed through a green filter and forms the green record. The aperture at right angles, which receives light by reflection at the cube interface, carries a bipack of which the front film is exposed through a magenta filter (subtracting green) to record the blue image, and the back film through an additional blue filter formed on the surface of the blue-sensitive emulsion to record the red. Thus, two panchromatic films are used (red- and green-sensitive) and one color-blind film. These films have been made to Technicolor specifications, and have low shrinkage characteristics.

The stringent lens requirements are met by the use of a specially designed set of lenses, of which the 25 mm. is notable because it requires a back focus much greater than its effective focal length,

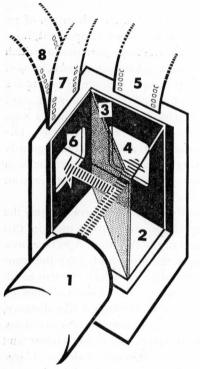

Fig. 9-8. Color separation in the Technicolor three-strip camera. The light beam entering the camera through the lens (1) passes into a glass cube (2) which is split diagonally to form two prisms. The common face of the prisms (3) is sputtered, so that it partially transmits and partially reflects the light beam falling on it. The transmitted part strikes the camera aperture (4), passes through a green filter, and thus makes the green record on the panchromatic film (5). The reflected part of the light beam strikes a second aperture (6) where it encounters a magenta filter which removes the green component. It then forms a blue image on a blue-sensitive film (7), and a red image on a panchromatic film (8), which is faced with a red filter layer to improve separation. Films 7 and 8 have emulsions in contact, as in bipack.

since the light path from lens to film is considerably lengthened by the inter-position of the cube.[13]

Animation.—Shorn of the problems of recording live action, two- and three-strip camerawork becomes much simpler. This is because the color-separation images can be recorded successively on a single emulsion, instead of requiring simultaneous recording on different strips or on a multilayer monopack. The three-color procedure is to equip the standard animation camera with a set of tricolor primary filters which can be brought in turn beneath the lens by some convenient mechanical device. Each motionless picture element (cell, cutout, scratch-off, puppet or whatever it may be), is recorded on three frames with the three filters. After exposure, the film is removed and processed, whereupon it is passed three times through an optical printer which is geared to print every third frame, the starting point being staggered one frame each time.

The filters and the mount form the only extra equipment needed. However, the camera registration must meet the rigorous standards set by three-strip cameras, and the lens or lenses must be of impeccable quality. Standard tricolor filters have equalized exposures, but the over-all exposure must be established by test and maintained exactly.

This technique may suggest to the experimentally minded the possibility of making color abstract films without colored objects and even without a camera. Three strips of film are placed in a synchronizer with the prerecorded sound track and considered as the yellow, magenta, and cyan separation negatives (or positives). By painting the tracks with greys of varying density, or using lengths of fogged film, different and determinable color combinations can be produced, while the shapes of the images can be designed to bear a rhythmical relationship to the sound track. Alternatively, the picture tracks may consist of wipe masks, which can be superimposed in complex patterns, the color changing as new overlappings take place. Films of this kind are cheap and easy to make, and provide excellent practice in the mechanism of color. Individual combined prints can be secured from the smaller three-color laboratories at a moderate price.

LIGHTING FOR COLOR

The black-and-white cameraman's most basic technical concern is with his exposure. The spectral composition of the light he shoots with is usually of little importance to him—and indeed is considered only if he wishes to

---

[13] A lens of *telephoto* construction is one in which the back focus is different from the effective focal length. In long-focus lenses, the back focus is less (for the sake of compactness); in the Technicolor wide-angle lens it is, of course, greater than the focal length.

use some unusual combination of filters. Change the film in his camera to a color stock, and the composition of the light must be his constant preoccupation. What kind of light is now just as important as how much light; if either of these questions is wrongly answered, the delicately balanced monopack or three-strip may yield unacceptable results.

The color quality of light sources having continuous spectra is measured by their *color temperature*. In daily life, temperature and color are seldom associated; yet their close connection will be apparent on a moment's thought. If a black poker is thrust into the fire, the heat of the fire will raise the poker to a temperature at which it begins to give off visible light—first a dull red, then bright cherry red and yellow, and ultimately a "white heat." This suggests that the temperature of the poker might be used to indicate the color of an unknown source whose radiations it was receiving. But if some of these radiations were reflected instead of being absorbed, the poker would not give a true indication. Therefore it is essential that the poker absorb all the radiation falling upon it. But this is the definition of a perfectly black body, and hence the color temperature of a source of light is defined as the temperature at which a *blackbody* must be operated to give a color matching the source in question. Since a blackbody radiates over a continuous region of heat and light frequencies, it is said to exhibit a *continuous spectrum*.

Since this is a basic definition, it is usual to express color temperature in basic temperature units, which are degrees Centigrade measured from absolute zero, or $-273°$ C. This scale is called the Kelvin scale (K).

Table 3 gives some common light sources and their color temperatures, but it must be remembered that sunlight varies according to geographical location and state of the atmosphere, so that the sunlight figures given may vary by 300–500° K.

Color stock can give accurate color reproduction only when the scene being photographed is illuminated with light of the color temperature for which it is balanced. The effective color temperature of a source can be raised or lowered by the use of filters placed over the source or over the camera lens. Therefore there exists a relationship between source temperature and film color-balance temperature which, when it departs from unity, must be corrected by the use of filters or—to a limited degree—by control exercised during processing.

Film color-balance temperatures and speeds for various available color stocks are given in table 4.

It is evident that the system of lighting will depend on the type of film chosen for shooting. The tungsten films, as we may call them, can be used with unfiltered lights, provided these are rated at 3200° K. Photoflood films, balanced for 3450° K, may be used satisfactorily with all types of Photoflood lamps. Daylight films are balanced for the mixture of sunlight and skylight

TABLE 3

LIGHT SOURCES AND COLOR TEMPERATURES

Source	Color Temperature (°K)
3200 K lamps	3200
Mazda CP	3380
No. 4 Photoflood	3415
No. 2 Photoflood	3430
No. 1 Photoflood	3450
Fluorescent white	3500
Daylight-blue Photoflood	4800
Morning sunlight plus skylight	2000–5000
White flame arc	5000
High intensity sun arc	5500
Sunlight (slightly overcast)	5800
Midday sunlight plus skylight	6100
Fully overcast	6500
Clear skylight alone	12000–26000

TABLE 4

COLOR-BALANCE TEMPERATURES AND SPEEDS, 16 MM. AND 35 MM. FILM

Sixteen Millimeter					
	Kodachrome			Ansco Color	
	Commercial	Daylight	Type A	Daylight	Tungsten
Color-balance temperature (°K)	3200	6100	3450	5000–6000	3200
Speed (ASA)					
Daylight	10	10	—	10	—
Tungsten	16	—	16	—	12

Thirty-five Millimeter			
	Technicolor 3-strip & Monopack	Kodak Type 5247	Ansco Color Type 735
Color-balance temperature (°K)	5400	6000	5400
Speed (ASA)	10	12	10

which falls on frontlighted subjects from approximately two hours after sunrise to two hours before sunset. High-intensity arcs fitted with straw-colored Y1 filters give a temperature of 5400° K, which is correct for Technicolor.

If mismatching is suspected, the color temperature of the light source must be read. Several color-temperature meters have recently been introduced which do not depend on color matching by eye when taking a reading. Notable among these is the Spectra meter, which measures with a photocell the radiation at both ends of the spectrum by means of red and blue filters which may alternately be slid over the cell. The latest type of Spectra meter enables a third measurement to be taken in the green region. Both meters are normally calibrated in degrees Kelvin, and give direct readings without calculation.

The least perceptible differences in color temperature do not, however, correspond to an equal number of degrees Kelvin throughout the scale. Much greater uniformity is obtained by substituting a reciprocal Kelvin unit, which may conveniently be arrived at by dividing Kelvin temperatures into 1,000,000. The resulting unit, called a Mired (micro-reciprocal degree) is expected to come into general use for color-temperature measurement. The maximum color-temperature tolerance throughout the usable scale is approximately ±5 Mireds, which corresponds to ±50°. K at tungsten temperatures, and ±200° K at daylight temperatures.

With the increasing use of light sources having outputs confined to a few narrow bands in the spectrum, the whole conception of color temperature —based on blackbody radiation—is beginning to undergo revision in its application to photography. Even daylight does not correspond closely to the light from a blackbody source, while fluorescent, mercury-vapor and concentrated-arc lamps bear little or no relation to it. What may eventually take the place of color temperatures in photography is a triple index based on the energy of a light source in the three primary-color regions of the spectrum. Until such an index is standardized, however, discussion must proceed in terms of color temperatures, but the qualifications mentioned above should be constantly borne in mind.[14]

---

[14] A simple and excellent statement of the color-temperature theory, which does full justice to many of its complexities, is published by the manufacturers of the Spectra meter, the Photo Research Corp., Burbank, California. Three members of the same corporation, Frank F. Crandell, Karl Freund, and Lars Moen have more recently published a paper of far-reaching importance, "Effects of Incorrect Color Temperature on Motion Picture Production," *JSMPTE*, July, 1950, pp. 67–87. The authors propose, on the basis of energy distribution, a Spectral Distribution Index (SDI) for light sources, a Spectral Sensitivity Index (SSI) for film emulsions, and a Spectral Absorption Index (SAI) for filters, which closely relate to the most recent thinking in color sensitometry. By the bold introduction of a decibel scale, the new ratio units are made directly additive and subtractive. See also O. E. Miller, "Color Temperature: Its Use in Color Photography," *JSMPTE*, Apr., 1950, pp. 435–444.

If the light source is incorrectly balanced to the film in the camera, it will, in general, contain excessive red (giving too "warm" a reproduction of color), or excessive blue (giving too "cold" a color reproduction). Correction can be accomplished by removing some of the excess color, adding some of the deficient color, or (if the source is not fluorescent) altering its supply voltage.

The first alternative is the commonest. If the color temperature of a lamp is too low (excess red), a blue filter will eliminate some of the red radiation, thus raising the color temperature as required, but at the same time greatly lowering the efficiency of the lamp. If the color temperature is too high (excess blue), a pinkish-yellow filter will eliminate some of the blue radiation, which is again what is required. Extreme corrections are very wasteful of light. For instance, the filter required to correct a 5-kilowatt spot for a certain daylight color film absorbs about 60 per cent of the light passing through it. When it is recalled that color film is already five times slower than the black-and-white emulsion most commonly used in studio shooting, it can be seen that the efficacy of the 5-kilowatt light (in black-and-white terms) is brought down to about 400 watts in terms of daylight-balanced color.

If all the light sources are equally mismatched to the film in the same direction, it is simpler to place a single correcting filter over the lens. (The loss of luminous efficiency will be exactly the same.) Such filters are at present employed as *batch* filters to match different rolls of commercial Kodachrome film.

The smaller production unit is therefore well advised to keep to tungsten and Photoflood types of film. The only really satisfactory artificial illuminant for daylight film is the arc, which has a very high luminous efficiency but draws large amounts of direct current because it is not available in small sizes. A fairly small set will require 700 to 800 amperes for color lighting—not an impossible current when drawn from most AC lines, but seldom obtainable in DC except at studios having their own generators.

Color temperature is also dependent on voltage. It is a familiar experience that a break in a power line causes the house lights to turn yellow and finally red before they go out. This drop in color temperature is measurable for voltage changes as small as one volt, the change being about 10° K. A change in color rendering resulting from a change in color temperature of 100° K is just noticeable in Kodachrome,[15] so that the voltage latitude is only 10 volts. Periods of heavy load, such as the early evening, should therefore be avoided for color shooting, if current is to be drawn off the city supply, since drops of 10 volts are often exceeded. Other sources of lowered color temperature are blackened bulbs, greenish glass in spotlight lenses, and incorrectly adjusted arcs.

---

15 A figure of 250° K has been quoted for three-strip Technicolor, because of its greater controllability in processing, and because the percentage is smaller on a higher balance temperature.

While limited use can be made of a set of lamps having different color temperatures, the film being balanced to the average temperature by filters, it is much better practice to decide on the color temperature first, and then arrange for all the lamps to operate at this temperature, with or without a lens filter according to the film color-balance temperature.

All these considerations apply only when standard or normal reproduction is expected—that is, accurate rendering of color within the limitations of present subtractive processes. To produce special effects, the color temperature may be intentionally raised or lowered. Raising the temperature gives a cold, hard, and bluish rendering to a scene; lowering it, a golden, warm, and ruddy tone. To these changes, the color film will respond much more sensitively than does the eye, so that there is plenty of scope for experiment in the non-literal use of color.

The shooting of exteriors presents fewer difficulties. The colors of the landscape have been seen under the aspect of all weathers and all seasons, shifting constantly and indeed never having the same appearance twice. Thus a faulty color rendering is much more likely to escape notice when it comes from the field than from the studio. Faces, however, which are likely to have appeared in other scenes lit by carefully controlled artificial light, will be recognized as having altered if their appearance is not made constant by the control of light out of doors. Reflectors are almost indispensable for exterior color shooting, and a judicious use of "cold" and "warm" reflectors (usually silver and gold respectively) will help to reduce an excessive color temperature by any desired amount. Increase of color temperature, when necessitated by the lowness of the sun, cannot usually be brought about by reflectors. Booster lights must be set up, and they of course draw current.

LEVEL AND CONTRAST OF LIGHT

Owing to the low sensitivity of color film, a very large amount of light is called for on the set. Assuming a uniform lens setting of T-2.3, the incident illumination required for Kodachrome (Type A) is 430 foot-candles, for British Tricolour 460 foot-candles, for Kodachrome (commercial) 650 foot-candles, and for Technicolor (three-strip and monopack) 700 foot-candles. Thus there is little more than half a stop difference between the fastest and slowest of these processes.

It is in the application of this light to the subject that the skillful cameraman is singled out. He knows that the brightness range of color film is much less than that of black and white, and should never exceed 20 to 1. Because of the varying reflectances of objects in the scene, the illumination ratio must not be nearly as great as the brightness ratio; a maximum of 4 to 1 is recommended, with 2 or 3 to 1 preferred for Kodachrome or Ansco Color duplication, which results in an unintended building up of contrast. In Technicolor, ratios of 8 to 1 or even higher may be used, since the printing process is under much better control. The illumination ratio is most easily measured by the reflecting-card method (see chapter iii), the key light and the fill-in light being switched on separately, and separate readings taken with a light meter. Out of doors, the card should be held well within the shadow reading.

This low degree of lighting contrast tends toward flat lighting, which the black-and-white cameraman takes the greatest pains to avoid. But the absence of color differentiation necessitates a modeling in light and shade created out of high brightness contrasts. The presence of color is itself a modeling factor, and therefore less contrast is needed to make objects stand out sharply. Obviously, where a choice of colors is possible, it can help greatly to produce this effect. Moreover, the more familiar the cameraman becomes with a color process, the more successful will be the liberties he can take. Several feature pictures (notably *Henry V*) have made highly dramatic use of brightly lighted figures moving against a background of velvety darkness, in which all the detail that could have been expected was to be seen.

The major recent improvements in color film have been, not toward increasing speed, but toward decreasing contrast. The effect of overexposure, whether over-all, or because of excessive local brightnesses, is to wash out color so that faces become white and chalky, and grass and trees appear bleached. General underexposure, or excessive shadow density, fills in dark areas and gives them a blue or bluish-green cast which is both unnatural and unpleasant. Films like Daylight and Type A Kodachrome were designed for the amateur who was interested only in direct reversal, and expected his original color film to project in brilliant color and contrast. As originals for making dupes, these materials gave an overcontrasty rendering, and for professional use they have been replaced by films like commercial Kodachrome, which are developed to a low contrast and do not give an accurate color rendering when projected. Duping, however, brings the contrast up to the proper figure, so that a *first-generation print,* as it is called, has as good a color rendering as original Kodachrome Type A, and a much better rendering of the brightness scale.

It is essential to shoot with lower contrast film materials in professional film making if results are to approach the standards set by the studios, using processes in which color contrast has long been accurately controlled.

LATER STAGES OF COLOR PRODUCTION

All the studio techniques which the producer is accustomed to ask for can now be realized in color. Process projection, trick photography, optical effects, though more difficult to contrive than their black-and-white counterparts, have all been achieved by the great resources thrown into color development.

The small unit, however, confined to 16 mm. color processes, often finds that even the necessities of production can only be secured with difficulty or delay. While editing with color prints is highly desirable for color matching and continuity, these prints cost four times as much per foot as 35 mm. black-and-white prints, or almost twice as much when the longer running time per foot of 16 mm. film is taken into account. For this reason, many units are forced to work with black-and-white prints, and do not see their color continuity until the film is finished.

Optical effects made on an optical printer also tend to be unsatisfactory in 16 mm. color. Since an effect is made on a piece of film one stage removed from the original, which in turn is a stage away from the release print, prints from opticals are called *second-generation prints*. These are apt to suffer very marked degradation of color. Fades and dissolves on Kodachrome and Ansco Color are therefore made by other processes. Chemical fades (made by immersing the camera original in a special solution) provide good quality, and can be washed off without damaging the film. For dissolves, the release prints are printed from A and B rolls, the optical effects being put in by fades during each printing, as described in chapter vi. This technique is not applicable to wipes. In order to speed up release printing, the A and B printing is sometimes made to result in a special color- and contrast-corrected dupe, from which the release prints are subsequently run off in a continuous printer. Owing to the cost and complication of these monopack effects, producers tend to avoid them wherever possible.

These objections do not apply to three-strip camerawork; but the producer of a 16 mm. monopack picture does well to work within the limitations of his process, and get satisfactory even if necessarily simple results.

Other aspects of production in color do not differ essentially from those met with in black and white. It is the difference between 35 mm. and 16 mm. techniques which now comes to the fore, for color has made such great strides that it almost monopolizes 16 mm. production.[16]

CHARACTERISTICS OF 16 MM. PRODUCTION

The 35 mm. standard of production and distribution had been established for more than thirty years before its technical supremacy was even remotely challenged by 16 mm. film. It is not surprising that the pretensions of this small competitor were at first greeted with ridicule. Critics complained that

[16] Laboratory practice in relation to color undergoes constant advance and change. Modern sensitometric techniques are well described in the Society of Motion Picture and Television Engineers' Color Sensitometry Subcommittee Report, "Principles of Color Sensitometry," *JSMPTE*, June, 1950, pp. 653–724, which also contains an extensive bibliography.

the screen image it provided was small and shaky; sound was either absent or unintelligible; projector breakdowns were so common that operators needed to be—though they seldom were—expert mechanics and electricians. Fifteen years ago, these criticisms may have been justified. In any event, the bad reputation they created stuck fast, and even today 16 mm. equipment and techniques are often patronizingly regarded in the larger production centers as little better than convenient makeshifts for classroom and vocational training.

The great advances in the possibility of securing professional quality in 16 mm. were due to the work of a few pioneers who held doggedly to their belief that the early ills of substandard production and projection were not inherent in the small size of the film, but could be eradicated by patient research into film fundamentals. Now that their findings have become common knowledge, it is the task of film makers and technicians to put them into wider practice.

Even today, the average 16 mm. projection in the field is more likely than not to be unsatisfactory. A recent survey of schools throughout the country disclosed that the schools least enthusiastic about the future of classroom films were those which had used them most; a part of their complaints must have been due to the technical troubles they had had.

The average moviegoer (and the movie maker can seldom escape being a moviegoer also) is not aware of the process of receiving impressions by film. The mechanical obstacles to his enjoyment have long ago been removed by a considerate industry. Lapped in the comfort of a resilient chair, his head automatically tilted to the angle of the screen, he is bathed in a melodious current of sound, and basks in the light of the images which flow past his eyes in liquid succession. Were he suddenly transplanted to an average 16 mm. screening, the moviegoer would be rudely shocked. He would find that the seat beneath him had become rigid and unyielding, and that he must dodge to and fro to get a glimpse of the screen past a moving sea of heads—a screen which dimly gives back an image fuzzy at the edges and lacking three-quarters of the photographic quality he has come to expect as a right. The sound, even if well recorded on 16 mm. film, must compete with the echoes which chase it from corner to corner of the room; and the light which leaks in from badly curtained windows does its best to blot out what little of the original picture actually reaches the screen.

These defects in reproduction are frictions to the receiving of information by film. If textbooks were dirty and torn, so that reading became a jigsaw puzzle of bits of paper; or if radio transmission were so inadequate that only the most patient ear could separate the program from the static, there would be some excuse for the poor performance of 16 mm. film.

The tools of improvement are now available. They must be put to work in the original 16 mm. production, in the design of new cameras and pro-

jectors, in the training of teachers and discussion-group leaders, in the utilization of film by people who, with the best will in the world, do not know how
to use what they have, let alone make the most of the new films and ideas
which the next ten years should bring forth.

The first thing the film maker must do is to dispel from his mind the notion
that, because 16 mm. film was created for the amateur, its use is straightforward and its techniques easy to understand and apply. Nothing could be
further from the truth. A 16 mm. frame is only one-quarter the area of the
35 mm. frame—only one-tenth of a square inch in size. Yet it must often be
projected on screens of eighty square feet, with good definition and contrast
and an over-all brilliance adequate to compete with far more stray light than
would be tolerated in a commercial theater. Sound is recorded on a track less
than one-tenth of an inch wide, traveling at less than half the speed of 35 mm.
film; nevertheless, it is expected to contain and faithfully reproduce all the
variations of volume and frequency in the original scene, which may have been
a whispered dialogue or the full sweep of a symphony orchestra.

The projector which must work these wonders on film cannot be a heavy
and rigid machine maintained at regular intervals by an expert, and daily
tended by a skilled operator. It must be portable and compact, strong enough
to be jolted all day over rough country roads, yet light enough to be lifted
onto a table by a school teacher. The loudspeaker which must render every
nuance of sound under varying acoustic conditions long brought under proper
control in the theater, cannot be designed as the engineer would wish, for it
too must be light and compact, and must match the case containing the rest
of the equipment.

In every department of 16 mm. procedure, there are the same contrasts between what is expected and what can be provided. Consequently, 16 mm.
production is extremely exacting. It demands work of the highest standard.
It calls for equipment built to minute tolerances, tolerances even closer than
can be permitted in 35 mm. practice. It is not a simplification of those practices, but rather an attempt to pack exactly the same capacities into much
smaller space. No one would suppose that, skill for skill, it was easier to build
a wristwatch than a grandfather clock. In film, however, the small and the
simple are commonly equated. The tradition of the amateur has died hard,
and it may yet be some time before 16 mm. techniques gain the attention and
respect they deserve.

The following sections discuss the differences between 16 mm. and 35 mm.
practice—differences which stem in part from the amateur beginnings of 16
mm. film, in part from alterations in process and equipment necessitated by
the narrower gauge of film. Many of them have already been embodied in a
series of American Standards which, though not obligatory, act as reference
points so authoritative that the industry as a whole gladly conforms to them.

World War II gave a great impetus to 16 mm. film as an instrument of the armed forces, and led to the setting up of the Z52 Committee of the American Standards Association on Photography and Cinematography. The work of the committee resulted in the issue of an important additional series of standards—the American War Standards—which remained effective until the war ended. The experience gained with these standards is now under review by committees of the A.S.A., which are determining the standards to be adopted, and the standards to be revised or dropped.

16 MM. FILM: REVERSAL

One of the most striking differences in 16 mm. technique lies in the film itself. For sixty years, 35 mm. film has been exclusively developed by the negative-positive process, in which the original film is a negative. These two terms—"original" and "negative"—have therefore come to appear synonymous, and the unconscious carry-over of this identity to 16 mm., where it seldom applies, is the cause of a great deal of muddled thinking.

It was more than twenty-five years ago that the Eastman Kodak Company introduced a new 16 mm. film which was to revolutionize amateur film making —*reversal* film. By achieving a positive image on the same piece of film on which the camera had recorded a negative, the company spared the amateur the cost of a second piece of film, and of the printing and developing processes otherwise needed to form the positive image. The original, in short, was not a negative. It had become a positive in the Kodak laboratory; the price of processing was now included in the cost of the stock, so that the manufacturer accepted responsibility for the final product. This difference of technique held fast with the introduction of color. Indeed, reversal became even more indispensable because of the high cost of color printing. It is true that the amateur was thus encouraged to project his original until destruction overtook it, and that in this way many millions of feet of original film—some of it of priceless documentary and historical value—have been ruined. But this cannot be laid at the door of the film manufacturer. A duplicating process has been available for many years, which, at a cost, would have preserved all that was valuable. It remains true that the professional who would shudder at the idea of projecting his uncut negative, thus risking irreparable damage to it, will project his reversal original with but the smallest misgiving. Unconsciously, he feels that a positive must be a duplicate and therefore replaceable.

The reversal process makes ingenious use of the photographic emulsion and the machinery of development (figure 9-9). The first stage of development results, as usual, in a negative image—that is, the exposed grains of silver halide are reduced to opaque silver, so that the greatest brightnesses in the

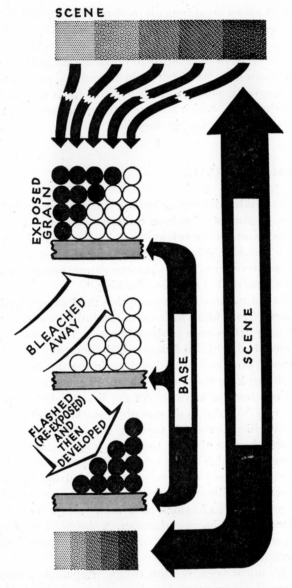

Fig. 9-9. Reversal development. The same piece of film followed through the stages of reversal development. The greatest depth of exposed grains (shown diagrammatically as four) corresponds to the greatest densities, and vice versa.

image formed by the camera lens correspond to the greatest densities on the negative. If, now, the surface of the emulsion—just developed and still in darkness—is visualized with its negative silver image, it will be seen that there is a complementary image formed of the grains of silver halide which have not been exposed and therefore not reduced to silver by the developer. In areas where the greatest number of grains has been exposed, the number of unexposed grains will be least, and vice versa. Thus this second image will be in tonalities opposite to those of the first. In other words, it will be a positive, and will correctly render the lights and shades of the original scene.

To form this positive image, the negative image must first be destroyed. It is therefore *bleached,* a process which reduces the opaque silver image to a transparent compound of silver. The film is then exposed to light for a period long enough to expose fully all the silver-halide grains left unexposed in the exposure of the original scene. This new image is then developed in the usual way. Thus, reversal development adds three processes to negative development: a bleach, a reëxposure, and a second development. Reversal has two important consequences: low latitude and fine grain. The danger of getting too great a highlight density as a result of the second exposure is obviated by the use of an extremely thin emulsion layer. This reduces exposure latitude, since the presence of many layers of grains in negative emulsions acts as a "cushion" which increases the usable range of exposure. And because the reversal process, with its two images, uses up almost all the sensitive grains in the emulsion, there is little latitude of development.

On the other hand, reversal film gives an image of excellently fine grain. The most sensitive grains in an emulsion tend to be the largest, and these are therefore the grains exposed in the original exposure, developed, and bleached out. The second exposure then forms an image in the smaller remaining grains —that is, a fine-grain image. In reversal color processes, this second image is formed in dyes which are altogether grainless, the black silver image having been bleached out.

Thus, black-and-white reversal film forms an excellent picture-recording medium. Instead, however, of release printing by a further reversal, correct practice is to make a fine-grain dupe negative from the original, and print from the dupe negative. The alternative plan of shooting on 16 mm. negative and printing directly is much less satisfactory, in spite of the saving of an intermediate stage. Graininess will be worse, and scratches and splices more visible. The deterrent to black-and-white reversal shooting has been the difficulty of getting quick and reliable processing service, even in the largest cities. It is to be hoped that this will be remedied soon.

Since original shooting in reversal film is normally followed by negative-positive duplication, and since an optical type of reversal can be applied to sound track, there is a great variety of ways of making every 16 mm. picture.

It is therefore imperative, at the beginning of each production, to detail the stages that the sound and picture films shall go through from the original in the camera to the combined release print. In the absence of a clear plan, the film may travel through unnecessary duplicating stages, with much loss of quality and accumulation of needless expense.

It is also important when starting a picture to make sure that the stock is footage numbered. Commercial Kodachrome is supplied already numbered in the same way as 35 mm. black-and-white negative. Other types of Kodachrome, however, are only supplied footage-numbered on request—another relic of amateur status—and delay is often experienced in getting the numbered film from the factory. Alternatively, the original and the print may be footage numbered after development from a corresponding starting frame. Even if this numbering has to be done by hand, it will save time in the long run because of the difficulty of matching the small 16 mm. frames by eye, and locating the needed shots among thousands of feet of unmarked film.

The perforation system for 35 mm. film was adopted more than fifty years ago, and was designed for film which expanded and shrank under varying conditions of temperature and humidity much more than the film in use today. Consequently, film needed to be repositioned in the camera and the projector by frequent engagement of sprocket teeth with perforations, and eight perforations were allotted each frame. Sixteen mm. silent film has only two perforations per frame, and one of these is eliminated on film designed for sound or sound and picture printing. The pitch, or distance from center to center of perforations, is 187 mils in 35 mm. film and 300 mils in 16 mm. film.

Camera film is usually provided with perforations along both sides for which most cameras (except those recording single-system sound) are designed. On the other hand, editing equipment—unless exclusively intended for the amateur—is furnished with single-sided sprocket teeth, so that it will accept film with single or double perforations. It will be evident that single-toothed sprockets will take both silent and sound film, whereas double-toothed sprockets will take only silent film. Disregard of this simple fact can lead to a number of expensive mistakes.

All substandard film (16 mm. and 8 mm.) is without exception made on a cellulose-acetate safety base which burns slowly and controllably like heavy paper. Acetate film has physical characteristics different from those of nitrate film, which affect its treatment in the lab and subsequent storage.

AMERICAN STANDARDS ON 16 MM. FILM

16 mm. silent film: Cutting and perforating negative and positive raw stock
. . . . Z22.5–1947
16 mm. sound film: Cutting and perforating negative and positive raw stock
. . . . Z22.12–1947

Motion picture safety film Z22.31–1946

PROPOSED AMERICAN STANDARD

Winding of 16 mm. sound film Z22.75–1949

[All American Standards and Recommended Practices may be obtained from the American Standards Association, 70 East 45th Street, New York 17, N.Y.]

THE 16 MM. CAMERA

The 16 mm. camera must be designed to the same limits of accuracy as its 35 mm. counterpart. It requires the same adjustments and the same skill in operation. Almost everything contained in the chapter on the camera applies with equal force to 16 mm. and 35 mm. cameras.

Differences of design flow chiefly from the smaller width and mass and lower running speed of the 16 mm. film, which result in a lighter and smaller camera. Since 400 feet of 16 mm. film runs as long as 1,000 feet of 35 mm. film, 400-foot magazines are the largest in common use.

Insufficient care has been exercised in the manufacture of amateur cameras to secure accurate placing of the camera aperture in relation to the film perforations. Since the perforations serve to position the film in the projector, an alteration in the placing of the camera aperture will result in a visible line at the top or bottom of the screen. If the whole picture has been shot with a single camera, a single framing adjustment on the projector will correct this error; but if, as more often happens, shots from several cameras have been intercut, an objectionable change in the framed area will occur. In fact, the picture will jump up and down from one shot to another. It is therefore important, when shooting a picture with cameras designed for the amateur (among which the Kodak Cine Special must be included), to have the aperture checked and corrected by the manufacturer to the new standard.

A common failing of 16 mm. cameras, including many of the latest types, is noisiness. Designers have apparently been content if all other features of the mechanism proved satisfactory—and have left it to the user to do his best in thinking out and building a soundproof blimp. Considering the very large amount of sync dialogue shot with 16 mm. cameras, this treatment by the manufacturer is rather cavalier. One of the best professional 16 mm. cameras, expensive enough as it is, requires the purchase of a thousand-dollar blimp before it is fit for sound recording. Another manufacturer has consistently refused to design a blimp for his machine on the grounds that it is already noiseless—an assertion easily contradicted by placing the ear some six feet from it when it is running. What is needed badly by 16 mm. film professionals is an advanced camera with the best type of through-the-lens viewfinding, self-blimped, and light enough not to risk confusion with a 35 mm. machine when it is necessary for the assistant to carry it on his shoulder from one set-up to another.

EDITING 16 MM. FILM

Most editors who have been trained on 35 mm. find 16 mm. film most inconvenient to cut, and refer to it contemptuously as "spaghetti." Editors who have never had experience with anything else get along as best they can without undue complaint. The truth is that the 16 mm. frame has to be looked at very closely to see what is on it, whereas the 35 mm. image can be recognized at some distance. This makes 16 mm. shot selection much more difficult. It might be thought that the standard moviola would be so designed that the image was brought up to 35 mm. viewing size, which is certainly none too big. But in fact all 16 mm. moviolas built before 1949 provide a wretchedly small image, tiring to the eyes and requiring great concentration to look at.[17] The many types of handviewer which are available on the market give a somewhat bigger image, but it is difficult to move the film steadily through any of these machines and hence difficult to gain the necessary "feel" of a shot for accurate dynamic cutting.

Other cutting equipment—synchronizers, bins, rewinds, etc.—is available in good designs, and "mixed" 35 and 16 mm. (sound and picture) production

[17] The latest model produced by the Moviola Company employs a greatly magnified image and is an improvement on anything hitherto available, but it is not yet in widespread use.

is now quite practical. Much of this equipment has been adapted from the 35 mm. size, and costs almost as much.

Owing to the popularity of the reversal process, the workprint presents the editor with a problem which is unknown in 35 mm. practice. If a picture is to be shot in monopack (Kodachrome or Ansco Color), the ideal solution is a color duplicate matching the original scene as closely as possible. (Note that a low-contrast color original film is not intended to match the original scene, but that a timed duplicate from it should do so.) However, as we have seen, a workprint of this kind is twice as expensive as a 35 mm. black-and-white print per minute of running time; moreover, timed color prints are produced very slowly owing to lack of printing and processing facilities. Various compromises reduce the cost but leave the critical editor unsatisfied. A one-light (untimed) color duplicate retains the advantage of color, is slightly cheaper and quicker to make, but of course lacks the fine balance of the timed print which is a commonplace of 35 mm. black-and-white production. Less cost and less wasted time, but less general satisfactoriness result from a black-and-white reversal print from the color original. This print must be made in the color laboratory, since reversal development is not normally procurable elsewhere. Lowest on the scale comes the simple black-and-white negative, a one-process step from the color original which can be carried out in the producer's own laboratory. This step on the scale can be further divided: the negative may be printed on a negative emulsion and developed in a negative bath, so that it will reproduce gradations of brightness on the black-and-white scale, albeit in reversed tonalities; or it may be printed on positive stock and developed in a positive bath, from which it will emerge as a contrasty rendering which has lost all its original softness.

The methods of producing workprints from 16 mm. monopack color originals, listed in descending order of cost, lost time, and satisfactory rendering of the original, can be conveniently grouped as follows:

1. Timed color duplicate
2. One-light (untimed) color duplicate
3. Black-and-white reversal print or print from negative
4. Negative print on negative stock, developed in negative developer
5. Negative print on positive stock, developed in positive developer

Negative workprints are difficult to edit, since they are so far removed from the original. They should be avoided whenever possible.

In all these methods of making workprints the utmost care must be taken to avoid damaging the color original by careless printing. Step printers, in particular, frequently cause scratching, as do continuous printers operated at high speed.

When the sound and picture workprints have been cut, and the editor needs interlock projection to screen them in synchronism, he may run into difficulties, unless his own organization is equipped for direct 16 mm. recording and re-recording. This is because 16 mm. sound equipment is still uncommon, even in major production centers. Three solutions are available: (*a*) Install a complete 16 mm. recording and re-recording system, (*b*) record the sound track on 35 mm. and use combined 16 and 35 mm. editing and sound equipment, the latter being somewhat commoner than all-16 mm. sound, or (*c*) adapt a standard 16 mm. sound projector for *double-headed* (separate sound and picture) projection.

The Bell and Howell projector is fairly simple to adapt to double-headed projection, requiring two additional reel arms, one of them with a take-up drive. This arrangement is cheap and convenient, provides a much larger picture than a moviola (but takes longer to thread), and does not interfere with the use of the machine as a normal projector.

MATCHING 16 MM. ORIGINALS

The requirements for matching 16 mm. originals are essentially no different from those discussed in chapter vii. Indeed, because of the small area of the 16 mm. frame, blemishes are even more noticeable, and the cutter cannot afford to relax any of the precautions familiar to her through cutting 35 mm. film. One additional problem presents itself. Because of its amateur origins, 16 mm. film is still often supplied without footage numbers, a situation which could be remedied overnight by a simple decision of the film manufacturers.

This means that the negative cutter must resort to "matching by eye," a technique familiar even to 35 mm. cutters, since shots are sometimes accidentally printed without numbers. Matching by eye means aligning two shots (one in the workprint, the other in the original) by a simple identity of the visual images, without guidance of edge numbers. The 16 mm. frame, less than half an inch wide and a third of an inch high, is difficult enough to examine in detail, even in the cutting room where it can be freely handled. In the negative room, handling must be kept to a minimum, yet frames of original and frames of workprint must be precisely matched to one another.

Matching by eye is sometimes called matching by action. It is clear that if a single frame, F, in the original can be matched with a single frame, F′, in the workprint, then $F + 1, F + 2 \ldots$ will match with $F' + 1, F' + 2 \ldots$, and the shots will coincide throughout their length. Thus the cutter need only look for the frame which is easiest to match. Where action is most rapid, there is the greatest displacement of an object between one frame and the next. Hence the cutter picks out a sharp frame in the workprint in a piece of fairly rapid action, slides the original along it (she has already picked out the original shots by eye from the camera material), and fairly easily identifies the piece of action. Then a few moments' close scrutiny enables her to pin down the exact matching frame, and a glance along the shots before and after this frame reveals whether the cycle of movement is indeed identical.

But suppose there is no rapid action in the shot. At the other extreme, where the shot is wholly stationary, it does not matter where it is matched, provided that the photographic quality and physical condition of the film are uniform. (The first and last frames of shots are always thrown out because of camera flashes—uneven exposure as the camera gets up to speed and slows down.) In between is the most difficult type of shot to match, that in which the movement is slow and affects only a very small part of the frame, like a girl's smile in a mid shot. It may take ten to fifteen minutes to match such a shot by eye, as contrasted with ten to fifteen seconds by edge number.

Matching originals by eye also places a great strain on the cutter's eyesight, since her work is so concentrated and close.

16 MM. SPLICING

Thirty-five mm. and 16 mm. splices have one important point of difference; 35 mm. splices normally are not visible when the film is projected, 16 mm. splices are always visible. Indeed, to the critical eye, the presence of visible splices is one of the most objectionable features of 16 mm. production, since a single reel is likely to contain between eighty and two-hundred splices, which, appearing on the screen every few seconds, distract the eye from the effect of cutting, which is due to the juxtaposition of images in time without perceptible time boundary. Those 16 mm. prints which have been reduced from 35 mm. originals, or printed from a spliceless 16 mm. dupe negative which has itself been reduced from a 35 mm. master positive, are of course free from this defect.

The tendency has therefore been toward ever narrower 16 mm. splices. These require more skill to make, and are therefore less well adapted to the amateur and his equipment; but this should not be regarded as an obstacle to their standardization. Diagonal splices are particularly objectionable, because of the distance they project into the picture area.

The current American Standard (Z22.25–1941) recognizes the diagonal splice, and calls for a 100-mil width of straight splice, but this width was reduced to a maximum of 70 mils in War Standard Z52.20–1944. An SMPE Committee has the old standard under current review.[18]

18 For an excellent survey of 16 mm. splicing practice, see W. H. Offenhauser, Jr., "Report of the 16 mm. Subcommittee on 16 mm. Film Splices," *JSMPE*, July, 1946, pp. 1–11.

Because of the visibility of 16 mm. film splices, they should be neatly and cleanly made, and carefully painted along the edges when the edited positive or negative is being assembled. Splices in workprints are of less importance, but a strong and neat splice is as quick to make as a weak and untidy splice, if the operator is skilled and the splicer in proper adjustment.

There is an opportunity for an enterprising manufacturer to build a splicer for making 16 mm. splices that are not visible. The maximum width of such a splice would be 16 mils, i.e. the distance between the lower edge of the projector aperture when properly centered on one frame, and the top of the projector aperture on the next frame. Even a 16-mil splice would be visible unless the picture image were properly centered with respect to the perforations.

AMERICAN STANDARDS ON 16 MM. SPLICES

16 mm. film splices—negative and positive—silent film Z22.24–1941
16 mm. film splices—negative and positive—sound film Z22.25–1941

AMERICAN WAR STANDARDS ON 16 MM. SPLICES

Positive and negative splices for processed 16 mm. sound
motion picture film Z52.20–1944

STORAGE OF 16 MM. FILM

Because 16 mm. film is slow burning and therefore not a fire hazard to the buildings in which it is kept, its proper storage is often disregarded. Sixteen mm. film is frequently stacked away in filing cabinets or bookcases, pushed into dusty corners, or piled on tables where the hot sun can strike directly on it. It is folly to spend several thousand dollars on a production, and then take so little care for the preservation of the original and the prints. Film is a much less retentive material than the printed page; but 16 mm. films are seldom given the care of a library of books.

Acetate film is at once more stable than nitrate film and more hygroscopic. Its long-term expectation of life is greater, but in the short term it absorbs or gives off more moisture to bring itself into equilibrium with the surrounding atmosphere. Therefore—apart from the absence of fire hazard—it needs more careful treatment.

The hygroscopic properties of substances are very often forgotten; that is, until the parched earth in the yard begins to crack under the summer sun, or the veneer on a favorite Sheraton cabinet peels off as a result of too much winter enthusiasm for the furnace. In between times, most people think of all materials as they think of metals—as providing an unyielding barrier to the penetration of the atmosphere. A very short observation of film will discourage this idea. Increase the temperature in the drybox of a developing machine, and the film will run off longitudinally curled like an engineer's steel tape; decrease the temperature and the film will be moist, tacky, and limp. Take a reel of film from a dry to a moist atmosphere at 100 per cent relative humidity, and it will gain 10 per cent in weight. Then rewind it tightly and take it back to the dry room; in a few hours the edges of the film will have become bent and warped owing to uneven transference of moisture back to the atmosphere. Some of the alterations are permanent, some temporary. The permanent changes result chiefly from loss of plasticizer, making the film hard and brittle; this is greatly accelerated by high storage temperatures. Temporary changes result from exposure to moderate differences of humidity and temperature. The film slowly takes in and gives out moisture, eventually reaching equilibrium with its surroundings. A lively appreciation of the fact that film is not an inert substance but constantly needs to absorb or release moisture will help the film maker to treat his reels of film more considerately.

Film is best handled at relative humidities (RH) of about 50 per cent and temperatures near 65° or 70° F, because it will then be pliable and easy to wind, clean, and inspect. Storage, on the other hand, requires temperatures as low as 40° to 50° F, the RH being about 40 per cent. The lower temperature will reduce shrinkage, but it is important when removing the film for printing or projection to let it rest for several hours at room temperature and humidity. Printing cold, dry film may photograph electric brush discharges, or static, on the print: projection may result in the film cracking from brittleness.

Color film is particularly susceptible to high temperatures and/or humidities. On location raw stock must never be stored during the summer in hot places like the glove compartments and trunks of cars. Rather, the full batch of film (except what is to be exposed during the day) should be kept in a shaded room or a refrigerator, often available in hotels. After exposure, the film should be sent to the processing plant as quickly as possible, since the latent image in color film deteriorates much more rapidly than in black-and-white.

Briefly summed up, acetate film base is more sensitive to moisture changes than nitrate (and gelatin emulsion is more sensitive than either). Either high temperature or high humidity can damage film permanently; low temperature and low humidity will do it no harm. Therefore, film storage is essentially a summer problem, though steam pipes and damp cellars must be avoided in winter. Air conditioning is useful but expensive. A well-placed vault building with a northerly aspect, ventilated by electric fans and well tree-shaded, will often maintain summer temperatures no higher than 65° F, which film can safely withstand. The greater the difference between conditions of storage and use, the longer must the film be allowed to rest under the new conditions before it is used, so that it may gain equilibrium with its surroundings.

DUPLICATION OF 16 MM. FILM

By duplication is here meant the preparation of intermediate materials from which the final release prints of a picture are made. Duplication is important in 35 mm. practice chiefly as a means to use library material not otherwise available, and also as a protection for the edited picture negative. The release prints themselves are not made from dupes, except in foreign countries. In 16 mm., the practice of release printing from a dupe is becoming increasingly common, as will be explained in a later section.

Today, most 16 mm. productions are shot on monopack color-original materials, and of these materials only two—Kodachrome and Ansco Color—are at present in extensive professional use. It is fortunate that both are very well adapted to the making of black-and-white prints, which cost one-fifth as much as color prints and therefore sell more rapidly in the competitive market. For all their popularity as color processes, Kodachrome and Ansco Color pictures cannot command a wide distribution when they cost $80 to $100 per reel. (The commercial price of a 16 mm. picture is commonly from two to three times its basic lab cost.) The color to black-and-white print process is as follows:

COLOR EDITED POSITIVE→FINE-GRAIN DUPE NEGATIVE→RELEASE PRINT

The chief disadvantage of Kodachrome and Ansco Color shooting lies in the very low speed of the stock, which necessitates heavy and cumbersome lighting equipment. Where portability and low current drain are of first importance, it may be better to shoot in black and white. A reversal material should be chosen on account of its low graininess, and duplication should be carried out as just explained, rather than by reversal, for negative-positive duplicating and printing emulsions are of finer grain than any available reversal materials.

Where color prints are to be made, it is common practice to make them from the original (reversal) positive, an *intermediate* or low-contrast print being taken off as a precaution against damage and stored for possible use as a parent of second-generation prints if the original becomes scratched or worn out. For reasons which will appear later, this procedure is not adequate when the film is expected to run to more than fifty color prints, or when its useful life exceeds one or two years. It is then advisable to make all the prints from intermediates, which in consequence assume a very great importance. Up to the present, owing to the color degradation caused by successive subtractive printings, this procedure has not had the success it deserves; but with the introduction of low-contrast commercial Kodachrome, it may enjoy wider use. If three-color timing, with or without masking techniques, were to become simple and practical, or if imbibition prints could be made from Kodachrome originals via separation negatives, there would be little need to print from the original, which could consequently be preserved against the rapid destruction wrought by step printers and frequent handling.

W. H. Offenhauser has drawn the apt analogy between the lab's duplicating materials and the factory's machine tools—automatic lathes, gear-cutting machines, drop presses, and the like. Just as mass production has proved the economy of an expensive machine tool to turn out a cheap and good product, so the lab has learned the wisdom of using the most expensive duplicating materials and printing equipment—providing only that they are the best.

Film of the finest grain, and usually therefore the slowest printing speed, is required for duplication. Contrast must be checked at every step, for printers, like developing processes, introduce gamma factors. Step-contact printers give the highest picture resolution at present, and in the best labs are also used for release printing, slow as they are. Finally, the lab must be on the watch for the smallest deterioration of its standards anywhere along the line. In 16 mm. practice, the margin between success and failure is very small.

AMERICAN STANDARDS ON DUPLICATION

Negative aperture dimensions and image size for duplicate negatives
made from 35 mm. positive prints Z22.47–1946
Printer aperture dimensions for contact printing 16 mm. reversal
and color reversal duplicate prints Z22.49–1946

16 MM. SOUND RECORDING

Methods of transferring sound to the 16 mm. release print are even more various than the methods of duplicating the picture. Table 5 lists some of the possible techniques.

TABLE 5

METHODS OF TRANSFERRING SOUND TO 16 MM. RELEASE PRINT

Original	Intermediate Processes	16 mm. Print
1. 35 mm. neg. . . . . . (P) . . . 35 mm. pos. . . . . (RP) . . reversal pos.		
2. 35 mm. neg. . . . . (RP) . . pos.		
3. 35 mm. neg. . . . . . (P) . . . 35 mm. pos. (RP) 16 mm. neg. . . . . (P) . . pos.		
4. 35 mm. neg. . . . . . (RP) . . 16 mm. pos. . . . . (P) . . reversal pos.		
5. 35 mm. neg. . . . . . (P) . . . 35 mm. pos. (RR) 16 mm. neg. . . . . . . (P) . . pos.		
6. 35 mm. neg. . . . . . (P) . . 35 mm. pos. (RR) 16 mm. direct pos. . . . (P) . . reversal pos.		
7. 35 mm. neg. . . . . . (P) . . . 35 mm. pos. . . . . (RP) . . reversal pos.		
8. 35 mm. direct pos. . . . . (RP) . . reversal pos.		
9. 16 mm. neg. . . . . . (P) . . . 16 mm. pos. . . . . (P) . . reversal pos.		
10. 16 mm. neg. . . . . . (P) . . . . (P) . . pos.		
11. 16 mm. direct pos. . . . . (P) . . reversal pos.		

NOTE: (P), Print to. (RP), Reduction print to. (RR), Re-record to.

When the film maker starts to pick from this list a process to suit his own special needs, he will probably find himself asking four questions:

a. Does standard 35 mm. re-recording need modification for 16 mm. release printing?

b. How good is direct 16 mm. sound recording?

c. What is a direct positive, and how does it improve 16 mm. sound quality?

d. Should variable-area or variable-density recording be used?

a. Does standard 35 mm. re-recording need modification for 16 mm. release printing?—Thirty-five mm. re-recordings are equalized to give a frequency response which conforms to the Motion Picture Academy's standard reproducing characteristic. This is shown in figure 9-10. The standard was established more than twelve years ago, when many theaters were still fitted with sound equipment manufactured when sound films were first introduced. Consequently, this characteristic results in a rendering of music, speech, and sound much inferior to what can be achieved today on, let us say, a good FM radio set. The industry, however, acting on the old theory of "giving the public what it wants" concludes from the absence of complaints that the public already has what it wants. Hence there is no effective movement toward a bettering of theater sound.[19]

Manufacturers of 16 mm. equipment do not suffer from the handicap of an Academy standard. Already, as we shall soon see, they are producing sound from their tracks which is superior in frequency range to the artificially worsened sounds heard in even the newest and most luxurious theaters. There is therefore no reason why they should be held down to current 35 mm. theater standards.

In the past few years, especially in Hollywood, there has been a tendency to re-record 16 mm. tracks from 35 mm. with a diminished frequency range, emphasizing the band of frequencies between 150 and 3,000 cycles which is chiefly responsible for the intelligibility of speech. Below 100 cycles and above 6,000 cyles there has been an almost complete cutoff. Behind this practice lies the belief that 16 mm. projectors and the places in which they operate are so much worse than movie theaters that 16 mm. film should be regarded simply as a means of conveying intelligence—not as an accurate reproducer of the world of music and sound.

[19] One of the industry's most influential authorities on sound recording, Wesley C. Miller of M.G.M. Studios, has expressed this point of view very clearly. "It is very doubtful," he says, "if frequencies above 7500–8000 cps will be required for a very long time to come, if ever. The industry is fully aware of the fact that this range is limited, but practical considerations over a number of years have all combined to produce what might almost be termed a standardized limited range. We need and want the closest practicable approach to perfection within this range, but we can very safely discard everything above it for commercial purposes. It seems extremely unlikely that public tastes will be so affected by any use of frequency modulation or stereophonic recording as to require much modification of this requirement." *JSMPE*, Jan., 1947, p. 62.

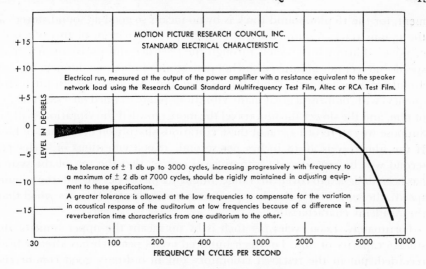

Fig. 9-10. Standard electrical characteristic for a typical 35 mm. theater reproducer system. (Courtesy Eastman Kodak Co.)

Today this attitude is beginning to change. It is realized that no harm is
done by putting on 16 mm. film the full width of the 35 mm. range.[20] In other
words, there should be a 1:1 transfer characteristic from the Academy track
to the 16 mm. track. The Academy standard should therefore be regarded as
the minimum specification to which all 16 mm. projectors should now be
designed.

If, then, 16 mm. recording now stands on an equal footing with 35 mm.
recording, is any good purpose served by recording on 35 mm. and reduction
printing to 16 mm., as has so long been standard practice? Would it not be
better to record direct on 16 mm. film?

b. How good is direct 16 mm. recording?—We have seen that the compactness and portability of 16 mm. camera equipment are often overshadowed
by the size of lights, parallels, dollies, and other shooting complications which
remain a constant factor in production. Sound recording, however, brings
only a microphone and a boom onto the studio floor. If the remainder of the
recording equipment could be kept light, compact, and cheap by 16 mm. design, film production would be valuably simplified.

Direct 16 mm. recording goes a long way to meet these needs. The combining of portability with high quality has been a notable engineering achieve-

---

[20] Recent recommended re-recording practice is detailed in John K. Hilliard, "35 mm.
and 16 mm. Sound-on-Film Reproducing Characteristic," *JSMPE*, Oct. 1949, pp. 389-395.

ment, for the 16 mm. sound track is by no means so good a "sound storer" as the 35 mm. track. A sound track is essentially a long, narrow picture of a train of waves. This picture travels through the recorder and projector at a fixed speed—90 feet per minute (18 inches per second) for 35 mm. film, 36 feet per minute (7.2 inches per second) for 16 mm. film. A sound of high pitch (frequency) will comprise a great many vibrations photographed on a short length of film, and the slower the film travel the more crowded the vibrations will be. Suppose we can record 1,000 of these vibrations sharply on every inch of film. If the film travels at 18 inches per second, 18,000 vibrations or cycles per second will be reproduced—assuming, of course, that the rest of the system has been designed to cover this range. But at 7.2 inches per second (the 16 mm. speed), the same film will only reproduce 7,200 cycles, which is less good than the Academy characteristic.

Fortunately, 1,000 cycles per inch is by no means the upper limit of the storage capacity of film. Fourteen hundred cycles per inch has already been recorded, not in the research laboratory but in ordinary good commercial practice. Multiplying 1,400 by 7.2, we arrive at an upper frequency limit of 10,000 cycles, which is more than enough to cope with the Academy characteristic. The recording and reproducing slits which must "see" each of these very narrow waves separately must necessarily be even narrower than the waves themselves. The width of each 10,000 cycle wave will be 7.2/10,000 inches, or 0.72 mils. The latest 16 mm. recorders achieve a slit width of only 0.11 mils, or less than one-sixth of the 10,000 cycle wavelength. The reproducer slit width is 0.3 mils—less than half this wavelength. In the laboratory, clean images have been obtained with standard 16 mm. film speed at 16,000 cycles, which is above the range of FM transmission, and close to the upper frequency limit of the ear. This represents a recording of 2,200 cycles per inch of film, which is much more than can be recorded per inch of magnetic tape or phonograph-record groove.

The next important characteristic of recorded sound is its *dynamic range:* if a very low sound is recorded so as to be just audible over the background noise, how loud can the loudest sound be made without overloading the system? The dynamic range of the best 16 mm. recordings is about 40 decibels, which is a satisfactory figure for 35 mm. tracks. Because of projector and outside noise in the average 16 mm. screening room, this range is normally reduced to 20 to 25 decibels, as compared with the movie theater range of 30 to 35 decibels.

Finally, all methods of recording introduce distortion. As we shall see in the next chapter, distortion is a veritable hydra, rearing up another head as soon as one has been cut off. Harmonic and intermodulation distortion do not increase appreciably when going down from 35 mm. to 16 mm., but the kind of distortion which results from *flutter*—unsteadiness of motion—is 2½ times as hard to correct. This is because a given speed variation is a larger percentage of a lower film speed, and thus is increased proportionately to the film speed ratio; in other words, 90:36, or 2.5:1. Even so, with precision workmanship, the flutter content of a 16 mm. recording can be reduced below audibility.

In short, sound can now be recorded, printed, and reproduced from 16 mm. film with a fidelity to the original which approaches the best theater 35 mm. reproduction, and markedly surpasses it in frequency range. If the reader finds this surprising, not to say incredible, he should remember that, as a "sound storer," 35 mm. film is being worked far below its maximum capacity. If the film moguls of Hollywood decided to give their audiences a sound quality equal to the best in FM (say, 40 to 15,000 cycles, and 50 decibel dynamic range), the 16 mm. experts would today find it difficult or even impossible to catch up with them. Protected, however, by its Academy characteristic and conservative approach to sound, the industry is content to coast easily along, while 16 mm., pressed to its limit as a "sound storer," forges ahead. The energetic tortoise has passed the indolent hare.

These results are commercially practicable, but they are certainly not commercially common. They call for excellent recording equipment, close processing tolerances, good optical printers, and reproducers built to the same high standards as the recorders. In 35 mm. production these high standards are taken for granted. In 16 mm., where they are even more necessary, progress is blocked by amateur-mindedness.

Thus 16 mm. recording is both practical and desirable for the highest quality of 16 mm. release, and it only remains to discuss the printing methods outlined in table 5 in the light of this conclusion. Up until the start of World War II, when there was no great bulk of 16 mm. printing, reduction of the 35 mm. track was standard procedure (methods 1 and 2). The slow speed of picture-reduction printers led to the development of 16 mm.–16 mm. continuous-contact printers, which encouraged the production of sound tracks by the roundabout method 3, and by method 4. In spite of the number of steps they involve, these two methods have the advantage of replacing the bulky and inflammable 35 mm. printing track with a 16 mm. track. And when optical sound printers were designed, it was possible to compute better lens systems for the narrower width of track.

However, the number of printer stages continued to lead to unnecessary printing losses, especially at the higher frequencies. Each stage, moreover, entailed handling of the sound track, and this, with the intrinsically poorer *signal-to-noise ratio* of 16 mm. tracks, often made residual noises objectionable. A solution to some of these problems was found in a new type of variable-area sound track.

c. What is a direct positive?—Just as a picture negative is an image in tonalities reversed from those of the original scene, which are also those desired, so a sound negative has tonalities reversed from those which produce desirable listening characteristics. It will be seen in the next chapter that variable-area noise reduction is so applied that in the negative it has a minimum effectiveness, and only becomes operative when the transparent areas of the track are printed to black. This was planned to meet the needs of the negative-positive process. A direct positive is simply a track which has the optical characteristics of a positive, generated in the recorder by a mask which makes the track opaque where it would normally be transparent and transparent where it would normally be opaque. This process is sometimes called "optical reversal"; but since the negative never exists and therefore cannot be reversed, the analogy with reversal development is rather misleading.

Reference to table 5 will show that a direct-positive track, and no other, will print a sound track on a reversal positive such as Kodachrome without intermediate processes (methods 8 and 11). This elimination of a complete step results in a marked improvement of quality, and the popularity of 16 mm. reversal materials (both in color and black and white) has encouraged wide use of the direct positive. Most modern 16 mm. sound recorders are therefore adaptable to direct-positive recording, as a rule by the movement of a simple manual control.

d. Variable-area or variable-density recording?—The type of track best suited to 16 mm. recording is widely debated, and a general discussion of the two systems must be deferred to the next chapter. Two special problems arise, however, in the final re-recording of a 16 mm. film—that is to say, the making of the release print sound track.

Variable-area tracks give a higher signal-to-noise ratio than variable-density tracks as at present recorded; in other words, a bigger dynamic range. The difference is about six decibels. Since the dynamic range of 16 mm. film under commercial conditions of print wear, etc. is already strained nearly to the limit, variable-density recording imposes a rather unwelcome limitation. It has one great advantage, however. The sound slits on 16 mm. projectors in the field are frequently out of line; that is to say, the slit, instead of "seeing" the track at an exact right angle to its length, sees it on the skew, as shown in figure 9-11. This is called *azimuth error*. Furthermore, projector slits are not always of uniform width. If a variable-area track is scanned with an azimuth error, distortion is set up, whereas a variable-density track merely suffers a reduced high-frequency response, which is much less disturbing to the ear.

Experimental work is going ahead to raise the signal output of the variable-density track. Meanwhile, early in 1950, the Maurer multiple variable-area track was announced. By subdividing the standard sound-track width into six parallel bilateral tracks, J. A. Maurer has substantially reduced the intermodulation distortion which results from errors in azimuth adjustment and lack of uniformity of the scanning beam of 16 mm. projectors. This device is

not new, having been employed for a
long time in Germany, notably by Tobis-
Klangfilm. However, the German tracks
were subdivided into so many parts that
noise reduction suffered, a fault which
has been obviated by the Maurer track.
Indeed, the exceptionally high signal-to-
noise ratio of 45 decibels is said to be
obtainable in commercial practice. Furthermore, both negative and direct-positive tracks can be recorded with only
minor modification to existing equipment, while processing techniques remain
unchanged. It would thus appear that
one of the greatest obstacles to obtaining
consistent high quality of 16 mm. sound
under commercial conditions has been
successfully overcome.

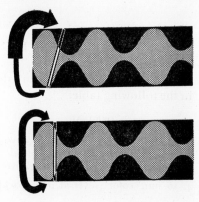

Fig. 9-11. Effect of azimuth
error on variable-area track.
The inclined slit in the upper
diagram "sees" a different
wave shape from the properly
adjusted slit shown in the lower
diagram, thus producing amplitude distortion. (For the sake
of clarity the maladjustment
of the slit is exaggerated.)

We can now briefly sum up the advantages and disadvantages of the 16 mm.
sound recording methods tabulated on
p. 247 above. Methods 1 to 4 have already
been discussed. Method 5 differs from
method 3 only in substituting re-recording for reduction printing; if the 35
mm. negative has a 35 mm. characteristic, this technique gives an opportunity
for altering it. Method 6 takes advantage of the direct positive, but so cir-
cuitously that its chief merits are wasted. Method 8 can be substituted for
method 6 without extra equipment. Method 5 and others of the same kind
are not in common use because recording equipment is scarce and expensive,
and cannot be tied in to release printing. Methods 8 and 11 (direct positive)
are well suited to reversal-positive prints and prints from negatives, respectively, provided that the special recording equipment is available. Method
9 is accepted practice for sound printing a reversal positive in the absence
of a direct-positive sound track. Method 10 is the best way of printing a
nonreversal positive, especially if 1:1 sound printers are available.

This list is by no means exhaustive. Its purpose is merely to suggest the sort
of considerations which the producer of a picture should have in mind when
he plans its release in 16 mm. Sound recording on 16 mm. film is still in its
early stages; in the next few years it may make natural sound and dialogue
available to a host of production units now confined to the straightforward
documentary type of film.

16 MM. RELEASE PRINTING

Most 16 mm. release prints are derived from six types of original, as shown in the following table:

ORIGINAL	16 MM. RELEASE PRINT
1. 35 mm. black-and-white negative	Black and white
2. 16 mm. black-and-white reversal	Black and white
3. 16 mm. black-and-white negative	Black and white
4. 16 mm. color (reversal monopack)	I. Black and white / II. Color
5. 35 mm. color (separation negatives)	Color
6. 35 mm. color (reversal monopack)	Color

The intermediate stages of release printing are outlined below.

BLACK-AND-WHITE RELEASE

1, *a. Reduction printing from the original negative* directly to the release print entails an increase of contrast (due to optical gamma) which often leads to an overcontrasty print. Since there are no intermediate processes, printer losses can be kept fairly small and further reduced by step printing. Step printers, however, impose a heavy wear on the 35 mm. negative. Consequently, the original is used only when the number of prints is very small, e.g., less than 25.

1, *b. Reduction printing from a 35 mm. dupe negative* to the release print increases contrast and wastes quality in extra processes, but does not destroy the original negative. There is little to recommend this method.

1, *c. Reduction printing from a master positive* of low gamma to a fine-grain 16 mm. dupe negative. When this dupe is printed in a step-contact printer to a fine-grain release print emulsion, it gives better results than either of the alternative methods. The graininess is less, the contrast not excessive, and the general appearance of the print is soft and smooth, like a good 35 mm. print. For best quality, however, it is essential to avoid high-speed continuous printers.

2, *a. Reversal printing direct to a reversal release print.* This method is used only for very small orders and by amateurs. The reversal process does not allow adequate control of contrast, is expensive, and does not lend itself to quantity production.

2, *b. Printing to a dupe negative* of fine grain, and step printing to the release prints, gives the best possible quality. Most labs, however, print by this method at much higher speeds on continuous printers.

3. *Printing from a 16 mm. original negative* to the release print is not recommended. See "16 mm. Film-Reversal," pp. 235–237.

4, I-a. Reversal printing direct to a black-and-white reversal release print (as in *2, a* above) is in practice confined to the making of positive workprints in one step, as explained on p. 241. Release prints are seldom or never made in this way.

4, I-b. Printing to a dupe negative, as in *2, b,* enables black-and-white prints of excellent quality to be made from monopack color originals. Again, step-contact printers give by far the best image quality, but are often replaced in commercial labs by continuous printers, which have higher speed.

COLOR RELEASE

4, II-a. Reversal printing direct to the release print is still the commonest method of obtaining color prints. Step printers, however, are unavoidably damaging to film, and 50 prints constitutes the average total before the original becomes unfit for further use. If $6,000 has been spent on a production and must be amortized over so small a number of prints, a cost of $120 must be added to the base price of each print, and will more than double the real cost of the prints of a 2-reel film. Furthermore, many films are in demand over a period of years. Like textbooks, they may not stir up a great initial demand, but as time goes on they become better known, until a gradually expanding market may absorb more prints in the third year of release than in the year when the picture was new. It is shortsighted, therefore, to throw away the whole life of an original in a year, and forfeit all possibility of increasing the number of prints beyond the second year's demands. Yet, until recently, this was the common practice. More prudent advice called for the making of one or more *protection prints,* which were kept in safe storage unprojected, and brought out when the original became irreparably worn, to be made the parents of second-generation prints. Even this practice may not meet the demand for prints of an important picture, since, with n protection prints, it only allows for a total of one more than 49 $(n + 1)$ release prints.

4, II-b. Reversal printing from intermediates. The logical conclusion is to regard the reversal original solely as a parent of intermediate duplicates, from which all the release prints are to be made. Since the original, by assumption, can print on an average 50 intermediates, each of which can in turn make 50 prints, a total of 2,500 release prints becomes possible. This would far exceed the largest foreseeable demand. Of course, not all these prints would be made at once. The original would be kept in a vault under the best possible storage conditions, and only as many duplicates would be struck off from it when it was brought out once a year as were necessary to meet the year's anticipated demand for prints.

This procedure has everything to recommend it except the quality of the prints. Owing to the degradation of color resulting from successive subtractive printings, a second-generation print is markedly inferior to its parent. In a competitive market, it might be harder to sell the poorer print with nothing but logic to support it. The logic belongs to the future; the color everyone can see.

New types of step printer, in which light changes affect the three color layers of the monopack separately by means of three printing lamps and three color filters, promise to give much greater control of color contrast than was available formerly, especially if combined with masks. A conformed dupe produced on such a machine would justify its heavy cost, since prints made from this dupe on a high-speed continuous printer would be better than prints made from the original.

4, II-*c. Imbibition printing from separation negatives.* This process entails no wear on the original, from which separation negatives alone have to be made. The number of prints can be multiplied indefinitely, and for bulk orders the cost falls to less than half that of monopack reversal prints. Kodachrome prints from 35 mm. Technicolor originals were first produced on a bulk scale during the war to satisfy the demands of the armed forces for feature pictures in distant theaters of operation. The Technicolor Corporation has never explained why this technique has not been applied to 16 mm. originals, so that the cost and wear-and-tear of reversal Kodachrome printing might be substantially reduced.

5. *Reduction printing from 35 mm. separation negatives.* Besides the Technicolor system mentioned in the last paragraph, the color-printing processes previously described can be adapted to 16 mm. printing from 35 mm. originals, but are not commonly so used because their quality is seldom as good as that of 16 mm. color originals.

6. *Reduction printing from 35 mm. reversal monopacks.* This process is technically quite feasible, since it merely calls for the production of separation negatives for subsequent printing. However, so few pictures have been shot on 35 mm. monopack that little reduction printing from them has been called for. If 35 mm. Ansco Color gains ground during the next few years, reduction processes adapted to it will doubtless be worked out.

EMULSION POSITION

A confusing feature of 16 mm. prints is that the emulsion must sometimes face the projector lamp, sometimes the lens, if the image is to appear the right way round on the screen. This derives from the many methods of printing which have just been described. The single negative-positive process standardized in 35 mm. practice results in the emulsion always facing the same way; this is known as the standard 35 mm. emulsion position. The emulsion in the camera faces the lens (as it must for direct exposure, except in bipack). When this negative is contact printed, the two emulsions are placed face to face, so that the print emulsion is opposite the negative emulsion. When the print is threaded in the projector, the base must consequently face the lens, and the emulsion face the light.

The normal 16 mm. original is a reversal, or direct positive, and therefore the emulsion position is the same in the camera and projector, that is, emulsion toward the lens. From the amateur custom of projecting the original, this became known as the standard 16 mm. emulsion position. It also results from a reversal original (color or black and white) which is printed to an intermediate negative and thence to a black-and-white print, and again results from an optical reduction from a 35 mm. negative, since in an optical printer the two emulsions face the same way, as contrasted with the contact printer in which they face one another.

Prints with nonstandard 16 mm. emulsion positions (i.e. emulsion toward the light, as in 35 mm.) occur whenever standard 35 mm. printing techniques are used: e.g. 16 mm. original negative to print, and original 16 mm. reversal to reversal. Thus, all first generation 16 mm. color prints have the nonstandard 16 mm. emulsion position.

Changing from one emulsion position to the other requires refocusing the projector; since the sound track must be on the same side of the film as the picture, it too should be refocused. Lack of provision for sound focusing is one of the unsatisfactory features of 16 mm. projectors discussed below.

GREEN FILM

Granted that the method of making release prints has been settled, and the sound and picture both accommodated on the strip of film with a minimum of loss, the film technician's worries are still not over. The processing of 16 mm. film is as yet not at all well standardized, and the end product is often what is euphemistically known in the trade as a *green print*. "The subject of green film," says W. H. Offenhauser, "is ordinarily considered 'delicate'; it is too often explained away rather than investigated." [21] The very term is unfortunate. The film user is encouraged to think that the greenness of film, like the greenness of youth, is an awkward but unavoidable stage on the path to maturity. As a film chatters and scratches its way through the projector, the owner of the print will remark happily, "Oh, it's just a little green; it'll get all right in a day or two," in the same way as he might remark of a friend's son, "Sure, he lost all his money at the horses his first year in college. He's green all right, but he'll get over it." This semantic parallel has little basis in fact. No matter how inevitable the greenness of youth, the greenness of film is easily remedied.

It stems from the amount of moisture which, as we have seen, is soaked up by the pores of the emulsion during development. Unless the film is adequately dried, the emulsion is very soft, and the slightest abrasion, usually

21 "The Commercial Film Laboratory," *JSMPE*, Aug., 1943, p. 177.

caused by the pressure shoes at the film aperture, is enough to peel off some emulsion, which clogs on the aperture plate and strips off more emulsion. Very soon the film is chattering merrily, the perforations are getting strained and torn by the extra tension, and scratches are beginning to appear which rapidly fill with dirt and show as black lines running from top to bottom of the screen. The print is ruined before its life is properly begun.

Prints from the better laboratories do not suffer from greenness; they can be projected immediately without *waxing, lubrication,* or *preservative.* It is the cheap print, produced on equipment never designed for the speeds at which it is run, which has to be treated before it can be projected. Adequate hardening in the fixing bath, thorough washing, and a drybox several times as long as the developing tank, will put an end to the myth of the green print.

AMERICAN STANDARDS ON 16 MM. PRINTING

16 mm. positive aperture dimensions and image size for positive
    prints made from 35 mm. negatives Z22.46–1946
Printer aperture dimensions for contact printing 16 mm. positive
    prints from 16 mm. negatives Z22.48–1946
Method of making intermodulation tests on variable-density
    16 mm. sound motion picture prints Z22.51–1946
Method of making cross-modulation tests on variable-area
    16 mm. sound motion picture prints Z22.52–1946

AMERICAN WAR STANDARDS ON 16 MM. PRINTING

16 mm. motion picture release prints, specification for Z52.3–1944
Leaders, cues, and trailers for 16 mm. sound motion picture
    release prints made from 35 mm. preprint material Z52.19–1944
Leaders and trailers for 16 mm. sound motion picture release
    prints made from 16 mm. original material Z52.31–1945
Method of determining signal-to-noise ratio of 16 mm. sound
    motion picture prints Z52.38–1945
Picture and sound synchronization marks for 35 mm. and 16 mm.
    sound motion picture release negatives and other preprint
    material Z52.53–1945

16 MM. PROJECTION

Of all the needle's eyes through which the 16 mm. film has to pass, the narrowest is the projector. For this the manufacturer has received more than his share of blame. Some of the impossible demands made on his skill have already been touched on. He is expected to provide a screen image as brilliant, as sharp, and as steady as the audience is accustomed to see in its neighborhood movie theater. Yet the picture frame he is given has only one quarter the area of the 35 mm. frame he has to compete with, and the sound travels at less than half the speed. He is not allowed to design a solid, heavily engineered machine like the theater projector; a frail schoolteacher must be able to lift his 16 mm. projector, and it is expected to give the same performance wherever it is set down. Perhaps the designer can hurdle all these fences by some miracle of engineering skill. But the buyer refuses to pay the price. He is affronted when he learns that 50 pounds of engineering in a projector costs half as much as the 3,000 pounds of engineering in his low-priced automobile. During the war, the dream of the hundred-dollar projector was supposed to be on the point of realization; today, with inflation only partly responsible, a standard machine costs five times as much.

Faced with these contradictions, design consists of a long series of compromises. In the future it may be possible to achieve high efficiency with lightness and low cost; but that day is as yet far off. The film maker cannot do better than understand the nature of the compromises, so that he knows what to look for in appraising a new machine, and what to recommend to a new user.

In 1941, a committee of the Society of Motion Picture Engineers, under the chairmanship of J. A. Maurer, issued a report on 16 mm. projection for educational groups which is still the most practical and useful summary available.[22] For the first time, fair and clear procedures were laid down for deciding the relative merits of different projectors in the classroom rather than in the laboratory. As a guide to the manufacturer, provisional specifications were drawn up for an educational projector which should take advantage of the better sound recording and printing then coming into general use.

During the war, the demands on projector design were intensified and carried forward by a committee composed of experts from all branches of the industry and the armed forces, which met to discuss full specifications for a new service 16 mm. projector. The machines then available had been designed before the war for the amateur market, and it was widely felt that much higher standards of strength and performance should be aimed at.

The new specifications were embodied in ASA Z52.1–1944, and accepted by the Army and Navy as JAN-P-49. By the end of the war, not a single projector design had met the specification, but it had profoundly influenced the thinking of the manufacturers. Barring precautions against extreme climatic conditions, which have little relevance in peacetime, JAN-P-49 is still the goal of 16 mm. projector design, and the following discussion is based on the performance it calls for.

MECHANICAL AND ELECTRICAL CONSTRUCTION

Strength of construction.—JAN-P-49 calls for testing under extremes of humidity and temperature, and dropping the projector ten times on a concrete

_____

[22] "Recommended Procedure and Equipment Specifications for Educational 16 mm. Projection," *JSMPE*, July, 1941. (Available as a reprint.) A revised set of recommendations may be issued in 1951 as a result of experience gained during and since the war.

floor from a height of eighteen inches. Though these conditions are not met with in the ordinary life of a projector, mechanical sturdiness is very important, since many machines are likely to be banged around in the course of their travels, and should not need major repair for at least two years. Careful inspection will show whether detachable reel arms are solidly dowelled in position, whether the case is securely fixed together at the corners, and whether the optical system from lamp house to lens has the rigidity needed to hold accurate alignment under stress. The strength of the main castings which carry the projector mechanism and usually protect the amplifier is also of first importance.

Independence of voltage variation.—If time and equipment allow, projectors should be tested for satisfactory running between 129 and 105 volts, the limiting voltages specified for proper running in JAN-P-49. Many projectors run slow at low voltages, and the amplifier volume drops, whereas at high voltages the electrical components overheat after a few hours of continuous operation.

Electrical layout and workmanship.—Very close specifications are set out in JAN-P-49. The average professional user may be content with an inspection of the wiring layout, looking for insecure connections, wires under tension which may break, binding posts which may rattle loose, components supported solely by wiring, and other evidences of bad electrical workmanship. Fuses should be fitted in all primary electrical circuits. The instruction book or the projector case should contain a complete schematic diagram, clearly cross-referenced to markings on the components themselves.

PICTURE PROJECTION

Speed controls.—There has been much discussion on the advisability of incorporating three devices in 16 mm. sound projectors: for stopping and reversing with the lamp on, and for running at silent speed. All these devices are specifically excluded in JAN-P-49; they add complication and they increase the lamp-house temperature. Stop clutches also lead to overheating of the film, which is one of the chief causes of film damage. Moreover, the projected quality of a single 16 mm. frame is so poor as to be almost useless for instructional purposes. Reverse and 16-frame speeds are of some value in projecting silent educational pictures; tests should be made to insure that the diminished or reversed current of air does not cause lamp-bulb distortion. After two hours of continuous forward running, no part of the projector save the top of the lamp house should be more than 50° F above the room temperature.

The film path.—Attention should next be paid to the design of the film path. Nowhere should the picture frame or sound track touch a stationary metal part; sprockets and rollers should be undercut, and the latter should revolve as freely as possible. A stuck roller is a common cause of scratching and of excessive film tension. Absence of end play and lack of friction in rollers are signs of good workmanship throughout the machine.

Reels and take-up.—The projector should be tested with 2,000-foot reels of film mounted on it. Does it become top-heavy at maximum tilt? Is there at least two ounces of take-up tension (easily measured with a letter balance) at the end of the 2,000-foot reel? Is there no more than five ounces of tension at the start? The film rewind should be examined for convenience. Is it necessary to shift reels and spring belts to start rewinding? Is there enough tension to maintain speed on a 2,000-foot reel, which should require less than four minutes (but more than two minutes) to rewind?

The intermittent mechanism.—As a result of projector wear, 16 mm. perforations often become broken. Unlike 35 mm. film, 16 mm. sound film is perforated on one side only, and has only one sprocket hole per frame. The breakage of a single perforation therefore leaves a whole frame without means to propel or position it. JAN-P-49 specifies that the film transport shall be able to pass film with three adjacent broken perforations, and to pass two adjacent broken perforations without resetting of the lower loop. It is important to notice what means, if any, are provided for resetting this loop without stopping the machine.

Film wear.—The sum of all these factors determines the wear which the projector inflicts on the film. This can conveniently be measured by making a 12-foot loop of new and well-processed sound film, supporting it on rollers in its return path and running it through the projector with a 750-watt lamp burning. According to the requirements of JAN-P-49, a well-made splice should last for an average of at least 400 passages through the machine. After 1,000 passages (remaking the splice when necessary), the projected picture and sound should show no deterioration.

Framing.—The framing lever is often awkwardly placed. It should be stiff enough not to creep during projection, but easy and smooth to move.

Screen illumination.—Standard projection lamps have a rating of 750 watts and 1,000 watts, with provision occasionally made for 1,200-watt lamps. More important to the user than the amount of light entering the system is the amount which emerges from it onto the screen, which will differ by the total of losses in the light collector (reflector and condenser lenses), in the shutter, and in the lens. The number of *lumens* of projector output is seldom stated by the manufacturer; JAN-P-49, however, calls for an output, with shutter running, of at least 275 lumens with a new 750-watt lamp, and at least 385 lumens with a new 1,000-watt lamp. These outputs are sufficient to illuminate matte-surface screens about 67 inches and 85 inches wide respectively, the corresponding figures for beaded screens being 84 inches and 114 inches.[23]

[23] Screen widths are given for the nearest standard size provided in ASA Z52.41–1945, for brightnesses lying as close as possible to the recommended brightness.

Screen brightness.—Carrying the argument a stage further, it can be seen that it is not the light falling on the screen, but the light reflected from it, which is of ultimate interest to the moviegoer—that is, the *brightness* of the screen, rather than its *illumination*. Brightness is commonly measured in *foot-lamberts* (ft-L), which equal the illumination of a surface in *foot-candles* multiplied by the reflection factor of the surface. It has been found that 9 ft-L is the minimum and 15 ft-L the maximum screen brightness for the most satisfactory tone reproduction of average prints.[24] However, the prevalence of beaded screens, giving a bright image at a central viewpoint with a sharp tapering off at the sides, persuaded the authors of the "Recommended Procedures" to adopt a wider set of limits—a maximum of 20 ft-L and a minimum of 5 ft-L.[25]

Uniform screen illumination.—Adequate screen brightness is not a final goal of design. It is merely the supply of the brute material—light—out of which the screen image will be built. Assuming a central viewing position, it is also important that the light be uniformly distributed. JAN-P-49 calls for an average screen illumination at the four corners of 65 per cent of the illumination at the center. There should be no objectionable bands or patches differing in brightness or color from the rest of the screen. To insure constant light transmission in the projector, neither the lamp holder nor the reflector should be adjustable.

The lens.—Of all the picture requirements, those relating to the lens and the image it forms are the hardest to meet within the rigid price limitations of the 16 mm. projector. A good 16 mm. camera lens will cost $250, but the user expects to pay only $15 for the equivalent lens on his projector. Though it is true that the more elaborate focusing mount and iris of the camera lens account for part of this difference, there is still a striking contrast between the lens which forms the image on film and the equally important lens which takes this image off the film and places it on the viewing screen. Ideally, these two lenses should have an equal performance, for otherwise the bad one will drag down the good. In practice, the projection lens falls far short of the taking lens.

The requirements for 16 mm. projector lenses are difficult to meet. They must be very fast, because of the limited light available from a compact incandescent source, and they must be very cheap because the lens is quite a large item in the total cost of the machine. Hitherto, these requirements have been met by modifications of the Petzval portrait lens, designed more than a hundred years ago. Speed and cheapness, however, have only been obtained

24 ASA Z22.39–1944 provides for a screen brightness at the center of 10 + 4 or − 1 ft-L when viewing 35 mm. film.

25 Screen brightness can readily be measured in foot-lamberts with a light meter calibrated in foot-candles, since the foot-lambert is an "apparent foot-candle."

at the cost of severe curvature of the field, which results in very poor definition at the edges. Recent research has shown that the shape of the sharp image is that of a deep bowl with its concave side toward the projector, the position of sharp focus at the edges being as much as 20 inches in front of a screen only 30 inches wide.[26] These extraordinary results, which the experimenters themselves found hard to believe, were obtained from tests of nine commercial projectors. Projectors fitted with *field flatteners* were appreciably better, but none the less produced about twice as much field distortion as standard 35 mm. machines.

The reason is not far to seek. More than fifteen years ago the old Petzval lenses were taken off theater projectors and replaced by anastigmatic types, in which both spherical and chromatic aberration, as well as astigmatism, are well corrected. To obtain these corrections at the large aperture of $f/1.4$ to $f/1.6$ at which 16 mm. projection lenses are expected to work is exceedingly difficult. After several years of calculation, however, such lenses were introduced early in 1949 at a retail price of about $80, or six times the price of standard lenses. The definition may be thus compared. The best Petzval lenses have an axial definition of about 90 lines per mm., but the definition tapers off rapidly toward the edges, where it seldom exceeds 40 lines per mm. And in fact this is all the definition called for by JAN-P-49. The new lenses have a central definition slightly better than 90 lines per mm., but nowhere over the whole surface of the frame does the definition fall below 90 lines. The improvement in picture quality is remarkable, the whole screen image having a sharpness which brings the picture suddenly to life.[27]

Though a sharp and clear image cannot be formed on the screen except by a well-corrected lens, the lens is by no means the only requirement. The positioning and movement of the film contribute importantly to the screen image. For instance, the researches on the shape of the image surface showed that, in comparison with the best available 16 mm. lens, the concavity increased to between 40 and 50 inches when the film was twisted around a vertical axis so that one edge was five-thousandths of an inch (5 mils) farther from the lens than the other. Even this small error is much larger than can be tolerated. To test its magnitude in an actual projector, project a film and focus the lens so that the corners on one side of the film are as sharp as possible. (The center of the image will now be fuzzy.) If the other two corners appear sharp when viewed from a distance equal to twice the picture width, the film is lying satisfactorily in the image plane of the lens.

Picture unsteadiness.—This test is made with a commercially available film,

[26] Kalb, Robertson, and Talbot, "A Method of Determining the Shape of the Image Surface in 16 mm. Projection," *JSMPE*, June, 1947, pp. 569–585.
[27] See A. E. Neumer, "New Series of Lenses for Professional 16 mm. Projection," *JSMPE*, May, 1949, pp. 501–508.

every frame of which has been punched with a hole made by an accurate perforator. Printing processes, which themselves introduce unsteadiness, are thus eliminated, and the chief residual error, film shrinkage, is held to a minimum by the manufacturer of the stock. With the projector securely mounted to avoid vibration, the test film is projected on a screen at least 40 inches wide, to which vertical and horizontal scales have been attached. The movement of the pattern relative to the two scales is then measured and expressed as a percentage of the width of the screen. JAN-P-49 allows 0.2 per cent horizontal unsteadiness and 0.3 per cent vertical unsteadiness in projectors which have operated for 500 hours.

Travel ghost.—A more elementary fault of projectors (and cameras) is travel ghost. This is easily recognized by vertical tails or light streaks, which accompany light parts of the image. It is due to maladjustment between shutter and intermittent mechanism, so that the shutter does not fully obscure the film as the latter starts and/or stops. Travel ghost is most clearly seen in the crudely designed moviola, which operates without a shutter, so that bright tails run vertically right across the screen, often destroying the appearance of the image. A travel ghost test film is available.

Flicker.—The shutter design should further be tested, without film in the gate, for flicker, which may be noticeable at full light output but should become imperceptible when the screen brightness is reduced to 3 ft-L.

Dynamic resolution.—The sharpness and clarity of the moving image on the screen are therefore the product of a complex of factors: the resolving power of the lens and its freedom from distortion, chromatic aberration, astigmatism, etc.; the positioning of the film in the image plane of the lens, and the flatness of the projected image; and the elimination of a series of defects arising in the film intermittent and shutter mechanisms. Picture unsteadiness will also be more or less objectionable as its period is short or long. The combination of all these factors is known as the *dynamic resolution* of the projector, and research and consultation are now going on in search of a satisfactory way of expressing it.

It appears that, with Petzval projection lenses, the current over-all dynamic resolution is about 30 to 40 lines per mm., and with anastigmat lenses about 60 lines per mm., or an improvement of 50 to 100 per cent.

SOUND PROJECTION

Several of the requirements of 16 mm. sound projection have already appeared in the discussion of recording. We have seen that the width of the scanning beam (or slit width) [28] should not be greater than 0.3 mil, and that the flutter content should be inaudibly low. It has also been taken for granted

[28] The terms "scanning-beam width" and "slit width" are not really identical, since the physical slit is imaged to a much smaller width on the film by means of a cylindrical lens.

that loudspeaker systems will be comparable to those used in small theaters of the most modern design. How far are these requirements met in commercial practice?

Unhappily, 16 mm. projector design shows signs of the same obstinate refusal to raise quality standards which in Hollywood takes shelter behind the wall of the Academy theater reproducing characteristic. As a result, 16 mm. sound is almost always thought of as poor sound, and the medium gets a bad name which it in no way deserves. Some of the steps to better sound are indicated in the paragraphs which follow. Most of them are not expensive, but even the costlier components could be provided in de luxe projector models if many manufacturers did not consider it better policy to plug an old design than to produce a new one. To attain a sound quality approaching the standard of 35 mm. projection requires close attention to many details which there is no space to describe here. An excellent summary will be found in the "Recommended Procedures" and the JAN-P-49 specifications.

Film motion.—Among the basic requirements is steadiness of film motion, to reduce flutter or wow. Slow-speed wow can best be detected from a piano recording, high-speed flutter from a cello or violin. A very high flutter content results in a gargling or bubbling quality in speech, but this can usually be traced to misthreading of the film round the sound sprocket, resulting in inadequate tension.

Projectors vary greatly in flutter content, not only from make to make but from one machine to another. Some designers have patented simple but excellent sound stabilizers, which continue to damp out unsteady motion even after years of hard service. Other machines make use of devices which in the showroom can just hold flutter down to an acceptable level. In use, however, the guide rollers become a little stiff, or the tension springs stretch, the frame warps and binds the stabilizing drum, and the narrow margin of safety disappears. This type of machine will give a shocking account of itself. Tests should therefore be carried out on a projector which has seen plenty of service. Some clue to the safety margin of a new machine may be gained by starting it from rest in the middle of a sound track with the volume in the normal position, and timing it to the moment when the sound "settles down" to a steady state. If this time is very short (one to two seconds), the sound stabilizing is good; if it is much longer (four to six seconds), the machine will probably give flutter trouble later on.

The scanning beam.—The width of the scanning beam should not exceed one-half mil, which is itself some concession to ease of manufacture from the 0.3 mil slits used in the best 16 mm. re-recorders. Commercial projectors today image the beam to a width of 0.6 to 0.75 mils. (The slit itself is 8 to 10 times this width, a cylindrical lens serving to narrow the image optically.) It appears that it would cost little more to reduce the image to 0.5 mils, since this would merely require better arrangements for setting up and aligning the optical system.

JAN-P-49 also calls for variable focus of the scanning beam, by means of a lever, onto either side of the film, the nonstandard as well as the standard emulsion position. If these and other beam requirements are not met, the higher frequencies which have been degraded can never be fully restored.

The audio amplifier.—After the sound modulations on the film have been converted, via the scanning beam, into current fluctuations, they pass through an audio amplifier of conventional design. The engineer can today design with the greatest ease an amplifier of adequate power output, low distortion, and a frequency range far greater than film reproduction requires. Again, however, compromises must be made on the score of weight and cost, and these compromises must be evaluated by the user to make sure that his own needs are met. In general, the greater the reserve of power (determined by the loudness with which a given track can be reproduced before audible distortion sets in), the better will be the quality at normal projection levels. Commercial distortion ratings are vague and unsatisfactory; the old limit of "5 per cent harmonic distortion" conceals a multitude of pitfalls. Subject to aural tests, it is wise to pick a projector with an output of at least 10 watts; this is ample for audiences of a hundred to two hundred in small auditoriums. These figures must, however, be related to the sensitivity of the loudspeaker, which can more than outweigh the difference between a 10- and a 15-watt amplifier output.

The over-all frequency response of the amplifier should be substantially uniform from 50 to 5,000 cycles, when the tone control is set to have no effect. Separate bass and treble tone controls (as required by JAN-P-49) are a great advantage, provided they are intelligently handled; they should enhance and attenuate at will both the bass and the treble response, and operation of one control should have no effect on the range of frequencies covered by the other.

The loudspeaker.—The design of small but efficient loudspeakers has made great strides in the last few years. With the development of more powerful magnetic materials and more flexible cone suspensions, modern eight-inch loudspeakers can produce a level and quality of sound fully adequate for a small 35 mm. review room. These loudspeakers, however, are not to be found in standard 16 mm. projectors, for their cost to a manufacturer lies between $15 and $50. A $500 projector is equipped with a loudspeaker which probably does not cost more than $5. The user, at very moderate cost, can much improve his 16 mm. sound reproduction by buying one of these small high-quality speakers and fitting it in an enclosed reflex baffle of simple design.

The goals of 16 mm. projector loudspeaker design are: a wide frequency response, low inherent distortion, high sensitivity, moderate directivity (so that sound is not wasted at the back of the screen), and low weight and cost. Practical designs involve more or less compromise. The user can easily test a loudspeaker for rattle and boominess, and he can check its weight and price; for its other qualities he must rely on the manufacturer's data, since they are difficult to determine without laboratory tests. Sixteen mm. projectors are furnished as standard equipment with nondirectional cone loudspeakers. For large auditoriums, *directional* loudspeakers are highly desirable. By concentrating the sound where it is wanted, they help to reduce unwanted room echoes which mar the intelligibility of speech. By economizing radiated acoustic power, they enable audio amplifiers to be operated at a lower distortion level. Where the extra expense is warranted, directional loudspeakers are an advantage even in classrooms and small halls.

The sound and picture projector is not an isolated mechanism; its function is to "couple" a film into an auditory and visual space. This simply means that the light and sound energy put out by the projector must be so adapted to the physical characteristics of the space in which the audience sits that there is an efficient transfer of modulated intelligence across this space. The projector is then satisfactorily coupled. Engineers have found that, where two determinate systems are to be coupled, the job can usually be done accurately and well. One element, the film, we have followed in some detail through its many energy transformations; ideally at least, its characteristics are not merely determinate but constant. The other element in the coupling, the visual and auditory space, is, in 16 mm. practice, both unpredictable and largely uncontrollable. Therefore, tests of 16 mm. equipment should take account of the full range of conditions likely to be met with in practice.

THE SCREEN

Just as the loudspeaker couples the sound image on film to the auditory space, so the screen couples the picture image to the visual space. Screens have widely different characteristics. The *matte screen,* used in all 35 mm. theaters, is of almost uniform brightness, no matter the angle from which it is viewed. If unlimited projector light is available, the matte screen gives by far the best performance. The *beaded screen,* the surface of which is covered with small glass beads, is designed so that a large proportion of the light which falls on it is returned in the direction from which it came. When the projector is mounted at or near the eye level of the audience, this construction insures a very brilliant picture for spectators in the center of the seating area. If the projector can be mounted low, the seats held within a 40 degree total angle measured at the screen center, and the nearest seat row placed at least two and a half screen widths from the screen, the beaded screen is the best. Its distributive area then matches the distribution of the audience and that of a directional loudspeaker.

The third type of screen is *metallic,* and its surface is usually coated with finely powdered aluminum, each particle of which reflects light like a mirror. This *semispecular* reflection produces a very pronounced *hot spot,* or over-brilliant area; to viewers at the ends of the front rows of seats, the near side of the screen may appear ten times as brilliant as the far side, completely over-setting the balance of lighting achieved by the cameraman. This objectionable effect can only be eliminated by greatly reducing the seating capacity of the hall. Hitherto, the simple metallic screen has alone had the property of re-taining, on reflection, the *polarization* of light thrown upon it. Matte and beaded screens both act as *depolarizers.*

Research in screen design is continually advancing, however, and it is now possible to build metallic screens with a controlled angle of reflectance in both vertical and horizontal planes. In almost all theaters an included angle of 90 degrees in these planes is fully sufficient to cover all seats in the house, and the screen gives an effective light gain of about three times over a uniformly diffusing matte screen. Furthermore, the gain on the axis is not sharply peaked, but is more or less uniform over the whole 90 degree solid angle, so that all the spectators get an equally good view of the picture. This high and uniform light gain is essential to the success of large-screen television, and if, as re-ported, these screens retain the polarization of incident light on reflection, they can be used for stereoscopic projection by the polarized light method.[29]

SIMPLE PROJECTOR TESTS

The design of projectors involves such a large number of interdependent factors that their evaluation by the user becomes a matter of difficulty. To run a sound film through one projector and then a second time through an-other will reveal only the grossest points of difference. Instead, the factors of design must be broken down as far as possible and separately estimated. Ac-curate analysis needs elaborate equipment only to be found in specialized laboratories. For these purposes a large number of test films and conditions have been devised, many of which are referred to in the list of standards at the end of this section. By following certain guiding lines, however, and employ-ing a few simple test films, the average user can make a fairly accurate evalua-tion of a 16 mm. projector. First he should investigate the chief electrical, mechanical, and optical characteristics of the projector, looking for the features already described. Some of these may be mentioned in the instruction manual, others must be traced on the machine, still others require tests.

29 For a fuller account of screen design and use, see the "Recommended Procedures," from which the figures given in this section have been drawn. There is very little reliable literature on screen design. Some of the most important screen characteristics are well discussed by France B. Berger, "Characteristics of Motion Picture and Television Screens," *JSMPTE,* Aug., 1950, pp. 131–146.

Next, picture tests can be run. As already explained, a special test film will enable unsteadiness to be determined. Then a normal film, known to be of excellent picture quality, should be projected with the sound switched off. Examine the picture carefully for haze or fog, and for sharpness of focus at different points on the screen, and determine how much refocusing is needed to shift the clearest area from center to side and corners of the image. Insist on a field flattener if it is available. Estimate whether the brilliance and contrast of the image are adequate on the largest screens to be used, and under the worst conditions of stray light. If these demands are too great to be met by incandescent lamps, an arc projector must be substituted. Light from the arc, after passing through the projector, will amount to about 1,100 lumens, sufficient for matte screens up to 14 feet wide.

Next, switch off the light source and project two sound tracks of known and excellent quality, one consisting of speech, the other of orchestral music. Listen carefully for uniformity of frequency response; flutes and cymbals should be adequately reproduced, speech sibilants should be audible but should not blast. The word "sibilant" will sound like "thibilant" if the high frequencies are weak, and like "sssibilant" if they are overemphasized or distorted.

Attention should then be directed to the bass frequencies. Speech should sound natural and not "tubby" at a normal setting of the tone control(s); drums and other bass instruments should come through with a full, rich sound, easily distinguished from false bass, or boominess. The volume should be turned up high and the ear and fingertips applied to the cabinet to detect traces of buzz, vibration, and rattle.

The next tests should be for distortion. Listen carefully to the instruments of the orchestral ensemble. If they can be heard separately and clearly, so that, for instance, a flute part can be easily followed as it twists its way through the surrounding orchestration, harmonic and intermodulation distortion are low at that sound level. Turn the volume level up to the loudest that may be expected with a large audience, and repeat the experiment. If the music now has a harsh and raspy quality, in which the tonal outlines of the instruments become blurred, distortion—either in the amplifier, or loudspeaker, or both—has reached an unacceptable level.

Finally, the effect of the tone control(s) should be noted. Accentuation of the bass will exaggerate hum, but this should never become objectionable when film is threaded in the projector and nearby lights have been switched off. (These may contribute an audible 60-cycle hum.) Accentuation of the treble will exaggerate phototube and film hiss, but an appreciable amount of residual noise is the price which has to be paid for good high-frequency reproduction in the present state of the art.

PRINTS AND PROJECTORS

The best projector available will not give good results if the film fed through it is unsatisfactory. We have followed the print up to its emergence from the lab; at this point it leaves the care of skilled technicians and often falls into inexperienced hands. Most of the damage to film occurs during passage through the projector. Loops which are too small will strain and tear the perforations. Gates and sprockets clogged with emulsion will scratch the delicate surfaces. Binding rollers will add to the tension on the film. The remedies are obvious. Proper cleaning, oiling, and threading of the projector are simple, but, like the handling of all machinery, need care and attention. Untrained or unskilled people should no more be allowed to operate a projector than any other complex and delicate instrument. A single cleaning of the aperture with a pin or a paper clip may cause enough damage to ruin a good many hundreds of dollars' worth of color prints in a single hour's projection.

Bad splices are a common cause of bad projection. If the emulsion has not been thoroughly and evenly scraped off, or if the base has been weakened by overscraping, or if too little or too much cement has been applied, or if the two ends of film are not correctly aligned, the splice may break and the projection be interrupted.

The second important source of print trouble is excessive drying and shrinkage of the film. This, as we have seen, often results from careless and improper storage near radiators and in overheated rooms with a dry atmosphere. Shrinkage may also result from frequent projection in a badly ventilated machine, or from rapid rewinding before the film cools. Shrinkage not only leads to perforation wear and a consequently unsteady picture; it increases the brittleness of film, which therefore tends to tear at the edges when going round curves of small radius, and during rewinding, inspection, and handling.

Tightly wound film will not absorb much moisture, except at the edges, when placed in a humid atmosphere. The simplest way of humidifying it is to rewind it slowly, cleaning it at the same time with carbon tetrachloride (Carbona) and winding it up on a large reel as loosely as possible. After leaving the film in a moist atmosphere (e.g., RH 60 to 70 per cent) for at least twenty-four hours, it may safely be rewound for projection or for returning to storage under normal conditions (i.e. RH 40 to 50 per cent, temperature 50 to 60° F).[30]

[30] See also Frank Wing, Jr., *Suggestions for Prolonging the Service Life of 16 mm. Prints,* available from the Allied Non-theatrical Film Association.

SUMMARY OF 16 MM. PRODUCTION CHARACTERISTICS

Sixteen mm. production, in short, can be considered as a special application of principles well known in professional 35 mm. practice. The main differences stem from five factors: the use of reversal film processes instead of negative-positive; the prevalence of color; the one-quarter ratio of frame area and the two-fifths ratio of film speed; the variability of projection conditions; and the narrow limits set to the cost of equipment. If a 35 mm. practice is looked at under all these headings, it will usually be seen to need extensive modification.

Sixteen mm. film is not, however, an inferior substitute for 35 mm. Rather, the development of 16 mm. film corresponds to the period in horological history in the early nineteenth century when watchmakers, not without some scorn from the older members of their craft, were trying to compress the accuracy, the reliability, and the longevity of the grandfather clock into a quarter of a cubic inch. The relative sales today of watches and grandfather clocks should give pause to those who doubt 16 mm. film's potentialities.

FILM WIDTHS: A SUMMARY

It may be convenient to sum up here the different gauges of film which are or have been in common use. Though 35 mm. and 16 mm. now have the professional field to themselves, 8 mm. film is used in certain high speed cameras, and periodic attempts are made to introduce gauges larger than 35 mm. in the theaters.

8 mm.—A popular amateur gauge of film. Maximum useful screen size is limited by the very small projected image (4.37 by 3.28 mm.). At 16 frames per second, the film velocity is 12 feet per minute, and at 24 frames per second it is 18 feet per minute. Since this is only one-half the already low speed of 16 mm. film, attempts to record sound on the narrow (36 mil) space outside the perforations have not been very successful. It is possible that magnetic recording may provide a sound track of adequate quality for the home. Eight mm. film is available both in color and black and white. One foot of film contains 80 frames.

AMERICAN STANDARDS ON 8 MM. FILM

8 mm. motion picture negative and positive raw stock, cutting and perforating dimensions for	Z22.17–1947
8 mm. film; 8-tooth projector sprockets	Z22.18–1941 *
8 mm. silent film: camera aperture	Z22.19–1941 *
8 mm. silent film: projector aperture	Z22.20–1941 *
Emulsion position in camera for 8 mm. silent motion picture film	Z22.21–1946
8 mm. silent film: emulsion position in projector—positive. For direct front projection	Z22.22–1941 *
8 mm. silent film: projection reels	Z22.23–1941 *

* Under revision.

9.5 mm.—Introduced by Pathe in 1923, 9.5 mm. film is still extensively used in Continental Europe. By employing a single, very shallow perforation between frames, the projected image (8.2 by 6.15 mm.) utilizes 70 per cent of the film area, contrasted with 57 per cent on 16 mm. The addition of a sound track, however, sacrifices this advantage, since it becomes necessary to reduce the projected image to 7.2 by 5.2 mm.

16 mm. (double 8).—Eight mm. film is available in double widths, with perforations on the outer edges only. The film is run twice through the camera, so that two bands of 8 mm. pictures are recorded, and the film is split after processing into two 8 mm. widths. Double-8 mm. film is identical with silent 16 mm. film save that it has twice as many perforations.

16 mm.—Introduced by Eastman Kodak in 1923, this has become the standard gauge for non-35 mm. professional production. Available with double or single perforations for silent shooting and recording and printing sound track. Its characteristics, dimensions and processes have already been described.

17.5 mm.—An obsolete substandard gauge of film formerly in use in Europe. Sound and silent.

17.5 mm. (split 35 mm.).—To economize stock, some studios, both in America and Europe, record sound on both sides of 35 mm. film, splitting it after printing to form two 17.5 mm. sound tracks. Since the perforations are standard, split film can be run on 35 mm. moviolas, synchronizers, and dubbers with only very small modifications to these mechanisms. In spite of the economies it introduces, split 35 mm. sound film has not won wide acceptance.

19 mm. and 20 mm.—Proposed standards (in France and the United States respectively) of a gauge of film on which the picture image would be of present 16 mm. dimensions, the sound track would be enlarged to the width employed on 35 mm. film, and a row of 16 mm. perforations would be provided on either side of the film. Interest in this hybrid seems to have waned.

28 mm.—An obsolete substandard gauge of film formerly in use in North America. It was the first film width to be supplied with an acetate base, and it lingered on in the Province of Ontario until 1937, long after new projectors and prints had ceased to be available.

32 mm. (double 16).—It is the practice of some of the larger release-printing labs to make dupe negatives on double 16 mm. stock, which is then printed, developed, and split to form two 16 mm. prints. Thirty-two mm. film is made with double or quadruple perforations, so that it splits into sound or silent 16 mm. film of standard dimensions.[31]

[31] See Frank La Grande, C. R. Daily, and Bruce H. Denney, "16 mm. Printing Using 35 mm. and 32 mm. Film," *JSMPE*, Feb., 1949, pp. 211–222.

35 mm.—Introduced by Edison in 1891, the width and perforation gauge of 35 mm. film have merely been standardized with more exactness during the succeeding 60 years. With the addition of sound track and waste space at top and bottom, the picture area has shrunk to three-quarters of what it was in Edison's time. The characteristics and processes of 35 mm. film are described in other chapters.

70 mm.—Between 1930 and 1932, when motion picture standards were in flux on account of the introduction of sound, many proposals were put forward for raising the standard gauge of film. The 70 mm. or "grandeur" film was the most widely advocated. The economic folly of building gigantic theaters, proved during the depression, followed by the introduction of fine-grain film emulsions which made it unnecessary to increase the size of the photographic image, resulted in the proposals being dropped. It is possible that large film might be reintroduced by the studios for process projection onto screens larger than any hitherto used.

[32] See discussion in *JSMPE,* Apr., 1949, pp. 447–452.

X

ЛЛЛЛЛЛЛЛЛЛЛЛЛЛЛЛЛЛЛЛЛЛЛЛ

Sound: Getting It onto Film

THERE ARE MANY materials on which sound can be satisfactorily recorded. One of these, wax, was well established twenty-five years ago when the Warner brothers undertook to commercialize sound with film. Consequently they turned to the disc, and it was several years before sound on film was able to compete in quality, although it had long been evident that storing the sound on a separate disc made synchronization clumsy and difficult. The sound belonged on the same piece of film as the picture; it must be conceived as a ribbon of the same length as the picture, printed alongside it and in some determinate synchronism—either parallel or ahead or behind.

But what property of the film to make use of? It is possible to emboss film with a running groove like a phonograph record, which is reproduced with a stylus; or else an opaque emulsion on the film can be cut away by a finely adjusted gouge, the resulting sound track being reproduced optically. These methods, which write the sound track by mechanical means, are called *mechanographic;* and the obscurity of the term testifies to the commercial failure of the principle.

Success was found in the adaptation of picture recording methods to the sound track.[1] The image on a piece of transparent film may be thought of as a variable light stopper. Where the picture is dense, the spectator sees a shadow on the white screen; and where it is light, he sees a bright area. Across the area of the frame, the variable light stopping of the film modulates the projection-lamp beam and so produces an image on the screen. Similarly, a traveling picture of the sound waves of a person speaking could be made to modulate another light beam which could then set up electrical impulses which would in turn be converted into sound. This is known as photographic or optical recording and reproduction, which today produces and plays back

[1] For a summary history of sound films, see E. I. Sponable's "Historical Development of Sound Films," *JSMPE*, pts. 1–2, April, 1947, pp. 275–303; pts. 3–7, May, 1947, pp. 407–422.

all the sound tracks in all the movie theaters and 16 mm. screening rooms throughout the world.

In recent years an entirely different method of recording and reproduction has come into use as a result of research in Germany and the United States in the period 1935–1945. In *magnetic recording,* none of the photographic properties of the film are made use of. The picture track (if there is one) and the sound track sit side by side on the same cellulose base, but instead of being partners in the various printing and developing processes, they have nothing to do with one another. The sound track, in fact, consists of powdered metallic particles bonded together and fastened to the base. The picture which the recording creates is not a picture in light and shade but in magnetization: thousands of little magnets are laid end to end along the ribbon of film, the lower frequencies being represented by longer magnets and the higher frequencies by shorter ones. The method of reproduction is also magnetic.

Since magnetic recording requires no processing and is thus immediately reproducible, it has very great advantages for all original or production registration of sound. None the less, there seems to be no compelling scientific or economic reason why movie theaters throughout the world should be converted to magnetic reproduction.

Thus for a long time the two systems are likely to coexist. In this chapter we shall perforce give more space to photographic recording, since its techniques are well established. The principles and uses of magnetic recording can only be sketched in briefly, since—like the magnetic particles themselves —they are in a state of flux.

WHAT IS SOUND?

Underlying all methods of recording are certain facts about the character of sound which should be familiar to every film maker. Sound is a basic and indefinable psychic sensation, aroused by vibrations of a certain character, received through the ear and the bones surrounding the ear, which are transmitted to the hearer through liquids, solids, and gases. Sound is also defined as the wave motion which gives rise to the sensation of sound, and which originates in the periodic vibration of waves, strings, vocal chords, reeds, diaphragms, moving columns of air, etc., as well as in the *aperiodic* vibration of many other structures.

Sound has three principal characteristics: frequency, intensity, and *phase.* Frequency, which is the scientific counterpart of the musician's *pitch,* is measured by the rate of vibration of the sound expressed in numbers of complete vibrations or *cycles* occurring per unit of time (i.e., one second). When wave motion in air has a frequency which lies between about 20 and 15,000 cycles per second (cps)—the exact limits depending on the individual—it produces a sensation of sound when it strikes the human ear. This is called the *audible spectrum* or audio spectrum. Below it, in the *infrasonic* region, air vibrations cannot be translated by the ear into sound, but, if powerful enough to exceed the *threshold of feeling*, they will excite a painful sensation in the nervous system. Above the audible range (the *supersonic* region), sounds are seldom intense enough to be felt; dogs and bats, however, respond up to frequencies of at least 25,000 cycles (e.g., the inaudible dog-whistle).

Since sound travels at about 1,100 feet per second in still air, the *wavelength* of an 1,100-cycle wave is one foot, and that of a 13,000 cycle wave, corresponding to a very high note, about an inch, while a 30-cycle wave, corresponding to a very low note, is about 36 feet long. The high note might be an overtone of the flute or violin, the low tone a pedal note on the organ. The second important characteristic of sound waves is their intensity. This is the measure of their displacement about a mean or middle position. If you press your finger lightly against the edge of a loudspeaker cone when the volume has been turned up very high, you will feel the motion, or *amplitude,* of the cone. If you then hold your hand in front of the loudspeaker, you will feel an appreciable wind caused by the amplitude transmitted from the moving cone to the molecules of air. However, it must not be thought that the molecules are blown from place to place; they merely oscillate about a mean position, and the sound wave travels through them, much as the impact of a locomotive shunting a long line of stationary freight cars may be said to "travel" from end to end, though none of the cars has moved more than a fraction of an inch. The small movement of the air molecules is longitudinal, like the movement of the freight cars, and not transverse, like waves on the surface of water. The greater the intensity of the sound, the more violently the air conveying the sound is displaced, and the larger is said to be the amplitude of the train of waves. Generated by a point source in free air, wave trains radiate out in a sphere, the compressions (or condensations) and rarefactions forming concentric shells.

If a train of sound waves, consisting of a series of alternate condensations and rarefactions of the air, is radiated in the direction of a solid surface like a wall, much of the sound energy will be reflected back from the wall toward the source. The sound waves will therefore be "traveling" in opposite directions (no material particles, of course, actually move from place to place), and there will be areas where an outgoing rarefaction will coincide with an inbound compression. Since the same molecules of air cannot at the same time be compressed and rarefied, it is evident that they will remain stationary and that no sound will be heard by an ear at this point. It is easy to verify the existence of these *nodes* with an oscillator and loudspeaker. They can, how-

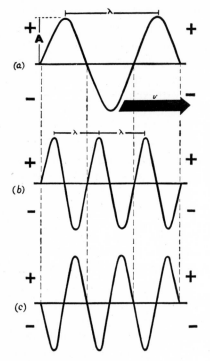

Fig. 10-1. Frequency, wave-length, amplitude, and phase. **a** shows a fundamental sine wave of wave length (λ) and amplitude (A) traveling at a given velocity (v). Hence v/λ equals the frequency (f); **b** shows the first harmonic of this sine wave, with a frequency 2f; **c** shows this first harmonic placed 180° out of phase with the wave of **b**, i.e. displaced along the axis one-half of a complete wave.

ever, only be detected by closing one ear, since it is unlikely that both ears will be situated at nodal points. Waves characterized by interference patterns caused by nodes are called *standing waves*.

When two waves interfere and cancel one another, they are said to be 180 degrees *out of phase;* and when their maxima and minima coincide, so that the energy of the two waves is additive, they are said to be *in phase*. Phase, therefore, is the third important characteristic of wave motion. While the ear does not detect a change of phase relationships within a complex wave train, it responds very noticeably to the phasing of separate trains of waves. The microphone, being a one-eared instrument, is even more sensitive to out-of-phase effects than the human being with his binaural hearing and his natural ability to place the source of a sound by integrating the phase relations of the wave-trains entering either ear (figure 10-1).

Complex as are the wave motions we have mentioned (and when the hundred instruments of a symphony orchestra are playing together, they are exceedingly complex), they are all superimposed on one another to produce a single wave motion which finally strikes the ears of the listener or the diaphragm of a microphone. This single complex wave motion (which can be uniquely represented by a curve in terms of its component frequencies, amplitudes and phases) is in fact all that the symphony orchestra finally has to show for itself. Eliminate the air through which the wave motion is propagated, and the thunderings of the orchestra will be in vain. The listener will hear nothing. No energy will have been conveyed to him. There will be nothing to carry the curve. Again, pass the curve through an electrical meat-chopper (like the average table radio), and so slice out some of the vibrations and mangle the shape of others, and you will find that the most magnificent creation of Bach or Stravinsky is reduced to such a horrible jangle of sound that you will rush to switch it off. Obviously, then, the precious curve must be preserved at all costs. The energy which sustains it must be efficiently transformed at each stage, and not allowed to die away. Above all, the curve must be carefully protected against maltreatments which would alter its shape.

These unwanted alterations of shape are called *distortions,* and it is the object of the sound engineer to see that they are held to a minimum in the various energy transformations through which the *signal* (as the energy curve is usually called) passes on its long electroacoustical travels.

SOUND—IMAGE—SOUND

Sound, as we have seen, is recorded on film for a very homely reason—to be next to the picture. And, like the picture, photographic recording makes use of the variable light-stopping capacities of a sensitive emulsion when it has been exposed and developed. In short, whereas the picture is an area which is density modulated in two space dimensions, the sound track is a ribbon modulated in the one time dimension. How, then, are the pulsations of a light beam passing through this variable light stopper to be retranslated into sound?

The phototube [2] consists of an evacuated space in which is set up a photosensitive *cathode* which emits electrons under the impact of light, and an *anode* to which a positive voltage is applied. The anode draws the negative electrons across the vacuum which separates it from the cathode, and thus enables them to flow through an external circuit as a very feeble electric current.[3] This current can be read directly on a microammeter. In a film reproducer, it is passed through an exceedingly high resistance—of the order of 0.1–1 megohms—across which it sets up enough voltage to be electronically amplified. If the light beam striking the tube cathode varies in intensity, the current flowing through the phototube will vary correspondingly.

Now, suppose we set up a light source and a phototube opposite one another, and run a piece of film between the two. If the light-obstructing quality of this piece of film is constant all the way along, its motion will not

---

[2] See Glossary under *photoelectric phenomena* for the distinction between different types of photoelectric device.

[3] It has been found that the sensitivity of the phototube can be increased five or six times if a very small quantity of an inert gas is introduced into the vacuum. This is due to the multiplying effect of ionic bombardment, called ionization, which is described in textbooks on electricity. The gas-filled phototube has a less good frequency response than the evacuated tube, but it is adequate to cover the audible spectrum and is therefore exclusively used in sound on film reproducers.

interfere with the constant current flow through the phototube because there will be no fluctuation of the incoming light. The needle of a micro-ammeter placed in series with the phototube will not move.

Suppose, however, that we place between the light source and the tube a piece of film having different amounts of light obstruction at different points along its length. If this piece of film is moved backward and forward, the microammeter needle in the phototube circuit will move up and down in an exactly corresponding manner. If now we take another piece of film and paint opaque blobs on it with marking ink at regular intervals, and if we replace the meter with an amplifier and loudspeaker and then pull the film rapidly to and fro, a musical note—or rather a rude noise—will be heard. The faster the piece of film is pulled, the higher the frequency (or pitch) of this sound will be, simply because more blobs will interrupt the passage of the light beam to the phototube in a given time. If fifty blobs pass in one second, the pitch will be very low (i.e., 50 cycles); if two hundred and fifty, the note will be close to middle C on the piano. Obviously, the closer the blobs are to-gether, the slower the travel of the film to produce any desired frequency; alternatively, if the speed of travel of the film is fixed, the closer blobs will pro-duce a higher frequency. If the speed varies, the pitch will vary, even though the blobs are all exactly the same distance apart. The process of introducing fluctuations into a steady light beam is called *modulating* it; and the fluctu-ations of amplitude themselves are called *modulations*.

We now have all the basic requirements of a sound reproducing system (figure 10-2). The light source of constant intensity is called the *exciter lamp*. Light from this lamp is focused on the sound-track area of the film. The film must travel at an absolutely constant speed (90 feet per minute for 35 mm. film and 36 feet per minute for 16 mm. film). If the speed fluctuates, as we have seen, a wavering of pitch, which is called *flutter* or *wow*, will be introduced. When the light beam has passed through the film, it strikes a phototube. The output of this tube is magnified by means of an amplifier called an *audio amplifier* because it passes the band of frequencies corre-sponding to the audio spectrum—20 to 15,000 cps. Finally, the output of this amplifier operates a loudspeaker.

One important part of this reproducer chain has been omitted. Suppose we have a field full of sheep which we wish to count while letting them out through a gate. If the gate is wide enough to let out a dozen sheep at once, it will be difficult to count them. It is sensible therefore to narrow the gate until it is just wide enough for one sheep to get through at a time. The individual waves as recorded on film,—the modulations—are represented by the sheep. If several of them were to get past the light beam simultaneously, it is obvious that the light-stopping effect of each modulation would be lost by becoming merged with that of other modulations. For this reason we

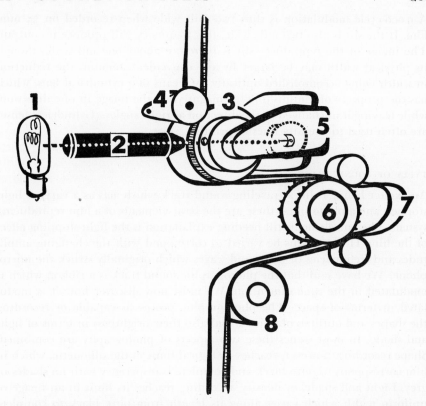

Fig. 10-2. Elements of the optical sound reproducer. An exciter
lamp (1) focuses a narrow beam of light through an optical system
(2) onto the film sound track, as it passes round a stabilizing roller
(3) attached to a heavy flywheel. These are driven by the motion
of the film itself, and the film is held in contact with the roller by
a spring-weighted guide roller (4). After passing through the
sound track, which projects beyond the edge of the roller, the beam
of light strikes the cathode of a phototube (5), thus setting up
varying electric currents, as explained in the text. The film thereafter passes over a sprocket (6), where a loop is formed at 7 to
reduce flutter at sprocket-hole frequency, and thence over another
guide roller (8) and so into the take-up magazine.

interpose a *slit* or light gate between the exciter lamp and the film. In this
way not more than one of even the thinnest modulations can get in front of
the phototube at one time.

We have already seen that the higher the frequency, the shorter the modulations. The normal speed of 35 mm. film is 18,000 mils (18 inches) per second.

A 9,000-cycle modulation is thus two mils wide when recorded on 35 mm. film. If the slit is also two mils wide, this frequency will produce no output. The image of the reproducer slit is therefore about one mil wide, though its physical width may be larger by any convenient amount, the reduction in width being accomplished optically by means of a cylindrical lens, which has the property of diminishing (or magnifying) the image in one direction, while leaving it unchanged in the direction at right angles. (Cylindrical lenses are often used to magnify lines of print.)

TYPES OF SOUND TRACK

An exciter lamp, a slit, a traveling sound track which acts as a varying light stopper, and a phototube—these are the basic elements of a film reproducing system. The one element still needing explanation is the light-stopping effect of the film. How can this be varied to correspond with the changing amplitudes and frequencies of the sound waves which originally struck the microphone? We have said that the photographic sound track is a ribbon which is modulated in the time dimension. We must now discover how it is modulated in terms of space. The photographic process is capable of recording the shapes and outlines of objects, and also their brightness in terms of light and shade. In most scenes these two aspects of photography are combined. Shape recording, however, reaches its logical limit in the silhouette, which in film corresponds to pure black and complete transparency with no shades of grey. Light and shade, or density, recording reaches its limit in an image of uniform width which varies along its length from pure black to complete transparency, with every shade of grey in between.

Thus we arrive at the two kinds of sound track, variable area and variable density. The variable-area track is a profile picture of a train of waves, looking as a rule like a cross-section of the Rocky Mountains. This is because the sounds of daily life are of extraordinary complexity, and are in fact called *complex waves*. Maximum modulation of the variable-area track occurs when an opaque wave blocking the slit is followed by a transparent area fully opening the slit. Some of the different types of variable-area track are shown in figure 10-5, p. 286. The choice of a certain track hinges more on the design of the recording instrument than on any significant advantage in the track itself.

The variable-density track is uniform across its width, but lengthwise forms an image of the track in densities. The resulting bands by which density tracks are recognized are called *striations*. Maximum modulation occurs when an opaque striation is followed by a transparent striation (the effective frequency being within the system *pass band*). A variable-density track thus modulated (which, for reasons discussed below, is not practicable) would

act as a variable light stopper of exactly the same efficacy as the maximally
modulated variable-area track.

The aim of photographic recording and reproduction is a linear relation
between the transparency of the print (which controls the light striking the
reproducer phototube) and the exposure of the negative (which is governed
by the intensity of the corresponding signal in the recording amplifier). In
the absence of wave-form distortion, this is not hard to accomplish in variable-
area recording, which is a simple painting in black on transparency. Variable-
density recording, however, must make use of the film characteristic itself,
which is markedly curved (i.e. nonlinear). Though much may be done in
printing by using the positive curvature to cancel the negative one, the
useful volume range is still somewhat lower than with variable-area recording. Both variable-area and variable-density track (the oscillogram and the
densogram) have interesting peculiarities, but before discussing them it will
be helpful to see how electric currents can be made to modulate light beams
and so record these modulations on film.

THE MODULATOR

It is convenient to have a general term to describe the device which impresses
the pulsations of current which have originally been generated in the microphone onto a beam of light. This is called a *modulator*. If a very small coil
of wire is delicately suspended between the poles of a strong magnet, and an
electric current passed through the coil, the coil will twist round in the
magnetic field. This is because the current forms magnetic poles in the coil
of wire, and these repel or attract the neighboring poles of the magnet according to whether they are of like or unlike polarity (north or south). Thus
the direction of movement of the coil will depend on the direction of flow
of the current through it. This principle is used in many electrical instruments, such as voltmeters and ammeters and the almost universal *moving-coil*
loudspeakers.

The same result is achieved if the coil carrying the signal current is wound
round the poles of the magnet, and the element which moves between the
poles is a simple piece of iron, or, more usually, an iron-nickel alloy. This
device is known as a moving-iron galvanometer in contrast to the moving-
coil galvanometer, the term galvanometer, colloquially shortened to "galvo,"
meaning simply a sensitive current indicator.

Suppose we pass the amplified current or *signal current* from a microphone
through the kind of galvanometer we have been describing. The moving element will then twist to and fro, or vibrate, according to the direction and
strength of this signal current. If the element is very light, it will vibrate even
when the frequency of the current is as high as 10,000 cps. Now suppose that
we fix an extremely small mirror to the moving element and focus a beam

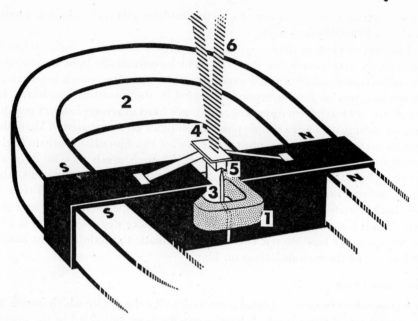

Fig. 10-3. A variable-area modulator. This highly simplified diagram shows the coil (1) carrying the audio current set over the pole pieces of the enclosing magnet (2) in such a way as to move the metal armature (3) which is clamped at its base to the magnet. As it moves, the armature deflects the mirror (4) through a knife-edge device (5), and so swings the beam of light (6) which falls on it. (Courtesy G. L. Dimmick, RCA, and SMPE.)

of light on it. As the mirror twists to and fro through a small angle, its movements will be magnified by the reflected beam of light acting as an optical lever. It is only necessary to direct the moving beam through a narrow slit onto the unexposed film traveling past, and regulate the amplitude of movement of the beam.

We now have the main elements of a recording galvanometer, the moving-iron type of which is in universal use for variable-area recording. A typical galvanometer is shown in figure 10-3, and the optical system used to form the light beam into a sound track in figure 10-4. In this drawing, noise reduction (discussed in the next section) is applied by means of a bias, as in the light valve. This bias deflects the mirror of the galvanometer, thus maximizing the negative exposure in the absence of a signal. However, in the variable-area system, the functions of modulation, track shaping, and noise reduction may all be separated. Modulation is effected by the galvanometer

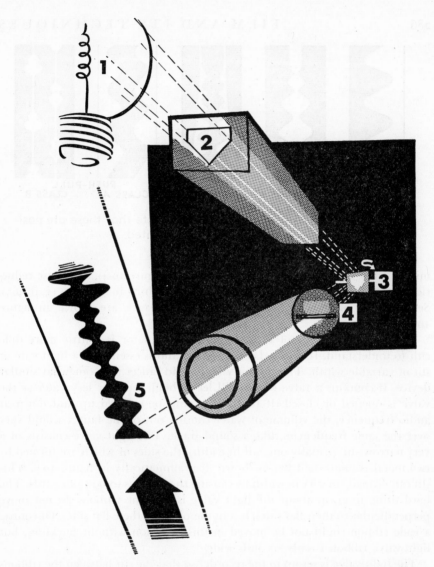

Fig. 10-4. Variable-area optical system. This diagram shows schematically how the light beam from the recording lamp (1) is shaped by a wedgelike mask (2) so that it assumes this wedge shape when it falls on the galvanometer mirror (3), shown as 4 in Figure 10-3. As the mirror oscillates, it moves the wedge-shaped beam up and down across the slit (4), thus causing the illuminated part of the slit to become narrower and wider alternately, producing the familiar bilateral track shown at 5. Noise reduction (see next section) is effected by biasing the mirror upward, so that minimum light strikes the negative, causing minimum transmission in the print.

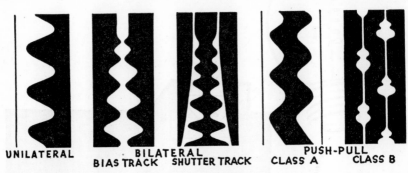

Fig. 10-5. Types of variable-area track. Note that these are positive tracks, whether directly recorded or printed.

mirror, track-shaping by a mask (shown at 2 in figure 10-4), and noise reduction by a pair of shutters (shown with vertical hatching in figure 10-13, p. 305). Several different types of variable-area sound track are shown in figure 10-5.

The commonest type of variable-density modulator is a little more difficult to understand. It is called a *light valve,* and is essentially a light gate or slit of variable width. The ordinary household faucet is a somewhat similar device. It contains a valve which will let through more or less water as the valve is opened or closed. If this valve could be screwed up and down at audio frequency, the volume of water coming out of the faucet would vary over the same frequencies, like a sound track. The light valve consists of a very narrow slit (usually one mil in width), the sides of which are formed by two metal ribbons, laid flat as shown diagrammatically in figure 10-6. This slit can be made to vary in width by causing the ribbons to bow outwards. The hard thing to grasp about the light valve is that the ribbons do not move perpendicular to their flat sides, but in the plane of these flat sides. Of course, a wide ribbon could not be moved in this direction without buckling; but light-valve ribbon is only six mils wide.

The light valve is set up in the recorder so that the slit between the ribbons is at right angles to the length of the sound track. That is, light passing through the ribbons illuminates evenly the full width of the sound track. (The length of the light-valve slit is greater than the width of the sound track, but masks are provided to prevent the sound track's trespassing onto other areas of the film.) In order to operate the light valve, it is necessary to mount it between the poles of a powerful magnet. The action is then just the same as that of the moving-coil galvanometer. When the signal current passes through the ribbons in one direction they move away from one another; in the other direction, toward one another. The usual initial spacing is one mil,

Fig. 10-6. The light valve. The light valve is set transverse to the axis of the sound track, so that when its ribbons (1) bow out and in, the track is exposed more or less intensely across its full width.

the maximum spacing is two mils, and the minimum spacing is zero. In the oldest and newest types of valve the ribbons are set in a single plane (forming a *monoplanar valve*), so that if they come together they strike one another and *clash*. Clashing may cause damage to the extremely delicate ribbons, so in certain types of valve the ribbons are set in slightly different planes so that they simply overlap after passing the zero position. These are called *biplanar valves*. The zero position is called the *clash point;* beyond it, further increases of the signal cannot let any less light through the valve—the light having already been reduced to nothing. Modulating beyond the zero point is equivalent to cutting off the troughs of the waves, as will be seen in more detail later in the discussion of distortion.

In the United States, the galvanometer is used principally by the Radio Corporation of America (RCA) to produce variable-area tracks, and the light valve by the Western Electric Company to produce variable-density tracks. However, with minor modifications, the galvanometer may be made to produce variable-density tracks, and the light valve variable-area tracks. These new arrangements are described in the technical literature.[4]

[4] See, for instance: C. W. Faulkner and C. N. Batsel, "Operation of the Variable-Intensity Recording System," *JSMPE*, Feb., 1941, p. 125; John G. Frayne, "Variable-Area Recording with the Light Valve," *JSMPE*, Nov., 1948, p. 501.

A film recorder thus consists essentially of a light source (to produce the beam), a slit, a modulator, and a driving mechanism to move the unexposed film along with extreme steadiness. It will be noticed that three out of these four components are the same as in a film reproducer, and exactly the same considerations govern their design. But in the recorder even higher standards of precision and workmanship are called for, since upon these depends the quality of sound on pictures in perhaps sixty-thousand movie theaters.

THE AMPLIFIER

The amplifier chain which leads from the microphone to the recorder is quite straightforward. It contains the volume controls (as on a radio set, but called *gain controls* or "pots") needed to vary the level of the output from each of several microphones to give the desired volume on the sound track. These are mounted on a mixing panel. It also contains a *V.I.* (*volume indicator*) *meter,* which registers the signal strength from moment to moment and so indicates whether the modulator is being overloaded. This meter is usually graduated in decibels (abbreviated to *db.*) which are the logarithmic units of gain and loss in level.[5]

Hence we now have a complete sound recording system which consists of one or more microphones, a mixing panel to adjust their relative levels, a main amplifier, and a recorder.

NOISE REDUCTION

There is one other important unit which cannot be overlooked even in an elementary account of the sound-recording process. This is the *noise reduction* unit. We have already seen that both in the variable-area and variable-density recording systems, the light beam throws a mean or middle amount of light onto the film when no modulation is being handled (i.e., when no sound waves are striking the microphone). The sound track is then said to be *unmodulated,* and it is able to receive both more and less illumination when the positive and negative halves of incoming waves are impressed on it. In this normal or mean condition, the variable factor in the track (area or density) can accept the full modulation which the track will take—which is therefore called *100 per cent modulation.* It follows that considerably more than the minimum amount of light—in fact about 50 per cent of the maximum—is transmitted to the film in the unmodulated condition. The more light that reaches the film, the higher the density (or the larger the opaque area) of the negative, and the lower the density (or the smaller the opaque area) of the print made from it. But if the print is of low density (minimum

---

[5] See pp. 177–178 above for a discussion of the advantages of logarithmic units.

opaque area), it will allow a large amount of light to strike the phototube, as it travels through the sound reproducer. This will make the phototube generate a high current, a condition in which its intrinsic noise—caused by irregular bombardment of electrons—is at a maximum. To these hissing noises are added the modulations set up by small opaque scratches and black particles of dirt in the print. All these factors are lumped together with the noise produced by the inherent graininess of the film and called *ground noise*. It is obvious that the higher the transmission of the print the worse will be the ground noise—worse too, the lower the wanted modulations, and worst of all where there is no modulation and the track is meant to be completely silent.

Hence it is desirable in variable-area recording to reduce the transparent area of the print as much as possible, and in variable-density recording to darken the print as much as possible. In both systems this must be done with due regard to the depth of modulation the system is carrying. When there is no modulation at all, a minimum amount of light needs to be passed; but when there is modulation, a sufficient amount of light must reach the film to carry the depth of modulation at that moment. And of course at full modulation, the maximum amount of light must reach the film—but then the signal will be so loud that the ground noise will be masked. In short, the light reaching the film plays the part of a *carrier* for the modulations impressed on it; while, if ground noise is to be reduced to a minimum, the light should act as a variable carrier. In other words, ground noise will be least when the light is at every instant 100 per cent modulated—that is, when there is no surplus light over and above what is needed to carry the signal. For reasons which will soon appear, it is usually difficult to realize this ideal in practice.

The idea of a variable carrier is rather abstract and hard to grasp. But a comparison may help to make it clearer. Suppose we are the operators of a canal doing a brisk business carrying barges and river steamers of different sizes. Owing to technical difficulties, the water for this canal has to be supplied from a neighboring city which charges for it. Water can be returned to, as well as drawn from the city mains, so that we are only obliged to pay for what we are actually using. Hence it is to our financial advantage to have at any moment as little water as possible in the canal.

Suppose that for a spell no boats are passing along the canal. We empty out all the water; any water left is waste, since it has no boats to carry. We then learn by phone that a barge is approaching. Its draft is given as two feet. Consequently, we let two feet of water into the canal to float the barge. But if the draft has been underestimated, or if a ripple on the surface depresses the level of the barge, it will go aground. Hence, to provide a margin of safety, an extra six inches of water may be let into the canal. If, when the barge has passed, a river steamer drawing five feet of water is signaled, another three feet of water should be run into the canal. If the steamer is followed by a canoe, all but about nine inches of water can be safely let out. In this way the depth of water is always proportioned to the draft of the boat which it is carrying.

In this comparison, the canal represents the sound track, the total depth of water at any time the amount of light reaching the track; the boats are the modulations, the draft of the boat representing the depth of modulation; the difference between the depth of water and the draft (if any) is the amount of free light or *margin*. When the canal is empty of boats it corresponds to an unmodulated sound track. When a boat enters the canal with a draft equal to the maximum depth of water which the canal will hold, this corresponds to 100 per cent modulation. Going aground represents overmodulation.

Variable-area and variable-density noise-reduction systems work on altogether different principles. In the variable-area system it is now universal to make a sound track in which the modulations are symmetrical about a center line running the length of the track. This kind of track resembles the children's game of making an ink blot near the fold in a piece of paper and then doubling over the paper before the ink is dry. The object of the noise-reduction unit is to mask off the part of the track not filled with modulations. This can be done by means of a mechanical shutter which closes in simultaneously from both sides like the blades of a pair of scissors and shuts off the surplus light. In the variable-density system no mechanical component is needed, since all that must be done is to keep the light-valve ribbons squeezed together as close as possible all the time—that is, compatible with providing a large enough carrier for the signal. In figure 10-7, *a*, a signal of different amplitudes is represented—first large, then gradually getting smaller. In figure 10-7, *b*, this signal is superimposed on a pair of vibrating light-valve ribbons. It will be noticed that the peak of a wave on one ribbon is exactly opposite a peak of a wave on the other ribbon, while the troughs are also opposite the troughs. If the ribbons are imagined to be simultaneously tracing out points opposite one another on the curves, it will be seen that they exactly reproduce the wave form of the first diagram, as they move toward and away from one another. The two lines through the centers of these oscillations represent the mean position of the ribbons—that is, the position to which the ribbons return when no signal is being applied to them. Figure 10-7, *c* shows how this mean spacing of the ribbons can itself be altered, since the ribbons can be brought together independently of whether a signal is being applied to them. This is done by applying a *bias* to the ribbons—that is, an electrical voltage which brings them nearer together. When their separation is thus reduced, the amount of light which can pass between them is also reduced.

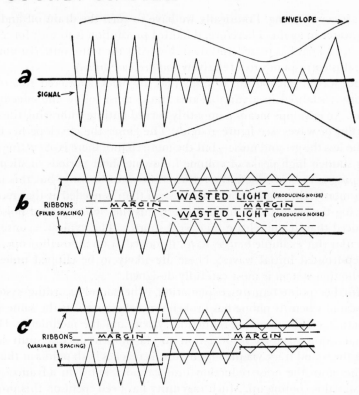

Fig. 10-7. How noise reduction is applied to variable-density light-valve recording.

Let us now go back to the comparison. Suppose our canal telephone gets out of order so that we have no advance notice of the draft of approaching boats. Imagine the canal to be dry (no modulation, maximum noise reduction). As soon as a boat reaches the entrance we hastily start letting water in. But to run it in takes time, and meanwhile the boat is beginning to go aground. To prevent any such accident, the first precaution must be to see that there is always some water in the bottom of the canal to give us a head start when filling it up. (In noise reduction, a small amount of light is always allowed to pass through the system, even when unmodulated.) The second precaution is to insure that the water flows in as rapidly as possible. (In noise reduction, the *attack time* must be reduced to the minimum.) Next, suppose that the first boat has reached the end of the canal. In the interests of economy we immediately start letting the water out (getting back to the position of maximum noise reduction). But suppose that a moment later a boat with a large draft comes along. Frantically we have to turn the drain off and start running water in again. Therefore, the third precaution is to wait for a short period after a boat has passed and then slowly let the water out. (In noise reduction, this corresponds to a relatively long *release time*.)

Another way of putting this is to say that the black, shuttered area (this is most easily visualized in a variable-area track) must follow the *envelope* of the waves. An envelope means a smoothly curved outline embracing the crests of the train of waves (see figure 10-9, *a*). The closer the envelope fits to the waves, the less the ground noise—but the more chance there is of cutting off or *clipping* sudden high peaks of volume following short periods of silence. If this clipping is to be avoided, the release time must be long; but this means allowing more light to go through the system than is needed at that moment for carrying the signal; and this in turn means that more ground noise will be produced than if the release time were shorter. The explosive consonants in particular (for example *b, d, g, k, p*), if looked at on an oscilloscope, show very steep-fronted initial waves. These are likely to be clipped unless the noise-reduction system is most carefully designed.

One further point requires explanation. The sound-recording system is like the canal when its phone has broken down because it is the same signal which actuates both the noise-reduction system and the modulator. Hence, the signal cannot get its information to the noise-reduction unit before reaching the sound track via the modulator. It reaches both points at the same time. Therefore the noise-reduction unit cannot "know in advance" what kind of signal is coming up. Much ingenuity has been spent on this problem of getting the signal to the noise-reduction amplifier before it reaches the modulator, so that at all times the maximum degree of noise reduction consistent with the modulation is being applied, and the margin (or amount of wasted light) reduced to a minimum. Devices of this kind are hence called *noise reduction anticipation* devices. But they have so far proved too complicated or too limiting in other ways to be applied extensively in practice, in spite of the advantages they would confer.

Clipping occurs not only on certain speech sounds. It is even more noticeable in piano playing when a series of heavy chords follow one another at short intervals. The noise reduction gradually comes into effect at the end of one heavy modulation and causes a hissing sound. Then another heavy modulation comes along and is partly clipped off before the noise reduction can sufficiently reduce itself (i.e., the boat bumps on the bottom before enough water can be let into the canal to float it).

We can now summarize the requirements of a noise-reduction system:

1. Very short attack time (5 to 15 milliseconds).
2. Comparatively slow release time (50 to 100 milliseconds). This time could be greatly reduced if a satisfactory noise-reduction anticipation device were available.

3. The smallest possible margin. The shorter the attack time, the smaller this can be made.

4. Maximum closing when no signal is passing (also dependent on the length of attack time).

5. Noise reduction to be operated strictly by the peaks of the waves and not by the average height of a train of waves. (This is necessary to avoid frequent clipping.)

6. Noise-reduction anticipation circuits if not too complicated.

It will be seen that much hinges on having a short attack time. But if this is too short, the noise-reduction system will itself generate frequencies within the audio range of the main amplifier—say above 40 cps. These frequencies (often called *shutter bumps*) will be audible as a thumping sound each time the noise-reduction system goes into operation at the onset of modulation.

Noise reduction has proved to be one of the most troublesome factors in sound-recorder design. It has a large literature which the interested reader can follow up for himself in the various technical journals.

DISTORTION

We have seen that two of the most important characteristics of sound waves— and of wave motion in general—are frequency and amplitude. The frequencies handled by a sound-recording system cover ideally the whole range of the human ear—that is, from about 20 to 15,000 cps. Amplitude is measured either in logarithmic decibel units or by the fraction of the available volume range of a system taken up by the particular modulation being considered: that is, it stretches from zero (unmodulated) to 100 per cent when the system is being modulated to full capacity. Both frequency and amplitude have their own peculiar forms of distortion—which is a matter of great importance, since distortion is one of the main limiting factors to be considered in the design of all sound-recording and sound-reproducing systems.

FREQUENCY DISTORTION AND MODIFICATION

Frequency distortion means that frequencies in the output of a system have relative amplitudes different from those they had in the input to that system. If we pass along from our microphone the full band from 20 to 15,000 cps., and find that our sound track contains no frequencies lower than 200 cycles and none higher than 7,000 cycles, frequency distortion is occurring. As we have already seen, commercial conservatism confines theater sound within an upper limit of 8,000 cycles.

The effect of frequency distortion is well known to all radio listeners. If the tone control of an average radio set is turned down to "bass," it is almost entirely the low frequencies which will be heard. Voices become gruff and

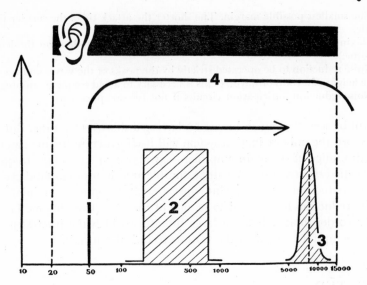

Fig. 10-8. Electrical filters (1-3) with idealized characteristics: (1) a high-pass filter, (2) a band-pass filter,
(3) a sharply tuned filter. A typical response curve of
an FM reproducer is shown at 4; above it appears the
audible spectrum.

boomy, music loses all its brilliance and instruments are easily confused with
one another. When the tone control is turned up to "treble," the high frequencies are accentuated at the expense of the low. Voices now become shrill
and emasculated, and music sounds tinny and lacking in body.

Some alterations in frequency response cannot, however, be classified as
distortions. They should rather be called *modifications*. Often it is desired to
emphasize some band of frequencies to produce a special effect—e.g., a voice
over a telephone or a loudspeaker. Often the object is to compensate for
known losses in other parts of the recording or reproducing system—e.g., high
frequencies in a sound printer or 16 mm. projector. These effects are produced by *filters* and *equalizers* (figure 10-8).

Electrical filters are very similar to the light filters we have already seen in
action. A blue filter is one which transmits a band of frequencies near the
upper frequency end of the visible spectrum, and absorbs all other light frequencies. A *high-pass filter* is one which passes all frequencies on the high
side of (or above) some stated frequency. Thus, a 50-cycle high-pass filter is
one which lets through all frequencies from 50 cycles to the top of the audible
spectrum. Conversely, a *low-pass filter* is one which passes all frequencies on
the low side of (or below) some stated frequency. Thus, a 6,000 cycle low-pass

filter is one which lets through all frequencies from 6,000 cycles to the bottom of the audible spectrum. A *band-pass filter,* as its name implies, lets through only a specific band of frequencies, whittling down or *attenuating* frequencies above and below this band. A *sharply tuned filter* is one with a response curve like an Alpine peak, which lets through only an extremely narrow band of frequencies and has a sharp *cutoff* on either side. A *broadly tuned filter* has an acceptance curve like a gentle hill with very slight gradients on either side. These filters are compounded out of elements present in every home radio set—the qualities of inductance, capacity, and resistance, and the components of coils, capacitors, and resistors. Equalizers and filters have their chief use in the re-recording process described in the next chapter.

AMPLITUDE DISTORTION

Amplitude distortion is more complicated than frequency distortion. It occurs when the shape or wave form of the original waves is altered in its passage through the electrical system. The wave form of most recorded signals looks much like a cross section of a mountain range. But no matter how jagged their profile, all such wave shapes can be broken down by mathematical analysis into fundamental *sine waves* and their *harmonics* or *overtones.* The sine wave is the simplest "natural" wave form in existence. It is the wave form traced out by the tip of a swinging pendulum on a piece of paper traveling at uniform speed in a direction at right angles to the motion of the pendulum. It is the wave form of the simplest mode of vibration of all reeds, diaphragms, and strings. But the majority of musical instruments are designed to produce more complicated vibrations. The *fundamental* sine wave is accompanied by harmonics, the frequencies of which are exact multiples of the frequency of the fundamental. If this fundamental has a frequency of 200 cycles, the *second harmonic* (which should really be called the first harmonic) will be 400 cycles, the *third harmonic,* 600 cycles, and so on (see figure 10-1).

The individual tone or *timbre* of musical instruments has been found to be due to the relative strength of different harmonics. Although the tones of both violin and flute may contain measurable harmonics up to the seventh, one instrument will be richer in second harmonics and the other in third. If the fundamental notes being played on both instruments correspond to 4,000 cycles, the second harmonic will be 8,000 cycles and the third harmonic 12,000 cycles. Hence a reproducer which has little response above 7,000 cycles will fail to distinguish between the two instruments when a 4,000-cycle note is played on them. Flute and violin will sound identical. This is why, when the tone control of a radio set is turned to "bass," instruments become confused and all sense of orchestration is lost.

So far we have been speaking only of wanted harmonics. But electrical devices have an unfortunate tendency to produce unwanted or *spurious har-*

monics, that is, frequencies which do not occur in the original signal. These of course are not separate harmonic frequencies traveling along with the fundamental frequency (like a cat and her kittens). They are alterations or distortions of the shape of the fundamental itself (as when we say of a man walking along the street that he has lumbago—not because we can see the lumbago but because we can see its distorting effect on his walk) . How are these amplitude distortions produced? We have already seen one example in the overloaded light valve in which the tops and bottoms of the waves are cut off because the valve closes before the bottom of the wave is reached, and cannot open far enough to permit the top of the wave to pass through. Thus, as the amplitude of the incoming wave increases and decreases beyond certain points, the valve goes on producing the same output, resulting in a flat-topped and flat-bottomed wave. This type of wave can be analyzed into its harmonic components, so that it is said to be the result of *harmonic distortion.* This does not mean that the harmonics of a given tone in the signal have been distorted; it means that spurious harmonics have been added. Another example already encountered is the clipping of wave fronts in noise-reduction systems. In each example the amplitude of the spurious harmonic can be expressed as a percentage of the amplitude of the fundamental, and this is the usual way of expressing harmonic distortion.

The audible effect of harmonic distortion is hard to describe, although it is familiar to every user of a radio set. When the volume is turned up so that the set is *overloaded,* a peculiar harshness and raspiness sets in. Musical instruments no longer sound clean in tone but become rough and ragged. Speech has an unpleasant edge to it, and the whole effect is jarring to the nerves.

Acceptance of harmonic distortion varies greatly from one individual to another. An uncritical listener will not complain about 10 per cent of spurious second harmonics and 5 per cent of third; a very critical listener would hardly tolerate 2 per cent of second harmonic and 1 per cent of third. As these harmonics lie for the most part in the higher frequency band, it is obvious that the wider the frequency spectrum which a system covers the more unpleasant will any given distortion sound. This is one reason why low-pass filters are essential in reproducing systems of poor or obsolete design.

INTERMODULATION DISTORTION

For a long time it was supposed that most of the amplitude distortion heard on radio receivers and in movie theaters was due to spurious harmonics. There are many reasons for thinking that much of this distortion has another source. Harmonics, as we have seen, are multiples of the fundamental, and as such produce the type of sound which is least offensive to the ear. If a French-horn player plays a passage once, and then plays it over again with an intentional introduction of additional harmonics, all he is doing, in technical terminology, is to introduce harmonic distortion. Yet we know perfectly well that in the second playing an extra richness would be added to the tone, and not the kind of unpleasant noise which is heard from a loudspeaker reproducing a signal suffering from amplitude distortion. Therefore the probability is that the spurious frequencies we hear are not exact multiples of fundamentals, but frequencies which bear some other and nonmusical relation to them. We have therefore to discover a type of distortion which introduces frequencies of this kind.

Intermodulation distortion has only been brought to light in recent years. When two or more tones of different frequencies are fed into a distorting or *non-linear* system, the different frequencies tend to modulate one another. This can easily be seen in the simple illustration of two frequencies (figure 10-9, *a–d*). In *a* is seen a high frequency of low amplitude; in *b* a low frequency of high amplitude. These signals are passing through the system at the same time. Let us suppose that, because of light-valve overloading or curvature of the film char-

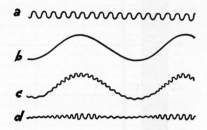

Fig. 10-9. Intermodulation of a high-frequency low-amplitude signal by a low-frequency high-amplitude signal in an overloaded modulating system.

acteristic, the troughs of the high amplitude wave are cut off; *c* shows how the high-frequency wave (which by itself would be quite incapable of overloading the system) is itself curtailed at these points by the failure of the system to respond any further because it has already reached its maximum modulation. The over-all effect, *d,* is that the high frequency is periodically interrupted or modulated by the low frequency. This modulation of one frequency by another is called intermodulation, and its effects were not appreciated so long as the testing of electrical systems was carried out with the aid of single frequencies.

All practical systems have to handle not merely two frequencies but dozens and perhaps hundreds simultaneously. As a result, whenever nonlinearity occurs (owing to curvature of modulation characteristics), innumerable intermodulations set in. These give rise to what are called *sum-and-difference tones,* frequencies corresponding to the sums and differences of the input frequencies. These sum-and-difference tones may in turn intermodulate, so that intermodulation frequencies may be said to breed like rabbits and turn up all over the frequency spectrum in relationships which are additive and subtractive, and therefore have no correspondence with musical intervals. Figure 10-10 shows what happens when two tones, one of 50 cps and one of

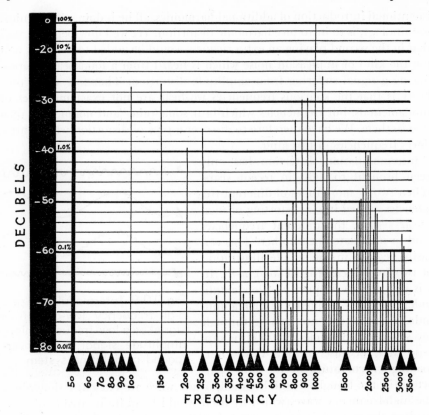

Fig. 10-10. Sum-and-difference tones and spurious harmonics generated in an overloaded amplifier. The two input tones (0 db. level) have a frequency of 50 and 1,000 cycles. All the other frequencies shown are spurious. (Courtesy J. K. Hilliard and the Institute of Radio Engineers.)

1,000 cps are fed together into an only slightly overmodulated amplifier.[6] Fifty-six spurious tones were produced in the band up to 3,150 cps, which was as far as the exploration was carried. Many of these fifty-six tones were of amplitudes too low to be audible, but a number of them were large enough to distort reproduction, and this number would grow rapidly with increase of overloading.

There is little doubt that intermodulation distortion is the main source of audible amplitude distortion. The spurious frequencies which it produces

[6] Data by courtesy of Dr. J. K. Hilliard and the Institute of Radio Engineers, in whose *Proceedings* this diagram appeared.

are hard to distinguish by ear from the spurious harmonics which usually accompany them. It is fairly easy to notice on most phonographs, however, that solo instruments sound sharp and clear, but that when more complex sounds are reproduced—even at the same level—harshness and roughness are introduced.

The light valve is a fruitful source both of intermodulation and harmonic distortion unless the normal ribbon spacing is reduced to a very much smaller image on the film by optical means. This is because of what is called the *ribbon velocity effect,* which is treated fully in the technical literature.

Much distortion analysis today consists of intermodulation tests, in which two widely separated frequencies are fed into the system simultaneously. The output from the system is then filtered so that any intermodulation of the high frequency by the low frequency can be measured.

CROSS MODULATION

This is a kind of distortion peculiar to variable-area recording. When a sharp exposed impression is being made on film by the light beam reflected from the recording galvanometer, the image of each wave is not confined to the area exactly under the beam. Because of the crystalline structure of the emulsion, the light scatters and the image spreads slightly. This is shown in figure 10-11. As a result, the transmission of the negative rises somewhat, and so produces lower-frequency components corresponding to the envelopes of groups of waves. Because speech usually consists of short bursts of modulations, cross modulation is more objectionable on speech than on music. Its effect has been vividly described

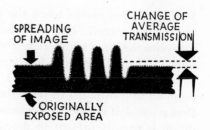

Fig. 10-11. The mechanism of cross-modulation. (Courtesy J. A. Maurer and Audio Engineering.)

by J. A. Maurer as producing "an extremely unpleasant distortion of 'ess' sounds which is as though two pieces of sandpaper were brushed together at the instant each sibilant is reproduced." The correction of cross modulation is discussed in the next section.

DYNAMIC DISTORTION

There are many other interesting kinds of distortion. (Distortion has the same kind of fascination to the electrical engineer as have wounds to a surgeon or fungus to a botanist.) One of these is *dynamic distortion.* Sounds like the human voice or the music of a symphony orchestra have a certain dynamic range, or normal range of amplitudes. (A big orchestra has a range of about eighty decibels.) When reproduced on film this range has to be chopped in half. One reason is that the many obsolete sound systems still in use in movie theaters would be hopelessly overloaded by a symphony orchestra's dynamic range, and would in consequence produce the most horrible noises.

Even if all sound systems were brought up to date, the random noise level in the average movie theater is so loud (owing to conversation, crackling paper, shuffling feet, etc.) that the lowest pianissimo would have to be set fairly high on the loudspeaker to rise above it. The loudest fortissimos would therefore be immensely loud and would cause moviegoers to protest that their sleep was being disturbed or their eardrums shattered. So a more cautious line is taken in Hollywood by squeezing the dynamic range and thus producing dynamic distortion. This is done by compressors or limiters, devices operating in slightly different ways which for a given increase of input produce a less than proportional increase of output.[7] Dynamic distortion of this kind reduces the physical impact of sounds—especially that of fortissimo musical passages and effects like gunfire or explosions.

SCALE DISTORTION

Scale distortion occurs when the whole level of reproduction is higher or lower than normal. This is because the frequency response of the human ear is not the same at different levels. If the reproduction level is lower than normal, the ear becomes less sensitive to the bass frequencies, and these will consequently seem to be lacking. (Try turning down the volume on a radio set and listening to the balance of frequencies.) If the level is higher than normal, it is the bass frequencies which seem to predominate. This condition is usually present in movie theaters, and must be compensated by equalization in the re-recording process.

DISTORTION AT WORK

We have now examined the chief forms of distortion which it is the object of the engineer to eliminate as far as possible from the energy transformer, which includes all the components of the recording and reproducing system from the microphone in the studio to the loudspeaker in the movie theater. It is in part because of the many changes of medium in this transformer that distortions are so difficult to get rid of altogether.

We can see in retrospect how many stages exist in the recording and reproduction of sound on film (figure 10-12). In the studio or on location, sound waves in air are converted into electrical impulses by a microphone (1). The electrical impulses are then amplified and suitably altered (2), and finally impressed on a modulator (3), which converts the electrical signal into fluctu-

---

[7] For a good summary of techniques, see W. K. Grimwood, "Volume Compressors for Sound Recording," *JSMPE*, Jan., 1949, pp. 49–76.

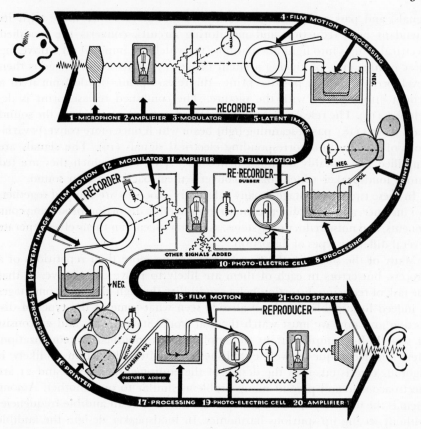

Fig. 10-12. The recording, re-recording and reproduction of sound on film by the optical method, from the speaker's voice to the listener's ear.

ations of a light beam. During amplification, various subsidiary actions take place, such as noise reduction and monitoring, which concern us only so far as they introduce distortion into the signal. The fluctuations of light are imposed on a traveling piece of film (4), producing a latent negative image (5). This latent image is developed (6), and a positive print made from it in a printer (7). The print is then developed (8). In normal studio practice, the print (or an exact duplicate made by printing again from the negative) is re-recorded. In this process, the print travels (9) past a scanning light beam which, modulated by the varying opacity of the film, produces corresponding electrical signals (10) in a phototube. These electrical signals are then suitably transformed (11), by frequency equalization or by being mixed with other signals, and pass again into a recorder. A modulator, once more with its attendant noise-reduction and monitoring circuits, converts the modified electrical signals into light fluctuations (12) which are imposed on a traveling piece of film (13), producing a latent image (14). This latent image is then developed (15), and a positive print—the release print—made from it in a printer (16) together with the picture. The combined release print is developed (17). The release print is then placed in a projector where the sound track travels (18) past a scanning light beam which once more converts variations of opacity into corresponding electrical signals (19). The signals are amplified and suitably modified if necessary (20), after which they are fed into a loudspeaker which finally converts them back (21) into sound.

In these twenty-one stages, many subsidiary processes are lumped together. For instance, audio amplifiers contain innumerable distortion-producing components, and noise-reduction systems, as we have seen, can themselves generate several different types of distortion.

Many of the stages in the transformer are no more than repetitions of a process, but errors in each of them are likely to prove cumulative, so that the task of reducing distortion below audibility through all twenty-one stages is indeed formidable. We have already seen what some of the types of distortion are; now we must watch them at work. Stages 2, 11, and 20 consist of straight-line amplifications or amplifications modified by equalization. Here the technique is well established, and little distortion is likely if rigorous care is taken in the design of the equipment. Stages 1 and 21 are electroacoustic and present many problems similar to one another. Among them is the difficulty of making diaphragms vibrate at all audible frequencies without setting up spurious harmonics. In loudspeaker design, the audible spectrum is usually split up into at least two parts. The high frequencies are covered by a very small and stiff curved diaphragm, which transmits its motion to the air through a multicellular horn designed to give wide distribution of sound. The lower frequencies radiate from a much larger diaphragm, which can move as much as half an inch, enabling it to push large masses of air. This bass speaker is mounted on a baffle, so that waves coming from the back of the diaphragm cannot interfere with and cancel out waves coming from the front.

Stages 5 and 12—the modulator—raise electromechanical difficulties related to mechanical stiffness and resonance. Stages 4, 9, 12, and 18 all involve steadiness of motion in the drives of recorders and reproducers. A vast amount of ingenuity has gone into the design of flutter-free drives with all sorts of fluid and electromagnetic damping systems. Stages 7 and 16 present greater difficulties, in that they are not only mechanical but photochemical in character. Printers require a high degree of mechanical accuracy in securing freedom from slippage in continuous machines, as well as freedom from scanning losses when an optical system is introduced. But as well as this there are photographic imperfections arising from the penetration of the exposing rays of light into the emulsion and base of the film, with a consequent loss of image sharpness due to multiple reflections. Stages 10 and 19, in which light is passed through film onto a phototube, are relatively straightforward, as the modern phototube has excellent characteristics and remains stable over long periods.

The remaining stages, 5, 6, 8, 14, 15, and 17 concern the transfer of an image to a light-sensitive emulsion, first by exposure, then by development. Here, some of the most interesting types of distortion occur, and here too they can be corrected.

Variable-area recording, as we have seen, gives rise to cross modulation, which produces harmonic distortion and spurious envelope frequencies in the original recording. It is normal practice to correct this by a careful choice of printing exposure, so that when the exposure takes place through the clear areas of track, the image spreads in the opposite direction and so cancels out the negative effect. This cancellation is rather critical, since the distortion components must be about 40 decibels down from maximum signal if they are to be inaudible. The direct-positive recording system discussed in the last chapter removes the very possibility of cancellation, because there is no printing stage. Hence, emulsions with a very low image spread must be used, and given a lower exposure.

With variable-density recording the problem is quite different. It is to match together the curvature of two curved characteristics (the negative and positive film) in such a way that the resultant over-all characteristic is straight. Only thus will negative exposure and print transmission be linearly related. A wrong choice of processing variables thus leads to a resultant curvature containing many harmonic and intermodulation components. The track sounds like an overloaded radio set, where the distortion springs from exactly the same cause—for the film characteristic has its counterpart in the well-known grid-volts–plate-current (E_g–I_p) tube curve. Intermodulation analysis was in fact developed as a practical tool to overcome the difficulties of variable-density processing.

However, even when negative exposure, negative development, and positive exposure have all been correctly set, the maximum output from a variable-density track is at present some six decibels below that of a properly processed variable-area track.

In the correct over-all procedure for variable-density processing the over-all gamma should be very close to unity, a condition we have already seen to apply to the picture. But the effect of departures from unity is very different. Gamma variations in the picture produce alterations in contrast, increasing contrast where the curve is too steep, lowering it where the slope falls away as in the toe and shoulder regions. But in sound recording the characteristic curves of the negative and positive film are part of the modulating system, and curvature results in nonlinear distortion. In such matters the ear is a great deal more sensitive than the eye—that is, the ear is more easily offended by spurious harmonics than the eye by errors of contrast.

METHODS OF IMPROVING THE SOUND TRACK

The last ten years have seen a great multiplication of proposals for improving the sound track and providing better sound in theaters. Of these proposals only a very short account can be given here; for further information the technical literature should be consulted.

Push-pull.—Readers familiar with electronics will have noticed the similarity between film and vacuum-tube characteristics. The grid-volts–plate-current curve has the same straight middle section and rounded shoulder and toe as the curve relating density and log exposure. Departures from linearity in the tube consequently produce the same kind of distortions as those found in film, when modulations are impressed on the two media. It is therefore not surprising that the *push-pull* method of tube coupling, with its cancellation of even-order harmonic distortion, should find a counterpart on film. The sound track, which may be of standard or of double width (the 200-mil track), is divided into two halves which are separately recorded by a double light valve or a double galvanometer mask, and separately scanned in the reproducer with the aid of a twin phototube.

In figure 10-13, the light beam has just returned to the unmodulated position, and the track appears identical to a normal bilateral track, as seen in figure 10-5. But, as soon as the shaped light beam starts moving up and down under the influence of modulation, a marked difference occurs. On the upstrokes, less of the left-hand and more of the right-hand side of the track is scanned by the slit, and on the downstroke, more of the left-hand side and less of the right-hand side. Thus, at all times, the total amount of exposing light reaching the film (in the absence of noise reduction) is constant. This is the condition for producing a Class A push-pull track—or two identical sound records 180° out of phase. It will be noticed that noise reduction must be applied, either by bias or movable shutters (the latter shown in figure 10-13).

Figure 10-14 shows a push-pull track. Suppose the narrow white line to be a reproducer slit, and let it be moved to and fro along the track. The transparent area of track under the slit, and therefore the transmission, remains constant. Hence, if the track is played through a normal reproducer, the sound

output is zero.[8] However, if the two
halves of the reproducing light beam are
"seen" by separate phototubes, the electrical outputs can be combined 180° out
of phase, so that they add instead of can-
celling. Now suppose that a splice comes
along, as shown in figure 10-14, in which
the whole track is crossed by a heavy
density followed by a thin transparent
line caused by excess scraping. When the
two sides of the splice are separately
scanned and added out of phase, the result is just the opposite to the effect of
the track itself. This is because the two
halves of the splice are alike, whereas
the two halves of the modulations are
always opposite. Differently expressed,
$(+4) + (-4)$, corresponding to the modulation, equals $+8$ if the central plus
sign is considered to be changed to a
minus in the reproduction. On the other
hand, $(+4) + (+4)$, the splice, equals
zero if the sign is similarly changed.

Thus push-pull recordings need no
blooping, a great convenience in sound
cutting, as will be seen in the next chapter.

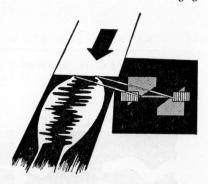

Fig. 10-13. How a class A
push-pull track is produced. As
the shaped light beam moves
upwards across the fixed slit,
less of the left-hand and more
of the right-hand side of the
track is scanned by the slit, and
on the downstroke more of the
left-hand side and less of the
right-hand side. Thus, apart
from noise reduction, the total
amount of light reaching the
film is always constant. Note
the noise-reduction shutters,
shown closed for an unmodulated passage.

Although the improved cancellation of distortion has not warranted replacing theater equipment with push-pull, the push-pull track is very extensively used in original recording. As we have seen, distortions in the energy
transformer are multiplicative; their reduction in the early stages is therefore
well worth the extra complication and cost.

---

[8] A standard width (100-mil) push-pull sound track cannot, for this reason, be reproduced
on a standard projector or moviola sound head; the better the balance of the track, the
more complete will be the silence. Two hundred-mil push-pull tracks (sound only, no
picture) are, however, reproducible in emergency on standard machines, for each half of
the double track behaves like a normal single track. However, a *Class B push-pull* track will
sound distorted when thus reproduced. Its chief advantage is that it provides automatic
noise reduction without additional equipment.

Stories are still told of the small-town projectionist who was sent a push-pull release
print by mistake, and soon learned from the reactions of the audience that the picture was
running in total silence. He frantically checked his equipment and found it in perfect
order, put on a test reel and was rewarded by a full volume of sound; then finally, having
assured himself that there were plenty of modulations on the new track, phoned the local
film exchange and told them that his theater must be jinxed.

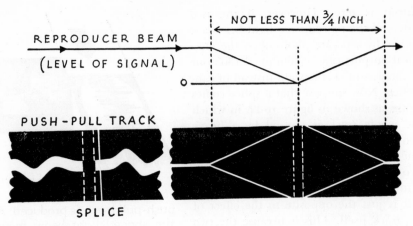

Fig. 10-14. The bloop, and why push-pull tracks do not need blooping.

CONTROL TRACKS

The sound channel today is a monaural device of limited volume range. The sounds it emits are not to be compared in variety and interest with those which strike the ears in ordinary life. Only habit has accustomed the movie-goer to an inferior substitute within the theater walls—habit and a wish to escape from life into a world of comforting sights and soothing and mellifluous sounds.

Only a few experimental attempts have been made, therefore, to improve strikingly what the listener hears. The most notable of these attempts was *Fantasia,* the joint achievement of Walt Disney and Leopold Stokowski, who had long been interested in the perfecting of musical reproduction. In *Fantasia,* the dynamic range of the original orchestra was restored in the theater by means of a *control track,* an additional sound track carrying electrical instructions which automatically expanded the range of loudnesses recorded on the regular tracks. Thus the volume range in the theater was made independent of the amplitude limitations of film recording (ground noise, etc.).

Great ingenuity has been expended on the positioning of control tracks on 35 mm. film, since the existing sound, picture, and perforations take up almost all the available space. None of the proposed systems, however, has so far been accepted in the industry, largely because there is supposed to be no popular demand for better reproduction of music or natural sounds.

STEREOSOUND

Stereophonic sound removes the other great disability of present day electrical reproduction—its one-eared character. We locate sounds in space by having two spaced-out ears, much as we locate objects in depth by having two spaced-out eyes. The location of sounds is quite complex, and even now is not fully understood.[9] When sound reaches a listener from an off-center position (i.e., when the source is at an angle to the perpendicular bisector of the line joining the listener's ears through his head), correct location of the source is partly a matter of phase discrimination between trains of waves at the two ears as to which "gets there fustest." This effect is most pronounced at frequencies below 1,000 cps. Next, the head acts as a barrier which favors the ear on the side of the off-center sound by partly blocking the other one. This causes a loudness difference between the two ears, which is interpreted directionally by the brain, reinforced by the fact that the shielded ear hears only an attenuated version of the higher frequency components of the sound. Thus by making use of the three characteristics of a train of sound waves— frequency, intensity, and phase—the ears most ingeniously transmit a variety of intelligence which the brain puts together as a localization of the sound source.

The necessity of simulating the two ears of the human auditor in the transmission of sound has long been recognized. Seventy years ago Clément Ader, a French scientist, gave a demonstration of stereophonic sound in Paris.[10] The following account, written by a contemporary, Amédée Guillemin,[11] may stand today as a model of clear exposition of the principles involved. "We cannot however pass over in silence the most remarkable, and the most decisive of these experiments; we mean the telephonic arrangements organized in the autumn of 1881 at the Palais de l'Industrie in Paris in four rooms at the Electrical Exhibition. A numerous and impatient public was able every evening to listen to the representations going on at the Opera, to hear the voices of the singers, the orchestral accompaniments, and even the murmurs and applause of the spectators."

After describing the electrical installation, which included no less than twelve microphones disposed around the footlights, Guillemin goes on,

[9] See, for instance, Bell System Technical Journal, April, 1934, describing the researches of Steinberg and Snow, and the following papers by K. de Boer in Philips Technical Review, "Stereophonic Sound Reproduction," V (April, 1940): 107; "The Formation of Stereophonic Images," VIII (Feb., 1946): 51; "Some Particulars of Directional Hearing," VI (Dec., 1941): 359 (with Th. van Urk).

[10] Ader was the first man to rise into the air in a powered flying machine. This was in 1890, fourteen years before the Wright brothers' first flight. The plane, however, was not under proper control and traveled only a few yards.

[11] Electricity and Magnetism, London: 1891.

"An interesting innovation made by Ader in the method of hearing is that which consists of putting each hearer into separate communication with the two sides of the stage. Whilst one of the receivers—that, for example, which the listener is to place to the right ear—is connected with a transmitter situated at one side of the stage, the other receiver, to be placed at the left ear, is connected with the transmitter placed on the other side of the stage. It is easy to see the reason of this arrangement. All the transmitters are simultaneously affected by the same sounds—for example, by the vibrations of the voice of a singer. But this singer, according to the place which he occupies on the stage, is not at the same distance from each of them; consequently the song will be reproduced with an intensity corresponding to its distance from the source of the sound. If the action is on the right of the stage, the sensation transmitted to the right ear, we may conclude, will be stronger than that transmitted to the left ear. Should the actor change his position, the sound would also change, and it would then be the turn of the left ear to be more strongly impressed. The result of these changes is to give the listener an idea of the respective positions of the singers on the stage, and of their movements; and thus a listener is led to feel as if he were present at the representation, but with his eyes shut."

The description is both clear and up-to-date; but it is evident that Ader's early anticipation of Fantasound was far ahead of its time, for Guillemin regretfully concludes, "The success of this device was great; but the laying down of such numerous wires was very expensive, and we doubt whether it excited any other interest than curiosity."

Perhaps Walt Disney might wryly admit that his own experience in *Fantasia* was not altogether different. Though *Fantasia* was the first, and up to now the only film to exploit commercially the resources of stereosound, its producers sacrificed many dramatic possibilities by concentrating exclusively on the reproduction of music. The average moviegoer knows little and cares less about the exact placement of the instruments of a symphony orchestra. If, however, he could hear a rifle bullet ricochetting toward him round the walls of the movie theater, a hailstorm beating down from its ceiling, footsteps which tiptoed across the screen without any visible person to produce them, he would assuredly react with the same surprise and excitement with which audiences greeted the first talking films. All these effects are possible with stereophonic sound.

Basically, this system calls for a multiplicity of loudspeakers. Three of them, as a rule, are situated behind the screen, left, center, and right, so that sounds may be made to traverse the screen without that effort of association with a noncentral visual image called for most of the time by the present centrally placed loudspeaker. The remaining speakers are mounted on the walls, the ceiling, and at the back of the auditorium, and all of them must be fed from separate sound tracks, so that any particular sound can be channeled exactly where it is needed. If the number of speakers exceeds the number of tracks, it is necessary to resort to complicated control tracks, as previously explained. It is impossible at present to accommodate even one extra sound track on a release print without sacrificing dynamic range. The use of six or seven sound tracks demands a separate band of film, with all the difficulties this entails in commercial projection.

However, if these problems could be overcome—and the laying of transparent sound tracks over the picture image would provide an elegant solution—there are various technical advantages which would flow from the use of stereophonic sound. The wide area from which music and sound are projected makes a much higher maximum loudness level acceptable to an audience, thus increasing the usable dynamic range of film. The separation of instruments (and sound effects) between different groups of speakers enables them to be reproduced with striking clarity because of the almost total absence of intermodulation. And for the first time in film history, invisible "presences" can be created on the screen and moved about at will. But the most significant difference to be anticipated is that sound would come out boldly into the audience, which it would envelop on all sides, as if they were, indeed, participants in the drama. When stereovision has been added, the shadowy surface of today's cinema screen, with all the images that have thronged it this last half century, will, we may hope, not become a thing of the past, but will take on a relationship to the new movies rather like that which a silhouette bears to a Van Gogh.[12]

VARIABLE-AREA AND VARIABLE-DENSITY RECORDING

Whether or not more versatile sound systems come into general use, methods of photochemical recording on film will still fall into two main groups—variable-area and variable-density. These two types of track are so markedly different, however, that the newcomer to film is often prompted to ask why the huge complication and expense of developing both systems in so small a field has been so long continued. He may suspect that large corporations use their resources to maintain an obsolete device because they have invested a great deal of capital in it. But this explanation happens to be far wide of the mark.

The two corporations which effectively command the 35 mm. sound recording field in North America have interests in both variable-area and variable-density systems, even though the former is always associated in the film-maker's mind with RCA, and the latter with Western Electric. More-

12 The technical and aesthetic issues thus briefly raised here will be fully discussed in the author's forthcoming book, *The Stereocinema*.

over, the manufacture of sound-recording equipment forms only a very small part of the business of both these corporations.

We must look elsewhere for the reasons why variable-area recording has not ousted variable-density, or vice versa. In the first place, both systems are capable of giving results of the highest quality, and both have been developed neck-and-neck. First one has led for a short time, then the other, in the race after improved sound fidelity. Second, any complex mechanical and electrical system bears the stamp or individuality of its own maker. Some equipment will be built relatively cheaply in forms which are frequently modified and improved. Other equipment will be more conservatively designed, and built with the most exacting and precise (and in some ways superfluous) craftsmanship. Engineers have very marked preferences for the kind of equipment they install; but these preferences are no more logical than a preference for Léger or Picasso.

More important than either of these reasons is the fact that one of the two systems excels in some important respects, the other in others, so that the balance of merit does not tip decisively in either direction. It is worth examining these merit factors in a little detail.

It is often said that variable-density recording requires more exacting laboratory standards than variable-area, because the latter system merely paints a wave form in the two tones of black and white (i.e., transparent film), whereas the former requires a perfectly correct gradation of tones over a wide range, thus introducing the well-known curvatures of the film characteristic. However, to get results of the best possible quality from variable-area recording, equally narrow processing tolerances must be maintained. And since these tolerances can easily be met in the modern laboratory, no great advantage results on this score from the use of variable-area track. It is true, however, that indifferent processing leads to distortion with variable-density more rapidly than with variable-area tracks.

The variable-area system in which the modulator, the beam-shaping aperture, and the noise-reduction vanes are all separate, is much more easily convertible to different types of track than the variable-density system which uses a light valve. The former requires only the changing of an aperture plate to go from standard bilateral to push-pull track, and from one kind of push-pull to another. The latter necessitates the substitution of one type of light valve for another, involving difficult optical and electrical changes.

The variable-area system is less liable to the kind of ground noise resulting from inherent graininess of the film. This is because the dense black of the shuttered areas can be made uniformly nontransmitting, whereas the corresponding scale of densities in the variable-density system cannot be made absolutely uniform, owing to the microscopic structure of the emulsion, especially at higher densities. This increases the inherent surface noise of the film.

Sound-track cutters usually prefer variable-area tracks because they are so much easier to "read," that is, they reveal the form of words and musical notes from the shapes of their modulations. This of course is because the variable-area track is a familiar oscillogram, whereas the variable-density track is an unfamiliar densogram. For the same reason, visual inspection of the quality of variable-area records is much simpler. Overmodulation can be checked instantly by examination, and the working of noise reduction is also easily visible. This is not so with variable-density tracks.

Some other points can be mentioned more briefly. In the variable-area system, a simple mechanical device will show the recordist the exact behavior of the galvanometer at all times, while recording is actually taking place. This is not so easily contrived with the light valve. The sound level from a release print is somewhat higher with variable-area recording. Not until 1949 was it possible to make a variable-density direct-positive track.[13] By making a positive image directly in recording, one stage of printing is avoided, and noise-reduction anticipation can be more easily secured.

This may seem a formidable list of advantages possessed by one system over the other. Yet the careful reader will have noticed that many of the seeming defects of variable-density recording with the light valve dwindle away as the efficiency of the system is improved. For instance, in a well-run studio, frequent checks for light-valve performance make it unnecessary to watch the modulator's behavior during recording, as is possible with the galvanometer. System checks, moreover, make visual inspection of overmodulation and noise-reduction action unnecessary. And the same sort of reasoning applies to the other factors.

Variable-density recording also has several inherent advantages. The variable-density track is much less susceptible to the kind of ground noise arising from "pinholes" and scratches in the positive film. This makes it less necessary to provide reprints of music and effects tracks for re-recording. Secondly, when correctly processed, the variable-density track has a smoother overload characteristic than the variable-area track, resulting in much less objectionable distortion when maximum modulation is exceeded. The reason is that the toe and shoulder bends of the film characteristic are gradually curved, so that though they introduce distortion, they compress the amplitude range before distortion becomes too audibly unpleasant. This automatic compression characteristic makes occasional overloads inoffensive, whereas with variable-area recording the abrupt cutting off of peaks sounds harsh and

[13] C. R. Keith and V. Pagliarulo, "Direct Positive Variable-Density Recording with the Light Valve," *JSMPE*, June, 1949, pp. 690–698.

grating at once. But with modern compressor amplifiers in circuit, this advantage becomes of less moment. Finally, the variable-density track gives rise only to a loss of higher frequencies and not to amplitude distortion, when it is scanned with a slit in incorrect alignment.

MAGNETIC RECORDING

There is no need for the film maker to forget the theory of photographic recording when he moves on to magnetic recording. Many of the concepts and many of the techniques are the same.

Consider first how the audio modulations are laid down. On the photographic track they appear either as wave silhouettes (variable-area) or as densograms (variable-density). On the magnetic track they appear as "magnetograms." A magnetic sound track, however, does not have a constantly changing gradient, like a variable-density record. Every magnet, no matter how small, has two separate and opposite poles, north and south, the basic law of which is that like poles repel and unlike poles attract one another.[14] If the magnet is very short, its north and south poles will be close to each other, the lines of force will leak around, and the magnet will tend to demagnetize itself. This effect is important in magnetic recording, where many of the magnets are no longer than a few thousandths of an inch.

Given, then, a piece of film and the object of creating on it an audio-wave pattern in tiny magnets. How can this best be done? Obviously the film emulsion is useless. It has no magnetic properties and can be scrapped at once. Another kind of flexible ribbon must be found to take its place.

About twenty years ago in Germany researchers discovered a way of minutely subdividing ferrous magnetic materials, out of which they proceeded to make highly efficient tuning inductances for radio sets. Soon afterwards it was discovered that this material could be coated on a paper tape and fixed or bonded to it. In this way a thin, flexible, and strong permanent magnet was produced for the first time, a magnet capable of being differently magnetized at different points along its length. Thus was realized in practical form the dream of Valdemar Poulsen, the Danish engineer who at the turn of the century conceived the idea of "a picture in magnetism" of sound waves along the length of a steel wire.

The magnetized medium is today a flexible ribbon of film or paper coated with a finely divided ferromagnetic powder of high retentivity—that is, ability to retain the magnetism induced in it. The audio signal is impressed

[14] Little magnetic toys, made out of the newer alloys like Alnico V, can now be bought at dime stores. They have convex bases, and will move one another by attraction and repulsion over distances as great as half an inch, if placed on a smooth table.

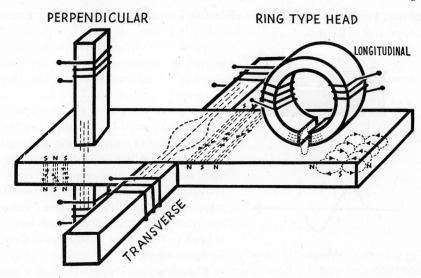

Fig. 10-15. Three methods of magnetic recording. (Courtesy Dorothy O'Dea, RCA, and SMPTE.)

on this ribbon by a magnet of opposite characteristics—a soft magnet, which gains and loses magnetism easily.

The modulating device which thus takes shape is not unlike the variable-area galvanometer sketched in figure 10-3. In this device the audio current was circulated through a coil wound over the poles of a soft magnet, and its effect was felt on an armature or thin strip of iron mounted in the narrow gap between the poles. If we were to remove this armature, and pass our ferromagnetic film strip through the gap, it would receive and retain a magnetic force varying from moment to moment with the fluctuations of the signal. Our "picture in magnetism" would be complete. To reproduce this "picture" from the magnetized film, it would merely be necessary to pass the film close to the narrow gap in another head, whereupon magnetic currents would be induced in the head, and electric currents in a coil wound round it. These currents would be amplified in the usual way and passed into a loud-speaker or another recorder. Thus the recording and reproducing heads are essentially similar in construction, and are sometimes identical.

There are three ways in which the magnetic gap can be placed in relation to the tape, thus producing three different types of recording: transverse, perpendicular, and longitudinal (figure 10-15). Each has its advantages and disadvantages. Transverse recording places the pole pieces much too far apart to secure a strong magnetic field in the gap, unless the tape is inconveniently narrow. On the other hand, the elementary magnets are of constant length, irrespective of frequency, so that there is no self-demagnetization at the higher

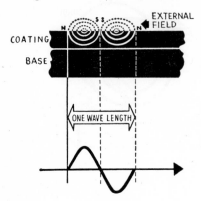

frequencies. Perpendicular recording demands an inconveniently thin tape, but also has the advantage of constant magnet length. Longitudinal recording, currently universal, places the magnetizing poles very close to one another, but only at the expense of a varying magnet length. The ring recording head shown in figure 10-15 has obvious analogies to the optical recorder: both require very narrow slits which must "see" less than one cycle on the track. How the magnetizing force is related to the signal wave form is shown in figure 10-16.

Fig. 10-16. Magnetic track and recorded signal. (Courtesy H. A. Howell, Indiana Steel Products Co., and SMPTE.)

The recording characteristic of a magnetic tape is not wholly unlike the film characteristic so often discussed in earlier chapters. It is based on the hysteresis curve of the magnetic material, which is explained in any standard textbook on electricity and magnetism. It must suffice here to say that the magnetic characteristic is by no means linear, but can be straightened out by applying along with the signal an alternating bias current of high frequency, usually between 25,000 and 100,000 cycles per second. The theory behind this procedure is still not generally agreed on, but the practice has been thoroughly investigated and brought under control.

Since magnetic devices respond less to the absolute value of the magnetic field at any instant than to its rate of change,[15] the output of a magnetic recorder will rise with increase of frequency until other factors such as self-demagnetization and gap loss combine to produce a drop.[16] This recording characteristic is not difficult to correct by the use of a mirror-image characteristic in the reproducing amplifier (figure 10-17).

[15] The theory of a rate-of-change device may be made somewhat clearer by an analogy. Let us imagine an electric fan having a small number of blades. In front of this fan a light card is suspended by one corner. The fan starts to revolve slowly. The suspended card remains almost motionless. Now the fan speeds up. The air molecules are rapidly accelerated; the rate of change of their motion increases. A steady wind is generated by the fan, and this wind becomes stronger the faster the fan rotates (i.e. the higher the frequency of the blades). The card blows out farther and farther, corresponding to a stronger and stronger current flowing through the magnetic coil windings with increase of frequency.

[16] The self-demagnetizing effect (arising from the smallest effective magnetic particle) has been compared with the resolving power of a photographic emulsion (arising from the smallest effective photographic particle). Gap loss is obviously analogous to slit loss in optical recording.

The requirement of extreme steadiness of motion affects equally the magnetic and the photographic track. This is the principal reason why professional magnetic recorders cost little less than conventional film recorders, and why the conversion of film to magnetic recorders has proved so simple. No more is required than the substitution or addition of heads, a change in the equalizing characteristics of the amplifiers, and the provision of a high-frequency generator for recording-bias and erasing.

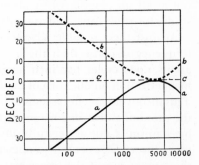

Fig. 10-17. Recording and reproducing characteristics. In this simplified diagram, curve **a** shows the magnetic recording characteristic, at first rising with frequency and then drooping. Curve **b** shows a mirror-image characteristic of curve **a** built into the reproducer, with the result that the final output curve (**c**) is flat within the effective pass band of the system. (Courtesy Earl Masterson, RCA, and SMPTE.)

Thus in drastically simplified form may be explained the methods of recording and reproducing magnetic tracks. There remains a third process which has won them great popularity—the wiping off or erasing of the magnetic record. Most people have experimented in childhood with small permanent magnets, and have discovered that the magnetism can be made to dwindle and finally disappear either by leaving off the magnet's "keeper" (a bar of soft iron joining the magnetic poles and preventing the leakage of flux), or by hammering the magnet repeatedly, or by stroking the magnet with another magnet in such a way as to induce an opposite magnetism. It is by making use of this last method of demagnetization that magnetic recording achieves one great advantage over photographic recording. If a suitable current (direct or alternating is passed through a special erasing head, the signal magnetization is destroyed and the tape is made ready to record again.

The first years of development of magnetic recording have shown that its principal technical advantage—apart from erasability and immediate playback—is the very high signal-to-noise ratio which it is able to achieve. A ratio of 60 to 70 decibels seems to be well within its capacity, if the system noise (tube hiss, etc.) can be held below this level. This compares with a ratio of about 55 decibels for photographic recording on film traveling at the same speed. This wide dynamic range, coupled with a smooth overload characteristic, makes it easy for comparatively inexpert operators in the field to come back with entirely usable sound tracks. Not only is monitoring less critical; the absence of exciter-lamp adjustments, and the handling of film in daylight, give confidence to the newly fledged sound man. Above all, the ability to hear what he has just recorded protects him against disastrous surprises which are not at all uncommon when photographic sound tracks are returned to the studio for processing, and are only listened to some days later.

Against these notable advantages must at present be set a rather poorer frequency response than the best photographic recording (a maximum of about 1,000 cycles per inch against about 1,500), and a tendency for the magnetization on one turn of tape to "print through" onto an adjacent turn. This inconvenient effect seems to be increased by increases of temperature and the proximity of strong magnetic fields, but it occurs only irregularly and its mechanism is not as yet fully understood. Finally, magnetic recorders and reproducers are essentially contact devices, that is, they must actually touch the tape or film if the frequency response is not to be seriously impaired.[17] This need for contact introduces a frictional drag into recorders and reproducers which will make it harder to eliminate flutter, especially if there are minute roughnesses in the tape coating. Also, some unavoidable wear is imposed on the film and the head.

Though practical magnetic techniques are still variable, the broad lines on which they will develop are already clear, and call for a brief summary.

PRACTICAL APPLICATION

Let us suppose that it is decided to make most or all original recordings on magnetic tape. The way is still not clear. Standards must be set up. There are two important areas of choice. One is tape speed; the other, perforations or no perforations. Each needs some examination.

Speed.—The faster a recording medium travels, the better (in general) is its high frequency response, because more space is allotted to each wave. Hence the proponents of a new medium will tend to set a very high speed of travel for it, since this is by far the simplest method of achieving high-frequency fidelity. Once it has been established that the medium is practical, engineers will not object to devising ways of improving it which result from self-imposed restrictions. We have seen that modern tape recording reaches easily up to 1,000 cycles per inch. This is not quite up to the level of photographic recording—but that has been under intense commercial development

---

17 Recent experiments have shown that, if the recording response is flat, and the reproducing head is spaced 1 mil from the film, the output will be 30 decibels down on a recorded wavelength of 1.75 mils. The same large drop in output is experienced when a 1.6 mil wave is separated from the head by a gap of only 0.75 mils. And finally, when the gap is 1 mil and the wavelength 5 mils, the drop in output is 12 decibels. (It will be recalled that, at a film speed of 18 inches per second [35 mm.], a 1.75 mil wave corresponds to 10,300 cycles, and a 5 mil wave to 3,600 cycles. At 7.2 inches per second [16 mm.], these frequencies are 4,120 and 1,450 cycles.) Data from Herr, Murphey and Wetzel, *JSMPE*, Jan., 1949, pp. 30–40.

for twenty-five years. Hence, whenever convenience demands it, tape and film speeds may be made equal. And this applies to 16 mm. film as well as to 35 mm.

However, there may well be occasions in the design of portable high-fidelity equipment when a higher tape speed is the simplest way of improving the frequency response. The designer (especially if he plans to use unperforated tape not suitable for film editing) will then feel free to raise the speed to any figure he thinks necessary, with the proviso that re-recording to film will be carried out on the same or an equivalent machine.

In short, the two speeds likely to be standardized for magnetic film are 36 feet and 90 feet per minute, but nonstandardized higher speeds for location recording may remain in use for several years.

Perforations.—The film perforation is an ancient and admirable device, whose invention by Edison and Eastman removed at a stroke the problems which had harassed Marey and other early workers in cinematography. It enables each frame of film to be registered with minute accuracy upon the same area in the camera and the projector. It holds the sound and picture in exact projected separation. But it has its disadvantages, which have loomed slowly larger as the obstacles to good sound quality have one by one been surmounted.

Briefly, these disadvantages stem from two causes, one chemical, the other mechanical. The passage of film through a developer is something like that of a chain of buckets through a tank. The buckets are the perforations, the chain the spaces between them. Because of the lifting action of the perforations on the developer, development is uneven and there tends to be impressed on 35 mm. film a 96-cycle modulation.[18] This defect is absent from magnetic recording on 35 mm. film, which makes no use of the developing process.

However, an analogous effect occurs when film is passed over sprockets. The engagement of the teeth with the perforations tends to push the film ahead slightly or hold it back slightly. This also causes a 96-cycle modulation, which must be removed, in both recorder and reproducer, by elaborate and expensive stabilizing devices. Since this disturbance is greatest in the area close to the perforations, some improvement would result by recording sound in the center of the 35 mm. film. However, it could be eliminated at the source by simply abolishing the perforations.

This raises the problem of synchronization. It was shown in chapter iv that an error of no more than one-fortieth of one per cent could be tolerated

18 At 24 frames per second, with 4 perforations on each side of each frame, 96 perforations pass the sound head each second, resulting in a 96-cycle frequency which is of course much closer to a square wave than to a sine wave, and therefore contains numerous higher harmonics.

in dialogue recording—which is much smaller than the best friction drive can assure. Hence, some self-synchronizing mechanism must be devised if perforations are to be eliminated. Among the many ingenious suggestions which have been put forward, the most workable seems to be that of recording on the tape (but on a separate control track) a pulse at 60 cycles, or any other convenient frequency. Now suppose that, owing to slippage during recording, the tape slows down slightly. The 60-cycle pulses will crowd a little more closely together (i.e., the recorded frequency rises). Next, the tape speeds up, perhaps due to a rise in line voltage. The pulses stretch out again (i.e., the recorded frequency falls). Thus on the sound track is impressed a slightly varying frequency, centering on 60 cycles. This track is played back through a head which picks up the control tone and uses it to operate its own synchronous drive motor. Thus if the control frequency falls slightly below 60 cycles, the motor momentarily slows down; and if the frequency increases, the motor turns faster. The signal is therefore reconstituted in exactly its original form, and will of course synchronize with any truly constant-speed picture recording made on perforated photographic film.[19]

Devices of this kind may compete successfully with perforated magnetic film outside the major studios, where advanced technique, developed over the years, has eliminated most of the flutter inseparable from the use of perforations. However, the existence of nonstandard speed recordings, and recordings on unperforated tape, raises acutely the problems of editing and re-recording. Before magnetic editing equipment became available, it was customary to re-record all good sound takes directly onto film, which was developed, printed, and edited in the usual way. Not only does this technique waste in second-stage processing all the time gained by initial magnetic recording; it throws away quality too. It cannot be regarded as anything but a makeshift. However, sound tracks which are nonstandard (whether because of speed or perforations) must be handled in this way, since they will not fit standard synchronizers and moviolas.

All standard magnetic tracks are likely in future to be edited on equipment specially designed for them. Invisible modulations present the cutter with obvious difficulties, since he has been accustomed for years to "reading" modulations by eye, and with increasing experience needs less and less to resort to the moviola. However, it is not difficult to design a moviola sound head which will stop instantly at the touch of a switch, so that the beginnings and ends of modulations can be accurately marked; moreover, substances are now available which may be applied to selected portions of the track to render the modulations faintly visible. Cutting tables will also be fitted with

[19] A full account of this interesting system is given in R. H. Ranger, "Sprocketless Synchronous Magnetic Tape," *JSMPTE*, Mar., 1950, pp. 328–336. See also Walter T. Selsted, "Synchronous Recording on ¼ Inch Magnetic Tape," *JSMPTE*, Sept., 1950, pp. 279–284.

portable magnetic sound heads, through which the film can be threaded and pulled by a rewinder, exactly as with a handviewer.

Thus it will not be hard for editors to accustom themselves to working with both kinds of sound track during the changeover period from optical to magnetic recording, which may indeed occupy several years, since effects and music libraries are well stocked with optical tracks which it would be too expensive to re-record all at once.

All modern re-recorders are built in such a way that they will mount magnetic heads, and most film recorders may also be so adapted. Thus the way is open for a gradual conversion of all production studios to magnetic recording. The laboratories will presumably be able to cut down their sound-processing facilities to the bare minimum required to develop the final re-recorded negative. At the same time re-recording facilities will have to be expanded, for all sound workprints and reprints must be produced by re-recording from the original track. The terms negative, positive, and dupe will become obsolete in sound recording, and will be replaced by "original" and "re-recorded track." Careful note will have to be taken of the number of re-recordings through which a track has passed, for there will be inevitable losses at each stage. Special devices for handling magnetic sound tracks more conveniently will doubtless be developed as experience is gained in their use.[20]

BASIC PROBLEMS OF RECORDING

Setting aside the digression on magnetic recording, we have now traced the signal back from the loudspeaker in the movie theater to the projector, to the sound track, to the recorder, to the main amplifier, to the mixer unit, and to the microphone. Throughout this long journey the techniques have been mainly electronic. But at either end of the chain acoustic problems are met with. Something will be said later about the acoustics of projection. Here we are concerned with the acoustics of recording, both indoors and outdoors.

Imagine the very simple example of two characters talking to one another. The camera is shooting over the shoulder of one against the full face of the other. Now the speech quality of these two sources of sound is quite different when heard from the position of the camera. The full-face character

[20] Progress in the development of magnetic recording, and in the formulation of its general theory, are reported principally in the *Journal of the Society of Motion Picture and Television Engineers, Audio Engineering,* and *Electronics.* The following general articles are recommended: "Magnetic Recording," *JSMPE,* Jan., 1947, pp. 1–62; W. W. Wetzel, "Review of the Present Status of Magnetic Recording Theory," *Audio Engineering,* Nov., 1947, pp. 14–17; Dorothy O'Dea, "Magnetic Recording for the Technician," *JSMPE,* Nov., 1948, pp. 468–480, and other articles in the same issue, pp. 481–500.

will be heard with plenty of brilliance in the sibilants and a high degree of intelligibility which comes with the higher frequencies. These frequencies, however, are very directional, that is, they tend to travel in straight lines; so the voice of the other character, whose head is turned away, will be lacking in higher frequencies and so will sound muffled and hard to understand. But the object of the shot is not merely to make a literal rendering of the scene: it is to make an intelligible rendering. Hence, a single camera angle calls for two microphone angles.

This notion of microphone angle is very important to grasp. Many directors and cameramen think in terms of the picture camera only. They regard the microphone simply as a convenient mechanical ear which can be placed anywhere outside the shot (no matter how far from the speaker), and which will then render perfectly all dialogue within range. It is also sometimes expected not to hear various sounds originating outside the set and having no bearing on the action.

Of course no mechanical instrument can possibly do all this. The microphone has limitations very similar to the camera. We saw our new director struggling with the camera's unfamiliar handicaps—many of which arose because it was only a one-eyed observer. In the same way the microphone is only a one-eared hearer. It is most unreasonable for a binocular, binaural human being to expect equal capacities from these limited machines. He must not complain of them; he must adjust himself to them. More, he must recognize that the technical characteristics of the microphone (just like those of the camera) can be studied with great profit and turned to creative advantage. It is often out of seemingly cramping limitations that the most brilliant effects can be produced.

So, in the example given above, the two necessary microphone positions must be taken for granted; and, as the actors speak in turn, the microphone must be cranked round in order to face first one, then the other. But before the mixer reaches this stage of refinement, he is likely to encounter more basic problems, especially if he is working on location. Few ordinary rooms are suitable for sound recording. Most of them suffer from sound reflections which mar the intelligibility of speech. In small places these reflections cause roominess or *room tone;* in very large spaces they cause *reverberation* and *echo.* The most fundamental measure of correction is to hang up sheets of sound-absorbing material (often plain blankets will do) around the area to be used for recording. The ceiling must not be forgotten, and it is sometimes necessary to sling a horizontal sound-absorbing curtain across the room, especially if the ceiling is very high. This, of course, must not interfere with any top lighting which the cameraman may wish to use. The floor, too, may need acoustic treatment. Parquet and other polished floors are especially live and reflective, but can be improved by ordinary carpeting.

Finally, the microphone itself can help much toward solving these problems. *Directional* microphones have a response which is different along different horizontal axes. If the response at the back is made less than at the front,
acoustic treatment can be confined to the front area and set noises from behind will also be automatically reduced. Among these set noises—except when
the latest or most carefully blimped cameras are used—is *camera noise,* which
is sometimes difficult to eliminate when small units are shooting on location
with cameras not designed for sound. Directional microphones, properly
placed, also help to remove a very unpleasant type of reflection which, traveling along a short path, arrives at the microphone in almost as great strength
as the directly radiated wave, but in opposite phase. This means that the direct
and reflected waves cancel one another, producing a *dead spot.*

The mixer is also concerned with the problem of signal strength. In other
words, he must insure that the sounds he wants are recorded sufficiently high
above the sounds he does not want. Recording dialogue at too low a level and
afterwards raising it to its proper volume will also amplify any unwanted
set noises, as well as ground noise in the recording system. In technical terms,
the signal-to-noise ratio must be kept as high as possible. This means moving
the microphone in close to the source of wanted sound—in other words, the
speaker. Sometimes this causes *microphone shadows* to be thrown on objects
in the camera's field of view. Again, this necessary closeness of the microphone
may make for difficulties in setting up the camera, because, each time it is
moved, the microphone must also be moved to keep it out of the shot. These
annoyances often upset the cameraman, but they are hardships which must
be tolerantly borne in the interests of good sound.

The mixer must also insure that the acoustic characteristics of the speech
he is recording are the same from shot to shot and from sequence to sequence,
in spite of the fact that the acoustic surroundings are changing continually.
To solve all these problems he needs the utmost coöperation from director
and cameraman, who must stoutly resist the temptation to think of the picture camera as alone being a selective and creative instrument.[21]

Up to this point we have supposed that we were making *live* or original
recordings, such as dialogue, music, songs, and sound effects like church bells
or gunfire. But there is another and equally important sound process called
re-recording or *dubbing* (a corruption of "duping"), which uses exactly the
same equipment save that the microphones are replaced by sound reproducers,
so that the input to the system comprises not live sounds entering a microphone, but dead sounds already recorded on film. Just as an optical printer
rephotographs the original picture image to produce modifications like fades
and zooms or mixtures of several images, such as dissolves and superimposi-

[21] Much good advice on all the practical problems of recording is to be found in Ken
Cameron, *Sound and the Documentary Film,* London: Pitman, 1947.

tions, so the dubber re-records the original sound image to produce modifications, such as equalizing and filtering, or mixtures of several sound images as in the blending of speech and music. This re-recording process is easier to understand after getting a grasp of sound cutting and the assembly of sound tracks for a film.

XI

⎍⎍⎍⎍⎍⎍⎍⎍⎍⎍⎍⎍⎍⎍⎍⎍⎍⎍⎍⎍⎍⎍⎍⎍⎍⎍⎍⎍⎍⎍⎍⎍

Sound:
Getting It onto the Screen

M OST PEOPLE who listen to an orchestra or a dance band hear only an over-all impression of the music, which will strike them simply as loud or soft, harsh or pleasant. They do not for the most part listen to the orchestration—picking out the parts devoted to each instrument or visualizing the music in terms of its different threads of melody and counterpoint. They see the fabric, not its texture. They accept and do not analyze. It is much the same when they go to the movies. To them the screen is as much a door to another world as ever was Alice's looking glass when she ventured through it; but, entering this world, they are far less interested in its bewildering mechanisms than was Alice, with her child's eager curiosity, in the complexities of the land beyond her looking glass.

But the professional must analyze as well as accept. He must be not only a creator, but a critic. His mind must work on two planes, hearing an effect as it is, and at the same time splitting it up into its component parts to see what makes it tick. In this matter of sound tracks he will soon realize that quite a complex synthesis is called for to produce even the most conventional scene.

BREAKING UP THE WORLD OF SOUND

Suppose that the hero and heroine of a movie drama are marooned together in a country cottage. A thunderstorm has been raging and is now dying away. Flickers of lightning play on the faces of the couple as they murmur to one another the conventional phrases of love making. The thunder still mutters in the distance, but now birds are beginning to sing outside and from far away a dog can be heard barking. The wind is subsiding and heavy raindrops fall from the branches. As the sugar-laden moment is prolonged, music enters with a glissando in the harps and begins to swell in a treacly crescendo. No more literal and unimaginative sequence could be conceived. Yet in technical terms what complication and trouble! The novice may rebel; but until he has mastered the routine—the machinery—of sound, he is not ready to explore its really exciting possibilities.

Suppose we had to produce the sequence just described. The most obvious way to do it would be the stage method of actually making everything happen at once. But before we could get the actors speaking their parts, the wind machine whistling away at the right level, the synthetic thunder rumbling in the distance, the dog barking (even if it was on a disc), the light playing on the faces, and so on, all in the right relationship to one another, an impossible problem of stage management would have arisen. And of course on the stage no such unwieldy effect would ever be attempted. Even if all the elements could with great effort be brought together for one movie shot, the necessity of repeating shots from several positions and angles—now nearer and now farther away—would involve repeating also this whole paraphernalia of sound. This technique just will not work. We must find another in the rich arsenal of film.

SELECTING THE SOUNDS THAT ARE WANTED

All the sound we actually need to record in the studio is the dialogue between the man and the girl. The remaining effects are left to be put in afterward, or *postsynchronized*.

The film maker thus has the unique advantage of not having to bother about living sound components; he can handle as many recorded components as he needs, separating them and using them simultaneously. All that this calls for is a large number of sound tracks and the necessary reproducers (called *re-recorders, film phonographs,* or *dubbers*) to play them on. By the simple machinery of synchronization, any desired relationship in time between any two or more sounds can be absolutely established and held. Impossible problems of time become problems of simple geometry in static space. A second of time is stretched out to become a linear foot and a half of film, containing no less than twenty-four separate frames.[1] So, when you hold one of these frames in your hand, you are holding the fractional interval of one twenty-fourth of a second. In this power to grasp the flying moment and transfix it in terms of easily handled space lies one of the keenest tools in the armory of film.

The lightning flickers over the girl's face. For a couple of seconds it plays, then for a moment it disappears; again it flashes brightly, this time dying slowly away. How can we manage to synchronize our synthetic thunder so ex-

---

[1] The following arithmetic applies to 35 mm. film.

actly with this visual effect? By rehearsal it might take half a day—not to mention the manipulation of the wind, the raindrops, the barking dog, and everything else. But in the cutting room all this becomes simple. The picture track shows us the girl's face with the light flickering over it. Since in each second of film travel there are twenty-four frames, each of which has four perforation positions, a very close analysis of the action is possible. We run the picture up and down on the moviola, first fast, then very slowly, until all the points of interest are exactly identified. A grease pencil mark, for instance, shows when the lightning first flashes, a line along the track shows its flicker continuing, and an **X** marks its end. And so on.

Now we take the shot of the girl and put it onto the nearest of the four sprockets of a four-way synchronizer. Next we take our thunder sound track, which was either recorded from real thunder or, more likely, from a thunder machine. We have had a lot of this track printed up because we are going to cut it around and probably throw a good deal of it away. This track goes on the sound head of the moviola. First we run it all the way through to get a general idea of what it contains. Then it has to be rewound. Next we run it through again, this time making grease pencil marks on the transparent area of the track as it whizzes past at ninety feet per minute. These marks indicate the thunder which seems to fit with the flickering of lightning on the girl's face. Now, as we rewind, we cut out these promising bits of film. This initial selection reduces the bulk of film to be handled, which is no small matter.

PUTTING THE SOUNDS TOGETHER

Now the real business of sound cutting begins. There may not be a single section of the thunder track which exactly fits the visuals. However, we pick out the likeliest looking piece. Running the film backward and forward, and grabbing the wheel at the end of the main shaft of the moviola to make it stop at an exact frame, we gradually mark up the sequence of the thunder, bearing in mind all the time what the visuals call for. When this is done, we wind the picture on a certain number of frames through the synchronizer. This is because the thunder should follow the lightning, not coincide with it. How many frames shall we wind on? While in reality the interval might amount to several seconds—especially as the storm is supposed to be far away—it is the usual dramatic convention to compress the time element considerably. A one-second lag will be quite enough here. Hence we wind on twenty-four frames and put the first loud crash of thunder marked on the thunder track over the second sprocket of the synchronizer. Now, unless one of the pieces of film comes off its sprocket (which frequently happens to the inexperienced cutter), both pieces of film are fixed in their relationship for as long as we need to keep them there.

Frame by frame we wind forward, watching the picture track to see when the flickering stops. The thunder should die down (i.e., the modulations fade out) twenty-four frames after this point. We wind on to see. The chances are that the modulations will run too far or not far enough. The remedy for this is sound cutting. If the sound needs to be longer, we must find a second piece which can be spliced onto the first. Its level must be the same (otherwise there will be an audible jump), and the effect of the dying away of the thunder must be continued over the splice. So we go back to the moviola and search through our selected pieces of sound to find one which seems likely to fit. But there is a difficulty here. Since the moviola takes a few frames of film to get up speed and cannot be stopped instantly, it is hard to judge the effect of beginning or ending a sound effect at a precise point in the middle of a piece of sound track. Of course the obvious solution is to cut the track at this point; but if the cut then proves to have been made in the wrong place, there is no way of splicing the film again without losing at least two sprocket holes (half a frame). Although this corresponds to only one forty-eighth second of running time, it will produce a noticeable bump in music and many kinds of sound. The remedy is to take a piece of opaque adhesive tape about six or eight inches long and fasten it lengthwise on the sound track. As the tape has been arranged to start or finish at exactly the wanted sprocket hole, it will blank out the sound after or before that point. By alternately running the track on the moviola and shifting the tape, the exact cutting point can be quickly determined.

This finishes the first job—finding a piece of sound track to match our section of thunder and carry it on down to the correct stopping point, as determined by the picture. We then continue on the synchronizer to match the rest of the thunder with the flickering on the girl's face. It may easily take two or three hours to construct fifteen or twenty seconds of screen time in this way. But once constructed it is permanently available.

Of course this is only a very small part of the task set at the beginning. We still have the bird sounds, the dog barking, the raindrops, and the entrance of the music to arrange for—not to mention the dialogue track which has already been cut. The first thing to decide is whether all these sounds are to be present at once, or whether they could perhaps occur only one at a time. If we took this second course we would only need one effects track, into which these different effects would be cut in succession. This was the practice twenty years ago at the very beginning of sound, when there were few facilities for running several sound tracks at the same time. But today even the smallest production outfit can handle three or four tracks, while most Hollywood studios have a maximum of more than thirty. The final re-recording or mixing process enables the sound engineer to select any sound on any track at will, decide the place where it will enter (provided the sound is on the track at that point), and control its volume.

For instance, as well as having the synchronous thunder, it might be a good thing to have a continuous reserve of thunder to reinforce other parts of the sequence. This can go on another track. The raindrops are not only a continuous but a monotonous sound, and they do not have to synchronize with anything in the visuals. They are therefore put on a *loop,* which is simply a piece of sound track, usually between fifteen and fifty feet long, which is joined end to end in a circle and placed on one of the re-recorders. The advantage of the loop over a single effect is that it makes the sound available all the way through the reel; its advantage over a complete track of the sound in question is that it saves a lot of footage and unnecessary cutting.

The dog's bark could also be put on a loop, but as the sound is essentially intermittent, it may be better to match it on the synchronizer with pauses in the dialogue between the man and the girl. The sound cutter soon learns which sounds will go well with one another and which will interfere. Thunder is a monotonous sound, low in pitch, which can easily be prevented from overriding dialogue. But a dog's bark is sharp and high-pitched and would conflict with speech. This means that it must be synchronized with the picture and dialogue tracks. If the cutter decides that the bark and the synchronous thunder will not be needed simultaneously, they can be cut into the same track. Otherwise, a separate track must be used. Last, the music will need still another track, since the effects are almost certain to have to overlap it, in order to produce a smooth transition from one to the other. We now have either five or six tracks, including loops; and these could easily be added to if we wanted to have wind sounds, say, and the noise of a car approaching the house. The sequence we have been imagining is a very simple one. In some sequences more than twenty tracks may be needed.

On the other hand, small organizations with no more than three or four channels are not debarred from producing effective sound tracks for their films. On the contrary, it is the literal and unimaginative tracks which as a rule are the most complicated. Imagination will often suggest a far simpler and more vivid method of producing the same mood in the audience. An English film made fifteen years ago showed that the faint and wandering sound of an S O S signal in the Morse code, heard over shots of an empty waste of sea, gave a sense of shipwreck much more intense than could have been conveyed by turgid "sea-music" and contrivances built up in studio tanks. It is in this field that the sound cutter can show as much originality as the director and cameraman. From miscellaneous oddments of sound—a steam whistle, the clank of a falling chain, the beat of a steam hammer, the grinding of automobile brakes—he can build up an exciting rhythmical sequence just as effective in conveying a mood as any piece of music.

NOISES OFF

Something needs to be said about the origin of all these sounds and noises. Of course in the first place they must have been recorded from real life or synthesized by some mechanical gadget like the ones used in broadcasting studios. In fact, film studios are always adding to their reserves of sound effects in this way. But a great mass of effects, ranging from the noise of a jet plane diving to the whistle of a French locomotive or the inevitable croaking of bull-frogs, is to be found in each studio's *effects library,* an organization exactly parallel to the picture library, although it does not as a rule contain so much footage. All the sounds in it are on negative track, which is footage-numbered to correspond with an analytical index. In this way, one effect can be picked out of thousands in a matter of seconds. As the negative must not be run on a moviola, the effects library provides *listening prints* numbered to correspond. These enable the sound cutter to pick out exactly the sound he needs, with a corresponding saving of footage to be printed in the lab.

FILM MUSIC

In news items and certain short films, where time precludes original music composition, music tracks are edited in the same way as effects from library footage.[2] The *music library* contains catalogued negatives and listening prints of all the music ever recorded for the studio. The full scores are filed away also, so that the music cutter—who is usually also a musician—can pick out in a few minutes passages in which the key relationship and mood enable sections of music which originally had nothing to do with one another to be cut together. Music cutting requires as much skill as sound cutting. Sometimes the cutter will pick out eight or ten separate bars of music from as many scores and join them all together to produce some special effect, with such success that the moviegoer would never know that they had not been played consecutively by a single orchestra.

If, as is more usual, a new score is to be written for a picture, the composer sees it in the workprint stage, takes down the footage of each sequence and notes any special effects which are needed. He then writes the score. It is much better, however, if he works closely with the film's director and cutter, learns how to operate a moviola and really gears his score to the nature of the film. The best movie music is often that which is least able to stand on its own feet when played on the concert platform. Music is only one of the contributory elements of film, and as such must subordinate conventional techniques and weave its way in and out of the cutting, the effects, and the various voices which may also be on the sound track.

This does not mean that film composers are constantly being thwarted and

2 This practice is subject to severe union restriction.

hampered by arbitrary demands. On the contrary, it means that just as eighteenth- and nineteenth-century composers tackled the fascinating problems of combining music with voice and dramatic action in opera, so the twentieth-century composer takes on a new problem of musical relationship in film. He too has sound and voice and action to contend with. But he has also new elements of time and rhythm, new problems of terseness derived from working with so condensed a medium, to consider—and above all, he is given a new necessity to write good music which is also popular.

MECHANICS OF SOUND CUTTING

As the sound cutter finishes assembling his tracks—his dialogue, music, and various kinds of effects—he must of course keep them in perfect synchronism with one another. This is insured where necessary by making sync marks in grease pencil on the blank areas of the tracks. Sync marks are made on frames level with one another across the synchronizer, so that if a piece of film accidentally slips out of the synchronizer it can be immediately put back in its proper place. The novice will waste hours winding tracks backward and forward once he has got *out of sync*. Nothing seems to fit. He starts the tracks off at one sync mark perfectly aligned; when they arrive at the next sync mark two or three of them are out of place by several frames—or even several feet. Feverishly he winds back again, but everything is still all right up the line; the second set of marks must have been inaccurately made. Perhaps he was trying to adjust several tracks simultaneously, carrying in his head all the consequent shifts in all the tracks which this alteration entailed. Perhaps he was just tired and muddled. Anyway, he soon finds out that sound cutters deserve their reputation for mathematical wizardry.

No sound cutter need be ashamed of making an adequate number of sync marks. It is far better to spend a few minutes making extra sync marks than an hour winding to and fro trying to reëstablish synchronism once it is lost. In fact, in all studio cutting of dialogue, sync marks every foot along the track are automatically assured. As soon as the print comes out of the lab, picture and dialogue are synchronized by clappers or whatever other device the studio uses. They then separately go through a device which prints a code number each foot along the edge, somewhat like the regular footage numbers printed on the stock, but appearing on the opposite side, and in black instead of white. By arranging that the same series of numbers goes on the synced sound and picture of each reel, any foot of sound or picture can afterward be matched to its corresponding picture or sound simply by hunting for a piece of film with the same number. This avoids the necessity of making sync marks on the dialogue track in grease pencil.

The starts of all reels to be re-recorded are synced with *standard leaders* (also called Academy leaders). These are the leaders used at the beginning of the reels of release prints in movie theaters, where they are occasionally noticed when projected on the screen by mistake. They contain a frame marked "Start," followed by frames at one foot intervals marked from "11" to "3." By standardizing the starts of all reels, whether in studios or in theaters, exact synchronism can be achieved under any conditions. Any of the numbers from 11 to 3 can be used for synchronization, and additional marks on the leaders indicate the 20-frame separation between corresponding sound and picture images which is entailed in 35 mm. projection (see pp. 358–360 below).

The sound tracks of a film have often been battered around in the cutting room during editing. They have been cut and recut, have fallen on the floor and have been handled without gloves. Before re-recording them, it is usual to make reprints at least of the dialogue and music tracks, so that no unwanted noises finally reach the screen. Two methods are available. Either the negative of the tracks may be cut and matched to the positive (as with picture), and a spliceless print made from the edited negative: or the track may be printed and the positive sections spliced together. In either case, unmodulated track (often called "unmod") must be spliced in to make up periods of silence. Variable-density unmodulated track must exactly match the density of the original dialogue track, otherwise an audible change of background level will occur in the re-recording at the splice between the two sections.

Sound tracks which are not to be reprinted must be carefully cleaned before re-recording. Carbon tetrachloride is an excellent solvent for dirt. It has no effect on the film emulsion and dries rapidly. (Inhalation of its fumes may, however, cause serious illness and even death; proper ventilation, preferably with forced-air fume extractors, is therefore essential.) It should be applied with a clean lintless cloth, which must be changed frequently as it becomes charged with dirt. Cleaning machines, which work on the same principle, save much handwork but are seldom so thorough.

Both the positive- and negative-spliced methods of preparing re-recording tracks call for *blooping*. When a film splice in a piece of sound track passes under the light beam of a reproducer, a noise is heard because of the extra density produced by the double film thickness, usually followed by a thin transparent line where the emulsion has been scraped away across slightly too great a width. Thus an unwanted sound is produced at a 100 per cent modulation level and at a frequency which is well within the pass band of the system. To eliminate this bump, it is necessary to reduce its frequency below the system pass band, which can be accomplished by gradually lowering the response of the amplifier as the center of the splice approaches, and then gradually restoring it to its normal value. The simplest way to do this is to place a triangular or diamond-shaped opaque patch over the splice, which gradually blocks off and then gradually restores the reproducer light beam, as shown in figure 10-13. This patch is called a *bloop*,[3] and its length on 35 mm. film should be at least one-half inch, so that the modulation frequency of the bloop itself is below the pass band of the system.[4]

Positive bloops are often cut out of Scotch tape and stuck on the film. Red tape is the best, since the dye is in the backing and not in the adhesive, so that there is no danger of black particles adhering to the track and causing noises if the bloop has to be taken off. The red tape is also not perfectly opaque, so that the blooped section of track does not sound altogether "dead." In the larger production centers, blooping patches are now seldom used. If re-recording tracks are to be printed from a cut negative, fog bloops may be made. A small light, set close to the printing aperture and tripped by a notch in the film, fogs the splice area as it goes through. Re-recorders are often fitted with automatic blooping devices. Usually these take the form of a control for reducing the amplifier gain to zero. The control is operated by the splice itself at an aperture ahead of the reproducing beam, or by a notch on the track or a punched hole in it, which trips a microswitch, this being a type of switch which can be released by a movement of only a mil or two. A refinement is to cut off the amplifier gain gradually and restore it gradually, so that the change from background sound to total silence shall not be too sudden.

Negative bloops are made by the simple process of punching a triangular or diamond-shaped hole in the track, which prints black on the positive.

THE FINAL SOUND TRACK

Now the tracks—between two and twenty in number—are all ready for re-recording, the last important creative process through which the film has to pass. Re-recording is the process of combining a large number of separate, simultaneous sound tracks into one. The machinery used is already familiar. If, for the multiple microphones used in a difficult piece of original recording, are substituted a number of special sound reproducers called dubbers, their output being fed into a mixing unit and thence to the main amplifier and recorder, we shall have all the basic elements we need, provided that the reproducers are synchronized with one another and with the picture projector.

---

[3] While the terminology used here is now universal, it may be recalled that the word "bloop" was originally applied to the sound made by an *unblooped* or plain splice. Thus blooping, as defined here, is really "de-blooping." But this word is now seldom used, and the term "bloop" is commonly confined to the device for eliminating the unwanted splice noise.

[4] At a film speed of 18 inches per second, a half-inch bloop will pass the reproducer slit in one thirty-sixth of a second. Bloops are usually made about an inch long to give an extra margin of safety.

Just as the camera had to be synchronized with the recorder so that a section of speech on the sound track was exactly the same length as its corresponding lip movements on the picture, so must the different dubbers be precisely synchronized with one another and with the workprint which is being projected at the same time. Otherwise, the cutter's mathematically established relationships will go astray, and the effect of the film will fall to pieces.

THE MIXER

The skilled part of re-recording lies in the *mixing,* which is much more complex than any mixing of an original recording, which requires only a few manipulations of the controls during each take. A reel for re-recording is generally a full ten minutes long. If there are between ten and twenty tracks, the mixer cannot possibly be constantly adjusting the level of all of them, for he has only the usual human complement of hands. The object of having so many tracks is to separate the different effects, so that each can be preset at the level at which rehearsal proves it to be most effective. For complicated studio jobs there may be assistant mixers handling the subsidiary tracks on which minor sound effects occur. The head mixer will then be responsible for dialogue, music, and perhaps the two chief effects tracks. For any given complexity of sound, the fewer the tracks the greater the mixer's difficulties, since he must then be continually altering his levels, cross fading from one track to another, keeping at all times one eye on the screen and the other on the V.I. meter. An expert mixer, working under these conditions, develops the bravura of a virtuoso pianist playing a Liszt concerto.

To keep all the tracks straight, and to have a definite record of which sound effects are coming through on which channels, the editor usually provides the mixer with a log, which consists of a series of vertical columns, one for each sound track. The effects are entered on horizontal lines opposite footage numbers, starting with 0.00 at the beginning of the reel, either at the Academy start mark or at the first frame of picture. Since the mixer is provided with a footage counter set to zero at the same point, he can easily determine, as the reels run through, which effects are coming up on which channels. Tracks may also be cued by "streamers," diagonal lines about four feet long marked on the workprint like wipes.

The re-recording process is so important that it can create or destroy the total effect of a film. Yet its elements often seem mechanical and crude. The individual sound tracks are no more inviting to the ear than are the ingredients of the most delicious dish to the eye or the palate, when laid out raw on the kitchen table. Re-recording, in fact, is a good deal like cooking. Just as a skilled chef will add the merest suspicion of seasoning to a dish, his object being to hint at a flavor rather than to overwhelm with a violent taste, so the mixer will use all the subtle resources of the sound tracks at his command to bring out every nuance of meaning which the producer and editor have put into them. In the cutting room, time was converted into space, studied at leisure, and precisely assembled. In the projection theater, space must be reconverted into time—time which is traveling headlong forward and cannot be held back. Any mistakes in a re-recording process make it necessary to do the whole thing over again until it is perfect. If the mixer cannot handle the complex tracks with sufficient speed, it means altering the tracks or getting another mixer, not slowing down the process. For we are back again now at the unrelenting speed of ninety feet a minute. A difficult reel will need many rehearsals before the crew is ready for a take; and often several takes before the producer is satisfied. Half a day may often be spent in getting not more than ten minutes of sound track onto the screen.

THE MIXING MACHINE

While the most important thing in a re-recording is what goes on in the mixer's head, his mechanical adjuncts are important too. Re-recording is best carried out in a room acoustically similar to the space where the film is ultimately to be projected, as this enables the producer to judge the proper balance between the tracks. If the film is destined for the theaters, the re-recording room should be of ample size; only 16 mm. pictures should be mixed in the smaller control rooms.

The actual mixing is done at a console, which is something like an organ console in that its face is covered with a large number of controls (figure 11-1). In addition to the gain controls for the various channels, there are banks of equalizers and filters, which serve to alter the frequency characteristics of any desired channel in one of a number of ways while the re-recording is actually taking place. Equalizers are used for bringing in special effects such as telephone voices, for emphasizing a commentator above music and effects, and for correcting electrical and optical losses in the over-all system. Finally, the console carries the main gain controls, a footage indicator, the V.I. meter, various other meters indicating the state of different parts of the system, and an intercommunication telephone which links the theater, the projection booth, and the dubber room.

This room contains the dubbers themselves, which are often mounted on ordinary projector stands, in spite of the fact that they comprise only a sound head and two magazines. Some modern designs are more compact, and are arranged horizontally like a sound camera instead of vertically like a projector. The sound camera is usually in another room, and is in charge of the recordist. Unless the dubbers have automatic high-speed rewinds, the crew in the dubbing room must rewind all the tracks at the end of each rehearsal and take, and put them back on the machines in sync with the least possible delay. Lastly, a projector projects the picture workprint from a booth above the re-

Fig. 11-1. A re-recording console. (Courtesy Reeves Sound Studios, New York.)

recording studio. The dubbers and the projector must run synchronously. They are generally connected by an electrical *interlock* system, which insures that any rotation of one motor is automatically communicated to all the rest. This avoids mechanical connection between the machines.

All this equipment funnels a multitude of separate sound signals through the mixing panel, where it is under the mixer's sensitive control. Thence it emerges as a single signal which is recorded as the final negative sound track of the film.

XII

⎍⎍⎍⎍⎍⎍⎍⎍⎍⎍⎍⎍⎍⎍⎍⎍⎍⎍⎍⎍⎍⎍⎍⎍⎍⎍⎍⎍⎍⎍⎍

Some Studio Techniques

UP TO THIS POINT, greatest emphasis has been laid on what takes place behind the camera—or rather, behind its lens, for the camera's own powers of molding actuality have been included. Now it is time to redress the balance, and examine some of those techniques whose place is in front of the camera and the microphone.

The camera has been called "a chisel of light." Were it not for the interplay of light and shade, the modeling of faces, the proper stress of feature and texture—in short, the aspect of the visible world which is placed before it—its other powers could accomplish little. This is true as much of outdoor as of indoor scenes. The cameraman may decide that there is only one period of fifteen minutes in a whole day when a shot is composed exactly to his liking. He may need the deep indigo which at evening gives a rich black shadow to a mountain range. He may choose the moment of dusk when a city's lights are on, but when the glow from the sky still reflects the detail of trees and masonry. He may find that only at dawn can he shoot from an airplane and get the right slanting of light to reveal every detail of the ground while avoiding the harshness of contrast which comes with high noon. Yet if he needs the pitiless glare of desert or prairie, he must shoot only when the sun is highest. Nor is the mere movement of the sun his only problem. The atmosphere is always changing. Cloud and haze will not merely affect the exposure. They will shift the emphasis, alter the scene, and change the whole scale of tonal values. It is little wonder that the documentary photographer, shooting a large part of the time under the open sky, works slowly and is subject to all kinds of capricious delays.

If the cycle of the sun and the weather were to determine the rate of shooting, commercial production schedules could not be accurately maintained. Although in recent years there has been a welcome increase of realism in Hollywood backgrounds, standard practice is and must be to portray as much as possible of the action indoors, to manufacture exteriors in the studio or on the *lot,* to synthesize living characters with dead exteriors already recorded on film, and finally, if these devices fail, to seek out a real setting and augment and modify the light of day by artificial illumination. We shall have something to say in turn about several of these techniques.

LIGHTING

The movie camera is at a great disadvantage compared to the still camera when it comes to taking pictures in the dark—and for practical purposes the great majority of interiors may be considered as initially dark, the lens and film having a sensitivity which even today is much inferior to that of the human eye. If the scene contains no movement, the still cameraman can give it a time exposure; if there is movement in it, he can burn one or more flashbulbs, which—for a period of a few microseconds—give off a light which would require fifty or more kilowatts to maintain continuously.

The movie cameraman seldom has a perfectly still scene to shoot; indeed, when there is no movement in the scene, he will usually supply movement by panning or dollying the camera. Shooting at less than 24 frames per second is therefore a virtual impossibility, though in emergency the characters in a shot may be asked to move slowly while the camera turns at 10 to 15 frames per second. However, for all practical purposes, a movie exposure is no longer than $\frac{1}{40}$ to $\frac{1}{70}$ second, depending on the angular opening of the camera shutter.

The still cameraman will appreciate how great is the amount of light called for by a minimum exposure of, say, $\frac{1}{50}$ second in a large interior, especially with slow emulsions such as those of color stocks. Consequently, the first task of the cameraman on location is to assure himself of adequate electric supplies. In estimating whether a source of power is adequate or not, he is helped by an elementary knowledge of three electrical units—the volt, the ampere, and the watt.

Electrical current is of two kinds, direct current (DC) and alternating current (AC). Flow of current can be understood with the help of a rough comparison. A source of DC is like a river with a perfectly even surface and a constant rate of flow, whereas AC resembles the ebb and flow of the tide through the mouth of a harbor, the energy of which resides in its periodic backward and forward movement.[1] The head or pressure which is driving the water corresponds to the electrical voltage, measured in *volts* (E); the amount or

---

[1] The rapidity of alternation is called the frequency (see chapter x), and is measured in cycles per second (cps). The standard AC frequencies throughout North America and Great Britain are 50 and 60 cycles.

volume of water flowing past a point in a given time corresponds to the current, measured in *amperes* (I); and the power which would be available to drive, say, a mill wheel, is the product of the pressure and volume of water— or, in electrical terms, the voltage and current. This electrical unit of power is called a *watt* (W). Thus E (volts) $\times$ I (amperes) = W (watts). Since the watt is rather a small unit, the *kilowatt* (kw), equal to one-thousand watts, is often used in power calculations.

It is worth remembering that the peak voltage of an AC supply is about 40 per cent higher than its rated voltage. As it is the peak voltage which determines the severity of electric shock, AC power must be handled with especial care.

Since most North American light sources are designed for 115 volt operation,[2] calculations of current are very simple when the number of kilowatts required is known. Multiply by 10 the number of kilowatts to be drawn from the power supply and the answer will be in amperes, with a safety margin of about 10 per cent provided automatically. An example will make this rule clear.

Suppose we have a 230-volt three-wire supply (which consists of two 115-volt lines with one wire in common), from which 200 amperes can be drawn on each side. We need to use four 5-kilowatt lamps and seven 2 kilowatts, and we want to know how many no. 4 *Photofloods* can safely be added to the circuit. All the lamps are rated at 115 volts. Applying the rule, the four 5-kilowatt lamps draw $4 \times 5 \times 10 = 200$ amperes, loading one side of the circuit to the full. The seven 2-kilowatt lamps draw $7 \times 2 \times 10 = 140$ amperes, leaving a surplus of 60 amperes on the other side. Since the no. 4 Photofloods are rated at about $8\frac{1}{2}$ amperes each, we could safely use seven of them. Reference to the table below will show that the actual drain of all these lamps together is 353 amperes, instead of the 400 amperes estimated by the rule. Thus the margin of safety—resulting from taking the voltage as 100 instead of 115—is approximately 10 per cent.

The following table shows the actual current drain of a number of commonly used lamps, when the voltage is 115.

LAMP	AMPERES
5 kilowatts	43.5
2 kilowatts	17
1 kilowatt	8.7
No. 4 Photoflood	8.4
750 watt	6.5
500 watt	4.3
No. 2 Photoflood	4.2
No. 1 Photoflood	2.1

2 The standard voltage in Great Britain is 215–230, and in France 110–115.

Arc lights must always be run off a DC source, and usually draw between 75 and 300 amperes each.

TECHNIQUES AND SOURCES

Working under studio conditions, it is possible to assume that no natural lighting exists. What is in front of a camera is invisible. It emerges out of darkness only as it is lighted at the command of the cameraman and the chief electrician, or gaffer. Three types of lighting can be conveniently distinguished:

1. *Frontlighting* consists of general illumination of the subject from the side toward the camera. It provides basic light intensity required for proper exposure within the latitude range of the negative emulsion.

2. *Crosslighting* provides the basic modeling which determines the general balance of light and relieves the uniformity of frontlighting.

3. *Highlighting* picks out important details in the subject and gives them added prominence.

Backlighting, important as it is as a technique, is not really a distinct type of lighting. If only the reverse side of an object were illuminated, the camera would notice no difference in its appearance, and the light would thus be thrown away. Actually, of course, back light becomes diffused and spread out so that it illuminates the sides of objects, throwing them into high relief. It is thus a kind of sidelighting. *Toplighting* is also as a rule a combination of frontlighting and crosslighting.

Wherever the basic lighting of a set is placed, it is known as key lighting. If the cameraman uses so small an amount of light that it produces a minimum acceptable exposure on the emulsion, he is said to work in a low key; if a relatively large amount of key light, in a high key. Low-key lighting has latterly come into wide use because of the dramatic effects of deep shadow and brilliant highlights which it helps to create. It demands much more exact coöperation with the laboratory than the less critical high-key lighting.

Coming now to the sources of light, we find that they are never used by themselves, any more than a bare bulb is used to light a sittingroom or office. It is only sensible to cut off waste light and direct it by a reflector into the limited area where it is needed. Two kinds of surfaces are used as reflectors; diffuse and specular. *Diffuse reflection* takes place when the reflecting particles in a material throw the light equally in all directions; *specular reflection* takes place when they throw it all in one direction. The same terms apply to substances which transmit light. Specular transmission goes with transparent substances; diffuse transmission with translucent substances which spread the light evenly over a wide field of view.

In the early days of movies, little was done with focused light sources, most of the light being provided by *scoops* and *broadsides,* lamps which covered a field 90° or 120° wide. When sets were small, and lighting placed as a rule close in to them, this was not such an important matter. Simple diffusing surfaces could be used, and no relative movement between the parts of the lamp was called for. On the other hand, the lighting which resulted was exceedingly flat and uninteresting. No camera could be called "a chisel of light" if it had such blunt instruments to work with.

Today the pendulum has swung the other way, and focusable spot lamps are used almost to the exclusion of the old broads and scoops. The two most common shapes of reflector—the sphere and the parabola—both have their applications. The parabolic reflector has the property of reflecting rays of light which originate at its focal point parallel to one another. If the source of the light rays is not a mathematical point, as it cannot be in a practical type of lamp, there will be some divergence of the beam, usually about 14°. This restricts lighting to very small areas, but some improvement can be gained by moving the light source away from the focal point. While this spreads the beam, it has the undesirable consequence of producing a dark spot at the center—the place it is hardest to fill in with adjacent illumination. Parabolic reflectors are thus confined to a useful angle between 14° and 24°, except in the case of very deep paraboloids of fixed focus, having a partially diffusing (semimatte) internal surface. These will give uniform lighting over an angle of about 30°, and are useful for front lighting. Fixed-focus lights with parabolic reflectors are called *rifles,* or rifle spots.

Frontlighting is accomplished with modern versions of the old broads and scoops, usually with angles in excess of 90° and arc sources to give extra intensity.

Most studio light sources today combine the lens and spherical mirror to produce a beam which can be made almost parallel or caused to converge or diverge over a smaller or larger angle, while still keeping the illumination uniform. Optically, the plano-convex lens behaves in exactly the same way as the parabolic reflector with a specular surface. It saves a good deal of space, however, while still collecting light from a wide angle. With very large collecting angles, the plano-convex lens becomes inconveniently thick and heavy. To avoid this, a Fresnel lens is often used—this consists of a number of partial surfaces of a lens of very high collecting power.

The spherical mirror behind the light sources usually plays no part in forming the beam. Its purpose is simply to redirect rays of light originating at its focus, or center, back to that focus again. The light source is in practice placed at this focus, and the mirror therefore redirects otherwise wasted light back to its starting point, where it then becomes part of the main beam going out through the lens. In a monoplane filament, the mirror "fills in" the spaces between the filament coils, producing a source of almost uniform intensity.

In this way, the efficiency of the source may be increased up to 75 per cent.

Light sources used in movie shooting today are almost exclusively of two kinds: incandescent and carbon arc. The popular fluorescent lamp has so far proved of little value in the motion picture studio. Outweighing the advantage of a cold light source is the fact that its large light-emitting area makes close beam concentration impossible, while the light output per unit area is not sufficient for adequate flood lighting.

Two important general characteristics of lighting need preliminary mention: color temperature and light output. Color temperature has already been discussed in chapter ix, but it is a concept not applicable to certain types of arc lamp (e.g., the mercury arc) which have *discontinuous spectra,* distinguishing them from the uniformly emitting, perfect radiator. The wide use of color has led to the rating of all other types of lamp by their color temperature, and this is a figure which must be ascertained by any cameraman who does not want false color rendering in his color shooting.

Lamps are further rated by their initial light output. (After a period of use, evaporated tungsten particles from the filament produce a blackening of the bulb which lowers the light output.) Light output is more scientifically called *luminous flux,* and is the time-rate flow of light. Its unit is the *lumen,* which is equal to the flux through a unit solid angle from a uniform point source of one candle. The lumen is quite a small unit. A no. 1 Photoflood has an output of about 8,500 lumens, and a 5-kilowatt lamp about 165,000 lumens.

INCANDESCENT LIGHTING

Incandescent lighting (or lighting produced by the raising of a metallic filament to a high temperature) has today been developed to such an efficiency that it will suffice for all small and medium-size sets, and will cover most of the interiors commonly met with on location.

It is a characteristic of incandescent light sources that the higher the color temperature, the larger the total luminous output, especially in the blue and violet regions to which even modern photographic materials are most sensitive. Tungsten is almost universally used as a filament material, since it has the highest melting point of any convenient conductor (about 3,650° K). By going right up to this limit, evaporation of the tungsten would take place so rapidly that the lamp would have an uneconomically short life. But since, unlike domestic bulbs, studio lamps are not expected to give an indefinitely long life, they can be designed with specific life expectations, these being deliberately balanced against luminous efficiency.

The *Photoflood* bulb has the highest color temperature practical with a tungsten filament (3,400° K), and a life which varies from about two to nine hours. (Larger wattage bulbs have a longer life, other things being equal, because the filament is thicker and does not evaporate so rapidly.) The advantage of the Photoflood is that it enables an extremely intense light source to be packed into a small space, with a consequent reduction in the size of the equipment. Photoflood lamps are mainly used for flood (general) lighting, but the smaller types are also employed in sets to replace actual light bulbs and give higher local illumination. The RFL-2 Photoflood is especially useful to small location units, since it contains a built-in reflector and is therefore a completely self-contained floodlight. When attached to a clamp-on holder, it can be set almost anywhere on a beading or window frame, and out of doors can be held by a spike driven into a tree or fence. A companion light is the newer RSP-2 Photospot, which concentrates its beam at a point about eight feet away. This spot lamp may be fitted with barn doors; with the aid of a clamp, a complete lighting unit which weighs only a few pounds can be assembled (figure 12-1). The development of less cumbersome lighting units has contributed much to the ease and speed with which the smaller unit can now tackle difficult interior shots on location.[3]

Other incandescent light sources operate at slightly lower color temperatures and have a correspondingly longer life. They can be had in sizes up to 10,000 watts (10 kilowatts), but the 750 watt, 1 kilowatt, 2 kilowatt, and 5 kilowatt are in most general use.

Lamps of lower color temperature can, however, be boosted to a higher temperature by the use of transformers such as the Color-Tran. By applying excess voltage to a normal lamp, such as is used for store window illumination, the color temperature and light output are raised and the life is shortened. To obviate rapid burning out, the Color-Tran is fitted with a convenient switch which enables normal voltage to be applied to the lamp until the cameraman is ready for a take, when excess voltage is applied only until the camera stops.

Finally, something must be said about the type of focusing lamps in which these light sources are most often used. These fit into the general category of *spot lamps* or spots, that is, lamps which can give either a very narrow or a comparatively wide beam, ranging usually from about 10 degrees to 45 degrees and having a good degree of uniformity. The smallest type of lamp is the *inky-dink*, which accommodates a 100- or 150-watt bulb and can easily be hidden behind quite small objects which appear in the camera's field. No great change occurs in the design of lamps with increasing size until the sun spots are reached. These are from two to three feet in diameter, are fitted with 5-kilowatt and 10-kilowatt lamps, and use glass mirrors instead of lenses.

---

[3] Some of these make use of an autotransformer which boosts the voltage to an ordinary lamp, thus raising its light output and color temperature at the expense of its useful life. See also Wayne Blackburn, "Study of Sealed Beam Lamps for Motion Picture Set Lighting," *JSMPTE*, July, 1950, pp. 101–112.

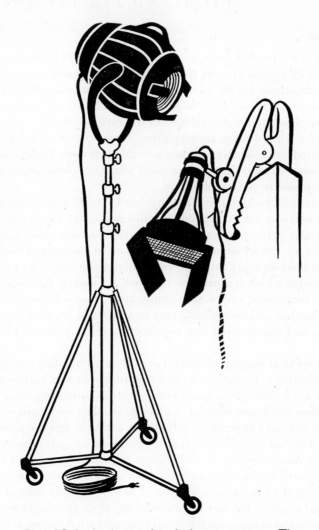

Fig. 12-1. Lightweight lighting units. The larger unit illustrated is a standard focusable 2 kilowatt spotlight. The smaller unit is a light clamp-on device fitted with an RFL-2 photoflood or an RSP-2 photospot, to which adjustable barn doors are mounted. This clamp-on unit can be attached to doors, windows, beading, and almost any other convenient object.

ARC LIGHTING

Arc lighting is a type of lighting produced by a bridge of incandescent vapor which carries an electric current from one electrode to another. This current sustains the luminous bridge so long as the distance between the electrodes does not exceed a critical limit. At present, carbon arcs are the only type of arc widely used in studios. Introduced in the earliest period of cinematography, they have since undergone very great improvement. Hand-fed carbons which sputtered and hissed were common in the early days. Today, carbons are invariably motor-fed and silenced to a point where no sound can be picked up by the microphone in normal shooting.

Since modern incandescent lighting has been raised to such high efficiency, there is less necessity for arcs in small-studio work. But where exceptionally long throw and great penetration are needed, together with high photographic efficiency, the arc comes into its own; and in commercial studios many arc units are used on every large set, especially in the shooting of color. The types of lamp for which arc units are designed are exactly the same as for incandescents: broadsides, scoops, spot lamps, and sun arcs. Owing to the size of the arc mechanism and motor feed, very small sizes of arc spot lamp are not economical; and the smallest size corresponds roughly to a 2-kilowatt incandescent.

Since the spectral output of carbon arcs closely resembles sunlight, little additional filtering is required for color shooting with film balanced for sunlight. Color work demands a much closer control of lighting color temperatures than does black and white. For whereas in black-and-white shooting, a dropping off of color temperature will merely affect the relative photographic contrast of different objects (which will be noticeable only when carried to extremes), in color shooting it will change the colors themselves in a most disturbing way. If, for instance, a type of color stock is balanced to give correct color rendering at a temperature of 3,200° K, a lower temperature of illumination will tend to give a warmer color rendering, since the longer wavelengths —corresponding to orange and red—will then prevail. A higher temperature, on the other hand, will stress the shorter-wavelength colors—blue and violet —and will give a cold rendering of the scene. A difference of color temperature of 100° K can be distinguished on color film balanced for tungsten light. Color temperature is very responsive to voltage changes, a change of one volt producing a temperature change of about 10° K.

Color temperature can be artificially raised by filtering, but only at the expense of absorbing a part of the emitted spectrum and so reducing the efficiency of the source. Daylight blue Photoflood lamps (4,800° K) have only about two-thirds of the efficiency of the corresponding white lamps. Hence, high intensity arc lamps, which with light-yellow filters give a color temperature of 5,400° K, have exceptionally high efficiency for color shooting with emulsions balanced to daylight.

Another type of arc lamp—the mercury arc—is beginning to give interesting results in studios, especially in England, where it reached a high state of development during the war.[4] Developed over a long period from the old-fashioned Cooper-Hewitt lamp, still to be seen in photoengraving plants, the mercury lamp has several excellent characteristics, among them high energy conversion of electricity into light, low radiation of heat, long life, and silent operation. Until very recently, however, the shape of the light source did not lend itself to use in focusable mountings; the very high pressure in the bulb made fracturing dangerous; starting voltages were inconveniently high; warming up and restarting periods of several minutes were required; the maximum available wattage was not great enough for studio lighting; a continuous flow of water was needed to carry surplus heat away from the small quartz containing cylinder; and the spectral distribution of the emitted light was confined to a few rather narrow bands which would not meet the needs of a color emulsion. These defects are now being remedied, and in the next few years the mercury lamp may become a powerful competitor to the carbon arc.

STUDIO ACCESSORIES

The lighting equipment described above needs many additional accessories before it can be brought into practical studio use. Some of these belong to the general field of electrical engineering; the rest are more specialized. Much of the lighting on each set is hooked up to *dimmer banks*—that is, banks of variable series resistances which can be made to reduce and thereafter increase the light intensity of the lamps connected to them. All manner of effects of emphasis can be achieved by modulating the intensity of set lighting to throw now one object, now another, into prominence. Light control is especially necessary on *follow shots,* or shots where the camera follows one or more characters through the set.

The disadvantage of dimmers is that they vary the color temperature of the lamps to which they are attached, while lamp life is also shortened by a fluctuating voltage. To remedy this, many studio lamps are now fitted with Venetian-blind shutters, which will smoothly reduce the illumination thrown on the set, and increase it again, without change of color temperature. An added refinement is a system of selsyn (self-synchronous) motors driving the shutters, hooked up to a central control lever. By moving this lever, a dozen or more lamps scattered high and low on the set may be opened or closed at

[4] For an excellent account of recent British developments of the so-called "compact source" mercury lamp, see F. E. Carlson, "New Developments in Mercury Lamps for Studio Lighting," *JSMPE*, Feb., 1948, pp. 122–138. See also H. K. Bourne and E. J. G. Beeson, "The Cine Flash," *JSMPTE*, Sept., 1950, pp. 299–312.

will. It is even possible to make some shutters open and others close by purely electrical means. Quick closing of the shutters will simulate the turning off of room lights, while still leaving enough key illumination to prevent the scene on the film from falling into total darkness.

Studio lamps are frequently combined with diffusers, the plentiful use of which marks one of the chief differences between the studio cameraman and his colleague who films the simpler documentaries and newsreels. Diffusers are screens of translucent material—cello glass, translucent glass, black net, spun glass, etc. Sometimes they are mounted on the lights themselves, sometimes on separate stands placed between the light and the subject. When set directly in front of the light, a diffuser softens and cuts down its intensity. But the most important use of diffusion is in reducing the intensity of a light over part of the area it covers—for instance, when the source light falls upon a set where the wall is too bright. Here a "half cello" may be used to cut down the light falling upon the upper part of the set. In a two-shot, it may be found that the costume of one person is too light to balance well; here a diffuser on a stand may be angled between the light and the subject to cut down the intensity of the light falling on the light dress. A flat area in the background or foreground of a shot may often be rendered more pleasing by introducing a new gradation with a diffuser affecting the light falling upon that part of the set alone. Again it may be that, when a set is well lighted, it is discovered that as an actor walks through a certain spot, he is directly in the beam of a light and therefore much too bright. Here the solution may be to station a person who will move a small piece of diffusion material into the beam of the light just as the actor walks through the bright area and withdraw it as he passes by.

The cost of a useful number of diffusers and stands is low in relation to the great improvement they can make in the quality of photography. Their use need not complicate the lighting of a set and can in fact accelerate it, since the quick placement of a proper diffuser may eliminate the necessity of moving a heavy light.

Where light is to be entirely cut off from an area, opaque screens are used instead of diffusers. When the screens are hinged to a lamp housing, they are known as *barn doors;* when mounted on separate stands, *gobos.*

Shooting exteriors, the most obvious source of light is the sun. (Because the moon cannot produce any useful exposure at one-fiftieth of a second, moonlight effects out of doors are often made in sunlight with a night filter.) But the sun is a single light source, and a very little experience in studio shooting will show the limitations of such a source, no matter how brilliant, when side- and backlighting (or front- and backlighting) depend simply on the reflective characteristics of objects in the scene. Studio location units therefore make use of arcs and incandescent lights, called booster lights, to balance the light of the sun; but to feed these necessarily powerful sources, motor generators must be provided, and these are often beyond the financial reach of a small unit.

Much can be done with the aid of *reflectors*, which redirect sunlight into areas in the scene where shadow illumination needs to be boosted. Often in brilliant sunlight the ratio of highlight to shadow far exceeds the latitude of the photographic process, especially when the scene is being recorded on color emulsions of limited scale. But even to the eye, the modeling of faces in sunlight is harsh and unsatisfactory, and reflectors are needed to add detail in shaded areas, especially under the eyes.

Just as the cameraman, when lighting an interior set, uses various types of lamp, so has he various types of reflectors when working out of doors. Most reflectors are about four feet square, made of plywood edged with inch boards for rigidity, and are coated with materials having the required reflective qualities. "Hard" reflectors (giving a specular or mirrorlike reflection) are coated with very bright silver or aluminum foil. These will reflect a very brilliant and penetrating beam of light, almost as bright as sunlight itself. They must therefore be used with great care, since they tend to produce hot spots or regions of intense brightness as unbalanced as the shadows they eliminate. "Soft" reflectors are coated with gold foil or less reflective aluminum foil and are given a pebbled surface which diffuses the reflected light. "Soft" reflectors are often used to fill in the shadow side of a face, while a "hard" reflector provides back- or edge-lighting—or lightens leaves or the side of a building.

Just as lights in a studio are set at different levels, some at eye level and others ten or fifteen feet above the floor, so are reflectors mounted at varying heights. While it is common practice in small units to put reflectors on the ground and lean them back upon a stick to get the proper angle, it is much better to have them mounted on large stands, like light stands, to enable them to be easily and quickly adjusted to the desired height and angle. A reflector resting on the ground and reflecting light from that angle into an actor's face produces the same unpleasant and unnatural effect as a single studio light set in the same position. Small reflectors held in the hand or concealed about the set are also useful items of equipment.

When working in color, it is necessary to consider not merely the reflective characteristics of the reflector but the changes in color temperature which it may introduce. Since reflectors normally pick up direct sunlight, which has a lower color temperature than skylight, they have a tendency to reduce the over-all temperature of illumination; and if the reflector is a golden color, this tendency is increased. Flesh tones must be carefully watched when reflectors are used in color photography. An over-warm and ruddy rendering may be lessened by reflecting bluish light from the sky, rather than warm sunlight, onto the subject's face.

Generally speaking, when shooting out of doors, the sun is the source light and reflectors are used to fill in shadows and to backlight. Sometimes, however, it is necessary or desirable to use the sun as backlight; the reflectors must then provide more than fill-light, they must in fact function as a source light.

The number of reflectors to be used on a unit will depend greatly on the cameraman, for in exteriors as in interiors, one man may need twenty lights to light a scene, another but ten. However, at least three to six reflectors of different types should be carried by even the smallest unit on location.

PROCESS PROJECTION

Process projection (also called back projection, background projection, and transparency process) is a composite technique whereby the actors and props in front of the camera are combined with a background which consists of a screen on which a picture (moving or still) is projected from behind. By the perfection of a large number of mechanical details, the foreground and background can be so fused together as to become one almost indistinguishable whole, a fusion which must also be effected in many kinds of trick photography, when different parts of the image have different origins.

The cost and complexity of film production frequently makes composite photography essential where large casts and elaborate equipment have to be brought into play. It would be impossible to transport the entire cast of a picture to all the locations called for in most scripts, if only for financial reasons; and having got them there, it would be impossible to make use of equipment which can only be operated in the largest studios. The remedy is to shoot the background separately and project it in the studio; then, by means of ingenious lighting and set design, to integrate it with the background action.

On the purely technical plane, remarkable advances have been made in background projection in the last few years. Yet its artistic limitations are serious and perhaps basic. One of the greatest assets of the movie camera is its ability to go anywhere and shoot anything. It is in the scene, and can therefore recreate the scene in all its living reality, unconfined by stage conventions. Process projection (and even more radically the English innovation known as Independent Frame) tends to reduce the actors to stage figures moving in front of conventional scenery—skies which cannot pour rain on them, trees from which no birds can fly. In short, the two parts of the scene occupy different worlds. Characters cannot pass from one to the other.

There cannot be absolute continuity across the boundary, even if the actual quality of the image does not suffer loss. The process screen has no depth. Hence, the camera cannot move across it or to and from it with any freedom, without making apparent the total lack of parallax movement between different objects in the background. These have been fixed in immutable relationship by the original camera, and cannot be changed by the movements of the camera which now rephotographs them.

Thus the audience, if only subconsciously, will gain a lesser impression of reality from the backgrounds which usually form the impersonal elements of a film—the social context—than from the actors who play their parts in front of these backgrounds. There will be a subtle psychological shift of emphasis, admirably adapted to support the present star system; less admirable if movies are to become an instrument for portraying the real world, with its factories, its political meetings, its farms and commerce—all the great explosive forces of life which must be shrunk into unreality to fit the back-projection screen.

Mechanically, process projection is accomplished with the aid of a projector or set of projectors employing very powerful arc lamps and throwing a picture of absolute steadiness onto a translucent screen. The need for screen images up to 36 feet or even 48 feet in width has overtaxed the capacity of single projectors, thus leading to the use of triple machines, run in synchronism, in which the three projected images are exactly superimposed. Not only is the light intensity thus greatly increased, but graininess and flicker are reduced. The projector mechanisms are fitted with registration pins, so that the slightest unsteadiness of image may be eliminated. The projector shutters are electrically synchronized with the camera shutters.

Back projection increases the size of the studio floor needed to shoot a scene, since the throw of the projector has to be added to the distance between the camera and the screen. In some modern sets, a total distance of 300 feet is thus included.

The techniques discussed so far mainly affect the picture image, and we have seen how—as so often in film—the tendency is to synthesize instead of recording actuality. The same tendency is at work in the field of sound.

PRESCORING AND PLAYBACK

While sound and picture are normally recorded simultaneously, there are many occasions when other techniques are desirable. The commonest of these is prescoring, with its corollary of playback. Prescoring means the recording of music prior to the shooting of the picture which is to accompany it; playback means the playing back of this music on the sound stage in order that the action may take place in absolute synchronism with it while it is being filmed.

At first sight it may seem strange that a sequence should be recorded before being photographed; but this is only a habit of mind inherited from the silent era, or from the knowledge that the visual record antedated the aural. There are many places where prescoring is much the more convenient method. In cartoon animation it is universal. It would be quite impossible to play a complicated musical score to a finished cartoon with the accuracy needed to bring out all the fine points of synchronism intended by the animator. Hence the music is recorded first, and analyzed into its constituents by marking the sound track and designing the animating cells to fit these markings. This procedure may even be used in very complex technical animation consisting of moving diagrams.

Solo songs also call for prescoring. The rendering of the human voice, if it is to be heard in a song or aria, must be as perfect as recording technique can make it, for blurring and distortion of the voice are exceedingly noticeable, especially in the upper register and at high amplitudes. The set on which the singer is to appear in the film cannot as a rule be designed for perfect recording characteristics, as a multitude of other demands have to be satisfied. Such are size, height, and obstructions called for by the set designer, space for the mounting of lights, presence of a camera which must often be mobile, and so on. Furthermore, sequences are invariably broken up into component shots, as establishing shots, approach shots, long, medium, and close shots, reaction shots, and others. If all these elements were to be shot synchronously with their accompanying sections of the song, the sound record would consist of a large number of separate small pieces which would have to be joined together to form the complete song. It would be well-nigh impossible to match levels, pitch, tempo, and acoustic quality to a degree which would render the abutting of all these sections unnoticeable. Moreover, the strain on the soloist of singing in full voice for all the rehearsals and takes of all the different angles would result in a gradual deterioration of voice quality, or would necessitate uneconomically short shooting periods. And lastly, the facial movements, not to say distortions, which are necessitated by singing fortissimo or in a very high or low register, are not particularly attractive when photographed in close-up.

All of these difficulties are removed by the technique of prescoring and playback (see figure 12-2). The first stage of shooting has no relation to the camera. It consists simply of sound recording. The singer (to continue the same example) stands in a small room acoustically treated to make it suitable for a single voice. Through a double-glass window the singer can see the stage where the orchestra is to play, and the conductor is so stationed that he can see both orchestra and singer. The space containing the orchestra is of course designed for recording of the utmost fidelity. In order that playing and singing may be in time with one another, the singer must be able to hear the orchestra,

Fig. 12-2. The technique of prescoring and playback with singer and orchestra. The conductor, tapped into the singer's recording line, is able to hear her voice through headphones, while she hears the orchestra by controlled acoustic leakage into the voice recording studio. Voice and orchestra are separately recorded, and additional discs or magnetic records of the voice part are played back on the studio floor to enable the actress (who may be beautiful but dumb) to synchronize her lip movements while appearing to sing. All equipment shown here must operate synchronously. (Many variations of this basic technique are in use in the studios.)

and the conductor the singer. Sometimes the singing studio is so designed that the orchestra can be heard in it at a very low level. Otherwise, the singer must wear headphones tapped into the line from the orchestral microphones and their associated amplifiers. In this way the singer keeps in time with the orchestra. Conversely, the conductor wears headphones tapped into the line from the singer's microphone and amplifier. The recording is consequently made on two separate channels, one for the singer and one for the orchestra. Sometimes, when these two channels are of the push-pull or direct-positive type, a third and fourth channel will be employed to make the recordings on normal track for editing purposes. At the same time discs will be cut, or a magnetic recording made, to enable the performance to be immediately played back to detect faults and errors. The purpose of separating orchestra and singer is to enable the balance between the two to be altered during the re-recording. Also, if at some later stage of the process the singer's performance should be found unsatisfactory, he can be recorded over again without incurring the cost and time of reassembling the orchestra. Indeed, the singer can be replaced without need to record the orchestra again.

The next stage is the playback process. A recording of the song, or combined song and orchestra, is played back on the set, either by magnetic tape or disc. A film dubber or dubbers can be used, but it takes some time to rewind and rethread a piece of film to a predetermined point, which may be in the middle of a song. The pickup can be placed instantly on the disc at a marked point. The pickup feeds to an amplifier and thence to a loudspeaker which is mounted close to the set. The singer then sings to his own voice coming from the loudspeaker but now he sings almost inaudibly—just loud enough in fact to form the words properly and give a reasonably good imitation of actual singing. Though this technique may sound difficult to master, it can be learned very rapidly by singers who have never attempted it before, and no hesitation need be felt about using the technique with inexperienced singers.

The camera which records this scene need not be fully silenced, as the sound records made at this time serve only an intermediate purpose and play no part in the final film. Synchronizing marks are placed on the sound and picture of each take in the normal way, and the film goes in for development and printing. It then becomes the editor's task to match it correctly. Let us call the picture track A, the intermediate record or guide track made on the set B, and the master record which was recorded first and is to be used last, C. The problem is to synchronize A and C. To do this, the assistant first synchronizes A and B by means of synchronizing marks as described before. He then screens these tracks to check their synchronism and enable the editor to select the takes he wishes used. The assistant next removes the unwanted takes, and matches modulations of each of the wanted B tracks with the corresponding sections of the C track. This is not difficult to do since, theoretically at least, the modulations are identical. In practice, however, there may be small disturbing set noises on the *B* tracks (which were disregarded by the director because these tracks are to be thrown away), or camera noise, or deterioration of disc quality owing to wear, or difference of level, or any combination of these factors. With variable-density track, in which modulations are always harder to match, some slight difficulty may be experienced from these sources. But practice makes very quick synchronizing by modulations possible.

The assistant then sends the song playback sequence to be coded, using a very convenient technique. Since there will be no sound cutting (the master track or tracks running without a break), the code letters and numbers for the track are established first. These might be 5A X00000 for the first foot, and 5A X00585 for the last foot, assuming the song track(s) to be 585 feet long. Next there may be an establishing shot of the singer, covering the entire song. This will be numbered 5A X01000-01585. Next let us imagine a close-up covering the first verse alone. This might be numbered 5A X03130-03590, and a reaction shot which tallied with certain selected words near the end of the song could be 5A X04545-04568. In this way the last three numerals will always synchronize with the corresponding numbers on the master sound track; while the two digits preceding these form an index designating the shot and corresponding with descriptions to be found in the editor's filing cards or loose-leaf book. Hence the cutting and recutting of playback sequences becomes technically a very simple matter.

The singer and orchestra we have followed through provide merely one example of a very wide application of prescoring and playback techniques. These techniques are used also for tap dancing and other dance routines, in which, besides the advantages mentioned before, there is the advantage of saving the director from having to concentrate on an impossible number of variable factors at a single time. A great deal of rehearsal goes into securing a perfect performance of a musical item, and a great deal into a perfect performance of a dance number. To secure simultaneously perfect performances of both would risk a prohibitive amount of time and money. By prescoring the music, the director can concentrate on perfecting the dance performance.

DUBBING

One of the most important applications of playback is to the *dubbing* of dialogue voices—that is, the subsequent fitting of voices to shots of people speaking either in the same or in another language. There are occasions when it is difficult to secure perfect sound recording in places where the picture must be shot. Sometimes there may be mechanical sounds which it is impossible to silence, not merely in factories but often in open country in the vicinity of airports, highways, and railroad tracks. Sometimes it is necessary to replace the recorded voice with another which better expresses the acted character; sometimes it is merely convenient not to be burdened with high-fidelity recording equipment on location.

The dubbing of English dialogue for reasons such as these is often resorted to even by large production units. The smaller unit should not be deterred by the apparent difficulties of the technique when dialogue is to be recorded under difficult and uncontrollable conditions; and if a dialogue track is spoiled by some fault like flutter or electrical interference, dubbing will prove indispensable in eliminating the need for reshooting.

The camera and recording requirements on the set or on location are simple. The camera need not be fully silenced, but it must run at synchronous speed. This rules out the use of spring-driven or *wild* DC motors. A single-phase synchronous motor driven from the regular 110-volt electrical supply is, however, perfectly satisfactory. The recording mechanism, used merely to provide an intelligible guide track, may take one of several forms. Like the camera, it must run at synchronous speed, and the same motor conditions apply. The recording medium may be shellac or acetate (a simple disc recorder), magnetic tape, magnetic wire, or film. The magnetic media must be positively driven by a capstan drive; otherwise, no matter how constant the motor speed, the tape or wire speed will vary. The film on which the picture is recorded may also be used to record the guide track by single-system, and several cameras (e.g. Bell and Howell and Standard Mitchell) may be converted without great difficulty to provide a recording of adequate quality for guide-track use and simple sound effects. An *aeolight* (glow lamp) makes a cheap and compact modulator, and modern B batteries will provide the necessary high-ignition voltage combined with low weight.

The editing and dubbing processes proceed as follows. The sound track, if single-system, is printed separately from the picture; if on disc or a magnetic medium, it is re-recorded. The picture and track are then synchronized. Next the dialogue sequences are edited to eliminate as much unwanted footage as possible. It is now necessary to mark the remaining sections of film for loops, continuous bands of film which may run from twenty to a hundred feet each. The planning of the loops is important, since misjudgments even at this early stage are difficult to correct later. Unless multiple microphone positions can be provided at the recording, long shots and close-ups of the same characters should not appear in a single loop, since they will need different acoustic treatment. A highly emotional passage should not be broken off in the middle. Not more than three or four characters should speak in each loop. If the loop is too long, it will be difficult to carry synchronization the full length, since the actors will tire or will concentrate on lip movements to the exclusion of natural acting.

Loops can be made up with separate sound and picture, but this doubles the amount of film to be threaded during projection, increases the likelihood of breakage, and introduces the chance of getting out of sync. It is therefore better to make a composite print with sound and picture in normal projection relationship. The loops are spliced together after inserting between the first picture frame and the last approximately fifteen feet of a special leader. This serves to make a pause of a few seconds between takes, giving the director a chance to instruct his actors; it provides a synchronizing mark punched in the sound track; and enables a diagonal line to be scratched down the picture track, ending at the corner of the exact frame at which the first character utters his first sound. This cues the actor when to start without introducing disturbing noises.

While the loops are being prepared, the speaking characters are selected and assembled. Since this discussion is confined to dubbing into the same language, little guidance need be given. The original characters will often be available; if not, the auditioning will proceed much as for an ordinary acted part, save that only the voice is of importance. A magnetic tape or wire recorder is a valuable help in enabling voices to be compared afterward "in the cold." If the number of loops is large, and the characters are not available for lengthy periods, it may be advisable to group the loops according to the characters they contain, rather than recording them in their order in the film. It is most important, however, not to upset the recording order of an emotional scene which has had to be broken down into several loops; this will inevitably disturb the actors' mood and call for much extra rehearsal.

The dubbing sessions should be conducted in as calm an atmosphere as possible, so that the actors are not overburdened by the complexity of the technical processes. They must memorize their parts and become perfectly familiar with them, which is helped by projecting each loop in the darkness of the recording studio, with the guide-track sound coming from the loud-speaker at a fairly low level. After a few repetitions, the actors will begin to say their lines over the projected sound, the first one taking his cue from the diagonal starting scratch, the others (if there is more than one part) picking up the rhythm of reply. It is here that the difficult aspects of dubbing present themselves. The mixer must try by proper microphone placement to reproduce (or improve on) the acoustic treatment of the original, which will in turn have depended on the position of the camera and the kind of acoustic space in which the scene was shot. Close-ups, medium and long shots can be simulated by the use of two or three microphones at different distances from the speaker, the change from one to another being made instantly with keys as the mixer takes his cue from the screen.

The director must at the same time strive to get the best possible performance out of his actors. The temptation will be to stress the need for lip synchronization at all costs, sacrificing every other quality to achieve this most basic requirement. Paradoxically, the skilled dubbing director seems on the surface to pay little attention to synchronization. He concentrates on catching the mood of the scene. If the screen character is smoking, he may give the actor a cigarette or a pipe; if the character gestures, he will make the actor gesture, for often a physical movement will alter the characteristics of speech. Indeed, if there is a tussle on the screen, the director may push the actor off his balance during the take, catching him unawares and so achieving naturalness of reaction. It may require ten or fifteen rehearsals of a loop, some with sound, others with sound switched off, before the acting is perfect and the wording and expression adjusted to proper synchronization. The director will signal to the mixer in his glass-paneled recording room in such a way that the actors do not know that the sound camera is turning as they continue speaking to the now silent loop. Usually, three or four takes will suffice, and the director watches the synchronization as carefully as the acting, using the break while the leader runs through to prompt the actors on any errors of timing he has noticed.

If all the technical preparations are well made, and the director and mixer are skilled, it should not be difficult to record four or five loops in an hour, and thirty to forty in a day. To exceed this number usually entails a heavy strain on the actors and the director. It must not be supposed, though, that previous acting experience in postsynchronization is essential. If untrained characters have spoken the dialogue in a film, there is no reason why their voices should not be satisfactorily used for dubbing. Most people pick up the apparently difficult technique very quickly, especially if the recording session is handled with an easy informality.

The director makes careful notes on the quality of each take of each loop as a guide to the editor, who may with great advantage be present at the recording. When the sound has been developed and printed, the editor breaks open each picture loop in turn, synchronizes it with the best take or combination of takes, and assembles his series of loops in script order, omitting the intervening sections of leader. This is only a trial synchronization. After a screening with the director, the difficult part of the sound cutting begins. To make an exact match, the editor may have to alter the position of individual words, shifting them a little up or down the track and juggling them until they match the lip movements as exactly as possible without doing violence to the stresses and rhythms of normal speech. This work is highly skilled and requires much practice and ingenuity.

Two or three further screenings and recuttings will complete the editing. If any loops are still unsatisfactory, they will have to be retaken. If all is well, the assembled picture and sound are once again broken down, this time to be placed in their proper position in the continuity of the film, which may contain many sequences not requiring dubbing. The new dialogue track takes its place among the various re-recording tracks, and the film moves toward completion as described in the previous chapter.

When a change of language is superimposed on the other difficulties of dubbing, many new problems are introduced which are beyond the scope of this study.[5]

The techniques described in this chapter—like many others mentioned in this book—are synthetic in character. They recreate reality from other than its ordinary elements. This is one of the most potent capacities of film, in that it prevents the medium from becoming tied to a naturalistic rendering of the world. But it is also one of its greatest dangers. The synthesis may become a feeble substitute for reality. The script writer, the set designer, even the director and producer, may have become so used to fabricating a world out of bits and pieces of studio shooting which afterwards become bits and pieces of celluloid, that they finally lose all touch with the world of living men and women. To be realistic without being naturalistic should be the movie maker's goal.

[5] An excellent account is to be found in W. A. Pozner, "Synchronization Technique," *JSMPE*, Sept., 1946, pp. 191–211.

XIII

⎍⎍⎍⎍⎍⎍⎍⎍⎍⎍⎍⎍⎍⎍⎍⎍⎍⎍⎍⎍⎍⎍⎍⎍⎍⎍⎍⎍⎍⎍⎍⎍

Journey's End

THE SOUND tracks of our picture have now been re-recorded, and the negative is developed and sent to be matched with the *picture release negative,* which has itself been matched to the workprint as described in chapter vii. Sometimes several sound takes of a single reel are developed, with instructions that one part is to be used for one section of the reel, another for another, and so on. When these cuts have been made, and the splices blooped, the sound release negative is ready for synchronizing with the picture.[1]

Hitherto we have been accustomed to a synchronism in which frames of picture and their accompanying sound occur opposite or parallel to one another. From its use in the cutting room and the re-recording process, this is called *parallel* or *editorial synchronism.* When the sound and picture are on separate tracks, this type of synchronism is convenient and serviceable. But when the picture finally goes out into the world, sound and visual image will be placed on the same ribbon of film. Again and again, however, we have encountered the basic contradiction: the picture must move intermittently, the sound steadily. If corresponding sound and picture were to be printed side by side, this requirement would be impossible to meet.

How much separation, then, and in which direction? Figure 13-1 shows how film travels from the top magazine of a projector to the bottom, the inverted image being turned right side up on the screen by the crossing of the light rays in the lens system. The necessity of a lower loop to take out the intermittent motion, and allowance for space to mount a separate sound head, led to the standardization of the 35 mm. sound track 20 frames ahead of the cor- .

---

1 Note that all the picture negative, except what has passed through an optical printer, is original negative. But none of the sound negative is original, every foot of it having been re-recorded. This is explained by the fact that the duping or optical printing of picture still involves more losses than the re-recording of sound. It is therefore not customary practice except for foreign 35 mm. release prints, and certain 16 mm. release printing procedures (see chapter ix).

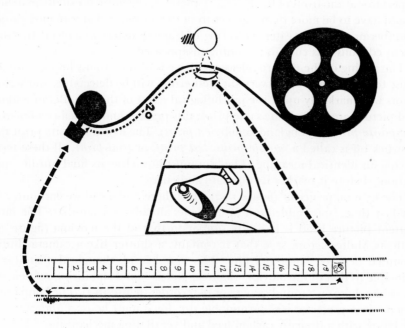

Fig. 13-1. Why corresponding sound and picture are not printed side by side. Because of the separation of sound and picture heads by 20 frames on the 35 mm. projector, and because film travels from the top of the projector to the bottom, the sound must precede the picture by 20 frames. The corresponding difference in 16 mm. projection is 26 frames.

responding picture, while in 16 mm. the separation was set at 26 frames because of the very much smaller height of the frame. This new synchronism is called *projection synchronism,* and is one of the most confusing relationships which the beginner encounters in learning the handling of film. An excellent handbook on film [2] made this surprising statement in its glossary. "Since light travels from screen to audience more quickly than the sound from the amplifiers, the sound precedes the image on the celluloid by some nine-

[2] Roger Manvell, *Film.* [1st ed.] London: Penguin Books, 1944, p. 173.

teen frames." A little arithmetic will show that, if this were the correct reason, a spectator at the front of the balcony (where synchronism is usually matched) would have to be more than 900 feet from the screen, and at a 16 mm. projection (because of the greater staggering of frames) almost 1,600 feet! In subsequent editions this curious reasoning disappeared.

The timing of the picture release negative is of the utmost importance, because to the expert eye the very slightest errors will be detectable, and serious errors will markedly upset the psychological effect of the film. Because sound and picture are now on the same print, this print is known as a *combined* or *composite print* (in England, a *married print*). The first composite print that is struck off is called a *sample print, test print,* or *trial print,* all these terms having an identical meaning. The film must now clear its final hurdle—projection—before it reaches its ultimate audience.

The 35 mm. projector (figure 13-2) which here at the end we encounter for the first time, is assembled out of elements already very familiar. The intermittent picture head is basically similar to that of the moviola (figure 4-3) with its Maltese cross, save that it contains a shutter like a camera shutter mounted between lamp and film. The sound head, though also similar in principle to that of the moviola (figure 4-5), has sound stabilizing refinements more like those on a sound camera or re-recorder (figure 10-2). The lamp house of a modern projector is of formidable size, for it must house a *high-intensity arc* lamp, with automatic carbon feed and ventilating mechanisms.

The film travels through the projector along the following path: The unprojected reel of film (standardized today at 2,000 feet) is placed in a fireproof magazine at the top of the machine. Thence the film travels over a *feed sprocket,* forms a loop and passes the picture aperture, where a pressure plate holds it in place. Here it is pulled down by an intermittent sprocket working on the Maltese-cross principle, a shutter obscuring the picture while this pull-down movement takes place. After passing the picture gate, the intermittent movement of the film is taken out by a loop and the film itself enters the sound head. Here it passes over a stabilizer to reduce the irregularities of film travel which would otherwise make themselves audible as an unpleasant flutter or *vibrato*. The stabilizer often consists of a freely turning drum attached to a flywheel and pulled round by the motion of the film itself. Other more complicated mechanisms are often employed, however. As the film passes over this drum, the sound track is scanned by a light beam originating in an exciter lamp. After passing through the track, the light beam is collected by a phototube, the output of which is amplified and fed to the loudspeaker. This loudspeaker is of the two-way type, in which the high and low frequencies are radiated from separate diaphragms in order to reduce distortions. Finally, after leaving the sound head, the film passes over another sprocket (the *take-up sprocket*), and is wound up into a second magazine.

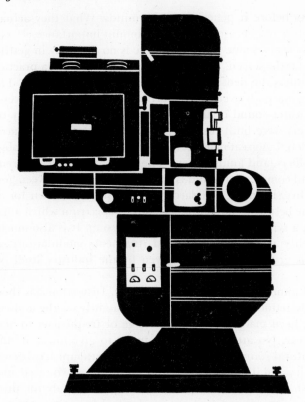

Fig. 13-2. A modern 35 mm. projector. This machine shows the influence of advanced industrial design in combining accessibility of the parts with clean and simple appearance.

The 16 mm. projector has already been adequately discussed in chapter ix. For reasons of cost and size, it is difficult to engineer it to the same high standards as the 35 mm. machine. The best 16 mm. projectors now on the market are approaching, at a very high price, the level of quality which all should attain at a much lower price. The circle of high prices limiting the market and the limited market keeping up the prices is akin to the situation in the American automobile market in 1907, before Henry Ford launched his Model T. The 16 mm. projector has not yet found its Henry Ford or its Model T. Their arrival is long overdue.

The limitations of projection are frequently overlooked by the film maker as being none of his business. His technical responsibility cannot stop, however, before the film reaches the eyes and ears of its audience, nor his social responsibility before it penetrates their minds. What they actually see and hear is therefore not of casual but of paramount importance.

With a modern 35 mm. projector, there is no difficulty in getting an excellent picture on the screen. The latest types of shutter give a practically flickerless image unless the density of the film is exceptionally low. This image is satisfactorily sharp all over, and its brilliance is adequate in even the largest theaters. Theater sound quality is much more variable. Many of the older movie theaters were built during the silent era, so that their acoustics were never considered. A great many of them are still equipped with obsolete sound heads, amplifiers, and loudspeakers. The result is that the difference between good and bad commercial sound is much greater than between good and bad picture quality. Even the standard characteristic laid down for all theaters, including the best, runs far below the audible spectrum which a listener hears at an opera, a symphony concert, or a jam session. It is also much below the level of fidelity achieved today in FM (frequency-modulation) radio broadcasts. This is grudgingly admitted even by the industry itself (see note, p. 248).

The level aimed at is that of acceptability. Distortion has therefore been painstakingly reduced, as likely to jar unpleasantly on the audience. But no attempt has been made to widen the range of frequencies to match that of the human ear. No attempt has been made to give music its full dynamic range, or natural sound its violent impact. No attempt has been made (save for the solitary and ill-fated Fantasound) to supply a two-eared audience with sounds which they can fix in space. There is no remedy for this so long as movie theaters are treated as a sort of glorified lounge in which people can talk, eat candies, and shuffle their feet to their heart's content. A movie audience would not survive ten minutes at a symphony concert, or even at a good musical comedy.

All these considerations are taken for granted by the group in the screening room waiting for the first projection of their new film. It may be a feature costing several million dollars. It may be a short film on which little money has been spent, but which is expected to make an important mark in the world. Those who have worked on a film for many months are conscious of its smallest imperfections, technical and creative, however little sign of this they may reveal in public. The first screening is likely, therefore, to be depressing. The timer will be present, if he has not already seen the film in the lab, to make notes on the numerous corrections which the sample print will call for. The mixer, or the head of the sound department, will be there to judge whether the balance will sound well in the theaters. Above all the producer will try to estimate what psychological effect the film will have on its audience, general or specialized as it may be. Will it hold their attention to the end? Will it make them laugh? Or cry? Or hold on to their seats? Or even think?

The producer seldom knows with any assurance. He may with advantage "sneak preview" the film, and if it is a comedy, retime it for laughs by shortening or lengthening the cutting, or if it is a drama, build up a greater suspense by re-recording it with different emphasis. All this becomes visible when the film and its audience at last enter into a living relationship through the currents of feeling generated when people gather together into a crowd. Sometimes the producer's confidence in his own judgment deserts him. Then he will allow a single audience to dictate to him, or worse still he will follow the advice of those pollsters and analysts who would reduce all human emotion and thought to a row of numbers, and sink every interesting individual difference under a specious average.

The producer of the film of ideas is saved from these seductions because he has less money at stake and therefore does not need to put such a premium on conformity. But he is even more in the dark about the ultimate effects of his film on people's minds and feelings. Hollywood has an answer; it can point to the eternal box office. The merchants of ideas on film have little or no cash to count and therefore no barometer of popularity. There is room here for investigation by the methods of mass observation, and by skilled analysis of individual reactions to controversial films.

Now that the film we have followed so far has at length reached its audience, it remains only to try to pierce a little way into the future and discover what innovations—what new paths in film—the economic structure of the industry will allow to be developed.

XIV

⊓⊔⊓⊔⊓⊔⊓⊔⊓⊔⊓⊔⊓⊔⊓⊔⊓⊔⊓⊔⊓⊔⊓⊔⊓⊔⊓⊔⊓⊔

Things to Come

THE MOTION PICTURE industry is intensely conservative, especially in the land of its birth. This is an inevitable consequence of its stature as a major industry, ranking among the first ten in the American hierarchy. Giants are seldom supple: they must expend too much energy to touch their toes. Thus, while Hollywood and other world film centers have made a legend of their technical progress, it has not in reality been very spectacular when compared with the development of, let us say, nuclear physics and antibiotics. Indeed, the coming of sound has been the only noteworthy break with an earlier technique; and the industry is certainly chary of repeating so drastic an experiment.

This conservative attitude is neither unreasonable nor unexpected. The big film studios are extremely efficient organizations, turning out pictures by means almost as time- and labor-saving as Detroit's assembly lines. Even Hollywood's fabulous private waste is used to advantage as a by-product. It becomes the fodder of a hundred movie magazines numbering their readers in millions, which glorify the star system and thus entrench the industry against its critics. The production processes described in this book correspond to the machine tools and capital equipment of other industries. These are scrapped only if their replacement cost can be amortized fairly quickly by manufacturing economies or the creation of new wants; they will never be scrapped at the vague behest of "artistic progress." Similarly, to scrap an actress whose charms (and contract) have expired costs the big studio nothing; but to convert to stereoscopic film would mean overhauling the whole capital structure of the industry.

Innovations like magnetic recording will scarcely cause a tremor on the financial seismograph, and there is therefore no obstacle to their introduction. It can be proved that within a very short time they will amortize their capital cost in reduced costs of production. Many writers on film have accepted Hollywood's myth of scientific progress at its face value, and have supposed that a technical revolution had only to issue from the research laboratory to win immediate acceptance. They have thus assumed that stereophonic sound, three-dimensional movies, the "feelies," the total cinema, were well on the way to realization—in fact, just around the corner.

No industry or business enterprise whose capital is counted in billions could afford to take so casual a view of its investments. Mass production stabilizes design, and a stabilized product creates a conformity of taste among its consumers which is itself an obstacle to change. Thus size becomes an enemy of progress.

There will always be a few small-scale experimenters who refuse to be thus bounded, and whose ideas, unsatisfied by the freedom of content which the film as a medium allows, must break its technical barriers and escape into new territories. There is little chance of these experiments finding their way into the theaters; but the nontheatrical film may give the iconoclast his chance, and prove—with modern painting and music—that the richest art-forms are those with ever new perspectives of growth.

In this chapter, therefore, we shall begin with something less ambitious than the total cinema; [1] something which may be realized within the given structure of the movie industry. From there we shall go on to explore certain possibilities of film which may never reach the theater screen, but which, if interest in them is awakened, may none the less form a kind of chamber music of the cinema.

FILM AND TELEVISION

Technically speaking, television is nothing more than a successive method of transmitting the intelligence which film transmits simultaneously. Also, television does not provide storage; film does. In other words, television breaks down an instantaneous cross-section in time of some visible continuum (a scene) into a large number of elements—usually about a quarter of a mil-

---

[1] The total cinema is by no means a recent idea. The French inventor, Grimoin Samson, was working toward it in 1899 with his Cinéorama. His audience gathered in the nacelle of a balloon, suspended in a global enclosure a hundred feet in diameter. Ten synchronized projectors, mounted in a star in the center of this space, cast upon its spherical white walls a continuous image, which had been shot by ten similarly mounted and synchronized movie cameras carried in a free balloon across Paris. This extraordinary machine, far ahead of its time and doubtless technically very imperfect, gave a few performances at the Paris Exhibition of 1900. Owing to defective installation, the ten arc projectors overheated, and the audience, in their gondola immediately above, ran grave risks of total incineration. The police intervened and closed down the Cinéorama. It was a financial disaster. (Description and illustrations in Sadoul, *Histoire générale du cinéma*, Vol. 2, chap. 6, and Jean Vivié, *Traité général de technique du cinéma*, Vol. 1, pp. 101–102.)

lion—and instantly transmits these elements one after another by wire or radio to some distant point. At the receiving end, these elements are reconstituted into a scene. Film, on the other hand, records the elementary units of a scene—usually between a quarter of a million and one million of them [2]— simultaneously upon a sensitive emulsion, which, having a physical existence in space, cannot be transmitted instantly to a distant point. On the other hand, because of its physical existence, film can be stored; the television image vanishes in the instant unless it is reproduced and stored by means of some other medium.

Now let us extend our analysis from the instantaneous cross-section and take in the dimension of time. Here film and television have found the same solution. Objects in the real world are not only infinitely modulable in the three space dimensions, but in the time dimension also. Thus, as we have pointed out in an earlier chapter, it is theoretically necessary to transmit an infinite number of images each second. Since this is impossible, researchers went to the other extreme to discover the lowest number of images per second required to recreate by persistence of vision the illusion of motion. The resulting figure (about sixteen) has been raised by various considerations to between twenty-four and thirty, and it is in this region that film and television have taken their stand.

Thus, in brief, we have the following situation. The world is an infinitely modulable continuum in four dimensions (three of space and one of time). Film abstracts two of the space dimensions and records them *simultaneously* as a modulated area of not much more than one million elements.[3] Television also abstracts two space dimensions and scans them into about a quarter of a

---

[2] Television and 16 mm. film today have approximately the same picture resolution, with about a quarter of a million elements. Thirty-five mm. film, with about one million elements, is still a long way ahead. Over-all resolution, however, is by no means completely defined in terms of picture elements.

[3] It has often been suggested that the intelligence conveyed on a movie film or a TV program could be stored much more conveniently and compactly on a magnetized wire. This bears investigation. Let us suppose that the standard 35 mm. film frame provides the standard of image resolution. A resolving power of 60 lines per mm. on the camera negative may be assumed. Since the picture space is approximately 22 mm. wide, $22 \times 60 = 1,320$ independently modulable areas (or picture elements) can be accommodated along it. The frame height being 16 mm., a vertical row will contain $16 \times 60 = 960$ picture elements. Thus the whole frame totals $1,320 \times 960 = 1,267,000$ modulable elements. But 24 frames of film must be transmitted (or stored) every second. Hence $1,267,000 \times 24$ or over 30,000,000 elements are required to store the intelligence in one second's worth of 35 mm. film. If three-color film is to be stored, there will be a further multiplier of 3. Engineers, using the most advanced recording techniques, can today crowd 2,000 modulations into one inch of sound track. Thus, 15,000 inches of track (on very fine wire, we may suppose) are required to record every second of black-and-white film, and 45,000 inches for every second of color film. It is true that these figures may be divided by 4 to reduce them to the capacity of the present television image or 16 mm. frame; neither, however, as yet provides really adequate resolution. For the time being, it is safe to assume that simultaneous storage of the picture image (film) will hold its own against successive storage (wire).

million successive elements which it then instantly transmits and recombines. Both film and television break down the time dimension into a mere sixteen to thirty equally spaced slices per second, which the eye conveniently blurs together by means of persistence of vision.

In much of what follows, we shall assume that the intelligence recorded by the two media is exactly the same; that television has achieved the same "quality" as film. Until this has happened, intelligence cannot be freely converted from one medium to another in the same way that an optical printer can transform the picture image or a re-recorder the sound image in current film practice. The loss of intelligence would be too great (the quality would deteriorate too much). However, there are various by-products of the film image which even today could be transmitted advantageously by television.

It is often necessary that a film image be dispatched to a distant point. The sound track can be dissected into a single time dimension and put on a wire or a radio carrier. As long as poor quality can be tolerated, the image can now be similarly dissected and transmitted. For instance, suppose a production unit wishes to record the score for a film in a hall, remote from the studio, where the acoustics are ideal. The composer prefers to conduct to the film itself, to keep the synchronism exact. It is only necessary to run the film in a TV scanning projector in the studio and place a TV receiver in the distant hall close to the composer, and the object is achieved, so long as both projector and film recorder are operated from the same supply frequency and linked by radio or wire. Since scanning projectors are now on the market, and AC/DC TV receivers are cheap and light, this solution is very simple.

Again, a producer in a major studio may wish to check on the morning's dailies of one of his productions without leaving his desk. If he is more interested in the dramatic action than the photographic quality, this is very easily achieved, even today, by feeding him a TV signal from the projection room. Furthermore, by the use of a dichroic prism or other image splitter, it would be possible for a single projector to deliver a photographic image to the cameraman in a screening room, and a TV image to the producer in his office.

Another example is the monitoring viewfinder in the camera. It has always been an inconvenience that only one person, the camera operator, can see the film image at the actual moment of shooting. Neither the chief cameraman nor the director can do more than imagine what the camera is seeing. Moreover, if the camera is on a crane, the director may have to remain on the studio floor, where his point of view will be altogether different. This problem is resolved today by much discussion between director and cameraman, and by a plurality of takes, which add up to a large waste of time and money. If the camera aperture could be scanned by a TV system during shooting, the image could be reconstituted on the studio floor at any convenient size and in any convenient place. Thus it could be watched by the director and his assistants, the chief cameraman, the dance director, or anybody else concerned, on one or several monitoring screens; and it could be piped into the producer's office to a receiver where, at the touch of a selector switch, all the other pictures for which the producer was responsible could be made to appear—whether they were on the set, in the projection room, or on a moviola in the cutting room.

The theoretical solution of the camera-monitoring problem is not difficult. The reflex shutter (figures 3-8) bleeds off an image identical to the film image, and of fairly good luminosity. Various French cameras have fed the faint image on the back of the film in the aperture into the operator's eye. However obtained, this image could be scanned by a very small iconoscope built into the camera. The practical problems are rather severe, since iconoscopes need preamplifiers mounted close to them, which might inconveniently increase the bulk of the camera. While this book was in the press, it was announced that such a device was being tested in England.

Many other applications will readily occur to the reader. All such nonrevolutionary devices will be developed and installed as soon as the industry considers that their savings will be worth their costs. They do not involve any unpredictable economic factors.

Next we come to the transmission of images by TV direct from the outside world to the theater screen. We have seen that TV is a nonstorage medium. Therefore, wholly TV methods involve breaking into theater programs, which raises economic problems outside the scope of this book. Technically, direct TV makes use of an iconoscope camera on location, a *microwave* transmitter to the theaters, and a TV receiver and projector in the theaters. This system is shown in highly simplified form in figure 14-1, *a*. The projector employs as a rule a projection-type cathode-ray tube and a Schmidt optical system of very high luminous efficiency and short throw (not more than 50 feet). Owing to the present low light output, the maximum screen size is about 24 by 18 feet, and a special design of lenticular screen is desirable.[4]

An alternative system, called intermediate-film television, is sketched in figure 14-1, *b*. Here the TV image, after reception in the theater, is reconstituted on a cathode-ray tube and photographed on film by an orthodox intermittent camera. The exposed film is passed from the camera into a 90 foot per minute developing machine, in which developing time is cut down to a few seconds by raising the developer to a high temperature. After fixing, washing, and drying, the film travels immediately into a normal film projector. Since

[4] Some of the most advanced work on theater television has been done in England. A good account is given by the late Captain A. G. D. West in "Development of Theater Television in England," *JSMPE*, Aug., 1948, pp. 122–168. For recent developments in the United States, see "Theater Television Today" and "FCC Allocation of Frequencies," *JSMPE*, Oct., 1949, pp. 321–353.

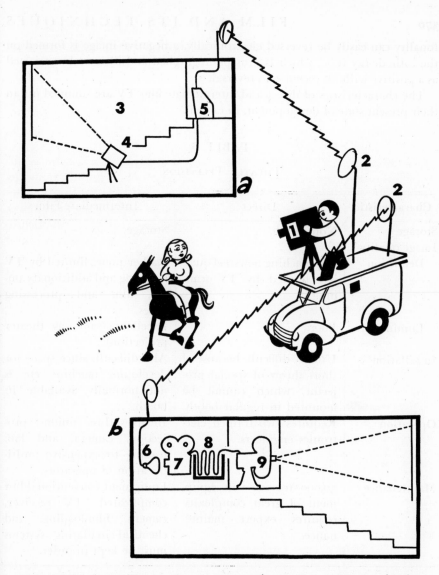

Fig. 14-1. Actuality in the theater: alternative systems of television. The upper diagram (**a**) shows how an actuality scene is picked up by the TV camera (1) and radiated via a microwave antenna (2) to a theater (3). Here the image is recreated and projected onto the screen by a short-throw Schmidt projector (4) controlled from a console (5).

Diagram **b** follows an identical route as far as the theater, where the image is recreated on a small cathode-ray tube (6) and photographed by a camera (7). The exposed film passes in darkness into a high-speed developing machine (8) running at 90 feet per minute, from which it travels to the projector (9), where it is projected in the ordinary way.

Thus, **a** shows direct TV, **b** intermediate-film TV.

tonality can easily be reversed electronically, a negative image is formed on the cathode-ray tube, which is thus photographed and ultimately projected as a positive without recourse to reversal.

The characteristics of direct and intermediate-film TV are summed up, in their present state of development, in table 6.

TABLE 6

THEATER TELEVISION

Characteristic	Direct	Intermediate-Film
Storage	Nonstorage.	Storage.
Image quality		
Definition	Approaching newsreel quality: limited by TV scanning.	Rather poor; limited by TV scanning and additional camera, film and processing losses.
Luminosity	Poor.	Excellent (same as theater projection).
Installation	Usually difficult, because of short throw of special projector, which cannot be mounted in regular booth.	Also difficult, since space for developing machine, etc. is not normally available in booth.
Operation	Requires two trained electronics engineers.	Involves three unions: projection, camera, and lab, leading to expensive multiplication of operators.
Maintenance	50,000–100,000 volt equipment of great complexity requires expert maintenance.	Equipment conventional but complicated. TV receiver, camera, film-loading, and chemical-circulating systems must be kept in order.

When and whether such systems are widely installed depends on (a) the rate of technical progress toward an interchangeability of film and TV images; (b) intensity of public demand to see events in the theaters as they happen; (c) the reaction of the motion picture industry to the threat of home television to diminish theater attendance. It appears as if a would come close to solution about 1953 or 1954, but b and c are factors outside the scope of this book, and will interact to accelerate or retard a.

Continuing in the same direction, we encounter the possibility of radiating complete film programs by TV to the theaters, probably with an admixture of actuality. This is sketched in figure 14-2, which indicates some possibilities in the New York area. Since no moviegoer would pay to see a tele-transmitted feature film of poorer quality than he could find around the block at a direct-view house, this development must await the complete solution of problem *a* and the allocation to the movie industry of adequate transmission channels.

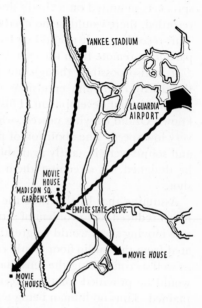

If all theater programs consisted of televised actuality and tele-transmitted movies, the cost of release prints would be virtually eliminated, projection staffs could be greatly reduced and many local film exchanges closed down. Even more important, costs of picture production could be amortized in a few weeks, instead of many months, by simultaneous teleprojection in several thousand theaters. If the industry thought that the conversion of theaters (a formidable expenditure) would be justified by these economies, it would still run up against a number of obstacles. The release-print laboratories would doubtless fight the threat of being driven out of business, and their capital investment is substan-

Fig. 14-2. How actuality and film programs may be fed by television to theaters in New York.

tial. The raw-film manufacturers would resist the loss of their most profitable market. And the well-unionized projectionists would undoubtedly oppose the change.

Assuming that in 1953 or 1954, the TV and film images become interchangeable, a very striking alteration of studio technique is possible.[5] The crude and noisy intermittent camera, which must be reloaded with film every ten minutes of operation, may disappear for sound shooting, its place being taken by the TV camera, which has no moving parts, is perfectly silent, and will run for long periods without attention. If the image were thus dissected electronically, it would be reconstituted line by line and frame by frame, and so recorded at once on continuously moving film. The narrow image-width slit and the moving beam of light rays have obvious analogies to the optical sound camera, as has the image-dissecting TV camera to the microphone.

[5] There is no technical reason why this development should be any longer delayed, since the studio TV channels would not be bounded by the low resolution limits set by radio waveband restrictions. Thousand-line channels could in fact be designed today, since amplification of 25 to 50 megacycle bandwidths is already possible, and the signal would presumably be transmitted from camera to floor by coaxial cable.

Picture- and sound-recording cameras would therefore be very similar in construction, and it is probable that the two film tracks would travel over sprockets mounted on a single shaft; since the sound would be magnetically recorded, there would be no need of a light-tight division between the tracks. This recording unit would be placed in what is now the sound-recording department, remote from the sound stage.

It is also possible, though not probable, that the next five years will see the discovery of film emulsions which will make the photographic image visible without development. This has already been accomplished in the well-known Ozalid copying process, which, however, is not panchromatic and has very low speed. The abolition of picture processing would mean that picture and sound were instantly available for projection, and means would at once be designed for screening them in the studio after each scene had been shot.

Assuming that by this time the size and weight of a TV camera had been much reduced, the problem of setting up and making crane and other elaborate moving shots would be greatly simplified. A series of selsyn motors operated from the studio floor would control the camera movements on the crane, as well as controlling the lens diaphragm and focus. TV monitoring screens would be provided for the director, cameraman, and others, as already explained. Thus no human being would have to ride the crane, which could in consequence be made much lighter, more flexible, and more mobile.

Lens focusing presents certain problems, since there is no means by which the camera can "know" how far away it is from its principal object in the absence of the camera operator, who usually judges this distance by marks or occasionally by a range finder. A built-in range finder, as on the Vinten Everest camera, could be coupled to a separate TV scanner, but this involves a second complete transmission channel, which is clumsy. More promising, because completely automatic, would be the use of a narrow-beam radar transmitter, mounted on top of the TV camera, which could be focused on the principal object of the shot, and revolved if necessary by a selsyn motor from below. The radar receiver would receive the "blips" reflected from this object, and would be coupled to the lens-focusing sleeve, which it would rotate to the proper position from moment to moment.[6] A third possible solution, requiring a very sensitive TV camera, is the replacement of the camera lens by a pinhole, which has infinite depth of focus and provides an unlimited range of magnifications. However, the definition afforded by even the smallest pinhole is mediocre, since diffraction effects impair the image.

6 Owing to the high velocity of radio waves, it might prove impossible to detect objects within a few feet by such means. The same principles could, however, be applied to a sonar device, or sound ranging by ultrasonic radiation, using air as the medium. The problem here would be to insure constant calibration of the focusing control with the temperature and barometric pressure of the air in the studio undergoing continuous changes.

A TV camera would require only a single lens if the resolving power of the image dissector were sufficiently high. This is because greater magnifications could be obtained simply by scanning smaller areas of the mosaic. When these smaller areas were reconstituted at fixed frame size in the recording camera, the same effect as optical magnification would be achieved. Since the scanned area could be diminished and expanded progressively, zoom-lens effects would become possible without any optical complications.[7] Finally, by trapezoidal and other nonrectangular types of scanning, interesting distortions of space could be produced which would baffle the ingenuity of a lens designer.

The sensitivity of a film camera is that of the emulsion which registers the image. Film speeds have, on the average, doubled every ten years under the intensive development of the manufacturers; but to maintain or improve resolving power while increasing speed is a chemical problem of quite exceptional difficulty. The TV camera, like the microphone, depends merely on electrical amplification for its sensitivity, and electronic techniques develop much more rapidly than emulsion chemistry. Though in quality the TV image is at present inferior to the 35 mm. photographic image, in sensitivity it is already ahead. Very great strides may be expected in the next few years. It is reasonable to anticipate, therefore, that the replacement of film emulsions in the camera by TV image dissectors will lead to a great simplification of studio lighting. Lighting for modeling must always remain; but with the virtual abolition of key lighting, the size and amperage of all studio lights could be scaled down by a very large factor.

This camera of the future would be worked wholly from the studio floor. The operator would sit at a console, which would look something like a re-recording console. On it would be grouped switches for starting the various crane movements, selsyn controls for panning and tilting the camera itself, the adjustment for the lens diaphragm, and the footage counter. Signal lights would show that the radar or sonar focusing device was in action. A log sheet would instruct the operator in the proper sequence of camera movements, and a small monitor screen would guide him in moving the controls. Nearby, the director and the chief cameraman would be in consultation over a much larger monitor screen, deciding whether any changes were needed to carry out the shot to better advantage. As the actors rehearsed their parts, the camera could be quickly moved in any direction, and the results immediately observed—all with a minimum of manpower and waste motion, and a consequent saving of time. Even more important, the conceptions of the director

---

[7] Since TV effects a space dissection into the time dimension, it is possible to intensity modulate the resulting signal according to any given pattern. Thus, for instance, "electronic highlights" may be introduced into the image, new shadows can be cast, and parts of the frame distorted or omitted, to be replaced by images from other cameras in masked effects.

and cameraman could be translated into action much more effectively than at present.

These predictions take us some distance into the future. The science of electronics advances quickly, but it has a long way to go before it can rival the old black box of the pioneers, which is essentially the camera of today. Moreover, movie cameramen are very conservative, and many of them have a deep-seated distrust of electronics. It took them a long time to become accustomed to gammas and sensitometric curves. No one knows if they will swallow a whole new terminology of scanning lines, flybacks, gamma amplifiers, time basis, X-, Y-, and Z-axis modulation, and the like.

The gains are clear. In live-action shooting, as in animation, much too much clumsy machinery stands between the artist and the execution of his designs. Paradoxically, it often takes more and better machinery, rather than none at all, to give rein to the imagination. Film is not yet a spontaneous art.

ADDING A THIRD DIMENSION

In this fragmentary glance at the future, we arrive now at one of those improbable revolutions which have long been prophesied but may never be achieved in commercial movies.

Three-dimensional photography (originating in Wheatstone's invention of the stereoscope in 1832) has come and gone and returned again as artistic fashion changed, only its scientific applications remaining in favor. At times its increased naturalism has been praised, at other times despised. Commercial movies, with their hankering after illusion, might have been expected to confer on it an enduring popularity. Yet in spite of the radical improvements introduced by Berthier, Lippmann, the two Ives, Kanolt, Dudley, and many another inventor, stereoscopic projection has gone aground on one formidable obstacle: the selection of the necessary left- and right-eye images must take place either at the audience's eyes (necessitating the wearing of viewing spectacles) or at the screen (necessitating an infinite number of projected images).

Since the start of this book we have been concerned with the transmission of one-eyed and one-eared intelligence. Two-eared intelligence, as we have briefly seen, demands for its recording a second microphone channel and sound track, and for its reproduction two sets of loudspeakers widely spaced on either side of the screen. Two-eyed intelligence requires more critical conditions for faithful transmission. The separate images destined for the left and right eyes of each member of the audience must be recorded on film through optical systems laterally spaced at a distance based on that of the average separation of the eyes (2.5 inches), but varying widely according to rather complicated geometrical considerations.

The most satisfactory method of projection whereby the proper sorting out of images is effected at the audience's eyes employs the substance known commercially as Polaroid, first produced in 1935 by E. H. Land. By creating appropriate molecular changes in a sheet of polyvinyl-alcohol plastic, impregnated in an iodine solution, Land was able to suppress all but one of the planes of vibration of a beam of light passing through it.[8] Thus if, for example, the projected left-eye image is passed through a Polaroid filter set to polarize in a vertical plane, it can be seen after reflection from a nondepolarizing screen by a person whose left eye is covered by a filter similarly oriented, the right eye remaining closed. If this filter is made to rotate, as in oculists' spectacles, the image will gradually darken, until at 90 degrees of rotation both image and screen disappear into total blackness. If, now, a second projector is switched on, with a filter polarizing in this new 90-degree plane over its lens, the image it throws will be clearly visible to the observer's left eye. In practice, therefore, the observer will wear filters over both eyes, mutually oriented at 90 degrees in exactly the same directions as the projector filters. This "light gate" achieves an almost perfect separation of images, thus realizing the fullest stereoscopic effect of which the projected images are capable. Since the transmission of Polaroid is almost constant throughout the visible spectrum, color film can be projected satisfactorily.

A later and even more striking invention by Land and Mahler (1939), the Vectograph, forms a kind of "stereoscopic sandwich" of the left- and right-eye images, which are produced in terms of percentage of polarization and afterwards superimposed with their polarizing axes at right angles. If Vectographic motion picture film were available (and no doubt much difficult research would be needed to reduce its thickness and make its processing commercially practical), it would be possible to project stereoscopic films with perfectly standard equipment, though of course the audiences would still need to wear polarizing viewers. That no commercialization is apparently planned is probably due to various psychological factors which need further discussion, because they affect all spectacle viewing systems.

The movie theater is primarily a place of relaxation, a place where people can go to gossip in undertones, make love, and chew candy. In this mood the donning of spectacles and the enforced concentration required to fuse stereoscopic images is regarded as annoying and difficult. For this reason the prewar

[8] Methods of polarizing light beams have been known for more than a century, and the present method of polarized projection was put forward as long ago as 1890 by J. Anderson, in England. Prior to the invention of Polaroid, however, polarizers were too cumbersome and expensive, or too difficult to manufacture, to be of much commercial value.

Pete Smith *Audioscopiks* were not conspicuously successful; many people did not even bother to put on their anaglyphic viewers, but contented themselves with a fuzzy and wholly nonstereoscopic image until the next item on the program appeared. There is also a good deal of apprehension in the industry lest it become involved in claims for medical damages which, whether genuine or frivolous, would be extremely hard to rebut because the physiology of eyestrain resulting from looking at stereoscopic pictures is still only imperfectly understood. On top of all this it is found with plane-polarized glasses that if the viewer's head is inclined from the vertical by no more than 15 degrees, the filtering action of both eyepieces falls off so much that the three-dimensional effect virtually disappears. Since the more fatigued and amorous members of movie audiences frequently incline their heads on one another's shoulders almost horizontally, there would be a great many demands at the box-office for ticket refunds. And finally, the distortion of the stereoscopic image which results from sitting at the extreme side and front of the theater (though not inherently worse than that suffered by a two-dimensional image) annihilates the appearance of solidity, so that the audience in these seats feels that it isn't getting its money's worth. Commercially, this entails reducing the seating capacity of theaters, thus lowering box-office receipts.

In short, the types of stereoscopic projection in which image selection occurs at the audience's eyes can make only a limited appeal to specialized groups who are prepared to concentrate on what they are seeing, and will accept special conditions. Virtually the same provisos apply to the present non-theatrical audience, which accepts the limitations of the 16 mm. medium for the sake of what it cannot see in any other form. There would thus appear to be a very real use for stereoscopic films projected by the polarized method, and at least one enterprising producer of short films has broken into this fascinating territory.

Economic conditions aside, however, the conversion of the feature film industry to three-dimensional projection must await the development of a satisfactory system which selects the images at the screen itself. Credit for the first full-scale public exhibition of films made by such a system, extending over a period of years, must go to the Soviet Union, though nothing could be more misleading than the Russian claim to the basic invention of parallax projection. Actually, the stereoscopic system of Semyon Pavlovich Ivanow is based on the work of many inventors in many countries, notably Berthier (1896) and Lippman (1908) in France, F. E. Ives (1903), Kanolt (1918), and H. E. Ives (1928–1933) in America. In its most elementary form, Ivanow's system consists of a grid of very fine wires or narrow slats called a raster, mounted in front of the screen in such a way that it blocks the observer's left-eye view of the right-eye picture, and his right-eye view of the left-eye picture, the two pictures being thrown in superimposition on the screen through the same grid. Thus the image separation depends on a precise positioning of the observer's eyes in relation to the screen. If he moves his head the least bit sideways, his lines of sight will go out of phase with the grid and the stereoscopic effect will disappear or become *pseudoscopic*. Though Ivanow greatly refined the wire screen by substituting for it a screen embossed in a fan-shaped pattern (this was a Belgian invention) with thousands of minute fluted lenses (due to a Swiss engineer), it was still found necessary to limit drastically the seating capacity of the special movie theater in order to eliminate the zones of blurred and pseudoscopic vision.[9]

The screen image formed in the Ivanow system (among many others) is known as a *parallax stereogram* from the fact that separation of the images is a result of the differences of parallax between the observer's eyes. Essentially, only two images are thrown on the screen, these being intercalated by the action of the grid, as already explained. Hence the pseudoscopic viewing zones are as wide as the *orthoscopic* zones, which is a great practical disadvantage. Moreover, since the eyes fuse the two component images into a single image, there is only one correct axis for viewing the parallax stereogram, the perpendicular bisector of the screen. Once the spectator moves to one side, the image becomes distorted, as indeed it does with all the other types of stereogram so far described.

Recognizing these drawbacks, inventors have set to work to develop more refined systems which produce pictures called *parallax panoramagrams*. Not only do these increase the ratio of orthoscopic to pseudoscopic viewing positions, but they create an image which can be viewed "in the round"; that is to say, when the spectator moves from side to side, he sees a different image, and not merely the same image from a different angle. This highly ingenious device, invented by Kanolt, achieves its object by subdividing the intercalated left- and right-eye strip images into still narrower strips forming a panorama of the subject, shot by a camera which slowly moves round it in the arc of a circle. Parallax panoramagrams are becoming familiar (though still in very imperfect form) in various types of advertising display, and their optical systems are of formidable complexity. The application of this idea to movies still further increases its inherent complications, often necessitating the use of multiple cameras and projectors.

Though much is accomplished by the panoramagram, it still does not

---

[9] Exact information on the Ivanow system is very scanty. The rise and fall of this inventor seem to have been equally meteoric. Two months after he had been awarded a Stalin prize for his outstanding contribution to science, he was denounced by Bolshakov, the Minister of Film, as a "faker and publicity seeker" and "a worrisome inventor," and was dismissed as scientific head of the stereoscopic studios in Moscow (*Pravda,* April 28, 1947). He completed one feature film, the famous *Robinson Crusoe,* which opened in Moscow in 1946 and remains to this day the only full-length stereoscopic film ever made. S. P. Ivanow is not to be confused with his colleague, B. T. Ivanow, author of a work mentioned in the Booklist. Diligent search in Russian film periodicals has failed to reveal any mention of either Ivanow since their eclipse, but a modest program of stereoscopic film production was announced for 1950.

amount to an optical reconstruction of events. For one thing, it cannot be observed from all sides, like objects in the real world. Hence proposals have been put forward for throwing multiple images onto layers of fog, and for creating massless lenticular screens of substantial depth by passing ultrasonic pulsations through various media. But if success is finally achieved along these lines, it will be far in the future.

No more can be said here of the vexed and complicated technical problems of stereoscopic film.[10] We would, however, like to challenge the commonly held assumption that adding a third dimension necessarily draws films toward a closer imitation of life. As we have argued extensively elsewhere,[11] it is the differences between film and life which give the medium its value. It is therefore the differentiating factors, those independent powers of the film on which the creative film maker will concentrate. But is the third dimension a differentiating factor? Is it not rather yet another chain binding the film to the solid floor of life? Here, in an old-fashioned one-eyed movie, two characters are sitting across a table arguing with one another. The camera is beginning to play miraculous tricks with them. The dominant character looms large in the frame, looking down at the camera with which we in the audience identify ourselves. His face appears tyrannously big, monstrous in its foreshortening and distortion. The other fellow, awkward and ill at ease, seems to have shrunk below his natural size. The camera catches small, nervous movements of his hands as he speaks. As the argument mounts, the camera cuts back and forth with uncanny skill, heightening the tension of the dialogue.

In a three-dimensional movie, it seems at first sight as if little of this emphasis by camera and cutting would be possible. On the analogy of the old-fashioned stereo still picture, each shot would be created as an exact reproduction of real life, whereupon effects of distorted perspective would vanish, and everything would appear as it does to the eye. Cutting likewise would seem like physically lifting up the spectator and bodily placing him in another position—not at all like the transference of attention so simply achieved in ordinary "flat" movies.

Doubtless, if stereoscopic films were introduced commercially, these considerations would be given the greatest weight. The camera would be slowed to a standstill, and long uninterrupted stretches of action would go on in front of it. This happened with the coming of sound; and it happened in the 1895–1915 period when the powers of the camera had not been explored. Each new discovery imposes itself at first to the exclusion of others. First it was the camera itself, then sound, and next possibly the third dimension of solidity.

10 Sources giving fuller information on stereoscopic methods of filming and projection are to be found in the Booklist, pp. 497–498.
11 Raymond Spottiswoode, *A Grammar of the Film*, Berkeley: University of California Press, 1950.

However, this hypnosis of the new gradually passes. It is no longer wonderful merely to watch action reproduced, or to hear actual dialogue, and eventually even the miracle of solid-seeming space will pall. Then at length the variable powers of the stereoscopic camera will come to be explored: the ability to alter the sensation of depth, either exaggerating or diminishing it, and the ability to produce inverted and distorted space perceptions at will. However, all this must await a very improbable revolution, and meanwhile there is a rich field of experiment which even now can be tapped by those willing to seek small audiences outside the theaters. It is to the animated film —that graphic world of the imagination—that the artist will look to find the most interesting possibilities of three-dimensional expression.

STEREOGRAPHIC ART [12]

Four general classifications of stereographic art—or art forms designed in pairs for right- and left-eye viewing—may be distinguished.

1. Stereographic Drawings.—These are simple stereoscopic drawings, in which any exaggeration, diminution, or inversion of the depth sensation may be introduced at will. These drawings are in two space dimensions, and create a third space dimension by stereosynthesis. The time dimension may be introduced by any convenient animation technique, as described in chapter vi.

2. Stereographic Paintings.—These resemble the drawings, save that they add the use of tone value and color in ways which may be quite nonrepresentational, as will appear later. They too may be generated in time by any of the techniques of animation.

3. Stereomobiles.—These start with two space dimensions and one time dimension, and by stereosynthesis create a third space dimension. By this means the remarkable effect of objects moving through solid space from infinity to the observer's eye without changing their size can be produced, thus contradicting the laws of normal space. Since this device introduces the time dimension, it may be filmed directly, without recourse to animation.[13]

4. Stereosculptures.—Carrying the stereomobile a dimension further, stereosculptures start with three actual space dimensions and one time dimension, and by stereosynthesis create a fourth spatial dimension, which is of course not observable as such by human eyes. Instead, as preliminary experiments have shown, this stepping up of solid form by another dimension results in a modulation of that form—a kind of optical variability of a solid of fixed volume and shape. In this way sculpture can be made to breathe with the

[12] This section owes much to ideas contained in an unpublished paper, "Stereographic Art," by Norman McLaren, who has already executed many of the projects experimentally.

[13] The stereomobile is a device, invented by the author, for imparting variable parallactic movements to a set of superimposed cells which forms one half of a steroscopic pair.

palpitation of life itself, yet with a bending and undulating movement which no living thing could compass, and which would be hard indeed to achieve by any kind of physical animation. And all this can be accomplished by a mere rotation of the stereosculptures, which may be filmed directly.

We have already discussed at some length the types and degrees of freedom which can be achieved by animation. Animation is not animated painting; it confers freedoms which are unknown to the painter on canvas. Similarly, stereographic art in motion is not animated sculpture; it creates effects unknown to the artist working in three real dimensions.

For instance, it dispenses with the force of gravity. Heavy objects, in all their solidity, may be made to balance in impossible positions, or float away and hang in space. Objects may be made to attain a vastness beyond all human construction. A man's figure can stretch from here to the horizon, a building overtop the Empire State; and the spectator, once accustomed to the stereoscopic world, will accept these things as being as real as life, for all his space perceptions will be satisfied.

Equally remarkable effects may be achieved with tone value and color. The use of these by Renaissance painters to build up a world of plastic solidity was an enormous release of the powers of expression; so too was the freeing by the cubists and others in this century of tone value and color from their earlier associations, but this freedom was only gained at the expense of the depth and space sensations which had come to be thought inseparable from painting. Stereographics for the first time combines the Renaissance sense of space with the modern freedom of tone value and color; for it enables space to be constructed at will without resort to chiaroscuro, which may then be introduced for quite different and even conflicting purposes.

Again, there are various devices like linear perspective and inferred opacity (one object partially blocking the view of another, which is thus assumed to be further away), which are generally used to reinforce one another to produce an impression of depth. In fact if, as in some modern painting, these two factors are set against one another, or both are dropped, the depth sensation becomes ambiguous and confused. However, in stereographics, the structure of space can be built without regard to linear perspective or inferred opacity, so that an object may be made to seem near and far away at the same time. Thus, in the stereomobile, it is possible to have one object partially blocked out by another, and yet advancing toward the eye, while the "nearer" object retreats into the far distance. In the example quoted above in describing the stereomobile, the object can be seen advancing through space; and yet, since it remains the same size, it also appears to be standing still. Furthermore, linear perspective can be pitted against stereographic depth, setting up a counterpoint between different elements in the image.

Moreover, the depth sensation may itself be made to vary in the time dimension. Far more easily than in the stereoscopic shooting of real objects can a stereoscopic variation be imposed on the drawings which, let us say, gradually reduces the feeling of depth and then increases it in the opposite direction, i.e. pseudoscopically, so that the world of vision is turned inside out. It has been discovered by experiment that if color and tone values are applied with slight differences between the left- and right-hand images, strange luminous and iridescent effects may be obtained within the area of a painting.

Enough has perhaps been said to show that stereographics can create new fields of visual experience of extraordinary richness and variety. It can combine the discoveries of the Renaissance with the revolution of twentieth-century painting, by accepting that revolution and restoring what it has largely sacrificed—the feeling of depth and space which Michelangelo and Tiepolo created in their soaring angel forms, and which Spengler has shown to be the great gift to civilization of the Gothic mind.

These are far horizons indeed, but the film may help to bring them nearer. Not, indeed, the commercial film of the theaters, but the nontheatrical film in which the artist can choose his subject, his technique and his audience. None of the possibilities we have described is physically difficult of execution. A few pioneers of genius may well within the next few years hack out a path through this unknown territory, which will afterward be widened and made familiar until the early experiments seem as commonplace as those timid angels which rose a few inches from the canvas of some early Renaissance painter, to whom, however, they must have seemed miraculously alive!

THE LIBERATION OF SOUND

If the visual image on film may be unchained from an imitation of life by exploiting the powers of the camera, of cutting, and of animation, so the sound track may also win a greater freedom than it has enjoyed for a long time. At the very beginning of the sound era, when studio cameras were immobilized by their heavy blimps, and the sound track was a literal record of dialogue, certain pioneers were exploring free and interesting possibilities of sound. As time passed, the studios became less conventional, the experimenters more so; a middle ground was established on which the film rests today.

Film music, in particular, is basically little different from concert music, as witness that the "best" film scores are frequently performed on concert platforms as suites, and are recorded for playing in the home. True, the composer will often have ingeniously adapted his music to the film—physically, to the length of sequences and their subdivisions, emotionally, to the mood of the scene. Nor need this imply a literal parallelism between the two, a hackneyed "mood music." The score may introduce leitmotifs or repeated phrases like the *idée fixe* in Berlioz' *Symphonie Fantastique* (e.g., the use of the theremin in Miklos Rosza's score for *Spellbound,* Hitchcock, 1944); or it may establish a deliberate counterpoint or conflict with the film; or it may eschew emotional effect altogether, and provide an abstract pattern equivalent to the complex of camera movements and cutting rhythms of which the visual film consists.

Whatever the relation to the film, such a score is essentially a score for concert performance, in that it is played by musical instruments and recorded exactly as it is played, the microphone interfering no more than to balance the pickup from different sections of the orchestra. Composers for film have almost all ignored one vital fact—that their music exists not only in the time dimension of performance, but in the space dimension of the sound track. A sound track, as we have seen in chapter xi, may be slowed down, speeded up, or reversed in direction; it may be cut and recombined in a different order; and it may be passed through filters and echo chambers which modify its quality.

It is possible to regard the musical score not as what goes into this process, but as what comes out of it; and this suggests that the composer should take account of all these potentialities from the very beginning, so as to incorporate them into his score. In this way the score would be less a conventional musical notation designed for performance by regular instruments, than an indication of how sounds were to be modeled, displaced, and altered by the many creative tools which the film maker, and therefore the film composer, have at their disposal. Pursuing this line of thought, we find that music, natural sound, and even voice lose their separate existences. The manipulative powers of film blur the dividing lines and blend one into another.

If, for simplicity of statement, we start with concert music, we arrive through the sound track at various interesting possibilities, which have long been known but are still surprisingly neglected.

Reversal of motion.—Many musical instruments produce sounds which start loudly, and then die away more or less quickly with more or less reverberation. This results from some kind of impact—a bow against a violin string, the hammer of a piano on a string, or a drumstick on a stretched membrane. When music or sound track is played backward, a totally different sound results. The crescendo is very gradual, but after the climax the sound dies away instantly. The reverberation seems inexplicable. It is at its loudest when the note is least audible, and after the crash which climaxes the note, when it should be most noticeable, it is nonexistent. If the note formerly rose in pitch, it now falls, and if it fell, it now rises. In this way a completely new musical sound is created, which composers for film have almost entirely ignored.[14]

Speeding up and slowing down.—If music tracks are accelerated, they alter in pitch as well as in tempo, and take on an excitable and nervous quality. If they are slowed down, the opposite effects occur. This has been used commercially in a recording of the guitar, in which four playings at different speeds are combined in synchronism to produce an effect not otherwise achievable.[15] Modern magnetic-tape recorders are easily fitted with drive capstans of different diameters, so that by an intermediate tape recording, any desired change of speed can be effected. Other interesting modifications can be achieved by gradually accelerating or slowing down the track. This has been used in an animation film to satirize the speech of a fast-talking salesman, who started off intelligibly at normal speed and was gradually accelerated into a nonsensical gabble which the poor veteran (who was being talked into buying a broken-down car) listened to with rapt attention.

Cutting.—On the cutting table the intractable time dimension is exchanged for the more manageable dimensions of space. It is thus possible to combine sound tracks which were recorded years or thousands of miles apart. The emphasis of passages can be altered by eliminating or inserting small pieces of silence in the form of unmodulated track. Duplicate tracks may be staggered by two or three perforations and re-recorded to give interesting effects of reverberation. Music may, in fact, be chopped up and recombined in as many ways as the ingenuity of the composer suggests, for it is the composer who should be the first to grasp these opportunities, since he has the technical skill to exploit them. Beethoven did not scorn to write a composition for Maelzel's panharmonicon, or mechanical orchestra, Haydn, Mozart, and Handel composed for several clockwork devices of their day, and in our own time Stravinsky, Malipiero, and others have written music for the player piano which was beyond the range of five-fingered human hands. Whether the composers of former times would have been as disdainful of film and its resources as the moderns we cannot know. But the almost total neglect of the sound track as a creative device in the writing of music will surely amaze the future historian.

Synthetic sound.—The last and most significant use of the sound track is as a tablet for writing or photographing trains of waves upon the film itself. Because the resulting sound never originated in any musical instrument or other source of sound, it is often called synthetic. Since it offers boundless opportunities to the musical-film maker, it deserves a section of its own.

---

14 One of the finest creative examples of this technique is in the climactic sequence of Basil Wright's *Song of Ceylon* (composer: Walter Leigh), where great Singalese gongs, with echo periods of 20 to 30 seconds, were made to sound and reverberate backward by reversing the sound track. See also *Challenge: Science Against Cancer* (music by Louis Applebaum).

15 *Brazil,* by Les Paul (Capitol 32082).

MUSIC WITHOUT INSTRUMENTS

Ever since sound waves began to be recorded on film, ingenious minds have realized that here for the first time the whole world of living music was presented in graphic and easily read form. The curve we have previously spoken of, into which is compressed all the resonant splendors of a symphony orchestra, all the most delicate nuances expressible on the violin, is indeed the profile of a variable-area sound track. Anyone who has examined a sound track closely will know that, though it is clear and legible, it is of surpassing complexity. In each inch of film there may be as many as five hundred changes of wave form. Their profile may be as jagged as that of a mountain range, or gentle and undulating, broken up into short staccato bursts, or continued in long and seemingly featureless passages.

It is to Hans Pfenninger that we owe the first close musical analysis of the sound track. This Austrian film maker, after several years of study of wave forms, was able to construct a sort of alphabet of large stencils which he photographed frame by frame to build up musical compositions. However, his ambition seems not to have outrun the imitation of existing music, and in 1932 he produced a synthesized version of Handel's "Largo" from *Xerxes*. This strange music, with an organlike timbre, which had never been played by musical instruments, produced a profound effect on the audiences which heard it.

Russian animators were pursuing similar experiments during the years 1931 to 1935. They laid down almost all the principles and techniques for producing synthetic sound tracks. Their films and tracks have apparently never been heard in the West, and the purge of formalistic art in 1936 seems to have put an end to their explorations.

Other experimenters, hampered only by lack of funds, have been urging forward the development of synthetic sound. Most important of these is Norman McLaren, whose first experiments in 1939 grew out of his discovery of the hand-animated film (chapter vi). It occurred to McLaren that, since any painted marks on a blank sound track would produce a noise, controlled marks could be made to produce music. In two early films, *Dots* and *Loops,* he built up ingenious and intricate rhythms of sound with no more elaborate equipment than pen and ink, and a length of blank film. Since the ink was applied directly to this 35 mm. film, the perforations (96 to the second) served as convenient time markers for his musical rhythms. The even spacing of the higher frequencies (i.e. fine lines painted close together) presented problems which would have baffled a less persistent person. McLaren developed a kind of "muscular memory" which enabled him to repeat wave shapes at very close intervals. Later, McLaren devised fan diagrams for the diatonic and equally tempered scales, which could be placed under the transparent film to help in spacing the modulations.[16]

In these simple experiments, volume was controlled by a combination of variable area (larger and smaller pen marks), and variable density (more and less opaque paints). Since wave shape controls timbre, different musical qualities could be produced by altering the shape of the stroke or blob, though not with any great refinement. In the films referred to, the sound is percussive, but with a peculiar squashy quality which does not correspond to that of any musical instrument.

In recent years, McLaren has developed methods of photographing under the animation camera, using cards similar in principle to Pfenninger's, but much refined in detail. The basic wave form is a variable-density sine wave which is repeated photographically on different scales to form a series of pitches corresponding to a musical scale. These are then cut into cards of convenient size, which are placed in registration under the animation camera so that they expose accurately on the sound-track area of the film. The timbre is controlled by black modulating masks placed over the cards; by moving these masks in and out across the track, volume can be raised or lowered. (This would of course be impossible if the wave forms were variable area.) If the music to be constructed consists of several parts or "voices," two methods present themselves; the parts may be physically intermixed frame by frame (an interval of only one twenty-fourth of a second), or they may be superimposed by multiple exposure in the camera, exactly as in animation.

The advantage of the animation camera lies in its being readily available to film makers. Its disadvantage is the repetition of the frame line twenty-four times in every second of film recorded. This produces a square wave, which contains an infinite number of harmonics and is heard as an unpleasant click. There are many ingenious ways of getting around this obstacle, or of absorbing it into the rhythmical structure of the synthetic music; but the most satisfactory solution is the development of a continuous-motion camera.

The composer needs to work slowly in order to build up his score note by note, and therefore the camera must be slowed down to a speed of not more than one frame every three or four seconds. Both glissandi and held notes of any of a very wide range of frequencies (seven or eight octaves) can be achieved with a well designed instrument, and there is a perfect control over volume and fairly good control of timbre by masking and other means. This machine lends itself particularly well to the construction of peculiar curves of attack and decay, which cannot be achieved on orthodox musical instruments.

It is not difficult to design such a camera from easily available elements.

16 These are reproduced in Robert E. Lewis and Norman McLaren, "Synthetic Sound on Film," *JSMPE*, March, 1948, pp. 233–47, figs. 2–7.

Very early intermittent-motion cameras of the 1905 to 1910 period may be picked up at junk stores and adapted to continuous drive. A governor-controlled phonograph motor provides a cheap variable-speed drive for the tone wheel, with a range of about one and one-half octaves. The tone wheel or cylinder which forms the actual frequency generator may conveniently be the variable-density card already referred to, bent into cylindrical form. Gearboxes and synchronous and selsyn motors which the designer will also need may be secured from army surplus. A useful and inexpensive source of standard frequencies is the Strobotac lamp (accuracy, ± 1 per cent), which will serve to set the pitch of the tone wheel stroboscopically.

Many more complicated synthetic-music machines have been projected. Carlos Chavez, Mexican composer and conductor, in his book *Toward A New Music*, has suggested an instrument not unlike an immensely diversified player piano, which would give the composer complete freedom to construct his score, and have it performed, outside the limitations of human executants. A Canadian physicist, O. K. Kendall, has devised an instrument which he calls a "Composertron" to take full advantage of the possibilities of magnetic recording. This enables the composer to check over his composition immediately, exactly as if he were playing it on a piano. A "magnetic eraser" is used to erase modulations from the track along the profile of a mask which determines the shape and time of a note's attack and decay. Tones are produced in this instrument by electronic oscillators, and ample provision is made for building up tracks by successive re-recordings on the instrument itself. With this composing machine, as with the others, the composer for film can make full use of speeding up the tracks, slowing them down, adding reverberation, reversing and cutting them, as well as adding to them by further re-recordings.

What, then, emerges from all this welter of machinery? Certainly, it will not supplant or even diminish composition by ordinary means. Certainly, it will not render orchestras obsolete. Composers may often have raged at the mutilation of their works by indifferent conductors and performers, but they have gained immeasurably by good execution over what they could have accomplished if every single detail of their scores could have been made scientifically precise. Interpretation can add to the composer's stature; it need not be a screen through which he hears a muffled and distorted rendering of his work.

The future of synthetic sound lies elsewhere. It does not invite separate performance, but is rather an integral part of a film. Film is a tangible substance, which in shooting and cutting compels very accurate control. Synthetic music likewise enables an exactitude of rhythm which would be impossible to the human performer. Furthermore, the manipulative elements we have discussed (cutting, reversal, change of tone quality, etc.) belong to the medium itself, like the script, the camera, the re-recording process, and all the other part-mechanical, part-creative processes of film. It is therefore reasonable to suppose that these new possibilities of sound should be explored, just as were those of the camera and the cutting bench thirty years ago.

What kind of music will emerge, we do not know. Whether its uses will be wide or limited is difficult to foretell. Yet assuredly this is another great area of the cinema's domain in which the scenery is rich and varied, the explorers brilliant but few.

Epilogue

W<small>E HAVE NOW</small> followed the film through some of its many successive transformations and alterations. We have seen how the first germ of the film idea comes to be worked out in ever greater and more concrete detail until the final shooting script gives instructions as to what is to take place before the camera. Next we have seen the photographic image emerge out of invisibility under the play of complex chemical reactions. We have examined the mechanisms which shaped this image until it conformed with the play of light and shade in which it was first brought into being. We have seen how film has the peculiar power of creating a new time and space, locked together out of pieces of celluloid which may have had their origins a world apart, and are now combined only by the scope of the cutter's imagination. In the cutting room, time becomes space, and space is fitted into a purposeful pattern which on the movie screen is converted back into time. We have seen how, in the same way, the world of natural sound is dismantled into its elements, to be recreated by a new and selective synthesis into a fresh kind of sound built with tools never before at the artist's disposal. And in the same way also, we saw that the physical air movements of sound waves were transformed again and again, first into electrical impulses, then into modulations of a beam of light, then into molecules forming a silver image less than a thousandth of an inch in thickness; and finally, after many more changes, back into electrical impulses and then into those movements of air molecules which finally strike the listener's ear. In the strokes of the artist's pencil, and under the time-analyzing eye of the animation camera, we saw a new world of action taking shape, in which dead lines and pictures, formless masses of pins, and static models were given a life of their own more vivid and varied than the old shadow shows and marionettes. Lastly, we have tried to peer into the future and discover some of the unmined riches of film which will give the artist more flexible control over his medium, and the audience a deeper response to the world beyond the screen.

In all this we have discovered that the technical processes of film making are not dull tools to be put in the hands of hacks and drudges, but are keen instruments for the minds of intelligent and creative film makers. They, just as much as the display of talent on the studio floor, help to mold the film into final shape.

Long as our survey has been, it has scarcely scratched the surface of the processes encountered in film making. But perhaps some of the technical and some of the human characteristics are now clearer to the reader.

Technically, film making is immensely complicated, by far exceeding any of the other arts in range of scientific processes and multiplication of mechanical skills. It therefore calls for very exacting standards. Physically, everything connected with it—sizes, speeds, properties—must be standardized to the closest limits. As a craft, there must be the most scrupulous attention to correct technique if flaws and faults are not to be magnified to unacceptable size, the multitude of processes accumulating small errors into large ones.

When the technical aspect of an art is predominant, there is a tendency to look on it as an end in itself. If a new color process is invented, or if sound is greatly improved, the movie industry hails these advances with rapture as marks of indisputable progress. But if an iron choice were to be set between freezing films at their present technical level and freezing them at their present mental level, not even the most ardent technician should hesitate a moment before making up his mind. The physical resources of music have advanced little in the last hundred years, of writing little in the last five hundred, of sculpture little in the last two thousand. Even such advances as have been made have not diminished the stature of what was done before. No one pities Scarlatti because he was born before the invention of the modern piano, or Sophocles because he never saw a revolving stage. Yet much film discussion seems to imply that film making is just a triumphal procession from one staggering technical improvement to the next, and that the quality of the ideas conveyed by film is immaterial.

We have seen that, on the plane of human endeavor, the film maker draws upon most of the sciences, many of the other arts. The actor, the architect, the composer, the scene designer, the writer, the painter, the mathematician, the chemist, the electrical engineer—these are just a few of the contributors to almost every movie shown on every screen.

Film making, in short, is a huge coöperative undertaking, requiring the dovetailing of innumerable skills. Never before has the task of artistic creation, so long considered the province of the individual, been parceled out among such a multitude of craftsmen, each with the power of making or marring the finished work. These bodies of skilled workers are concentrated into a comparatively few centers, perhaps no more than fifty in the whole world, yet dispersed as far as from Washington to Shanghai, Moscow to

Montreal, Sydney to Buenos Aires. There is every outward reason why the strong bands of common interest should unite all these film makers into a single close fraternity, much like the guilds of the Middle Ages with their apprentices, journeymen, and master craftsmen. And indeed in the documentary-film movement, this collective spirit is living and vigorous. Between documentary-film workers there is a bond of social purpose, a community of aim and idea. That is their strength.

Commercial production has developed quite differently. It has fed and fattened on bitter competition. Each national center, each company, each group, each individual has had to beat a way to the front, thrusting competitors aside, scrupling nothing to achieve supremacy. The result has been a sensational rapidity of growth.

To the sober investigator the limitations may appear equally sensational. True, Hollywood produces two or three good pictures every year. A few directors are big enough to impose themselves on the system. But under that system there can in general be no respite for reflection, since the unrelenting pace of production must be kept up; little experiment, since an experiment not immediately justified by the box office will be abandoned. The individual can survive only by pushing others out of his way, only by conforming to the popular stereotypes of thought, many of them minted by the film itself and stamped, to its loss and theirs, upon a whole generation. Hollywood may now and then believe privately in a cause, but can never afford to appear publicly as its champion, if that cause is unpopular. Organized as it is, Hollywood must be content to have the courage of its conventions.

The very year that World War II was declared, film producers could not portray on the theater screen the evils of Nazi dictatorship, for fear of giving offence to the dictators or of being dubbed "premature anti-Fascists." (No doubt the twelve disciples and their Master would have been condemned by Hollywood as "prematurely anti-pagan.") Finally, when everyone else had been long persuaded, Hollywood was persuaded too. Film had been far outrun by reality.

Ten years later, the position is outwardly different. Everyone recognizes the necessity of fighting political dictatorship. But there will be other unpopular causes to fight for. Can the commercial film prove that it has both convictions and courage? Or will it be left to that small but growing army of film makers outside the studios, who are not chained to the support of the status quo, to make film an instrument of honest social purpose? In the development of film as an art, they have the advantage of closeness to the medium, and unlimited chance to experiment. As yet, they do not reach audiences a hundredth as large as those which cluster nightly in the dark theaters to see their private fantasies projected on twenty thousand screens. Film is today predominantly an imitation of life, an instrument of illusion.

It could be, as the other arts have been in their eras of influence, a means of awakening people to life itself, of piercing through illusions. The great names of the cinema—Chaplin, Clair, Pudovkin, Griffith, Vigo, Grierson—are those of men who in comedy, in satire, and in social document have struck the springs of truth. Film has often been called the art of the future. And in fact the rare truths, the many falsehoods, which films purvey, reach and influence a greater number of people than any art form which man has created, for radio and television are little more than means of sending information to a distance.

It is within living memory that Louis Lumière gave the first public screening of films at the Grand Café in Paris. To us he is a pioneer, and we are moderns. A century hence, these last fifty years will be foreshortened into the flat perspective of history. We too will have become pioneers. And on our shoulders will be squarely placed the responsibility for the film of tomorrow. Will it still be today's great sprawling infant, a century older but not a year wiser? Or will it have grown to take its real place in the world?

Glossary

THERE ARE many glossaries of film; rare indeed is the film book which does not contain one. Very often they are confined to terms like "cut," "lap-dissolve," and "dolly" which are the peculiar province of film; and this lends them a rather threadbare look, for the medium is a great borrower, and much of its language is not original but is derived from established arts and sciences. Longer glossaries, on the other hand, run the risk of losing the reader in a forest of technicalities remote from his own field of interest. Among these the present glossary cannot claim immunity on the basis of any profound principle of selection. Here are gathered up merely the terms used in the body of the book, cross-referenced by the use of italics and augmented by a few important words which escaped inclusion in the text.

No claim can be made to completeness. The thousand words defined represent only a small part of the vocabulary of film, when account is taken of the many branches of film technology, like make-up and set designing, which are not represented here at all, and of the differences of terminology between production centers and between one English-speaking country and another. Nor are the definitions as rigorous as the scientist might wish. Some current technical glossaries give definitions almost as incomprehensible to the layman as the terms themselves, for they are addressed to specialists whose language must be mathematically exact. Here the aim has been descriptive as much as definitive, and the needs of the newcomer to film have often guided the choice of phrase.

The most that can be hoped for is that the reader, not seeking illumination on his own topic, will find that a little light has been shed on neighboring parts of the subject and on some of the more distant reaches of film technique —that seemingly limitless expanse of scientific endeavor.

A relatively small number of terms, for the most part not concerned with film but with allied branches of science, has been drawn from the following sources, all of them publications of the American Standards Association.

American Standard Definitions of Electrical Terms, C42–1941

American Standard Acoustical Terminology, Z24.1–1942
Illuminating Engineering Nomenclature and Photometric Standards, Z7.1–1942
Nomenclature for Motion Picture Film Used in Studios and Processing Laboratories, Z22.56–1947

Definitions from these sources are quoted in the standard form; e.g. ASA C42–1941:05.45.155.

The new proposed American Standard, *Acoustical Terminology,* published early in 1949 for trial and study, has also proved useful. The few definitions drawn from this source are marked ASA Z24.1–1949. The many electroacoustic definitions to be found in this glossary owe much to the work of the Electro-acoustics Committee of the Institute of Radio Engineers, on which the proposed standard is based. Early drafts of the committee's glossary, made available through the courtesy of Mr. E. Dietze, its co-chairman, have supplied a number of definitions which are more descriptive than those embodied in the published text, though doubtless less rigorously accurate.

When italicized words appear in the ASA definitions printed here they have been italicized by the author to indicate a cross-reference; they are not italicized in the original definition. Alternative designations and explanatory details added by the author have been enclosed in brackets.

Readers concerned with the translation of film textbooks and technical papers may find it helpful to consult Van Santen, *Amalux Fototolk* (Bloemendaal, Holland, Focus N. V.), an excellent glossary in four languages, English, French, German, and Dutch.

A

AGN
Anti-ground-noise. A term sometimes used to describe the *noise reduction* unit in an *optical sound recorder.*

Aberration
A deviation from the ideal in the performance of *lenses* which impairs the quality of the images they form. (For discussion of specific kinds of aberrations see p. 55 of text.)

Abrasions
Unwanted marks and slight *scratches* on the surface of film caused by the rubbing action of film on film, or of film on metal, hardened emulsion, or some other substance.

Academy aperture
See *Academy mask.*

Academy leader
A type of *leader,* standardized throughout the industry, which is placed on the beginning and end of all reels of *release prints,* and contains *threading* and other information useful to the projectionist. Named after the Academy of Motion Picture Arts and Sciences.

GLOSSARY

Academy mask

The introduction of sound altered the shape of the 35 *mm. frame* by cutting off a strip at the side where the *sound track* runs. To restore the rectangularity of the screen proportions, it was agreed to adopt a camera *mask* which would reduce the height of the camera image, as well as cutting off the sound track area. This mask, named after the Academy of Motion Picture Arts and Sciences, which secured its standardization, frames an image 0.631 inches high by 0.868 inches wide, giving a screen proportion of approximately 3:4. The area enclosed by an Academy mask is known as an Academy aperture.

Acceptance angle

Applied to an *exposure meter*. The angle of the cone of rays which the optical design allows to strike the *cathode* of the *photocell*.

Acetate base

A *base* or support for motion picture film composed principally of cellulose acetate. Synonymous with *safety base*.

Acetic acid: CH_3COOH

The acid in vinegar which gives it its characteristic odor. Manufactured from the pyroligneous acid obtained in the destructive distillation of wood. A clear, colorless liquid with a pungent odor. Often called "glacial" because in one process for its manufacture the material is frozen to crystallize out the acid. Acetic acid is often added to a *fixing* bath to neutralize the *alkaline developer* carried over.

Properties:
Specific gravity: 1.049
Melting point: 16.7° C
Boiling point: 118.1° C
Soluble in alcohol, water, and ether

Achromatic lens

A lens corrected for *chromatic aberration* by bringing light of two wavelengths to a common *focus*. All high-quality camera lenses are achromatic.

Action

A term sometimes used to designate *picture* in contrast to sound in a *reel* of film.

"Action!"

The order given by the director of a film when the sound and/or picture cameras are running to *speed*, indicating that the action within the shot is to begin.

Additive method

Applied to color reproduction, a method of recombining the *separation* images into which a colored scene has been analyzed by employing the same *primary* colors used in the analysis.

Aeolight

A glow lamp employing a hot cathode and a mixture of permanent gases, the intensity of illumination varying with the applied signal voltage. See also *variable-intensity recording*.

Alkalies

Salts of certain alkaline earth metals such as sodium and potassium. The word is now used to embrace the hydroxides and carbonates of sodium, potassium, and calcium, and the bicarbonate and hydroxide of ammonia.

Properties:
Neutralize acids and form salts
Change colors of certain organic indicators: red litmus to blue, methyl orange to yellow, etc.
Impart soapy feeling to their aqueous solutions
Yield negatively charged hydroxyl ions in solution

Alternating current (AC)

An alternating current is a periodic current the average value of which over a period is zero. A periodic current is an oscillating current the values of which recur at equal intervals of time. An oscillating current is a current which alternately increases and decreases in magnitude with respect to time according to a definite law.

American standard exposure index

Defined as 1/4E or Speed/4, where "speed" is the *American standard speed,* and E is the minimum satisfactory exposure on which it is based. See also *exposure index.*

American standard speed

This method of measuring emulsion *speed,* now universally accepted in America, is based on a minimum useful exposure at the toe of the *D log E curve* of the emulsion under given conditions of *development.* More precisely, the American standard speed number is inversely proportional to the minimum exposure which must be incident upon the negative material, from the scene element of minimum brightness in which detail is visible, in order that a print of excellent quality can be made from the resultant negative. The rating of quality is based on statistical evaluation by expert observers. If E is the minimum satisfactory exposure under these conditions (more precisely defined in ASA Z38.2.1–1947), the American standard speed is given by 1/E. It is applicable only to daylight illumination.

Ampere

The unit of electrical current flow, equivalent to one coulomb per second. Usually abbreviated "I" for intensity. Related to voltage and resistance in the manner described by *Ohm's Law.* The ampere is one-tenth of the absolute ampere, or abampere.

Amplifier ASA C42–1941:05.45.155

An amplifier is a device for increasing the power associated with a phenomenon without appreciably altering its quality, through control by the amplifier input of a larger amount of power supplied by a local source to the amplifier output.

Amplitude of a simple sinusoidal quantity ASA C42–1941:05.05.275

The amplitude of a *simple sinusoidal quantity* is the largest value that the quantity attains. [Mathematical section of the definition omitted.]

Animation

The bringing to apparent life and movement of inanimate objects set before the camera by employing the joint capacity of film and eye to fuse disparate images into an apparently continuous flow. Among the objects set before the *animation camera* are *cells, cutouts* and *puppets.*

ABC ANIMATION: A method of shooting in which each phase of an object in front of the *animation camera (cell, puppet, cutout,* etc.) is recorded on three successive frames of film (A, B and C), each through one of the three primary color filters, which are usually mounted on a rotating device in front of the lens. Thus when frames A, D, G . . . , B, E, H . . . , C, F, I . . . have been sorted out by *optical printing,* they form the three *separation negatives* required for color printing onto a single strip of film. It is because the different color images can be shot successively that color shooting is so much easier in animation than in actuality. This of course is due to the essentially static character of animation techniques. Also called 1-2-3 animation.

CAMERALESS ANIMATION: A group of animation techniques in which the animator uses the film itself as a tablet on which to paint or draw. Some techniques call for repeated drawing of similar images on successive *frames,* i.e. frame = cell (see figure 6-3); others use the strip of film itself for the drawing of extended designs, which the *intermittent movement* of the projector then breaks up into sections (see figure 6-4).

Both methods, as well as eliminating the cost of the camera, make color animation very simple: it is only necessary to construct three parallel animation tracks to the required designs and densities, which then become the *separation negatives* for color printing.

CELL ANIMATION: A type of animation in which apparent movements are produced under the camera by drawing or painting objects in successively displaced positions on transparent *cells.* One *frame* of film is then as a rule exposed for each cell, causing an appearance of movement in the final film due to *persistence of vision.*

DOUBLE-FRAME ANIMATION: A type of animation in which two frames of film are exposed to each object or phase of an object before the camera, thus reducing the labor of animation but increasing the risk of jerkiness on the screen.

PUPPET ANIMATION: A group of animation techniques in which the objects before the camera are three-dimensional, though the reproduction is normally *planoscopic.* For this reason, the illusion of reality is seldom superior to that achieved by the best cell animation, for the same *pseudostereoscopic* devices are available to both. In the rendering of movement puppets are usually much inferior to cells, and this contributes to the jerkiness which is characteristic of puppet animation.

SCRATCH-OFF ANIMATION: A type of animation technique in which lines or areas which are to appear to extend themselves on the screen are drawn in their entirety, and then progressively scratched off, while the camera operates a frame at a time, running backwards.

SINGLE-FRAME ANIMATION: The usual type of animation, in which only a single frame of film is exposed to each object or phase of an object before the camera.

TABLE-TOP ANIMATION: A type of animation in which small objects are photographed in close-up and moved along a frame at a time to produce magical effects.

TRIPLE-FRAME ANIMATION: As compared with double-frame animation, the exposure of three frames at a time (not to be confused with ABC animation) still further reduces the labor and increases the risk of jerkiness.

Animation camera

The camera used for filming *animation.* It is usually mounted on an *animation stand* with its optical axis vertical, so that it looks down on the objects being photographed. The *drive* is so constructed that the film can be moved forward one frame at a time.

Animation photography

The photographic aspects of *animation.*

Animation stand

A mount for an *animation camera,* built with great rigidity and usually designed for *zooming* the camera and for traversing and rotating the material to be filmed by determinate small amounts which can be accurately set with the aid of calibrations.

Animators

Those who lay out the sequence of action and draw the key movements in an animated film are called animators.

Anode (of a vacuum tube)   ASA C42–1941:70.15.005

An anode of a vacuum tube is an electrode to which a principal electron stream flows.

Antinode   ASA C42–1941:05.05.422

An antinode of a *stationary* wave is a point in a line of propagation at which the *amplitude* is a maximum.

Antireflective coating

A transparent coating applied to the surfaces of *lens elements,* which is ideally one-quarter of the *wavelength* of the incident light in thickness, and of such a refractive index that unwanted reflection from the surface is cancelled out.

Aperiodic quantity

An *oscillating quantity* which is not a *periodic quantity.*

Aperture, Lens

The orifice through which light is admitted to a *lens.* The diameter of the aperture in relation to the *focal length* and *transmission* of the lens determines its effective *speed.*

Aperture plate

The plate in a camera or projector in close proximity to which the photographic image is exposed or projected. For each gauge of film, the projector aperture is slightly smaller than the camera aperture in order to mask imperfections at the edges of the image and simplify the task of *framing* it correctly.

Apochromatic lens

A *lens* corrected for *chromatic aberration* by bringing light of three wavelengths to a common *focus.* Lenses designed for accurate copy work are often apochromatic.

Arc light

Light produced by a bridge of incandescent vapor which carries an electric current from one electrode to another. In the carbon arc, the electrodes are made principally of carbon, and the arc is unenclosed and therefore at atmospheric pressure. In the mercury arc, the electrodes are mounted in a space which contains mercury vapor, sometimes at a pressure as high as one hundred atmospheres. Arcs are normally supplied with *direct current.* The following terms apply to carbon arcs:

FLAME ARC: The light source is the entire arc stream made luminescent by the addition of flame materials consisting of rare earths such as thorium.

HIGH-INTENSITY ARC (H.I.): In addition to the light from the incandescent crater, light originates in the gaseous region in front of the carbons, where it is intensified by high current density and an atmosphere rich in flame materials.

LOW-INTENSITY ARC: The principal light source is incandescent solid carbon at or near its sublimation temperature, i.e. the temperature at which solid particles pass directly into the gaseous state.

Artificial head

A sphere or other shape approximating to the size and configuration of the human head, with small microphones mounted at either extremity of a horizontal diameter, may be set up to form a receiver for *stereophonic recording* which simulates the human method of laterally localizing sounds. See *binaural hearing*.

Assembly
The putting together of the shots of a film into approximately the right order. See also *rough cut* and *fine cut*.

Assistant director
An assistant to the *director* of a picture. In a small *unit,* his chief function is to act as liaison with authorities and with suppliers of services. In a large unit, he is responsible for the presence of actors at the right time and place, and for carrying out the director's instructions.

Attack time
In a *noise reduction* circuit, the time taken by the noise-reduction elements to move away from their normal position of rest by a predetermined amount. See also *release time*.

Attenuator   ASA C42–1941:65.20.690
An attenuator is an adjustable *transducer* for reducing the *amplitude* of a wave without introducing appreciable *distortion*.

Audio amplifier
An amplifier characterized by having a *pass band* which comprises the *audio frequencies*.

Audio frequencies
The *frequencies* embraced within the audible *spectrum* are called audio frequencies.

Azimuth error
As applied to *scanning slits,* azimuth error is an angular deviation between the axis of the slit and a line at right angles with the direction of travel of the film. Azimuth error causes waveform *distortion* in film recorders and reproducers.

B

Background projection
See *process projection*.

Barn doors
Hinged doors mounted on a studio lamp, which may be swung to block off light from an area where it is not wanted.

Barrel distortion
Distortion in a lens characterized by convex curvature of the lines of a rectangular grid image; it is caused by magnification which is greater at the center than at the edges of the field. See also *pincushion distortion*.

Base, Film
The transparent material on which a photographic *emulsion* is coated is called film base; it serves no photographic purpose, but merely acts as a support for the very thin emulsion layer. For this reason it is sometimes called the support. *Safety base* will soon be in universal use; hitherto, *nitrate base* has been standard for 35 mm. film.

Batch

The quantity of *emulsion* which is manufactured at any one time for the production of *raw stock* is substantially homogeneous, and the stock on which it is coated is called a batch. Different batches of film, however, may differ appreciably in their characteristics. *Sensitometric* tests are therefore always made on a piece of film (a *gamma strip*) from the same batch as the film to be processed, and preferably from the same roll. Batch variations in color film often necessitate the use of correction filters to standardize the color response.

Beaded screen

A *directional* projection screen surfaced with small glass beads. These beads reflect the incident light internally, finally refracting much of it back toward the light source, even when the rays of light have struck the screen at an angle. See also *matte screen* and *metallic screen*.

Beam splitter

A device for splitting a light beam to form two or more separate lens images. Used in certain types of color camera and in *push-pull* recording and projecting systems. Beam splitting can be accomplished by prisms, rotating mirrors, *semireflecting* surfaces, and other devices.

Bell and Howell perforations

See *negative perforations*.

Bias

A steady voltage applied to an element in an electrical circuit, causing it to take on a different from normal potential.

Bias recording

A recording producing a type of variable-area track in which the noise reduction is effected by *biasing* the *galvanometer*. A bias track is illustrated in figure 10-5, where it is contrasted with a *shutter track*.

Bilateral sound track

A type of symmetrical variable-area sound track recognizable by the fact that, in the print, the central axis and surrounding modulated area are transparent, whereas in the equally common duplex type of track they are opaque.

Bin

A container for film, usually made of fire-resisting material, which is placed in cutting rooms and other rooms where film is handled. Scrap film is dumped in a waste bin.

Binaural hearing

The possession by human beings of two ears separated by a distance of about eight inches and by a fairly solid and more or less spherical head is of great assistance in localizing the source of a sound. Though it contributes little to the estimation of distance (derived principally from an estimate of the ratio of direct to reverberant sound), binaural hearing is remarkably effective in fixing the direction from which a sound comes. The two ears provide separate information about the *frequency*, intensity, and *phase* of incoming trains of *waves*, which the brain synthesizes into a "fix" of the source. The brain is even able to give accurate answers from data far outside its normal range of experience, as when listening to *stereophonic reproduction* from loudspeakers. See also *artificial head*.

Binaural reproduction

A transmission and reproduction system in which the conditions of *binaural hearing* are reproduced as closely as possible. Sometimes this term is applied to a two-channel system, the term *stereophonic reproduction* being reserved for systems employing three or more channels.

Binocular vision

The possession by human beings of two eyes separated by a distance of about two and a half inches (known as the *interocular distance*) and having overlapping fields, is of great assistance in fixing the distance of objects as near or far from the observer. While there are many *pseudostereoscopic* means of accomplishing this, the ability to "see round" an object by reason of the *parallax* between the eyes is of primary importance. A transmission system based on binocular vision is called *stereoscopic;* one not so based, *planoscopic.*

Bipack

Usually refers to the running of two films simultaneously through a camera or printer *aperture,* either to expose both, or to expose one through the other, using the latter as a mask. In a color process, bipack denotes the location of two color-sensitive *emulsions* on separate films which are exposed simultaneously.

Bipack printing

A method of printing in an *optical printer* in which the printing and printed films are in contact with one another and are therefore not optically printed. Essentially the same as *contact printing.*

Biplanar valve

A type of *light valve* construction in which the ribbons move in separate planes.

Black-and-white print

See *print.*

Black-and-white reproduction

A form of photographic reproduction in which color is translated into a scale of monochromatic *densities* ranging from near-opacity to near-transparency. When the photographic image is viewed on a white screen, it appears in the scale of near-black to near-white, the range of tonalities determining the *contrast* of the image.

Blackbody   ASA Z7.1–1942:10.055

A blackbody is a temperature radiator of uniform temperature whose radiant flux in all parts of the spectrum is the maximum obtainable from any temperature radiator at the same temperature.

Such a radiator is called a blackbody because it will absorb all the radiant energy that falls upon it. All other temperature radiators may be classed as nonblackbodies. They radiate less in some or all wavelength intervals than a blackbody of the same size and the same temperature. [Note omitted.]

Blank

The blank or imageless piece of film which receives successive color imprints by *dye transfer* in the *imbibition printing* process. Sometimes, however, the blank carries a sound image prior to picture printing.

Bleaching

The process of converting the metallic-silver photographic image into a transparent compound of silver which is not sensitive to light.

Blending valve
A device for combining two streams of fluid (usually at different temperatures) in predetermined proportions.

Blimp
The soundproof housing which surrounds a camera used to record dialogue, and which prevents the noise of the camera from being superimposed on the recorded dialogue.
SELF BLIMPED: A term sometimes applied to cameras in which the normal housing silences the noise of the mechanism without the addition of an external blimp.

Bloom
A term used in England to denote *antireflective coating.*

Bloop
Originally, the noise generated in a *film reproducer* by the passage of a *splice* (or occasionally some other interruption) in a piece of *sound track,* the noise being due to a sudden and unwanted *modulation* of the light beam caused either by the greater opacity of the splice or by a transparent line resulting from scraping the emulsion at the splice over too wide an area.
The derived meaning of the term describes the patch, fogging mark, painted area, or stencil by which the bloop is rendered inaudible. The process of applying the bloop (in the second sense) is therefore known either as *blooping* or deblooping, the meaning of the two terms being identical.

Blooping
Less commonly called "deblooping." Any method of silencing the unwanted noise produced by the passage of a *splice* through a sound reproducer.

Blooping patch
A small opaque piece of material of special shape fixed over a sound *splice* in order to *bloop* it.

Blow-up
The optical printing process by which a picture image on a larger gauge of film is produced from a picture image on a smaller gauge of film. A common application is the production of 35 mm. *separation negatives* from 16 mm. *monopack* color originals. Sometimes also refers to the enlargement of the film image in an optical camera.

Blueprint
See *lavender.*

Blur circle
See *circle of confusion.*

Boom, Camera
A mobile camera mount, usually of large size, on which the camera may be projected out over the *set* and/or raised above it. Provision is made for counterbalancing, raising and lowering, rotating, and bodily moving the boom, these motions being effected either by electric motors or by hand.

Boom, Microphone
A simple version of the *camera boom,* designed to project the *microphone* over the *set* and twist it in any direction required by the *mixer.*

Boom boy
See *mikeman.*

Booster light

Light, usually from an *arc* source, which is used to augment daylight in the lighting of an exterior scene.

Borax: $Na_2B_4O_7.10H_2O$

Sodium tetraborate, found principally in the marshes of certain shallow lakes in California, Nevada, and Oregon. Used as a mild activator in negative developing baths and combined with boric acid to form *buffered* baths.

Properties:

Specific gravity, 1.69–1.72

Hardness, 2.0–2.5

Breaking down

In *cutting*, the act of reducing a roll of film into its component shots. The term is usually applied to *rushes*, when a single roll of picture or sound may contain thirty or more separate scenes and takes.

Breathing

1) The audible coming into operation and going out of operation of the *noise reduction* system in sound recording, as heard on the *sound track*.

2) Another term for camera *flutter*.

Brightness: $B = dI/ (dA \cos \theta)$ ASA Z7.1–1942:05.065

Brightness is the luminous intensity of any surface in a given direction per unit of projected area of the surface as viewed from that direction. [See also *illumination*.]

In the defining equation, θ is the angle between the direction of observation and the normal to the surface.

In practice, no surface follows exactly the cosine formula of emission or reflection; hence the brightness of a surface generally is not uniform but varies with the angle at which it is viewed. Brightness can be measured not only for sources and illuminated surfaces, but also for virtual surfaces such as the sky.

In common usage the term brightness usually refers to the intensity of *sensation* * which results from viewing surfaces or spaces from which light comes to the eye. This sensation is determined in part by the definitely measurable "brightness" defined above and in part by conditions of observation such as the state of adaptation of the eye.

Broadside

See *scoop*.

Buffering agent

A system of acids or bases which ionizes in aqueous solution to restrain large changes in the hydrogen ion activity (*pH*) of the solution on the addition or subtraction of strong acids or *alkalies*. Very often a solution of a weak acid and its salt is used for this purpose, e.g. boric acid and sodium tetraborate (*borax*).

C

Calibrations

1) The markings on *lens* barrels and rings used to set the effective *aperture* of the lens *diaphragm* and to control the *focus*.

2) The markings, invisible to the camera, which are sometimes required in *cutout*

* Italicized in the original.

animation to determine the distances through which the cutouts are to be moved between successive exposures.

Callier quotient

The ratio of *specular* to *diffuse density*. Cannot be less than unity, and—owing to the scattering of light by photographic emulsions—is in practice always greater than unity. Specular density is approached in *optical printing*, diffuse density in *contact printing*.

Camera angle

The field of view of a camera when it is set up to shoot. The qualifying terms "high," "low," and "wide" are based on an imaginary norm which more or less corresponds to a 35 mm. camera with a 2-inch lens pointed at a scene from shoulder height.

Camera, Motion picture

An instrument for making a series of intermittent exposures on a strip of sensitized film which, after development, can be projected in such a way as to produce an illusion of movement.

COMBAT CAMERA: A camera designed primarily for hand-held shooting under combat conditions.

FIELD CAMERA: A nonsilenced camera adapted primarily to shooting *exterior* scenes with a small production *unit*, where portability is of first importance.

HAND CAMERA: A field camera light enough to be held in the hand for emergency shooting.

STUDIO CAMERA: A massive camera designed for studio use, fully silenced and carrying every refinement needed for complicated shooting.

Camera movement

1) Movement of the camera as a whole (i.e. not pivotal movement on its horizontal or vertical axes) while shooting a scene.

2) Same as *intermittent movement*.

Camera noise

Noise produced when a camera is running. Highly undesirable when recording sound. See also *blimp*. A standard method of determining the noise level of cameras is proposed in ASA Z52.60–1945.

Camera tracks

Tracks of wood or metal laid down to carry a *dolly* or camera *boom* in order to insure smoothness of *camera movement*.

Cameraman

A person who operates or contributes to the operation of a *motion picture camera*.

FIRST CAMERAMAN (sometimes called Director of Photography or chief cameraman): The person who is responsible for the movements and settings of a camera, and for the lighting of the scene which is being shot. Except in small units, the chief cameraman does not as a rule manipulate the controls of the camera, either when making preliminary adjustments or during the actual shooting.

SECOND CAMERAMAN (assistant cameraman or camera operator): The person who, acting on instructions from the first cameraman, carries out the preliminary adjustments to the camera, and *monitors* the scene during shooting.

FIRST ASSISTANT CAMERAMAN: Chief assistant to the camera operator. Often responsible for *following focus*.

SECOND ASSISTANT CAMERAMAN: Second assistant to the camera operator.

STILL CAMERAMAN: Is responsible for the taking of publicity and production still
photographs.

Carrier wave   ASA C42–1941:05.05.460
A carrier wave is a wave having those characteristics which are essential in order
that the modulated wave may be transmitted through a particular physical system.
[See also *modulation*.]

Cathode (of a vacuum tube)   ASA C42–1941:70.15.015
A cathode of a vacuum tube is an electrode which is the primary source of an
electron stream.

Cathode-ray tube
A type of vacuum tube in which a beam of electrons is directed at a fluorescent
screen by an electron gun. The resulting emission of light may be, but seldom is, used
to produce a sound track. Cathode-ray tubes are sometimes used as *V. I. meters*.

Cell
One of the transparent pieces of celluloid used in cell *animation*. It contains two
or more holes or slots which mount on pins under the *animation camera* to secure
perfect *registration*.

Cello
A type of glass having an indented cellular pattern which enables it to act as a
diffuser. The term cello is often applied to the diffuser made of this substance.

Cement, Film
A liquid used for dissolving film *base* in order to make two pieces of film unite in
a *splice*.

Change focus
See *follow focus*.

Changing bag
A black bag fitted with light-tight sleeves through which the cameraman puts his
hands when loading unexposed film into *magazines,* or unloading exposed film.
Changing bags are often used on *location,* when darkrooms are not available.

Chemical fade
A type of fade made by immersing a negative in a chemical reducer or a positive
in an intensifier in such a way that the scene to be faded progressively disappears.
Though commonly shorter and somewhat less even than optical fades, chemical fades
have the advantage of requiring no intermediate processing steps, so that they are
quicker to make, and often, in the case of color originals, actually superior in quality.

Chromatic aberration
A lens *aberration* characterized by the failure of a lens to bring light of different
wavelengths to the same *focus*.

Cinch marks
Lateral *scratch* marks on the surface of a piece of film, usually made by pressing
down on the edges of a tightly wound roll of film.

Cinex printer
A device for printing a series of exposures from adjacent *frames* of a piece of negative, these exposures corresponding to standard *printer lights*. A cameraman is thus

able, by looking at his *cinex strips,* to see in a few moments how his day's shooting will appear on different printer lights.

Cinex strip
The strip of positive film, about eight inches long, which is developed from exposure to the negative in a *cinex printer.*

Circle of confusion
The spot of light of finite size which constitutes the optical image of an object point when formed by a practical *lens.* The maximum acceptable circle of confusion governs the useful *depth of field,* and is itself governed by the magnification and viewing conditions under which the film image is to be seen.

Circulating system
The flow system consisting of pumps, *tanks, interchangers,* pipes, etc. which supplies developing and fixing solutions to continuous *developing machines.*

Citric acid: $C_3Hy(OH)(COOH)_3.H_2O$
Prepared by extraction from citrus fruits such as lemon and lime as calcium citrate, which is in turn decomposed by a mineral acid. Used as a *restrainer.*
Properties:
Specific gravity: 1.542
Melting point: 153° C

Clapper boards
A pair of hinged boards which are clapped together in dialogue shooting before or after each *take,* when the picture camera and *sound camera* are running at *synchronous speed.* The first frame of closure on the picture is afterwards synchronized in the cutting room with the modulations resulting from the bang, thus establishing synchronism between sound and picture tracks. See also *slate board.* Clapper boards have been dispensed with in modern types of sound recording system.

Clashing
In a *variable density* recording system using a *light valve,* clashing is the act of arriving at the *clash point.*

Clash point
As applied to *light valves,* denotes the position of zero light transmission which results from the coming together of the ribbons.

Claw
A device used in cameras and *substandard* projectors for providing *intermittent motion.* The claw engages one or more *sprocket holes,* and thus pulls down the film a distance equal to the height of one frame; it then withdraws to go back to the initial position. The claw is an example of a *pull-down mechanism.*

Clipping
In a *noise reduction* circuit, the mutilation of one or more *waves* by failure on the part of the noise-reduction elements to open sufficiently rapidly at the onset of a *signal.*

Clumps
The aggregations of light-sensitive grains which occur in a photographic *emulsion.* The resulting nonhomogeneity of the photographic image is called *graininess.*

Coating, Lens
See *antireflective coating.* Sometimes also called "bloom."

Code numbers

Identical numbers printed during the *editorial process* along the edges of synchro-nized positive picture and sound tracks, thus in effect providing *sync marks* at inter-vals of one foot from the start to the end of a *reel*. To be carefully distinguished from *negative numbers*.

Coding machine

A machine for printing *code numbers*. Consists of a revolving printing head and a series of spaced-out rollers over which the film passes after coding while the ink dries.

Color

Color is a basic and indefinable mental sensation resulting from the stimulation of the retina of the eye by electromagnetic radiations, called *light,* which lie within the *wavelength* range of approximately 400–700 *millimicrons*. The term "colored" is ap-plied to objects by virtue of their power of reflection or transmission of light falling within this band of wavelengths. See also *colorimetry*.

Colorblind film

Describes a type of *black-and-white emulsion* which responds only to one region of the *spectrum,* usually the blue, and is therefore unable to distinguish colors on a monochromatic scale.

Colorimetry

1) The science which deals with the specification and measurement of *color*. It is based on Young's three-color theory which states that the sensation produced by any one color can be matched by a proper mixture of three fundamental colors called *primaries*. Colors are also distinguished in colorimetry by hue, brightness, and satura-tion, the last quality referring to vividness of hue. Colorimetry, making use of tri-stimulus values, gives quantitive meaning to these three variables, which can be represented by chromaticity diagrams.

2) A method of determining quantitatively the extent of chemical reactions by means of corresponding color changes in indicator dyes. Using a controlled light source and *photocell* unit, the changes in over-all transmission of solutions may be studied. Changes in specific *wavelengths* may also be ascertained by using selective *filters*.

Color response

In photography, the relative magnitude of the *photochemical reaction* of an emul-sion or system of emulsions to light of different *wavelengths* falling within the *visible spectrum*.

Color temperature ASA Z7.1–1942:25.030

The color temperature of a source of *light* is the temperature at which a *blackbody* must be operated to give a color matching that of the source in question.

NOTE.—Color temperatures are usually assignable only for sources which have a spectral distribution of energy not greatly different from that of a blackbody. [Color temperatures are measured on the Kelvin scale, which reads in degrees Centigrade with its zero at ab-solute zero, or −273° C.]

Combined print

See *composite print*.

Complementary colors

The *colors* which result from subtracting in turn the three *primary* colors from the *visible spectrum.* The three complementary colors are therefore minus-green (magenta), minus-red (blue-green or cyan) and minus-blue (yellow).

Complex wave

More correctly called a complex sinusoidal quantity. It is the result of combining two or more *simple sinusoidal quantities.*

Composite

The presence on one piece of film of corresponding sound and picture images, either in *editorial, camera,* or *projection synchronism.*

Composite dupe negative   ASA Z22.56–1947:2.4.2

A composite dupe negative is a *composite negative* which, after exposure and processing, produces a *dupe negative* picture and sound-track image.

NOTE.—The sound and picture may be in *editorial, projection,* or *camera synchronism,* depending upon the manner in which the composite negative is made and its intended use.

Composite master positive   ASA Z22.56–1947:3.4.5

A composite master positive is a *composite print* usually made for the purpose of producing composite or picture and sound *dupe negatives* which would be used for printing *release prints.*

NOTE.—It is usually made on *duplicating raw stock* and may be in *editorial* or *projection synchronism.*

Composite negative   ASA Z22.56–1947:2.4

A composite negative is a *negative* film which is exposed and processed to produce both *sound track* and picture negative images on the same film.

NOTE.—The sound and picture may be in *editorial, projection,* or *camera synchronism,* depending upon the manner in which the composite negative is made and its intended use.

Composite print   ASA Z22.56–1947:3.4

A composite print is a *positive* film having both picture and sound track images on the same film which may be in *editorial* or *projection synchronism.*

Compression

The function of a device which transfers a *wave motion* from its input to its output and at the same time reduces the span of *amplitudes* of the wave motion.

Compressor

A device for effecting *compression.* See also *volume compressor.*

Conformed dupe

In color printing, a color *dupe* which has been printed by a *masking* technique to reduce *degradation* of color. The conformed dupe is used for making *release prints.* In black-and-white printing, conformed means synchronized to superimposed *subtitles.*

Console

A control panel, used for *sound recording* and *re-recording,* which enables the input from one or more *microphones* or *dubbers* to be varied in respect of *amplitude* and *frequency pass band.* It also makes provision for the *mixer* to *monitor* the *signal* at the console output. Re-recording consoles are often of impressive appearance and carry fifty or more controls (see figure 11-1).

Continuity cutting

A style of *cutting* marked by its emphasis on maintaining the continuous and seemingly uninterrupted flow of action in a story, as if this action were being observed by the audience as spectator. Contrasted with *dynamic cutting*.

Continuity girl

See *script girl*.

Continuous motion

A term characterizing a device used in *viewers* and certain high-speed cameras which, without *intermittent motion,* renders the image of each frame stationary for a short period, so that there is an intermittent succession of images presented to the eye or the film. See also *optical compensator*.

Contrast

In a scene, this term popularly denotes the difference between the *brightness* of the most illuminated and the least illuminated areas; and, in a negative or print, the difference between the *densities* of the most exposed and least exposed areas. Contrast is technically measured by *gamma*. See also *point exposure*.

Contrasty

See *reproduction, contrasty*.

Control track

An auxiliary *sound track* used to manipulate the volume of the main track according to some predetermined plan or to bring additional loudspeakers into play. Control tracks are most commonly used to increase the *dynamic range* of reproduced sound.

Control strip

See *gamma strip*.

Control unit

The unit in a *sound recorder* which varies the *signal* input of one or more *microphones* or *dubbers*.

Cookie

A variegated *flag*, perforated with a pattern of leaves, branches, flowers, etc., which is set so as to cast a shadow on an otherwise uniform and monotonous surface. Cookies are sometimes opaque, sometimes translucent like a *scrim*.

Cording off

When a *cutter* or his assistant wishes a *print, master positive,* or *dupe* to be derived by single or double printing process from a *negative* or other *original,* he ties thin pieces of string through the *perforations* of the original just before the point where he wishes printing to start and just after the point where he wishes it to stop. This marking up is called cording off. See also *papering*.

Core

Cores are centers, usually made of plastic but sometimes of wood or metal, upon which *raw stock* is wound. It is customary to store developed negative in rolls on cores, rather than wound on reels. Cores are classified by their width (35 mm., 16 mm., etc.), and by their gender. The male core has a protruding keyway along its length which engages in a shallow slot on a *rewind* or *flange,* whereas the female core has a shallow slot which engages with a corresponding keyway on male attachments.

Corrective network   ASA C42–1941:65.20.735
A corrective network is an electric network designed to be inserted in a network to improve its transmission characteristics, its impedance properties, or both.

Crane
A large *camera boom.*

Cut
The instantaneous transition from any *shot* to the immediately succeeding shot which results from splicing the two shots together. The cut, a simple and timeless occurrence, is at the root of many of the creative powers of the film, and is primarily responsible for its ability to construct a new framework of time and space. See also *filmic space.*

"Cut!"
The order given by the director of a film when the action in a shot is completed, to indicate that the sound and/or picture cameras are to be shut off.

Cutoff
In *wave filter* design, the critical frequency at which the response of the filter starts to fall sharply.

Cutout
Applied to *animation,* the use of small cutout figures, usually jointed, which by means of *calibrations* may be made to assume successive positions prescribed in a *shooting script,* so that, when photographed a frame at a time, they give the illusion on the screen of continuous movement.

Cuts
See *trims.*

Cutter
The person who is responsible for assembling the raw material of a film (the individual shots) into a coherent and compelling whole. He progresses gradually from an *assembly* to a *rough cut* and thence to a *fine cut,* usually deputing the preparation of music and *sound effects* tracks to a *sound cutter.* The cutter's style will differ greatly according to the nature of his material, from *dynamic cutting* in a *documentary* to *continuity cutting* in an orthodox story film. The terms cutter and editor are synonyms.

Cutting
In analytical terms, the succession of shots as they appear on the movie screen. In synthetic terms, the assembling and piecing together of shots according to the script or some predetermined idea. See also *cutter.*

Cutting copy
See *workprint.*

Cutting room
A room where the positive *cutting* or editing of films is carried out. Cutting rooms must be of fireproof construction when *35 mm. nitrate* film is to be handled in them.

Cutting sync
See *editorial synchronism.*

Cycle   ASA C42–1941:05.05.190
A cycle is the complete series of values of a *periodic quantity* which occur during a *period.*

D

D log E curve

The curve relating *density* with the logarithm of *exposure* which exhibits the photographic response of a given *emulsion* under given conditions of development. The D log E curve is a type of *response curve*. It is the same as the H & D curve.

Dailies

The *prints* delivered daily from the *laboratory* of negative shot on the preceding day. Also called *rushes*.

Dark end

The developing end of the majority of continuous *developing machines,* in which the undeveloped film would become fogged if it were exposed to light. Also called "wet end." In some machines, the wet end is enclosed, so that the operator can work in the light.

Dead spot

In acoustics, a place at which a train of sound waves is cancelled by reflections arriving *out of phase* with the wanted *signal,* thus creating an area of silence or poor audibility. See also *standing wave* and *node*.

Decibel (db)

The human sense organs receive a subjective impression of magnitude of many physical quantities which is approximately proportional to the common *logarithms* of these magnitudes. Accordingly, they are often more conveniently compared on a logarithmic than on a linear basis.

The decibel is one-tenth of a bel, the number of decibels denoting the ratio of two amounts of power being ten times the common logarithm of this ratio.

Degradation

Applied to the photographic image, degradation means the deterioration of the image from the original scene to the photographic reproduction, or from the latter to some more removed image arrived at by *duplication*. The degradation may be in terms of *contrast, resolving power,* or any other image characteristic, but the term is most frequently applied to the reproduction of *color,* which in the present state of the art suffers from many imperfections generically referred to by this term.

Densitometer

A densitometer is a device for measuring photographic *density*.

COMPARATOR DENSITOMETER: A densitometer in which light passing through the film sample is compared in intensity with light from the same source which has passed through an optical wedge. This wedge is as a rule a block of wax, the opacity of which varies progressively and logarithmically from a minimum at one end to a maximum at the other.

INTEGRATING-SPHERE DENSITOMETER: A type of densitometer in which the light to be measured is perfectly diffused by being thrown hither and thither inside a sphere with a diffusing lining.

PHOTOELECTRIC DENSITOMETER: A densitometer in which light passing through the film sample is measured by its effect on a *photoelectric cell*.

PROJECTION-TYPE DENSITOMETER: A densitometer distinguished by the fact that the light passing through the film sample is collimated, or projected in a parallel beam.

Density

The common logarithm of *opacity*, which in turn is the reciprocal of the *transmission factor* of a substance. The value of density depends on the experimental conditions under which it is read. See *Callier quotient*. For a short explanation of the use of logarithmic units, see *decibel*.

DIFFUSE DENSITY: The value of density as measured with diffused light. Conditions approximating to those of diffuse density are met with in *contact printing*.

SPECULAR DENSITY: The value of density as measured with a parallel (collimated) beam of light. Met with in *optical printing*.

SPECULAR-DIFFUSE DENSITY: A density intermediate in value between a specular and a diffuse density.

Depolarizer

In optics, a device for eliminating the *polarization* of a polarized ray of light, that is, for restoring the vibrations of the ray in all directions at right angles to the ray itself. *Matte* and *beaded* projection *screens* act as depolarizers.

Depth of field

The range of object distances within which objects are in satisfactorily sharp focus, the limits being the production of a *circle of confusion* of greatest acceptable size.

Depth of focus

The range through which the image plane (the *emulsion* surface of the film) can be moved backward and forward with respect to the camera lens, as defined under *depth of field* and *circle of confusion*. The term depth of focus is often colloquially used when depth of field is meant.

Developer

A solution containing a *developing agent,* in which film *development* takes place. Also called a developing solution. Practical developers also contain, as a rule, a *preservative,* an *alkali,* a *buffering agent,* and a *restrainer*.

Developing agent

Any chemical compound, organic or inorganic, which, in aqueous solution, will reduce light-sensitive silver salts proportionally to the amount of light that has acted upon them.

Developing formula

A specification giving the kinds and amounts of the chemicals which are mixed to form a *developer*.

Developing machines, Continuous

A machine in which the film to be developed travels continuously from end to end, usually through tanks. The most important of these tanks contain solutions for *developing, fixing,* and *washing* the film, but machines designed for developing *black-and-white* film may have other alternative or subsidiary tanks, while color developing machines require many more tanks.

SPRAY DEVELOPING MACHINE: A developing machine in which the film is not immersed in tanks, but is subjected to the action of the developer, fix and wash by means of jets which spray these liquids onto the *emulsion* surface at close range.

SPROCKETLESS DEVELOPING MACHINE: A developing machine in which the film is propelled by friction rollers instead of by *sprockets*.

See also *rack-and-tank development*.

Developing streaks

Visible streaks in the developed photographic image which are directly traceable to the developing solution(s). They may be caused by the presence of solid matter in the *developer,* or by localized overconcentration due to insufficient *turbulation,* or by a specialized fault of this kind called *directional development.*

Development   ASA Z52.56–1947:1.7

Development is the process of treating an exposed photographic emulsion to make the *latent image* visible.

NOTE.—This term is sometimes incorrectly used in the trade to include both *fixation* and *washing* of the developed image and *drying* of the film. The correct term for these operations as a group is *processing.*

OVERDEVELOPMENT: Development to a higher than normal *gamma* and *density* for a particular photographic *emulsion.*

UNDERDEVELOPMENT: Development to a lower than normal *gamma* and *density* for a particular photographic *emulsion.*

Diaphragm, Lens

An adjustable opening formed by thin overlapping plates, usually placed between the *elements* of the camera *lens* to alter the amount of light reaching the film. Also called an *iris* because its action resembles the iris of the eye.

Diaphragm, Printer

The variable opening in the aperture of certain types of *printer,* through which light is admitted to the film.

Differential reëxposure

A type of color *development,* currently applied to Kodachrome, whereby, after development of the three black-and-white images in the *monopack,* the three layers, which retain their selective spectral sensitivities, are separately reëxposed to colored light and developed in a *dye-coupling* developer.

Diffuse reflection

Reflection characterized by scattering of the reflected light in many directions.

Diffusers

Pieces of a cellular diffusing composition placed in front of studio lamps to soften the light. Also called jellies.

Dimmer banks

Banks of rheostats (variable resistances) used to adjust the voltage, and thus the light intensity, of lamps connected to them.

Direct current (DC)   ASA C42–1941:05.20.057

A direct current is a *unidirectional current* in which the changes in value are either zero or so small that they may be neglected. A given current would be considered a direct current in some applications, but would not necessarily be so considered in other applications.

Direct playback positive   ASA Z22.56–1947:1.2

A direct playback positive is a sound film which is so originally exposed that upon development in a single developer bath, the resulting image is in positive form available for normal sound reproduction.

NOTE.—It is often a variable-area sound record.

Directional

Applied to certain optical and acoustic devices like *screens,* loudspeakers, *exposure meters,* and *microphones,* this term denotes a limitation of the angle of reflection, radiation, or acceptance.

Directional development

In the absence of adequate *turbulation* in a *developing machine,* the by-products of development tend to accumulate near the surface of the film, thus restraining the development of the areas of the image which the film movement next brings in front of them. As a result, in negative development, directional streaks tend to appear on light (less exposed) image areas which abut on dense (heavily exposed) areas. The process of duplication intensifies this effect by two further repetitions of the developing process producing visible "tails" and streamers.

Directional loudspeaker

A loudspeaker characterized by its ability to confine acoustic radiation within a more or less narrow horizontal and vertical angle. This is normally accomplished by means of a *horn,* usually of the *multicellular* type.

Director

The person who controls action and dialogue in front of the camera, and who is therefore responsible for realizing the intentions of the *producer* through the medium of the *shooting script.* See also *assistant director.*

Director of photography

See *cameraman.*

Discontinuous spectrum

A *spectrum* consisting not of a continuous region of radiation, but of a comparatively few widely spaced bright lines. Sources with discontinuous spectra—e.g. mercury-vapor lamps—are not in general suited to color photography or to the projection of color film.

Dissolve

An *optical effect* between two superimposed shots on the screen in which the second shot gradually begins to appear, the first shot at the same time gradually disappearing. Also called lap dissolves, and, in England, mixes.

Distortion, Acoustic

Unwanted changes in the *frequency, amplitude,* or *phase* of an electrical *signal* or a sound wave. Distortion is a change in wave form occurring in a *transducer* or transmission medium. Distortion results from: (a) A *nonlinear* relation between input and output at a given frequency (*amplitude distortion*). (b) Nonuniform transmission at different frequencies (*frequency discrimination*). (c) Phase shift not proportional to frequency, or not zero or 180 degrees at all frequencies (*phase distortion*).

AMPLITUDE DISTORTION: If frequencies occur in the output of a system which do not occur in the input, amplitude distortion is said to be present. This is generally due to a nonlinear relationship between input and output, and is characterized by the presence of spurious *harmonics* and *intermodulation* frequencies.

DYNAMIC DISTORTION: Distortion characterized by an alteration in the dynamic range or *volume range* of a program when it becomes a signal and passes through a transducer or transmission medium.

FREQUENCY DISCRIMINATION (or distortion): The exaggeration or diminution of certain frequencies in relation to other frequencies during the passage of a signal through a transducer or transmission medium.

INTERMODULATION DISTORTION: A type of amplitude distortion characterized principally by the presence of *sum-and-difference tones* related inharmonically to the frequencies present in the original signal.

PHASE DISTORTION: The shifting of the phase of the output voltage or current relative to the input voltage or current by an amount that is not proportional to frequency. Usually unobjectionable in the amplification of sound because not detectable by ear, but objectionable in television amplifiers and in amplifiers designed for wave-form analysis.

SCALE DISTORTION: The rendering of a program so that it strikes the listener's ear at a volume level higher or lower than is normal for that particular series of sounds (e.g. when a voice sounds too loud in the front seats of a movie theater). Since the *frequency response* of the ear is different at different volume levels, frequency distortion results.

Documentary
A type of film marked by its interpretative handling of realistic subjects and backgrounds. Sometimes the term is applied so widely as to include all films which appear more realistic than conventional commercial pictures; sometimes so narrowly that only short films with a spoken narration and a background of real life are included.

Dolly
A light and compact wheeled mount for a camera, often used by small *units* for making *dollying* shots, and for moving a camera from place to place on a set. See also *boom, camera* and *velocilator*.

Dollying
Movement of the whole camera when making a *shot*. Sometimes called trucking and tracking.

Dope sheet
An analysis of film material prepared for purposes of *library* classification.

Double exposure
Successive exposure of a light-sensitive *emulsion* to two scenes, so that two superimposed images are visible after development. When more than two images are exposed on the same emulsion, as in some types of *animation*, the term multiple exposure is used.

Double-headed projection
A colloquial term for synchronous *projection* of a picture track and a *sound track*.

Double-system sound recording
A method of sound recording in which the sound is originally recorded on a separate piece of film from that which records the picture image. See also *single-system sound*.

Drive, Camera
The mechanism through which motion is conveyed from the motor to the film in a motion picture *camera*. See also *intermittent movement*.

Dryboxes
See *drying cabinets*.

Dry end
See *light end*.

Drying cabinets
The sections of a continuous *developing machine* through which warm air is cir-

culated to dry the film. More or less elaborate arrangements are necessary to dehumidify and reheat the air after it has absorbed moisture from the film.

Dubber
A *sound reproducer* of high quality, the output of which is *mixed* in a *console* with the output of other dubbers and/or *microphones,* and finally recorded in a *sound camera,* the whole process being known as dubbing or *re-recording.*

Dubbing
1) Synchronization with the lip movements of an actor of a voice not originally recorded in synchronism with the picture track. The voice may or may not be that of the original actor, and it may or may not be in the same language. Dubbing is usually accomplished by means of *loops,* consisting of short sections of the dialogue in *composite print* form, while the actors are guided by *playback.* Dubbing is used to record songs and prepare foreign versions of films.

2) Same as *re-recording.*

Dubray-Howell perforation
An experimental *perforation* for 35 mm. film, designed eventually (if successful) to supersede both the *negative* and the *positive* perforation, thus unifying the 35 mm. perforating standard.

Dupe
Colloquial term for *dupe negative.* See also *dupe print, color.*

Dupe (duplicate) negative   ASA Z22.56–1947:1.3
A dupe (duplicate) negative is a negative film that is produced by printing from a *positive.*

NOTE.—A dupe negative is used for producing prints which are, in effect, duplicates of prints which might be made from the original negative.

Dupe print, Color   ASA Z22.56–1947:4.5.2
A color dupe print is a color *reversal* which is printed from a color reversal *original* and processed to obtain a *positive* color image.

Duping
See *duplication.*

Duplex track
A common type of *variable-area* track which can be recognized in the print by its two narrow transparent bias lines (when unmodulated) and by its symmetrical opaque modulations down the center. *Push-pull* sound tracks can always be distinguished by the fact that they are not symmetrical about the center line.

Duplicating negative
A type of *raw stock* having characteristics adapted to the making of *dupe negatives.*

Duplication
The process of reproducing picture film; one method of reproducing sound film. The simplest type of duplication is *printing.* In the *negative-positive process,* however, the term is reserved for the sequence of printing a *dupe negative* from a *master positive,* which in turn has been printed from the original *negative.* Any further removal from the original is also called duplication. In the *reversal process,* the term duplication is often applied to printing from the original, as well as to printing from *first-generation dupes.*

Duplitized

A *film* consisting of a *base* coated with *emulsion* on both sides, commonly used for obtaining *two-color* prints by the *dye-toning* process. An extension of this idea leads to a film with two emulsions on one side and one emulsion on the other, by which *three-color* prints may be obtained.

Dynamic range

The dynamic range of a sound system is the difference in *decibels* between the *noise level* of the system and its *overload level*.

Dye coupling

Colored dye images may be obtained by adding groups such as amines and phenols to certain *developers*, the image being formed by the coupling or condensation of the oxidized *developing agent* and the amine or phenol. The couplers may either be incorporated in the emulsion or added during *processing*. See also *tripack*.

Dye toning

The production of a dyed photographic image by converting the silver image into an inorganic compound called a *mordant* which will cause the dye to come out of solution and precipitate proportionally to the amount of silver present in the image.

Dye transfer

A color-printing process in which a dyed image, usually formed by *imbibition* of dye into a *relief* film, is transferred onto a *blank* film.

Dynamic cutting

A term used in film aesthetics to mean a type of *cutting* which, by the juxtaposition of contrasting *shots* or *sequences*, generates ideas in the mind of the spectator which were not latent in any of the synthesizing elements of the film.

Dynamic resolution

The *resolution* of a projected image on a screen. In addition to the individual *resolving powers* of the film, lens, and screen, dynamic resolution takes into account losses of resolution caused by X-, Y-, and Z-axis image unsteadiness of different periodicities.

E

Echo   ASA Z24.1–1949:1.210

A wave which has been reflected or otherwise returned with sufficient magnitude and delay to be perceived in some manner as a wave distinct from that directly transmitted.

Edge fogging

Light *fogging* along the edge of a piece of film, often caused by light leakage in a *magazine* or by inadequate taping of the lid of a film can.

Edge number

One of a series of numbers, combined with key lettering, printed at intervals of a foot along the edge of a number of types of *raw stock*. These numbers, incorporated in the film, print through to positive stock not so marked. Same as footage number and negative number.

Editor

See *cutter*.

Effects filter

An optical *filter* which distorts the rendering of natural objects to such an extent that a special effect, like a night or fog effect, is produced.

Effects library

See *sound effects library.*

Eight mm. film

A *substandard* gauge of film in extensive use by amateurs. Its cutting and perforating dimensions are given in ASA Z22.17–1947, or latest revision thereof.

Electrician

A person responsible for the placing and adjustment of lights, and for the supply of electricity to them. See also *gaffer.*

Elements, Lens

The individual lenses (either separate or cemented together) which in combination form a photographic objective corrected for *aberrations.* Lens elements are also called components.

Elon

See *metol.*

Emulsion

In photographic terminology, the emulsion is the light-sensitive coating supported by a base of cellulose *nitrate* or *acetate* which together form *film.* A photographic emulsion is not a true emulsion, but a suspension of a light-sensitive solid in a colloid, which for all practical purposes is gelatin. The term emulsion is often extended to represent the film itself, since it alone has photographic qualities. See also *halide.*

End sync marks

Synchronizing marks placed at the ends of reels of sound and picture film, usually to enable printing to be effected in both directions. End sync marks can also be usefully applied to *re-recording sound tracks.*

Envelope

The profile of a train of *waves.* The envelope can either fit closely to the crests of the waves or follow a more general outline.

Equalizer

See *corrective network.*

Equalizer, Attenuation

A network whose insertion loss varies in some desirable manner with change of *frequency.* Such networks are usually inserted into *transmission systems* to compensate for defects in the transmission-frequency characteristics of the systems.

Exciter lamp

A lamp which excites a current in a *phototube* is called an exciter lamp. Often the lamp output is *modulated* by placing a light *modulator* such as a *sound track* between the lamp and the tube.

Exposure

Exposure is the process of subjecting a photographic film to any given intensity of light in such a manner that it may produce a *latent image* on the *emulsion.* According to the *reciprocity law,* exposure is determined by the product of time and intensity of illumination. See also *point exposure.*

OVEREXPOSURE: An exposure greater than the optimum for a particular photographic *emulsion*, developing condition, and range of object *brightnesses*.

UNDEREXPOSURE: An exposure less than the optimum for a particular photographic emulsion, developing condition and range of object *brightnesses*.

Exposure index

A number based on *emulsion speed* and *latitude, exposure meter* characteristics and technique, and expected conditions of *development,* which enables the user of a film emulsion to determine the correct *exposure* under different light conditions estimated by an *exposure meter* or from tables.

Exposure meter

A device for determining the light flux incident upon or reflected from a scene which is to be photographed, the corresponding instruments being known as incident-light meters and reflected-light meters. Exposure meters are read (a) by exposing a piece of light-sensitive paper until it has taken up a prescribed color; (b) by rotating an optical wedge until a density is matched or a light extinguished (extinction-type meter, see also *densitometer, comparator*); (c) by noting the reading on a calibrated microammeter actuated by a *photovoltaic cell.* The third type of meter is by far the commonest.

Exposure number

See *exposure index.*

Exposure scale

The range of *point exposures* projected by a lens onto an *emulsion* when forming a photographic image. The greatest exposure corresponds to the most brilliantly illuminated point in the original scene, the least exposure to the point in deepest shadow. See also *object brightness scale.*

Exteriors

Outdoor scenes.

F

F/number

A number denoting the geometrical determination of *lens speed.* It is arrived at by dividing the *focal length* of the lens by its effective *aperture.* See also *T-number.*

Fade

An *optical effect* occupying a single shot, in which the shot gradually disappears into blackness (fade-out) or appears out of blackness (fade-in). See also *chemical fade.*

Fast motion

Motion of the film through the camera slower than the standard rate, which therefore results in action appearing faster than normal when the film is projected at the standard rate. See also *slow motion.*

Feed sprocket

See *sprocket, feed.*

Field flattener

An auxiliary lens which helps to correct for curvature of field, the lens *aberration* which causes a photographic image to assume a curved shape in contrast to the shape of *emulsion* surfaces and projection *screens,* which are usually flat.

Filler light
Filler light is the light which builds up shadow illumination. The ratio of *key light* to filler light establishes in general terms the lighting contrast of a scene.

Film bank
As used in continuous *developing machines*, a film bank consists of two parallel spindles, mounted several feet apart, on which the film is wound like a skein over spools or rollers so that it can travel continuously.

Film, Motion picture   ASA Z22.56–1947:1.1
Motion picture film is a thin flexible ribbon of transparent material having *perforations* along one or both edges and bearing a sensitized layer or other coating capable of producing photographic images.

NOTE.—The term "film" may be applied to unexposed film, to exposed but unprocessed film, and to exposed and processed film.

Film exchanges
Regional centers from which films are distributed to movie theaters.

Film library
An organization of the film material in the possession of a studio, correlated by means of a more or less elaborate reference and cross-index system.

Film loader
The member of a camera team whose function is to load unexposed film into *magazines* and unload exposed film into cans. Except in a very large unit, the functions of loader are discharged by an *assistant cameraman*.

Film phonograph
See *dubber*.

Film reproducer   ASA Z24.1–1949:8.320
A film reproducer is an instrument in which film is the medium from which a recording is reproduced.

NOTE.—In many cases, the term "film reproducer" is erroneously used synonymously with *optical sound reproducer*.

Filmic space
The power of the film medium which enables it to combine shots of widely separated origin into a single framework of space.

Filter factor
A numerical factor by which the length of a photographic *exposure* must be increased to compensate for the absorption of an optical *filter* through which the exposure is to be made.

Filter, Wave
A device, of whatever character, for varying the transmission of a system in accordance with some predetermined spectral response. In film technology, the two spectra of principal interest are the *visible spectrum* and the *audible spectrum*. The most commonly used filters are *optical filters* and *electrical filters*, for the manipulation of sound is most conveniently handled electrically.

OPTICAL FILTERS: Light transmitters, usually made of glass or gelatin, which transmit freely waves having frequencies within one or more frequency bands and which attenuate substantially waves having other frequencies. The optical frequency band for most film purposes corresponds to wavelengths between 360 and 900 *millimicrons*. The term filter is also applied to light transmitters which affect the polarization of light or absorb it non-selectively.

i) Sharp-cut filters have low transmittance throughout a part of the spectrum and higher transmittance throughout the balance of the spectrum. The transition from low to high transmittance occurs within a narrow wavelength interval.

ii) Medium-cut filters differ from sharp-cut filters only in that the transition from low to high transmittance occurs within a moderately narrow wavelength interval.

iii) Band-transmission filters have low transmittance throughout the spectrum except for a single wavelength band where the transmittance is considerably greater.

iv) Band-absorption filters have high transmittance throughout the spectrum except for a single wavelength band where the transmittance is considerably lower.

v) Neutral-density filters show relatively small variations in transmittance throughout the spectrum, but vary in *density* as required. They are used in camerawork for increasing the lens aperture at a given illumination level without altering color values, and for reducing the effective contrast of a scene.

vi) Polarizing filters have the property of *polarizing* light, and are used for reducing certain types of unwanted reflection, and for certain types of stereoscopic projection.

ELECTRICAL FILTERS: Selective networks which transmit freely electric waves having frequencies within one or more frequency bands and which attenuate substantially electric waves having other frequencies. The audio frequency band ranges from approximately 30 to 15,000 cycles. Electrical filters are built with the same general characteristics as optical filters, but can be designed with greater accuracy and for more specialized purposes.

i) Low-pass filters have a single transmission band extending from zero frequency up to some critical or *cutoff* frequency, not infinite.

ii) High-pass filters have a single transmission band extending from some critical or cutoff frequency up to infinite frequency.

iii) Band-pass filters have a single transmission band, neither of the critical or cutoff frequencies being zero or infinite.

iv) Band-elimination filters have a single attenuation band, neither of the critical or cutoff frequencies being zero or infinite.

v) Broadly tuned filters have a wide transmission or attenuation band, characterized by a single peak.

vi) Sharply tuned filters have a narrow transmission or attenuation band, characterized by a single peak.

Fine cut

The version of the workprint of a film which follows the *rough cut* stage in the film's progress toward completion. At each successive stage the cutting is refined and unnecessary footage eliminated.

Fine-grain ASA Z22.56–1947:1.1.4

Fine-grain is the term used to designate film *emulsions* in which the *grain* size is smaller or finer than in the older type emulsions commonly employed prior to about 1936. [Later outside the United States.]

NOTE.—This term is relative as there is a wide variation in grain size among various fine-grain films. It is probable that the term will become obsolete when all film emulsions become fine grain. There is no inverse term such as coarse grain.

First generation dupe

A *reversal print* made from a reversal *original,* often for the purpose of producing further prints, which are known as *second generation dupes.*

Fishpole

A long and light pole from which a *microphone* can be suspended, the whole being swung round to provide the best pickup of sound. Fishpoles are often used by small and medium-size units on location, where the size and weight of a *boom* would prove inconvenient.

Fixing   ASA Z22.56–1947:1.7.1

Fixing (fixation) is the process of removing the residual sensitive silver *halides* from a developed film to render the developed image permanent.

NOTE.—During the process of fixation, films are customarily treated to preserve and harden the developed image.

Flag

A miniature *gobo,* made of plywood or of cloth mounted on a metal frame and usually set on a stand. See also *scrim.*

Flange

A disc, usually made of metal or bakelite, against which film is wound on a *core* mounted on a *rewinder.*

Flares

Areas of spurious highlight intensity in the negative film image, caused by internal reflections in the camera *lens* or by stray reflections from bright objects in the *camera.*

Flat

See *reproduction, flat.*

Flicker

In film *projection,* a cyclical fluctuation in the intensity of light thrown on the screen, caused by the passage of the *shutter* across the light beam. Flicker is also caused by a projection rate of fewer frames per second than *persistence of vision* can fuse into a continuous mental image.

Flipover wipe

A kind of *wipe* in which the image appears to turn over, revealing another image on the "back," the axis of rotation being either vertical or horizontal.

Flutter, Picture

A term applied to unwanted movement of the film at right angles to its plane when it is located in the camera, projector, or printer aperture.

Flutter (wow)   Proposed SMPE Standard Specification, 2.0

The term "flutter" relates to any deviation of frequency which results, in general, from irregular motion in the recording, duplication, or reproduction of a tone, or from deformation of the record.

The term "wow" is colloquial and usually refers to deviation of frequency occurring at a relatively low rate as, for example, a "once-a-revolution" speed variation of phonograph turntables.

Flutter rate Proposed SMPE Standard Specification, 3.0

Flutter rate is the number of excursions of frequency per second in a tone which has flutter.

NOTE.—(1) Each excursion is a complete cycle of deviation, for example, from maximum frequency to minimum frequency and back to maximum frequency at the rate indicated. (2) Flutter is usually periodic with a dominant rate. (3) Two or more flutter rates may be present simultaneously each of which is regarded as a component of the complex variation. (4) Flutter which occurs at random rates close to zero cps is generally termed drift.

Focal length

The constant of a *lens* upon which the size of the image depends. In a thin lens, it is the distance from the center of the lens to either principal *focus*. The equivalent focal length of a thick lens is the focal length of a thin lens of identical magnifying power.

Focal plane

The locus of the foci of different systems of parallel rays refracted through a *lens*.

Focal point

The intersection of a *focal plane* with the axis of a lens.

Focus

The point at which parallel rays meet after passing through a convergent *lens;* also called the principal focus. More generally, that position at which an object must be situated in order that the image produced by a lens may be sharp and well defined; hence, an object may be said to be in focus or out of focus. The term is also used to denote the sharpness of the photographic image as affected by the relation between the *focal plane* of the lens and the plane of the *emulsion* surface. When these two planes are coincident, the image is said to be in focus; when they are out of coincidence to such an extent that the emulsion plane is outside the *depth of focus,* the image is said to be out of focus.

Focusing

The art of moving a camera lens toward or away from the *emulsion* plane to bring the image on this plane into *focus.*

Focusing microscope

An optical device employed in many *cameras* of superior design for magnifying the image formed on a *ground glass* by the camera *lens*. Sometimes incorrectly called a focusing telescope.

Fog blooping

A popular method of *blooping re-recording prints* by triggering a small light in the printer to cause it to come into action at a *splice,* thus fogging the splice and eliminating the audible bump when it is reproduced.

Fog density

A density produced on a piece of film by causes other than *exposure* to light, or a greater density than such exposure would normally produce.

Fogging, Chemical

Any increase in *emulsion density* not caused by exposure to light. Metallic salts of tin or copper present in minute quantities in a *developer* will cause fogging (developer fog). Exposure to air during development will, if excessive, also cause fogging. This is particularly noticeable with *hydroquinone* developers.

Fogging, Light

An unwanted *exposure* of a piece of film caused by exposing it to stray light. See also *edge fogging*.

Follow focus

A continuous change in camera *focusing* necessitated by relative movement between the camera and its subject greater than can be accommodated by *depth of field*. Following focus is usually a function of the *first assistant cameraman*.

Follow shots

Shots in which the camera moves around following the action of the scene. Also called *dollying* and trucking shots.

Footage number

See *edge number*.

Foot-candle (ft-c)　　　　　　　　　　　　　　　　ASA Z7.1–1942:05.040

The foot-candle is the unit of *illumination* when the foot is taken as the unit of length. It is the illumination on a surface one square foot in area on which there is a uniformly distributed flux of one *lumen,* or the illumination produced at a surface all points of which are at a distance of one foot from a uniform point source of one candle.

Foot-lambert (ft-L)　　　　　　　　　　　　　　　　ASA Z7.1–1942:05.085

The foot-lambert is a unit of *brightness* equal to $1/\pi$ candle per square centimeter, and, therefore is equal to the uniform brightness of a perfectly diffusing surface emitting or reflecting light at the rate of one lumen per square foot, or to the average brightness of any surface emitting or reflecting light at that rate.

The average brightness of any reflecting surface in foot-lamberts is, therefore, the product of the illumination in *foot-candles* by the *reflection factor* of the surface.

The foot-lambert is the same as the "apparent foot-candle."

Frame

The individual picture on a strip of film.

FRAME LINES: The horizontal bands between *frames* of film, which divide frames from one another.

IN FRAME: So framed that the *frame lines* do not trespass on the image area.

OUT OF FRAME: So framed that the frame lines trespass on the image area.

TO FRAME: To make an adjustment to certain film mechanisms such as *projectors* and *step printers* whereby the frames of film coincide with an *aperture plate*. If there is no such coincidence, the *frame lines* will appear in the image area and the image will be out of frame.

Framing

The act of adjusting a film mechanism to make the film *in frame*. Also, the setting up of a camera in such a way that the image framed by its lens and aperture plate is precisely that required by the *director* and *cameraman*.

Framing device

A mechanical device incorporated in *projectors* and *moviolas* for adjusting the image until it is *in frame*.

Freezing

If the *cutter* desires to lengthen a shot, he may arrange for a single *frame* (usually close to but not at the end) to be printed over and over again in the *optical printer* to make up the required footage. This is called freezing frames. To reduce graininess, it is better to repeat a cycle of three frames, but this is only possible if there are three successive frames without appreciable motion.

Frequency (f)
The number of *cycles* occurring per unit of time, or which would occur per unit of time if all subsequent cycles were identical with the cycle under consideration. The frequency is the reciprocal of the period in seconds. The unit is the cycle per second (cps or c/s). Since the second is invariably the unit of time, frequencies are often loosely denoted in cycles.

Frequency-response characteristic
A curve denoting the relative response of a system (often an *amplifier*) to changes of *frequency*. The band of frequencies covered by the curve is usually the entire *pass band* of the system; often it is the *audible spectrum*.

Friction head
A type of *panning* and *tilting head* set on a tripod or other camera support which incorporates a smoothly sliding friction device to secure smoothness of camera movement. Also called a free head. See also *geared head* and *gyro head*.

Fringing
When a photographic image results from the superimposition of two or more antecedent images, and when these images are not in perfect *registration,* the final image is said to exhibit fringing. Fringing is particularly objectionable in color syntheses, since the fringes will then be of different colors from adjacent parts of the image.

Fundamental frequency
The lowest sinusoidal component *frequency* of a *periodic quantity.* See also *harmonic.*

G

Gaffer
In studio parlance, the chief electrician who is responsible, under the *first cameraman,* for the lighting of *sets.*

Gain control
A control on a recording console which enables the amplification or gain of the system to be varied, so that the *signal* level may be raised or lowered at will. A master gain control is one which alters the gain of a number of channels simultaneously.

Galvanometer
A sensitive device for indicating the passage of electric current. In film recording, the moving member of a galvanometer may be made to produce fluctuations of a beam of light corresponding with its electrical input.

Gamma
The slope of the straight part of the *D log E curve* of a photographic *emulsion,* as measured by the tangent of the angle which this part of the curve makes with the exposure axis. In other words, gamma equals the *density* increase divided by the log exposure increase. Gamma is a convenient measure of photographic contrast, a basic element in pictorial reproduction. The determination of gamma is a fundamental in the science of *sensitometry.*

GAMMA INFINITY: The limiting gamma beyond which a given film *emulsion* in a given *developer* will not develop, even if immersion is continued indefinitely.

GAMMA STRIP: A strip of film exposed in a *sensitometer* for the purpose of controlling development gamma.

LIGHT VALVE GAMMA: A gamma factor introduced in a *light valve* by variations in the film exposure consequent on the opening and closing of the valve. These exposure variations tend to fall on that part of the emulsion sensitivity curve which shows a progressive departure from the *reciprocity law*, thus causing alterations of contrast.

NEGATIVE GAMMA: The gamma resulting from the development of the *negative* image in a photographic process.

POSITIVE GAMMA: The gamma resulting from the development of the *positive* image in a photographic process.

PRODUCT GAMMA: The result of multiplying together the individual gammas of two or more of the various steps through which the image passes from the original exposure to the viewing of the final print.

VISUAL GAMMA: A gamma plotted from densities read visually.

Gammeter

A device like a protractor which indicates the tangents of angles, and thus may be calibrated to read *gamma* directly, when placed against the straight part of the *D log E curve*.

Gate

A term sometimes applied to the *aperture* unit of cameras and projectors, perhaps because they often swing outwards on hinges for *threading* and cleaning.

Geared head

A type of *panning* and *tilting head* set on a tripod or other camera support which incorporates two geared drives for the two movements, operated by crank handles. See also *friction head* and *gyro head*.

Glow lamp

See *aeolight*.

Gobo

A wooden screen, painted black and so placed that it screens the light from one or more studio lamps, thus preventing it from entering the camera lens. Gobos are usually mounted on adjustable stands, and are of many shapes and sizes. See also *flag, target,* and *scrim*.

Gradient

The instantaneous value of the slope of a curve.

Graininess

The characteristic of an *emulsion* brought about by its being composed of microscopic particles called grains, which are irregularly clustered together into *clumps*. If these clumps are visible when the image is projected, the image is said to be grainy.

Grey-back antihalation stock

A film stock which has a grey dye mixed in the *base* for the purpose of absorbing light which has passed through the *emulsion* and would otherwise cause *halation*. Formerly, a grey backing served the same purpose; it was water soluble and dissolved off during development. Also called grey-base stock.

Green print

A *positive print* which has been improperly *hardened* and/or *dried,* resulting in a tacky condition of the film which leads to damage in projection.

Grip

The person who, on the studio *set,* has charge of minor adjustments and repairs to *props,* camera tracks, and the like.

Ground glass

A piece of glass with a finely ground surface on which an image can be formed. Ground glass is used in the *viewfinders* of cameras, and the image is often enlarged by means of a *focusing microscope.* Ground film may also be placed in the camera aperture to form an image.

Gyro head

A type of *panning* and *tilting head* set on a tripod or other camera support which incorporates a heavy flywheel driven at high speed by gearing from the moving camera platform. The inertia of the flywheel insures the steady movement of the camera. See also *friction head* and *geared head.*

H

H and D Curve

See *D log E curve.*

HQ

See *hydroquinone.*

Halation

A halo or ghost image surrounding the true image of a brightly lighted object on a photographic *emulsion.* Frequently caused by light rebounding from the under-surface of the film *base* and once again entering the emulsion, thus producing a spurious image. See *grey-back antihalation stock.*

Halide

Any salt of the halogen family comprising chlorine, fluorine, bromine, and iodine. Examples: sodium chloride, potassium bromide, silver iodide. The light-sensitive constituents of all practical *emulsions* are halides, and more particularly silver halides.

Handviewer

See *viewer (or reader).*

Hardening

Film emulsion, which is softened during *development,* is normally hardened so that it can be *fixed,* washed, and *dried* without damage from *scratches, abrasions,* or *reticulation.* Hardening (or tanning) of the gelatin emulsion may take place before or after development, but is customarily combined with fixation by adding some form of alum to the bath.

Harmonic

A sinusoidal component of a *periodic quantity* having a frequency which is an integral multiple of the *fundamental frequency.* For example, a component the frequency of which is twice the fundamental frequency is called the second harmonic. See also *distortion, amplitude.*

Harmonic distortion

See *distortion, amplitude.*

Head, Camera

The revolving and tilting mount on which a camera is fixed, and which is in turn fixed to a *tripod, high hat, dolly, velocilator,* or *boom.* See also *friction head, geared head,* and *gyro head.*

Head-up

A term applied to a reel of film so wound that the first frame is on the outside of the reel, which is accordingly ready to project. The opposite term is *tails-up.*

High hat

A very small *tripod* of fixed height which can be attached to the floor of an airplane or to any place where it is desired to set the camera as low on its mounting as possible.

Horse

A simple device consisting of two parallel hinged arms mounted vertically on a cutting bench and carrying a spindle midway up. The arms are separated by a distance just greater than the width of the film to be mounted, and this film, wound in a roll, is supported on the horse spindle for unwinding or *breaking down.*

Hot spot

A small area in a scene which has been lighted excessively brightly. The excessive brilliance of part of an illuminated *screen,* usually caused by *metallic* reflection characteristics, is also called a hot spot.

Hydroquinone (Parahydroxybenzene): $C_6H_4(OH)_2$

Prepared by oxidizing and reducing aniline, or by reducing quinone with sulphuric acid. Used as a *developing agent* giving high density and contrast.

Properties:
   Specific gravity: 1.33
   Melting point: 176° C
   Boiling point: 285° C
   Soluble in water, alcohol, and ether.

Hyperstereoscopy

In *stereoscopy,* the taking of a pair of photographs with a camera *interaxial* greater than the *interocular* of the person who views them results in an enhanced sense of relief and a corresponding reduction in the apparent size of an object. This is called *hyperstereoscopy.* The increased interaxial distance may amount to a few inches or many thousands of miles, according to the subject chosen. Among the objects (to the eye appearing flat) which may be made to appear in depth by this method are distant mountain ranges and celestial bodies such as comets and the moon. See also *ortho-stereoscopy.*

Hypo

Popular term for sodium thiosulfate ($Na_2S_2O_3.5H_2O$), the most commonly used photographic fixing agent. Sometimes incorrectly called sodium hyposulfite.

I

Illumination: $E = dF/dA$ ASA Z7.1–1942:05.035

Illumination is the density of the luminous flux on a surface; it is the quotient of the flux by the area of the surface when the latter is uniformly illuminated.

NOTE.—The term illumination is also commonly used in a qualitative or general sense to designate the act of illuminating or the state of being illuminated. Usually the context will indicate which meaning is intended, but occasionally it is desirable to use the expression *amount of illumination* * to indicate that the quantitative meaning is intended.

Imbibition
A color printing process in which *relief matrices* are caused to absorb or imbibe dyes in proportion to the depth of the relief, which is in turn proportionate to the intensity of a *primary* color component in the original scene. The imbibed dye is transferred from the matrices onto a *blank* which becomes the *release print*.

In-betweeners
The persons in an *animation* studio who draw the sketches for the *cells* which, in the sequence of action, fill up the gaps between the significant moments drawn by senior *animators*.

Incandescent light
Light produced by the raising of a metallic filament, usually containing tungsten, to a high temperature by means of an electric current.

Incident-light exposure meter
See *exposure meter*.

Infra-audible sound (Infrasonic sound)
Sound whose *frequency* is below the lower *pitch* of hearing. This is generally assumed to be 15 cps.

Infrared
The infrared region of the *spectrum* ranges upwards from 700 *millimicrons,* eventually merging into heat waves. The band which is of photographic interest ends at about 1,350 mμ, and most practical infrared photography is confined to the 700–860 mμ region. Infrared motion picture film is chiefly used for haze penetration and for producing special nonpanchromatic effects.

Inkers
The persons in an *animation* studio who trace the outlines of drawings prepared by *animators* onto *cells*.

Inky-dink
A popular term for a miniature *incandescent* lamp.

Inspection
Periodic inspection of film to insure that it is in proper physical condition, or to report on defects. Essential to accurate *laboratory* control.

Integral tripack
A three-layered *emulsion,* having three different spectral sensitivities, enabling each layer to respond to one of the *primary* colors of the *spectrum*. Since, in an integral tripack, the three emulsion layers are superimposed (with or without intervening filters or other separators) on a single *base*, the term monopack is often used.

Interaxial distance
In *stereoscopy,* the horizontal distance between the two lens axes of the camera. If a shot is made with an interaxial distance less than the human *interocular,* the

* Italicized in the original.

resulting *stereogram* will represent an object larger than actual, removed to a greater distance; but if the interaxial is greater, the effect will be that of a smaller object seen at a lesser distance. This is called *hyperstereoscopy*. The term interocular is sometimes applied to the camera when interaxial is meant; this may lead to serious confusion.

Interchanger

A device for interchanging heat between two or more liquids. In its film application it usually consists of a cylinder containing an outer jacket or series of pipes through which hot or cold water flows, and an inner part of the cylinder containing a *developing* or *fixing solution*, the temperature of which is thereby raised or lowered.

Interface

The boundary surface between two adjacent pieces of glass or other transparent material. Interfaces are to be found in compound *lenses* and prisms, and sometimes are given *semireflecting* characteristics.

Interiors

Indoor scenes.

Interlock system

A system of interdependent motors which are so controlled electrically that all turn at precisely the same speed. In some types of interlock control, rotation by hand of one motor shaft will turn the other motors correspondingly. AC, DC, and *selsyn* interlock systems are available.

The term interlock is sometimes loosely applied to any system by which picture and sound tracks may be projected synchronously, even when synchronism is obtained by the use of *synchronous motors* or mechanical coupling.

Intermediate

A color *dupe print* which is intended for use as a parent of release prints, which are called *second generation dupes* (or prints).

Intermittent movement

A stop-and-go movement of film which in a *camera* or *projector* enables each picture or *frame* to be exposed or viewed at rest and then replaced by the next picture. The term is applied also to the mechanism by which this effect is secured, usually a *claw* or a *Maltese cross*. See also *persistence of vision, shutter,* and *motion, continuous.*

Intermittent pressure

The application of pressure to film in a *camera aperture* during the periods in the cycle of *intermittent movement* when it is at rest. In certain camera designs, intermittent pressure is applied in order to steady the film during exposure.

Intermodulation ASA C42–1941:65.11.215

Intermodulation is the modulation of the components of a complex wave by each other, as a result of which are produced waves which have frequencies equal to the sums and differences of those of the components of the original complex wave.

Intermodulation Distortion

See *distortion.*

Iris

See *diaphragm, lens.*

J

Jellies
    See *diffusers*.

Jump cut
    If a section is taken out of the middle of a shot, and the film respliced across the gap, a jump cut is said to result, since there is a jump in the shot's continuity. When the shot is motionless, this is a useful device for eliminating dead footage. Shots, however, are seldom perfectly static, and if there is movement, an unpleasantly visible jump will usually occur.

K

Key light
    The main light used for the illumination of a subject. See also *filler light*.

    HIGH-KEY LIGHTING: A lighting technique in which the *key light* forms a very large proportion of the total illumination of the set, resulting in a low lighting contrast and an effect of general brilliance in the scene. Before 1939 or thereabouts, this was the method of lighting universally favored in Hollywood, and it is still recommended for color shooting.

    LOW-KEY LIGHTING: A lighting technique in which the key light forms, in comparison with *high key lighting,* a lower proportion of a smaller total illumination. The result is that many objects are allowed to fall into semi-darkness or even total blackness, thus throwing others into correspondingly stronger relief. This more dramatic style of lighting, which has now won general acceptance in Hollywood for certain types of film and is advancing even in color photography, makes greater demands on *emulsion* characteristics and on *processing* techniques than does high key lighting.

Key number
    See *edge number*.

Kilowatt (kw)
    One thousand *watts*.

L

Laboratory
    In film technology, the place where film is *processed,* and where the attendant operations of *sensitometry, inspection,* chemical analysis, etc. are carried out. Commonly abbreviated to lab.

Lap dissolve
    See *dissolve*.

Latensification
    A means of intensifying the *latent image* on film by subjecting the film, after photographic exposure but before development, to a protracted fogging exposure of very low brightness. This has a greater effect on the emulsion grains which have received a subthreshold exposure in the camera than on the totally unexposed grains. Thus, at the cost of a slight increase in *graininess* and *fog density,* shadow detail in

the negative can be very greatly improved under conditions of extreme under-exposure.

Latent image ASA Z22.56–1947:1.4.1

A latent image is the invisible image registered on a photographic *emulsion* due to the reaction produced in the emulsion by exposure to light.

NOTE.—This image becomes visible after *development.*

Latitude

The range of *exposure* of an *emulsion* within which, for any given conditions of *development,* the *gradient* of its *D log E curve* is constant (i.e. the curve is straight). Latitude of exposure is normally greater than the latitude of an emulsion as here defined, since portions of the *shoulder* and *toe* of the curve can be successfully used in practical photography.

Lavender

Colloquial term for an obsolescent type of *master positive* stock, distinguished by having a lavender-tinted *base.* Sometimes called blueprint.

Leader

Film consisting of a coated or uncoated *base* which is used for *threading* through continuous *developing machines* and sometimes for assembling workprints and *re-recording sound tracks* which contain only short lengths of modulated film. Different kinds of leader are designated by their color. See also *Academy leader.*

Leader, Standard

See *Academy leader.*

Lens

A photographic lens consists of a piece or series of pieces called *elements* of transparent substance, bounded by two curved surfaces (usually spherical), or by a curved surface and a plane. In cinematography it is a converging lens which forms a real image of greater or less magnification, usually on the *emulsion* surface or the projection *screen.* See also *focus, focal length, aperture, f/number, T-number,* and *anti-reflective coating.*

LONG-FOCUS LENS: A relative term describing lenses of longer focal length than normal, and consequently giving greater than normal magnification. See also *telephoto lens.*

SHORT-FOCUS LENS: A relative term describing lenses of shorter focal length than normal, consequently giving lower than normal magnification and a wider field of view. Hence also called wide-angle lens.

Lenticular process

A color process in which the film *base* is embossed with a multitude of small *lenses* or *lenticules,* each of which images the *primary* components of a small colored patch in the object through a three-banded filter covering the lens. Since projection of the original film or a duplicate takes place through an identical filter and set of lenticules, an *additive* color synthesis results.

Lenticular screen

A screen having a surface embossed or coated with *lenticules* is called a lenticular screen. Such a screen is formed on the film base in a *lenticular process* for color reproduction, and also in many direct vision systems of *stereoscopy.* The lenticules are not necessarily parts of spherical surfaces. They may be portions of minute cylinders or prisms, extended lengthwise the full height or width of the screen.

Lenticule

A minute lens such as may be embossed or otherwise formed in large numbers on a transparent plate or film. See *lenticular screen*.

Library vaults

Film *storage vaults* under the control of the *film library*. Their contents are usually indexed in detail, shot by shot.

Light

Light is radiant energy traveling in the form of electromagnetic waves and evaluated according to its capacity to produce visual sensation.

Light box

An item of *cutting room* equipment which consists of a box containing a light source and covered with opalescent glass. By holding up film in front of a light box, the cutter makes the images on it easily visible. In some places, light boxes are prohibited by local fire regulations in rooms where *nitrate* film is handled.

Light-change board

A board containing a series of fixed resistors used to alter the intensity of light in certain types of *printer* for purposes of *timing*. The light changes can usually be preset on the board, but the change of light intensity is not instantaneous with *incandescent* sources because of *thermal lag* in the filament.

Light end

The end of a continuous *developing machine* which follows the *fixing* and *washing* tanks, and so makes possible the exposure of the developed film to white light. Also called the dry end.

Lighting

The illumination of a scene in front of a camera. In the studio, it is convenient to think of the scene as totally dark, so that its appearance is created solely by the color, disposition, and intensity of the light which falls upon it. Photographic lighting is designated, like wind, by the direction from which it comes. See also *filler light* and *key light*.

  BACK-LIGHTING: Lighting from behind the set, or toward the camera, the actual light source(s) being shielded so as not to shine into the lens. Backlighting increases lighting contrast up to the extreme condition of silhouette (no front light).

  CROSSLIGHTING: Lighting intermediate in its direction and effect between frontlighting and backlighting.

  FRONTLIGHTING: The main lighting of a *set* is directed on it from behind and beside the camera, i.e. from in front of the set. The greater the proportion of front light to other kinds of light, the flatter in general will the lighting be, i.e. the lower will be the lighting contrast.

  HIGHLIGHTING: Additional illumination applied to a small area. Extreme highlighting may result in a *hot spot*.

  TOPLIGHTING: Light resulting from sources mounted above the subject and shining down onto it. According to whether toplighting is mounted in front of, behind or to one side of the subject, its effect will fall into one of the above categories.

Light meter

See *exposure meter.*

Light trap

A mechanical device for excluding light. Applied to film *magazines,* dark-room entrances, and ventilators.

Light valve

A *modulator* consisting of a narrow slit or gate of variable width which modulates a beam of light directed onto a light-sensitive film. If the light valve is set transversely to the axis of the *sound track* (which is normal), it produces a *variable-density* sound record. If it is mounted longitudinally and suitably masked, it may be made to produce a *variable-area* record. See also *light-valve gamma* and *ribbon-velocity effect.*

Limiter

A simple type of *compressor* in which the peaks of the waves in a wave train are sliced off at some predetermined *amplitude* level.

Lining up

The process by which a *cameraman* sets up his *camera* to cover the desired field of view. Also the adjustment of the *monitor viewfinder* to correct for *parallax.* Lining up is often called *framing.*

Listening prints

Sound-track prints kept intact in a *sound effects library* to enable users of the library to hear what effects are available.

Live recording

Recording of actual sounds in the physical world, as contrasted with *re-recording.* Also called original recording.

Location

Any place, other than the studio or studio *lot* of a film producing organization, where one of its *units* is shooting pictures.

Logarithm

A logarithm is the exponent of the power to which a number, constant for each system and called the base of the system, must be raised in order to produce the natural number, or antilogarithm. The base of the common logarithm is 10.

Loop

1) A slack section of film designed to provide play when film is being fed from a continuously moving to an *intermittently moving* sprocket, or vice versa.

2) A continuous band of film which passes through a *projector* or film *reproducer* in order to repeat a piece of action or sound over and over again. Loops are used for instructional purposes, as *guide tracks* in *dubbing,* and as convenient vehicles for continuous *sound effects* in *re-recording.*

Lot

The area of land adjacent to a studio which is used for the erection of exterior *sets* and for other exterior shooting.

Lubrication

The treatment of film with *preservative* to reduce excessive dryness and therefore limit *shrinkage.* See also *waxing.*

Lumen (lm)   ASA Z7.1–1942:05.015
The lumen is the unit of luminous flux. It is equal to the flux through a unit solid angle (steradian) from a uniform point source of one candle, or to the flux on a unit surface all points of which are at unit distance from a uniform point source of one candle.

Luminous flux (F)   ASA Z7.1–1942:05.010
Luminous flux is the time rate of flow of light.

M

M. E. track
When several foreign language versions of a film are to be produced, it is often convenient to combine all but the dialogue and/or narrative *sound tracks* into a single *re-recording* track. This is done by mixing together the Music and Effects into a single track known as an M. E. track, which may then be conveniently combined with each of the foreign language tracks in turn by a subsequent re-recording process, with much saving of time and trouble.

MQ developer
A *developing solution* composed principally of *metol* and *hydroquinone*.

Macrocinematography
The filming of objects intermediate in size between those requiring magnification by a microscope and those which can be *focused* by lenses of normal *focal length*.

Magazines, Film
Film containers forming part of *picture cameras, sound cameras,* and *projectors*. Camera magazines are light tight, the film entering and leaving them through *light traps*.

Magnetic head   ASA Z24.1–1949:8.140
In *magnetic recording,* a magnetic head is a *transducer* for converting electric variations into magnetic variations for storage on magnetic media, for reconverting energy so stored into electric energy, or for erasing such stored energy.

Magnetic recorder   ASA Z24.1–1949:8.095
A magnetic recorder is equipment incorporating an electromagnetic *transducer* and means for moving a ferromagnetic recording medium relative to the transducer for recording electric signals as magnetic variations in the medium.

NOTE.—The generic term "magnetic recorder" can also be applied to an instrument which has not only facilities for recording electric *signals* as magnetic variations, but also for converting such magnetic variations back into electric variations.

Magnetic recording
Recording by effecting magnetic variations in a ferromagnetic medium, usually a coated tape or a wire.

Magnetic recording medium   ASA Z24.1–1949:8.100
A magnetic recording medium is a magnetizable material in a magnetic recorder for retaining the magnetic variations imparted during the recording process. It may have the form of a wire, tape, cylinder, disk, etc.
MAGNETIC TAPE: Magnetic tape is a magnetic recording medium having a width

greater than approximately 10 times the thickness. This tape may be homogeneous or coated. ASA Z24.1–1949:8.105

MAGNETIC WIRE: Magnetic wire is a magnetic recording medium, approximately circular in cross-section. ASA Z24.1–1949:8.120

Maltese cross

An intermittent driving mechanism, the essential part of which is a slotted wheel resembling in appearance a Maltese cross. The Maltese cross is a form of Geneva movement, so called from its use by watchmakers in Switzerland. See *intermittent movement* and *claw*.

Margin

The amount of free or wasted light reaching the film in a sound recording system undergoing *modulation;* that is, the light transmitted to the film in excess of that required to carry the modulation at any instant. Margin is required by the limitations of practical *noise reduction* systems.

Married print

A term used in England to denote a *composite print*.

Mask

A form of light *modulator* consisting of a strip of film containing opaque areas designed to exclude or reduce the transmission of light. Masks are commonly used in trick photography and color printing.

Masking

A technique of color printing by means of *masks* designed to reduce color *degradation* by compensating for the imperfect transmission characteristics of the dyes used in *subtractive* color synthesis.

Master positive

A *positive* film with special photographic characteristics making it suitable for acting as a master from which a series of *dupe negatives* can be printed with minimum loss of quality.

PICTURE MASTER POSITIVE: A picture duping print usually made for the purpose of producing a picture dupe negative for release printing. ASA Z22.56–1947:3.2.5.1

SOUND MASTER POSITIVE: A sound print on special film stock, usually made from a sound *release negative* for the purpose of producing sound dupe negatives for release printing. ASA Z22.56–1947:3.3.8

Matrices

In color-film printing by the *imbibition* process, matrices are the films made from *three-color separation negatives,* in which the photographic image is formed in *relief* in tanned (hardened) gelatin.

Matte

A matte is a light *modulator* which consists of an obstruction to the passage of light on its way to form a photographic image. Thus mattes are not essentially different from *masks,* but the former term is applied more often to the camera, the latter to the color printer and the *optical printer*.

MATTE BOX: A box mounted in front of a camera lens and designed to hold camera mattes used in trick photography, as well as *filters*. The matte box is usually combined with a sunshade.

MATTE ROLLS (traveling masks): A pair of film rolls used as light *modulators*. ASA Z22.56–1947:1.15

NOTE.—Matte rolls are complementary in that where one roll is clear, the other is effectively opaque. They are usually matched to rolls of original black and white, or of color reversal positives in the printing of black and white or color duplicates.

Matte screen
A projection *screen* having a reflection characteristic such that the *brightness* is substantially the same at all angles of view. See also *beaded screen* and *metallic screen*.

Matting down
The process of *masking* or blocking out part of the image, as in a *monitor viewfinder*, which must be adjusted to match lenses of different *focal length*.

Mechanographic recording
A type of sound recording in which *modulation* is obtained by mechanically indenting or embossing the film, reproduction then being effected by a stylus; or by gouging out a transparent *sound track* from an opaque coating, the track then being reproduced optically.

Mercer clip
See *patch*.

Metallic screen
A projection *screen* coated with finely divided particles of metal, usually aluminum, which reflect the light more or less *specularly* because they act as so many small mirrors, instead of diffusing it as does the *matte screen*. Metallic screens thus tend to produce unpleasant *hot spots*. They do not *depolarize* the light which falls on them, and are therefore useful for *stereoscopic* projection by polarized light.

Metol: $HOC_6H_4NHCH_3.\frac{1}{2}H_2O$
Methyl para-aminophenol sulphate is prepared by methylation of paraminophenol and conversion of the methylated base by neutralization with sulphuric acid. A rapid, low contrast *developing agent* with a long useful life. Also known as Elon, Pictol, and Photol.
Properties:
  Soluble in water
  Insoluble in alcohol and ether

Microammeter
An instrument for measuring very small electric currents of the order of one microampere, or one-millionth of an *ampere*.

Microcinematography (Cinemicrography)
The filming of objects so small that they require preliminary magnification by a microscope before they can be recorded by a normal camera lens.

Microphone
A device whereby sound waves produce substantially equivalent electric waves. The term telephone transmitter is employed to represent a microphone used in a telephone system.
  CARBON MICROPHONE: A microphone which depends for its operation upon the variation in resistance of carbon contacts.
  CONDENSER MICROPHONE: A microphone which depends for its operation upon variations in electrostatic capacity.
  CRYSTAL MICROPHONE: A microphone which depends for its operation on the gener-

ation of an electromotive force by the deformation of a crystal having piezoelectric properties.

DIRECTIONAL MICROPHONE: A microphone the response of which is designed to vary with the direction of sound incidence.

LAPEL MICROPHONE: A microphone adapted to positioning on the lapel of the wearer's coat.

MOVING-COIL MICROPHONE: A microphone which depends for its operation on the currents which are set up when a coil of wire is moved across the lines of force in a magnetic field.

RIBBON MICROPHONE: A moving-conductor microphone in which the moving conductor is in the form of a ribbon which also serves as the moving acoustic element.

UNIDIRECTIONAL MICROPHONE: A microphone which is essentially responsive to sound incident from one hemisphere only.

VELOCITY MICROPHONE: A microphone which is essentially responsive to the particle velocity resulting from the propagation of a sound wave through an acoustic medium. A velocity microphone is inherently directional.

Microphone shadow

The shadow which may be cast by a *microphone* onto some object in the field of view of the camera. Microphone shadows must be eliminated before shooting can begin by altering the position of the microphone, the camera, or the lights.

Microwave

Electromagnetic (radio) waves of very high frequency corresponding to a range of *wavelengths* of approximately 50 cm. to 1 mm.

Mike boom

See *boom, microphone.*

Mikeman

Familiar term for the operator who controls the physical movement of the microphone(s) in the studio or on *location,* either by means of a *boom* or a *fishpole.*

Mil

One one-thousandth of an inch.

Millimicron (mμ)

One one-millionth of a millimeter, or 10 Angstroms (A).

Mislighting

The incorrect *timing* of a *shot* or a *reel* of film. Often used to describe the result when one *printer light* in a reel is missed, so that all the subsequent lights are thrown out of step.

Mix

See *dissolve.*

Mixer

The senior member of a sound-recording crew, who is in charge of the balance and control of the dialogue, music, or *sound effects* to be recorded.

Mixing

The process of combining a number of separate sound tracks into a single track, the *frequency pass band* and relative *amplitude* of the different sound components being under the accurate control of a *mixer.*

Mixing console
See *console.*

Modification
Any desired alteration in the waveform of a *signal* in its passage through an electrical system. The term *distortion,* though strictly comprising modifications as here defined, is usually reserved for undesired alterations in the signal.

Modulation   ASA C42–1941:65.10.300
1) Modulation is the process whereby the *amplitude* (or other characteristic) of a wave is varied as a function of the instantaneous value of another wave. The first wave, which is usually a single-frequency wave, is called the "carrier wave"; the second wave is called the "modulating wave."

   MODULATION CAPABILITY: The maximum percentage modulation that is possible
   without objectionable distortion.   ASA C42–1941:65.11.080

   ONE HUNDRED PER CENT MODULATION: The maximum signal *amplitude* which a system will transmit without severe distortion. Often undesirable distortion is present, however, and 100 per cent modulation is accordingly avoided except on *transients.*

2) A single *cycle,* or small group of cycles, photographically recorded on a *sound track,* is familiarly referred to as a modulation.

Modulator
1) In optical *sound recording,* a device for converting an electrical *signal* into corresponding *modulations* of a beam of light, which are subsequently impressed photographically on a moving strip of film. See also *galvanometer* and *light valve.*
2) A light modulator is a *masking* or *matting* device or an optical wedge which imposes some predetermined pattern or *modulation* on the light which it transmits.

Monaural reproduction
Complementary to its *planoscopic reproduction,* the motion picture of today renders the world of sound through a single transmission channel and a single point source loudspeaker (save that high and low frequencies are normally made to issue from different units). Though sound location in depth is retained, the sense of lateral localization is lost, and this greatly impairs the reproduction of music and somewhat increases the effort of association of speech and sound effects with an image which can move to and fro across the screen.

Monitor viewfinder
See *viewfinder.*

Monitoring
The process of checking by eye or ear the picture or sound image which is to be recorded on film.

Monomethylparaminophenol
See *metol.*

Monopack
See *integral tripack.* An integral bipack would also be called a monopack.

Monoplane valve
A type of light valve in which the ribbons move in the same plane. See also *biplanar valve.*

Montage

1) See *dynamic cutting*.

2) As used in commercial studios, the term montage means a type of cutting using numerous *dissolves* and *superimpositions* rapidly following one another to produce a generalized visual effect.

Motion, Film

1) The movement of film whereby the visible continuum of the external world is reproduced through a series of discrete images recorded at regular intervals which are not infinitesimal. This movement must be actually or apparently intermittent.

2) The movement of film whereby the audible continuum of the external world is reproduced through a continuous recording. This movement must approximate as closely as possible to absolute steadiness.

See also *intermittent movement, continuous motion*, and *optical compensator*.

Mordant

An inorganic compound into which a silver photographic image is transformed, having the property of causing a dye to come out of solution and precipitate on it, the dye being then said to be mordanted. Silver ferrocyanide is a typical mordant. See also *dye toning*.

Moving coil

A coil of wire suspended in a magnetic field. If the coil is moved across the lines of force in the field, a current is set up in it. This is the principle of the moving-coil *microphone*. If the coil conducts a fluctuating current, it will be made to move to and fro in the magnetic field. This is the principle of the moving-coil (dynamic) loudspeaker.

Moviola

The trade name of a particular kind of portable motor-driven film-viewing machine used in *cutting*. The name is often applied generically to any such machine.

Multicellular horn

A cluster of horns having a common throat and separate mouths which lie in a common surface and are contiguous. The purpose of the cluster is to control the directional pattern of the radiated power.

A multicellular horn is often attached to a loudspeaker designed to radiate the higher audible frequencies.

Multiplane

A device for securing *parallactic* and thus *pseudostereoscopic* effects in *animation* by mounting a series of *cells* one beneath the other in different planes, the whole set being placed beneath the lens of the *animation camera*.

Music library

An index or catalogue of the music *sound tracks* of which a studio may wish to make repeated use; also the music sound tracks themselves.

Mutilator

A device for making a deep scratch along the *emulsion* surface of a film, thus effectively rendering it unusable. See *scratched print*.

N

N.G.

A colloquialism for "No Good." The term may unhappily be applied very widely and often to film processes, and bears witness to the essential wastefulness of the medium.

Naturalism

In aesthetic theory, a belief in a rendering of the external world which tends to exclude artistic interpretation and aims at simple and literal reproduction.

Needle valve

A valve with a small orifice which is often used to supply *replenisher* from the *bleed tank* into the *circulating system* of continuous *developing machines* in a *laboratory*.

Negative   ASA Z22.56–1947:2.1

The term "negative" is used to designate any of the following: (a) the *raw stock* specifically designed for negative images, (b) the negative image, (c) negative raw stock which has been exposed but has not been *processed,* (d) film bearing a negative image which has been processed.

NEGATIVE, ORIGINAL PICTURE: The original picture negative is the negative film which is exposed in the camera and subsequently processed to produce an original negative picture image.   ASA Z22.56–1947:2.2.1

NEGATIVE, ORIGINAL SOUND: The original sound negative is the sound negative which is exposed in a film recorder and after processing produces a negative sound image on the film.   ASA Z22.56–1947:2.3.1

NEGATIVE, PICTURE: A picture negative is any negative film which, after exposure to a subject or positive image and subsequent *processing,* produces a negative picture image on the film.   ASA Z22.56–1947:2.2

NEGATIVE, SOUND: A sound negative is any negative film which, after exposure to a positive sound image and subsequent processing, produces a negative sound track on the film.   ASA Z22.56–1947:2.3

NEGATIVE CUTTING (matching): The cutting of the original negative of a film to match the edited positive, *shot* by shot and *frame* by frame. The term is usually extended to include the preparation of the *sound release negative* as well as the *picture release negative.* The term is also applied to the process of searching out and sorting the negative. The large footage to be catalogued, the necessity for exact correspondence of frame with frame, and the irreplaceability of the negative, impose very exacting conditions on negative cutters.

NEGATIVE IMAGE: A negative image is a photographic image in which the values of light and shade of the original photographed subject are represented in inverse order.   ASA Z22.56–1947:1.4.4

A negative color image is usually understood to mean an image in *complementary* colors, from which an image in the original colors can be printed.

NEGATIVE NUMBERS: Same as *edge numbers,* but the term *negative number* is more commonly used by manufacturers of *raw stock.*

NEGATIVE PERFORATIONS, 35 MM.: A 35 mm. negative perforation is the perforation used for negative and some special-purpose 35 mm. films.

ASA Z22.56–1947:1.1.3.1

NOTE.—It is a perforation with sharp corners, curved sides and a straight top and bottom, and its dimensions are as shown in American Standard for Cutting and Perforating Negative Raw Stock, Z22.34 (under revision).

Cameras, optical printers, projectors designed for *process projection,* and certain other specialized 35 mm. equipment intended to provide great accuracy of *registration,* have been designed for negative perforated film.

NEGATIVE-POSITIVE PROCESS: Generic term for the normal process of 35 mm. black-and-white image reproduction (which also covers a much less common form of color reproduction) whereby *positive images* are printed from *negatives,* and vice versa. In other words, any film image generates unlikes, whereas in the *reversal process* it generates likes.

Night filter

An *optical filter* which attenuates those parts of the *spectrum* which are predominant constituents of daylight—i.e. the blue from the sky and the green reflected from trees and grass. Night filters are consequently red, and are used to produce night effects by day on *black-and-white* film. They require a large *filter factor* to compensate for the amount of light they absorb. Night filters are a type of *effects filter.*

Nitrate base

Since George Eastman first manufactured 35 mm. *raw stock* for Edison in 1891, the standard gauge of film has been supplied on nitrate *base,* except for special purposes. Cellulose nitrate is, however, a rapidly burning substance which under different conditions will ignite spontaneously, explode, or give off large volumes of toxic fumes. Today, sixty years after its introduction, and with millions of feet still in existence, nitrate base finds itself superseded by a new tri-acetate base having excellent wearing qualities and improved shrinkage characteristics.

Nodes

The points, lines, or surfaces in a *stationary wave* system which have a zero *amplitude,* pressure, or velocity.

Noise ASA C42–1941:65.11.200

1) Noise is any extraneous sound tending to interfere with the proper and easy perception of those sounds which it is desired to receive.

2) Noise is any undesired sound. ASA Z24.1–1942:1.42

GROUND NOISE (background noise): Residual system noise predominantly caused by film *grain* in reproduced sound records. May also include *amplifier* noises such as tube noise or noises generated in resistive elements in the input of the reproducer amplifier system.

NOISE LEVEL: The value of noise integrated over the frequency range of interest, expressed in *decibels* vs. a given reference level.

NOISE REDUCTION: A process whereby the average *transmission* of the print *sound track* (averaged across the track) is decreased for *signals* of low level and increased for signals of high level. The background noise introduced by the film emulsion being less at low transmission, this process reduces film noise during soft passages. It is normally accomplished automatically through *rectification* of the signal and application of the *envelope* to the *light valve* or shutters operating in the light beam.

NOISE-REDUCTION ANTICIPATION: A noise-reduction system in which the signal is transmitted so as to reach and actuate the noise-reduction elements before it reaches the *modulator.* In this way these elements "know in advance" how much they will be required to open to admit a signal of rapidly increased *amplitude,* without *clipping.*

Nonlinear

Any transmission system, or component of such a system, which imposes on the transmitted *signal* a *distortion* of *wave form* is described as nonlinear when the distortion results from the curvature of a characteristic curve (e.g. the *D log E curve*) which carries the modulation of the signal. The term nonlinear is also used more generally to denote a system in which some scalar quantity in the input is internally expanded or compressed, and is not merely magnified or attenuated as a whole as in a normal *amplifier or attenuator*. See also *volume compressor*.

Nonlinear distortion ASA C42–1941:65.11.440

Nonlinear distortion is that form of distortion which occurs when the ratio of voltage to current, using root-mean-square values (or analogous quantities in other fields), is a function of the magnitude of either. [See also *distortion*.]

Nontheatrical

A term applied to the showing of films outside commercial movie theaters.

Notch

A shallow depression cut in the edge of a piece of film, usually with a hand punch, for releasing a *printer diaphragm* to a predetermined position, or actuating a warning buzzer so that the operator can move the diaphragm-setting control. The correct *printer light* is thus brought into play to effect a desired change in *timing*.

Numbering machine

A machine for printing *edge numbers* at regular intervals on *raw stock*. The term is sometimes used when *coding machine* is meant.

O

Object brightness scale

A scale of point *brightnesses,* abstracted from a photographed scene, which ranges from the brightest to the least bright point or small area in the scene. See also *exposure scale*.

Ohm's Law ASA C42–1941:05.40.025

Ohm's Law states that the current in an electric circuit is directly proportional to the electromotive force in the circuit.

Ohm's Law does not apply to all circuits. It is applicable to all metallic circuits and to many circuits containing an electrolytic resistance.

Ohm's Law was first enunciated for a circuit in which there is a constant electromotive force and an unvarying current. It is applicable to varying currents if account is taken of the induced electromotive force resulting from the self inductance of the circuit and of the distribution of current in the cross-section of the circuit.

[If the voltage is represented by E, the current by I, and the resistance in the circuit by R, Ohm's Law states that $E = IR$.]

One-light dupe negative

A *dupe negative* in which the *timing* has been so perfectly corrected that prints can be made from the negative without change of *printer light* from beginning to end.

Opacimeter

An instrument consisting essentially of a controlled light source, sample and filter compartments, and a *photocell* unit with which changes in light *transmission* due to chemical reactions may be quantitatively measured. Opacimetric analysis is often used to determine the condition of *developing solutions.*

Opacity
The opacity of the photographic-silver deposit is defined as the ratio of the incident to the emergent light. See also *density.*

Optical compensator
A commonly used *continuous motion* device, in which a rotating slab of glass displaces the image in the same direction and at the same speed as the film motion, so that over a short distance there is no relative movement between the two. In many high-speed cameras, a glass polygon with parallel faces replaces the two-sided slab of glass.

Optical dupe
A *dupe negative* printed in an *optical printer,* usually containing *optical effects.*

Optical effects
Modifications of the photographic image as filmed in a motion picture camera of the normal type, produced in an *optical printer.* See also *fade, dissolve, wipe,* and *superimposition.*

Optical lever
A weightless lever for magnifying very small movements, consisting of a beam of light reflected from a mirror or a delicately suspended *galvanometer* coil.

Optical positive
A *master positive* having special characteristics adapted to printing from it in an *optical printer.* It is sometimes printed with a lower than normal *gamma* to compensate for the higher than unity gamma introduced by optical printing (see *Callier quotient*).

Optical sound recorder (Photographic sound recorder) ASA Z24.1:8.230
An optical sound recorder is equipment incorporating means for producing a modulated light beam and means for moving a light-sensitive medium relative to the beam for recording *signals* derived from sound signals.

Optical sound reproducer ASA Z24.1–1949:8.315
An optical sound reproducer is a combination of light source, optical system, photoelectric cell, and a mechanism for moving a medium carrying an optical sound record (usually film), by means of which the recorded variations may be converted into electric signals of approximately like form. [See figure 10-2.]

Original
A generic film term applied either to a filmed scene (whether visible or audible or both), or to the first recording of that scene. Since film processes are marked by sequential *modification* or *degradation* of a scene, the concept of an original is of great importance in setting up standards of comparison.

Orthochromatic
Applied to *emulsions,* orthochromatic means a type of emulsion sensitive to blue and green, but not to red. Applied to photographic reproduction, orthochromatic means the true reproduction of colors in *black and white.*

Orthoscopic
When a *stereoscopic* image is viewed correctly, i.e., when the left eye sees the left-

eye image and the right eye the right-eye image, the resulting mental image is said to be orthoscopic. When the constituent images are reversed, the resulting mental impression is said to be *pseudoscopic*.

Orthostereoscopy

When the image viewed in a system of *stereoscopy* is in all geometrical respects identical with the original object or drawing photographed, it is said to be orthostereoscopic. The conditions for orthostereoscopy are often extremely complex, but it is essential to realize them in many scientific applications of stereoscopy.

Oscillating quantity ASA C42–1941:05.05.165

An oscillating quantity is a quantity which, as a function of some independent variable (such as time), alternately increases and decreases in value, always remaining within finite limits. [Example omitted.]

Oscillogram

The trace or recording made by an *oscillograph*.

Oscillograph ASA C42–1941:30.40.065

An oscillograph is an apparatus for producing a continuous curve representing the instantaneous values of a rapidly varying electrical quantity as a function of time or of another electrical quantity.

Outline

An early *treatment* of the idea of a film, in which the film maker's intended approach to his subject is roughly sketched.

Out of phase

Two *periodic quantities* are said to be out of phase when their *phases,* measured from the same origin, differ.

Outs

Rejected shots (or *takes* of a single shot) which do not find a place in the completed version of a film.

Overlap

In dialogue cutting, the extension of a dialogue *sound track* over a shot to which it does not belong, usually a *reaction shot* of the person being addressed on the overlapping sound track. Also, the use of multiple-dialogue tracks which are overlapped to avoid cutting close to modulations.

Overload level

The level at which *distortion* becomes noticeable.

Overloading

The impression on a transmission system of a *signal* of greater *amplitude* than it is designed to carry, resulting as a rule in more or less severe *amplitude distortion,* often accompanied by other kinds of distortion.

Overtone ASA Z24.1–1942:1.12

An overtone is a *partial* having a *frequency* higher than that of the basic frequency.

P

pH

pH is the measure of the acidity or alkalinity of a solution, and is defined as being the logarithm of the number of units which contain one gram of hydrogen ion. Since pH is a logarithmic function, it can be seen that a change of 1.0 pH units means a change of relative concentration of 10 times, while a change of 2.0 units means a change of 100 times. pH units are so designed that 7.0 units represents the neutral point, so that pure water will have a pH value of 7.0. pH values below 7.0 represent increasing acidity as they grow smaller, while pH values above 7.0 represent increasing alkalinity as they become larger.

pH meter

An instrument for measuring the *pH* value of a solution, usually consisting of a hydrogen electrode, and another electrode immersed in the solution under test, the two being connected by a salt bridge, which is a glass tube filled with a conducting liquid. The voltage of the battery thus formed is very accurately measured by a null method using a *galvanometer,* and the pH of the solution is then read off.

Panchromatic

A type of light-sensitive *emulsion,* recording in *black and white,* which is almost equally responsive to all colors of the *visible spectrum.* Other common types of emulsion are *orthochromatic* and *colorblind.*

Pan; Panning

Movement of the camera in a horizontal plane. Sometimes the term is used generally to describe movements of the camera in any plane.

Papering

Marking up a *negative* or *master positive* for *duping* or *printing* selected sections, by means of small pieces of paper folded over the film, or by *patches.* See also *cording off.*

Parallax

The apparent displacement of an observed object, due to a real displacement of the observer, so that the direction of the object in relation to the observer is changed. The effect of parallax may be most easily seen by looking past a near object at a far object with the left and right eye alternately, the other eye being closed.

Parallax panoramagram

A more advanced type of *parallax stereogram* in which the interlaced strip images are themselves composed of even narrower strips forming a panorama of the subject. Thus, when the viewer moves sideways across the subject, he sees it "in the round," i.e., from different viewpoints.

Parallax stereogram

A type of *stereogram* consisting of interlaced strips of the stereoscopic pair of pictures, which is viewed through a grid (called a raster) in such a way that the observer's left eye sees and sums together only the strips belonging to the left-hand picture, the right-eye strips being blocked by the slats of the grid. Similarly, the right eye sees only the right-eye picture. Thus the conditions of *stereoscopic reproduction* are met. The raster may be replaced by a suitable *lenticular screen,* with a great saving of light otherwise lost in the system.

Parallel

A fixed platform which can be set up in the studio or on location to raise the camera and crew above the ground for high shots.

Parallel synchronism

See *editorial synchronism.*

Partial ASA Z24.1–1942:1.11

A partial is a component of a complex tone. Its *frequency* may be either higher or lower than that of the basic frequency and may or may not bear an integral relation to the basic frequency.

Pass band

A pass band is a *frequency* band of free transmission; that is, a band in which the attenuation approximates to zero.

Patch

1) A small piece of cardboard, celluloid or metal with projecting teeth on either side which engage in the *perforations* of two pieces of film to be assembled, thus temporarily joining them together. Sometimes called a Mercer clip, after the inventor.

2) A film overlay cemented to two abutting pieces of film to join them together. The purpose of a patch is usually to repair a damaged negative, or to *splice* two lengths of negative without losing *frames*.

Perforations, Film ASA Z22.56–1947:1.1.3

Film perforations are the regularly and accurately spaced holes that are punched throughout the length of motion picture film. These holes are engaged by the teeth of various *sprockets* and pins by which the film is propelled and positioned as it travels through cameras, processing machines, projectors and other film machinery. [See also *negative, positive,* and *16 mm. perforations.*]

Period (Primitive Period) ASA C42–1941:05.05.175

The period of a *periodic quantity* is the smallest value of the increment of the independent variable which separates recurring values of the quantity. [Mathematical section of definition omitted.]

Periodic quantity ASA C42–1941:05.05.170

A periodic quantity is an *oscillating quantity* the values of which recur for equal increments of the independent variable. If a periodic quantity, y, is a function of x, then y has the property that $y = f(x) = f(x + k)$, where k, a constant, is a *period* of y. The smallest positive value of k is the primitive period of y, generally called simply the period of y. [Mathematical section of definition omitted.]

Persistence of vision

A phenomenon which causes an image on the retina to be mentally retained for a short period, so that if a second similar image takes its place within a period of about one-sixteenth of a second, no visible discontinuity or *flicker* will be noticed.

Phase ASA C42–1941:05.05.280

The phase of a *periodic quantity,* for a particular value of the independent variable, is the fractional part of a period through which the independent variable has advanced measured from an arbitrary origin. In the case of a *simple sinusoidal quantity,* the origin is usually taken as the last previous passage through zero from the negative to positive direction. The origin is generally so chosen that the fraction is less than unity.

Photochemical reaction

A complex of reactions caused by exposure of substances to light. Among these reactions are: synthesis, decomposition, oxidation-reduction, hydrolysis, and polymerization. The exact mechanism by which the *latent* photographic image is produced is still a matter of uncertainty.

Photoelectric phenomena

The phenomena through which electric voltage and current can be generated or controlled by the incidence of radiation on a light-sensitive surface. The three types of photoelectric phenomena are:

PHOTOCONDUCTIVE EFFECT: The change of resistance of semiconductors by the action of incident radiation.

PHOTOEMISSIVE EFFECT: The emission of electrons from metallic surfaces as the result of incident radiation.

PHOTOVOLTAIC EFFECT: The production of a potential difference across the boundary between two substances that are in close contact, by illumination of the boundary.

The three types of practical device which make use of these phenomena are respectively:

PHOTOCONDUCTIVE CELL: A nonevacuated cell containing a single element, usually of selenium, the resistance of which varies according to the intensity of the incident illumination. Since the photoconductive cell has a poor frequency response, but requires an outside voltage to operate it, it has little application in motion pictures.

PHOTOTUBE (photoelectric cell; photocell): A vacuum tube (into some types of which a small quantity of inert gas has been introduced), which contains two electrodes: a photoemissive *cathode* and an *anode* to which a positive potential is applied in order to draw off the photoemitted electrons in the form of a current. Because of their excellent *frequency response* over the *audible spectrum,* phototubes are well adapted to the optical reproduction of modulated *sound tracks.*

PHOTOVOLTAIC CELL (barrier-layer cell): A nonevacuated cell consisting as a rule of a thin layer of cuprous oxide or iron selenide deposited on a plate of copper, gold, platinum, or iron, the junction being illuminated by light passing through the thin layer. Though the photovoltaic cell has a poor frequency response, it can generate current without the application of external voltage, and is therefore well adapted to use in compact photoelectric instruments such as *exposure meters.*

Photoflood

Trade name for a type of light bulb in which the *color temperature* and light output are raised to an abnormally high figure by the application of excess voltage, thus also shortening the life of the lamp.

Photographic recorder

See *optical sound recorder.*

Photol

See *metol.*

Picture (Picture image)

The visual image or likeness of an object recorded photographically on film.

PICTURE DUPING PRINT: A picture print made on a special film for the purpose of producing a *duplicate negative,* or for producing *dissolves, montages, titles,* etc.

ASA Z22.56–1947:3.2.5

NOTE.—Duping print is synonymous with master positive except that duping print is the term used in the *editorial process,* while master positive is used in *release.*

PICTURE HEAD: A term sometimes used in contrast to *sound head* to denote the intermittent device through which picture track is run in order to project the picture image in motion. The term is also applied to the printing head of a *printer*.

PICTURE PRINT: A picture print is any *positive* printed from a picture *negative*.

ASA Z22.56–1947:3.2

PICTURE RELEASE NEGATIVE: A *release negative* used for printing the picture portion of *release prints*. ASA Z22.56–1947:2.2.6

NOTE.—It may consist of intercut original picture negatives, picture dupe negatives, etc., depending upon the choice of available material or the intended use of the release print.

Pilot pins

Stationary positioning pins set close to a camera, printer or projector *aperture* to engage accurately with film *perforations* and thus provide precise *registration* of the film at the aperture.

Pilot print

Owing to the high cost of color printing, the *dailies* for pictures shot in color are often supplied in black-and-white, but they are accompanied by short strips, a foot or two in length, printed in color from the end of each shot. These strips are called pilot prints or pilots.

Pincushion distortion

Distortion in a *lens* characterized by concave curvature of the lines of a rectangular grid image; caused by magnification which is less at the center than at the edges of the field. See also *barrel distortion*.

Pitch (Acoustic) ASA Z24.1–1942:3.1

1) Pitch is that subjective quality of a sound which determines its position in a musical scale. Pitch may be measured as the frequency of that pure tone having a specified sound pressure, or specified loudness level, which seems to the average normal ear to occupy the same position in a musical scale. The unit is the cycle per second.

2) Pitch is a sensory characteristic arising out of *frequency*, which may assign to a tone a position in a musical scale. [Note omitted.] ASA Z24.1–1942:6.2

Pitch (Film)

The perforation pitch of film is the longitudinal distance between corresponding points on adjacent *perforations*.

Planoscopic reproduction

A visual transmission system employing a single camera and projector (or print), by which the representational advantages of *binocular vision* are lost, though compensating artistic advantages may be gained. Depth in space may still be imaged by *pseudostereoscopic* means.

Plasticizers

Substances added to photographic film *base* to keep it supple and retard its decomposition.

Plate

The print which is used in *process projection* is called a plate. It must be shot in a camera having an *intermittent movement* of the utmost steadiness, employing *pilot pins*, and must be projected in an equally steady projector, also fitted with pilot pins. Processing conditions must be established with the greatest accuracy, since the plate is one stage farther away from reality than the actors who move before it, when the two are combined onto a single film. Sometimes two or even three plates are printed and projected in a triple projector when the utmost magnification must be combined with perfect freedom from *graininess*. Also called process plate.

Playback

1) An expression used to denote immediate reproduction of a recording. The term "instantaneous" is sometimes applied to playback, so that there shall be no doubt of the immediacy of reproduction.

2) A method of filming singing and other types of musical action in which the music is recorded first (called *prescoring*) and afterwards played back through loudspeakers on the sound stage, thus enabling the singers or dancers to perform to the music while being filmed with an unsilenced camera under imperfect acoustic conditions. This *action* is afterwards synchronized with the original recording made under substantially perfect acoustic conditions.

Point exposure

The *exposure* on a photographic *emulsion* corresponding to a point or very small area in the subject.

Polarization

A normal beam of light may be supposed to consist of electromagnetic vibrations occurring in all possible planes at right angles to the axis of the beam. Certain crystalline materials, some of them natural (e.g., tourmaline, calcite), others synthetic (e.g., Polaroid), have the property of stripping the light beam of all vibrations save those in a single plane. The beam is then said to be plane polarized, or simply polarized, and the crystalline materials are called *polarizers*.

Polarizer

A substance which is able to effect the *polarization* of a light beam or ray. Since polarizers act as light gates, transmitting light which has been polarized in the appropriate plane, but blocking light polarized at 90 degrees to this plane, they are of great service in separating two images projected on the same screen, as in *stereoscopy*. It is essential that this screen retain the polarization of the light falling on it, and not act as a *depolarizer*.

Positive (Print)   ASA Z22.56–1947:3.1

The term "positive" or "print" is used to designate any of the following: (a) the *raw stock* specifically designed for positive images, (b) the positive image, (c) positive raw stock which has been exposed but has not been *processed*, (d) film bearing a positive image which has been processed.

    POSITIVE IMAGE: A photographic replica in which the values of light and shade of the original photographed subject are represented in their natural order.

ASA Z22.56–1947:1.4.5

    NOTE.—In a positive image, the light objects of the original subject are represented by low *densities* and the dark objects are represented by high densities.

    POSITIVE PERFORATION, 35 MM.: A 35 mm. positive *perforation* is the perforation used for positive 35 mm. film.

    NOTE.—This perforation is rectangular in shape with fillets in the corners, and its dimensions are as shown in American Standard, Cutting and Perforating Dimensions for 35 mm. Motion Picture Positive Raw Stock, Z22.36–1947 or latest revision thereof.

See also *master positive*.

Postsynchronization

The addition of speech or *sound effects* to synchronize with picture images which have already been shot. See also *dubbing (1)*.

Potentiometer

A variable resistor (usually of the constant impedance type) used for altering the *signal* level in a *control unit,* console or similar device. Familiarly known as a "pot."

Pre- and post-equalization

In sound recording, a system of complementary filtering at the recording and reproducing stage respectively which serves to improve the over-all *signal-to-noise* ratio and reduce *breathing* and other audibly unpleasant consequences of *noise reduction.*

Prescoring

Recording of music or other sound prior to the shooting of the picture which is to accompany it, and in predetermined *synchronism.* This technique is almost always used in the making of *animation* pictures.

Preservative

Any kind of waxy substance which, when applied to the surface of film, tends to lengthen its life by protecting it from scratching, or by helping it to retain its plasticizer so as to prevent it from becoming dry and brittle. Also called lacquer.

Pressure plate

In a *camera, projector,* or *optical printer,* a plate which presses on the back of the film in order to keep the *emulsion* surface in the *focal plane* of the lens.

Primary colors

Red, green, and blue are called primary colors because their *additive* mixture will reproduce almost all *saturated* colors.

Print

See *positive.*

Printer

A device for carrying out the process of *printing.* Film printers can be classified according to one or more of the following types:

CONTACT PRINTER: A device for *contact printing.*

CONTINUOUS PRINTER: A printer in which the printing and printed (i.e. modulating and modulated) strips of film are moved continuously along.

OPTICAL PRINTER: A printer in which the printing image is transferred to the film to be printed via an optical system. Optical printers are used in the production of *optical effects* because they allow modification of the original image.

STEP PRINTER: A printer in which the modulating and modulated strips of film are moved intermittently *frame* by frame as in a camera or projector.

Printer light

A light setting (determining either the length or the intensity of the *exposure*) on a *printer.* Usually, twenty-one printer lights are provided, the higher numbers corresponding to the higher light intensities.

Printing   ASA Z22.56–1947:1.8

Printing is the process of exposing *raw stock* by using the image of another film as the *light modulator.*

NOTE.—Through printing, one may produce a *positive* print from a *negative* film; a negative film from a positive film; or, if the *reversal process* is employed, printing may be used to produce positives from positives or negatives from negatives. When the verb "to print" is used, any of the above processes may be implied.

CONTACT PRINTING: That method of printing in which the raw stock is held in intimate contact with the film bearing the image to be copied.

ASA Z22.56–1947:1.8.1

PROJECTION PRINTING (optical printing): Printing by projecting the image to be copied on the raw stock.   ASA Z22.56–1947:1.8.2

NOTE.—When projection printing, the image being copied may be enlarged, reduced, or made the same size.

Process projection

A composite studio technique whereby the actors, sets, and props in front of the camera are combined with a background which consists of a translucent screen on which a picture (moving or still) is projected from behind. Also called back projection, background projection, and transparency process.

Processing

The group of operations comprising the *developing, fixing, hardening, washing* and drying of black-and-white film, together with the reëxposing, *bleaching,* and redeveloping of color film, with any other processes required to produce a *negative* or *positive* with a satisfactory visible image from a strip of film carrying a corresponding *latent image.*

Processing equipment

The equipment required for *processing.* Includes continuous *developing machines,* a *circulating system,* and subsidiary apparatus for the control of temperature, humidity, *pH,* etc.

Producer

The person who carries ultimate responsibility for the original shaping and final outcome of a film.

Production   ASA Z22.56–1947:1.10

Production is the general term used to describe the processes involved in making all the original material that is the basis for the finished motion picture.

Production unit

A self-contained group consisting of *director,* camera crew, sound crew, electricians, etc. which works on a sound *stage* or on *location* to shoot an assigned picture or section of a picture.

Projector

A device by which films are viewed. The term is usually confined to film-viewing devices which throw an image on a large *screen.* Projectors are classified as sound or silent according as they are able or unable to project a *sound image* accompanying the picture image.

Props

Properties. The term has the same meaning in film production and theater production.

Protection print

A *print* (sometimes in *master positive* form) which is made from an original negative or positive and kept in storage so that, in the event of loss or damage to the original, it may be used for the production of further release prints.

Pseudoscopic

In a system of *stereoscopy,* the transposition of the left- and right-hand components of a *stereogram* will lead to an inversion of the normal depth perceptions, which is described as pseudoscopic. This often sets up extremely complicated physiological and mental reactions, the nature of which is still not fully understood; for the pseudoscopic appearance of an object conflicts with the *pseudostereoscopic* indications, which may be equally strong or even stronger.

Pseudostereoscopic

If the world be viewed with one eye, it loses all *stereoscopic* sense of depth, but a surprisingly strong impression of depth none the less remains. Many factors contribute to this. Chiaroscuro, or the play of light and shade, perspective, color, parallactic displacement when the eye or the object moves—all these form a mental synthesis of depth which compensates for the loss of *binocular vision.* It is for this reason that the movies of today, *planoscopic* as they are, provide an acceptable illusion of reality and do not pass before the eyes as a mere set of fleeting and bodiless shadows.

Pull-down mechanism

A device for advancing a strip of film in a camera, projector, or printer one *frame* at a time. See also *intermittent movement.*

Punch, Film

A device for punching holes in film. These holes may be used for cueing the picture, or for making identifying marks in sound track recording, or for *blooping* negative sound tracks, or for making a plop or *bloop* in a positive track.

Push-over wipe

A type of *wipe* in which the first image moves horizontally across the screen, as if propelled by the second image which immediately follows it, much as in a lantern slide projector when slides are being changed.

Push-pull channel

A *sound track* divided into two equal parts, the two halves being exposed to light modulated oppositely (180 degrees *out of phase*). The sound track may be either *variable area* or *variable density.*

Push-pull channels may be either Class A, Class B, or Class A-B (see *sound track*). Push-pull sound tracks require modification of the *film reproducer* for proper reproduction.

<h1 style="text-align:center">Q</h1>

Q factor

See *Callier quotient.*

<h1 style="text-align:center">R</h1>

Rack-and-tank development

A noncontinuous system of film *development* in which the film is wound on racks and immersed in tanks containing solutions. Rack-and-tank development is an obsolete process for the development of motion picture film, except under emergency conditions in the field.

Raw stock   ASA Z22.56–1947:1.1.1

Raw stock is *film* which has not been exposed or processed.

Reader, Sound
See *viewer*.

Realism
In aesthetic theory, an attempt to render the naturalistic elements in the external world with a freer play of interpretation than is allowed in strict *naturalism*.

Reciprocity law
This law states that the *photochemical effect* (or conversion to metallic silver) produced by a photographic *exposure* is proportional to the product of time and intensity of *illumination*—i.e. time is reciprocal to illumination and vice versa. Photographic emulsions show slight deviations from the reciprocity law when exposure is very long (e.g. in astronomical photography) or very short (e.g. in the *light valve*). Only the latter deviation is important in film technology. See also *gamma*.

Reconditioning
Treatment of *negatives* and *prints* with the object of removing oil, *scratches,* and *abrasions* from their surface. While the exact methods are trade secrets, they are based on wax applications, and sometimes localized heating of the emulsion to cause it to close over the scratch.

Recording
The act of producing a copy of a visible or audible event in the external world.

Recording, Live
A *recording* of an original sound, as distinguished from *re-recording*. Also called an original recording.

Recording system
A combination of *microphones, mixer, amplifiers,* and a film recorder, which is often used for recording sound with a picture.

Recordist
The actual operator of the *sound camera*. He is in charge of changing and reloading *magazines,* switching the sound camera on and off, etc. Sometimes, however, the term is used in the sense of *mixer*.

Rectification   ASA C42–1941:60.41.005
Rectification is the conversion of *alternating* current into *unidirectional current* by means of electric valves.

Reduction
Essentially a transfer of electrons resulting in a change of valence of a chemical compound. This reaction is always accompanied by oxidation as the reaction seeks to establish electrochemical equilibrium. *Development* is an example of a reduction process.

Reel (of film)
The standard unit of film measurement: the amount of film which will project for ten minutes (i.e. 900 feet of 35 mm. film and 360 feet of 16 mm. sound film). Standard *reels* are designed to hold these lengths of film, but will accommodate up to 1,000 feet of 35 mm. film and 400 feet of 16 mm. film.

Reels
Metal spools, carrying a small positioning notch and spoked flanges or side pieces, on which film is wound: 35 mm. reels are commonly of 1,000 and 2,000 feet capacity; 16 mm. reels are of 50, 100, 200, 400, 800, 1,200, 1,600, and 2,000 feet capacity. Accord-

ing to American practice, *positive* film is at all times kept wound on reels after it has left the *laboratory*. According to European practice, positive film is often wound in rolls, without external support.

Reflectance
See *reflection factor*.

Reflected-light exposure meter
See *exposure meter*.

Reflection factor; Reflectance ASA Z7.1–1942:30.100
The reflection factor of a body is the ratio of the light reflected by the body to the incident light.

Reflector
A reflecting surface, frequently silver in color, which is used to reflect light where it is needed. For *exteriors,* reflectors are often used to direct sunlight onto the actors or some other part of the scene. For *interior* lighting, reflectors are incorporated in lamps to reflect light coming from the back of the bulb.

> HARD REFLECTOR: A reflector coated with silver and aluminum foil and having a *specular* or mirrorlike reflection characteristic. In bright sunlight it produces a brilliant and intense light which may cause *hot spots*.
>
> SOFT REFLECTOR: A reflector coated with a silver or gold surface which is softer in color than that of the hard reflector and pebbled to diffuse the reflected light.

Register pins
Same as *pilot pins*.

Registration
The precise positioning of an object, usually a strip of film (or superimposed strips of film) in a camera, projector, or printer *aperture,* or else a cell on a drawing board or under an *animation camera*. Since both film and cell depend for their effect on the exact repetition of positions, registration is of first importance in motion picture photography.

Release ASA Z22.56–1947:1.13
Release is a generic term used to designate films used for or intended for general distribution or exhibition.

> NOTE.—Unless specifically stated, release refers only to the normal or domestic release of 35 mm. motion picture production through agencies within the United States [or other country of origin].

> FOREIGN RELEASE: A foreign release is any release made to agencies outside the United States [or other country of origin].
>
> RELEASE NEGATIVE: A release negative is a complete negative prepared specifically for printing release prints. ASA Z22.56–1947:1.13.3

> NOTE.—A release negative may consist of separate picture and sound negatives and may be in either *projection* or *editorial synchronism,* depending upon the film processing technique to be employed in making release prints.

> RELEASE PRINT: A *composite print* made for general distribution and exhibition after the final trial composite or sample print has been approved. It is in projection synchronism. ASA Z22.56–1947:3.4.6
>
> SIXTEEN MM. RELEASE: A 16 mm. release designates any or all the releases made on 16 mm. film. ASA Z22.56–1947:1.13.1

Release time

In a *noise reduction* circuit, the time required by the noise-reduction elements to return from their maximum light-transmitting position to the position they occupy when the sound track is *unmodulated.*

Relief process

A photographic process in which the gelatin *emulsion* is *tanned* or hardened proportionately to the depth of the developed positive silver image, so that when the unhardened gelatin is washed off, a tanned-gelatin relief image is left. This may be used as a *matrix* to absorb or imbibe dyes, which are then transferred to a *blank.* This process may be repeated for two other matrices derived from the remaining *separation negatives,* and a *three-color imbibition* print is the result.

Replenisher

The *developing solution* used for *replenishment;* its composition is usually somewhat different from that of the original developer, and is determined experimentally by analysis and *sensitometry* as that which will give the most constant and reliable development.

Replenishment

The supplying of fresh *developer* to a developing machine to replace that used up in developing film or carried away to waste. An automatic overflow device keeps the total quantity of developing solution constant.

BATCH REPLENISHMENT: A system of replenishment in which the replenisher is dumped at intervals into the system. Common in small labs.

CONTINUOUS REPLENISHMENT: A system of replenishment in which the replenisher is fed continuously into the *circulating system* through a *bleed tank.* Universal in large labs.

Report sheet

A data sheet filled out by *assistant cameramen, recordists,* etc., listing the *scenes* and *takes* which have been shot, and adding such technical information as may be necessary for a *laboratory, cutting* department, or any other agency which is handling the film.

Reprints

Reprints are replacement sections used to make good damaged *workprints* or *release prints.* Reprints may be sound, picture, or *composite.*

Reproduction

The reproduction of the world of colors in the convention of black and white is usually accompanied by an effort to record the tones in their proper relation to one another. This is one kind of normal reproduction.

CONTRASTY REPRODUCTION: Pictorial reproduction which departs from normal reproduction in such a way that the *contrast* of the observed image is excessive and objectionable.

FLAT REPRODUCTION: Pictorial reproduction which departs from normal reproduction in such a way that the contrast of the observed image is insufficient and objectionable.

NORMAL REPRODUCTION: In film technology, normal reproduction is a reproduction of visible and audible elements in the external world, either with greatest possible fidelity to the original, or with such modifications to the original as are necessary—owing to imperfections in the reproductive process—to produce an illusion of fidelity.

See also *gamma* and *sensitometry*.

Re-recorder
See *dubber*.

Re-recording ASA Z22.56–1947:1.12
Re-recording is the electrical process of transferring sound records from one or more films or discs to other films or discs.

NOTE.—Re-recording may be used to combine different sound records into a single record; to adjust the *response-frequency* characteristic; or to adjust the relative levels between different *scenes* and *sequences*.

RE-RECORDED NEGATIVE: A sound negative which is exposed by re-recording and
    when processed produces a negative sound-track image. ASA Z22.56–1947:2.3.5
RE-RECORDED PRINT: A sound print from a re-recorded sound track negative.
    ASA Z22.56–1947:3.3.6
RE-RECORDING PRINT: A sound print prepared specifically for use in re-recording to
    produce a re-recorded negative. ASA Z22.56–1947:3.3.5

NOTE.—It may be a print from a sound cut negative, a specially intercut print, or a combination of both. A re-recording print may consist of several sound records on separate films including dialogue, sound effects, music or any other required material. The term is used interchangeably to designate the entire group of associated films or any individual film which is part of the group.

Réseau
If the screen in a *screen-plate process* is of regular geometrical pattern, it is called a réseau (French for grid or network). The Dufaycolor system uses a réseau.

Reserve tank
A tank forming part of the *circulating system* of one or more *continuous developing machines,* which maintains a constant flow into the *bleed tank*.

Resolution; Resolving Power
The ability of a *lens* or *emulsion* to render fine detail in a photographic image. Resolving power is most conveniently measured by photographing a series of narrow parallel black lines separated by interspaces equal to their width. The resolving power of lens or emulsion is then expressed as the maximum number of lines per millimeter which can just be distinctly separated. Resolving power is not an absolute measurement, but varies with the contrast of the lines, the composition of the developer and the time of development, and is dependent on the resolving power of previous stages through which the photographic image has passed.

Response curve
A curve connecting any two characteristic factors in a transmission system, or in some part of such a system. Often the response of the output of the system or component part to a change in its input is measured in the standard *decibel* unit of power, which may be converted into voltage at a stated or assumed impedance. The other variable may then be *frequency* (e.g. in an *amplifier*), or angle of incidence of sound (e.g. in a *microphone*). See also *frequency-response characteristic*.

Response-frequency characteristic
See *frequency-response* characteristic.

Restrainer

A substance such as potassium bromide which restrains photographic development and thus reduces *chemical fogging,* the bromide having a greater effect on the fog than on the latent photographic image.

Reticulation

The breaking up of the film *emulsion,* and thus the photographic image, into wrinkles or fissures, resembling the grain of leather. Reticulation is usually caused by a sudden change of temperature during development or drying. The process is irreversible.

Reverberation

The persistence of sound at a given point due to repeated reflections.

Reversal film   ASA Z22.56–1947:4.1

A reversal film is one which after exposure is *processed* to produce a positive image on the same film rather than the customary *negative* image. If exposure is made by printing from a negative, a negative image is produced directly.

NOTE.—Reversal films may be black and white, or color, and either sound or picture or both, and they are usually 16 mm. films.

> REVERSAL ORIGINAL: The film which is originally exposed in a camera or [*sound*] *recorder* and is processed by reversal to produce a positive image.
>   ASA Z22.56–1947:4.3

> NOTE.—This positive image is not the same as a print from a negative inasmuch as right and left are transposed. A reversal original may be a black and white, or color, film.

> REVERSAL PRINT: A print which is made on reversal film and developed by the reversal process.   ASA Z22.56–1947:4.5

> NOTE.—A reversal print is usually a positive.

> REVERSAL PROCESS: The reversal process is the photographic process which reversal films undergo. It is a process in which a latent image is developed to a silver image by primary *development,* destroyed by a chemical *bleach,* and the remaining sensitized material exposed and developed in a second developer bath before *fixing* and *washing.*   ASA Z22.56–1947:4.2

Reversal, optical

A method of reversing the direction of motion of a shot by turning it over and rephotographing it in an *optical printer,* so that the *emulsion* side becomes the base side, and vice versa. Adjustment is made for *Academy masking,* if any, by recentering the shot. If the shot contains lettering, it will of course be turned into "mirror writing" by optical reversal.

Rewinds

Geared rewinding devices on which a *reel* or *flange* may be mounted and rotated rapidly by hand or by electric motor.

> MOTOR REWIND: An electrically-driven rewind used in places like projection rooms where large reels of positive film have to be rewound rapidly.

> NEGATIVE REWIND: A hand-driven rewind for rewinding *negative* which is provided with a low gearing-up ratio to discourage over-rapid rewinding which might damage the film.

POSITIVE REWIND: A high-geared hand-driven rewind used for rewinding positive film which can safely travel at high speed.

Rhodol
See *metol*.

Ribbon velocity effect
A type of *distortion* arising in a *light-valve modulator* on account of the fact that the vibrating ribbons travel sometimes in the same, and sometimes in the opposite direction to the film moving past them, and with a velocity comparable to that of the ribbons. This causes a spurious variation of exposure.

Rifle spots
A type of spot lamp in which the light is concentrated by a parabolic reflector of fixed focus.

Rigging
Rigging a set means placing the lights in their preliminary positions, prior to accurate adjustment when the action and camera angle or movement are determined.

Riser
A low platform, a few inches in height, for raising a prop, an actor, or the camera-man above the studio floor.

Rough cut
The version of the *workprint* of a film which follows next after the *assembly* in the film's progress toward completion. See also *fine cut*.

Room tone
A type of sound-reflection pattern, frequently met with in small rooms, which causes a boominess in recorded speech. See also *echo* and *reverberation*.

Run up
The footage which passes through a film mechanism before it gets up to the desired speed.

Rushes
Prints rushed through the *laboratory*, usually the day after the negative has been exposed. Rushes may be picture, sound, or *composite*. Rushes are also called *dailies*.

S

Safety base   ASA Z22.56–1947:1.1.2.1
Safety base is the slow-burning film base used in motion picture film.

NOTE.—At the present time, safety base and acetate base are synonymous and 16 mm. film manufactured in the United States is of this form. All safety base must comply with American Recommended Practice for Motion Picture Safety Film, Z22.31–1941.

Sample print (Final trial composite)   ASA Z22.56–1947:3.4.4
A *composite* print, approved for release, in which all corrections found necessary in previous *trial composite prints* have been incorporated.

NOTE.—The final trial composite may be any one of the various trial composite prints, depending upon the type and extent of corrections required.
[In current commercial practice, the terms sample print, *trial print* and *test print* are used interchangeably, without regard to the distinctions laid down in ASA Z22.56–1947.]

Saturation

The characteristic of color which refers to distinctness and vividness of hue. A color is considered most saturated when it is purest, least saturated when it is pale and appears to be mixed with a large quantity of white.

Scanning

Scanning is the process whereby a fine pencil of electromagnetic waves (as a rule, *light* or cathode rays) is made to pass sequentially over a *scene* or the image of a scene, whether visible or audible, in order to become modulated, or to convert its *modulations* into a more useful form. Since most electrical transmission systems are sequential, scanning is a very important process. In film technology, a modulated scanning beam records the *sound track,* which in turn, after processing, serves to modulate a second scanning beam to provide aural reproduction by optico-electronic means.

Scene

In film parlance, a scene is a piece of the external world, regarded visually or audibly, or both, which is being recorded by a picture and/or sound camera. More technically, the term is confined to the one or more renderings (called *takes*) of an identical scene in the general sense, as delineated in a script, recorded in a camera, or rendered visible on the film itself.

Scoop

A nonfocusable kind of lamp used for general *lighting* and covering a horizontal angle of about 90 to 120 degrees.

Scratched print

A *print* which has been deliberately scratched, usually in a *mutilator,* to prevent its unauthorized duplication. Scratched prints are normally supplied by *stock shot* libraries for viewing purposes. Sometimes called "scratch prints."

Scratches

Scored lines which penetrate the *emulsion* surface of film or seriously indent its *base* are called scratches, and are distinguished from *abrasions* by their greater severity. Scratches usually run vertically on the screen, and are caused by the gouging effect of hard particles in *cameras, developing machines, printers,* and *projectors.* Horizontal scratches are usually *cinch marks.* Scratches may sometimes be rendered invisible by heat treatment which softens the emulsion, or by a wax which fills in the indentations in emulsion or base. This is called *reconditioning.*

NEGATIVE SCRATCH: This is the most serious type of scratch, because it damages *negative* or *original* material. It can often be identified from a print by the fact that it is lighter than any part of the image.

POSITIVE SCRATCH: A type of scratch which is usually of secondary importance, and can often be identified because it is black, having collected particles of dirt during *projection* and *rewinding.*

Screen

In film, the projected photographic image is formed on a white screen, which may have a *matte, beaded,* or *metallic* surface, and is often perforated in order to transmit sound freely from loudspeakers mounted behind the screen.

Screen-plate process

An *additive* color process in which the image is both recorded and viewed through a screen of minute *primary color* filters, indistinguishable to the eye at a distance, and either distributed at random in a mosaic, or arranged in a regular pattern called a *réseau.*

Scrim

If a *flag* is made of translucent material, it is called a scrim. Its effect is partly to cut off, partly to diffuse the source of light near which it is placed. It is thus midway between a *gobo* and a *diffuser.*

Script

The written prescription for the making of any film is called a script. In its early stages the script is often known as a *treatment,* while the finally revised script is distinguished as a *shooting script.*

Script girl

The person responsible on a *set* or on *location* for keeping a record of all *scenes* and *takes* which are shot, recording technical notes on them, and putting all this information in a form useful to the *cutter.* Also called a continuity girl.

Second generation dupe (Print)

A *dupe* (print) from a *first generation dupe* (print) is called a second generation dupe (print). If in color, such a print usually suffers from a more or less severe *degradation* unless it has been *conformed* by *masking.*

Second harmonic

See *harmonic.*

Secondary colors

See *complementary colors.*

Selective response

As applied to a wave-transmission system (usually electromagnetic), selective response signifies a markedly nonuniform transmission characteristic, such as that of a resonant amplifier.

Selsyn motor

Trade name (now in generic use) for a brand of self-synchronizing motor which, when suitably connected to other motors and distributors, provides an *interlock system.* Since rotation of the armature of one motor so connected results in similar rotation of the other armature(s), selsyn motors are often used to provide remote focusing of cameras, both in the studio and on the *animation stand.*

Semimatte

A type of surface having reflection characteristics intermediate between *specular* and *diffuse.* The term is used of *reflectors* for lighting purposes.

Semireflecting

A semireflecting surface is one which partly reflects and partly transmits the incident light, the proportions either being equal or having some predetermined ratio.

Semispecular

See *semimatte.*

Sensitometer

A precision instrument for producing a graduated series of *exposures,* usually in *logarithmic steps,* on a sample strip of film. See also *gamma, control strip,* and *sensitometry.*

INTENSITY SCALE SENSITOMETER: A sensitometer in which exposure is varied by varying the intensity of illumination.

TIME SCALE SENSITOMETER: A sensitometer in which exposure is varied by varying
the time factor.

NOTE.—Under noncritical conditions, the two types of sensitometer will give the same
readings. However, where deviations from the *reciprocity law* become important, the readings will be different.

Sensitometry, photographic

Basically, the science of measuring the sensitivity of photographic materials. The
term also includes the quantitative measurement of all the characteristic responses
of a photographic material to radiant energy, together with the effects of *developers*
in converting the *latent image* into a visible image.

Separation negatives

A set of photographic *negatives,* usually representing the three *primary colors,*
which form the intermediate stage of a number of color-reproduction processes, since
in combination and often in *subtractive* synthesis, they are used to produce the final
release prints.

Sequence

A section of a film which is more or less complete in itself, and which sometimes
begins and ends with a *fade.* However, sequences frequently end with dissolves or
even cuts, which give a better flow of action than fades. In a comparison with writing, a shot may be taken as equal to a sentence; a scene, a paragraph; a sequence, a
chapter.

Set

An artificial construction which forms the *scene* of a motion picture shot or series
of shots.

Sharpness of image

Applied to photographic *emulsions,* sharpness of image means the ability to render
accurately sharp boundaries between opaque and transparent areas. This property is
related to *resolving power,* but is by no means identical with it.

Shooting script

The final working *script* of a film which details the shots one by one in relation to
their accompanying dialogue or other sound.

Shot

The elemental division of a film into sections, within which spatial and temporal
continuity is preserved. Synthetically, shots are the basic elements by which a framework of *filmic space* is built up. In commercial practice, a shot is more often called a
scene, especially in referring to the *script.* Shots are characterized according to *camera
angle,* distance between camera and subject, and subject matter, but their common
descriptions are necessarily relative to the kind of picture of which they form part;
e.g., a close shot from an airplane might be taken fifty feet away, whereas a long shot
of a beetle might be taken five inches away from the subject.

CLOSE SHOT (close-up): A shot taken with the camera close, or apparently close, to
the subject, which is often a human face filling the field. Abbreviated CS or CU.

DOLLY SHOT: A shot in which the camera moves bodily from one place to another on a special camera support such as a *dolly* or *boom*. Also called a trucking or tracking shot.

ESTABLISHING SHOT: Long shots, usually in *exteriors*, which establish the whereabouts of a scene.

HIGH SHOT: A shot which looks down on the subject from a height.

INSERT SHOT: A shot of some object, usually a piece of printed matter, which is cut into a sequence to help explain the action.

LONG SHOT: A shot in which the object of principal interest is, or appears to be, far removed from the camera. Abbreviated LS.

LOW SHOT: A shot which looks up at the subject, often from ground level.

MEDIUM CLOSE SHOT: A shot intermediate in distance between a close shot and a medium shot. Abbreviated MCS.

MEDIUM LONG SHOT: A shot intermediate in distance between a medium shot and a long shot. Abbreviated MLS.

MEDIUM SHOT (mid shot): A shot which shows a person at full height, or views a scene at normal viewing distance. Abbreviated MS.

MOVING SHOT: A shot from some normally moving object such as an airplane or automobile.

PAN SHOT: A shot in which the camera *pans* across the scene.

REACTION SHOT: A shot inserted in a dialogue sequence to show the effect of an actor's words on other participants in the scene, usually in close-up. More generally, any shot displaying the reaction of anything.

TWO SHOT: A shot containing two characters, as a rule close to the camera. The term three shot has a corresponding meaning.

ZOOM SHOT: A shot taken with a *zoom lens*.

Shot listing

The *library* procedure of enumerating shots in completed films or other film material such as *outs*, along with a description of their contents.

Shoulder

The curved part at the upper end of an S-shaped response curve; often refers to that part of the *D log E curve*, which corresponds to the region of supernormal *nonlinear* exposure. See also *toe*.

Shrinkage

A term sometimes generically and loosely applied to all changes in the mass of film, whether *emulsion* or *base*, which result from the hygroscopic (moisture-absorbing) character of the materials composing them. More strictly, the terms swelling and shrinkage are distinguished, the latter being confined to the loss of moisture which occurs rapidly during the latter stages of *processing*, and much more slowly throughout the subsequent life of a piece of film. Significantly affects *registration*.

Shutter bumps

When *noise reduction* elements are allowed to move toward or away from one another at an *audio frequency*, the thumping sounds which are thereby recorded on the sound track are known as shutter bumps.

Shutter track

A type of variable-area *sound track* in which *noise reduction* is effected by movable shutters which, during periods of low modulation, move in such a way as to cut off the recording light beam, thus reducing the area exposed in the negative and correspondingly reducing the transmission of the print. See also *bias recording.*

Signal

The form or variation with time of a wave whereby the information, message, or effect is conveyed in communication.

SIGNAL CURRENT: An electrical current, the fluctuation of which conveys a signal.

SIGNAL STRENGTH: The *amplitude* of a series of impulses (or signal) passing through an electrical system. The term is properly applied to wanted impulses, the term *noise* being reserved for unwanted impulses. See *signal-to-noise ratio.*

Signal-to-noise ratio

The ratio of the *amplitudes* of the wanted *signal* to the unwanted noise in an electrical transmission system. Since the signal-to-noise ratio sets an upper limit to the *dynamic range* of a system, it is a factor of prime importance in design.

Silent aperture

A camera aperture standardized and in use prior to the introduction of the sound film. Its measurements were 0.720 inches × 0.969 inches. See also *Academy mask.*

Silent camera

An ambiguous term, usually denoting a *camera* designed for silent shooting (i.e. picture without concurrent sound), and therefore unsilenced and noisy. In a purely descriptive sense, the term means the exact opposite: i.e. a camera which is silent.

Silent speed

A standard frame-repetition rate for shooting and projecting films not accompanied by sound. Whatever the gauge of film, silent speed is normally set at the minimum repetition rate which can be fused by the average observer into a continuous image: i.e. 16 frames per second. Silent speed is contrasted with *sound speed.* See also *motion, film* and *persistence of vision.*

Silver halide

A metallic salt consisting of silver combined with one of the halogens—bromine, iodine, chlorine, fluorine. A silver halide is the most important constituent of light-sensitive photographic *emulsions.*

Silver recovery

The removal of silver, derived from the cleared away *silver halide,* which accumulates in a photographic *fixing* bath. This removal is accomplished as a rule by chemical precipitation or electrolytic deposition.

Simple sinusoidal quantity   ASA C42–1941:05.05.220

A simple sinusoidal quantity is a quantity which is the product of a constant and the sine or cosine of an angle having values varying linearly with the values of the independent variable. Thus $y = A \sin (\omega x + d)$ and $y = A \cos (\omega x + d)$ are simple sinusoidal quantities, where A, d, and ω are constants.

NOTE.—Any quantity that can be represented by a sine function can also be represented by a cosine function.

Sine wave

The representation of a *simple sinusoidal quantity* as exemplified, for instance, by the line traced by the tip of a swinging pendulum on a piece of paper or film moving at right angles to it. See also *wave.*

Single-frame mechanism

A device attached to a motor-driven or hand-driven camera which moves the film through the *aperture* a single *frame* at a time, giving it a uniform exposure at each operation.

Single-system sound recording

A method of sound recording in which the sound is originally recorded on the same strip of film as the picture image. Owing to difficulties in cutting caused by the difference between camera and editorial *synchronism,* and to sensitometric disadvantages, single-system sound has been almost wholly abandoned in favor of *double-system sound recording,* except for newsreels.

Sinusoidal

Having the form of a *sine wave.*

Sixteen mm. film

The principal nontheatrical standard gauge of film, sometimes called *substandard.* The principal dimensions of 16 mm. silent film are given in ASA Z22.5–1947, or latest revision thereof; and the principal dimensions of 16 mm. sound film in ASA Z22.12–1947, or latest revision thereof.

Slate board

A board placed in front of the camera at the beginning or end of each *take* of each *scene,* which identifies the scene and take, and gives the name of the picture, the director, and the cameraman. See also *clapper board.*

Slit

A narrow aperture allowing the passage of a fine pencil of rays for purposes of *scanning* in film devices such as *sound recorders* and *reproducers.* It is important that the width of a slit be less than that of the narrowest wave to be scanned. See also under *wave motion.*

Slow motion

Motion of the film in the camera faster than the standard rate, which therefore results in action appearing slower than normal when the film is projected at the standard rate.

Slug

A piece of leader inserted in a picture or sound *workprint* to replace damaged or missing footage.

Sodium Bisulfite: $NaHSO_3$

Prepared by saturating sodium hydroxide solution with sulfur dioxide which crystallizes the solution. Its principal function in *developing solutions* is that of a mild *restrainer.*

    Properties:
      Specific gravity 1.48
      Soluble in water

Sodium Carbonate: Na_2CO_3

Used as an activating agent in developers. Available with varying amounts of combined water.

Sodium Sulfite: Na_2SO_3

Sodium disulfite solution is saturated with sodium carbonate, concentrated and allowed to crystallize. Principally used as an oxidation inhibitor in *developers.*

    Properties:
      Specific gravity 2.6334

Melting point 150° C

In its hydrated form ($Na_2SO_3 \cdot 7H_2O$) it has a specific gravity of 1.5939, and loses its $7H_2O$ at 150° C.

Sodium Tetraborate

See *Borax*.

Sodium Thiosulfate: $Na_2S_2O_3 \cdot 5H_2O$

The principal chemical used for *fixing* film. Commonly called *hypo*.

Soft-edge wipe

A kind of *wipe* in which the boundary line between the two shots is softened or blurred, often by shooting the wipe masks out of focus. The degree of softness can be brought perfectly under control.

Sound   ASA Z24.1–1942:1.1

a) Sound is an alteration in pressure, particle displacement, or particle velocity propagated in an elastic material or the superposition of such propagated alterations.

b) Sound is also the sensation produced through the ear by the alterations described above.

NOTE.—In case of possible confusion the term "Sound wave" may be used for concept (a), and the term "Sound sensation" for concept (b).

Sound camera

A camera designed for sound shooting (i.e. picture and concurrent sound), and therefore silenced so as not to produce *camera noise*. The term is also applied to the recording camera in which the *sound image* is transferred to film via a *modulator* and a modulated beam of light, or its magnetic equivalent.

Sound effects

All sounds, other than synchronized voices, narrative, and music, which may be recorded on the sound track of a film. Prior to *re-recording*, these effects usually occupy a separate *sound track* or tracks called sound effects track(s).

Sound effects library

An indexed or catalogued collection of the most commonly used *sound effects* which may be required by the *editing* department of a studio. Sound effects are most conveniently recorded on film, but are often *re-recorded* from discs, and from unperforated magnetic tape.

Sound head

The section of a *projector, dubber,* or other *film reproducer* which contains the constant-speed film propulsion mechanism, the *exciter lamp* and *phototube*. The term is also applied to the sound-printing head of a printer.

Sound image   ASA Z22.56–1947:1.4.3

A sound image is a photographically obtained *sound track* or sound record.

Sound print   ASA Z22.56–1947:3.3

A sound print is any *positive* printed from a sound *negative*.

Sound recorder

A generic term for the complete sound-recording chain from the *microphone* to the *sound camera* (in the second sense of the definition). This chain is more properly called a sound-recording channel. The term sound recorder is sometimes limited so that it becomes synonymous with sound camera.

Sound reproducer
See *film reproducer.*

Sound speed
A standard *frame*-repetition rate and film velocity for shooting and reproducing films accompanied by sound. In standard 35 mm. and 16 mm. practice, the frame-repetition rate is 24; the film velocity is 90 and 36 feet per second respectively. No standard repetition rate and film velocity have been adopted for 8 mm. film accompanied by sound.

Sound stages
Stages used for sound shooting, and therefore silenced and air conditioned to isolate them acoustically from their surroundings.

Sound track
A narrow band, along one side of a sound film, which carries the sound record. In some cases, several such bands may be used.

CLASS A SOUND TRACK: A sound track which carries both positive and negative sound waves.

CLASS A-B SOUND TRACK: A type of sound track characterized by being class A recording for low-percentage *modulation,* and generally becoming class B for high-percentage modulation.

CLASS B SOUND TRACK: A sound track in which one side carries only negative half waves, and the other side positive half waves.

CONTROL TRACK: A supplementary sound track, usually placed on the same film with the sound track carrying the program material, the purpose of which is to control, in some respect, the reproduction of the sound track. Ordinarily it contains a single frequency of varying amplitude or a varying frequency of constant amplitude, and it is at present most commonly used to control the gain of the reproducing system in order to increase the effective *dynamic range* of the reproduced sound.

MULTIPLE SOUND TRACKS: A group of sound tracks, generally independent, as used for *stereophonic* sound recording.

SQUEEZE TRACK: A sound track, generally of the variable-density type, wherein, by means of variable masking, the width of the track is varied at a slow rate throughout the length of the track, thus controlling the reproduced *signal amplitude.*

Sound truck
A mobile conveyance fitted up with a sound-recording channel. It usually carries drums on which microphone and other cables are wound, a small darkroom for loading film, and a battery system rendering it independent of external power supplies.

Special effects
A generic term for trick effects which are artificially constructed, as a rule in a studio separate from the main shooting *stages.* Special effects include split screens and other forms of matting, models, and combination foregrounds and backgrounds.

Spectral response
The *pass band* of a transmission system or some part of such a system (e.g. a photographic *filter* or *emulsion*). In photography, the *spectrum* in question is usually the *visible spectrum;* in sound recording, the *audible spectrum.*

Spectral selectivity
Where the *pass band* of a transmission system is not infinite, it can be said to have spectral selectivity. See also *spectral response.*

Spectrogram

A graphical representation of the *spectral response* of a substance such as a photographic *filter* or *emulsion*.

Spectrum

If a series of *wave phenomena* is susceptible of a continuous variation of *frequency* over a band of frequencies which may be finite or may range from zero to infinity, the band is called a spectrum.

AUDIBLE SPECTRUM: The band of *sound* frequencies which affect the normal human ear and range from about 15 cps to about 20,000 cps. The audible spectrum is bounded at its lower limit by the region of *infra-audible sound,* and at its upper limit by the region of *ultra-audible sound*. Also called the audio spectrum.

ELECTROMAGNETIC SPECTRUM: The spectrum comprising radiation, which obeys electrical and magnetic laws and travels through the universe at a uniform speed of approximately 186,000 miles per second. This radiation ranges in frequency from cosmic rays through X-rays and visible light to radio waves of increasing wavelength and of a frequency which approaches zero.

VISIBLE SPECTRUM: The band of frequencies, forming part of the electromagnetic spectrum, which affect the normal human eye and produce the sensation of *light*. The visible spectrum ranges from about 400 to about 700 *millimicrons* in *wavelength*. It is bounded at its lower (frequency) limit by the *infrared* region, and at its upper (frequency) limit by the *ultraviolet* region.

See also *discontinuous spectrum.*

Specular reflection

Specular reflection is the type of reflection resembling that of a mirror—i.e. in which the angle of incidence of a beam of light is equal to the angle of reflection. Specular reflection is contrasted with *diffuse reflection.*

Speed

1) Speed is a generic term for the magnitude of light transmission of some part of a photographic system, usually an emulsion or a lens.

EMULSION SPEED: Emulsion speed is the sensitivity of a photographic *emulsion* to *light,* the latter term being defined spectrally with as much precision as may be needed. Speed is more easily defined than measured, since it is normally required to be a practical aid to photographic reproduction, rather than a method of laboratory standardization. In recent years, especially in the U.S., emulsion speed has come to be measured by the minimum gradient method, which determines the point of least gradient in the *toe* of the *D log E curve* which will give satisfactory photographic reproduction. Emulsion speed, however, is markedly affected by variations in development (see *gamma*), and by the constitution of the developer. See also *American standard speed, American standard exposure index, exposure index.*

LENS SPEED: The light-admitting index of a *lens* is usually measured by its *f/number,* which, however, is based on purely geometrical considerations and does not take account of the light absorbed, reflected or uselessly scattered during its passage through the lens. The transmission of the lens, as well as its light-gathering power, is now measured by a *T-number.*

2) The correct speed at which a film mechanism is designed to run. The cry "Speed!" means that a sound or picture camera has reached *synchronous speed.* It is the signal for the director to call *"Action!"*

Splice; Splicing

The joining together of two pieces of *film*, end to end, in such a way that they form one continuous piece of film is called splicing, and the joint so produced is called a splice. Splices are of two kinds: butt splices and lap splices.

BUTT SPLICE: When the ends of two pieces of film are made to abut against one another, they may be joined by fastening a patch across the line of abutment. This type of splice tends to be insecure, and is seldom used except in the cutting of *picture release negatives* when it is important to retain frames which would be lost in a lap splice.

LAP SPLICE: When the ends of two pieces of film are made to overlap on one another, they may be united by applying film *cement* to the overlapped area, any emulsion present having been removed. The cement then partly dissolves the base over the area in contact and produces a joint which is in effect a weld. Lap splices are of various widths, the wider splices being known as positive splices and the narrower as negative or sound splices.

NEGATIVE SPLICE: A narrower type of lap splice invariably used for splicing negative or positive original-picture material, in order to make the printed-through image of the splice invisible (or, in 16 mm., as little visible as possible) under all normal projection conditions. Negative splices are also used in making *re-recording prints*.

POSITIVE SPLICE: A wider type of lap splice, often used by film exchanges in the repair of *release prints,* and mistakenly supposed by many projectionists and editors to be stronger than a negative splice.

Splicer

A machine for more or less automatically effecting the operations needed to *splice* two lengths of film. All practical splicers are at present confined to making *lap splices,* and none is fully automatic. Splicers are often classed as hot or cold, according to whether heat is or is not applied to the film joint to hasten the drying of the *cement.*

HAND SPLICER: A splicer in which the motions required in splicing are effected exclusively by the operator's hands.

MACHINE SPLICER: A splicer in which the motions required in splicing are effected by the operator's hands and feet.

Split reels

Standard reels having one removable side, so that a *core* may be mounted on the spindle and wound film taken off at will and transferred to a *flange* or a can without having to undergo rewinding.

Spotlamps

Focusable lamps, the beam of which can be narrowed to a spot, or widened to a flood. Also called spots.

Spotting

The process whereby the location of individual words or *modulations* on a *sound track* can be accurately determined. This is accomplished with a sound *moviola,* and, since 35 mm. film travels eighteen inches in a second, calls for some manual dexterity. In a narrower sense, spotting means the determination of the distances from a *start mark* of the beginnings and ends of phrases and sentences on a film in a foreign language which is to be translated with *subtitles.*

Sprocket

A wheel carrying regularly spaced teeth of the correct pitch and separation to engage with film *perforations* and to propel the film through various types of mechanism while maintaining proper *synchronism,* and, where necessary, *registration.*

FEED SPROCKET: A driven sprocket which feds film from a compartment or *magazine* into a piece of mechanism such as a *camera, moviola, projector, printer,* or *sound camera.*

INTERMITTENT SPROCKET: A stop-and-go sprocket, frequently driven by a *Maltese cross* or other form of Geneva movement, which provides the *intermittent movement* in many types of film mechanism.

TAKE-UP SPROCKET: A driven sprocket which moves film out of a piece of film mechanism and into a magazine or onto a spool at the completion of a process.

Sprocket holes
Same as *perforations.*

Spurious harmonics
Unwanted harmonics introduced into a transmission system by *distortion.*

Sputtering
A process of spraying or otherwise depositing finely divided particles onto a surface. E.g., the sputtering of glass with metal to produce a *semireflecting* surface.

Square wave
A wave whose oscillographic profile is rectangular. It can be shown mathematically that a perfect square wave contains sinusoidal components from zero to infinite *frequency,* so that comparison of a single square wave as it enters and leaves a transmission system will yield rapid and interesting information on the *pass band* of the system and the distortion it is introducing.

Stabilizer
1) A substance used in the manufacture of *nitrate* film base to give it a greater chemical stability and reduce its explosiveness. Stabilizers tend to evaporate gradually, especially if film is stored at a high temperature. See also *plasticizer.*

2) A revolving drum in the film path of a *sound recorder* or *reproducer* which imparts smoothness to film motion, and thus helps to eliminate flutter, through attachment to a heavy flywheel or by making use of magnetic drag or oil damping to increase inertia.

Stage
The floor of a studio on which shooting takes place is called a *stage.* If it is designed for sound shooting, it is called a *sound stage.*

Standard leader
See *Academy leader.*

Start mark
A *sync mark* on one or more film *tracks* designating the point from which an operation such as printing, projection, or synchronizing is to begin. *Academy leaders* incorporate two start marks, one for picture and one for sound, the difference being explained under the term *synchronism.*

Static
If a discharge of static electricity takes place in a camera or contact printer, it will record on the film emulsion as a series of jagged lines, often in the form of a brush or crowsfoot pattern. This is called static, and its occurrence is favored by low temperatures, low humidities, absence of grounding, and excessive rubbing friction between the film and the *aperture plate.*

Stationary wave (standing wave)

The *wave* system resulting from the interference of progressive waves of the same *frequency* and kind. They are characterized by the existence of *nodes* or partial nodes in the interference pattern. In order to obtain standing waves the interfering waves must have components traveling in opposite directions.

NOTE.—This definition broadens the ideal classical concept which is limited to a wave system characterized by zero sound-energy flux at all points.

Step printing

Printing in a step *printer.*

Steps

In *sensitometry,* a series of graduated exposures, the lengths or intensities of successive exposures being in a fixed ratio which obtains throughout the series. In this way, a logarithmic series of exposures is obtained.

Stereogram

A stereoscopic pair of images meeting the requirements of *stereoscopic recording* is known as a stereogram. If the rendering it gives is *pseudoscopic,* it may be called a pseudogram. The pair of images forming a stereogram may be broken down into narrow strips and interlaced to form a *parallax stereogram;* or the left and right eye images may be multiplied and interlaced, as in the *parallax panoramagram.* Finally, there may be an infinite number of subdivided images, as was proposed by Lippmann for the integral photograph.

Stereophony

The removal of the limitations of *monaural reproduction* is called stereophony. Stereophonic transmission systems have been experimentally evolved for film, radio, and the duplication of concerts by wire, but the fact that they double or treble the demands made on the transmission band width (in film the sound *storage factor*) has hitherto prevented their commercial introduction.

> STEREOPHONIC RECORDING: The employment of an *artificial head* (requiring two channels), or two or three laterally spaced microphones (two or three channels) enables *binaural hearing* to be simulated electronically. The choice of microphone positions is governed by fairly well understood physical factors, but little practical experience has been amassed. Additional channels may be used for *"wild" recording.*

> STEREOPHONIC REPRODUCTION: Ideally, the twin outputs of an artificial-head type of recording system should be fed separately into headphone units worn over each ear of each member of the audience (cf. the close parallel to *stereoscopy*). In practice, it is usual to employ two loudspeakers set as far as possible apart behind the screen, in order to reduce their mutual interference and increase the angle subtended at the ears. If a third channel is employed, it usually feeds a central loudspeaker. Additional channels feed "wild" sound into speakers which may be placed behind and above the audience, in order to bring the sound image out into the theater itself.

Stereoscopy

The removal of the limitations of *planoscopic reproduction* is called stereoscopy. Stereoscopic systems have been experimentally evolved for film, but the fact that image separation, if accomplished at the spectator's eyes, requires the wearing of viewing spectacles, and if at the screen, the multiplication of images to a theoretically infinite number, has hitherto retarded commercial development.

STEREOSCOPIC RECORDING: The conditions of *binocular vision* are met if the camera takes two pictures which are simultaneous, identical in size and shape, and horizontally spaced apart. The proper lens spacing, called the *interaxial distance,* is governed by the effect desired and by the geometry of the ultimate projection system; exaggerated depth effects are called *hyperstereoscopic.*

STEREOSCOPIC REPRODUCTION: The one basic condition is that the spectator's left eye must receive the film left-eye image, and his right eye the right-eye image. This may be accomplished with viewers by *polarization,* by flicker projection, and by anaglyphic methods; without viewers, by *parallax stereograms, parallax panoramagrams,* and integral photographs.

Stock footage

The material in a *film library* which consists of shots such as *establishing shots,* historical material, and footage of other general application, which is likely to be used on many productions over a period of time.

Stock shots

Shots which are kept in stock for general studio use. They record historical events, famous places, and in general whatever it would be impracticable to shoot for each production.

Stop

A fixed aperture designed to limit the amount of light passing through a *lens.* The term is applied also to any specific setting of a movable lens *diaphragm,* and thus designates the effective *speed* of a lens which is working at other than its full *aperture.* In a still more general sense, the term stop is applied to any optical transmission system not containing lenses.

Stopping down

The process of reducing the *aperture* of a lens by means of a stop or *diaphragm.*

Storage cabinet

A cabinet in which film is stored in *cutting rooms.* If used to house *nitrate* film, storage cabinets must be equipped with sprinklers and vents of approved design.

Storage factor

Since film is an imperfect transmission medium, it is important to be able to gauge it in terms of the number of elements from the worlds of sound and vision which it is able to store and reproduce. Such a measure may be called a storage factor.

PICTURE STORAGE FACTOR: The area of the image may be multiplied by a factor based on the *dynamic resolution* of the film; but since there is as yet no agreed method of measuring dynamic resolution, it is necessary to substitute the *resolving power* of the static image.

SOUND STORAGE FACTOR: A convenient comparison between different gauges of film may be made by multiplying the velocity of the film by the width of the sound track to be recorded on it.

Supersonic

See *ultra-audible sound.*

Story board

In the preparation of an *animation* film, and sometimes of other types of film, it is often convenient to make sketches of key incidents in the action, which are then arranged in order on a board called a story board and suitably captioned.

Striations

Narrow adjacent bands. In *variable density* sound recording, the term is applied to the transverse bands of differing densities forming the *sound track*.

Stroboscopic cinematography

The recording of successive images on continuously moving film by intermittent flashes of light of such short duration that the subject moves only an imperceptible distance during each period of illumination. This method allows of high-speed cinematography with relatively simple camera equipment.

Substandard

A term used to describe all gauges or widths of film smaller than the theater standard, which is *35 mm*. The most important substandard gauges for photography and projection are *16 mm.* and *8 mm.*

Subtitles

See *title*.

Subtractive process

A process of color reproduction in which, after analysis into *primary colors*, a scene is recombined by filtering out (i.e., subtracting) from white light each of the three pairs of primaries, thus in each case transmitting the remaining primary.

Sum and difference tones

See *intermodulation*.

Swish pan

A type of *panning* shot in which the camera is swung very rapidly on its vertical axis, the resulting film producing a blurred sensation when viewed, which is quite unlike that produced by a corresponding movement of the eyes.

Synchronism   ASA Z22.56–1947:1.5

Synchronism is the relation between the picture and sound films with respect either to the physical location on the film or films, or to the time at which corresponding picture and sound are seen and heard.

[NOTE.—The term synchronism is almost universally abbreviated in film parlance to "sync" (pronounced "sink"). Though there is no agreed spelling for this word, it is commonly written as "synch," perhaps to reproduce the Greek letter χ, which could not, however, have terminated a Greek word. Furthermore, there is no English analogy for the corresponding pronunciation (cf. lynch and finch). It would therefore seem logical to standardize the spelling "sync" with a final "c" as in "zinc."]

CAMERA SYNCHRONISM: Camera synchronism is the relationship between picture and sound on an original composite negative. [See *single-system sound*.]
                                                                     ASA Z22.56–1947:1.5.3

NOTE.—Camera synchronism is generally not the same as *projection synchronism* and is never the same as *editorial synchronism*. The relationship between picture and sound may vary among different type cameras.

CUTTING SYNC: See *editorial synchronism*.

EDITORIAL SYNCHRONISM: Editorial synchronism is the relationship between the picture and sound film during the editorial processes.   ASA Z22.56–1947:1.5.2

NOTE.—During the editorial process, the sound track and corresponding picture, whether on the same or separate films, are kept in alignment and not offset as for projection. Thus, cutting a picture and sound can be a simultaneous operation. Many composite release negatives are supplied in editorial synchronism.

IN SYNC: Picture and/or sound tracks are said to be in sync when synchronism has been established.

OUT OF SYNC: Picture and/or sound tracks are said to be out of sync when synchronism has not been established or has been lost.

PARALLEL SYNC: See *editorial synchronism.*

PRINTING SYNC: See *projection synchronism.*

PROJECTION SYNCHRONISM: Projection synchronism is the time relation between picture and corresponding sound in a projection print.　　ASA Z22.56–1947:1.5.1

NOTE.—Correct projection synchronism is indicated by exact coincidence of picture and sound as seen and heard. To attain this result, it is necessary to place the sound track 20 frames ahead of the center of the corresponding picture for 35 mm. film and 26 frames ahead of the center of the corresponding picture for 16 mm. film, since sound motion picture projection equipment is designed for projection synchronism with this relationship existing between the locations of the projected picture and corresponding sound.

SYNC MARKS: A general term for all marks placed on picture and sound *tracks* to denote their synchronous relationship. On positive film, sync marks are usually applied with a grease pencil or brush pen; on negative, they are scratched with a scriber. See also *start marks, end sync marks,* and *code numbers.*

Synchronizer

A device used in the cutting room for maintaining *synchronism* between film *tracks.* It consists of two or more *sprockets* rigidly mounted on a revolving shaft. The tracks are placed on the sprockets and accurately positioned by their *perforations,* so that they can be wound along by *rewinds* while maintaining a proper synchronous relationship.

Synchronous motor

A type of *alternating current* electric motor in which the rotation of the armature is automatically locked to the *frequency* of the power supply, which in central generating stations is in turn determined by a clock motion of a very high order of accuracy. For most practical purposes, including film drive, a synchronous motor insures constant speed. See also *interlock system.*

Synchronous speed

The rate of film travel of sychronized sound and picture cameras, which must be identical with the standard rate of projection in order that recorded sounds should be reproduced at the right pitch and recorded actions at the right tempo. Synchronous speed for 35 mm. film is 90 feet per minute, and for 16 mm. film 36 feet per minute, the picture repetition rate being 24 *frames* per second in both gauges.

Synopsis

1) A short or preliminary version of the *script* of a film.

2) A summary of a completed film, often intended to catalogue its contents for a *film library.*

T

T-stop

A system of lens calibration, now coming into general use but not yet fully standardized, which makes allowance for the varying *transmittance* of different lenses, and of the same lens at different periods. The most widely accepted definition of the T-stop corresponding to any *diaphragm* opening (d) is the quotient of the *focal length* (F) of the lens divided by the diameter (D) of the fixed circular opening having the same transmittance. If the lens transmittance is k; $f = F/d$; $T = F/D$; and $(d/D)^2 = k$. Hence, if $k = 1$ (100 per cent transmittance), the T-stop and the f-stop will be the same. See also *f/number*.

Tachometer

A speed-measuring device. Tachometers are often fitted to cameras equipped with *"wild" motors,* so that the operator can assure himself that the camera is running at the desired speed, or take steps to correct it.

Tailgate

The section of an *optical printer* in which the printing film is run. It is usually mounted so that it can slide on rails like a lathe bed toward or away from the optical camera, in order to produce enlargement or diminution of the photographed image.

Tails-up

A *reel* of film so wound that the last frame in the image sequence is on the outside of the roll. Contrasted with *head-up*.

Take

Each performance of a piece of action in front of a camera which is exposing film is called a take, the successive takes usually being numbered from one upward and recorded by photographing a numbered *slate board*.

Take board

See *slate board*.

Take-off spool

The spool or *reel* from which film is unwound and fed into film machinery such as projectors, cameras, printers, developing machines, etc. Also called a feed spool.

Take-up spool

The spool or *reel* on which film is wound after being run on film machinery such as projectors, cameras, printers, developing machines, etc.

Take-up sprocket

See *sprocket*.

Tank

Containers, usually rectangular in shape, for holding developing and other solutions used in *developing machines,* whether of the *continuous* or *rack-and-tank* type. Some developing machines carry solutions in tubes; spray developing machines require neither tanks nor tubes.

BLEED TANK: A tank from which *replenisher* is fed into the *circulating system* of a developing machine.

CIRCULATING TANK: A tank forming part of the *circulating system* of a *developing machine,* and containing that part of the developing solution which is in actual circulation.

MIXING TANK: A tank forming part of the *circulating system* of a developing machine in which the chemicals are mixed and dissolved to form the *developing* and fixing solutions before passing into the bleed and circulating tanks.

Tanning

In the *imbibition* printing process, the hardening of the *emulsion* gelatin in proportion to the *density* of the photographic image is called tanning.

Target

A type of *gobo* even smaller than a *flag*, circular in shape and from three to nine inches in diameter. Half-targets are semicircular.

Tea wagon

Colloquial term for a small wheeled *console* sometimes used by *mixers* when controlling sound on a *sound stage.*

Telephoto lens

A lens, usually of greater than normal *focal length,* so constructed that the back focus is different from the effective focal length of the lens: usually less, in order to increase compactness; sometimes more, in order to allow for the use of a wide-angle lens in a camera where a prism must be interposed between lens and film. More generally, a lens of any construction which is of more than normal focal length.

Temperature radiator   ASA Z7.1–1942:10.050

A temperature radiator is one whose radiant flux density (radiancy) is determined by its temperature and the material and character of its surface, and is independent of its previous history.

Temporary picture dupe negative   ASA Z22.56–1947:1.3.1

A temporary picture dupe negative is a low quality *dupe negative* and is made on positive stock.

NOTE.—It is used to make low-quality prints for use in editing. It usually contains picture only, but may also have the sound track on the same film.

Test print

Any trial composite print (see under *sample print*) is often called a test print.

Test strip

A strip of film, held over as a general practice at the end of all rolls of film exposed in sound and picture cameras, which is used by the laboratory for *sensitometric* purposes. In sound recording, part of this strip is occupied by a *bias* track to check the working of the *noise reduction* unit.

Thermal lag

The lag in the temperature drop of a filament when the heating current is suddenly reduced, or in the temperature rise when the current is suddenly increased. Thermal lag renders it impossible to *modulate* normal filamentary light sources at *audio frequencies,* and also creates difficulties in the design of certain kinds of *light-change boards.*

Thermostatically operated valve

In a *circulating system,* a valve operated by a thermostat and arranged to stop or release a flow of liquid at a predetermined temperature.

Third harmonic

A component of a periodic *wave* having a *frequency* which is three times the *fundamental frequency.*

Thirty-five mm. film

The standard gauge, or width, of motion picture *film.* The dimensions of 35 mm.

negative film are given in ASA Z22.1–1941, or latest revision thereof; and the dimensions of 35 mm. *positive* film in ASA Z22.36–1947, or latest revision thereof.

Threading
The act of placing film on the proper *sprockets* and rollers, aligning it in *gates* and forming *loops,* and doing whatever else is necessary to insure its proper passage through a camera, projector, printer or other film mechanism.

Three-color process
A process of color reproduction involving analysis and synthesis by means of the three *primary* colors. See also *three-strip* and *integral tripack.*

Three-strip
A process of color photography in which the initial *three-color* analysis takes place on three separate strips or *tracks* of film. Contrasted with *integral tripack.* See also *separation negatives.*

Threshold of feeling
At any specified frequency, the minimum value of the sound pressure of a sinusoidal wave of that frequency which will stimulate the ear to a point at which there is the sensation of feeling. The point at which the pressure is measured must be specified in every case. It is expressed in dynes per square centimeter.

Tilting
Pivotal movement of the camera in a vertical plane. Contrasted with *panning.*

Timbre
A term more often used by musicians than by scientists to denote the peculiar tone quality of different musical instruments. It is now known that differences of timbre result from the presence of different *harmonics* of different relative *amplitudes.*

Time-gamma curve
The curve connecting developing time with *gamma* for a particular *emulsion, developing solution,* temperature and *developing machine.*

Timer
1) The person who determines the *printer lights* to be used in printing negatives in order to produce a visually satisfactory print *density,* and, as a rule, to compensate for different negative densities in successive shots of the completed picture.

2) A device for making a series of exposures from eleven successive *frames* of a negative or master positive corresponding to alternate *printer lights* in the scale from 1 to 21. This provides a guide to the *timer (1)* in selecting the proper printer light. Also called by the trade names of *Cinex printer* and sensitester.

Timing card
A card on which the *printer lights* are noted in printing from a negative or master positive.

Title
Any written material which appears on a film and is not a part of an original scene is called a title.

CREDIT TITLES: The titles which enumerate the actors in a film and the technicians who made it.

CREEPER TITLE: A title, often carrying the names of the cast of a film, which creeps slowly round on a large unseen drum in front of the camera. Sometimes called a roll-up title.

END TITLES: The title(s) which bring the film to an end.

MAIN TITLES: All the titles which occur at the beginning of a film, which as a rule include the credit titles. The term sometimes refers solely to the title card carrying the name of the film itself.

PAN TITLE: A title, often carrying the names of the cast of a film, which is *panned* slowly past the camera lens in a flat plane. Sometimes called a creeper title.

STRIP TITLES: Superimposed titles placed near the bottom of the frame, usually to translate dialogue from a foreign language into the language of the audience.

SUBTITLES: Titles appearing in the main body of a film, to make a comment, explain or summarize, or to present the dialogue or commentary in a silent film, or most commonly to translate dialogue into the language of the audience.

SUPERIMPOSED TITLE: Any title which is superimposed on an actual shot, and not on an artificial background.

Title stand

A camera stand designed principally for shooting titles. Specially designed title stands are now seldom built, their place having been taken by *animation stands* on account of the growing complexity of title shooting.

Toe

The curved part at the lower end of an S-shaped *response curve;* often refers to that part of the *D log E curve* which corresponds to the region of low *nonlinear* exposure. See also *shoulder.*

Tolerance

Maximum allowable limits of error in the setting up or running of any physical or chemical system.

Tracking

See *dollying.*

Tracks

A useful generic term for the bands of sound and picture film which play an important and complicated part in all processes of film making. The term is used most often in *cutting* and *re-recording.*

Transducer   ASA C42–1941:65.20.600

A transducer is a device by means of which energy may flow from one or more transmission systems to one or more other transmission systems.

NOTE.—The energy transmitted by these systems may be of any form (for example, it may be electric, mechanical or acoustical), and it may be of the same form or different forms in the various input and output systems.

Transfer process

In *imbibition* printing, transfer consists of the application of a *matrix,* in which dye has been absorbed or *imbibed,* to a *blank* piece of film onto which, as a result of suitable treatment, the dye readily transfers, thus producing a colored image.

Transient

A sound or electrical signal of nonrepeating character, marked by a steep-fronted waveform which is difficult to reproduce faithfully in an electrical transmission system. See also *square wave.*

Transmission factor   ASA Z7.1–1942:30.125

The transmission factor of a body is the ratio of the light transmitted by the body to the incident light.

Transmittance   ASA Z7.1–1942:30.126

The transmittance of a body is the ratio of the light reaching the second surface of the body to the light which enters the surface where it is incident.

NOTE.—This definition of transmittance as distinguished from *transmission factor* is adopted tentatively. The distinctive use of the two terms is not generally accepted.

Transparency process
See *process projection.*

Travel ghost
A ghostlike image, produced either in a camera or projector, which sometimes accompanies the wanted photographic image and is caused by movement of the film while not obscured by the *shutter.* It is caused by incorrect shutter adjustment.

Traveling masks
See *matte rolls.*

Traveling shot
A shot in which the camera moves bodily in relation to its object. Sometimes called a *dolly* shot.

Treatment
A more or less detailed preparation of a story or idea in film form, which has not yet been clothed in the technical terms which convert it into a *script.*

Trial print
A trial composite print is a composite print made from the picture and sound *release negatives* for the purpose of checking and correcting picture and sound quality, *negative cutting* and assembly, *timing,* etc. Also frequently known as a *sample print,* test print or answer print.

Triangle
A triangular or three-pointed star-shaped device which receives the three legs of a tripod in order to prevent their slipping apart.

Trims
Sections of shots which are left over when the wanted parts of the shots have been incorporated in a finished picture. See also *outs.*

Tripack
See *integral tripack.*

Tripod
A simple type of three-legged camera support, often used to hold field cameras. See also *head, camera.*

Trucking
See *dollying.*

Turbulation
Agitation of a developing solution near the surface of the film undergoing development, to produce more uniform development and combat *directional development* effects.

Turret, Lens
A revolving mount attached to the front of a camera, carrying three or more *lenses,* and enabling them in turn to be swung into position in front of the photographing *aperture.*

Two-color process

A process of color reproduction involving an unsatisfactory analysis of the spectrum into two bands of color. According to the modern tristimulus theory, three *primary* color elements are required to reproduce colors accurately. See also *bipack* and *three-color process*.

Two-strip

See *bipack*.

U

Ultra-audible sound

Sound whose *frequency* is above the upper audible limit. This is generally assumed to be 20,000 cps, but there are large individual variations, and the limit as a rule varies inversely with the age of the listener. The more common term supersonic sound is now deprecated.

Ultraviolet

The ultraviolet region of the *spectrum* ranges from about 100 to 400 *millimicrons* in wavelength. The chief usefulness of the ultraviolet in cinematography lies in the recording and printing of *variable-area* sound tracks.

Ultraviolet recording and printing

Ultraviolet light, being of very short *wavelength,* suffers little scattering in the film *emulsion,* and produces a surface image of increased sharpness which is often of value in sound recording, where the aim is to produce a sharp image form.

Unblooped

A *spliced* sound track, to which *bloops* have not been applied, either during printing or subsequently, is described as unblooped. *Push-pull* sound tracks do not normally require blooping.

Unexposed

Film which has not undergone an *exposure* is called unexposed.

Unidirectional current   ASA C42–1941:05.20.056

A unidirectional current is a current which has either all positive or all negative values. [See *direct current;* also diagram under *wave motion*.]

Unit

See *production unit*.

Unit manager

The person in business control of a *production unit* on *location*.

Unmodulated track

Sound track recorded in a *sound recorder* without the application of modulation to the *modulator,* usually with *noise reduction* in effect (biased track), but occasionally without it (unbiased track). Unmodulated track (often abbreviated to "unmod") is used for filling up the soundless spaces in re-recording and other tracks, thus avoiding the complete silence or deadness produced by opaque *leader*.

Unsteadiness

A general term for unwanted movement or shake of the photographic image as recorded in a camera or projected on a screen.

V

Variable-area recording
Recording by means of an *optical sound recorder* designed to produce a *variable-area track*, normally using a *galvanometer* as *modulator*. See also *sound track, shutter track,* and *bias recording*.

Variable-area track   ASA Z24.1–1949:8.295
A variable-area track is a sound track divided laterally into opaque and transparent areas, a sharp line of demarcation between these areas forming an oscillographic trace of the wave shape of the recorded *signal*.

Variable-density recording
Recording by means of an *optical sound recorder* designed to produce a *variable-density track*, normally using a *light valve* as *modulator*. See also *sound track*.

Variable-density sound track
A method of sound recording on film in which the sound is recorded as a number of *density* gradations perpendicular to the edge of the sound track, and extending across its full width. The distance between gradations is determined by the recorded *frequency,* and the difference in density between the lines and the spaces between the lines is determined by the *signal amplitude*. The gradations are often referred to as *striations*.

Variable-intensity recording
A type of sound recording (e.g. with an *aeolight*) in which the intensity of the recording beam is varied to produce a *variable-density sound track*.

Velocilator
A movable camera mount intermediate in size between a *dolly* and a *boom*. It will carry a heavy camera up to a height of about six feet, but is not intended to be raised or lowered rapidly while the camera is running. The movement is usually hand operated.

Viewer
A simple viewing device, based on the *optical compensator,* which enables film to be seen with the proper intermittency without the complication of a *moviola*. Since the one working spindle of the viewer revolves continuously, not intermittently, the device may be mounted between two *rewinds,* and the film pulled through at any desired speed. The image, however, is much inferior to that provided by a moviola. The term "reader" is sometimes applied to an analogous device for listening to sound track, which consists of a small *sound head* placed between two rewinds and connected to an amplifier and loudspeaker or headphones. Also known as hand-viewer or reader.

Viewfinder
An optical device forming part of a camera, or attached to it, which provides an image (usually magnified) approximating that which is formed by the lens on the film.
   DIRECT VIEWFINDER: This type of viewfinder, which usually incorporates a *focusing microscope,* enables the cameraman to scrutinize the image which the lens is actually forming on the film. It therefore requires no correction for *parallax*.
   MONITORING VIEWFINDER: A viewfinder external to the camera and often to the *blimp* (if one is used), which enables the cameraman to watch his scene while

the camera is turning. It is usually equipped with accurate compensation for parallax, and in some designs gearing is provided to couple the finder to the lens-focusing mount.

REFLEX VIEWFINDER: A type of direct *viewfinder* used in some advanced cameras. The front surface of the *shutter* is silvered and set at an angle of 45° to the film plane. When the shutter obscures the film, the image-forming light rays are reflected from it through an optical system onto *ground glass,* where they are observed by the cameraman through a *focusing microscope.* Thus an accurate image, devoid of all *parallactic* error, is seen while the camera is actually shooting on film. This image is intermittent, and, being formed by the shooting lens, varies in brilliance with the setting of the lens *aperture.*

Viewing print

A print kept in a *film library* to enable the library users to see what negative material is available.

V. I. meter

A volume indicator (which may or may not be a meter) is a device used for monitoring the *amplitude* of *signals* which are being recorded on film. V. I. meters may consist of vacuum tube voltmeters, a series of neon lamps, or a *cathode-ray tube.* They can be designed with different degrees of damping to read instantaneous peaks or more gradually changing *envelopes.*

Visuals

The picture images of which a film is composed are often called visuals in technical discussion to direct attention to the picture as contrasted with the sound elements of a film.

Volt, International   ASA C42–1941:05.35.185

The international volt is the voltage that will produce a current of one international ampere through a resistance of one international ohm. One international volt equals 1.00033 absolute volts.

Volume compressor

A device used in sound recording to reduce the *dynamic range* of a program by recording any given span of *decibels* in some lesser span. Volume compressors are often designed to come into operation only when the *signal* level has reached some predetermined value.

Volume range

The volume range of a program is the total variation in volume during the program, expressed in *decibels.*

W

Washing

The removal of the *hypo* and soluble by-products which remain in the film after fixation is called washing. It is normally carried out in ordinary running water.

Watt, International   ASA C42–1941:05.35.205

The international watt is the power expended when one international ampere flows between two points having a potential difference of one international volt. One international watt equals 1.00018 absolute watts.

Wave
1) A propagated disturbance, usually periodic, such as an electric wave or sound wave.
2) A single *cycle* of such a disturbance.
3) A periodic variation represented by a graph.

Wave form
The shape or outline of a *wave*.

Wave motion
The principal characteristics of simple harmonic wave motion (the sine wave) can be conveniently shown in a diagram:

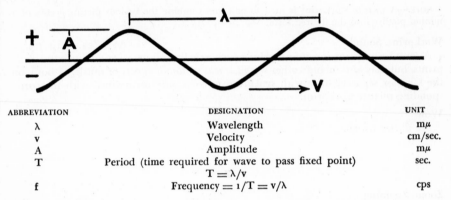

ABBREVIATION	DESIGNATION	UNIT
λ	Wavelength	mμ
v	Velocity	cm/sec.
A	Amplitude	mμ
T	Period (time required for wave to pass fixed point)	sec.
	$T = \lambda/v$	
f	Frequency $= 1/T = v/\lambda$	cps

NOTE.—In electrical engineering, amplitude is usually measured in *decibels* above a stated or assumed reference level based on absolute power units.

Wavelength
See *wave motion.*

Waxing
The application of wax to the edges of film which is to be projected, in order to prevent chattering and consequent piling up of the *emulsion,* especially when the film has been improperly dried.

Weave
Unwanted lateral motion of the film in the camera or projector.

Wet end
See *dark end.*

Wide-angle lens
See *lens, short focus.*

"Wild" motors
A camera or other motor (usually a *direct current* electric motor), which does not run at a fixed *synchronous speed* is called a "wild" motor. Such motors are used for silent shooting which does not require very precise speed control, since they may be operated very simply from batteries.

"Wild" recording
Any sound recording which is not made synchronously with a picture record is

called a "wild" recording. Sound effects and random voices are usually recorded "wild," narration and music sometimes so. Also called non-sync.

Wipe

An *optical effect* between two succeeding shots on the screen in which the second shot appears and wipes the first off the screen along a visible line, which may run from top to bottom or side to side, or in any one of a large number of patterns.

Workprint, Picture   ASA Z22.56–1947:3.2.2

A picture workprint is a positive print which usually consists of intercut picture daily prints, picture library prints, prints of dissolves, montages, titles, etc., and has synchronism constantly maintained with the corresponding sound workprint.

NOTE.—A picture workprint is used to edit and combine the various picture scenes of a motion picture into the desired form.

Workprint, Sound   ASA Z22.56–1947:3.3.2

A sound workprint is a sound print which usually consists of intercut sound *daily* prints, but may also include other *sound tracks* of *sound effects* or music, or both, on the same or separate films with synchronism constantly maintained with the corresponding picture workprint.

Wow

See *flutter (wow)*.

Z

Zoom; Zooming

Real or apparent rapid motion of the camera toward its object is known as zooming.

Zoom lens

A lens of variable magnification which enables *zooming* effects to be simply achieved without moving the camera toward its object. Parallactic effects, which usually accompany real movement, are of course absent from zoom lens shots, which are therefore most useful when the object is at a great distance, e.g., a football field.

Zoom stand

Colloquial term for a type of stand mounting an *animation camera*, in which the camera can advance toward and recede from the objects being photographed. An automatic cam device for *following focus* is sometimes incorporated, or the focus may be remotely controlled by a *selsyn motor*.

Booklist

LITERATURE on film art is becoming more voluminous; literature on film science is still surprisingly scanty. This is not, as might be supposed, because rapid advances in technology quickly makes books out of date. Compared with progress in other branches of applied science, advance in film has been rather slow. The real reason is that there have been so few film-production centers in any one country that there has been no need to collect specialized knowledge into books; it could be communicated more quickly and effectively by technical journals and by personal contact. Today, however, the resources of production are everywhere expanding; new units of moderate size are springing up in places which would never before have considered making their own films. With this the demand for books on the science of film increases.

In France this need has been met by a remarkable upsurge since the war in books on film, technical as well as aesthetic and historical. This accounts for the relatively large proportion of French books in the following list, which makes no claim to completeness but merely suggests certain starting points for further reading in the subjects already discussed in the text. In each group the books mentioned first are those likely to be of most interest to the reader.

PHOTOGRAPHY: HISTORY AND THEORY

Almost all cinematography has its roots in the prior science of photography, and a knowledge of the photographic process is essential to an understanding of film.

Photography, Its Principles and Practice, by C. B. Neblette. 4th ed. New York: Van Nostrand, 1942. 865 pp.

Among the many comprehensive and up-to-date studies of photography, this book is outstanding for its authority and for the lucid and attractive style in which it is written.

Fundamentals of Photographic Theory, by T. H. James and George C. Higgins. New York: Wiley, 1948. 286 pp.

This short and up-to-date book gives an admirable condensed account of modern ideas about the latent image, the theory of development, and the principles of sensitometry.

The Theory of the Photographic Process, by C. E. Kenneth Mees. New York: Macmillan, 1946. 1,124 pp.

A rigorous study, by the greatest living authority, of theoretical photography in monochrome. Contains important chapters on the theory of tone reproduction and on sensitometry, but has little to say on the important subject of emulsion manufacture, which remains a closely guarded commercial secret.

The Encyclopedia of Photography. General editor, Willard D. Morgan. New York: National Educational Alliance, 1942–43 (reprinted 1949). 3,924 pp.

A voluminous source of reference to almost all the subjects included in photography, with some treatment of the motion picture, written by experts in each field.

Basic Photography. War Department Technical Manual, No. 219. Washington, D.C.: Government Printing Office, 1941. 342 pp.

A very inexpensive manual of still photography, which also contains some underlying photographic theory.

History of Photography, by J. M. Eder; translated by Edward Epstean. New York: Columbia University Press, 1945. 860 pp.

This classical but chauvinistic work traces the history of photography from Aristotle down to the year 1925, with particular emphasis on the achievements of German scientists. Illustrations are to be found only in the German editions.

Histoire de la photographie, by Raymond Lécuyer. Paris: Baschet et Cie, 1945. 455 pp.

Though popular in style, this book is produced on a magnificent scale, and includes an outstanding collection of pictures on the art and science of photography.

CINEMATOGRAPHY: THEORY AND PRACTICE

Under this heading are general sources of reference which treat all or most of the topics detailed in the following sections of the booklist.

Society of Motion Picture and Television Engineers; Transactions (prior to 1930) and *Journal* (1930–   ), published monthly by the Society, New York.

The bound volumes of the *Transactions* and *Journal* form the best library of scientific information of film available in any language. The published papers have maintained a high standard throughout the years, and strike a good balance between the theoretical and the practical. Important papers are accompanied by detailed references to the technical literature. Standardization is reported through subcommittees of the Society. Before January, 1950, the name of the Society was the Society of Motion Picture Engineers.

The Technique of Motion Picture Production. New York: Interscience Publishers, 1944. 150 pp.

A Society of Motion Picture Engineers symposium by many noted Hollywood technical authorities on studio methods of production. An invaluable guide to modern large-scale techniques.

Filmlexicon, comp. by Francesco Pasinetti. Milan: Filmeuropa, 1948. 715 pp. (In Italian.)

This useful compilation (of which there is a shorter German version published at Zurich in 1946) consists of nearly 200 pages of technical film dictionary, followed by 450 pages of international film biography. This includes almost everyone of note connected with film—from Edison, Armat, and Méliès to Rita Hayworth and Gregory Peck. There is also a 37-page bibliography of writings on film.

Films in Business and Industry, by Henry Clay Gipson. New York: McGraw-Hill, 1947. 291 pp.

A part of this study of the methods and uses of the sponsored film is devoted to techniques of production. Though uncritical in its approach, it gives many useful pieces of advice on the making of industrial films.

Cine Data Book, compiled by R. H. Bomback. London: Fountain Press, 1950. 286 pp.

An invaluable sourcebook of numerical and descriptive data on almost all branches of cinematography, much of it difficult to procure elsewhere.

École technique de cinéma par correspondance, by Yvan Noé, Henry Laks, and Leo Laks. Nice: 1944–46.

This correspondence course, in more than twenty parts, covers all processes of film making, and has at present no parallel in any other language. The style is vigorous, the information accurate and up-to-date, and the many illustrations are imaginative and amusing. An English translation is badly needed.

Technique du cinéma, by Lo Duca. 2d ed. Paris: Presses Universitaires de France, 1948. 128 pp.

This is the shortest as well as the cheapest of the technologies of film. Though it sometimes sacrifices logic in favor of wit, it gives a good bird's-eye view of the subject.

Le Cinéma: son art, sa technique, son économie, by Georges Sadoul. Paris: La Bibliothèque Française, 1948. 222 pp.

An even more comprehensive view of the cinema is packed into little more space in this readable but biased and not always accurate book.

The Cinema Today, by D. A. Spencer and H. D. Waley. New York: Oxford University Press, 1940. 191 pp.

A brief but well-illustrated account of a large number of technical processes used in modern film making.

Working for the Films, ed. by Oswell Blakeston. London and New York: Focal Press, 1948. 204 pp.

This English work brings together nineteen authorities on the different branches of film making. The approach is conversational rather than technical, but the book conveys very well the "feel" of the film business in its many aspects.

Le Cinéma, par ceux qui le font, ed. by Denis Marion. Paris: Librairie Artheme Fayard, 1949. 410 pp.

Approaching its subject from the same direction as Blakeston's work, this book treats it rather more fully and comprehensively.

Foto-Kino-Technik. Berlin, 1946–   . Published monthly.

The German tradition of thoroughness is well exemplified in the large range of technical film articles presented in this general photographic magazine. Proceedings of the Deutsche Filmtechnische Gesellschaft (German equivalent of the Society of Motion Picture and Television Engineers) are fully reported.

Bulletin de l'Association Française des Ingénieurs et Techniciens du Cinéma. Paris, 1947–   . Published at irregular intervals.

The Frenchman's love of ingenious, but perhaps not always practical, mechanisms is given full scope in papers which are often very interestingly off the beaten track.

Journal of the British Kinematograph Society (British Kinematography) London, 1937–   . Published monthly.

Despite its mediocre editorial standards, this journal occasionally publishes an interesting paper.

SCRIPT WRITING

Theory and Technique of Playwriting and Screenwriting, by John Howard Lawson. New York: G. P. Putnam, 1949. 464 pp.

In this scholarly and able analysis of the dramatic arts, the screen receives (as it probably deserves) less than one-third of the total space. However, in this space the author concentrates the best account yet given of the problems of the script writer in relation to the film itself and to society.

THE CAMERA

The camera as an instrument is described in most of the works listed in the section on Cinematography, but there exists no good recent study of its creative techniques.

The Cinema as a Graphic Art, by Vladimir Nīlsen; trans. by Stephen Garry. London: Newnes, 1934. 227 pp.

Though out of date, out of print, and limited in its subject matter to Soviet silent films, this book still stands out as the most vigorous and imaginative projection of the art of the camera. Dedicated to Eisenstein, it brilliantly expounds that breakaway from the orthodox theories of camera composition which was initiated by the Russians and later followed by the documentary film makers of other countries, until finally even the commercial studios began to take notice of it.

American Cinematographer's Handbook and Reference Guide, by Jackson J. Rose. 7th ed. Hollywood: The author, 1950. 299 pp.

Often called "The Cameraman's Bible," this databook contains a mass of useful information on lenses, cameras, filters, exposure meters, film emulsions, etc. Periodically revised.

The American Cinematographer. Hollywood: American Society of Cinematographers. Published monthly.

This journal is often ahead of all other sources of information in releasing details of new equipment and techniques relating to the camera.

Optics: The Technique of Definition, by Arthur Cox. 6th ed. London and New York: Focal Press, 1946. 365 pp.

No study of the camera is complete without some knowledge of photographic optics. This popularly written introduction is admirably designed for the general reader who is shy on mathematics. The many tables and illustrations are outstandingly good.

High-Speed Photography: A Symposium of Papers. New York: Society of Motion Picture and Television Engineers. Vol. I, March, 1949, 129 pp.; Vol. II, November, 1949, 163 pp. [Published as supplements to the *JSMPE*.]

Methods of shooting at all speeds between one hundred and ten million frames per second are described in a group of papers by well known authorities who deal also with the analysis and application of high-speed motion pictures.

ANIMATION

There is great need for an up to date study in the English language of all kinds of animation technique—not simply cell animation.

Le Dessin animé, by Lo Duca, introduction by Walt Disney. Paris: Editions Prisma, 1948. 178 pp.

Though summary in its treatment, this book discusses with critical insight the many styles of animation which have flourished in different parts of the world. It is thus a useful corrective to the books which explain cell animation alone—the technique which has hitherto monopolized the attention of American animators.

The Art of Walt Disney, by Robert D. Feild. New York: Macmillan, 1942. 290 pp.

A popular introduction to Walt Disney's production methods, which throws light on the techniques of cell animation, though not in sufficient detail to be of much use to the professional film maker.

How to Make Animated Cartoons, by Nat Falk. New York: Foundation Books, 1941. 79 pp.

A brief history of the animated film is followed by an equally brief survey of animation studio techniques. The best part of the book is an essay on the creation of character in cartoon drawing.

La Technique de dessin animé, by Jean Regnier. Les cahiers de la technique cinématographique, vol. 40. Paris: Editions Film et Technique, 1947. 27 pp.

No better (or cheaper) introduction to cell animation could be found than this condensed but precise little book, which ranges all the way from Leonardo da Vinci to "le gag" and a complete set of American illustrations.

The Animated Film, by G. Roshal and others. Moscow: 1936. 288 pp. (In Russian.)

This untranslated work contains the best and fullest published account of puppet animation (by Ptushko, of *New Gulliver* fame), and a description of early methods of synthesizing sound. Most of the animation examples are drawn from films unfamiliar to Western audiences, and the book does not carry its subject beyond 1934.

Le Cinéma scientifique, by P. Thevenard and G. Tassel. Paris: 1948. 214 pp.
   A study of the scientific applications of the motion picture, which, however, contains a chapter on animation.

FILM AS A SUBSTANCE

Motion Picture Laboratory Practice. Rochester: Eastman Kodak Company, 1936.
   The standard textbook on laboratory practices and problems. Written before the introduction of fine-grain emulsions and the widespread adoption of chemical analysis, it none the less contains a wealth of useful data on the management of laboratories. Should be supplemented on almost every point by more recent Society of Motion Picture and Television Engineers papers.

Motion Picture Films for Professional Use. Rochester: Eastman Kodak Company, 1942.
   A databook on the characteristics of Eastman Kodak motion picture film which is comprehensive and thorough. Contains notes on sensitometric procedure, use of filters, tropical handling of film, etc. Revised periodically by the addition of loose-leaf pages.

Photo-Lab Index, ed. by Willard D. Morgan. New York: Morgan and Lester, n.d.
   An index, periodically revised and supplemented, on photographic formulae and materials.

Kodak Reference Handbook. Rochester: Eastman Kodak Company, n.d.
   An invaluable collection of the excellent databooks published by the Eastman Kodak Company on emulsions, filters, lenses, infrared film, films for television, etc. A loose-leaf binding enables it to be progressively expanded.

Photographic Chemicals and Solutions, by John I. Crabtree and G. E. Matthews. Boston: American Photographic Publishing Co., 1939.
   The standard work on the preparation and mixing of photographic solutions.

Film Hazards, by C. A. Vlachos. New York: Vlachos and Co., 1930.
   A useful summary of the hazardous characteristics of cellulose-nitrate film, together with recommendations on fire prevention in laboratories and studios.

COLOR: THEORY AND TECHNIQUES OF REPRODUCTION

An Introduction to Color, by Ralph M. Evans. New York: Wiley, 1948.

A lucid and stimulating analysis of color, its physics and psychology. Excellently illustrated and embodying the recently introduced international color terminology, this book tackles most of the difficult problems of color, but does not concern itself with color reproduction. An outstanding achievement.

The Measurement of Colour, by W. D. Wright. London: Adam Hilger, 1944. 223 pp.

The best available general text on the principles and methods of the new science of colorimetry, written by one of the leading workers in the field.

Colour Cinematography, by A. Cornwell-Clyne (A. B. Klein). 3d ed. London: Chapman and Hall, 1951.

An exhaustive survey, now brought fully up to date, covering the whole range of color patents as they relate to the motion picture, with many illustrations. Color camera mechanisms are fully described, and the history of the development of individual color processes is recounted in detail.

The History of 3-Color Photography, by E. J. Wall. Boston: American Photographic Publishing Co., 1925. 747 pp.

The earliest comprehensive work on the subject, now long out of print, but well deserving of study in tracing the early history of today's color processes, and of many others which still await development.

History of Color Photography, by Joseph S. Friedman. Boston: American Photographic Publishing Co., 1945. 514 pp.

A thorough historical analysis of color processes through a survey of patent disclosures, conducted by an eminent authority. The treatment of lenticular processes is outstandingly good. Difficult reading for the beginner.

British Technicolour Films, by John Huntley. London: Skelton Robinson, 1949. 224 pp.

A wealth of detail about methods of production in Technicolor is scattered through these notes on the Technicolor films produced in England between 1936 and 1948.

The Agfacolor Process, by Wilhelm Schneider. FIAT Final Report No. 976. Office of Military Government for Germany (US), 1946. 165 pp.

A clear and detailed account of the chemistry and optics of the Agfacolor process, as developed in Germany up to 1945, written for the general technical reader and fully illustrated. For more specialized information see FIAT Final Reports Nos. 721, 943, 977, and Microfilm Reels D2–D7.

Farbenfilm und Farbenphoto, by Max Feiss. Geneva: Editions K. Meister, 1949. 196 pp.

For the reader of German, this book provides a thorough analysis of color reproduction, magnificently illustrated in color.

Le Secret des couleurs, by Marcel Boll and Jean Dourgnon. Paris: Presses Universitaires de France, 1946. 128 pp.

An inexpensive and brilliantly succinct analysis of the physics and psychology of color, which necessarily omits a great many refinements and qualifications because of its small compass.

Three Monographs on Color. New York: International Printing Ink Co., 1935.

A brief but magnificently illustrated introduction to color analysis, based on the Munsell system.

16 MM. TECHNIQUES AND PRACTICES

A great many books are now available addressed to the amateur film maker. The books listed here, however, while of great value to the really keen amateur, are designed to guide the professional in the production and use of small-gauge films.

16 mm. Sound Motion Pictures, by W. H. Offenhauser, Jr. New York: Interscience Publishers, 1949. 580 pp.

The standard work on all technical aspects of the 16 mm. film has been written by an authority whose lively and imaginative approach is in refreshing contrast to the orthodox textbook style. The book contains a vast quantity of practical detail indispensable to the user of small-gauge film. The author's insistence on high technical standards cannot help but improve the quality of 16 mm. production wherever the book's recommendations are scrupulously followed.

Le Cinéma sur formats réduits, by Georges Acher, Raymond Bricon, and Jean Vivié. Vol. I. Paris: Editions B. P. I., 1948. 493 pp.

Less rigorous in approach than Offenhauser, but even more encyclopedic in scope, this work sets out to describe all aspects of small-gauge film making, the creative no less than the purely technical. In this it succeeds notably well. By comparison with the text, however, the illustrations are weak in conception and poorly executed. Volume II will appear in 1951.

Recommended Procedure and Equipment Specifications for Educational 16 mm. Projection, by a Society of Motion Picture Engineers Committee under the chairmanship of John A. Maurer. New York: The Society, 1941. 54 pp.

Though compiled before the advances in 16 mm. technique which resulted from World War II, these brief and clear recommendations still form an admirable guide to the nontechnical film user in the choice of projectors, screens, and loudspeakers.

Joint Army-Navy Specification, Projection Equipment, Sound Motion Picture, 16 mm. Class I (Jan-P-49). Washington, D.C.: Government Printing Office, 1945. 58 pp.

This elaborate specification for a service 16 mm. sound projector is still in force, and was in fact not met by the manufacturers until 1948. Almost all commercial machines fall below its requirements in certain respects, some of them in very many, so that it continues to be a useful guide in the evaluation of current designs.

Cine-Film Projection, by Cecil A. Hill. London: The Fountain Press, 1948. 167 pp.

Though some of this book on 16 mm. projection is applicable only to English conditions, it contains a large amount of practical detail on good and bad practices, and on overcoming acoustical problems, which is not elsewhere to be found in print.

Manual of Sub-Standard Cinematography, edited by Arthur Pereira, based on *Le Cinéma d'amateur* by Jean Vivié, Raymond Bricon, and Georges Acher. London: The Fountain Press, 1949. 455 pp.

Though written from a European point of view, and including information on the 9.5 mm. film which does not exist in America, this book, based on an earlier and shorter version of *Le Cinéma sur formats reduit,* contains much valuable information on the art of production as well as on small-gauge technical processes.

SOUND RECORDING AND REPRODUCTION

Elements of Sound Recording, by John G. Frayne and Halley Wolfe. New York: Wiley, 1949. 686 pp.

This new standard work on recording for film covers all modern techniques, including magnetic recording and stereophonic sound. The analysis of processing techniques is extremely thorough. The book is fully illustrated, and makes only sparing use of mathematical analysis.

Physik und Technik des Tonfilms, by Hugo Lichte and Albert Narath. Leipzig, 1943. (Reprinted by Edwards Bros., Ann Arbor, Mich., 1945.) 411 pp.

For the reader of German, this book provides a clear and thorough physical background to sound recording for film; it employs mathematics wherever necessary to compress the analysis.

Magnetic Recording, by S. J. Begun. New York: Murray Hill Books, 1949. 238 pp.

Although undue weight is perhaps given to the now obsolescent system of recording on steel wire, this book furnishes the first comprehensive account of magnetic recording theory and practice, including a lucid treatment of the difficult subject of high-frequency bias. The author is a pioneer in the development of all forms of magnetic recording.

Sound and the Documentary Film, by Ken Cameron. London: Pitman and Sons, 1947. 157 pp.

A thoroughly practical account of microphone techniques, acoustic treatment, and other aspects of sound recording for the documentary film. The style is popular and attractive, and the book is written by England's foremost exponent of documentary recording.

The ABC of Photographic Sound Recording, by E. W. Kellogg. New York: The Society of Motion Picture Engineers, 1945. 44 pp.

A crystal-clear account of the elements of sound-recording mechanics, optics, and processing techniques, followed by an admirable bibliography broken down into 54 divisions of the subject.

Sound Reproduction, by G. A. Briggs. Bradford, Yorkshire, England: Wharfedale Wireless Works, 1949. 143 pp.

A simple introduction to the nature of sound, and the problems of recording and reproducing it. The companion volume entitled *Loudspeakers* is also worth reading.

FILM MUSIC

Film Music, by Kurt London. London: Faber and Faber, 1936. 280 pp.

A history and analysis of the place of music in film, with a study of contemporary European film composers and a discussion of the instruments of the orchestra and their adaptability in different combinations to the peculiarities of the sound track.

Composing for the Films, by Hanns Eisler. New York: Oxford University Press, 1947. 165 pp.

In this report for the Rockefeller Foundation Film Music Project, the well-known composer delivers a rough but not unmerited blast at Hollywood's conception of film music, and advances his own theories of the complementary character of the sound track.

British Film Music, by John Huntley. London: Skelton Robinson, 1947. 247 pp.

A comprehensive but not very critical study of the place of music in British films, popularly written and thoroughly documented up to the end of 1946, with biographies of composers.

STUDIO TECHNIQUES

These are well described in *The Technique of Motion Picture Production,* listed on p. 487, which gives a picture of the whole studio process as practised in Hollywood.

Painting with Light, by John Alton. New York: Macmillan, 1949. 191 pp.

A breezily written account of the techniques of lighting (exterior as well as interior) employed by Hollywood. With the aid of almost three hundred finely reproduced illustrations, and a wealth of detailed information about equipment, the author, a well-known director of photography, is able to explain clearly almost all the photographic effects (including trick work) to be found in studio films.

Designing for Moving Pictures, by Edward Carrick (Edward Craig). London and New York: Studio, 1947. 104 pp.

An excellent short book on the design of studio sets and properties, well illustrated from the work the author has himself executed both in feature and in elaborate documentary films.

Art and Design in the British Film, comp. by Edward Carrick. London: Dennis Dobson, Ltd., 1948.

A series of biographies of British art directors, accompanied by handsome illustrations of their work, and prefaced by a short essay on the place of design in films.

PROJECTION AND THEATER DESIGN

References to 16 mm. projection will be found in the section on 16 mm. techniques and practices.

Bluebook of Projection, by F. H. Richardson. 7th ed. New York: Quigley Publishing Co., 1942. 706 pp.

This "Projectionist's Bible," now in circulation for more than thirty years, answers all the questions the projectionist may ask, encourages him to maintain high standards, and helps him to locate breakdowns in his equipment. The latest edition contains chapters on television.

The Complete Projectionist, by R. Howard Cricks. 4th ed. London: Odhams Press, 1949. 335 pp.

An extremely clear and scholarly account of projection equipment and associated electrical theory, intended for the British projectionist, but much of it of general application. Well illustrated. Contains a chapter on television.

The Motion Picture Theater. New York: Society of Motion Picture Engineers, 1949. 428 pp.

A symposium of SMPE papers on such subjects as theater design, acoustics, the use of color, air conditioning, lighting, screen brightness, black light, and large-screen television.

Das Lichtspieltheater, by Werner Gabler. Halle: Wilhelm Knapp, 1950. 113 pp.

A compact and copiously illustrated treatment of most of the optical and acoustical problems encountered in the design of motion picture theaters.

THE STEREOCINEMA

A complete bibliography will be included in the author's forthcoming book, *The Stereocinema.* References to stereophonic sound should be looked for in the *Journal of the Society of Motion Picture Engineers,* principally between 1938 and 1942, and in *Philips Technical Review* between 1940 and 1949. See also the last chapter in Frayne and Wolfe, *Elements of Sound Recording,* listed above.

Stereoscopic Photography, by A. W. Judge. 3d ed. London: Chapman and Hall, 1950. 480 pp.

Now that it has been fully brought up to date in a new edition, this book ranks as by far the best study of three-dimensional pictorial reproduction, both in still pictures and movies. With more than three hundred illustrations and an extensive bibliography, it will serve as an admirable introduction to all branches of stereoscopy.

Stereoptics: An Introduction, by L. P. Dudley. London: MacDonald, 1951.

The author, a well-known inventor and engineer, reveals his complete mastery of this difficult subject in the lucidity and simplicity of his approach. After carrying the reader through the anaglyphic and polarized systems of stereoscopy, the author breaks new ground with a very full discussion of parallax stereograms, parallax panoramagrams, and integral photographs, assembling a mass of material hitherto available only in the patent literature. The book is well illustrated, but suffers somewhat from the author's preoccupation with systems of his own invention.

Principles of Stereoscopy, by Hubert J. MacKay. Boston: American Photographic Publishing Co., 1948. 191 pp.

This study of stereoscopic photography is directed mainly at the amateur, and is therefore confined to processes he is able to carry out. Though up to date, it needs to be supplemented by references to current technical literature.

Raster-Stereoscopy, by B. T. Ivanow. Moscow: 1945. 172 pp. (In Russian.)

This untranslated handbook is at present the standard work on raster (grid) methods of stereoscopic film projection, which do not require the audience to wear viewing spectacles. In welcome contrast to much popular Soviet technical writing, this book is clear and detailed, and the author does not indulge in bombastic claims.

CINEMATOGRAPHY: HISTORY

There is no adequate technical history of the development of the motion picture from the early nineteenth century to the present day comparable to the many excellent studies of its growth as an art and as an article of commerce. It is therefore necessary to fall back on a series of books, each of which reviews the progress of the science up to the date of its publication, and describes in detail the level of technique prevailing at that time. From 1917 onward, the *Transactions* and *Journal* of the Society of Motion Picture Engineers form an invaluable source of reference.

GENERAL

A Million and One Nights, by Terry Ramsaye. New York: Simon and Schuster, 1926. 868 pp.

This lively history of the film presents with great accuracy and a wealth of interesting detail most of the technical developments up to the end of the silent era. The author does less than justice, however, to Muybridge, Marey, the Gaumonts, the Lumiéres, and other European pioneers.

Traité général de technique du cinéma, by Jean Vivié. Vol. I, *Historique et developpement de la technique cinématographique.* Paris: B.P.I., 1946. 135 pp., XXIV plates.

Though too brief to be considered more than an introductory study, this first volume of a projected twelve volume work gives a useful bird's-eye view of film mechanisms and processes as they have developed over the last seventy years. The most valuable part of the book is its admirable series of illustrations drawn from contemporary sources and reproduced large enough for careful study.

Cent ans d'image, by Roger Simonet. Paris: Calmann Levy, 1947. 287 pp.
   Another rapid glance at the history of photography, a large but still insufficient part of which is devoted to the motion picture.

THE PRECURSORS OF THE CINEMA

Histoire générale du cinéma, by Georges Sadoul. 2d ed. Vol. I, *L'Invention du cinéma: 1832–1897.* Paris: Editions Denoel, 1948. 438 pp.
   This first volume of Sadoul's magnificent general history achieves in the revised edition an outstanding level of impartiality in its investigation of the many competing claims to have "invented the cinema." Authoritative and fully documented as it is, the book is written with an infectious enthusiasm which carries the reader through all the complexities of the subject. There are over two hundred contemporary illustrations, a full chronology, and filmographies of Reynaud, Lumière, and Edison.

Descriptive Zoopraxography, by Eadweard Muybridge. Phila.: University of Pennsylvania, 1893. 92 pp.
   This curious little work, full of the author's addiction to self-praise, is included because it contains the only extant description in his own words of the apparatus which may truly be said to be the foundation of all attempts to record life in movement.

The Horse in Motion, by Jacob D. B. Stillman. Boston: 1882. 127 pp.
   This rare and magnificently produced book is illustrated from Muybridge's original photographs of the horse in motion, and shows the scientific purposes to which "successive photography" was being put.

Animal Locomotion, by James B. Pettigrew. Phila.: Lippincott, 1888. 136 pp.
   Taking a step forward from the work of Muybridge, this book documents the outstanding contribution to the birth of the scientific film which was made by the University of Pennsylvania. It has an additional interest in that it records the part played by Thomas Eakins, the painter, in the development of movies.

THE PRIMITIVE CINEMA

History of the Kinetograph, Kinetoscope and Kineto-Phonograph, by W. K. L. Dickson and Antonia Dickson. New York: 1895.
   A lively anecdotal history of the first true American movies by their director and Edison's collaborator, this is the first book to have been illustrated by

frames of perforated film. It is also noteworthy that the sound film figures prominently in its title.

Movement, by E. J. Marey, trans. by Eric Pritchard. London: Heinemann, 1895. 323 pp.

A lengthy and beautifully presented record of the work of one of the great pioneers of movie photography and the scientific film, the French inventor and physiologist, Edouard Marey.

Living Pictures, by Henry V. Hopwood. London: The Optician and Photographic Trades Review, 1899. 275 pp.

An extremely detailed and very well-illustrated account of all the motion picture equipment available in England at the end of the last century. A bibliography of more than one hundred entries is of much historical value.

THE ERA OF EXPANSION

Motion Picture Work, by David S. Hulfish. Chicago: American School of Correspondence, 1913. 579 pp.

This very considerable study of film production, copiously illustrated by film stills as well as diagrams, throws a great deal of light on how movies were produced before World War I. Chapters on scripting and the sound film are of especial interest.

Moving Pictures: How They Are Made and Worked, by Frederick A. Talbot. Phila.: Lippincott, 1912. 340 pp.

By the time the cinema had come of age, most of its basic principles, technical as well as artistic, had been established, and this book gives a good account of them. Many interesting trick techniques are described which have long fallen out of use, but which might in certain circumstances merit revival.

THE SUMMIT OF THE SILENT FILM

Moving Pictures: How They Are Made and Worked, by Frederick A. Talbot. Rev. ed. Phila.: Lippincott, 1923. 429 pp.

The new chapters and revisions in this edition enable the reader to trace the progress of film in the decade prior to 1923.

Histoire du cinématographe, by Georges-Michel Coissac. Paris: Editions du "Cinéopse," 1925. 604 pp.

An encyclopedic work which charts the technical history of the film up to 1924, mostly from the French point of view, and throws some light on the controversies of the time about the priority of early inventions.

La Technique cinématographique, by Leopold Lobel, 3d ed. Paris: Editions Denoel, 1927. 342 pp.

Records the technical level of the film industry at the summit of the silent era. Starting with projection, the book discusses in turn the various stages of film making.

THE COMING OF SOUND

Cinematographic Annual. Hollywood: American Society of Cinematographers. Vol. I, 1930, 606 pp.; Vol. II, 1931, 425 pp.

A very complete account, by various contributors, of the technology of film as it stood on the threshold of the sound era. Contains a discussion of "Grandeur" film, and other abortive efforts to break away from the 35 mm. standard.

* * * * * * * * * * *

The final twenty years of development belong to the present day, and may be traced in technical journals and in earlier references given in this bibliography.

BIBLIOGRAPHY

There does not appear to exist (save in reference to the German cinema) any complete technical bibliography of film. The indexes to the Journal of the Society of Motion Picture and Television Engineers, however, are conveniently subdivided into the many branches of film technology, and the more important of the papers referred to contain extensive sectional bibliographies.

Index of Films

T_{HIS} index of films mentioned in the text is preceded by a table giving names of the distributors of these films and addresses of their head offices. All films are available in 16 mm. gauge save those marked with an asterisk, which can be obtained in 35 mm. only. Films no longer extant, or of which no prints are at present in circulation in the United States, are marked thus: °. The name of the director of each film and the year in which it was produced are given in parentheses.

AR	American Rolex Corp., 580 Fifth Ave., New York
BR	Brandon Films, Inc., 1600 Broadway, New York
BIS	British Information Services, 30 Rockefeller Plaza, New York
CF	Castle Films, Inc., 450 West 56th St., New York
CC	Cine-Classics, Inc., 117 West 48th St., New York
FPS	Film Program Services, 1273 Sixth Ave., New York
FR	Film Rights, Inc., 1600 Broadway, New York
IFB	International Film Bureau, 6 North Michigan Ave., Chicago
IFF	International Film Foundation, 1600 Broadway, New York
LP	Lopert Films, Inc., 148 West 57th St., New York
MoT	March of Time, 369 Lexington Ave., New York
MB	Mayer and Burstyn, Inc., 113 West 42d St., New York
MGM	Metro-Goldwyn-Mayer, 1540 Broadway, New York
MMA	Museum of Modern Art Film Library, 11 West 53d St., New York
NFB	National Film Board of Canada, 620 Fifth Ave., New York
RKO	RKO Theaters, 1270 Sixth Ave., New York
S	Superfilm, Inc., 52 Vanderbilt Ave., New York
UA	United Artists Corp., 630 Ninth Ave., New York
UWF	United World Films, 445 Park Ave., New York

American Scene, The (OWI, 1942–1945). A series continued up to the present by the U.S. State Department but not generally released domestically. It now has no series title. A few pictures available from MMA, CF, BR, 21

°*Apropos de Nice* (Vigo, 1930), 24 n. 10

Bambi (Disney, 1942), RKO, 138
Banknote Story, The (1948). [Obtainable from the Security Banknote Company, 52 Wall St., New York], 8, 12

Battleship Potemkin, The (Eisenstein, 1925), MMA, 104
Begone, Dull Care (McLaren, 1949), 24 n. 11, 141
*Body and Soul (Rosson, 1947), UA, 30 n. 14
Boundary Lines (Stapp, 1947), IFF, 24 n. 13, 129, 130, 132

C'est l'aviron, in *Chants populaires*, no. 6 (McLaren, 1944), NFB, 24 n. 11, 128, 129
Chalk River Ballet (McLaren, 1949), NFB, 24 n. 11, 141-142

General Index

(In this index, titles of periodical articles, as well as titles of books and periodicals, are italicized for the reader's convenience.)